# HARCOURT
# · TROPHIES ·

## A HARCOURT READING/LANGUAGE ARTS PROGRAM

### LEAD THE WAY

## TEACHER'S EDITION

AUTHORS

Alma Flor Ada ◆ Marcia Brechtel ◆ Margaret McKeown
Nancy Roser ◆ Hallie Kay Yopp

SENIOR CONSULTANT
Asa G. Hilliard III

CONSULTANTS
F. Isabel Campoy ◆ David A. Monti

## Harcourt

Orlando   Boston   Dallas   Chicago   San Diego

Visit *The Learning Site!*

www.harcourtschool.com

Permission is hereby granted to individual teachers using the corresponding student's textbook or kit as the major vehicle for regular classroom instruction to photocopy Copying Masters from this publication in classroom quantities for instructional use and not for resale. Requests for information on other matters regarding duplication of this work should be addressed to School Permissions and Copyrights, Harcourt, Inc., 6277 Sea Harbor Drive, Orlando, Florida 32887-6777. Fax: 407-345-2418.

Acknowledgments appear in the back of this book.

Printed in the United States of America

ISBN 0-15-325040-2

2 3 4 5 6 7 8 9 10    030    10 09 08 07 06 05 04 03 02

# Program Authors

## SENIOR AUTHORS

### Isabel L. Beck

Professor of Education and Senior Scientist at the Learning Research and Development Center, University of Pittsburgh

**Research Contributions:** Reading Comprehension, Beginning Reading, Phonics, Vocabulary

### Roger C. Farr

Chancellor's Professor of Education and Director of the Center for Innovation in Assessment, Indiana University, Bloomington

**Research Contributions:** Instructional Assessment, Reading Strategies Staff Development

### Dorothy S. Strickland

The State of New Jersey Professor of Reading, Rutgers University

**Research Contributions:** Early Literacy, Elementary Reading/Language Arts, Writing, Intervention

# AUTHORS

**Alma Flor Ada**
Director of Doctoral Studies in the International Multicultural
Program, University of San Francisco

**Research Contributions:** English as a Second Language,
Bilingual Education, Family Involvement

**Marcia Brechtel**
Director of Training, Project GLAD, Fountain Valley School District,
Fountain Valley, California

**Research Contributions:** English as a Second Language,
Bilingual Education

**Margaret McKeown**
Research Scientist at the Learning Research and Development Center,
University of Pittsburgh

**Research Contributions:** Reading Comprehension, Vocabulary

**Nancy Roser**
Professor, Language and Literacy Studies, University of Texas, Austin

**Research Contributions:** Early Literacy, Phonics, Comprehension,
Fluency

**Hallie Kay Yopp**
Professor, Department of Elementary Bilingual and Reading
Education, California State University, Fullerton

**Research Contributions:** Phonemic Awareness, Early Childhood

# SENIOR CONSULTANT

**Asa G. Hilliard III**
Fuller E. Callaway Professor of Urban Education, Department of Educational Foundations, Georgia State University, Atlanta

**Research Contributions:** Multicultural Literature and Education

# CONSULTANTS

**F. Isabel Campoy**
Former President, Association of Spanish Professionals in the USA

**Research Contributions:** English as a Second Language, Family Involvement

**David A. Monti**
Professor, Reading/Language Arts Department, Central Connecticut State University

**Research Contributions:** Classroom Management, Technology, Family Involvement

# PHONEMIC AWARENESS

Research clearly shows that phonemic awareness is one of the primary predictors of success in learning to read, and instruction in phonemic awareness significantly supports students' reading and writing achievement.

**P**honemic awareness is the awareness of sounds in spoken language. It is recognizing and understanding that speech is made up of a series of individual sounds, or phonemes, and that the individual sounds can be manipulated. A phonemically aware child can segment and blend strings of isolated sounds to form words. Phonemic awareness falls under the umbrella of phonological awareness, which also includes recognizing and manipulating larger units of sound, such as syllables and words. Phonemic awareness can be difficult for young children to attain because it demands a shift in attention from the *content* of speech to the *form* of speech. It requires individuals to attend to the sounds of speech separate from their meanings. Primary grade teachers will find that a handful of children enter school with well-developed phonemic awareness. Other children have only a rudimentary sense of the sound structure of speech. With extended exposure to a language-rich environment, most children develop phonemic awareness over time.

**R**esearch has shown that phonemic awareness is significantly related to success in learning to read and spell. The relationship is one of reciprocal causation or mutual facilitation. That is, phonemic awareness supports reading and spelling acquisition, and instruction in reading and spelling, in turn, supports further understanding of the phonemic basis of our speech. The relationship is so powerful that researchers have concluded the following:

- Phonemic awareness is the most potent predictor of success in learning to read (Stanovich, 1986, 1994).
- The lack of phonemic awareness is the most powerful determinant of the likelihood of failure to learn to read (Adams, 1990).
- Phonemic awareness is the most important core and causal factor separating normal and disabled readers (Adams, 1990).

Phonemic awareness is central in learning to read and spell because English and other alphabetic languages map speech to print at the level of phonemes. Our written language is a representation of the *sounds* of our spoken language. It is critical to understand that our speech is made up of sounds. Without this insight, written language makes little sense.

**D**irect instruction in phonemic awareness helps children decode new words and remember how to read familiar words. Growth and improvement in phonemic awareness can be facilitated through instruction and practice in phonemic awareness tasks such as these:

- **Phoneme isolation,** which requires students to recognize individual sounds in words. For example, "What is the last sound in *hop*?" (/p/)
- **Phoneme matching,** which requires students to recognize the same sound in different words. For example, "Which two words begin with the same sound—*bed, bike, cat*?" (*bed, bike*)
- **Phoneme blending,** which asks students to form a recognizable word after listening to separately spoken sounds. For example, "What word is /a/ -/p/ -/l/?" (*apple*)
- **Phoneme segmentation,** which has students break a word into its individual sounds. For example, "What sounds do you hear in the word *dog*?" (/d/-/ô/-/g/)
- **Phoneme deletion,** which requires students to identify what word remains when a specific phoneme has been removed. For example, "Say *spin* without /s/." (*pin*)
- **Phoneme addition,** which requires the identification of a word when a phoneme is added. For example, "Say *row* with /g/ at the beginning." (*grow*)

**Q** What types of phonemic awareness activities or tasks are children exposed to in the program?

**A** Phonemic awareness instruction in *Trophies* is strongly supported by the finding that phonemic awareness is one of the most potent predictors of success in learning to read. Activities for stimulating phonemic awareness are incorporated throughout the program. There are two types of phonemic awareness instruction in *Trophies*. The first is word-play activities that draw attention to sounds in spoken language, recited poems, and read-aloud literature. The second type is more formal instruction that focuses on single phonemes to prepare students for studying the letter-sound correspondences for those phonemes.

**Q** What phonemic awareness skills are taught in kindergarten and grade 1?

**A** Phonemic awareness instruction in *Trophies* follows a systematic, developmental sequence progressing in difficulty from an awareness of words, syllables, and onset/rimes to isolating medial phonemes, substituting phonemes, and other manipulating tasks.

**Phonemic Awareness Skills Sequence**

- Word Segmentation
- Rhyme Recognition and Production
- Syllable Blending
- Syllable Segmentation
- Syllable Deletion
- Onset and Rime Blending
- Initial Phoneme Isolation
- Final Phoneme Isolation
- Medial Phoneme Isolation
- Phoneme Blending
- Phoneme Segmentation
- Phoneme Substitution
- Phoneme Addition
- Phoneme Deletion

**Q** How do the phonemic awareness lessons relate to the phonics lessons in *Trophies*?

**A** In kindergarten and grade 1, each phonemic awareness lesson is tied to a phonics lesson. A phonemic awareness lesson, for example, could focus on blending phonemes in words with the /i/ sound, featuring such words as *sit, lip,* and *if.* The subsequent phonics lesson would be the short sound of the letter *i.*

> " A growing number of studies indicate that phonemic awareness is not simply a strong predictor, but that it is a necessary prerequisite for success in learning to read. "
>
> — Hallie Kay Yopp
>
> Professor
> Department of Elementary
> Bilingual and Reading Education,
> California State University,
> Fullerton

## Look for

✓ Daily phonemic awareness lessons in Kindergarten and Grade 1
✓ Additional Support Activities to Reteach and Extend
✓ Point-of-use suggestions for Reaching All Learners

# EXPLICIT, SYSTEMATIC PHONICS

Decoding is the process of translating written words into speech. Phonics instruction gives students the knowledge of letter-sound correspondences and strategies they need to make the translations and to be successful readers.

**Explicit, systematic phonics instruction can help children learn to read more effectively.** Current and confirmed research shows that systematic phonics instruction has a significant effect on reading achievement. Research findings clearly indicate that phonics instruction in kindergarten and first grade produces a dramatic impact on reading achievement. In phonics instruction letter-sound correspondences are taught sequentially and cumulatively and are then applied. The individual sounds represented by letters are blended to form words, and those words appear in decodable text. At grade 2, more complex letter patterns are introduced and practiced. This type of instruction allows students to continually build on what they learn.

**Word Blending and Word Building are essential aspects of phonics instruction.** Word Blending is combining the sounds represented by letter sequences to decode and pronounce words. In phonics instruction beginning in kindergarten or first grade, students are explicitly taught the process of blending individual sounds into words. They begin with VC or CVC words, such as *at* or *man,* and progress to words with consonant blends, as in *tent* and *split*. In contrast to Word Blending, which focuses on decoding a particular word, Word Building allows students to practice making words by using previously taught letter-sound relationships. Word Building activities require children to focus attention on each letter in the sequence of letters that make up words. This helps children develop a sense of the alphabetic system of written English.

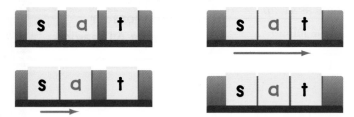

**As students progress through the grades, they receive direct instruction in decoding multisyllabic words.** Direct instruction in recognizing syllables will help students develop effective strategies to read longer, unfamiliar words. Research shows that good readers chunk letter patterns into manageable units in order to read a long, unfamiliar word. Effective strategies include

- identifying syllable boundaries
- identifying syllable types
- isolating affixes
- applying phonics knowledge to blend syllables in sequence

Direct instruction in these strategies helps students recognize word parts so they can apply phonics generalizations to decode unfamiliar words.

> **Decoding is important because this early skill accurately predicts later skill in reading comprehension.**
>
> — Isabel L. Beck
> **Professor of Education and Senior Scientist at the Learning Research and Development Center, University of Pittsburgh**

**Q** **How is Word Blending taught in *Trophies*?**

**A** The purpose of Word Blending instruction is to provide students with practice in combining the sounds represented by letter sequences to decode words. *Trophies* employs the cumulative blending method, which has students blend sounds successively as they are pronounced.

**Q** **How does *Trophies* use Word Building to help students with decoding (reading) and encoding (spelling)?**

**A** In the decoding portion of Word Building, teachers first tell students what letters to put in what place. For example, students are told to put *c* at the beginning, *a* after *c,* and *t* at the end. They are asked to read the word *cat* and then are asked to change *c* to *m* and read the new word, *mat.* In Word Building activities that help encoding, students are asked which letter in the word *cat* needs to change to make the word *mat.* This encoding approach is used to build spelling words throughout the first grade program.

**Q** **How are students taught to decode multisyllabic words?**

**A** Students are taught to see words as patterns of letters, to identify long words by breaking them down into syllable units, and to blend the syllables to form and read long words. Decoding lessons throughout grades 2–6 directly and explicitly provide students with various strategies, including understanding syllable types and patterns and recognizing such word structures as prefixes, suffixes, and root words, to decode multisyllabic words.

## Look for

- ✔ Phonics and spelling lessons
- ✔ Word Blending
- ✔ Word Building
- ✔ Decoding/Phonics lessons in Grades 2–6
- ✔ Additional Support Activities to reteach and extend

# WHAT RESEARCH SAYS ABOUT
# READING ALOUD

Reading aloud to students contributes to their motivation, comprehension, vocabulary, fluency, knowledge base, literary understanding, familiarity with academic and literary terms, sense of community, enjoyment, and perhaps to a lifetime love of literature.

**Sharing and responding to books during read-aloud time helps develop communication and oral language skills and improves comprehension.** Literature that is read aloud to students serves as the vehicle for developing literary insights, including sensitivity to the sounds and structure of language. Students learn how powerful written language can be when fluent readers read aloud, interpreting a text through appropriate intonation, pacing, and phrasing. Comprehension skills are developed as students ask and answer questions and share their personal understandings. More advanced students who are read to and who get to talk with others about the best of written language learn both to discuss texts knowingly and to interpret their meanings expressively.

**Reading aloud exposes students to more challenging texts than they may be able to read independently.** Vocabulary development is fostered by listening to both familiar and challenging selections read aloud. Texts read aloud that are conceptually challenging for students can effectively improve language and comprehension abilities. Listening to challenging texts also exposes students to text structures and content knowledge that are more sophisticated than they may encounter in their own reading.

**Listening skills and strategies are greatly improved during read-aloud activities.** When students are encouraged to respond to stories read aloud, they tend to listen intently in order to recall relevant content. When students listen responsively and frequently to literature and expository texts, they hone critical-thinking skills that will serve them in many other contexts. In sum, reading aloud

- models fluent reading behavior
- builds students' vocabularies and concepts
- creates an interest in narrative structures
- builds background knowledge by introducing children to new ideas and concepts and by expanding on what is familiar to them
- exposes students to different text structures and genres, such as stories, alphabet books, poetry, and informational books

**"** Sharing literature with children increases their vocabulary and their understanding of how language works. Sharing stories, informational books, and poetry with children has become increasingly valued for its cognitive contribution to children's literary development. **"**

— **Dorothy S. Strickland**
The State of New Jersey
Professor of Reading,
Rutgers University

**Q** **How does *Trophies* provide opportunities for teachers to read aloud to their students?**

**A** *Trophies* provides a comprehensive collection of read-aloud selections for all levels of instruction. In kindergarten through grade 2, the program includes read-aloud options for students every day. In grades 3–6, a read-aloud selection accompanies every lesson in the *Teacher's Edition.* Read-aloud selections are available in *Read-Aloud Anthologies* for kindergarten through grade 2, the *Library Books Collections* for kindergarten through grade 6, and several other formats.

**Q** **What genres can students meet through read-alouds?**

**A** Students encounter a wide variety of literary genres and expository texts through read-aloud selections in all grades. Expository nonfiction becomes more prevalent as students move up the grades. Other genres include poetry, finger plays, folktales, myths, and narrative nonfiction. In lessons in grades 3-6 with focus skills, such as narrative elements or text structure, the genre of the read-aloud selection matches the genre of the reading selection.

**Q** **What kind of instruction accompanies read-aloud selections in *Trophies*?**

**A** In kindergarten and grade 1, the instruction that accompanies Sharing Literature includes three options:
- Build Concept Vocabulary
- Develop Listening Comprehension
- Listen and Respond

In grade 2, options include Develop Listening Comprehension, Set a Purpose, and Recognize Genre. The instructional focus in kindergarten centers on concepts about print and beginning narrative analysis (characters, setting, important events). As students move up the grades, they are taught more complex literary skills, such as following the structure of stories, recognizing their beginnings, middles, and endings, and even occasionally generating alternative endings. In grades 3–6, read-alouds also serve as a vehicle for exploring expository text structures.

## Look for

✓ Daily "Sharing Literature" activities in Kindergarten through Grade 2
✓ Read-aloud selections and instruction with every lesson in Grades 2–6
✓ *Library Books Collections* at all grades
✓ *Read-Aloud Anthologies* in Kindergarten through Grade 2

# COMPREHENSION

Reading comprehension is the complex process of constructing meaning from texts. Recent comprehension research has been guided by the idea that the process is strategic and interactive.

**Comprehension is the construction of meaning through an interactive exchange of ideas between the text and the reader.** Comprehension strategies are interactive processes that allow readers to monitor and self-assess how well they understand what they are reading. These processes include determining the purpose or purposes for reading, such as to obtain information or to be entertained. After the purpose is determined, readers activate prior knowledge about the content of the text and its structure. Research has shown that the more readers know about the content of a particular text, the more likely they will understand, integrate, and remember the new information. Familiarity with the genre or text structure also fosters comprehension.

**Most students need explicit instruction in comprehension skills and strategies.** Research shows that comprehension skills and strategies are necessary for student success and that they do not develop automatically in most students. Without explicit instruction and guidance, many readers fail to acquire automatic use of these skills and strategies and show little flexibility in applying them to understand a variety of texts. Research shows that poor readers who are directly taught a particular strategy do as well as good readers who have used the strategy spontaneously. Typically, direct instruction consists of

- an explanation of what the skill or strategy is and how it aids comprehension
- modeling how to use the skill or strategy
- working directly with students as they apply the skill or strategy, offering assistance as needed
- having students apply the skill or strategy independently and repeatedly

Students need extensive direct instruction, guidance, and cumulative practice until they can independently determine the method of constructing meaning that works for them.

**Students need to learn strategies for comprehending a wide variety of texts, including both fiction and nonfiction.** In kindergarten, students should be taught to understand narrative structure. They should learn to identify the beginning, middle, and ending of a story and other literary elements, such as characters and setting. Then they can use their knowledge of these elements to retell stories they have listened to. In first through third grade, readers deepen their knowledge of these narrative elements and interact with others as book discussants and literary meaning makers. They learn to use the specific language of literature study, such as *point of view* and *character trait*. By grades 4–6, students must have the skills, strategies, and knowledge of text structures to comprehend complex nonfiction texts, including those in the classroom content areas. Students need to be explicitly and systematically taught the organizational structure of expository text, e.g., compare/contrast, cause/effect, and main idea and details. These organizational structures should be taught systematically and reviewed cumulatively.

**" One of the fundamental understandings about the nature of reading is that it is a constructive act. Specifically, a reader does not extract meaning from a page, but constructs meaning from information on the page and information already in his/her mind. "**

— Isabel L. Beck
Professor of Education and Senior Scientist at the Learning Research and Development Center, University of Pittsburgh

**Q** How does *Trophies* provide explicit instruction in comprehension?

**A** *Trophies* features systematic and explicit comprehension instruction grounded in current and confirmed research. Comprehension instruction in kindergarten focuses on helping students construct meaning from stories read to them. From the earliest grades, teachers guide students before, during, and after reading in the use of strategies to monitor comprehension. Guided comprehension questions ask students to apply a variety of comprehension skills and strategies appropriate to particular selections. Each tested skill is introduced, reinforced, assessed informally, retaught as needed, reviewed at least twice, and maintained throughout each grade level.

**Q** How does comprehension instruction in *Trophies* build through the grades?

**A** Comprehension instruction in *Trophies* is rigorous, developmental, and spiraled. Students gain increasingly sophisticated skills and strategies to help them understand texts successfully. In the instructional components of the earliest grades, emergent and beginning readers develop use of strategies as they respond to texts read by the teacher, and more advanced students begin to apply skills and strategies to texts they read themselves. Students demonstrate their comprehension through asking and answering questions, retelling stories, discussing characters, comparing stories, and making and confirming predictions. As students progress through the grades, they build upon their existing skills and read a more extensive variety of texts.

**Q** How is instruction in genres and text structures developed in the program?

**A** The foundation of *Trophies* is a wide variety of fiction and nonfiction selections, including many paired selections to promote reading across texts. Instruction in both the *Pupil Edition* and *Teacher's Edition* helps students develop a thorough understanding of genre characteristics and text structures. In kindergarten, students explore story elements, such as characters, setting, and important events. As students move up the grades, they analyze both literary elements and devices and expository organizational patterns, such as cause/effect and compare/contrast, to understand increasingly difficult texts.

## Look for

- ✔ Focus Strategies and Focus Skills
- ✔ Diagnostic Checks
- ✔ Additional Support Activities
- ✔ Guided Comprehension
- ✔ Strategies Good Readers Use
- ✔ Ongoing Assessment
- ✔ Comprehension Cards

# VOCABULARY

A large and flexible vocabulary is the hallmark of an educated person. The more words students acquire, the better chance they will have for success in reading, writing, and spelling.

**S**tudents acquire vocabulary knowledge through extensive reading in a variety of texts. The amount of reading students do in and out of school is a strong indicator of students' vocabulary acquisition. Research supports exposing students to rich language environments through listening to literature and reading a variety of genres independently. Their vocabulary knowledge grows when they hear stories containing unfamiliar words. As students progress through the grades, their reading of books and other materials contributes more significantly to vocabulary knowledge than viewing television, participating in conversations, or other typical oral language activities. In other words, increasing students' volume of reading is the best way to promote vocabulary growth.

**S**tudents need multiple encounters with key vocabulary words in order to improve comprehension. Current and confirmed research has shown that students need to encounter a word several times before it is known well enough to facilitate comprehension. Direct instruction in vocabulary has an important role here because learning words from context is far from automatic. After being introduced to new words, students need opportunities to see those words again in their reading and to develop their own uses for the words in a variety of different contexts, in relationship to other words, and both inside and outside of the classroom. For instruction to enhance comprehension, new words need to become a permanent part of students' repertoires, which means instruction must go well beyond providing information on word meanings.

**S**tudents can benefit from direct instruction in vocabulary strategies. Although estimates of vocabulary size and growth vary, children likely learn between 1,000 and 5,000 words per year—and the average child learns about 3,000 words. Since wide reading provides a significant source for increasing word knowledge, it is imperative that students learn key strategies to help them learn new words as they are encountered. Vocabulary strategies students should know by third grade include

- using a dictionary and other reference sources to understand the meanings of unknown words
- using context to determine the meanings of unfamiliar words
- learning about the relationships between words (synonyms, antonyms, and multiple-meaning words)
- exploring shades of meaning of words that are synonyms or near-synonyms
- using morphemic analysis—breaking words into meaning-bearing components, such as prefixes and roots

At grades 3 and above, morphemic analysis becomes an even more valuable dimension of vocabulary instruction. For example, learning just one root, *astro*, can help students unlock the meanings of such words as *astronaut*, *astronomy*, *astrology*, and *astrological*.

**❝** Research on vocabulary shows that for learners to come to know words in a meaningful way, they need to engage with word meanings and build habits of attending to words and exploring their uses in thoughtful and lively ways. **❞**

— Margaret C. McKeown
**Research Scientist**
**Learning Research and Development Center,**
**University of Pittsburgh**

**Q How does *Trophies* provide exposure to a wide variety of texts?**

**A** *Trophies* provides students with a wealth of opportunities to read a rich variety of texts. The *Pupil Editions,* the nucleus of the program in grades 1–6, feature a variety of high-quality literature selections that help students build vocabulary. *Trophies* also provides students with extensive reading opportunities through such components as these:

- *Big Books* (kindergarten and grade 1)
- *Read-Aloud Anthologies* (kindergarten through grade 2)
- *Library Books Collections* (kindergarten through grade 6)
- *Books for All Learners* (grades 1–6)
- *Intervention Readers* (grades 2–6)
- *Teacher's Edition* Read-Aloud Selections (grades 2–6)

**Q How does the program provide multiple exposures to key vocabulary?**

**A** Students are given many rich exposures to key vocabulary through the following program features:

- Vocabulary in context on *Teaching Transparencies*
- *Pupil Edition* and *Teacher's Edition* Vocabulary Power pages
- *Pupil Edition* main selections
- Word Study pages of the *Teacher's Edition* (grades 3–6)
- Additional Support Activities in the *Teacher's Edition*
- *Practice Books*
- *Books for All Learners*
- *Intervention Readers*

**Q How does *Trophies* facilitate the teaching of vocabulary-learning strategies?**

**A** Lessons include explicit teaching and modeling of vocabulary strategies. Specific lessons in both the *Pupil Edition* and *Teacher's Edition* provide direct instruction that helps enable students to increase their vocabulary every time they read. Strategies include using a dictionary, using context to determine word meaning, and understanding word structures and word relationships.

## Look for

- ✓ Building Background and Vocabulary
- ✓ *Big Book* lessons
- ✓ Listening Comprehension
- ✓ Word Study (grades 3–6)
- ✓ Lessons on word relationships and word structure (grades 3–6)
- ✓ Additional Support Activities

# FLUENCY

Research recognizes fluency as a strong indicator of efficient and proficient reading. A fluent reader reads with accuracy at an appropriate rate, attending to phrasing. When the reading is oral, it reflects a speech-like pace.

**O**ral fluency is reading with speed, accuracy, and prosody—meaning that the reader uses stress, pitch, and juncture of spoken language. Researchers have repeatedly demonstrated the relationship between fluency and reading comprehension. If a reader must devote most of his or her cognitive attention to pronouncing words, comprehension suffers. It follows then that students who read fluently can devote more attention to meaning and thus increase their comprehension. This is why oral reading fluency is an important goal of reading instruction, especially in the elementary grades. Word recognition must be automatic—freeing cognitive resources for comprehending text. If word recognition is labored, cognitive resources are consumed by decoding, leaving little or no resources for interpretation. In kindergarten and at the beginning of grade 1, oral reading may sound less like speech because students are still learning to decode and to identify words. Nevertheless, with appropriate support, text that "fits," and time to practice, students soon begin to read simple texts in a natural, more fluent, manner. By the beginning of grade 2, many students have come to enjoy the sounds of their own voices reading. They choose to read and reread with the natural sounds of spoken language and have few interruptions due to inadequate word attack or word recognition problems.

Fluent readers can
- recognize words automatically
- group individual words into meaningful phrases
- apply strategies rapidly to identify unknown words
- determine where to place emphasis or pause to make sense of a text

**F**luency can be developed through directed reading practice, opportunities for repeated reading, and other instructional strategies. The primary method to improve fluency is directed reading practice in accessible texts. Practice does not replace instruction; it provides the reader opportunity to gain speed and accuracy within manageable text. One form of directed reading practice is repeated reading, which gives a developing reader more time and chances with the same text.

Repeated reading
- provides practice reading words in context
- produces gains in reading rate, accuracy, and comprehension
- helps lower-achieving readers

**❝** Children gain reading fluency when they can read at a steady rate, recognizing words accurately and achieving correctness in phrasing and intonation. **❞**

— Nancy Roser
Professor, Language and Literacy Studies
The University of Texas at Austin

**(Q) How does *Trophies* teach and assess oral reading fluency?**

**(A)** Toward developing fluent readers, *Trophies* provides explicit, systematic phonics instruction to build word recognition skills that enable students to become efficient decoders. (See the Phonics section of these pages for more information.) *Trophies* also provides the following tools that enable teachers to assess student progress on an ongoing basis:

- Oral reading passages in the back of each *Teacher's Edition* (Grades 2–6)
- Guidelines teachers use these passages to help (Grades 2–6)
- *Oral Reading Fluency Assessment*

**(Q) How does *Trophies* provide intervention for students who are not developing oral reading fluency at an appropriate pace?**

**(A)** In the grades 2–6 *Intervention Resource Kit*, every day of instruction includes a fluency builder activity. Students are assigned repeated readings with cumulative texts. These readings begin with word lists, expand to include multiple sentences, and eventually become extended self-selected passages. Fluency performance-assessment activities are also provided in the *Intervention Teacher's Guides*.

**(Q) How does *Trophies* provide opportunities for repeated readings?**

**(A)** In grades 1–6, the Rereading for Fluency features offer a wide variety of engaging activities that have students reread with a focus on expression, pacing, and intonation. These activities include

- **Echo Reading**—Students repeat (echo) what the teacher reads aloud.
- **Choral Reading**—Students read aloud with the teacher simultaneously.
- **Repeated Reading**—The teacher models, and students reread several times until fluency is gained.
- **Readers Theatre**—Students assume roles and read them aloud from the text.

## Look for

✓ **Rereading for Fluency**
✓ **Oral reading passages in the *Teacher's Edition***
✓ ***Oral Reading Fluency Assessment***
✓ ***Intervention Teacher's Guides***

# ASSESSMENT

Assessment is integral to instruction. By choosing the appropriate assessment tools and methods, you can find out where your students are instructionally and plan accordingly.

**Assessment is the process of collecting information in order to make instructional decisions about students.** Good decisions require good information and to provide this information, assessment of students and their learning must be continuous. Because the reading process is composed of many complex skills, such as comprehension, word attack, and synthesis of information, no one assessment tool can evaluate completely all aspects of reading. Teachers need to gather information about their students in many ways, both formally and informally. Assessment helps them plan instruction, and ongoing assessments throughout the instructional process should guide their decisions and actions.

**Assessment must systematically inform instruction and help teachers differentiate instruction.** The first tool the classroom teacher requires is an entry-level assessment instrument to identify students' instructional level and potential for participating in grade-level instruction. This diagnostic instrument should be sensitive to gaps and strengths in student learning. After placement, teachers need differentiation strategies that are flexible and that can be easily adapted according to continual monitoring of student progress.

**Assessments for monitoring progress should be used to determine ongoing priorities for instruction.** The use of both formal and informal tools and strategies, including formative and summative assessments, provides a comprehensive picture of students' achievement as they progress through an instructional program. Informal assessments encourage teachers to observe students as they read, write, and discuss. These assessments provide immediate feedback and allow teachers to quickly determine which students are having difficulty and need additional instruction and practice. Formal assessments

provide opportunities for teachers to take a more focused look at how students are progressing. Whether formal or informal, monitoring instruments and activities should be

- frequent
- ongoing
- easy to score and interpret

Teachers should be provided with clear options for monitoring and clear pathways for providing intervention and enrichment as needed. Less frequent summative assessments may be used to gauge long-term growth.

**Student progress needs to be communicated to parents and guardians on a regular basis.** As students become more accountable for their learning through standards-based testing, teachers are becoming more accountable not only to administrators but also to families. A complete instructional program should offer means for teachers to communicate with families about how their students are progressing and how families can contribute to students' growth.

> **" Knowing how well a student can use literacy skills such as reading, writing, listening, and speaking is vital to effective instruction. "**
>
> — **Roger Farr**
> Chancellor's Professor and Director of the
> Center for Innovation in Assessment,
> Indiana University, Bloomington

**Q** **How does *Trophies* integrate entry-level group and individual assessments with instruction?**

**A** The *Placement and Diagnostic Assessment* provides an overview of specific diagnostic information about prerequisite skills for each grade level. In addition, *Reading and Language Skills Assessment* pretests can be used to determine whether students need additional instruction and practice in phonics, comprehension skills, vocabulary, writing, and writing conventions.

**Q** **What monitoring instruments are included with *Trophies*?**

**A** Formative assessments that facilitate monitoring student progress include

- Diagnostic Checks at point of use for immediate assessment of understanding, with follow-up Additional Support Activities in the *Teacher's Edition*
- Ongoing Assessment to assess and model the use of reading strategies, in the *Teacher's Edition*
- *Intervention Assessment Book*
- Performance Assessment activities in the *Teacher's Edition*
- *End-of-Selection Tests* to monitor students' comprehension of each selection

In each theme's *Teacher's Edition*, the Theme Assessment to Plan Instruction section provides a clear road map for using assessment to adapt instruction to student needs.

**Q** **What other assessment instruments are used in *Trophies*?**

**A** The *Reading and Language Skills Assessment*, which includes posttests for end-of-theme assessment and Mid-Year and End-of-Year Tests, provides information about students' mastery of reading skills. Other assessment instruments in *Trophies* include

- *Holistic Assessment*, which uses authentic, theme-related passages and provides a more global, holistic evaluation of students' reading and writing ability
- *Oral Reading Fluency Assessment*, which monitors accuracy and rate
- *Assessment Handbook* (Kindergarten)

## Look for

**In the *Teacher's Edition***
- ✓ Diagnostic Checks
- ✓ Ongoing Assessment
- ✓ Performance Assessment
- ✓ Theme Assessment to Plan Instruction

**Other Components**
- ✓ *Placement* and *Diagnostic Assessments*
- ✓ *Reading and Language Skills Assessment* (Pretests and Posttests)
- ✓ *Holistic Assessment*
- ✓ *Oral Reading Fluency Assessment*
- ✓ *Assessment Handbook* (Kindergarten)

# WRITING

Good writing skills are critical both to students'
academic achievement and to their future success
in society.

**W**riting instruction should incorporate explicit modeling and practice in the conventions of written English. All students can benefit from systematic instruction and practice in spelling, grammar, usage, mechanics, and presentation skills, such as handwriting and document preparation. Mastering these conventions enables students to communicate their ideas and information clearly and effectively.

- In kindergarten, children should use their growing knowledge of language structure and the conventions of print to begin expressing their ideas through words and pictures and putting these ideas into writing, with words spelled phonetically.

- In grades 1–3, students should continue to transfer their developing reading skills to writing conventions by using their knowledge of word structure and phonics to spell new words. They should learn and apply the fundamentals of grammar, mechanics, and sentence structure.

- In grades 4–6, instruction should build advanced spelling, grammar, and mechanics skills and should apply them in student writing of narratives, descriptions, and other extended compositions. Students should be systematically taught to apply writing conventions in purposeful writing activities.

**S**tudents should learn about and practice the process skills that good writers use. Many students do not realize, until they are told, that most stories and articles are not written in one sitting. Good writers plan, revise, rewrite, and rethink during the process of writing. Instruction in writing processes can spring from author features and interviews with the writers whose works students are reading. The teacher's modeling of effective prewriting, drafting, revising, proofreading, and publishing techniques should build upon this understanding. Particular attention should systematically be paid to revision strategies such as adding, deleting, clarifying, and rearranging text. Students

should apply these strategies to their own work repeatedly and should learn new techniques gradually and cumulatively.

**S**ystematic instruction in writer's craft skills should be applied to the process. Students should be taught that, whatever the form of their writing, they must determine a clear focus, organize their ideas, use effective word choice and sentence structures, and express their own viewpoint. These writer's craft skills should be taught through focused exercises and writing tasks and should be reinforced cumulatively in lessons that teach the elements of longer writing forms.

> **“** Effective writing is both an art and a science. The ability to generate interesting ideas and a pleasing style characterizes the art side; mastering the craft and its conventions characterizes the science side. Good instruction judiciously attends to both. **”**
>
> — **Dorothy S. Strickland**
> **The State of New Jersey**
> **Professor of Reading,**
> **Rutgers University**

**Q How does *Trophies* provide instruction and practice in the conventions of written English?**

**A** *Trophies* provides systematic, explicit instruction and abundant practice in spelling, grammar, usage, and mechanics in daily, easy-to-use lessons. Transparencies, activities, and practice sheets are provided for modeling and practice. Presentation skills are also formally taught, with an emphasis on handwriting at the lower grades. Spelling instruction, especially at the primary grades, is closely linked to phonics instruction. All skills of conventions are applied in purposeful writing activities.

**Q How does *Trophies* teach the process of writing?**

**A** From the earliest grades, students using *Trophies* learn that good writers plan and revise their writing. Students are guided through the prewriting, drafting, revising, and proofreading stages with models, practice activities, graphic organizers, and checklists. Instruction in presentation skills, such as handwriting and speaking, guides the publishing stage. Teacher rubrics for evaluation are provided at point of use, and reproducible student rubrics are provided in the back of the *Teacher's Edition*.

**Q How does *Trophies* apply writer's craft instruction to the writing process?**

**A** In kindergarten, students begin to write sentences and brief narratives about familiar experiences. Students also engage in shared and interactive writing in kindergarten through grade 2. In grades 1 and 2, instruction in story grammar and sentence types becomes more sophisticated, with students learning about and applying one component, such as capitalization, at a time. In grades 2–6, explicit writer's craft lessons are built into the writing strand and follow this format:

- Weeks 1 and 2 of the unit present writer's craft skills, such as organizing, choosing words, and writing effective sentences. Students complete targeted exercises and apply the craft in relatively brief writing forms.
- Weeks 3 and 4 present longer writing forms, emphasizing the steps of the writing process. The writer's craft skills learned in Weeks 1 and 2 are applied in longer compositions.
- In grades 3–6, Week 5 presents a timed writing test in which students apply what they have learned.

## Look for

✔ Writer's Craft lessons
✔ Writing Process lessons
✔ Timed or Tested Writing lessons
✔ 5-day grammar and spelling lessons
✔ Traits of good writing

# LISTENING AND SPEAKING

Increasingly, young people must comprehend, and are expected to create, messages that are oral and visual rather than strictly written. Listening and speaking skills are essential to achievement in both reading and writing.

**Listening to narratives, poetry, and nonfiction texts builds thinking and language skills that students need for success in reading and writing.** The domains of the language arts (listening, speaking, reading, and writing) are closely connected. Listening instruction and speaking instruction are critical scaffolds that support reading comprehension, vocabulary knowledge, and oral communication skills. Classroom instruction must be focused on these skills and must also strategically address the needs of students with limited levels of language experience or whose language experiences are primarily in languages other than English.

**Listening instruction and speaking instruction should progress developmentally through the grades.** In the primary grades, instruction should focus on

- listening to and retelling stories, with an emphasis on story grammar (setting, characters, and important events)
- explicit modeling of standard English structures, with frequent opportunities to repeat sentences and recite rhymes and songs
- brief oral presentations about familiar topics and experiences
- developing familiarity with academic and literary terms

**As students move up the grades, they should develop increasingly sophisticated listening and speaking skills, including the more complex production skills.** By grades 4–6, students should be increasingly capable of

- delivering both narrative and expository presentations using a range of narrative and rhetorical devices
- modeling their own presentations on effective text structures they have analyzed in their reading
- orally responding to literature in ways that demonstrate advanced understanding and insight
- supporting their interpretations with facts and specific examples
- interpreting and using verbal and nonverbal messages
- analyzing oral and visual messages, purposes, and persuasive techniques

" Oral response activities encourage critical thinking and allow students to bring their individuality to the process of responding to literature. "

— **Hallie Kay Yopp**
Professor
Department of Elementary Bilingual
and Reading Education,
California State University, Fullerton

**Q** **How does *Trophies* provide rich listening experiences that build understanding of language structures and texts?**

**A** From the very first day of kindergarten through the end of grade 6, *Trophies* provides abundant and varied texts, support, and modeling for listening instruction. With resources such as *Big Books, Read-Aloud Anthologies,* and Audiotext of the reading selections, the teacher has every type of narrative and expository text available. *Trophies* also provides direct instruction and engaging response activities so that teachers can use each listening selection to its full advantage. The *English-Language Learners Resource Kit* provides additional opportunities for students with special needs to develop an understanding of English language structure, concept vocabulary and background, and listening comprehension skills.

**Q** **How does *Trophies* develop listening through the grades?**

**A** Listening is developed through the Sharing Literature features in kindergarten through grade 2 with such options as Build Concept Vocabulary, Develop Listening Comprehension, and Listen and Respond and through the *Read-Aloud Anthologies.* In grades 3–6, read-alouds serve as a vehicle for setting a purpose for listening and develop listening comprehension and listening strategies.

**Q** **How does *Trophies* provide instruction in speaking and in making presentations?**

**A** *Trophies* provides instruction to guide students in making both narrative and expository presentations. In kindergarten, each lesson offers formal and informal speaking opportunities through the Share Time feature. In grades 1 and 2, speaking activities are included in the Rereading for Fluency and in the Wrap-Up sections of the lesson. The Morning Message feature in kindergarten through grade 2 provides additional informal speaking opportunities. In grades 3–6, presentation skills become more sophisticated. Students are asked to make such presentations as extended oral reports, multimedia presentations, debates, and persuasive speeches.

## Look for

- ✓ **Develop Listening Comprehension**
- ✓ **Daily "Sharing Literature" activities (Kindergarten through Grade 2)**
- ✓ **Read-Aloud selections and instruction with every lesson (Grades 2–6)**
- ✓ **Morning Message (Kindergarten–Grade 2)**
- ✓ **Author's Chair presentations (Kindergarten–Grade 2)**
- ✓ **Rereading for Fluency**
- ✓ **Listening and Speaking Lessons (Grades 3–6)**
- ✓ **Presentation Rubrics (Grades 2–6)**
- ✓ ***Read-Aloud Anthologies* (Kindergarten–Grade 2)**

# RESEARCH AND INFORMATION SKILLS

Today's increasing amount of accessible information and ideas mandates an explicit approach to research and information skills and strategies.

**Information is more widely available to the general public than ever before, and having the skills and strategies to effectively access and produce information is increasingly important.** Evaluating and producing electronically transmitted information is becoming a basic literacy skill, as well as a skill that can lead to a more rewarding working life. Students who do not receive instruction in information skills are at a clear disadvantage. The goal of such instruction should be to prepare students to carry these skills into many areas so that students can be independent seekers, consumers, and providers of information throughout their lives.

**Instruction in research and information skills should begin at an early age.** By grade 2, students should be learning to choose reference sources for specific purposes, such as to clarify word meanings or to find colorful, exact words for their own writing. In grade 3, students should refine their dictionary skills and become familiar with the structure of other reference sources, such as atlases and encyclopedias. In grade 4 and above, students should become more proficient with

- using a variety of print and electronic information media, such as newspapers, almanacs, library catalogs, and other online sources
- basic keyboarding and word processing skills
- computer usage skills, such as efficient Internet searching and document creation
- using tables of contents, indexes, and other document features to locate information
- taking notes efficiently
- evaluating the quality of information
- finding information in a library
- using reference sources as an aid to writing

**As students move up the grades, they should learn to produce and deliver increasingly lengthy, well-researched informational reports.** Because the language arts domains (reading, writing, listening, and speaking) are closely interrelated, the text structures students learn through their reading become structures they can use to effectively present their own research. Skills such as identifying the main idea of a nonfiction selection should be explicitly incorporated into writing assignments at the upper grades. Students should be able to compose, revise, edit, and publish their research findings by using a computer. Other skills for students in the upper grades include substantive inquiry, framing questions to develop the research logically, identifying and securing multiple reference sources, analyzing and synthesizing information, and summarizing and evaluating the research results.

**Q** How does *Trophies* provide instruction in using reference sources, including computer-based resources?

**A** Direct instruction is provided through explicit skill lessons. Instruction includes such skills as recognizing authoritative sources and evaluating information. These lessons include

- Using a Dictionary
- Locating Information: Online Information
- Locating Information: Text Features/Book Parts
- Locating Information: Newspapers, Magazines, and Reference Sources
- Search Techniques

**Q** What technological resources are available for use by students with *Trophies*?

**A** *The Learning Site* (www.harcourtschool.com) offers, among many other features, motivating, interactive activities that challenge students to practice and apply skills taught in the *Pupil Edition* and *Teacher's Edition*.

Other resources available for students include

- *Writing Express™ CD-ROMs* (activities that provide reinforcement of language and writing skills)
- *Mission: Comprehension™ Reading Skills Practice* (practice and reinforcement of comprehension skills)
- *Phonics Express™ CD-ROM* (captivating games and activities that reinforce phonics skills)
- *Media Literacy and Communication Skills Package™* (a set of videotapes and accompanying Teacher's Guides that reinforce listening, speaking, viewing and presentation skills)

**Q** How are students taught to develop research reports and other informational projects?

**A** In grades 1–2, the Making Connections sections in the *Pupil Edition* and the Cross-Curricular Centers in the *Teacher's Editions* offer activities that require students to gather and present. In grades 3–6, students engage in a full theme's worth of instruction in all stages of writing a research report, including gathering information, note-taking, outlining, drafting, revising, and publishing. Students also have the opportunity to use information and research skills to complete a theme project, which involves formulating research questions and recording and presenting their research findings.

## Look for

- ✔ Skill lessons with Teaching Transparencies
- ✔ Research Report Writing lessons
- ✔ Theme Projects
- ✔ Presentation Rubrics
- ✔ Technology Integrated with the lesson plans

# REACHING ALL LEARNERS

Students come to school with diverse experiences and language backgrounds. Teachers, who are charged with providing universal access to high-quality instruction, require specially designed plans and materials to help all students meet or exceed grade-level standards.

**Curriculum and instruction must be carefully planned to provide for students who need varying levels of intervention and challenge.** Students require additional instruction, practice, and extension at different times and in different degrees. Some students need occasional reteaching and slight modifications in pacing, while others are at greater risk and require more intensive intervention. Research shows that students with learning difficulties need more review and practice to perform a new task automatically. Instruction should cumulatively integrate simpler or previously learned tasks with newer, more complex activities. In addition, research shows the following:

■ Reading difficulties can stem from inaccuracy in identifying words.

■ Intervention should be geared toward a student's level of reading development.

■ Diagnostic testing results should show what students know and what they need to know; frequent assessment is critical.

■ Instruction should be direct and explicit.

**Curriculum and instruction must be structured to meet the needs of English-language learners.** The 2000 U.S. Census confirmed what many educators already knew: more and more students do not speak English as their first language. Widely ranging levels of English proficiency in mainstream classrooms present special challenges and opportunities for teachers. Depending on their level of English acquisition and their grade placement, English-language learners need varying degrees of additional support in areas such as oral language, English phonology, vocabulary, background information, and the academic language of school.

**Students who already meet or exceed grade-level expectations need opportunities for enrichment or acceleration.** They need to be challenged by vocabulary extension study and exposure to sophisticated literature in a variety of genres. Students may also be encouraged to carry out investigations that extend their learning. Such activities should promote sustained investigative skills: raising questions, researching answers, and organizing information. Several research studies have shown the importance of setting high standards for advanced learners. An instructional program that clearly provides for differentiation at a variety of levels can be the tool teachers need to provide universal access to high-level standards.

> " In the process of helping students learn, we want to support them in discovering that each person is unique and has a unique contribution to make towards creating a better world for all. "
>
> — **Alma Flor Ada**
> Director of Doctoral Studies in the
> International Multicultural Program
> University of San Francisco
>
> — **F. Isabel Campoy**
> Former President, Association of
> Spanish Professionals in the USA

**Q** **How does _Trophies_ provide differentiated instruction at a variety of levels?**

**A** _Trophies_ was designed to accommodate a diverse student population, with tiers of differentiation for different needs. Diagnostic Checks, with brief activities, are positioned at point of use within each lesson in the _Teacher's Edition_ so that specific needs of students can be identified and addressed. Additional Support Activities, tied closely to the lessons, are provided for further differentiation. The three types of activities address below-level readers, advanced students, and English-language learners. In addition, Alternative Teaching Strategies are provided for students who perform below level on the _Reading and Language Skills Assessments._ The _Library Books Collections_ and the _Books for All Learners_ also provide students at all levels with a wealth of reading opportunities in a variety of genres.

**Q** **What additional support does _Trophies_ provide?**

**A** An _Intervention Resource Kit_ and an _English-Language Learners Resource Kit_ are available for students with greater needs. Both kits

- align closely with the core program
- provide rigorous daily lessons
- provide abundant cumulative, spiraled practice

For below-level readers, the _Intervention Resource Kit_ preteaches and reteaches the same skills and concepts that are taught in the core program. The _English-Language Learners Resource Kit_ builds background, vocabulary and concepts, academic language, comprehension, and language arts. Finally, to guide teachers in making instructional decisions, _Trophies_ provides a complete assessment program, with instruments for entry-level assessment, monitoring of progress, and summative assessment. (See the Assessment section of these pages for more information.)

## Look for

- ✓ **Reaching All Learners**
- ✓ **Diagnostic Checks**
- ✓ **Additional Support Activities**
- ✓ **Practice pages for all levels**
- ✓ **_Books for All Learners_**
- ✓ **_Intervention Resource Kit_**
- ✓ **_English-Language Learners Resource Kit_**
- ✓ **_Library Books Collections_**
- ✓ **_Placement and Diagnostic Assessments_**

# CLASSROOM MANAGEMENT

The task of managing the classroom is becoming increasingly complex. Teachers are seeking to maximize instructional effectiveness for students with a diverse range of skills and backgrounds.

**Classroom management is a critical variable related to student achievement.** Research shows that the more time teachers spend dealing with student behavior and interruptions in instruction, the more student achievement suffers. A classroom environment that promotes student growth and learning results from making effective decisions about the organization and scheduling of instruction and the physical arrangement of the classroom.

**Effective organization includes differentiating instruction to engage all students in instructional-level activities.** Grouping strategies are important for addressing diverse needs, but grouping must never be treated as an aim in itself. Flexible grouping can help ensure that all students meet instructional goals, and it can be effective in helping students participate and contribute in a learning environment. Grouping should be fluid and temporary, varying according to individual students' progress and interests and should allow time for students to function independently and be responsible for their own work. The types of instruction that are most successful in the major grouping patterns include

### Whole Group

- Sharing literature
- Developing concepts
- Providing modeling
- Presenting new knowledge

### Small Group

- Developing skills
- Practicing processes
- Collaborating on projects
- Providing challenge activities

**After flexible work groups are established, effective classroom organization should focus on scheduling classroom activities and creating a classroom arrangement that facilitates learning.** Initially, teachers might establish one or two learning centers based on tasks that are familiar to students. Then teachers can develop other centers and routines as needed. Before beginning a routine, teachers should introduce students to the procedures for using each area, ensuring that students understand what they are to do and how much time they should spend in each area. A rotation schedule should be established so that students can easily move from one area to another as tasks are completed. Helping students become familiar with schedules and routines enables the teacher to devote more time to individual and small-group instruction.

> **The organization of the classroom should provide students with many opportunities to share with teachers and other students the things they are reading and writing.**
>
> — **Roger Farr**
> Chancellor's Professor and Director of the Center for Innovation in Assessment, Indiana University, Bloomington

**Q** **How can teachers keep other students engaged in meaningful experiences while providing instruction to students with special needs?**

**A** *Trophies* provides an abundance of productive materials and ideas for independent and small-group work

- Managing the Classroom sections in the back of the *Teacher's Editions* that provide clear instructions in arranging the classroom with centers or stations, using a Work Board with center icons to help organize routines and schedules, and tracking student progress.
- Classroom Management and Reading and Writing Routines sections in the *Teacher's Editions* (grades 1–2) that provide suggestions for individual, whole-group, and small-group activities.
- Cross-Curricular Centers and Stations with pacing suggestions to regulate student participation
- Lesson-specific Workboards to help teachers manage groups and individuals simultaneously
- Integration of content from social studies, science, and other content areas
- *Books for All Learners* to allow students to read independently at their own level
- Practice pages for students with diverse skills and language backgrounds
- Theme Projects for extended group work
- Comprehension Cards, *Library Books Collections,* and other resources to facilitate group and independent reading

**Q** **How does *Trophies* help teachers manage its instructional pathways for classrooms with diverse learners?**

**A** *Trophies* provides a clear, manageable system of diagnostic assessment checkpoints, ongoing formal assessment and performance-based opportunities, and instructional pathways for teachers to follow based on results. In addition to easy-to-use lesson planners that include suggested pacing, the system provides

- Diagnostic Checks and customized activities at point of use
- Additional Support Activities to reinforce, reteach, and extend key concepts in every lesson
- *Intervention Resource Kits* and *English-Language Learners Resource Kits* for more intensive instruction
- Alternative Teaching Strategies for additional options to modify instruction

For more information, see Theme Assessment to Plan Instruction in each *Teacher's Edition.*

## Look for

✔ Diagnostic Checks
✔ Cross-Curricular Centers or Stations
✔ Work Boards
✔ *Books for All Learners*
✔ *Library Books Collections*
✔ Practice pages
✔ Theme Projects
✔ Comprehension Cards
✔ Managing the Classroom

# Contents

Contents   **xxxi**

# Reference Materials

## School-Home Connections

## Additional Reading

## Additional Resources

# Introducing the Book

## Discuss the Title and Cover Illustration

Invite students to discuss the title and the cover illustration. Ask what the title, *Lead the Way,* might mean. Discuss how the horse on the cover might be leading the way and what feelings the cover illustration conveys.

## Discuss the Book's Organization

**Discuss the letter to the reader.** Have students read the letter on page 3 of the *Pupil Edition.* Invite volunteers to give examples of hopes and dreams that people might have for the future and how their goals might be achieved.

**Examine other parts of the book.** Have students turn to each feature. Briefly discuss how each part helps readers use the book and understand the literature.

- Table of Contents—shows titles, authors, and page numbers
- Using Reading Strategies—describes tools readers can use
- Theme Table of Contents—lists literature in that theme
- Vocabulary Power—introduces selection vocabulary words
- Genre Notes and Labels—describe the different types of literature
- Making Connections—provides questions and activities relating to the literature
- Focus Skill—provides instruction in skills relating to the literature
- Test Preparation—reinforces the Focus Skill with sample test questions
- Writer's Handbook—explains the writing process and how to use reference sources
- Glossary—contains all vocabulary words and their definitions
- Index—provides page numbers of alphabetized literature titles and authors

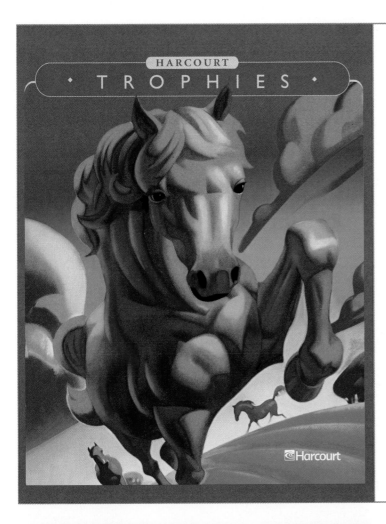

### HARCOURT
· T R O P H I E S ·

A HARCOURT READING/LANGUAGE ARTS PROGRAM

LEAD THE WAY

SENIOR AUTHORS
Isabel L. Beck ◆ Roger C. Farr ◆ Dorothy S. Strickland

AUTHORS
Alma Flor Ada ◆ Marcia Brechtel ◆ Margaret McKeown
Nancy Roser ◆ Hallie Kay Yopp

SENIOR CONSULTANT
Asa G. Hilliard III

CONSULTANTS
F. Isabel Campoy ◆ David A. Monti

**Harcourt**
Orlando  Boston  Dallas  Chicago  San Diego

Visit *The Learning Site!*
www.harcourtschool.com

Requests for permission to make copies of any part of the work should be addressed to School Permissions and Copyrights, Harcourt, Inc., 6277 Sea Harbor Drive, Orlando, Florida 32887-6777. Fax: 407-345-2418.

HARCOURT and the Harcourt Logo are trademarks of Harcourt, Inc., registered in the United States of America and/or other jurisdictions.

Acknowledgments appear in the back of this book.

Printed in the United States of America

ISBN 0-15-322478-9

1 2 3 4 5 6 7 8 9 10  048  10 09 08 07 06 05 04 03 02 01

### HARCOURT
· T R O P H I E S ·

A HARCOURT READING/LANGUAGE ARTS PROGRAM

LEAD THE WAY

**Dear Reader,**

We all can think of people who inspire us. They may be historical figures, friends, or family members. We look up to people who are not afraid to move ahead in a new direction.

In **Lead the Way,** you will read about people who are working toward their goals by taking bold strides. Some travel to distant lands to study rare plants, while others simply plant a garden in their neighborhood. Some help those around them, while others work to improve themselves. Some even brave the dangers of the frontier to lead the way west.

As you read this book, you will see how both real people and story characters solve problems and make the most of changes. You may find someone here to inspire you!

Now, keep your eyes and your mind wide open, turn the page, and prepare to read about people who lead the way.

Sincerely,

*The Authors*

The Authors

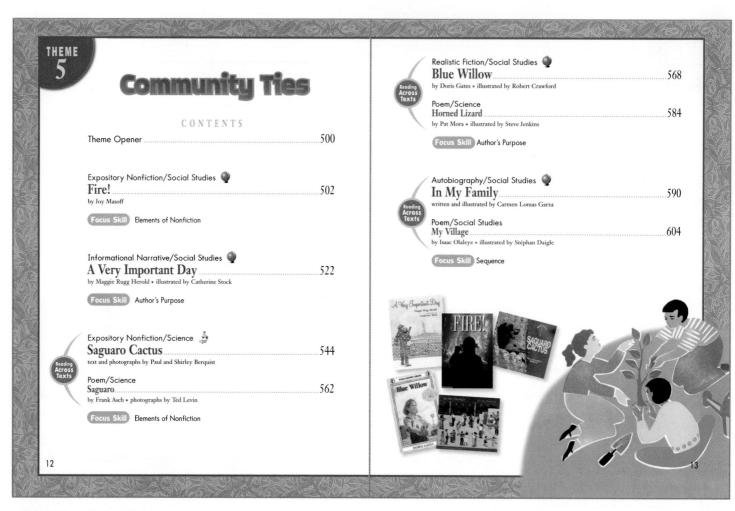

12

13

---

14

15

# Using Reading Strategies

## Introduce the Concept

Discuss with students what they do when they read. They may mention things that they do before, during, or after reading. Ask questions such as these: **What do you do to get yourself ready to read? What do you do when you don't understand something you are reading? What do you do when you come to a word you don't know?** Make a list on the board of students' answers. Tell students that they have named some good reading *strategies.* Explain that a strategy is a plan for doing something well.

## Explain Strategies Good Readers Use

Have students read pages 16–17. Explain that these are the strategies they will be focusing on as they read the selections in this book. Discuss with students a brief explanation of each strategy:

- **Use Decoding/Phonics**   Look for familiar spelling patterns and word parts to help you decode longer words as you read.

- **Make and Confirm Predictions**   Think about what might happen next in a story. Read to find out whether you are right. Make new predictions as you read.

- **Create Mental Images**   Sometimes, picturing in your mind what you are reading can help you understand and enjoy a selection. Pay attention to descriptive details.

- **Self-Question**   Have you ever found that you have questions as you are reading? Learn to ask yourself good questions as you read. This will help you check your understanding and focus on important ideas in the selection.

- **Summarize**   Tell or list the main points of the selection or the main things that happened. This will help you understand and remember what you read.

- **Read Ahead**   If you are having trouble understanding something in a selection, such as who a certain character is, don't give up. Keep on reading. The meaning may become clearer when you have more information.

- **Reread to Clarify**   If something doesn't make sense, you may have missed an important point. Try reading the passage again or going back to an earlier part of the selection.

- **Use Context to Confirm Meaning**   After you read an unfamiliar or difficult word, ask yourself whether what you read makes sense in the sentence and whether it fits what is happening in the selection. By paying attention to the words around unfamiliar words, you can learn many new words and become a stronger reader.

- **Use Text Structure and Format**   Find clues to meaning by looking at how the author organized the information. Is it arranged in time order? By main idea and details? Look at headings and captions.

- **Adjust Reading Rate**   Think about the type of selection you are reading. A selection that has a lot of facts and details, such as a selection about volcanoes, may have to be read more slowly than a story about a character your age.

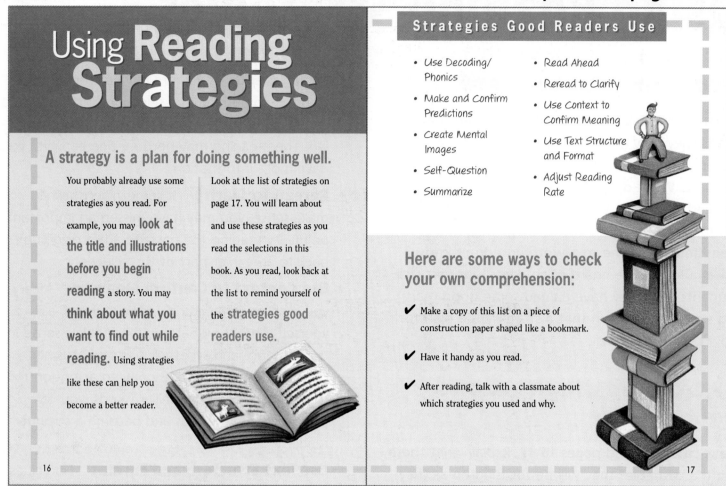

# Using Reading Strategies

**Monitor Comprehension** Distribute copies of Thinking About My Reading and Writing and My Reading Log, pages R38–R39. Have each student begin a personal reading portfolio. Students can use the forms to record how they choose self-selected books, the strategies they use during reading, how long they read outside of class each day, and other reading behaviors.

**Strategy Bookmark** Have students make a bookmark from a sheet of heavy paper and write the strategies on the bookmark. Invite students to decorate their bookmarks. As they read, they should refer to the bookmark to help remind them of the strategies they can use.

**Response Journal** Explain to students that they should keep a journal to record their responses to selections and to monitor their progress as readers. They may use a spiral-bound notebook or sheets of paper stapled together. In the notebook, they should create sections to write about which strategies work best for them and to develop their own plans for reading different kinds of selections. You may want to have them record here rather than on the My Reading Log copying master how long they read each day. They should also set aside a section of the notebook for a Word Bank, where they will list new or interesting words they come across in their reading.

# Side by Side

This theme explores situations that highlight the benefits of teamwork. Students learn that cooperation strengthens relationships, and they are encouraged to apply this concept to their own lives.

# Theme Resources

## PUPIL EDITION READING SELECTIONS

▲ **"The Baker's Neighbor,"** pages 152–169

PLAY

▲ **"The Garden of Happiness,"** pages 232–245

REALISTIC FICTION

**READING ACROSS TEXTS**

**"I do not plant my garden,"/"The City,"** pages 246–247

POETRY

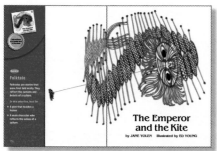

▲ **"The Emperor and the Kite,"** pages 176–197

FOLKTALE

**READING ACROSS TEXTS**

**"Kite Festivals,"** pages 198–201

MAGAZINE ARTICLE

▲ **"How to Babysit an Orangutan,"** pages 254–267

NONFICTION

▲ **"Nights of the Pufflings,"** pages 208–219

NONFICTION

**READING ACROSS TEXTS**

**"Caring for Crocs,"** pages 220–225

MAGAZINE ARTICLE

See also Intervention Reader: *Moving Ahead*

- "Can-Do Kid"
- "Small but Brave"
- "Bringing Back the Puffins"
- "Green Tomatoes"
- "A Day with the Orangutans"

 All the above selections are available on *Audiotext 2.*

## INDEPENDENT/SELF-SELECTED READING

*These books are available through Harcourt.*

### Library Books Collection

Teaching plans for the **Library Books Collection** can be found on pages **27 IQ–27 IT**.

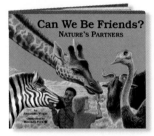

▲ **Can We Be Friends? Nature's Partners** by Alexandra Wright

▲ *The Canada Geese Quilt* by Natalie Kinsey-Warnock

## Books for All Learners

**BELOW-LEVEL**

**ON-LEVEL**

**ADVANCED**

**ELL**

Teaching suggestions for the Books for All Learners can be found on pages **173M–173P, 205K–205N, 229M–229P, 25IK–25IN, 27IK–27IN.**

**30 Minutes**

**Reading Outside of Class** Additional trade book titles can be found on page T67. Have students complete the "My Reading Log" form on page R38 for each book they read.

## TECHNOLOGY RESOURCES

*Available at The Learning Site!* www.harcourtschool.com

- *Mission: Comprehension*™ *Skills Practice* CD-ROM
- *Writing Express*™ CD-ROM
- *Grammar Jingles*™ CD-ROM
- *Media Literacy and Communication Skills Package* (Video)
- *Reading and Language Skills Assessment* CD-ROM

**Resources for Teachers**
- Graphic Organizers
- Language Support
- Classroom Management
- Lesson Planner

**Resources for Parents**
- Helping Your Child Learn to Read
- Helping Your Child Learn to Write
- Helping Your Child Take Tests
- Internet Safety
- Homework Helper

**Student Activities**
- Author/Illustrator Information
- Skill Activities
- Test Tutor
- Writing Activities
- Grammar Activities

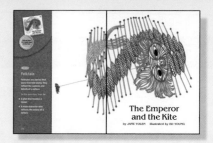

| | The Baker's Neighbor pp. 152–169 | The Emperor and the Kite pp. 176–197 |
|---|---|---|
| • **Reading**<br>• **Comprehension**<br>• **Vocabulary** | **Read** Play<br>**Guided Comprehension**<br>**Cause and Effect** T<br>**Figurative Language** T<br>**Prefixes, Suffixes, and Roots** T<br>**Selection Vocabulary**<br>*ad lib, shiftless, luxury, privilege*<br>*elated, shamefacedly, indignantly, assent* | **Read** Folktale<br>**Guided Comprehension**<br>**Read Across Texts**<br>"Kite Festivals" MAGAZINE ARTICLE<br>**Narrative Elements** T<br>**Figurative Language** T<br>**Selection Vocabulary**<br>*insignificant, plotting, twined, steely*<br>*encircling, loyal, neglected, unyielding* |
| • **Independent Reading** |  **Books for All Learners**<br>**Below-Level:** *Wise Queen Catherine*<br>**On-Level:** *Honest Neighbors*<br>**Advanced:** *The Story of Wheat*<br>**English-Language Learners:**<br>*Tea with Jam* |  **Books for All Learners**<br>**Below-Level:** *Young Jose and His Paint Box*<br>**On-Level:** *Three Kite Tales*<br>**Advanced:** *The Crystal Radio*<br>**English-Language Learners:**<br>*Inside and Outside Together* |
| • **Writing**<br>• **Grammar**<br>• **Spelling** | **WRITER'S CRAFT: Effective Paragraphs**<br>**WRITING FORM: Paragraph of Information**<br>**Complete and Simple Predicates**<br>**Words with /är/** | **WRITER'S CRAFT: Effective Paragraphs**<br>**WRITING FORM: Written Directions**<br>**Compound Subjects and Predicates**<br>**Words with /ôr/** |
| • **Cross-Curricular Stations** |  **Social Studies**<br>Participating in Government<br> **Science**<br>The Nose Knows |  **Social Studies**<br>Research Government in the United States<br> **Math**<br>Find the Perimeter and the Area |

**T** = tested skill

## Nights of the Pufflings
### pp. 208–219

**Read** Nonfiction

**Guided Comprehension**

**Read Across Texts**
"Caring for Crocs" MAGAZINE ARTICLE

**Summarize** T

**Search Techniques**

**Locate Information**

**Selection Vocabulary**

uninhabited, burrows, venture

stranded, nestles, instinctively

 **Books for All Learners**

**Below-Level:** *The Bird on the Beach*

**On-Level:** *Summer Mystery*

**Advanced:** *Fire and Ice*

**English-Language Learners:**
*Beaks and Wings*

**WRITING PROCESS: Summary** T

**APPLYING WRITER'S CRAFT:**
**Effective Paragraphs**

**Simple and Compound Sentences**

**Words with /är/**

 **Science**
Volcanoes

 **Social Studies**
Comparing Locations

## The Garden of Happiness
### pp. 232–245

**Read** Realistic Fiction

**Guided Comprehension**

**Read Across Texts**
"I do not plant my garden"/ "The City"
POEM

**Cause and Effect** T

**Figurative Language** T

**Selection Vocabulary**

inhaled, lavender, mural, skidded, haze

 **Books for All Learners**

**Below-Level:** *Growing a City Garden*

**On-Level:** *Faces to the Sun*

**Advanced:** *Home Grown*

**English-Language Learners:**
*Sunshine Place*

**WRITING PROCESS: How-to Essay**

**APPLYING WRITER'S CRAFT:**
**Effective Paragraphs**

**Clauses**

**Words with /ûr/**

 **Science**
Growth Journal

 **Writing**
A Plant's Perspective

## How to Babysit an Orangutan
### pp. 254–267

**Read** Nonfiction

**Guided Comprehension**

**Summarize** T

**Search Techniques**

**Selection Vocabulary**

displeasure, jealous, endangered

smuggled, facial

coordination

 **Books for All Learners**

**Below-Level:** *The Rain Forest Is Their
Home*

**On-Level:** *Bravo!*

**Advanced:** *Adopting a Wild Horse*

**English-Language Learners:**
*Kid Care*

**TESTED OR TIMED WRITING:**
**Summary** T

**Complex Sentences**

**Words with /ou/**

 **Science**
Where in the World?

 **Math**
Solve a Problem

# Theme Assessment
## to Plan Instruction

## Entry-Level Assessment *Assesses essential prior knowledge and skills*

*PLACEMENT AND DIAGNOSTIC ASSESSMENT*
**Use to diagnose individual students and to make placement decisions.**

- **End-of-Selection Tests (in Practice Book)**
- **Oral Reading Fluency Assessment**

### Administer the Pretest

| Diagnosis | Prescription |
|---|---|
| **IF** performance is | **THEN** use these available resources: |
| **BELOW-LEVEL** | • Core Instruction in the Teacher's Edition<br>• Below-Level Reaching All Learners notes (at point of use in the Teacher's Edition)<br>• Extra Support Copying Masters<br>• Intervention Resources Kit |
| **ON-LEVEL** | • Core Instruction in the Teacher's Edition<br>• Cross-Curricular Stations<br>• Practice Book |
| **ADVANCED** | • Core Instruction in the Teacher's Edition<br>• Advanced Reaching All Learners notes (at point of use in the Teacher's Edition)<br>• Challenge Copying Masters |

## Monitoring of Progress *Lesson resources and assessment instruments*

- **Holistic Assessment**
- **Reading and Language Skills Assessment: Posttest**

### Assess progress and customize instruction

| Diagnosis | Prescription |
|---|---|
| **IF** students do not perform well on the<br><br>• Performance Assessments<br>• Diagnostic Checks (at point of use in the Teacher's Edition)<br>• End-of-Selection Tests (in Practice Book)<br>• Oral Reading Fluency Assessment | **THEN** choose from these available resources:<br><br>• Additional Support Activities, pp. S34–S63<br>• Books for All Learners<br>• Intervention Resources Kit<br>• Extra Support Copying Masters |
| **IF** students do perform well on the<br><br>• Performance Assessments<br>• Diagnostic Checks (at point of use in the Teacher's Edition)<br>• End-of-Selection Tests (in Practice Book)<br>• Oral Reading Fluency Assessment | **THEN** choose from these available resources:<br><br>• Additional Support Activities, pp. S34–S63<br>• Books for All Learners<br>• Challenge Copying Masters |

## Summative Assessment *Assesses mastery of theme objectives*

### Administer Theme Posttests

| Diagnosis | Prescription |
|---|---|
| **IF** performance is | **THEN** use these available resources: |
| **BELOW-LEVEL** | • Alternative Teaching Strategies, T36–T43<br>• Intervention Resources Kit<br>• Chart their progress. See pages R36–R37. |
| **ON-LEVEL** | • Chart their progress. See pages R36–R37. |
| **ADVANCED** | • Provide accelerated instruction in higher-grade-level materials.<br>• Chart their progress. See pages R36–R37. |

• **Holistic Assessment**

• **Reading and Language Skills Assessment: Posttest**

### Technology

#### Reading and Language Skills CD-ROM

Use this CD-ROM to

• administer assessments electronically
• customize assessments to focus on specific standards
• track students' progress

# Reaching All Learners

## ■ BELOW-LEVEL

### Levels of Support

**Point-of-use notes**

in Teacher's Edition, pp. 150K, 172, 173G, 174K, 204, 205E, 206K, 228, 229G, 230K, 250, 251E, 252K, 270, 271E

**Extra Support Copying Masters**

pp. 24–26, 29–30, 33–35, 38–39, 42–43

**Additional Support Activities**

Vocabulary, pp. S34–S35, S40–S41, S46–S47, S52–S53, S58–S59

Comprehension and Skills, pp. S36–S37, S42–S43, S48–S49, S54–S55, S60–S61

Grammar and Writing, pp. S38–S39, S44–S45, S50–S51, S56–S57, S62–S63

**Intervention Resources Kit**

## ■ ENGLISH-LANGUAGE LEARNERS

### Levels of Support

**Point-of-use notes**

in Teacher's Edition, pp. 150K, 172, 173G, 174K, 204, 205E, 206K, 228, 229G, 230K, 250, 251E, 252K, 270, 271E

**English-Language Learners Copying Masters**

pp. 24–26, 29–30, 33–35, 38–39, 42–43

**Additional Support Activities**

Vocabulary, pp. S34–S35, S40–S41, S46–S47, S52–S53, S58–S59

Comprehension and Skills, pp. S36–S37, S42–S43, S48–S49, S60–S61

Grammar and Writing, pp. S38–S39, S44–S45, S50–S55, S56–S57, S62–S63

**English-Language Learners Resources Kit**

Visit *The Learning Site:* www.harcourtschool.com
See Language Support

## ■ ADVANCED

# Levels of Support

### Point-of-use notes
in Teacher's Edition, pp. 150K, 172, 173G, 174K, 204, 205E, 206K, 228, 229G, 230K, 250, 251E, 252K, 270, 271E

### Challenge Copying Masters
pp. 24–26, 29–30, 33–35, 38–39, 42–43

### Additional Support Activities
Vocabulary, pp. S34–S35, S40–S41, S46–S47, S52–S53, S58–S59

Comprehension and Skills, pp. S36–S37, S44–S45, S50–S51, S56–S57, S62–S63

Grammar and Writing, pp. S38–S39, S44–S45, S50–S51, S56–S57, S62–S63

### Accelerated Instruction
• Use higher-grade-level materials for accelerated instruction.

• Theme Project, pp. 148J, 271O

# Combination Classrooms
## Reader Response Groups

Reader Response Groups meet to respond to and reflect upon a reading passage. Their purpose is to examine concerns, situations, or questions, and to clarify and share information and viewpoints on text. Readers understand text, at least initially, in terms of prior experiences. Reader Response Groups invite readers to reflect upon their reaction to and interpretation of a text and to examine the emotions, memories, associations, and ideas that reading the text provokes.

• **Before each group meeting, write several discussion starters on the board.**

• **After the group meeting, have students record their ideas in a reader response journal.**

The teacher's role in the Reader Response Group is that of facilitator. If students lack experience working in student-directed groups, you may initially need to direct the Reader Response Group discussions. Model effective methods of asking questions and probing for opinions. Find points of contact and agreement among students, but support respect for alternative opinions and interpretations. As time goes on, help students assume greater responsibility for group discussion. Then, have groups meet concurrently as you circulate among them.

# Students with Special Needs
## Using Visual Aids and Models

Using visual aids and models can aid acquisition of language and reading skills for many special-needs students. Visual aids can include diagrams, charts, maps, graphs, illustrations, videos, Web sites, photographs, and graphic organizers. When significant content is delivered through visuals, adaptations must be made for students with visual impairments. In some instances you might want to pair students who are strong visual learners with those who have visual limitations.

• **When introducing selection vocabulary** to special-needs students, draw on students' prior knowledge and experiences.

• **Relate new words** to known words, comparing semantic features, such as roots, suffixes, and prefixes.

• **Draw concept maps** to graphically portray the relationship between words and meanings.

• **Pair words with pictures or props** to teach meaning. (For instance, teach **rough** with a piece of sandpaper and **light** with a feather.)

• **Provide tactile experience** by having students build words from syllable cards and letter tiles, substituting Braille letter tiles or syllable cards, if possible, for visually impaired students.

SCIENCE

# Save a Species

## OBJECTIVE

*To research an endangered species and find out what people can do to help protect it.*

45-90 Minutes per Week

### Materials

- pencil
- note cards
- paper
- encyclopedia and nonfiction books
- computer with Internet (optional)
- poster board or chart paper

## Research Question

*Living things depend upon their environment and on other living things to survive. Endangered species are plants and animals whose survival is threatened. What can people do to help?*

**1** **CHOOSE A TOPIC** Have students find out what species are threatened or endangered. Then have them choose one species to study.

**2** **FORMULATE RESEARCH QUESTIONS** Have students write a list of research questions upon which to focus their research. Students should concentrate on learning why the species is threatened and what people can do to help.

**3** **RESEARCH** Have students research their chosen species using encyclopedias, nonfiction books, and the Internet. Tell students to take notes as they research.

**4** **ORGANIZE FINDINGS** Tell students to use an E-chart to organize each main idea and its supporting details.

| | |
|---|---|
| Manatees are endangered. | Boat propellers can cut manatees. |
| | Pollution harms water in which manatees live. |
| | |

**5** **PRESENT** Allow time for student presentations. Students might present posters or persuasive dialogues. You may wish to use the Rubric for Presentations on page T58 for evaluation.

# Additional Homework Ideas

Visit *The Learning Site:* www.harcourtschool.com See Resources for Parents and Teachers: Homework Helper.

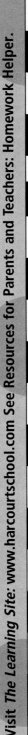

| | Vocabulary | Comprehension | Literature Response | Grammar/Writing | Spelling |
|---|---|---|---|---|---|
| **WEEK 1** | **Write a conversation** between two people. Use vocabulary words in the dialogue. " " | **Compare and contrast** Manuel and Pablo. Record your ideas in a Venn diagram. | **Explain how** the stage directions help you understand the thoughts and feelings of the characters. | **Rewrite one scene** from the play as a story. Then use what you learned about complete and simple subjects to help you proofread your work for correct grammar and usage. | **Cut out letters** from junk mail or old magazines to spell five spelling words. Then glue your letters to a large sheet of paper to create a colorful word poster. |
| **WEEK 2** | **Make a thesaurus** for the vocabulary words. Write at least two synonyms for each word. | **Identify the main problem** in the story. How is the problem solved? | **Find three similes or metaphors** in the story. Explain what each one means. | **Write a new ending** to the story. Then use what you learned about compound subjects and predicates to help you proofread your work for correct grammar and usage. | **Race against time.** Write each word on a slip of paper. Then mix up the words and time yourself to see how long it takes you to put the words into alphabetical order. |
| **WEEK 3** | **Change each word** by adding or deleting a prefix, suffix, or verb ending. Then write a sentence with each new word. re- | **Write a summary** to tell how people helped the puffins. | **Explain how the author feels** about the work that Halla and the other children do with puffins. How can you tell? | **Write a journal entry** for Halla. Tell how she feels after a night searching for pufflings. Then use what you learned about simple and compound sentences to help you proofread your work for correct grammar and usage. | **Play concentration.** Write each word on two cards. Turn the cards face down, then draw two and try to make a match. Keep going until you match each pair. |
| **WEEK 4** | **Make a poster** from the vocabulary words. Use each word in a way that shows its meaning. | **Draw a chain of events chart** to show how one event in the story caused multiple effects. | **Write a paragraph explaining why** the painting of the sunflower is so important to Marisol. | **Write a newspaper article** about the community garden. Then use what you learned about clauses to help you proofread your work for correct grammar and usage. | **Scramble the letters** in each word. List the correct spellings at the bottom of the page. Give your puzzle to someone else to solve. |
| **WEEK 5** | **Write headlines** containing vocabulary words. Use the words in a way to catch the reader's interest. | **Predict** what you think will happen to Nanang. ? ? ? | **Identify the narrator** of the story. What words in the story show you who is telling the story? | **Make a list** of at least ten things you learned about orangutans from this selection. Use at least three complex sentences in your writing. Then proofread your work for correct grammar and usage. | **Build new words.** See how many new words you can write by rearranging the letters in each spelling word. own |

© Harcourt

# Build Background

**Discuss how people and other living things live side by side.** Tell students that this theme is called *Side by Side.* Ask students what ideas come to mind when they think of people working together. Write their ideas on the board. Then, have students scan the Table of Contents and discuss authors or titles listed that are familiar to them.

**Preview the Theme.** Have students preview the selections. Ask:

• Which selections might give information about how people work together to solve problems affecting people and other living creatures?

• Which selections might be about the value of teamwork?

# Develop Concepts

**Make a Cause and Effect Chart.** Work with students to develop a cause and effect chart that shows how people's actions have an effect on others. Draw the chart on a large sheet of paper, and record students initial ideas. Post the cause and effect chart in the room. Tell students to add to the chart as they read the unit selections and develop their understanding of the unit theme, Side by Side.

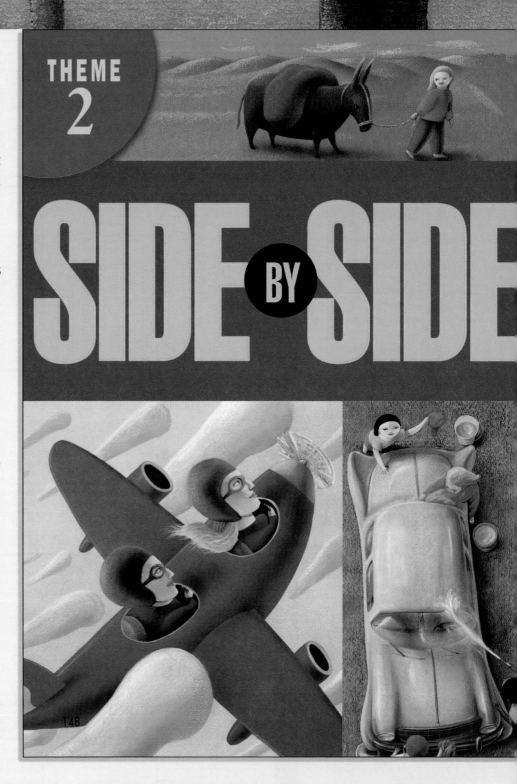

THEME
2

SIDE BY SIDE

148

| Cause | Effect |
|---|---|
| Students hold a bake sale. | School earns money to buy playground balls. |
| Students pick up litter. | School grounds looks nice. |
| Child helps parent fold laundry. | |

# CONTENTS

149

# Build Theme Connections

**Begin an ongoing concept web.** Have students create a concept web on which to record their thoughts about how people work together to accomplish their goals. You may want to store the organizer on a computer or post it on a bulletin board. Students can return to it to add new ideas as they read.

Working Together

 **QUICKWRITE**

**Ask students to list in their journals** three different tasks they have accomplished by working with another person or group of people. They can add new ideas to their lists as they progress through the theme. Remind students also to add to their Word Banks after they finish each reading selection.

 **Apply to Writing**

Tell students to check for words with /är/, /ôr/, /âr/, /ûr/, and /ou/ sounds to be sure they have spelled them correctly.

# Teacher Notes

**THEME CONNECTION:**
*Side by Side*

**GENRE:**
*Play*

**SUMMARY:**

A conflict arises between a baker and his neighbor. When it is resolved, the community learns that good friends and neighbors are worth more than gold.

 Selections available on *Audiotext 2*

# Books for All Learners

*Lesson Plans on pages 173M–173P*

## BELOW-LEVEL

- Lesson Vocabulary
- Focus Skill: Cause and Effect

## ON-LEVEL

- Lesson Vocabulary
- Focus Skill: Cause and Effect

## ADVANCED

- Challenge Vocabulary
- Focus Skill: Cause and Effect

## ELL

- Concept Vocabulary
- Focus Skill: Cause and Effect

## MULTI-LEVEL PRACTICE

**Extra Support,** pp. 24–26

**Practice Book,** pp. 24–28

**Challenge,** pp. 24–26

**English-Language Learners,** pp. 24–26

## ADDITIONAL RESOURCES

**Spelling Practice Book,** pp. 27–29

**Language Handbook,** pp. 30–33, 67, 108–110

**Audiotext 2**

**Intervention Resource Kit,** Lesson 6
- Intervention Reader, *Included in Intervention Resource Kit*

**English-Language Learners Resource Kit,** Lesson 6

 **technology**

- *Mission: Comprehension™ Skills Practice* **CD-ROM**

- *Media Literacy and Communication Skills Package* (Video)

- *Grammar Jingles™* **CD**, Intermediate

- *Writing Express™* **CD-ROM**

- *Reading and Language Skills Assessment* **CD-ROM**

- *The Learning Site:* www.harcourtschool.com

## ORAL LANGUAGE
5-15 Minutes

- **Question of the Day**

- **Sharing Literature**

## SKILLS & STRATEGIES
15-30 Minutes

- **Comprehension**

- **Vocabulary**

## READING
30-45 Minutes

- **Guided Comprehension**

- **Independent Reading**

- **Cross-Curricular Connections**

## LANGUAGE ARTS
45-90 Minutes

- **Writing**

  *Daily Writing Prompt*

- **Grammar**

  *Daily Language Practice*

- **Spelling**

### Daily Routines
- Question of the Day
- Daily Language Practice
- Daily Writing Prompt

---

# Day 1

**Question of the Day,** p. 150H
*Name a privilege or a luxury you enjoy. Why do think it is a privilege or a luxury?*

**Literature Read-Aloud,** pp. 150G–H

**Comprehension:**

 (Skill) Cause and Effect, p. 150I **T**

(Strategy) Use Decoding/Phonics, p. 150J

**Vocabulary,** p. 150L

**Read: Vocabulary Power,** pp. 150–151
Vocabulary Power Words:
*privilege, luxury, elated, assent, ad lib, shiftless, indignantly, shamefacedly*

 **Independent Reading**
Books for All Learners

**SOCIAL STUDIES** Participating in Government
**SCIENCE** The Nose Knows
**INQUIRY PROJECT** Extending the Selection

**Writing:** Writer's Craft, p. 173E

 **Writing Prompt:**
*All of us have had a problem to solve. Think about a time when you had a problem. Now write about how you solved it.*

**Grammar:**
Complete and Simple Predicates, p. 173G **T**

*Daily Language Practice*

1. Neighbors and friends. Sometimes argue or disagree. (friends sometimes)
2. Are you in a bad moode. (mood?)

**Spelling:**
Words with /är/, p. 173I **T**

---

# Day 2

**Question of the Day,** p. 150H
*Which character in the story do you think is right—Manuel or Pablo? Explain your reasoning.*

**Think and Respond,** p. 168

**Comprehension:**

(Skill) Cause and Effect, pp. 152–168 **T**

**Decoding/Phonics:**
Letter Patterns: Consonant /s/c and Consonant /j/g, p. 173C

**Reading the Selection,** pp. 152–168
GENRE: Play

 **Independent Reading**
Books for All Learners

**LITERARY ANALYSIS** Play Format and Structure
**MATH** How Much Does It Cost?

**Writing:** Writer's Craft, p. 173E

**Writing Prompt:**
*Think about the first time you saw or read a play. Write a paragraph explaining what you liked and disliked about the play.*

**Grammar:**
Extend the Concept, p. 173G

*Daily Language Practice*

1. how noisy the chidren are (How; are!)
2. Mr. Adams sweeps. the stop with a broom. (sweeps the stoop)

**Spelling:**
Word Sort, p. 173I

---

**Objectives of the Week:**

- To identify cause-and-effect relationships in a literary text and use them to understand plot development
- To read and understand a play
- To use complete and simple predicates correctly
- To use effective paragraphs in writing a paragraph of information

# Day 3

**Question of the Day,** p. 150H
*Think about the way in which Manuel and Pablo resolve their disagreement. How else could they have solved the problem without going to the Judge?*

**Oral Grammar,** p. 173H

**Comprehension:**
 Cause and Effect, pp. 172–173 **T**
Test Prep

**Word Study:**
Homophones, p. 173K

**Rereading for Fluency,** p. 167

 **Independent Reading**
Books for All Learners

**MATH** Fractions and Decimals
**SOCIAL STUDIES** Branches of Government

**Writing:** Writer's Craft, p. 173F

**Writing Prompt:**
*Think about the relationship between Pablo and Manuel. Write to explain how it would be different if Pablo was the baker and Manuel sniffed the pies.*

**Grammar:**
Same Subject, p. 173H

**Daily Language Practice**
1. I carry the garbage out. And put it by the street (out and; street.)
2. In the afternon! Mona and My sister walk the dog. (afternoon Mona and my)

**Spelling:**
Guessing and Checking, p. 173J

# Day 4

**Question of the Day,** p. 150H
*How would you describe something in the classroom, using figurative language?*

**Comprehension:**
 Cause and Effect, pp. 173M–P **T**

**Figurative Language,** pp. 173A–B **T**
**Prefixes, Suffixes, and Roots,** p. 173D **T**

**Self-Selected Reading,** p. 150F

 **Independent Reading**
Books for All Learners

**SOCIAL STUDIES** Courts, Officials, and Citizens
**TECHNOLOGY/WRITING** Writing a Script

**Writing:** Writer's Craft, p. 173F

**Writing Prompt:**
*Most of us have a favorite store or restaurant. Write about your favorite store or restaurant, telling why you like it.*

**Grammar:**
Unity, p. 173H

**Daily Language Practice**
1. People crowded Around our both? (crowded around; booth.)
2. My brother. and I. painted and set it up. (brother and I painted)

**Spelling:**
Think and Spell, Ten Questions, p. 173J

# Day 5

**Question of the Day,** p. 150H
*The United States Constitution guarantees every citizen the right to a fair trial. What other rights does the Constitution guarantee? Which right is most important to you and why?*

**Speaking and Listening**
Performing in a Dramatic Presentation, p. 173L

**Comprehension:**
 Cause and Effect, pp. 173M–P **T**

**Word Study:**
Word Origins, p. 173K

**Self-Selected Reading,** pp. 167, T67

**Independent Reading**
Books for All Learners

**WRITING** Write an Ad
**SCIENCE** Conduct Experiments
**SOCIAL STUDIES** Create a Pamphlet

**Writing:** Writer's Craft, p. 173F

**Writing Prompt:**
*Do you think the play "The Baker's Neighbor" is a good way to teach about the importance of being a good neighbor? Write to explain your answer.*

**Grammar:**
Subjects and Predicates, p. 173H

**Daily Language Practice**
1. Who wants? to have a booth next year! (wants to; year?)
2. sign up now for the neighborhood fair (Sign; fair! or fair.)

**Spelling:**
Posttest, p. 173J

# Cross-Curricular Stations

**MANAGING THE CLASSROOM** While you provide direct instruction to individuals or small groups, other students can work on ongoing activities such as the ones below.

## SOCIAL STUDIES

### Materials

- library resources and/or computer with Internet access
- social studies textbook
- poster board
- markers

### Participating in Government

**OBJECTIVE: To understand the importance of citizen participation in government**

Find out how citizens take part in court cases.
- Gather information about juries and jury trials.
- Make a flowchart showing the steps in a jury trial.
- Give an oral report explaining what goes on in a jury trial.

| Jury selection | → | Lawyers give opening statements, present evidence, and sum up. | → | Judge gives jury instructions. | → | Jury discusses case. | → | Jury gives decision. |

## SCIENCE

### Materials

- a print or online encyclopedia
- pencil
- paper
- butcher paper
- drawing materials

### The Nose Knows

**OBJECTIVE: To understand the function of various body systems**

Find out how humans smell odors.
- Learn about the olfactory system of the body from an encyclopedia. Look under the entry *nose*, or use *nose* as a keyword for your search.
- On a sheet of paper, list the parts of the olfactory system and their different jobs.
- Draw a diagram showing how odors enter the body and how information about them reaches the brain. Label the parts of the olfactory system. Use color and symbols in your diagram as needed, and include a key explaining any colors or symbols you use.

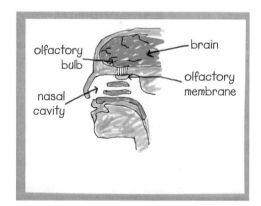

 Use the Internet or an online encyclopedia to gather information.

## LIBRARY CENTER

### Self-Selected Reading

**OBJECTIVE: To select and read books independently**

Look for these books that deal with communities and people's roles and relationships with one another.

- *Wanda's Roses* by Pat Brisson. Boyds Mills, 1994. **FICTION**
- *In My Momma's Kitchen* by Jerdine Nolan. Lothrop, Lee & Shepard, 1999. **FICTION**
- *Market!* by Ted Lewin. Lothrop, Lee & Shepard, 1996. **NONFICTION**

- Use appropriate reading strategies.
- Keep track in your Reading Log of what you read each day.

**20 Minutes a day**

**Materials**
- self-selected book
- *My Reading Log* copying master, p. R38

## INQUIRY PROJECT

### Extending the Selection

**OBJECTIVE: To select a focus for an inquiry project**

"The Baker's Neighbor" can lead to inquiry into a variety of topics and ideas. Brainstorm a list of topics you would like to know more about. Choose one, and use one of the books below for your inquiry project.

- *Wise Queen Catherine: A Play*
- *The Honest Neighbors*
- *The Story of Wheat*
- *Tea with Jam*

**30 Minutes**

**Materials**
- research materials
- pens or pencils
- paper

## TECHNOLOGY/WRITING

### Writing a Script

**OBJECTIVE: To use word processing software to format a script for a play**

Choose a favorite story, and write a script for a short play based on it, using a word processing program. Include all the elements of a play you saw in "The Baker's Neighbor."

- List the characters.
- Provide stage directions with the dialogue.
- Use parentheses and italics to set off stage directions.

**45 Minutes**

**Materials**
- computer with word processing software

# Read Aloud

## SET A PURPOSE

### Listen for Enjoyment

Emphasize that people often read poetry for enjoyment. Ask students what they like about reading or listening to poetry. Then read the poem aloud twice. After the first reading, point out the elements that help poetry come alive and make sense when read aloud: pacing, rhythm, intonation, and phrasing. As you read the poem aloud a second time, ask students to listen for words that are repeated at the beginnings of lines. Discuss with students how the repetition affects the rhythm and tone of the poem.

## LISTENING STRATEGY

### Self-Question

Tell students to check their understanding of the poem during the first reading by jotting down questions they have about words, images, or events. Then have students listen for answers to their questions about the poem's content as you read the poem a second time.

## Tortillas Like Africa

**by Gary Soto**

When Isaac and me squeezed dough over a mixing bowl,
When we dusted the cutting board with flour,
When we spanked and palmed our balls of dough,
When we said, "Here goes,"
And began rolling out tortillas,
We giggled because ours came out not round, like Mama's,
But in the shapes of faraway lands.

Here was Africa, here was Colombia and Greenland.
Here was Italy, the boot country,
And here was México, our homeland to the south.

Here was Chile, thin as a tie.
Here was France, square as a hat.
Here was Australia, with patches of jumping kangaroos.

We rolled out our tortillas on the board
And laughed when we threw them on the *comal*,
These tortillas that were not round as a pocked moon,
But the twist and stretch of the earth taking shape.

So we made our first batch of tortillas, laughing.
So we wrapped them in a dish towel.
So we buttered and rolled two each
And sat on the front porch—
Butter ran down our arms and our faces shone.

I asked Isaac, "How's yours?"
He cleared his throat and opened his tortilla.
He said, "¡Bueno! Greenland tastes like México."

***comal*: a clay dish used for baking tortillas**

- **What do the speaker and Isaac do before rolling out the tortillas?** (They squeeze the dough over a mixing bowl, dust the cutting board with flour, and hit and press their balls of dough.) SEQUENCE

- **Do the speaker and Isaac enjoy making tortillas? How do you know?** (Yes; they laugh, giggle, and tell jokes.) IMPORTANT DETAILS

- **What makes the speaker and Isaac laugh?** (Their tortillas aren't the usual round shape but have the shapes of different countries.) CHARACTERS' EMOTIONS

- **What does the poet say tortillas usually look like?** (They are round like the moon.) UNDERSTAND FIGURATIVE LANGUAGE

- **What makes this poem interesting to listen to?** (Possible responses: repeated words at the beginning of lines) POET'S CRAFT

# Question of the Day

## DEVELOP ORAL LANGUAGE

- Show students the first question on Transparency 48, or write it on the board. Tell them to read it to themselves.

- **Response Journal** Explain to students that they should think about the question throughout the day and write their responses in their journals. Tell students to be prepared to discuss their responses to the question by the end of the day or at another time you choose.

- You may want to repeat this process daily for each of the remaining discussion questions.

▼ **Teaching Transparency 48**

**QUESTION OF THE DAY**

**DAY 1:** Name a **privilege** or a **luxury** you enjoy. Why do you think it is a privilege or a luxury? Responses will vary; students should explain their responses. SELECTION CONNECTION

**DAY 2:** Which character in the story do you think is right—Manuel or Pablo? Explain your reasoning. Responses will vary; students should support their ideas. SELECTION CONNECTION

**DAY 3:** Think about the way in which Manuel and Pablo resolve their disagreement. How else could they have solved the problem without going to the Judge? Possible response: They could have compromised; they could have asked the other customers to help them find a solution. SELECTION CONNECTION

**DAY 4:** How would you describe something in the classroom, using figurative language? Responses will vary. FIGURATIVE LANGUAGE

**DAY 5:** The United States Constitution guarantees every citizen the right to a fair trial. What other rights does the Constitution guarantee? Which right is most important to you and why? Possible responses: freedom of speech; freedom of religion, freedom of the press. Responses to the second part of the question will vary; responses should be supported by specific reasons. CROSS-CURRICULAR CONNECTION

"The Baker's Neighbor"
Side by Side, Theme 2 — 48 — Question of the Day Harcourt

## Focus Skill — Cause and Effect

## OBJECTIVE

*To identify cause-and-effect relationships in a literary text and use them to understand plot development*

### SKILL TRACE

#### CAUSE AND EFFECT

| Introduce | p. 150I |
|-----------|---------|
| Reteach | pp. S36, S54, T36 |
| Review | pp. 172, 230I, 250 |
| Test | Theme 2 |
| Maintain | p. 397B |

▼ **Teaching Transparency 49**

---

**CAUSE AND EFFECT**

- A **cause** is an action or event that makes something happen.
- An **effect** is what happens as the result of an action or event.
- Authors sometimes use signal words and phrases such as *because, so, since,* and *as a result.* Looking for signal words and phrases helps readers identify causes and effects.

**EXAMPLES:**

| CAUSE | EFFECT |
|-------|--------|
| Mrs. Li's dog, Jake, ran away last week. | She put an advertisement in the paper describing him. |
| A man saw a similar dog in his neighborhood. | He called Mrs. Li. |
| The man reads the paper every day. | He knew Mrs. Li's dog was missing. |

Because her dog Jake ran away last week, Mrs. Li put an advertisement in the paper describing him. A man saw a similar dog in his neighborhood, so he called Mrs. Li. Since the man reads the paper every day, he knew Mrs. Li's dog was missing.

"The Baker's Neighbor"
Side by Side, Theme 2

**49**

Focus Skill: Cause and Effect
Harcourt

---

### BELOW-LEVEL

**Additional Support**
- *Intervention Teacher's Guide,* p. 60

### ENGLISH-LANGUAGE LEARNERS

**Additional Support**
- *English-Language Learners Teacher's Guide,* p. 33

---

### INTRODUCE THE SKILL

**Access prior knowledge.** Ask students how they would dress if it was cold outside. (Possible responses: put on a sweater or jacket; put on gloves and a hat.) Then ask them why they would dress in this way. (Possible response: to stay warm.) Tell students that dressing appropriately for the weather is an example of a cause-and-effect relationship. The desire to stay warm is the cause. Wearing warm clothing is the effect. Explain that a **cause** is why something happens. An **effect** is what happens as the result of an action or event.

### TEACH/MODEL

Explain to students that recognizing cause-and-effect relationships can help them understand how and why events in a story happen.

- **Have a volunteer read aloud the bulleted items.**

- **Guide students through the examples of causes and effects.**

- **Point out that words and phrases often are used to signal cause-and-effect relationships. Ask: Why does Mrs. Li put an ad in the paper?** (because her dog ran away)

**Text Structure** Explain that authors often use cause-and-effect relationships to show how events in the plot are related.

### PRACTICE/APPLY

Suggest that students use a chart like this to record causes and effects in "The Baker's Neighbor."

| Cause | Effect |
|-------|--------|
|  |  |

To apply and reinforce the skill, see these pages:

**During reading:** pages 154, 156, 158, and 166
**After reading:** *Pupil Edition* pages 172–173

# Focus Strategy: Use Decoding/Phonics

## OBJECTIVE

*To use decoding and phonics to determine the pronunciation of words*

## REVIEW THE STRATEGY

Remind students that **using decoding and phonics** will help them read long or unfamiliar words. Tell them that breaking a longer word into word parts such as prefixes, suffixes, roots, and root words and blending the parts together will help them read longer words.

## TEACH/MODEL

Use the example on Transparency 49 to model the strategy.

> **MODEL** When I come to a longer word, such as *advertisement*, I try breaking it into smaller parts. When I read this word, I see the root word *advertise* and the suffix *-ment*. I know how to say each word part separately, so I blend them together to read the word *advertisement*.

advertise     ment

### SKILL ⟷ STRATEGY CONNECTION

Tell students that thinking about **cause-and-effect** relationships and **using decoding and phonics** to read longer words will help them better understand the selection.

## PRACTICE/APPLY

Remind students to use the Use Decoding/Phonics strategy when they come to some of the long or unfamiliar words in the selection. For opportunities to apply and reinforce the strategy **during reading**, see pages 155 and 161.

## Strategies Good Readers Use

- **Use Decoding/ Phonics**   Focus Strategy
- Make and Confirm Predictions
- Create Mental Images
- Self-Question
- Summarize
- Read Ahead
- Reread to Clarify
- Use Context to Confirm Meaning
- Use Text Structure and Format
- Adjust Reading Rate

# Building Background

## ACCESS PRIOR KNOWLEDGE

Ask students what it means to be a good neighbor. Prompt them to name characteristics of a good neighbor and give examples of how a good neighbor acts. Organize students' ideas in a concept map.

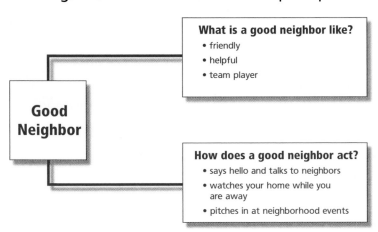

**Good Neighbor**

**What is a good neighbor like?**
- friendly
- helpful
- team player

**How does a good neighbor act?**
- says hello and talks to neighbors
- watches your home while you are away
- pitches in at neighborhood events

## technology

**VIDEO** *Tall Tales, Yarns, and Whoppers,* ©1991. Library Video Company, 35 min.

## DEVELOP CONCEPTS

Help students use prior knowledge to develop concepts by asking the following questions:

- **When do people in your neighborhood or community get together?** (Possible responses: to play or watch sports; for street fairs, barbecues, block parties, or other special events)

- **How do people in your neighborhood solve problems or disagreements?** (Possible responses: They talk with each other; they ask someone else in the neighborhood or from outside the neighborhood for help.)

- **What do you like most about your neighborhood?** (Possible responses: There are lots of people nearby to have fun with.)

Discuss why it is important to be a good neighbor.

### REACHING ALL LEARNERS

## Diagnostic Check: Vocabulary

**If** . . . students do not understand at least 6 of the 8 words . . .

**Then** . . . duplicate the word cards on page T59, have students write the definitions on the back, and have pairs of students use them as flash cards.

### ADDITIONAL SUPPORT ACTIVITIES

| BELOW-LEVEL | Reteach, p. S34 |
| ADVANCED | Extend, p. S35 |
| ENGLISH-LANGUAGE LEARNERS | Reteach, p. S35 |

# Vocabulary

## TEACH VOCABULARY STRATEGIES

**Use reference sources.** Direct students' attention to the phrase *ad lib* on Transparency 50. Tell students that when they are unsure about the meaning of a word, they can look it up in a reference source such as a dictionary, glossary, or thesaurus. Model using this strategy to determine the meaning of the phrase *ad lib*.

**MODEL** The words and sentences around the phrase *ad lib* don't give me enough clues to figure out its meaning, so I look for the phrase in a dictionary. The dictionary tells me *ad lib* means "to make up lines or music on the spot." The meaning "to make up lines or music on the spot" makes sense for *ad lib* in the passage.

As students encounter other unfamiliar words, have them use a dictionary or thesaurus to determine the words' meanings. Then, have them check to see if it makes sense in the sentence.

## Vocabulary

**privilege** a special benefit enjoyed under special conditions

**luxury** anything of value that gives comfort but is not necessary for life

**elated** filled with joy or pride

**assent** to agree or approve

**ad lib** to make up lines or music on the spot

**shiftless** not motivated, lazy

**indignantly** being angry about something that does not seem right

**shamefacedly** a way that shows shame for having done something bad

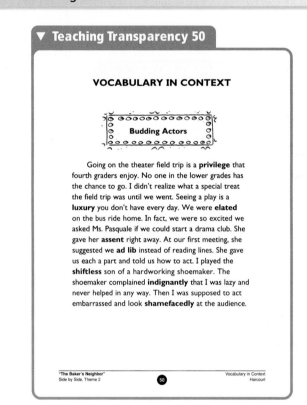

▼ **Teaching Transparency 50**

### VOCABULARY IN CONTEXT

**Budding Actors**

Going on the theater field trip is a **privilege** that fourth graders enjoy. No one in the lower grades has the chance to go. I didn't realize what a special treat the field trip was until we went. Seeing a play is a **luxury** you don't have every day. We were **elated** on the bus ride home. In fact, we were so excited we asked Ms. Pasquale if we could start a drama club. She gave her **assent** right away. At our first meeting, she suggested we **ad lib** instead of reading lines. She gave us each a part and told us how to act. I played the **shiftless** son of a hardworking shoemaker. The shoemaker complained **indignantly** that I was lazy and never helped in any way. Then I was supposed to act embarrassed and look **shamefacedly** at the audience.

"The Baker's Neighbor"
Side by Side, Theme 2
**50**
Vocabulary in Context
Harcourt

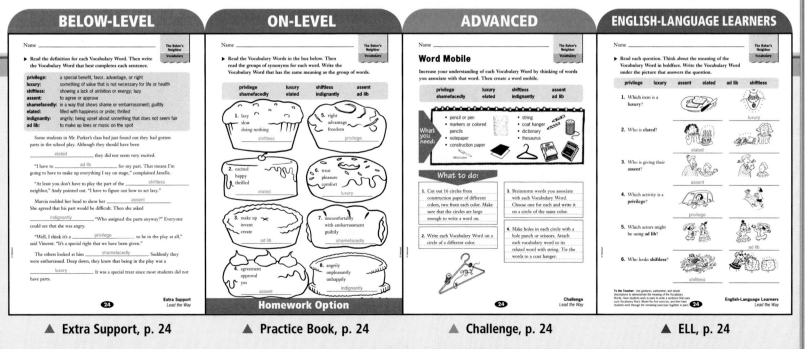

▲ Extra Support, p. 24     ▲ Practice Book, p. 24     ▲ Challenge, p. 24     ▲ ELL, p. 24

# Vocabulary Power

## APPLY STRATEGIES

Ask a volunteer to read aloud the first paragraph on page 150. Then tell students to read the remaining text silently. Remind students to use context or reference sources to determine the meanings of unfamiliar words.

## EXTEND WORD KNOWLEDGE

**Practice other vocabulary strategies.**
Direct students to answer the questions below with sentences that show what the vocabulary words mean. MEANINGFUL SENTENCES

- **When have you felt *elated*?** DESCRIPTION

- **Is food a *luxury* or a necessity? Explain.** EXAMPLE

- **Would you act *shamefacedly* if you had just done a good deed? Explain.** EXPLANATION

- **What is a *privilege* you have?** EXAMPLE

- **How would you show your *assent*?** EXPLANATION

- **What is a synonym for *shiftless*?** SYNONYM

- **In what types of situations might someone have to *ad lib*?** CLASSIFY/CATEGORIZE

- **When might someone act *indignantly*?** PRIOR KNOWLEDGE

▲ The Baker's Neighbor

| shiftless |
| indignantly |
| ad lib |
| shamefacedly |
| luxury |
| assent |
| privilege |
| elated |

150

# Vocabulary Power

The next selection you will read is written in the form of a play. Here are some descriptions of other plays put on by fourth-grade classes.

This play is about a farmer who believes that his donkey is lazy and **shiftless**. In this scene, the farmer speaks **indignantly** to the donkey. He speaks angrily because the donkey won't carry the sack for him. The other actors **ad lib**, or make up lines on the spot, telling the farmer they think the sack is too heavy for the little donkey.

In this play, a boy has taken a hat that doesn't belong to him. He stands **shamefacedly** before the queen, showing by the expression on his face how ashamed he is for what he has done. The queen tells him he must return the hat to its owner. Such a wonderful hat is a **luxury** because it is costly and gives pleasure but isn't really necessary. The queen says she will give the boy a plain wool cap to keep him warm. Her advisors agree and nod in **assent**.

The main character in this play is a boy who longs for the **privilege**, or special favor, of carrying the American flag in a parade for the very first Independence Day celebration. In this scene, the boy has just found out that he may carry the flag and lead the parade. He is **elated**, filled with joy.

**Vocabulary–Writing CONNECTION**

**D**o you think television is a **luxury** or a necessity in our modern world? Write a sentence expressing your opinion. Then give three reasons to explain why you feel as you do.

151

**QUICKWRITE**

**VOCABULARY–WRITING CONNECTION**

Suggest that students brainstorm a list of reasons for their opinion. Students should then choose the three strongest reasons to support their opinion statements. Have students add the Vocabulary Power words to their Word Banks for future use.

# Prereading Strategies

## PREVIEW AND PREDICT

Have students read the **genre** information on page 152. Then have them preview the play. Ask them what they think this play is about, based on their preview and the characteristics of plays. Then have them record predictions about the setting, characters, and plot of the play. Students can begin a cause-and-effect chart to help them understand plot development. See Transparency F.

| Cause | Effect |
|-------|--------|
| Pablo smells Manuel's pastries instead of buying them. | Manuel gets upset. |

Award-Winning Illustrator

### Genre

## Play

A play is a story that can be performed for an audience.

In this selection, look for

● Acts that are divided into scenes

● Text telling the reader where the characters are positioned on stage

152

| **BELOW-LEVEL** | **ON-LEVEL** | **ADVANCED** | **ENGLISH-LANGUAGE LEARNERS** |
|-----------------|--------------|--------------|-------------------------------|
| Guide students' preview of the play. To ensure comprehension, discuss the meanings of such words as *fragrance, pastries, miser,* and *trial.* Help students set a purpose for reading through page 160. **SMALL GROUP** **ADDITIONAL SUPPORT**  *Intervention Reader: Moving Ahead. Intervention Reader Teacher's Guide, pp. 60–63.* | Have students read the play in small groups. Use the Guided Comprehension questions to gauge students' understanding and the Ongoing Assessments to provide additional support. **SMALL GROUP/PARTNER** | Have students read the selection in small groups. Ask them to take notes about how their responses to the characters change as they read. **SMALL GROUP** | Read aloud the play, or have students listen to it on *Audiotext 2.* Then have students take parts and read aloud portions of the play to develop oral fluency. **SMALL GROUP** **ADDITIONAL SUPPORT** See *English-Language Learners Resource Kit,* Lesson 6. *English-Language Learners Teacher's Guide,* p. 33 |

# Neighbor

adapted by Adele Thane
illustrated by Mary GrandPré

### Characters

| | |
|---|---|
| Manuel Gonzales, *a baker* | Judge |
| Pablo Perez, *his neighbor* | Three Women |
| Carlos, *a boy* | Villagers |
| Ramona ⎱ | |
| Inez ⎬ *his sisters* | |
| Isabel ⎰ | |

## SET PURPOSE

**Read to enjoy.** Encourage students to set their own purposes for reading the play. If students have difficulty, remind them that one purpose for reading is to be entertained. Offer this suggestion:

**MODEL** The illustrations make the play seem entertaining. They also show that the baker and his neighbor disagree about something, and other people have strong feelings about the disagreement. I'll read to learn about the problem between the main characters and to enjoy the play.

(**Focus Strategy**) **Use Decoding/Phonics**
Remind students to use decoding and phonics to help them figure out the pronunciation of long or unfamiliar words.

"The Baker's Neighbor" is available on *Audiotext 2.*

## COMPREHENSION CARD 6

**Theme** Have students use Comprehension Card 6 to discuss theme in "The Baker's Neighbor."

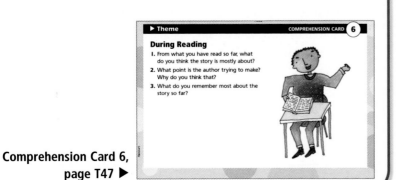

▶ Theme                    COMPREHENSION CARD **6**

**During Reading**
1. From what you have read so far, what do you think the story is mostly about?
2. What point is the author trying to make? Why do you think that?
3. What do you remember most about the story so far?

Comprehension Card 6,
page T47 ▶

# Guided Comprehension

**1** (Focus Skill) **CAUSE/EFFECT** **Why is Manuel the baker angry at Pablo?** (because Pablo always smells Manuel's pastries but never buys any)

**2** **SUMMARIZE** **Why doesn't Pablo accept Manuel's solution to the problem between them?** (If he buys a pie or cake and eats it, he won't be able to enjoy its fragrance.)

**3** **CHARACTERS' EMOTIONS** **What word best describes Manuel? Pablo?** (Possible responses: Manuel: grouchy; Pablo: pleasant)

**4** **MAKE PREDICTIONS** **Do you think Manuel and Pablo will be able to solve their disagreement on their own? Why or why not?** (Possible responses: No, because both Manuel and Pablo have strong ideas that they probably won't give up; Yes, because Pablo seems nice, and he will probably finally give in to Manuel.)

SETTING: *A street in an old town. Manuel's Bakery is at right. There is an outdoor counter with shelves for the display of pastries in front of the bakery, and a wooden table and stool near the counter. Across the street, at left, is the patio of Pablo's house, with a bench and chairs on it. At the rear of the stage, there is a flowering tree with a circular seat around the trunk.*

AT RISE: *It is early morning.* MANUEL *comes out of bakery with a tray of pies which he carries to counter. As he is putting the pies on a shelf,* PABLO *steps out onto his patio, sniffs the air and smiles with delight.*

## BELOW-LEVEL

Remind students that the plot of a play usually involves a problem faced by the main character(s) and then shows how the problem is solved by the character(s). Focus on the dialogue on page 155 to help students identify the problem between Manuel and Pablo. Then have students continue to read to find out how the problem is solved.

| Problem | → | Solution |
|---|---|---|
| | | |

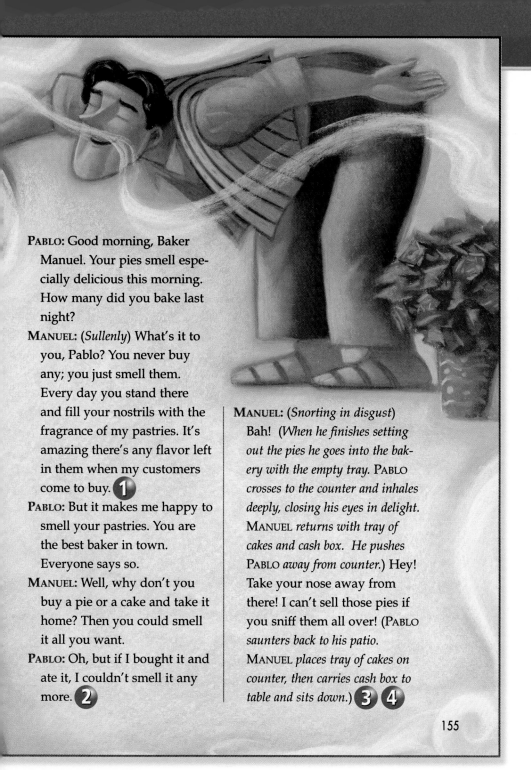

PABLO: Good morning, Baker Manuel. Your pies smell especially delicious this morning. How many did you bake last night?

MANUEL: (*Sullenly*) What's it to you, Pablo? You never buy any; you just smell them. Every day you stand there and fill your nostrils with the fragrance of my pastries. It's amazing there's any flavor left in them when my customers come to buy. **1**

PABLO: But it makes me happy to smell your pastries. You are the best baker in town. Everyone says so.

MANUEL: Well, why don't you buy a pie or a cake and take it home? Then you could smell it all you want.

PABLO: Oh, but if I bought it and ate it, I couldn't smell it any more. **2**

MANUEL: (*Snorting in disgust*) Bah! (*When he finishes setting out the pies he goes into the bakery with the empty tray.* PABLO *crosses to the counter and inhales deeply, closing his eyes in delight.* MANUEL *returns with tray of cakes and cash box. He pushes* PABLO *away from counter.*) Hey! Take your nose away from there! I can't sell those pies if you sniff them all over! (PABLO *saunters back to his patio.* MANUEL *places tray of cakes on counter, then carries cash box to table and sits down.*) **3** **4**

155

**ONGOING ASSESSMENT**

Monitor Progress

(★ Focus Strategy) **Use Decoding/Phonics**

Have students read Pablo's first speech on page 155. Listen for their pronunciation of *especially*.

Ask students to model using decoding and phonics to pronounce *especially*. If students have difficulty, model the strategy:

**MODEL** When I look at the word *especially*, I see the root word *special* and the suffix *-ly*. I know how to pronounce each part separately, so I blend the parts together to read the word. When I do this, I read the word /is′•pesh′əl•ē/.

## LITERARY ANALYSIS

**Play Format and Structure** Discuss the genre and format of this selection. Draw students' attention to the list of characters (page 153), the description of the general setting and of the specific scene when the curtain rises (page 154), the lines of dialogue preceded by the name of the character speaking, and the stage directions (in italic and parentheses). Prompt students to compare and contrast the structure of a play with the structures of other forms of literature, leading them to observe that plays have the same elements as other forms of fiction: setting, characters, and a plot with a beginning, middle, and end.

# Guided Comprehension

**5** **DRAW CONCLUSIONS** **Why do you think Pablo is amused as he watches Manuel count his money?** (Possible response: because Pablo doesn't care about money the way Manuel does)

**6** **CHARACTERS' TRAITS** **How can you tell that Manuel is a miser?** (Possible responses: He is completely focused on his money and does not want to be bothered when he is counting it; he carefully checks each coin and writes down every coin he takes in.)

**7** (Focus Skill) **CAUSE/EFFECT** **According to Carlos, why doesn't Manuel smile?** (Manuel doesn't smile because he is a miser and does not like people.)

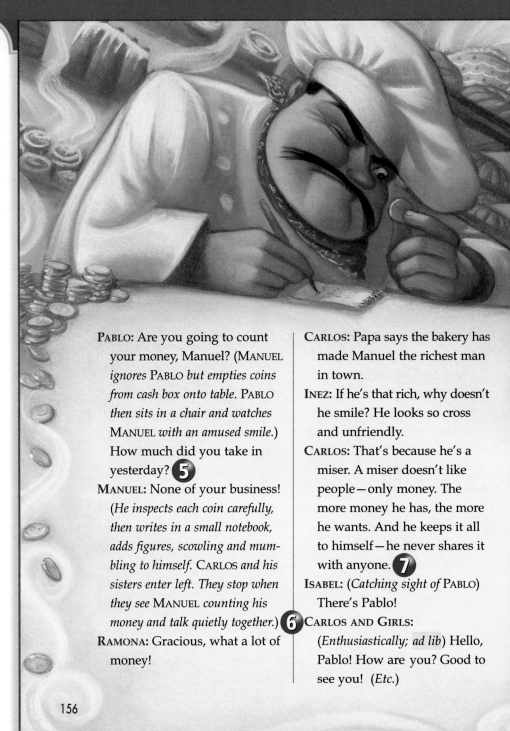

PABLO: Are you going to count your money, Manuel? (MANUEL *ignores* PABLO *but empties coins from cash box onto table.* PABLO *then sits in a chair and watches* MANUEL *with an amused smile.*) How much did you take in yesterday? **5**

MANUEL: None of your business! (*He inspects each coin carefully, then writes in a small notebook, adds figures, scowling and mumbling to himself.* CARLOS *and his sisters enter left. They stop when they see* MANUEL *counting his money and talk quietly together.*) **6**

RAMONA: Gracious, what a lot of money!

CARLOS: Papa says the bakery has made Manuel the richest man in town.

INEZ: If he's that rich, why doesn't he smile? He looks so cross and unfriendly.

CARLOS: That's because he's a miser. A miser doesn't like people—only money. The more money he has, the more he wants. And he keeps it all to himself—he never shares it with anyone. **7**

ISABEL: (*Catching sight of* PABLO) There's Pablo!

CARLOS AND GIRLS: (*Enthusiastically; ad lib*) Hello, Pablo! How are you? Good to see you! (*Etc.*)

156

**REACHING ALL LEARNERS**

## Diagnostic Check: Comprehension and Skills

**If** . . . students are having difficulty understanding a character's motivation . . .

**Then** . . . ask them to write a series of "why" questions about the character's actions. Have students put the questions and answers together into cause-and-effect statements.

### ADDITIONAL SUPPORT ACTIVITIES

| BELOW-LEVEL | Reteach, p. S36 |
| ADVANCED | Extend, p. S37 |
| ENGLISH-LANGUAGE LEARNERS | Reteach, p. S37 |

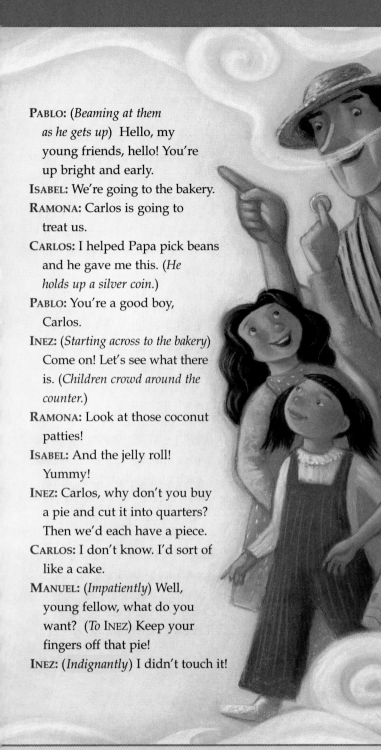

PABLO: (*Beaming at them as he gets up*) Hello, my young friends, hello! You're up bright and early.

ISABEL: We're going to the bakery.

RAMONA: Carlos is going to treat us.

CARLOS: I helped Papa pick beans and he gave me this. (*He holds up a silver coin.*)

PABLO: You're a good boy, Carlos.

INEZ: (*Starting across to the bakery*) Come on! Let's see what there is. (*Children crowd around the counter.*)

RAMONA: Look at those coconut patties!

ISABEL: And the jelly roll! Yummy!

INEZ: Carlos, why don't you buy a pie and cut it into quarters? Then we'd each have a piece.

CARLOS: I don't know. I'd sort of like a cake.

MANUEL: (*Impatiently*) Well, young fellow, what do you want? (*To* INEZ) Keep your fingers off that pie!

INEZ: (*Indignantly*) I didn't touch it!

157

Monitor Progress

# Use Context to Confirm Meaning

**What is a miser?** (A miser is someone who likes money more than anything else and does not share his or her money.)

**If students are unable to answer the question, use this model:**

**MODEL** When I first see the word *miser* on page 156, I am not sure what it means. As I continue to read, though, I see that Carlos goes on to explain exactly what a miser is. He says that a miser is someone who likes having a lot of money but will not share it with anyone.

# Guided Comprehension

**8 CHARACTERS' TRAITS   Is Manuel a good neighbor to the children? How do you know?** (No, he is very unneighborly. He is impatient, mean, and ungenerous toward them when they are deciding on pastries to buy.)

**9 (Focus Skill) CAUSE/EFFECT   Why won't Pablo share Carlos's tart?** (Pablo thinks that since Carlos earned the money to buy the tart, Carlos should eat it.)

**10 SYNTHESIZE   How do the children play their game?** (By imagining they are something that can be experienced through one of the five senses: sight, sound, smell, taste and touch.)

---

MANUEL: Come now, hurry up and decide. This isn't a waiting room. I have to make a living. What with rent and taxes, it's as much as I can do.

CARLOS: How much is that cake with the pink frosting?

MANUEL: You can't afford that. How much money do you have? (CARLOS *holds out his hand to show him*.) Not enough. That cake costs three times what you can pay.

CARLOS: What *can* I buy with my money? I want something for all of us.

MANUEL: You can have four tapioca tarts—and I'm giving them away at that price. (*He hands tarts to* CARLOS.) Here you are. Now take your tarts over to Pablo and let him smell them. (*He puts* CARLOS'S *coin with others on table, sits down and makes entry in his notebook.* CARLOS *passes out tarts to his sisters as they cross to the patio*). **8**

CARLOS: (*Offering tart to* PABLO) Have a bite?

PABLO: No, thank you, Carlos. You earned it—you eat it. **9**

ISABEL: Pablo, why did Manuel say we should let you smell our tarts?

PABLO: Oh, he's annoyed, because every morning I stand here and enjoy the smell of his freshly-baked pies and cakes when they are right out of the oven. Ah, what fragrance! It's as if the bakery has burst into bloom.

RAMONA: If you could be a beautiful smell, Pablo, instead of a man—would you like to be a beautiful bakery smell?

PABLO: (*Laughing*) Well, that's a new one on me! If I were a *smell* instead of a man? Of all the comical ideas!

INEZ: (*Explaining*) It's a game we play among ourselves. We ask each other what thing we'd like to be if we weren't a person—what color, what sight, what sound? **10**

RAMONA: What sound would *you* like to be, Pablo, if you weren't a person?

PABLO: This minute?

RAMONA: Any minute.

158

---

Below · On-Level · Advanced · ELL

## ADVANCED

Have students write brief descriptions of what they would like to be if they weren't people. Tell students that the thing they name must be something that can be experienced through one of the five senses: sight, smell, sound, touch, or taste. In their descriptions, students should provide reasons for their choices. Encourage students to draw pictures to illustrate their choices. Display students' descriptions and illustrations in the classroom.

I'd like to be the taste of a fresh orange.

---

159

Monitor Progress

# Read Ahead

**Why does Ramona ask Pablo if he would want to be a beautiful bakery smell?** (Possible response: because she wants him to take part in a game that she often plays with her friends.)

**If students were unable to answer the question, model the strategy:**

**MODEL**  I am not sure why Ramona asks Pablo such an unusual question, so I read ahead to find more information. When I get to Inez's part, she explains to Pablo the reason for Ramona's question. By reading ahead, I learn that the children play a game in which they ask each other what things they'd like to be if they weren't people. Ramona asks Pablo the question because she wants him to take part in the game.

## MATH

**How much does it cost?**   Manuel and Carlos try to determine what Carlos can afford to purchase with his money. Tell students to suppose that Carlos has four dollars. Ask: **How much does the cake with pink frosting cost if it costs three times more than what Carlos can pay?** (12 dollars) **How much more money does Carlos need to be able to buy the cake?** (8 dollars) Then ask students how they would figure out the cost of an individual tart if they know that Carlos is able to purchase four of them with four dollars. (division)

$12.00

# Guided Comprehension

**11** **MAKE COMPARISONS** **How is Manuel different from Pablo and the children? How do you know?** (Possible response: He is serious and does not seem to enjoy life; he thinks their game is stupid and he refuses to play it.)

**12** **IMPORTANT DETAILS** **What is more important to Pablo than money?** (the simple pleasures of life that he can enjoy every day, such as smelling freshly baked pastries)

**13** **MAKE JUDGMENTS** **Do you agree with Manuel that Pablo is a thief? Explain.** (Possible response: No; Pablo doesn't take the pastries or do damage to them, and Manuel can still sell them to someone else.)

PABLO: Let me think. (*Suddenly he slaps his knee.*) I have it! If I were a sound instead of a man, I'd choose to be a song! A happy little song in children's hearts. Or turning up in a boy's whistle—like this! (*He whistles a merry tune.*)

ISABEL: What sound do you think Manuel would like to be?

CARLOS: That's easy. He'd be the sound of gold pieces jingling in his own pocket.

ISABEL: I'm going to ask him. (*She goes to the table where* MANUEL *is putting his money back into cash box.*) Manuel, may I ask you a question?

MANUEL: (*Scowling*) What is it?

ISABEL: If you were a sound instead of a baker, what sound in the whole wide world would you choose to be?

MANUEL: Well, of all the idiotic nonsense! Clear out of here and stop bothering me! I have better things to do than to answer stupid questions. (ISABEL *returns to patio, and* PABLO *goes center.*)

PABLO: It has taken you a long time to count your money, Manuel.

160

## BELOW-LEVEL

When students have read through page 161, have them summarize what has happened to that point:

- Manuel catches Pablo sniffing his pastries.

- Manuel calls Pablo a thief because he doesn't pay for the pastries he smells.

- Manuel goes to get the Judge to make Pablo pay.

Help students set a purpose for reading the rest of the selection. (to find out whether Pablo has to pay Manuel)

MANUEL: (*Sneering*) It wouldn't take *you* long to count yours.

PABLO: That's right. I don't care much for money.

MANUEL: You're too lazy to earn it.

PABLO: (*Good-naturedly*) Oh, I work. But I'd rather sit in the sun and take advantage of all the small, everyday pleasures that life has to offer. **12**

MANUEL: Like smelling my pastries, I suppose—without charge?

PABLO: (*Shrugging*) The air is free.

MANUEL: It's not as free as you think.

PABLO: What do you mean?

MANUEL: I'm going to make you pay for all the pastry smells I've supplied you with for many years.

PABLO: (*Smiling in disbelief*) You can't mean that!

MANUEL: But I do! You stand outside my bakery every day and smell my pies and cakes. To my mind, that is the same as taking them without paying for them. You are no better than a thief, Pablo Perez!

PABLO: (*Mildly*) I never took anything that didn't belong to me, and you know it. What's

more, I haven't done your business any harm. Why, I've even helped it. People often stop when they see me standing here and go in to buy something. (*Children giggle, then begin to taunt* MANUEL *and run around him, sniffing.*) **13**

ISABEL: I smell raisins!

RAMONA: I smell spice!

INEZ: How much does it cost to smell the flour on your apron?

CARLOS: May I smell your cap for a penny? (*He snatches baker's cap from* MANUEL'S *head and sniffs it, laughing.*)

MANUEL: (*Angrily, snatching it back*) You'll laugh on the other side of your face when I get the Judge!

161

## ONGOING ASSESSMENT

### Monitor Progress

**Focus Strategy**

## Use Decoding/Phonics

Have students read Pablo's second part on page 161. Listen for their pronunciation of *pleasures*.

Ask volunteers to model using decoding and phonics to read *pleasures*.

**MODEL** I am not sure how to pronounce the first part of this word. I know that the letters *ea* can stand for the /ē/ sound or the /e/ sound. I try saying this word with each vowel sound. When I say /plezh´ər/, it sounds like a word I know.

## MATH

### Fractions and Decimals

Draw a circle on the board. Tell students the circle represents a pizza. Then divide the circle in half. Call on students to describe the pieces of the pizza in equivalent forms of fractions and decimals. Repeat for thirds, quarters, tenths, and other parts of the pie. Then have students plot the equivalent forms of fractions and decimals on a number line.

# Guided Comprehension

**14** **MAKE AND CONFIRM PREDIC-TIONS** **Was your prediction correct about whether Manuel and Pablo would be able to solve their disagreement on their own? Explain.** (Possible responses: Yes; I knew their strong ideas would not lead to an agreement, and now Manuel is getting a judge to solve their disagreement. No; I thought Pablo would give in and pay Manuel something or buy a pastry, but now I see Pablo is certain that what he is doing is not unfair.) **What do you think will happen now?** (Responses will vary.)

**15** **SEQUENCE** **What must take place before Pablo is proved to be a thief?** (He must be given a fair trial.)

**16** **GENERALIZE/CHARACTERS' EMO-TIONS** **How do people in the village feel about the case Manuel is bringing against Pablo? Why?** (Possible responses: They think it is unfair because it is not possible to steal the smell of something.)

---

PABLO: When you get *who*?

MANUEL: The Judge. I'm going to tell him the whole story. I'll show you I'm not joking. The Judge will make you pay me. (*He grabs his cash box from table and exits left as* THREE WOMEN *enter right. They come downstage and question the children.*) **14**

1ST WOMAN: What's the matter with Manuel?

2ND WOMAN: Will he be back soon? I want to buy a cake.

3RD WOMAN: So do I. What happened?

1ST WOMAN: He looked so angry. Where's he gone?

GIRLS: (*Excitedly, ad lib*) He's gone to get the Judge! He is angry! He is furious! (*Etc.*)

1ST WOMAN: The Judge! What for?

CARLOS: He says Pablo will have to pay for smelling his cakes and pies.

2ND WOMAN: (*To* PABLO) He wants you to pay him for doing that?

3RD WOMAN: He can't be serious!

PABLO: Oh, yes, he is! But I think it's very funny. (*He laughs, and the* WOMEN *join in.*)

1ST WOMAN: It's ridiculous! Everyone who goes by the shop smells his pastry.

2ND WOMAN: Is he going to take everyone in town to court? (*They are all in gales of laughter when* MANUEL *returns with* JUDGE, *followed by several* VILLAGERS.)

MANUEL: (*To* JUDGE) There he is! (*Points to* PABLO) There's the thief!

JUDGE: Calm yourself, Manuel. It has not yet been proved that Pablo is a thief. First he must have a fair trial. (*He sits down at table and motions for two chairs to be placed facing him.* VILLAGERS *and* THREE WOMEN *gather under tree and on patio with children. They whisper and talk together as they seat themselves.*) **15**

1ST VILLAGER: In all my days, I've never heard of a case like this before.

2ND VILLAGER: How can a man steal the *smell* of anything?

3RD VILLAGER: I'm surprised the Judge would even listen to the baker's story. Money for smelling his cakes! How absurd! **16**

162

---

**ENGLISH-LANGUAGE LEARNERS**

Students may be unfamiliar with the words *thief* and *trial*. Point out both words, pronounce them, and have students repeat them after you. Tell students that a thief is a person who takes something that does not belong to him or her. Then tell students that when a person has a trial, he or she goes before a court so that the court can decide if he or she did something wrong. Explain that if someone is charged with being a thief, he or she would have a trial to determine if that charge can be proven to be true.

---

**ONGOING ASSESSMENT**

Monitor Progress

# Read Ahead

**What is the Judge going to decide?** (Possible responses: The Judge may decide that Manuel doesn't have a case and that Pablo owes him nothing; the Judge may decide that Pablo must pay Manuel for sniffing his pastries.)

**If students are unable to answer, use this model:**

**MODEL** When Manuel returns with the Judge, it isn't clear what the Judge will decide. If I keep reading, though, I will probably find out how the Judge will handle the disagreement between Manuel and Pablo.

## SOCIAL STUDIES

**Branches of Government**   Tell students that local, state, and federal, governments in the United States have three branches: legislative, executive, and judicial. Discuss the functions of each. Ask students which branch of government the Judge would be part of. (the judicial branch) Then have students make simple diagrams showing the branches of government and their duties.

| Legislative Branch | Executive Branch | Judicial Branch |
|---|---|---|
| makes the laws | makes sure the laws are carried out | judges people accused of breaking the law and makes sure the laws are fair |

# Guided Comprehension

**⑰ DRAW CONCLUSIONS** Why do you think the Judge asks Manuel specific questions about what Pablo does at the bakery? (Possible response: to show that Pablo is not doing harm to business by standing outside the bakery)

**⑱ UNDERSTAND FIGURATIVE LANGUAGE** When Manuel describes Pablo as "fresh as a daisy," is he using a simile or metaphor? How do you know? What does Manuel mean? (He is using a simile because he is making a comparison using the word *as*. Manuel means that Pablo doesn't work very hard, has no concerns or worries, and gets plenty of sleep so that he is bright and well rested in the morning.)

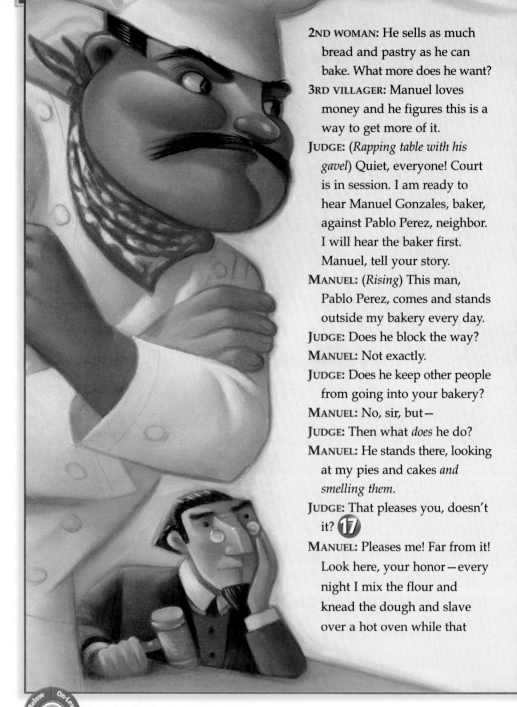

**2ND WOMAN:** He sells as much bread and pastry as he can bake. What more does he want?

**3RD VILLAGER:** Manuel loves money and he figures this is a way to get more of it.

**JUDGE:** (*Rapping table with his gavel*) Quiet, everyone! Court is in session. I am ready to hear Manuel Gonzales, baker, against Pablo Perez, neighbor. I will hear the baker first. Manuel, tell your story.

**MANUEL:** (*Rising*) This man, Pablo Perez, comes and stands outside my bakery every day.

**JUDGE:** Does he block the way?

**MANUEL:** Not exactly.

**JUDGE:** Does he keep other people from going into your bakery?

**MANUEL:** No, sir, but—

**JUDGE:** Then what *does* he do?

**MANUEL:** He stands there, looking at my pies and cakes *and smelling them.*

**JUDGE:** That pleases you, doesn't it? ⑰

**MANUEL:** Pleases me! Far from it! Look here, your honor—every night I mix the flour and knead the dough and slave over a hot oven while that

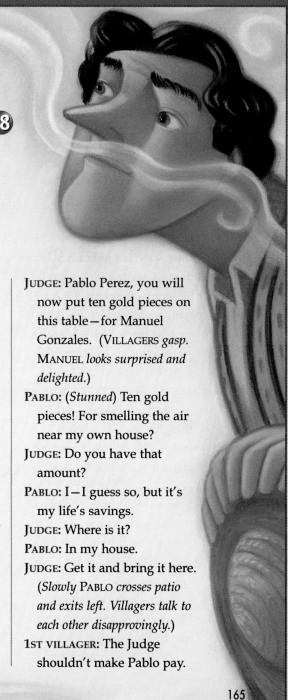

shiftless, good-for-nothing Pablo sleeps. Then he gets up in the morning, fresh as a daisy, and comes out here to **18** smell the fine sweet pastry I've baked. He takes full value of this free, daily luxury. He acts as if it's his privilege. Now I ask you, Judge—is it right that I should work so hard to provide him with this luxury, without charge? No! He should pay for it!

JUDGE: I see. You may sit down, Manuel. Now, Pablo Perez, it is your turn. (PABLO *stands.*) Is it true that you stand in front of Manuel's bakery and smell his cakes and pies?

PABLO: I can't help smelling them, your honor. Their spicy fragrance fills the air.

JUDGE: Would you say you *enjoy* it?

PABLO: Oh, yes, sir. I am a man of simple pleasures. Just the smell of a bakery makes me happy.

JUDGE: But did you ever pay the baker for this pleasure?

PABLO: Well, no, sir. It never occurred to me that I had to pay him.

JUDGE: Pablo Perez, you will now put ten gold pieces on this table—for Manuel Gonzales. (VILLAGERS *gasp.* MANUEL *looks surprised and delighted.*)

PABLO: (*Stunned*) Ten gold pieces! For smelling the air near my own house?

JUDGE: Do you have that amount?

PABLO: I—I guess so, but it's my life's savings.

JUDGE: Where is it?

PABLO: In my house.

JUDGE: Get it and bring it here. (*Slowly* PABLO *crosses patio and exits left. Villagers talk to each other disapprovingly.*)

1ST VILLAGER: The Judge shouldn't make Pablo pay.

165

Monitor Progress

## Make and Confirm Predictions

**Will Pablo have to give Manuel his life savings as payment? Explain your prediction.**
(Possible responses: Yes, because the Judge orders Pablo to bring his savings to the court after listening to Manuel's side of the story; No, the Judge wants Pablo to bring his savings to the court so that he can make a point about Pablo's side of the story.)

**If students were unable to answer, use this model:**

**MODEL** The Judge asks Pablo to bring his savings to the court. It seems as though Pablo is going to have to pay Manuel. The Judge does not say anything about Pablo paying Manuel the money, though. Maybe the Judge wants Pablo to bring his money to court for another reason. I will keep reading to confirm my prediction.

## SOCIAL STUDIES

**Courts, Officials, and Citizens** Identify the current members of the U.S. Supreme Court. Explain that Supreme Court justices are appointed by the President and serve a life term. Then identify the various state courts and the people who officiate over them. Ask students what level of government the Judge in "The Baker's Neighbor" represents. (local) Discuss how the judicial branch of the local government is similar to the judicial branch of the national government.

# Guided Comprehension

**19** (Focus Skill) **CAUSE/EFFECT  How do the villagers react when the Judge orders Pablo to get his life savings? What causes them to react that way?**
(Possible response: They are shocked and disapproving; they think that the Judge is going to make Pablo give the money to Manuel.)

**20 STORY EVENTS  What conclusion does Manuel draw about the money Pablo brings? How can you tell?**
(Possible response: Manuel thinks that Pablo has brought the money to pay him; he picks up Pablo's purse and begins to put it into his cash box.)

**21 MAKE JUDGMENTS  Has Pablo been a good friend and neighbor? In what ways?** (Possible responses: Yes, he has enjoyed and been thankful for the smell of Manuel's pastries; he gets along well with others in the town; and he respects others' ideas and possessions.)

---

1ST WOMAN: Pablo is an honest man.

2ND VILLAGER: I don't see how the Judge could rule in the baker's favor.

3RD VILLAGER: Why, he's richer than the Judge himself.

2ND WOMAN: And now he's going to get poor Pablo's savings.

3RD WOMAN: It's not fair! **19**

JUDGE: (*Rapping with his gavel*) Silence in the court! (PABLO *returns sadly with purse, puts it on table before* JUDGE. MANUEL, *elated, rubs his hands together greedily.*)

MANUEL: (*To* JUDGE) I knew your honor would do the right thing by me. Thank you, Judge. (*He picks up purse and starts to put it into his cash box.*) **20**

JUDGE: (*Rising*) Not so fast, Manuel! Empty that purse on the table and count the gold pieces, one by one.

MANUEL: (*Grinning craftily*) Ah, yes, your honor. I must make sure I haven't been cheated. How kind of you to remind me! (*He empties purse and begins to count, excitedly.*

JUDGE *watches* MANUEL *as he lovingly fingers each coin.*)

JUDGE: It gives you great pleasure to touch that gold, doesn't it, Manuel? You *enjoy* it.

MANUEL: Oh, I do, I do! . . . Eight . . . nine . . . ten. It's all here, your honor, and none of it false.

JUDGE: Please put it back in the purse. (*Manuel does so.*) Now return it to Pablo.

MANUEL: (*In disbelief*) *Return* it! But—but you just told Pablo to pay it to me.

JUDGE: No, I did not tell him to pay it to you. I told him to put it on this table. Then I instructed you to count the money, which you did. In doing so, you enjoyed Pablo's money the way he has enjoyed your cakes and pies. In other words, he has smelled your pastry and you have touched his gold. Therefore, I hereby declare that the case is now settled. (*He raps twice with his gavel.* MANUEL *shamefacedly shoves purse across table to* PABLO *and turns to leave.* JUDGE *stops him.*)

166

**REACHING ALL LEARNERS**

## Diagnostic Check: Comprehension and Skills

**If** . . . students are having difficulty identifying cause-and-effect relationships in the plot . . .

**Then** . . . work with them to make a cause-and-effect chart starting with the first action of the plot (cause) and the outcome of that action (effect).

### ADDITIONAL SUPPORT ACTIVITIES

**BELOW-LEVEL**  Reteach, p. S36

**ADVANCED**  Extend, p. S37

**ENGLISH-LANGUAGE LEARNERS**  Reteach, p. S37

## related books

You may want to recommend to students these titles.

### LIBRARY BOOKS COLLECTION

***Under the Lemon Moon***
by Edith Hope Fine.
1999.

### ADDITIONAL READING

- ***City Green***
  by Dyanne Di Salvo-Ryan. Morrow, 1994. **EASY**

- ***In My Momma's Kitchen***
  by Jerdine Nolan. Lothrop, Lee & Shepard,
  1999. **AVERAGE**

- ***Don't Read This Book Whatever You Do!***
  ***More Poems About School***
  by Kalli Dakos. Aladdin, 1998. **CHALLENGING**

## REREADING FOR FLUENCY

**Radio Play**   Assign small groups sequential portions of the selection to prepare as a radio play. Students should rehearse reading their lines accurately and with appropriate pacing, intonation, and expression.

Then have the groups perform their portions of the play in sequence, or tape them performing their portions in sequence. "Air" the complete play for the entire class.

**Note:** For assessment of oral reading accuracy and fluency, see pages T44–T46.

*The Baker's Neighbor*    **167**

# Guided Comprehension

**RETURN TO THE PREDICTIONS/PURPOSE**

**What problem do the characters face? How is it solved?** Discuss with students whether their purposes for reading were met.

# Think and Respond

## Answers:

1. Possible response: Manuel wants Pablo to pay for smelling his pies and cakes. The Judge tells Pablo to bring ten gold pieces. After Manuel counts the money, the Judge has him give it back to Pablo. **SUMMARIZE**

2. Possible responses: The author would use quotation marks and include information in the sentences to tell who is speaking. **AUTHOR'S CRAFT**

3. Possible response: to show that Manuel has learned his lesson **AUTHOR'S PURPOSE**

4. Responses will vary. **MAKE JUDGMENTS**

5. Responses will vary. **READING STRATEGIES**

## OPEN-ENDED RESPONSE

What did you like and dislike about reading this play? Would you like to read other plays? Write a paragraph answering these questions. Support your ideas with reasons.

---

Just a moment, Manuel! I hope this has been a lesson to you. In the future, think less about making money and more about making friends. Good friends and neighbors are better than gold. And now, if you please—my fee! **21**

MANUEL: Yes, your honor. (*He opens his cash box willingly but* JUDGE *closes the lid.*)

JUDGE: Put away your money. There's been enough fuss over money already today. The fee I am asking is this—pies and cakes for everyone here—free of charge! (MANUEL *nods his head vigorously in* assent. VILLAGERS *and children cheer, then they rush to pastry counter and help themselves.*

MANUEL *goes into bakery and reappears with more pastry piled high on tray.* PABLO *and* JUDGE *hold a whole pie between them and start to eat from opposite edges toward the center of pie, as the curtain closes.*)

THE END

## Think and Respond

1. What is the problem between Manuel the baker and his neighbor Pablo? How does the judge solve it?

2. How would this story be different if the author had not told it in the form of a play?

3. Why does the author have Manuel nod in **assent** at the end of the play?

4. Do you think the judge's solution is fair? Explain your answer.

5. When did you use a reading strategy as you read this play? Tell how the strategy helped you.

---

## COMPREHENSION

**End-of-Selection Test**

To evaluate comprehension, see *Practice Book*, pages A21–A24.

---

## Meet the Illustrator

# Mary GrandPré

Mary GrandPré is well known for her lively, colorful illustrations. She has received awards from The Society of Children's Book Illustrators, and the magazines *Communication Arts*, and *Art Direction*. She now is thinking about writing her own books. "I already have lots of ideas written down for stories," she said.

Mary GrandPré grew up in Minnesota, where she still lives with her two dogs and one cat. In her spare time she likes to cook and to remodel houses. She loves her illustrating work and said she likes to create books that people of all ages can enjoy.

**Visit *The Learning Site!***
www.harcourtschool.com

169

### RETELL

Use these questions to guide students as they retell "The Baker's Neighbor."

- **What is the problem between the baker and his neighbor?**
- **How do other people in the story feel about how the baker wants to solve the problem?**
- **How does the Judge solve the problem?**

### SUMMARIZE

Have students summarize the selection, using their completed cause-and-effect charts. See Transparency F on page T52.

#### ▼ Teaching Transparency F

| Cause | Effect |
|---|---|
| Pablo smells Manuel's pastries instead of buying them. | Manuel gets upset. |
| Pablo refuses to pay Manuel for smelling his pastries. | Manuel takes the case to the Judge. |
| The Judge asks Pablo to bring his gold coins to the courtroom. | Pablo brings his money. |
| The Judge asks Manuel to count the money. | Manuel enjoys counting the money. |
| Manuel enjoys counting the money. | The Judge declares the case settled because Manuel enjoyed counting Pablo's money just as Pablo enjoyed smelling Manuel's pastries. |

"The Baker's Neighbor"
You Can Do It!, Theme 1          **F**          Graphic Organizer
Harcourt

### WRITTEN SUMMARY

Have students use their completed cause-and-effect charts to write a summary of the plot of the play. PERFORMANCE ASSESSMENT

---

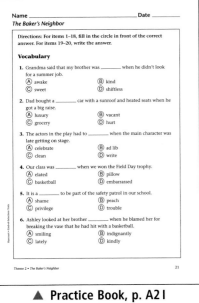

Name _____ Date _____
*The Baker's Neighbor*

Directions: For items 1–18, fill in the circle in front of the correct answer. For items 19–20, write the answer.

**Vocabulary**

1. Grandma said that my brother was _____ when he didn't look for a summer job.
   Ⓐ awake   Ⓑ kind
   Ⓒ sweet   Ⓓ shiftless

2. Dad bought a _____ car with a sunroof and heated seats when he got a big raise.
   Ⓐ luxury   Ⓑ vacant
   Ⓒ grocery   Ⓓ hurt

3. The actors in the play had to _____ when the main character was late getting on stage.
   Ⓐ celebrate   Ⓑ ad lib
   Ⓒ clean   Ⓓ write

4. Our class was _____ when we won the Field Day trophy.
   Ⓐ elated   Ⓑ pillow
   Ⓒ basketball   Ⓓ embarrassed

5. It is a _____ to be part of the safety patrol in our school.
   Ⓐ shame   Ⓑ peach
   Ⓒ privilege   Ⓓ trouble

6. Ashley looked at her brother _____ when he blamed her for breaking the vase that he had hit with a basketball.
   Ⓐ smiling   Ⓑ indignantly
   Ⓒ lately   Ⓓ kindly

Theme 2 • *The Baker's Neighbor*          21

▲ **Practice Book, p. A21**

Name _____ Date _____

17. Why do the children ask Manuel how much it costs to smell the flour on his apron or cap?
   Ⓐ They are making fun of him because they don't like his bakery.
   Ⓑ They think that his apron and cap are dirty.
   Ⓒ The flour that Manuel uses smells very tasty.
   Ⓓ They are teasing him because he is acting so silly.

18. Why does Manuel become excited when the judge orders Pablo to put the ten gold pieces on the table?
   Ⓐ Manuel needs to buy more flour for his bakery.
   Ⓑ He thinks the judge means to give him the gold as his payment.
   Ⓒ The gold looks pretty on the table.
   Ⓓ He has been stung by a bee.

19. Why do you think the judge's decision was a wise one?
   _____
   _____
   _____
   _____

20. How is a play different from a story? List at least two ways.
   _____
   _____
   _____

24          Theme 2 • *The Baker's Neighbor*

▲ **Practice Book, p. A24**

# Making Connections

▲ The Baker's Neighbor

# Making Connections

## COMPARE TEXTS

**Answers:**

**1** Possible response: It shows that neighbors can get along with one another by being fair and understanding one another's point of view. **THEME**

**2** Possible response: In the beginning, stage directions have Manuel speaking "sullenly" and "snorting in disgust." At the end of the play, the stage directions have him open the cash box "willingly" and nod his head "vigorously in assent." **TEXT STRUCTURE**

**3** Possible response: At first, he is happy and friendly. He thinks it is funny when Manuel goes to get the Judge, but he is surprised and disappointed when the Judge tells him to put gold on the table for Manuel. At the end, he is happy again because the Judge has settled the case fairly. **CHARACTERS' EMOTIONS**

**4** Possible response: It would not have stage directions or separate parts for each character. **GENRE/TEXT STRUCTURE**

**5** Possible responses: interview a business owner; read a book about starting your own business **INQUIRY**

## Compare Texts

**1** Why does "The Baker's Neighbor" belong in a theme about working with others?

**2** How does the author use stage directions to show a change in Manuel from the beginning of the play to the end?

**3** How and why do Pablo's feelings change during the play?

**4** How would "The Baker's Neighbor" be different if it were written as a story instead of a play?

**5** In the play, Manuel owns a bakery. How could you find out more about what it takes to start a business?

### Write an Ad

**S**uppose Manuel the baker asked you to write an ad to persuade people to go to his bakery. Use information from the play to write your ad. Include words and phrases that appeal to the senses. Organize your ideas in a web like this one.

**Writing CONNECTION**

170

## Conduct Experiments

**Science CONNECTION**

Manuel bakes pies and cakes in his bakery. The ingredients he uses probably include flour, sugar, and salt. Find out which of these substances dissolve in water. Conduct an experiment in which you stir 1 teaspoon of each substance into 1 cup of water. Write a prediction about the outcome of each experiment, keep a record of what happens, and then draw a conclusion.

| Substance | Prediction | Results When Stirred | Results After One Hour | Conclusion |
|-----------|-----------|------|------|-----------|
| salt | | | | |
| sugar | | | | |
| flour | | | | |

## Create a Pamphlet

**Social Studies CONNECTION**

The neighbors in "The Baker's Neighbor" ask the Judge to settle a disagreement. Research your state's court system. Create a pamphlet about the court system in your state. Include written information and illustrations.

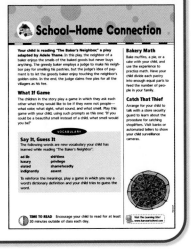

171

### HOMEWORK FOR THE WEEK

Students and family members can work together to complete the activities on page T62. You may want to assign some or all of the activities as homework for each day of the week.

**TECHNOLOGY**
**Visit *The Learning Site:***
**www.harcourtschool.com**
See Resources for Parents and Teachers:
Homework Helper.
**Teacher's Edition p. T62 ▶**

**🏫 School–Home Connection**

**Your child is reading "The Baker's Neighbor," a play adapted by Adele Thane.** In this play, the neighbor of a baker enjoys the smells of the baked goods but never buys anything. The greedy baker employs a judge to make his neighbor pay for smelling his pastries, but the judge's idea of payment is to let the greedy baker enjoy touching the neighbor's golden coins. In the end, the judge claims free pies for all the villagers as his fee.

**What If Game**
The children in the story play a game in which they ask each other what they would like to be if they were not people—what color, what sight, what sound, and what smell. Play this game with your child, using such prompts as this one: "If you could be a beautiful smell instead of a child, what smell would you be?"

**Say It, Guess It**
The following words are new vocabulary your child has learned while reading "The Baker's Neighbor":

VOCABULARY

ad lib            shirtless
luxury           privilege
elated           shamefacedly
indignantly      assent

To reinforce the meanings, play a game in which you say a word's dictionary definition and your child tries to guess the word.

**Bakery Math**
Bake muffins, a pie, or a cake with your child, and use the experience to practice math. Have your child divide each pastry into enough equal parts to feed the number of people in your family.

**Catch That Thief**
Arrange for your child to talk with a store security guard to learn about the procedure for catching shoplifters. Visit banks or automated tellers to show your child surveillance cameras.

**TIME TO READ** Encourage your child to read for at least 30 minutes outside of class each day.

---

## WRITING

**Write an Ad** Ask students to write down ideas as they look back through the play. Have them choose the ideas that are most persuasive to include in their ads.

**📁 PORTFOLIO OPPORTUNITY**
Students may choose to place their ads in their working portfolios.

## SCIENCE

**Conduct Experiments** Tell students to keep accurate records of their observations and to place their data in the correct spaces in the chart. Remind them to use what they observe and their prior knowledge to make predictions about the results.

| Substance | Prediction | Results When Stirred | Results After One Hour | Conclusion |
|-----------|-----------|------|------|-----------|
| Salt | | | | |
| Sugar | | | | |
| Flour | | | | |

## SOCIAL STUDIES

**Create a Pamphlet** Tell students that their social studies book and their state government's website may have information about the state court system. Have students categorize the information they find. Tell them to include a page in their pamphlets for each category.

# Cause and Effect

## SKILL TRACE

### CAUSE AND EFFECT

| Introduce | p. 150I |
|---|---|
| Reteach | pp. S36, S54, T36 |
| **Review** | **pp.172, 230I, 250** |
| Test | Theme 2 |
| Maintain | p. 397B |

### RETURN TO THE SKILL

Have students read page 172 in the *Pupil Edition.* You may want to use this model:

**MODEL** When I look at the chart on page 172, I see that the plot of "The Baker's Neighbor" is made up of causes and effects. Thinking about causes and effects helps me understand the relationships among events in the plot.

### PRACTICE/APPLY

Students can work in pairs or small groups to think of events or actions, such as a birthday party or hitting a ball. Then have them create cause-and-effect charts to illustrate the causes of each event or action.

**PERFORMANCE ASSESSMENT**

**TECHNOLOGY** ■ *Mission: Comprehension™ Skills Practice* CD-ROM provides additional practice with reading comprehension and focus skills.

**Visit** *The Learning Site*: www.harcourtschool.com
See Skill Activities and Test Tutors: Cause and Effect

---

▲ The Baker's Neighbor

# Cause and Effect Focus Skill

**A** **cause** is an action or event that makes something happen. An **effect** is what happens as a result of an action or event.

Sometimes authors use signal words such as *because* or *so* to help readers identify a cause and an effect. Other times, readers must figure out causes and effects on their own.

INEZ: If Manuel is that rich, why doesn't he smile?
CARLOS: That's because he's a miser. A miser doesn't like people—only money.

| **Cause** Manuel doesn't like people—only money. | → | **Effect** Manuel doesn't smile. |
|---|---|---|

Understanding causes and effects can help you better understand the plot of a story. Sometimes an effect has more than one cause. A cause can also have more than one effect.

| **Cause** Pablo enjoys smelling Manuel's pastries. | **Cause** Manuel wants Pablo to pay him. |
|---|---|

↓ ↓

| **Effect** Manuel calls the judge. |
|---|

**Visit** *The Learning Site!*
**www.harcourtschool.com**

See *Skills* and *Activities*

172

### REACHING ALL LEARNERS

## Diagnostic Check: Comprehension and Skills

**If** . . . students are having difficulty understanding cause-and-effect relationships . . .

**Then** . . . have them work in pairs. Pairs should write simple cause-and-effect statements such as "I overslept, so I missed the bus and was late for school."

### ADDITIONAL SUPPORT ACTIVITIES

| **BELOW-LEVEL** | Reteach, p. S36 |
| **ADVANCED** | Extend, p. S37 |
| **ENGLISH-LANGUAGE LEARNERS** | Reteach, p. S37 |

## Test Prep
Cause and Effect

▶ **Read the passage. Then answer the questions.**

Kevin decided to bake his dad a cake for his birthday. He took out the recipe book and gathered the ingredients. He did not understand the part of the recipe that told him to sift the flour, so he dumped the flour into the bowl. When he went to add the sugar, he realized that he didn't have enough, so he added extra salt. Then he poured the batter into the pan and called his mom to turn on the oven. After the cake was in the oven, he realized that he had forgotten to grease the pan. He hoped the cake would turn out.

1. **What causes Kevin to decide to bake a cake?**

   A  He has never baked a cake before.

   B  He wants dessert.

   C  The recipe looks easy.

   D  It is his father's birthday.

**Tip**

The question gives the effect and asks you to find the cause. To find a cause, ask yourself, *Why did this happen?*

2. **If the cake turns out poorly, which of these actions will *not* be a cause?**

   F  following the recipe

   G  not sifting the flour

   H  adding more salt instead of sugar

   J  forgetting to grease the pan

**Tip**

Read the question carefully. Remember that you are looking for the one action that will *not* cause the cake to turn out poorly.

173

# Test Prep

**Cause and Effect**   Have students read the passage carefully. Remind them that an effect is *what* happens and a cause is *why* something happens. Use the Tips to reinforce good test-taking strategies.

(1.D; 2.F)

---

| **BELOW-LEVEL** | **ON-LEVEL** | **ADVANCED** | **ENGLISH-LANGUAGE LEARNERS** |
|---|---|---|---|

▲ Extra Support, p. 25    ▲ Practice Book, p. 25    ▲ Challenge, p. 25    ▲ ELL, p. 25

# Figurative Language

## *Literary Analysis*

### INTRODUCE THE SKILL

**Discuss figurative language.**   Tell students that writers of fiction sometimes use special descriptive phrases to help readers picture what they are describing. These phrases often include *figurative language.* Figurative language is a group of words whose individual meanings are different from their meaning as a group. Discuss these examples of figurative language:

> It is raining cats and dogs. (idiom)
>
> His smile was like the sun after a storm. (simile)
>
> The rainbow was a brightly colored ribbon in the sky. (metaphor)
>
> The banner shouted at passersby. (personification)
>
> I've told you a million times not to do that. (hyperbole)

### TEACH/MODEL

**Model how to interpret figurative language.**   Direct students' attention to the following sentence on page 158 of the selection: *It's as if the bakery has burst into bloom.* Model interpreting the sentence figuratively.

**MODEL**  I know that a bakery can't actually burst into bloom. I think the sentence really means that the fragrance of freshly baked pies and cakes is similar to the strong, sweet smell of flowers that have just bloomed.

## GUIDED PRACTICE

**Display Transparency 51.** Use the transparency to make sure students understand figurative language.

- **In figurative language, the words have a literal meaning that is different from the intended meaning.**

- **There are different types of figurative language.**

- **Guide students through the examples pointing out the characteristics of each type of figurative language.**

## PRACTICE/APPLY

**Hunt for figurative language.** Encourage students to look for examples of figurative language in other stories. Have them use context or a dictionary to find literal meanings. Then have small groups discuss what each expression means. Have students fill in a chart like the one below. **PERFORMANCE ASSESSMENT**

| Figurative Language | What Each Word Means By Itself | What the Words Mean Together |
|---|---|---|
| | | |

▼ **Teaching Transparency 51**

**FIGURATIVE LANGUAGE**

In figurative language, the meaning of a group of words often is different from the meaning of each word in that group. Writers use figurative language to create vivid images in the mind of the reader.

**Types of Figurative Language**

| | |
|---|---|
| **Idiom:** a group of words with a special meaning |
| **Simile:** a comparison signaled by the use of *like* or *as* |
| **Metaphor:** a comparison that says one thing *is* something else |
| **Personification:** a figure of speech that gives human qualities to animals, abstract ideas, or nonliving things |
| **Hyperbole:** an obviously exaggerated statement made for dramatic effect |

**EXAMPLES:**

**Idiom:** She spilled the beans about our neighbor's new baby.
**Simile:** The baby's cheeks are as smooth as a peach.
**Metaphor:** Mom says our neighbor's baby is a little lamb.
**Personification:** The toys in the baby's room begged us to play with them.
**Hyperbole:** The baby's sweater was the tiniest thing I've ever seen.

"The Baker's Neighbor" Side by Side, Theme 2 — 51 — Figurative Language Harcourt

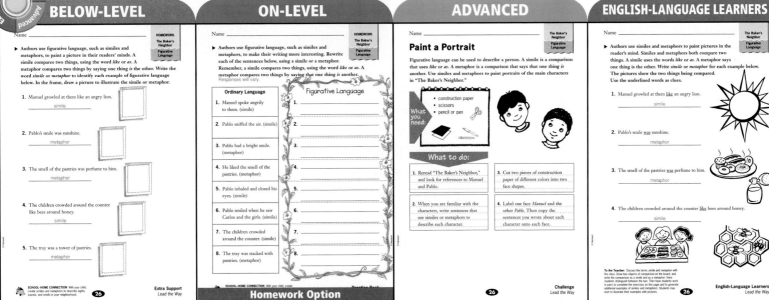

▲ Extra Support, p. 26     ▲ Practice Book, p. 26     ▲ Challenge, p. 26     ▲ ELL, p. 26

*The Baker's Neighbor* **173B**

# Phonics

## OBJECTIVE

*To decode words with /s/c and /j/g*

### SKILL TRACE

| LETTER PATTERNS: CONSONANT /s/c; /j/g | |
|---|---|
| Introduce | Grade 2 |
| **Maintain** | **p. 173C** |

### ONGOING ASSESSMENT

**If** students are not able to read fluently approximately 99 words per minute, **then** they require phonics instruction and will also benefit from fluency practice.

**NOTE:** For assessment of oral reading accuracy and fluency, see pages T44–T46.

*Phonics Practice Book,* Intermediate, pp. 202–218

# Decoding/Phonics

*Letter Patterns: Consonant /s/c and Consonant /j/g*

### MAINTAIN THE SKILL

**Decode words with the letter patterns /s/c and /j/g.** Write the words *center* and *gem* on the board, and have students read them aloud. Ask students what sound the *c* stands for in *center*. /s/ Then ask students what sound the *g* in *gem* stands for. /j/ Review with students that when the letter *c* is followed by the vowel *e*, *i*, or *y*, it has the /s/ sound. When *g* is followed by *e*, *i*, or *y*, it has the /j/ sound.

Write the word *city* on the board. Ask students to identify the letter that stands for the /s/ sound. Have them explain how they know that the *c* has the /s/ sound. (It is followed by the letter *i*.)

Repeat the procedure with the word *general*.

### PRACTICE/APPLY

**Pronounce words with the letter patterns /s/c and /j/g.** Write the words below on the board. Have students copy the list.

| candy | coffee | gentle |
| gymnastics | city | pencil |
| gasoline | genuine | ageless |
| center | golf | actress |

Ask students to underline the words that are pronounced with the /s/ or /j/ sound. Then have students break the underlined words into syllables and pronounce them. Ask students how they decided whether to pronounce the *c* with the /s/ sound or the /k/ sound. Then ask how they decided whether to pronounce the *g* with the /j/ sound or the /g/ sound. Encourage students to make a list of other words with *c* that have the /s/ sound and words with *g* that have the /j/ sound. **PERFORMANCE ASSESSMENT**

century    generous

# Prefixes, Suffixes, and Roots

*Vocabulary and Concepts*

## OBJECTIVE

*To use prefixes, suffixes, and roots to decode words and understand their meanings*

### SKILL TRACE

**PREFIXES, SUFFIXES, AND ROOTS**

| | |
|---|---|
| Introduce | p. 50I |
| Reteach | pp. S10, S22, T4 |
| Review | pp. 76, 102I, 122 |
| Test | Theme I |
| **Maintain** | p. 173D |

## MAINTAIN THE SKILL

**Discuss prefixes, suffixes, and roots.** Remind students that knowing the meanings of prefixes, suffixes, and roots can help readers figure out unfamiliar words. Ask volunteers to explain what prefixes, suffixes, and roots are. (prefix: a word part that is added to the beginning of a word to change its meaning; suffix: a word part that is added to the end of a word to change its meaning; root: the basic part of a word that gives the word its meaning) Remind students that longer words are often made up of a prefix, a root word or root, and a suffix.

Then use the word *disbelief* on page 161 to model how to use prefixes and suffixes to figure out the meanings of unfamiliar words.

**MODEL** I see a prefix I know at the beginning of the word *disbelief.* If I cover up the prefix *dis-*, I see the root word *belief.* I remember that *dis-* sometimes means "lack of," and I know that *belief* means "a feeling that something is true or real." When I put the meanings of the prefix and the root word together, I understand that *disbelief* means "lack of belief."

## ADVANCED

Have students make root clusters. Students should write a root at the center of a cluster and around it write words that can be developed by adding prefixes, suffixes, or other roots to it.

## PRACTICE/APPLY

**Use word parts to determine meaning.** Have each student find three other words in "The Baker's Neighbor" or another story that contain prefixes, suffixes, and roots. Then ask them to break each word into its parts and show the word as an equation:

### quiet + ly = quietly

Have students write their equations and tell how the meanings of the root words have been changed. **PERFORMANCE ASSESSMENT**

**Summarize.** Have students explain why knowing the meanings of prefixes, suffixes, and roots is useful. (Possible response: You can use prefixes, suffixes, and roots to figure out the meaning of the word.)

# Paragraph of Information

## Writer's Craft: Effective Paragraphs

## TRAITS OF GOOD WRITING

| | INTRODUCE AND PRACTICE | APPLY TO LONGER WRITING FORMS |
|---|---|---|
| Focus/Ideas | 421E–F | 453E–F, 471C–D |
| Organization | 521E–F, 543E–F | 567C–D, 589E–F |
| Voice | 49E–F, 77E–F | 101C–D, 123C–D |
| Word Choice | 637E–F, 667E–F | 689C–D, 713C–D |
| Development | 421E–F, 437C–D | 453E–F, 471C–D |
| Effective Sentences | 299E–F, 325C–D | 349C–D, 371C–D |
| Effective Paragraphs | 173E–F, 205C–D | 229E–F, 251C–D |
| Conventions | (See Grammar and Spelling Lessons.) | (Applied to all writing lessons.) |

## technology

**Writing Express™ CD-ROM**
Visit *The Learning Site*:
www.harcourtschool.com
See Writing Detective:
Proofreading Makes Perfect.

## TRAITS OF GOOD WRITING

- **Focus/Ideas:** The writer has a clear task and audience in mind.

- **Organization/Effective Paragraphs:** The first sentence states the main idea of the paragraph. The writer provides three examples in a logical order. The main idea is restated.

- **Voice:** The writer thinks cooperation on a camping trip is important.

- **Word Choice:** The writer uses specific verbs such as *carry, pack* and *clean* to describe duties.

- **Development:** The writer supplies details about each task to support the main idea. Signal words and phrases are used to identify the stages of the trip.

- **Effective Sentences:** Transition words help the sentences flow together.

**173E    Side by Side**

### DAY 1 — TEACH/MODEL

**CONNECT READING TO WRITING** Remind students that cause-and-effect relationships are one way the author of "The Baker's Neighbor" organizes events. Tell students that ordering ideas is an important part of writing effective paragraphs.

**ORGANIZATION: ORDERING IDEAS** Explain to students that it is important for writers to organize their ideas in a logical order. Some ways to organize ideas include time order, and order of importance. Guide students in determining the order of ideas in the model.

▼ **Teaching Transparency 52**

**STUDENT MODEL: PARAGRAPH OF INFORMATION**

The topic sentence of a paragraph of information states the main idea. The writer then develops the main idea with supporting facts or examples. The following paragraph of information was written by a student for a friend whose family plans to go camping.

**topic sentence** — Everyone on a camping trip has to cooperate to make the trip a success. For

**first fact or example with details** — example, campers need food, water, and equipment. On the way to the campsite, each camper must carry part of the load. When you arrive at camp, everyone helps set up the tents. Making a fire, cooking,

**second fact or example with details** — and washing dishes are some of the tasks that can be shared while camping. Finally,

**third fact or example with details** — when it is time to leave, everyone must help pack up and clean the campsite. That includes carefully putting out the fire. A

**main idea restated** — camping trip can be fun if all the campers do their share.

"The Baker's Neighbor"
Side by Side, Theme 2    52    Writing: Paragraph Information    Harcourt

### DAY 2 — EXTEND THE CONCEPT

**ORDERING IDEAS** Display Transparency 53, and have students use the graphic organizer in Part A to arrange the examples from the student model in time order.

**APPLY TO WRITING** Point out that order of importance is another logical way to order ideas. When a writer arranges ideas according to their importance, the most important idea may be presented first or last. Have students use the graphic organizer in Part B of Transparency 53 to write the examples in the student model in order of importance, with what they consider the most important example at the top.

▼ **Teaching Transparency 53**

**ORDERING IDEAS**

Good writers present ideas in a logical order.

A. Organize the examples from the student model in time order, using this diagram.

**Sequence Chart**

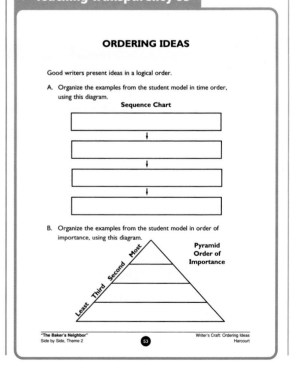

B. Organize the examples from the student model in order of importance, using this diagram.

Pyramid Order of Importance

Most  Second  Third  Least

"The Baker's Neighbor"
Side by Side, Theme 2    53    Writer's Craft: Ordering Ideas    Harcourt

# 5 Day Plan

DAY **3** PREWRITE

**APPLY TO LITERATURE** Have students look back at "The Baker's Neighbor" to determine the way in which the author ordered her ideas. (Possible responses: sequence of events; cause and effect)

**WRITING PROMPT:** *Think about an activity that involves several people, such as doing a school project. Then write a paragraph of information that tells the responsibilities of each person for the activity. Present the responsibilities in a logical order.*

**PREWRITE** Tell students to state their focus (topic, audience, and purpose). Then have them list the responsibilities of each person involved in the activity.

DAY **4** DRAFT

**DRAFT** Have students draft their paragraphs:

1. **Introduce** the topic in the first sentence.

2. **Organize** the responsibilities in time order, order of importance, or another logical order.

3. **Develop** the main idea by providing details about each responsibility.

4. **Conclude** by restating the main idea.

DAY **5** REVISE AND REFLECT

**REVISION FOCUS: DELETING**
Explain that one part of revising is deleting unnecessary facts, examples, or details. Information that does not support the main idea should be deleted.

**PEER CONFERENCE CHECKLIST**
Have student pairs use this checklist to discuss their paragraphs. Students may want to keep their revised paragraphs in their work portfolios. Provide these questions:

✓ **Is there a clear topic sentence?**

✓ **Is the main idea supported by facts or examples?**

✓ **Are the ideas presented in a logical order?**

✓ **Do any details need to be deleted because they don't support the main idea?**

| SCORING RUBRIC | | | |
|---|---|---|---|
| **4** | **3** | **2** | **1** |
| **FOCUS/IDEAS** Completely focused, purposeful. | Generally focused on task and purpose. | Somewhat focused on task and purpose. | Lacks focus and purpose. |
| **ORGANIZATION/ PARAGRAPHS** Ideas progress logically; transitions make the relationships among ideas clear. | Organization mostly clear, but some lapses occur; some transitions are used. | Some sense of organization but inconsistent or unclear in places. | Little or no sense of organization. |
| **DEVELOPMENT** Central idea supported by strong, specific details. | Central idea with adequate support, mostly relevant details. | Unclear central idea; limited supporting details. | Unclear central idea; little or no development. |
| **VOICE** Viewpoint clear; original expressions used where appropriate. | Viewpoint somewhat clear; few original expressions. | Viewpoint unclear or inconsistent. | Writer seems detached and unconcerned. |
| **WORD CHOICE** Clear, exact language; freshness of expression. | Clear language; some interesting word choices. | Word choice unclear or inappropriate in places. | Word choice often unclear or inappropriate. |
| **SENTENCES** Variety of sentence structures; flows smoothly. | Some variety in sentence structures. | Little variety; choppy or run-on sentences. | Little or no variety; sentences unclear. |
| **CONVENTIONS** Few, if any, errors. | Few errors. | Some errors. | Many errors. |

**REPRODUCIBLE STUDENT RUBRICS** for specific writing purposes and presentations are available on pages T56–T58.

Language Handbook, pp. 30–33, 67, 108–110, 198–199

# Grammar

## Complete and Simple Predicates

### SKILL TRACE

**COMPLETE AND SIMPLE PREDICATES**

| | |
|---|---|
| Introduce | pp. 173G–173H |
| Review | p. 205F |
| Test | Theme 2 |
| Reteach | pp. S39, T38 |

### REACHING ALL LEARNERS

## Diagnostic Check: Grammar and Writing

**If** . . . students are unable to locate the simple predicate in the complete predicate . . .

**Then** . . . have them work in pairs. One student should cover the subject and ask, "What did the subject do?" The response should be the simple predicate. Have student reverse roles.

### ADDITIONAL SUPPORT ACTIVITIES

| | |
|---|---|
| **BELOW-LEVEL** | Reteach, p. S38 |
| **ADVANCED** | Extend, p. S39 |
| **ENGLISH-LANGUAGE LEARNERS** | Reteach, p. S39 |

## technology

**Grammar Jingles™ CD,**
Intermediate: Track 3
Visit *The Learning Site:*
**www.harcourtschool.com**
See Grammar Practice Park,
Go for Grammar Gold,
Multimedia Grammar Glossary.

---

### DAY 1 — TEACH/MODEL

**DAILY LANGUAGE PRACTICE**

1. **Neighbors and friends. Sometims argue or disagree.**
   (friends sometimes)
2. **Are you in a bad moode.**
   (mood?)

**INTRODUCE THE CONCEPT** Use Transparency 54 to show that:

- The **complete predicate** includes words that tell what the subject of the sentence is or does.
- The **simple predicate** is the main word or words in the complete predicate of a sentence.

Have students add subjects to items 4–6. Ask them to circle the simple predicate.

▼ **Teaching Transparency 54**

**COMPLETE AND SIMPLE PREDICATES**

1. Manuel and Pablo disagreed. complete: disagreed; simple: disagreed
2. Manuel and Pablo disagreed with each other.
   complete: disagreed with each other; simple: disagreed
3. They had an argument. complete: had an argument; simple: had
4. asked the Judge
5. shoved the purse across the table
6. counted the money excitedly

4–6. Responses will vary. Students should circle *asked*, *shoved*, and *counted*.

"The Baker's Neighbor"
Side by Side, Theme 2

54

Grammar
Harcourt

---

### DAY 2 — EXTEND THE CONCEPT

**DAILY LANGUAGE PRACTICE**

1. **how noisy the children are** (How; are!)
2. **Mr. Adams sweeps. the stop with a broom.** (sweeps the stoop)

**BUILD ORAL LANGUAGE** Write these words on the board: *walk, help, jump, love.* Tell students that some words can be part of either the subject or the predicate of a sentence, depending on how they are used. Say a sentence in which you use one of the words as a simple subject—for example, *The walk was fun.* Then ask students to say sentences in which the same word is used as the simple predicate—for example, *We walk to school.*

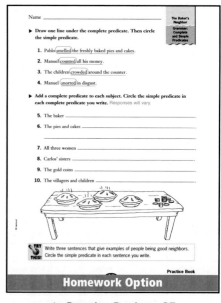

▲ **Practice Book, p. 27**

---

## DAILY LANGUAGE PRACTICE

1. **I carry the garbage out. And put it by the street** (out and; street.)

2. **In the afternon! Mona and My sister walk the dog.** (afternoon Mona and my)

**SAME SUBJECT** Write on the board sentences that contain the same subject. Have students identify the complete and simple predicates in each.

### Test Prep Tip

"If you have trouble locating the predicate, remember that these forms of *be* are always the simple predicate or part of it: *am, is, are, was, were.*"

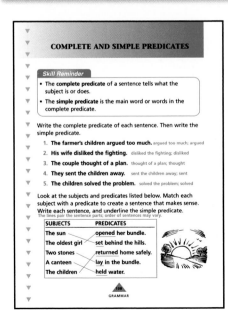

▲ Language Handbook, p. 108

## DAILY LANGUAGE PRACTICE

1. **People crowded Around our both?** (crowded around; booth.)

2. **My brother. and I. painted and set it up.** (brother and I painted)

**UNITY** Have students write a paragraph about why people working together is important at home, at school, or in a neighborhood. Ask students to exchange papers and identify the complete and simple predicates in each other's work.

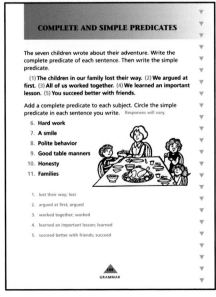

▲ Language Handbook, p. 109

## DAILY LANGUAGE PRACTICE

1. **Who wants? to have a booth next year!** (wants to; year?)

2. **sign up now for the neighborhood fair** (Sign; fair! *or* fair.)

**SUBJECTS AND PREDICATES** Have students copy these sentences and draw one line under the complete subject and two lines under the complete predicate. Ask them to write *S* above each simple subject and *P* above each simple predicate.

1. Our neighbors volunteered for next year.

2. They want a food booth.

3. The woman next door plans to bake pies and cakes.

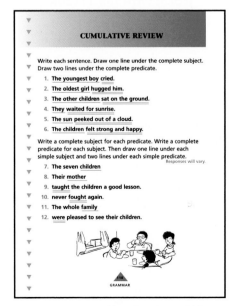

▲ Language Handbook, p. 110

*The Baker's Neighbor*   **173H**

## Spelling Words

1. carved
2. garden
3. harm*
4. farther
5. barked
6. alarm
7. chart
8. starved
9. harder
10. parked
11. smartest
12. charge*
13. guard
14. argument
15. hardware
16. garbage
17. harsh
18. parts
19. radar
20. harbor

* Selection Words

### Challenge Words

21. tapioca*
22. gourmet
23. delicious*
24. delicatessen
25. pastry*

# Spelling

## Words with /är/

**DAY 1 — PRETEST/SELF-CHECK**

**ADMINISTER THE PRETEST** Use the Dictation Sentences under Day 5. Help students self-check their pretests using Transparency 55.

### ADVANCED

Use the Challenge Words in these Dictation Sentences:

21. The **tapioca** tart was a sweet end to the meal.
22. The **gourmet** expected the food to be perfect.
23. The food was **delicious**.
24. We bought something for lunch at the **delicatessen**.
25. The freshly baked **pastry** was still warm.

**DAY 2 — TEACH/MODEL**

**WORD SORT** Display Transparency 55. Make sure students know the meanings of the words. Then ask them to copy the chart and to write each Spelling Word where it belongs.

Point to and read a five-letter word on the chart. Ask a volunteer to circle the letters that make the /är/ sound. Do the same with longer words. Ask students what vowel sound they hear in all the words and which letters stand for that sound.

**HANDWRITING** Advise students to close the circle along the top line when they write the letter *a*.

*a*

▼ **Teaching Transparency 55**

### WORDS WITH THE /är/ SOUND

**Spelling Words**

| | | | |
|---|---|---|---|
| 1. carved | 6. alarm | 11. smartest | 16. garbage |
| 2. garden | 7. chart | 12. charge | 17. harsh |
| 3. harm | 8. starved | 13. guard | 18. parts |
| 4. farther | 9. harder | 14. argument | 19. radar |
| 5. barked | 10. parked | 15. hardware | 20. harbor |

| 4 letters | 5 letters | 6 letters | 7 letters | 8 letters |
|---|---|---|---|---|
| harm | alarm | carved | farther | smartest |
| | chart | garden | starved | argument |
| | guard | barked | garbage | hardware |
| | harsh | harder | | |
| | parts | parked | | |
| | radar | charge | | |
| | | harbor | | |

The vowel sound you hear in car is usually spelled ar.

"The Baker's Neighbor"
Side by Side, Theme 2          55          Spelling Harcourt

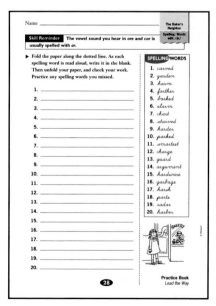
▲ Practice Book, p. 28

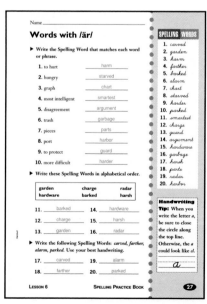
▲ Spelling Practice Book, p. 27

**GUESSING AND CHECKING**   Write the following on the board:

**barege  start  farm**

Suggest that when students encounter a word they are not sure how to spell, they take a guess. Ask a volunteer to write any misspelled words correctly. *(barge)*

If students are still not sure about the spelling, they should look up the word in a dictionary.

### Apply to Writing

Have students use their writing and look for words with the /är/ sound that they are unsure of how to spell. Have them guess how to spell them and then check them in a dictionary.

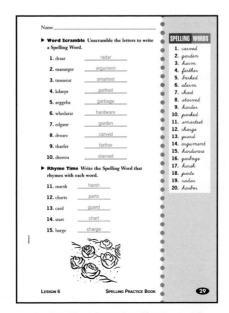

▲ Spelling Practice Book, p. 28

**THINK AND SPELL**   Organize the class into small groups. Have one person think of a Spelling Word and write it on a sheet of paper. The other students in the group guess the word by spelling it within a given number of turns. They start by guessing the first letter, the second, and so on. The student who is It records the correct letters on a sheet of paper. The student who completes the word then becomes It.

**TEN QUESTIONS**   To play Ten Questions, have a student write a Spelling Word on a sheet of paper. His or her partner asks up to ten yes-or-no questions to determine which word has been written. One point is scored for each question the partner asks.

▲ Spelling Practice Book, p. 29

**DICTATION SENTENCES**

1. We **carved** a pumpkin for the fall festival.
2. Mrs. Carter's **garden** has many beautiful flowers.
3. Try not to **harm** the plants when you paint the fence.
4. Can you run **farther** than Joan?
5. Our dog Mattie **barked** at the letter carrier.
6. Is the smoke **alarm** working?
7. We made a **chart** of the heights of all students in our class.
8. The winter has been so bad that the squirrels look **starved**.
9. The **harder** you practice, the better you will learn to spell.
10. We **parked** near the gym.
11. My mother is the **smartest** woman I know.
12. What do you **charge** to fix a flat tire?
13. The crossing **guard** told us to wait.
14. I had an **argument** with my best friend.
15. We are going to the **hardware** store.
16. I take out the **garbage** every night.
17. They live in a **harsh** climate.
18. I like **parts** of the book.
19. The **radar** showed that he was speeding.
20. There are no boats in the **harbor**.

*The Baker's Neighbor*   **173J**

# Word Study

## Determine Meanings

**OBJECTIVE**

*To use context and reference sources to determine the meanings of homophones*

Write on the board these words:

peace          night

Discuss the words and their meanings. Then, under each word, write its homophone: *peace/piece*; *night/knight*. Have students explain how the words in each pair are alike and different. Point out that homophones are words that sound the same but are spelled differently and have different meanings.

| Homophones | Sentences |
|------------|-----------|
| wood | The table is made of wood. |
| would | Would you help me look for my coat? |
| sun | The sun is covered by clouds today. |
| son | Her son plays soccer on Saturdays. |

Have students figure out the meaning of a homophone by using a dictionary or context clues. Pairs of students can work together to fill in the chart by looking up the words in a dictionary and writing context sentences. You might take this opportunity to have them practice writing commonly confused words such as *its* and *it's*.

## Find Meanings

**OBJECTIVE**

*To apply knowledge of word origins to determine the meanings of words and phrases*

Explain that many words in English come from Latin, an ancient language. Point out, for example, that the term *ad lib* comes from the longer Latin expression *ad libitum*, meaning "as one wishes." Have students use a dictionary to find the meanings of these commonly used words of Latin origin.

agenda

consensus

curriculum

data

extempore

vice versa

**BELOW-LEVEL**

Students may be unfamiliar with the parts of a dictionary entry. Guide students as they look up the word *agenda*. Point out the part of speech, the word origin, the definition, as well as any synonyms or antonyms that are given.

# Speaking and Listening

## Performing a Dramatic Presentation

**OBJECTIVE**

*To use clear diction, tempo, volume, and phrasing to represent several characters in a dramatic performance*

Have one group of students perform a dramatic reading of "The Baker's Neighbor" while another group watches as an audience. Then have the groups change roles.

**Organization**   Share these **organizational tips**.
- Assign each group member a part. Choose a narrator to introduce the show and set the scene.
- Rehearse reading and performing as a group. During the rehearsal, decide matters such as where each person will sit and where props will be kept.

**Delivery**   Share the following **practice tips** with students.
- Speak clearly and project your voice so that the audience can hear you.
- Adjust pitch, tone, and stress to express different characters' feelings.
- Show characters' feelings with gestures and movements on the stage to enhance meaning.

## Audience Behavior

**OBJECTIVE**

*To listen and respond to a dramatic performance*

Have students listen carefully to the performance of each character in "The Baker's Neighbor."

Share the Listening Tips with students.

### Listening Tips
- Notice voice cues that signal important feelings and ideas.
- Watch to interpret nonverbal cues, such as gestures and movements.
- Show your appreciation by applauding at the end of the performance.

**GOOD-LISTENER PAMPHLET**   Have each group compose a pamphlet for their audience titled "How to Get the Most Out of a Dramatic Presentation." Students should include listening and watching tips specifically for a play as well as general tips for responsive audience behavior. Have students distribute their pamphlets before their group's performance.

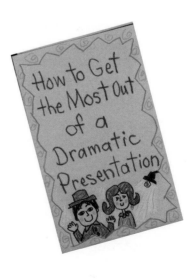

*The Baker's Neighbor*   **173L**

# Books for All Learners

*Reinforcing Skills and Strategies*

## ■ BELOW-LEVEL

adapted by Cynthia Benjamin
illustrated by Tatjana Mai-Wyss

 **Focus Skill: Cause and Effect**

 **Focus Strategy: Use Decoding/Phonics**

 **Vocabulary:** *privilege, luxury, elated, assent, ad lib, shiftless, indignantly, shamefacedly*

**Genre:** Play
**Language Arts Connection:** Understand the Elements of a Play

**SUMMARY** A king is outsmarted and learns some lessons from his new queen.

For additional related activities, visit *The Learning Site* at
**www.harcourtschool.com**

---

### BEFORE READING

**Preview/Set Purpose** Have students preview the book. Discuss how reading a play is different from reading other fiction.

**Reinforce Cause and Effect** Have students create a cause-effect chart to track events in the play. CAUSE AND EFFECT/GRAPHIC SOURCES

| Cause | Effect |
|-------|--------|
|       |        |

**Reinforce Vocabulary** Ask students which vocabulary word best matches the King's expression in the illustration on page 12.

### READING THE BOOK

**Page 2** Why does the King wish to meet Catherine? (He heard that she is known to be very wise.) IMPORTANT DETAILS

**Page 9** Why do you think Queen Catherine tries to help the farmer? (She is a nice person who is fair.)
EXPRESS PERSONAL OPINIONS

**Pages 14–16** How does the King end up in the hut of Queen Catherine's father? (He falls asleep after a heavy meal, and servants carry him there for Queen Catherine.) CAUSE AND EFFECT

**Reread for Fluency** Have students choose a favorite scene in the play and reread it aloud to you.

### RESPONDING

**Cause and Effect** Students can complete their charts by writing events from the play under the heading *Effect*. Then they can write why the event happened under the heading *Cause*.

 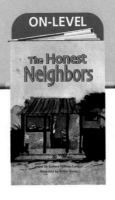  

▲ page 173O    ▲ page 173P

**Managing Small Groups**

While you work with small groups have other students do the following:

- Self-Selected Reading
- Practice Pages
- Cross-Curricular Centers
- Journal Writing

## ■ ON-LEVEL

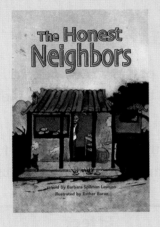

 **Focus Skill: Cause and Effect**

 **Focus Strategy: Use Decoding/Phonics**

 **Vocabulary: *privilege, luxury, elated, assent, ad lib, shiftless, indignantly, shamefacedly***

**Genre:** Folktale

**Social Studies Connection:** Understand the importance of participation through community service, civic improvement, and political activities.

**SUMMARY** This story tells of five neighbors who learn from a stranger a lesson about honesty and dishonesty.

For additional related activities, visit *The Learning Site* at **www.harcourtschool.com**

### BEFORE READING

**Preview/Set Purpose** Have students preview the book. Have them explain what the illustrations might reveal about the book.

**Reinforce Cause and Effect** Have students make a chart like the following to keep track of the causes of some of the events in the story. GRAPHIC SOURCES

| Cause | → | Effect |

### READING THE BOOK

**pages 4–10** What are each of the five neighbors talking about before the stranger comes? (They each tell a story of how honest they are and accuse one another of dishonesty.) **MAIN IDEA AND DETAILS**

**pages 12–15** How is Chang's dishonesty shown? (He does not touch the bell, and this eventually shows his fear of being caught lying.) **CAUSE AND EFFECT**

**Rereading for Fluency** Have groups of students perform dramatic readings of passages from the story that they liked or found interesting.

### RESPONDING

**Story Map** Have students complete a story map to summarize the story.

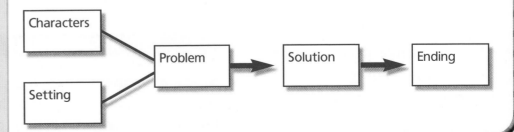

# Books for All Learners

*Reinforcing Skills and Strategies*

## ■ ADVANCED

 **Focus Skill: Cause and Effect**

 **Focus Strategy: Use Decoding/Phonics**

 **Vocabulary: *privilege, luxury, elated, assent, ad lib, shiftless, indignantly, shamefacedly, germinate, humus***

**Genre:** Nonfiction
**Science Connection:** Distinctions are made among observations.

**SUMMARY** This story tells how wheat is grown and harvested, and it explains all the food products that can be made from wheat.

For additional related activities, visit *The Learning Site* at **www.harcourtschool.com**

## BEFORE READING

**Preview/Set Purpose** Have students preview the book's illustrations and photographs. Then have them tell why they think the information in this book might be important.

**Reinforce Cause and Effect** Have students begin a chart to track the causes and effects of the events from the book. GRAPHIC AIDS

| Cause | Effect |
|-------|--------|
|       |        |

**Expand Vocabulary** Write the words *germinate* and *humus* on the board and discuss their meanings. (*germinate*: begin to grow or develop from seed; *humus*: decaying plant and animal matter that becomes food for plants)

## READING THE BOOK

**pages 4–16** What information does this book give? (how wheat is planted and harvested, food that can be made from wheat) SUMMARIZE

**pages 8–10** How does wheat become flour? (It is harvested, stored, and then ground into flour at a mill.) CAUSE AND EFFECT

**Rereading for Fluency** Have students choose a passage from the book that they liked or found interesting. Then have students read aloud the passage the way they believe it should be read.

## RESPONDING

**Share a Recipe** Tell students to think of a favorite food or dish that is made with wheat as an ingredient. Have them present instructions for preparing and eating that food or dish.

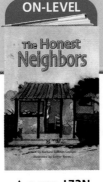
**Managing Small Groups**

While you work with small groups have other students do the following:
- Self-Selected Reading
- Practice Pages
- Cross-Curricular Centers
- Journal Writing

▲ page 173M     ▲ page 173N

## ■ ENGLISH-LANGUAGE LEARNERS

 **Focus Skill: Cause and Effect**

 **Focus Strategy: Use Decoding/Phonics**

 **Concept Vocabulary:**
*Saturday, party, learn, something, can't, surprise*

**Genre:** Fiction
**Social Studies Connection:** Describe American Immigration

**SUMMARY**   Natasha and her friends have a tradition-sharing party.

For additional related activities, visit *The Learning Site* at **www.harcourtschool.com**

### BEFORE READING

**Tap Prior Knowledge**   Write the word *tradition* on the board. Explain that traditions are customs or beliefs that are passed from one generation to the next.  Ask students to give examples of traditions that they or their families have.

**Total Physical Response**   Have students draw a picture of foods they like to eat at celebrations.

**Display Vocabulary Concept Words**   Write the words on the board. Use the illustrations in the book to discuss their meanings.

**Preview the Book**   Read the title, and ask students to predict what the book may be about. Help students preview the book by pointing out and discussing the illustrations.

### READING THE BOOK

**Page 5**   Why has Chun learned English but her grandmother hasn't? (Her grandmother's friends are all Chinese, so it hasn't been necessary to learn a new language.) FOCUS SKILL: CAUSE AND EFFECT

**Pages 9–10**   What food will be served at the tradition-sharing party? (coconut macaroons, Scottish shortbread cookies, che, sweet rice cakes, empanadas, vareniki, tea with jam) IMPORTANT DETAILS

**Pages 2–16**   What is the main idea of this story? (Students share traditional foods from their homelands.) MAIN IDEA/SUMMARIZE

**Rereading**   Reread the book aloud with students. Have volunteers reread and summarize sections of their choice.

### RESPONDING

**Concept Web**   Use a Web to help students retell the story.

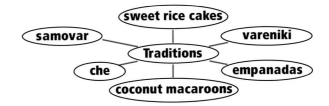

# Teacher Notes

**THEME CONNECTION:**
*Side by Side*

**GENRE:**
*Folktale*

PAPERSTAR

Caldecott Honor
ALA Notable
SLJ Best Book

The Emperor
and the Kite

by JANE YOLEN    illustrated by ED YOUNG

Comparing Folktales and
Magazine Articles

▲ **READING ACROSS TEXTS:** "Kite Festivals"
**GENRE:** Magazine Article

## SUMMARY:

Djeow Seow is so tiny that her father, the Emperor, hardly knows she exists. His attitude changes when she saves his life.

 Selections available on *Audiotext 2*

# Guided Reading OPTIONS

# Books for All Learners

*Lesson Plans on pages 205K–205N*

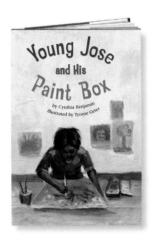

## BELOW-LEVEL

- Lesson Vocabulary
- Focus Skill: Narrative Elements

## ON-LEVEL

- Lesson Vocabulary
- Focus Skill: Narrative Elements

## ADVANCED

- Challenge Vocabulary
- Focus Skill: Narrative Elements

## ELL

- Concept Vocabulary
- Focus Skill: Narrative Elements

## MULTI-LEVEL PRACTICE

**Extra Support,** pp. 29–30

**Practice Book,** pp. 29–32

**Challenge,** pp. 29–30

**English-Language Learners,** pp. 29–30

## ADDITIONAL RESOURCES

**Spelling Practice Book,** pp. 30–32

**Language Handbook,** pp. 30–33, 111–113

**Audiotext 2**

**Intervention Resource Kit,** Lesson 7
- Intervention Reader, *Included in Intervention Resource Kit*

**English-Language Learners Resource Kit,** Lesson 7

 **technology**

- *Mission: Comprehension™ Skills Practice* **CD-ROM**
- *Media Literacy and Communication Skills Package* (Video)
- *Grammar Jingles™* **CD**, Intermediate
- *Writing Express™* **CD-ROM**
- *Reading and Language Skills Assessment* **CD-ROM**
- *The Learning Site:* www.harcourtschool.com

### ORAL LANGUAGE

• **Question of the Day**

• **Sharing Literature**

### SKILLS & STRATEGIES

• **Comprehension**

• **Vocabulary**

### READING

• **Guided Comprehension**

• **Independent Reading**

• **Cross-Curricular Connections**

### LANGUAGE ARTS

• **Writing**

  *Daily Writing Prompt*

• **Grammar**

  *Daily Language Practice*

• **Spelling**

**Daily Routines**
• Question of the Day
• Daily Language Practice
• Daily Writing Prompt

---

## Day 1

**Question of the Day,** p. 174H
*When you are unwilling to change your mind, you are unyielding. What is something you are unyielding about?*

**Literature Read-Aloud,** pp. 174G–H

---

**Comprehension:**
 Narrative Elements, p. 174I **T**
 Self-Question, p. 174J

**Vocabulary,** p. 174L

---

**Read: Vocabulary Power,** pp. 174–175
Vocabulary Power Words:
*insignificant, plotting, twined, steely, encircling, loyal, neglected, unyielding*

 **Independent Reading**
Books for All Learners

**SOCIAL STUDIES** Research the United States Government
**MATH** Find the Perimeter and the Area
**INQUIRY PROJECT** Extending the Selection

---

**Writing:** Writer's Craft, p. 205C

**Writing Prompt:**
*Write a shape poem about a kite. Include specific details about the kite, such as its color, size, and shape.*

**Grammar:**
Compound Subjects and Predicates, p. 205E
**T**

*Daily Language Practice*
1. Do you have a kite fetsival at your school. (festival; school?)
2. Last year Marta made the prettyist kite (prettiest; kite.)

**Spelling:**
Words with /ôr/, p. 205G **T**

---

## Day 2

**Question of the Day,** p. 174H
*What things bring family members closer together?*

**Think and Respond,** p. 194

---

**Comprehension:**
 Narrative Elements, pp. 176–195 **T**

**Decoding/Phonics:**
Word Structure: Compound Words, p. 205A

---

**Reading the Selection,** pp. 176–195
GENRE: Folktale

 **Independent Reading**
Books for All Learners

**LITERARY ANALYSIS** Figurative Language
**LITERARY ANALYSIS** Haiku
**SCIENCE** Plains

---

**Writing:** Writer's Craft, p. 205C

**Writing Prompt:**
*Everyone has taken a test. Think about the reasons why you take a test. Explain why it is sometimes necessary to take a test.*

**Grammar:**
Extend the Concept, p. 205E

*Daily Language Practice*
1. Joel and Jenny. Want to enter a kite. Inn the festival. (Jenny want; kite in)
2. It is two late. the places are all taken. (too; The)

**Spelling:**
Word Sort, p. 205G

---

**Objectives of the Week:**

- To identify ways in which narrative elements impact one another in a literary text
- To read and understand a fiction/folktale selection; to compare fiction/folktale with nonfiction
- To use compound subjects and predicates correctly
- To use effective paragraphs in writing written directions

## Day 3

**Question of the Day,** p. 174H
*What part of a kite festival would you enjoy the most? Why?*

**Oral Grammar,** p. 205F

**Comprehension:**
 Narrative Elements, pp. 204–205 **T**
Test Prep

**Word Study:**
Analogies, p. 205I

**Reading Across Texts,** pp. 198–201
GENRE: Magazine Article
**Rereading for Fluency,** p. 193

 **Independent Reading**
Books for All Learners
**SOCIAL STUDIES** Kites
**SOCIAL STUDIES** Wind Patterns

**Writing:** Writer's Craft, p. 205D

 **Writing Prompt:**
*Imagine that you own a special kite that can take you anywhere in the world. Now write a story about the day your special kite took you to that place.*

**Grammar:**
Make a Compound, p. 205F

*Daily Language Practice*

1. The Park is an open plase. Where people walk dogs? (park; place where; dogs.)
2. We shouldnt' fly. Our kites there. (shouldn't; fly our)

**Spelling:**
Smaller Words, p. 205H

## Day 4

**Question of the Day,** p. 174H
*What simile would you use to describe a kite? Why?*

**Comprehension:**
 Narrative Elements, pp. 205K–N **T**

**Figurative Language,** p. 205B **T**

**Self-Selected Reading,** p. 174F

 **Independent Reading**
Books for All Learners
**SOCIAL STUDIES** Cultural Gestures
**TECHNOLOGY** Information Search

**Writing:** Writer's Craft, p. 205D

 **Writing Prompt:**
*Write a journal entry that Djeow Seow might have written the day she rescued her father.*

**Grammar:**
Article, p. 205F

*Daily Language Practice*

1. Will kyle's kite fly for a long time. (Kyle's; time?)
2. He wonders if the whether will be good for flying? (weather; flying.)

**Spelling:**
Memory, Word Constructions, p. 205H

## Day 5

**Question of the Day,** p. 174H
*Think of stories and legends about historical figures. How are the heroes of those stories similar to and different from Djeow Seow?*

**Speaking and Listening**
Giving Directions, p. 205J

**Comprehension:**
 Narrative Elements, pp. 205K–N **T**

**Word Study:**
Connotations, p. 205I

**Self-Selected Reading,** pp. 201, T67

 **Independent Reading**
Books for All Learners
**WRITING** Write to Explain
**SCIENCE** Create a Display
**MATH** Measure Perimeters and Areas

**Writing:** Writer's Craft, p. 205D

**Writing Prompt:**
*Write a character sketch of Djeow Seow. Include specific details from the story.*

**Grammar:**
Subjects and Predicates, p. 205F

*Daily Language Practice*

1. Everyone liked Kyles kite last year (Kyle's; year.)
2. People on the street stopt, and smiled. (stopped and)

**Spelling:**
Posttest, p. 205H

# Cross-Curricular Stations

**MANAGING THE CLASSROOM** While you provide direct instruction to individuals or small groups, other students can work on ongoing activities such as the ones below.

## SOCIAL STUDIES

### Research Government in the United States

**OBJECTIVE: To understand the similarities and differences among the local, state, and federal branches of government in the United States**

In "The Emperor and the Kite," the emperor's four sons help him rule different parts of the empire. The United States government is divided into federal, state, and local governments.

- Choose a branch of government to research.
- Find out how the responsibilities for the branch you chose are similar and different at the local, state, and federal levels.
- Make a poster to show the similarities and differences.

### Materials
- research materials
- paper
- pen or pencil
- poster board
- colored pencils or markers (optional)

60 Minutes

---

## MATH

### Find the Perimeter and the Area

**OBJECTIVE: To understand that rectangles that have the same area can have different perimeters**

Imagine that you are making a kite. The kite-making manual says that the kite tail should have an area of 108 square inches.

- Copy the chart below, and use the given lengths to find the widths needed to make an area of 108 square inches. Remember that the formula for area is *length x width = area*. To find the width, divide the area by the given length. Record each width in the chart.
- Use the length and the width to calculate the perimeter of each kite tail. Do all rectangles that have the same area have the same perimeter? Discuss your conclusion.

| Length | Width | Area | Perimeter |
|--------|-------|------|-----------|
| 12 inches | (9 inches) | 108 square inches | (42 inches) |
| 18 inches | (6 inches) | 108 square inches | (48 inches) |
| 27 inches | (4 inches) | 108 square inches | (62 inches) |
| 36 inches | (3 inches) | 108 square inches | (78 inches) |
| 54 inches | (2 inches) | 108 square inches | (112 inches) |

Use a computer to make your chart. Remember to save your chart to a disk.

### Materials
- paper
- pen or pencil

20 Minutes

## LIBRARY CENTER

### Self-Selected Reading

**OBJECTIVE: To select and read books independently**

Look for these books about family relationships:

- *Dreamcatcher* by Audrey Osofsky. Grolier, 1992. FICTION
- *When I Am Old with You* by Angela Johnson. Orchard Paperbacks, 1993. FICTION
- *Love as Strong as Ginger* by Lenore Look. Atheneum, 1999. FICTION

**Remember to**

- select a book that interests you.
- use reading strategies as you read.
- keep track in your Reading Log of what you read each day.

### Materials

- self-selected book
- *My Reading Log* copying master, p. R38

## INQUIRY PROJECT

### Extending the Selection

**OBJECTIVE: To select a focus for an inquiry project**

Use the ideas in "The Emperor and the Kite" to brainstorm with a partner related topics to explore. Choose a topic and use one of these books for your project.

- *Young José and His Paint Box*
- *Three Kite Tales*
- *The Crystal Radio*
- *Inside and Outside Together*

### Materials

- research materials
- pen or pencil
- paper

## TECHNOLOGY

### Information Search

**OBJECTIVE: To use technology resources to research the setting of "The Emperor and the Kite"**

Use the Internet or a CD-ROM encyclopedia to find facts about one of the ancient Chinese dynasties, such as the Ch'in or Han Dynasty. Write a paragraph about what you learned. Remember to quote or paraphrase the information you find.

### Materials

- computer with Internet access or CD-ROM encyclopedia
- pen or pencil
- paper

# Read Aloud

## SET A PURPOSE
### Listen for Enjoyment

Remind students that one purpose for reading or listening to poetry is for enjoyment. Point out that many poets use rhyme in their poetry. Rhyme makes a poem pleasurable to listen to and creates an emotional response in the reader or listener. Read the poem in an animated voice, conveying excitement about flying a kite. Let your voice show surprise when the kite is caught in the tree. Ask volunteers to tell what rhymes they noticed. Then discuss whether the poem would have been more or less enjoyable without the rhymes.

## LISTENING STRATEGY
### Concentrate on the Speaker

Explain that one way to understand a poet's feelings is to pay attention to the way the speaker reads it. Tell students to face the speaker, making eye contact and watching facial expressions. Remind them to listen for changes in the speaker's voice.

Oh, what a wonderful feeling
what a tremendous delight
you can feel so light, so fresh, so free
when you are outside flying a kite.

You make it with glue and some paper
you tie on a tail at the end
then you get some string (a whole lot of string)
and you find a big place with some friends.

One friend holds the kite very gently
you walk out twenty paces or so
then you hold the string tight and with all of your might
you shout to your friend to let go.

And then you start running and running
and your heart's pounding out of your chest
and the kite slowly, steadily rises—
right about now you are feeling your best.

Then you see your friends shouting and waving
and you know they're as thrilled as can be
but as it turns out what the shouting's about . . .
your kite has been eaten by a tree.

Oh, what a wonderful feeling
so light, so fresh, so free
hold the string tight as you run with your kite
but please . . . don't fly kites near a tree.

- **How does the narrator feel about flying a kite?** (Possible response: The narrator is excited and happy about flying a kite.) CHARACTERS' EMOTIONS

- **Where is the best place to fly a kite?** (in a large, open space without trees) DRAW CONCLUSIONS

- **Why do you think the kite got stuck in the tree?** (The narrator is so excited about flying the kite that he or she doesn't pay attention to the surroundings.) SYNTHESIZE

# Question of the Day

## DEVELOP ORAL LANGUAGE

- Display the first question on Teaching Transparency 58, or write it on the board. Ask a volunteer to read it aloud.

- **Response Journal** Explain to students that they should think about the question throughout the day and write their responses in their journals. Tell students to be prepared to discuss their responses to the question by the end of the day or at another time you choose.

- You may want to repeat this process daily for each of the remaining discussion questions.

▼ **Teaching Transparency 58**

**QUESTION OF THE DAY**

**DAY 1:** When you are unwilling to change your mind, you are **unyielding**. What is something you are unyielding about? Responses will vary. VOCABULARY AND CONCEPTS

**DAY 2:** What things bring family members closer together? Possible response: spending time together, solving problems together SELECTION CONNECTION

**DAY 3:** What part of a kite festival would you enjoy the most? Why? Responses will vary. READING ACROSS TEXTS

**DAY 4:** What simile would you use to describe a kite? Why? Responses will vary. FIGURATIVE LANGUAGE

**DAY 5:** Think of stories and legends about historical figures. How are the heroes of those stories similar to and different from Djeow Seow? Responses will vary. CROSS-CURRICULAR CONNECTION

"The Emperor and the Kite"
Side by Side, Theme 2                     58                    Question of the Day
                                                                Harcourt

## OBJECTIVE

*To identify ways in which narrative elements impact one another in a literary text*

### SKILL TRACE

**NARRATIVE ELEMENTS**

| | |
|---|---|
| Introduce | pp. 20I |
| Reteach | pp. S4, S16, T2 |
| Review | pp. 48, 78I, 100 |
| Test | Theme I |
| **Maintain** | **pp. 174I, 204** |

▼ **Teaching Transparency 59**

### NARRATIVE ELEMENTS

- The narrative elements of a story include **characters, setting,** and **plot.**
- The narrative elements of a story work together.
- Changing one narrative element causes changes in the others. This results in a different story.

**Example:**

A hard working tortoise and a lazy hare were in a race. The tortoise ran as fast as he could, while the hare stopped to rest and didn't put forth his best effort. The tortoise easily won the race.

| A Change in Character | → | A Change in the Events | → | A Change in the Ending |
|---|---|---|---|---|
| A hard-working tortoise and a **hard-working** hare were in a race. | | **Both** the tortoise and the hare **ran as fast as they could.** | | The **hare** easily **won the race.** |

Alison was nervous about moving to the country. She was not sure how she would spend her time, but she was determined to make the best of the situation. Soon after she arrived, her fears went away. There was plenty to do! She planted her own garden in the backyard, and her new friends taught her how to ride a horse.

- How would this story be different if Alison had moved to the city?
- How would this story be different if Alison did not think positively about new situation?

"The Emperor and the Kite"
Side by Side, Theme 2          **59**          Writing
Harcourt

### BELOW-LEVEL

**Additional Support**
- *Intervention Teacher's Guide,* p. 70

### ENGLISH-LANGUAGE LEARNERS

**Additional Support**
- *English-Language Learners Teacher's Guide,* p. 39

---

## ☆ Focus Skill Narrative Elements

### MAINTAIN THE SKILL

**Access prior knowledge.** Ask students to discuss a time when they have worked as members of a team. Remind them that a story is made up of narrative elements—plot, character, and setting—that work together.

### TEACH/MODEL

Explain that each narrative element affects the story as a whole. If any narrative element changes, the story also changes.

- **Have a volunteer read aloud the bulleted items.**

- **Read aloud the example. Point out how a change in one of the characters affects the rest of the story.**

- **Read aloud the second passage. Discuss the questions.**

### PRACTICE/APPLY

Have students use a story map to keep track of the narrative elements as they read.

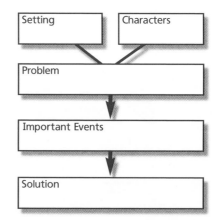

To apply and reinforce the skill, see the following pages:

**During reading:** pages 178, 184, 186
**After reading:** *Pupil Edition* pages 204–205

**Focus Strategy** ## Self-Question

### INTRODUCE THE STRATEGY

Tell students that good readers use strategies such as **self-questioning** when they read. Explain that asking and answering their own questions as they read will help them better understand what is happening in the story.

### TEACH/MODEL

Use the first example on Transparency 59 to model the strategy.

> **MODEL** If I am confused about why Alison is nervous about moving to the country, I can ask myself questions such as *How would I feel if I had to move to a new place? What things would worry me about moving?*

#### SKILL ⟷ STRATEGY CONNECTION

Explain to students that when they read and are not sure why something happens, they should use **self-questioning** to determine whether they have understood the **narrative elements** of plot, character, and setting correctly.

### PRACTICE/APPLY

Remind students to use the Self-Question strategy if they are confused about any parts of the plot as they read. For opportunities to apply and reinforce the strategy **during reading**, see pages 181, 191 and 193.

**OBJECTIVE**

*To understand that self-questioning while reading can help a reader understand important ideas*

## Strategies Good Readers Use

- Use Decoding/Phonics
- Make and Confirm Predictions
- Create Mental Images
- **Self-Question**
- Summarize
- Read Ahead
- Reread to Clarify
- Use Context to Confirm Meaning
- Use Text Structure and Format
- Adjust Reading Rate

*The Emperor and the Kite* **174J**

# Building Background

## ACCESS PRIOR KNOWLEDGE

Tell students that in "The Emperor and the Kite," they will read about a ruler who learns an important lesson from his smallest daughter.

Discuss with students how they think a good leader should act. Then guide them to develop a web like the one below.

rule wisely

listen to the people they lead

**Good Leaders**

treat people equally

act fairly and kindly

## technology

**VIDEO** *Tall Tales, Yarns, and Whoppers,* ©1991. Library Video Company, 35 min.

## DEVELOP CONCEPTS

Help students use prior knowledge to develop concepts by asking the following questions:

- **What kinds of responsibilities does an emperor have?** (Possible response: He makes laws and enforces them. He maintains peace in his kingdom.)

- **Why would someone want to be an emperor?** (Possible response: to have the opportunity to make rules)

- **Why should an emperor treat people equally?** (Possible response: because he is responsible for the well-being of everyone in the kingdom)

Discuss with students what kinds of things adults can learn from children.

### REACHING ALL LEARNERS

## Diagnostic Check: Vocabulary

**If** . . . students do not understand at least 6 of the 8 vocabulary words . . .

**Then** . . . have them write original sentences for the vocabulary words and share them with the class.

### ADDITIONAL SUPPORT ACTIVITIES

| BELOW-LEVEL | Reteach, p. S40 |
| ADVANCED | Extend, p. S41 |
| ENGLISH-LANGUAGE LEARNERS | Reteach, p. S41 |

# Vocabulary

## TEACH VOCABULARY STRATEGIES

**Use affixes and root words.** Point to the word *steely* on Transparency 60. Explain that students can sometimes figure out the meaning of an unfamiliar word by looking for prefixes, suffixes, roots, and root words. Model using affixes and root words to determine the meaning of the word *steely*.

**MODEL** This is a word I do not recognize. As I look at the word, I see a smaller word I know, *steel*. I also see the suffix *-y*. I know that steel is a hard combination of metals and that *-y* is a suffix used to describe things. Maybe *steely* means "like steel" or "hard."

Have students use this strategy as they encounter other unfamiliar words when they read. Remind them to use a dictionary or a glossary to confirm word meanings.

**plotting** planning in secret to do something, often something evil

**loyal** constant and faithful to people or ideals

**neglected** failed to care for or attend to

**insignificant** lacking in importance, meaning, size, or worth

**encircling** forming a circle around; surrounding

**unyielding** constant and never-ending; not giving way

**steely** like steel, as in strength, hardness, or coldness

**twined** twisted around

▼ **Teaching Transparency 60**

### VOCABULARY IN CONTEXT

Dear Diary,

I'm really excited about what happened today at day camp. When I got there this morning, I noticed that all my friends were acting strangely. They seemed to be **plotting** something. Even my most **loyal** friends whispered together and wouldn't let me in on their secret. When I sat down for lunch, I noticed a big box in the middle of the table. At first I thought it was **insignificant**, because it looked like the box that holds our craft supplies. Then I realized that all my friends were **encircling** the table and smiling at me. The camp counselor tried to open the box. At first it was **unyielding**, but then, with a **steely** grip on a plastic knife, she was able to cut through the heavily taped edges. It was a big cake, with different colors of frosting **twined** together along the border. The message on it read, "Happy 10th Birthday, Kirsten!" I ate a big piece and even brought some home for Mom and Dad. Dad would have been upset if I had **neglected** to bring him home his favorite—chocolate cake!

Your friend,
Kirsten

"The Emperor and the Kite" — Side by Side, Theme 2 — 60 — Vocabulary in Context — Harcourt

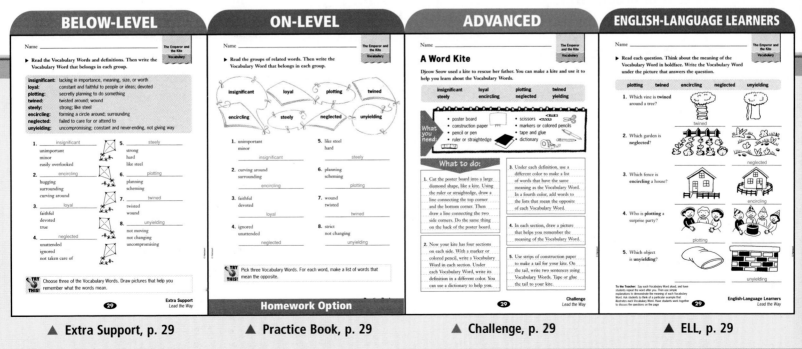

| BELOW-LEVEL | ON-LEVEL | ADVANCED | ENGLISH-LANGUAGE LEARNERS |

▲ Extra Support, p. 29     ▲ Practice Book, p. 29     ▲ Challenge, p. 29     ▲ ELL, p. 29

# Vocabulary Power

## APPLY STRATEGIES

Have a volunteer read aloud the first paragraph on page 174. Then ask students to follow along as you read the remaining text aloud. Remind students to use affixes and root words, as well as context clues, to determine or confirm the meanings of unfamiliar words.

## EXTEND WORD KNOWLEDGE

**Practice other vocabulary strategies.**
Ask students to answer questions with sentences that show what the vocabulary words mean. MEANINGFUL SENTENCES

- Would you expect someone who is *unyielding* to give in easily? Why or why not? EXPLANATION

- Is something small always *insignificant*? Explain. EXPLANATION

- If you and a group of your friends are *encircling* the water fountain, are you standing next to it or around it? DEFINITION

- Which word could you replace with the word *scheming*? SYNONYMS

- If someone *neglected* a plant for three weeks, what might happen? EXAMPLE

- If someone has a *steely* expression, what does he or she look like? DESCRIPTION

- Which word describes what someone might have done to make a rope? EXAMPLE

▲ The Emperor and the Kite

insignificant

steely

unyielding

twined

neglected

loyal

plotting

encircling

174

# Vocabulary Power

The main character in "The Emperor and the Kite" is very small. It is sometimes surprising what someone or something small is able to do.

**Spiders**  Although most spiders are less than a half inch long, it would be a mistake to think of these tiny creatures as **insignificant**, or unimportant. Many thousands of types of spiders are found all over the world.

Spiders produce silk threads from their bodies. They use the silk to make webs for catching their food. The silk threads of a spider-web may look delicate, but they are **steely** strands. Some people say that spider threads, if twisted into a string as thick as a pencil, could stop a jet plane in the sky! What other material is so **unyielding** that it would not give way under that kind of force?

In a spiderweb, the silk threads are not **twined**, or twisted together. Instead, they are held together by tiny drops of glue. When the glue begins to loosen, the spider eats its old web and makes a new one. If the spider **neglected** this task, or ignored it, the spider would soon go hungry.

Some stories picture spiders as **loyal** friends. However, many stories picture evil spiders **plotting**, or secretly planning, to capture things in their webs. In fact, spiders make webs just to catch insects for food. Some spiders also use their silk to wrap up their food for later. They move around and around an insect's body, **encircling** it in silk.

**Vocabulary–Writing CONNECTION**

**T**hink about what makes someone a **loyal** friend. Then write to describe someone you think of as a loyal friend.

175

## QUICKWRITE

**VOCABULARY–WRITING CONNECTION**

Tell students to focus their writing on one person. Encourage them to combine short, related sentences with adverbs or adjectives. Students should add the adjectives, adverbs, and Vocabulary Power words to their Word Banks to use in future writing assignments.

# Prereading Strategies

## PREVIEW AND PREDICT

Have students read the **genre** information on page 176. Ask them what they think this selection is about, based on their preview and the characteristics of folktales. Then have them record predictions about what role the kite will play in the story. Remind them to confirm their predictions as they read. Ask students to begin a story map. See Transparency D.

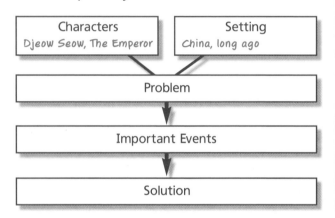

| Characters | Setting |
|---|---|
| Djeow Seow, The Emperor | China, long ago |

Problem

↓

Important Events

↓

Solution

*The Emperor and the Kite*
by JANE YOLEN  Illustrated by ED YOUNG

Caldecott Honor
ALA Notable Book
*SLJ* Best Book

### Genre

## Folktale

**Folktales are stories that were first told orally. They reflect the customs and beliefs of a culture.**

**In this selection, look for**

● **A plot that teaches a lesson**

● **A main character who reflects the values of a culture**

176

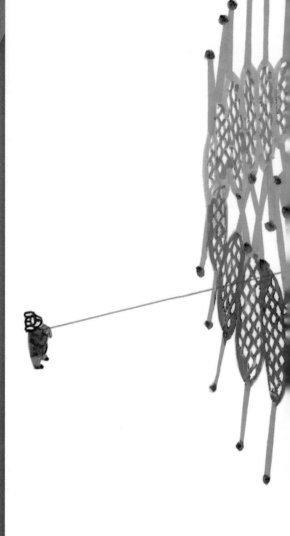

| BELOW-LEVEL | ON-LEVEL | ADVANCED | ENGLISH-LANGUAGE LEARNERS |
|---|---|---|---|
| Guide students as they preview the selection. Discuss the meaning of these words: *Emperor, monk, kingdom, mortar,* and *billowed.* Help students set a purpose for reading through page 182. **SMALL GROUP** | Students can read the selection with a partner. Use the Guided Comprehension questions and Ongoing Assessments to gauge students' understanding. **WHOLE GROUP/PARTNER** | Tell students to read the selection independently. Have them add to their story maps as they read. Remind them to think about how the narrative elements work together as they complete their story maps. **INDEPENDENT/SMALL GROUP** | Read aloud the selection, or have students listen to it on *Audiotext 2.* Then have students read aloud selected pages as a group to develop oral fluency. **SMALL GROUP** |

**ADDITIONAL SUPPORT**

*Intervention Reader: Moving Ahead Intervention Reader Teacher's Guide* pp. 70–73

**ADDITIONAL SUPPORT**

See *English-Language Learners Resource Kit,* Lesson 7. *English-Language Learners Teacher's Guide,* p. 39

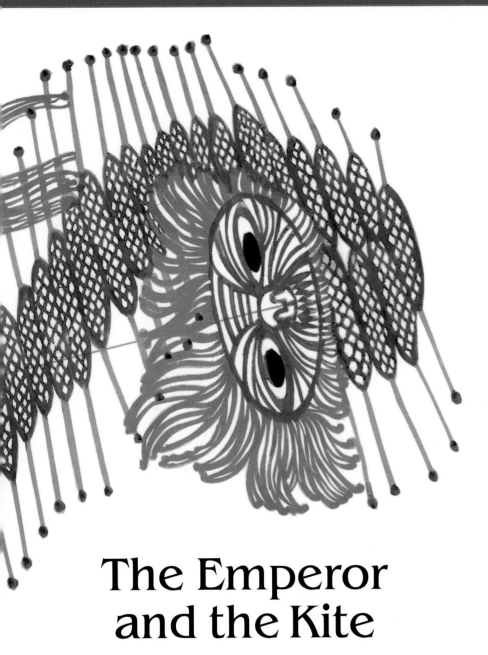

# The Emperor and the Kite

by JANE YOLEN    illustrated by ED YOUNG

**Read to understand.** Remind students that one purpose for reading a folktale is to understand the lesson that is being taught. Ask students to set their own purposes. Offer this suggestion:

**MODEL** Because this is a folktale, I think a lesson will be taught. I will read to find out which character learns a lesson and what lesson he or she learns.

**Focus Strategy** **Self-Question** Have students use this strategy to help them monitor their comprehension as they read.

**"The Emperor and the Kite" and "Kite Festivals" are available on *Audiotext 2*.**

## COMPREHENSION CARD 7

**Setting** Have students use Comprehension Card 7 to discuss **setting** in "The Emperor and the Kite."

▶ Setting                                    COMPREHENSION CARD **7**

**During Reading**
1. Describe where the story takes place.
2. When does this story take place—long ago, in the present, or in the future? What clues helped you decide?
3. Have you ever been to a place like this? If you have, how was it like the place in the story?

**Comprehension Card 7, page T48▶**

*The Emperor and the Kite*    **177**

# Guided Comprehension

**1** **(Focus Skill)** **NARRATIVE ELEMENTS**
**What is the setting of the story?** (The story takes place in ancient China.)

**2** **COMPARE AND CONTRAST How is Djeow Seow different from her brothers and sisters?** (Djeow Seow's brothers are big and strong. They help their father, the emperor, run the kingdom. Her sisters are also big and strong. They bring their father his meals. Djeow Seow is very tiny, and her father does not notice her.)

**3** **DRAW CONCLUSIONS/IDENTIFY WITH CHARACTERS How do you think Djeow Seow feels? How would you feel if you were she?** (Possible answer: I think she is lonely. I know I would feel lonely if I ate by myself and talked to myself every day.)

Once in ancient China there lived a princess who was the **1** fourth daughter of the emperor. She was very tiny. In fact she was so tiny her name was Djeow Seow, which means "the smallest one." And, because she was so tiny, she was not thought very much of—when she was thought of at all.

Her brothers, who were all older and bigger and stronger than she, were thought of all the time. And they were like four rising suns in the eyes of their father. They helped the emperor rule the kingdom and teach the people the ways of peace.

178

**BELOW-LEVEL**

If students have difficulty visualizing the difference between Djeow Seow and her older sisters, remind them that looking at the illustrations can help them picture what they read. Then discuss how Djeow Seow is treated because of her small size.

- She is not thought of.
- She is not allowed to bring food to the table.
- She is often forgotten.

Tell students to read to find out how Djeow Seow's small size affects the plot of the story.

Monitor Progress

# Make and Confirm Predictions

**Based on what you have read, what do you think will happen to Djeow Seow by the end of the story?** (Possible response: She will be appreciated by her father.)

**If students were unable to answer, use this model:**

**MODEL** I know that characters in stories often solve their problems. Djeow Seow's problem is that her father does not notice her. I think she will solve this problem by the end of the story.

Even her three sisters were all older and bigger and stronger than she. They were like three midnight moons in the eyes of their father. They were the ones who brought food to his table.

But Djeow Seow was like a tiny star in the emperor's sight. She was not even allowed to bring a grain of rice to the meal, so little was she thought of. In fact she was so insignificant, the emperor often forgot he had a fourth daughter at all. **2**

And so, Djeow Seow ate by herself. And she talked to herself. **3**

179

## LITERARY ANALYSIS

**Figurative Language**  Remind students that authors sometimes compare two unlike things to describe characters and objects to readers. Read the description of Djeow Seow's brothers on page 178: *They were like four rising suns in the eyes of their father.* Tell students that this is a **simile:** the author uses the words *like* or *as* to say that one thing is like another. Then ask students:

• What does the author mean when she compares Djeow Seow's brothers to rising suns? (She means that Djeow Seow's brothers are easy for the emperor to notice, just like the rising sun is easy to notice.)

Ask students to find other similes on pages 180–181.

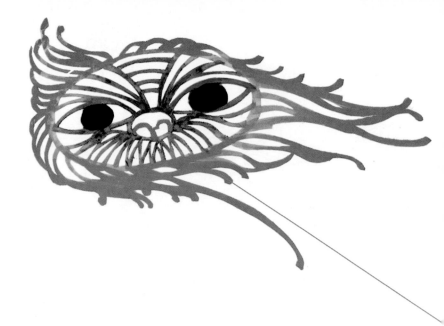

# Guided Comprehension

**4 CHARACTERS' MOTIVATIONS   Why does Djeow Seow fly her kite every day?** (Possible response: Flying the kite makes her feel less lonely; she doesn't have any other job to do in her father's palace.)

**5 FIGURATIVE LANGUAGE   What comparison does the monk make in his poem? What do you think it means?** (The monk compares Djeow Seow's kite to her soul. When Djeow Seow flies her kite, her soul feels light and she is happier than usual.)

**6 CONTEXT CLUES   What does the word *trouble* mean in the sentence, "For the wind can trouble the waters of a still pond"? How do you know?**

(In this sentence, *trouble* means *disturb* or *ripple*. I know this because the wind on the pond is being compared to the men who plot against the emperor. The wind and the men both disturb a peaceful situation.)

And she played by herself, which was the loneliest thing of all. Her favorite toy was a kite of paper and sticks.

Every morning, when the wind came from the east past the rising sun, she flew her kite. And every evening, when the wind went to the west past the setting sun, she flew her kite. Her toy was like a flower in the sky. And it was like a prayer in the wind.

In fact a monk who passed the palace daily made up a poem about her kite.

> *My kite sails upward,*
> *Mounting to the high heavens.*
> *My soul goes on wings.* **5**

But then he was a monk, and given to such thoughts. As for Princess Djeow Seow, she thanked him each day for his prayer. Then she went back to flying her toy.

180

**ENGLISH-LANGUAGE LEARNERS**

Help students put these examples of figurative phrases in their own words:

- *Her toy was like a flower in the sky.* (Her kite was beautiful.)

- *It was like a prayer in the wind.* (The kite goes up toward the heavens.)

Discuss with students why the author would describe Djeow Seow's kite as a flower. (Possible responses: It is beautiful and brightly colored like a flower.)

But all was not peaceful in the kingdom, just as the wind is not always peaceful. For the wind can trouble the waters of a still pond. And there were evil men plotting against the emperor. **6**

181

## ONGOING ASSESSMENT

**Monitor Progress**

(Focus Strategy) **Self-Question**

**How do you think the monk feels about Djeow Seow?** (I think the monk likes Djeow Seow. He does not think she is insignificant.)

**If students are unable to answer the question, model the strategy:**

**MODEL** **To decide how the monk feels about Djeow Seow, I ask myself, *How does he treat Djeow Seow?* The monk creates a poem about the way she flies her kite. He shares the poem with her. These actions make me think that he likes her.**

## LITERARY ANALYSIS

**Haiku** Tell students that the monk's poem about the kite is called a haiku. A haiku is an unrhymed, three-line poem, usually about nature. Explain to students that a haiku has a specific format. The first and third lines in a haiku have five syllables. The second line has seven syllables. With students, count the number of syllables in the monk's haiku. Then invite students to write their own haikus about something in nature or a topic of their choice.

My kite sails upward,
Mounting to the high heavens,
My soul goes on wings.

# Guided Comprehension

**7 DRAW CONCLUSIONS** Why don't the plotters kidnap Djeow Seow along with her father? (She is so small that the plotters do not notice her sitting in the corner.)

**8 CHARACTERS' MOTIVATIONS** Why do the plotters seal the door to the tower with mortar and bricks? (The plotters do not want the emperor to escape. They think that if they seal the door, they can keep him in the tower.)

**9 SUMMARIZE** How does Djeow Seow help her father survive in the tower? (She builds a hut near the tower. Every morning and every night she fills a basket with food. She uses the kite to send the basket to her father.)

They crept up on him one day when he was alone, when his four sons were away ruling in the furthermost parts of the kingdom and his three daughters were down in the garden. And only Princess Djeow Seow, so tiny she seemed part of the corner where she sat, saw what happened.

The evil men took the emperor to a tower in the middle of a wide, treeless plain. The tower had only a single window, with an iron bar across the center. The plotters sealed the door with bricks and mortar once the emperor was inside. **8**

Then they rode back to the palace and declared that the emperor was dead.

182

**BELOW-LEVEL**

Work with students to summarize what they have read so far.

- Djeow Seow is tiny. Her father, the emperor, does not notice her.

- Every day Djeow Seow flies a kite, and a monk makes up a poem about her kite.

- Evil men kidnap the emperor. Djeow Seow sees them do it, but because she is so small, they do not see her.

- Djeow Seow keeps her father alive. She uses her kite to send him food.

Help students set a purpose for reading through the end of the selection.

When his sons and daughters heard this, they all fled to a neighboring kingdom where they spent their time sobbing and sighing. But they did nothing else all day long.

All except Djeow Seow. She was so tiny, the evil men did not notice her at all. And so, she crept to the edge of the wide, treeless plain. And there she built a hut of twigs and branches.

Every day at dawn and again at dark, she would walk across the plain to the tower. And there she would sail her stick-and-paper kite. To the kite string she tied a tiny basket filled with rice and poppyseed cakes, water chestnuts and green tea. The kite pulled the basket high, high in the air, up as high as the window in the tower. And, in this way, she kept her father alive. **9**

So they lived for many days: the emperor in his tower and the princess in a hut near the edge of the plain. The evil men ruled with their cruel, harsh ways, and the people of the country were very sad.

183

## SCIENCE

**Plains**  Plains, like the one on which Djeow Seow builds her hut, are large, mostly treeless areas where grass is the dominant plant. These areas get very little rain, so grasses have adaptations to help them live without much water. Their roots are spread out and grow just beneath the soil's surface to take in the little rain that does fall. Plains play an important role in agriculture. Many grasses, such as corn, rice, wheat, and other grains, are grown in these areas.

# Guided Comprehension

**10** **(Focus Skill)** **NARRATIVE ELEMENTS**
**How does the monk change his poem? What effect does this have on Djeow Seow?** (He changes the last line to "My emperor goes on wings." Djeow Seow realizes that she can use her kite to rescue her father.)

**11** **SEQUENCE** **What does Djeow Seow do after she finishes making her rope?** (She attaches the rope to the string of her kite. She brings the kite to the tower where her father is being held prisoner.)

**12** **MAKE PREDICTIONS** **What do you predict Djeow Seow will do next?** (She will use the kite to rescue her father with the rope.)

One day as the princess prepared a basket of food for her father, the old monk passed by her hut. She smiled at him, but he seemed not to see her. Yet as he passed, he repeated his prayer in a loud voice. He said:

*My kite sails upward,*
*Mounting to the high heavens.*
*My emperor goes on wings.* **10**

184

**REACHING ALL LEARNERS**

## Diagnostic Check: Comprehension and Skills

**If** . . . students have difficulty with Question 10 . . .

**Then** . . . help them restate the conflict by asking, "What is the problem Djeow Seow is facing?" Then ask, "How can the emperor's poem help her solve this problem?"

**ADDITIONAL SUPPORT ACTIVITIES**

**BELOW-LEVEL** Reteach, p. S42

**ADVANCED** Extend, p. S43

**ENGLISH-LANGUAGE LEARNERS** Reteach, p. S43

**ONGOING ASSESSMENT**

Monitor Progress

# Read Ahead

**What message is the monk trying to give Djeow Seow?** (Possible response: She can use her kite to rescue her father.)

**If students were unable to answer the question, model the strategy:**

**MODEL** The meaning of the poem isn't clear at first, so I read ahead to see if the author gives more clues to its meaning. As I continue reading, I find out that once Djeow Seow understands the poem, she makes a rope which she attaches to her kite. The monk's poem must have given Djeow Seow an idea about how to rescue her father.

The princess started to thank him. But then she stopped. Something was different. The words were not quite right. "Stop," she called to the monk. But he had already passed by. He was a monk, after all, and did not take part in things of this world.

And then Djeow Seow understood. The monk was telling her something important. And she understood.

Each day after that, when she was not bringing food to her father, Djeow Seow was busy. She twined a string of grass and vines, and wove in strands of her own long black hair. When her rope was as thick as her waist and as high as the tower, she was ready. She attached the rope to the string of the stick-and-paper kite, and made her way across the treeless plain. When she reached the tower, she called to her father. But her voice was as tiny as she, and her words were lost in the wind. ⓫ ⓬

185

## SOCIAL STUDIES

**Kites** The Chinese have flown kites for approximately 3,000 years. The first kites were made of wood. Then they were made of silk and bamboo and, later, paper. Popular kite designs include dragons, centipedes, and birds.

The traditional kite colors are red, yellow, and blue because these were the main colors of the robes the emperors wore. Kite flying season in China usually begins in January or February and ends in March or April.

# Guided Comprehension

**⑬ CHARACTER'S TRAITS** **What do Djeow Seow's actions tell you about her character?** (The fact that she uses her kite to help her father escape tells me that she is clever and loyal.)

**⑭ (Focus Skill) NARRATIVE ELEMENTS** **How does the emperor's attitude toward Djeow Seow change? How do you know?** (At the beginning of the story, the emperor did not notice Djeow Seow. When she sends him the rope, he understands how valuable Djeow Seow is to him.)

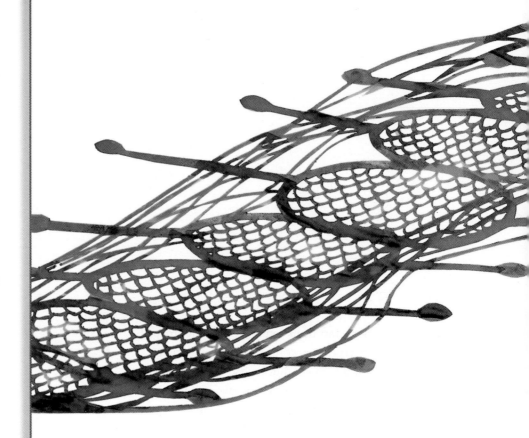

186

**ENGLISH-LANGUAGE LEARNERS**

Students may have difficulty with the phrase *The wind was raging above, holding the kite in its steely grip*. Explain to students that this sentence means that the wind was blowing hard and helping the kite stay up in the air. Students may also be unfamiliar with the word *thy*. Tell them that *thy* is an old-fashioned word for *your*. Have students read the sentence aloud, substituting the word *your* for *thy*. Point out that substituting *your* doesn't change the meaning of the sentence, but it does make it less formal.

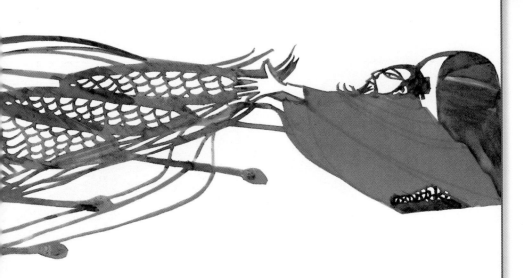

At last, though, the emperor looked out and saw his daughter flying her kite. He expected the tiny basket of food to sail up to his window as it had done each day. But what should he see but the strand of vines and grass and long black hair. The wind was raging above, holding the kite in its steely grip.

And the princess was below, holding tight to the end of the rope. **13**

Although the emperor had never really understood the worth of his tiniest daughter before, he did now. And he promised himself that if her plan worked she would never again want for anything, though all she had ever wanted was love. Then he **14** leaned farther out of the tower window and grasped the heavy strand. He brought it into his tower room and loosened the string of the kite. He set the kite free, saying, "Go to thy home in the sky, great kite." And the kite flew off toward the heavens.

187

Monitor Progress

# Make and Confirm Predictions

**How will the emperor use the rope?** (He will tie it to something in the tower and climb down to the ground.)

**If students have trouble answering, model how they can use the Make and Confirm Predictions strategy to answer the question.**

**MODEL** **I know that the emperor must want to escape and return to ruling his kingdom. I also know that there is a window with an iron bar across it. I predict that the emperor will tie the rope to the iron bar and use the rope to climb down to the ground.**

## SOCIAL STUDIES

**Wind Patterns** For centuries people have relied upon the wind to help them. Knowing the location of favorable wind currents and ocean currents was essential to the early explorers. Discuss with students why knowing where wind and ocean currents are would be important to an explorer. (Possible response: Knowing the path of a particular wind or ocean current would help explorers sail their boats toward their intended destinations.)

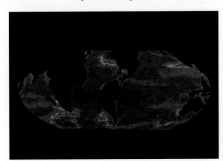

# Guided Comprehension

**15** **CONFIRM PREDICTIONS** **What does the emperor do with the rope? Is this what you predicted he would do?** (Possible response: He ties the rope to the iron bar and slides down it. Responses will vary.)

**16** **SEQUENCE** **What does the emperor do before he slips under the iron bar?** (Possible response: He steps to the windowsill.)

**17** **FIGURATIVE LANGUAGE** **How is the emperor like a kite?** (As the emperor slides down the rope, his robes look like the wings of a kite.)

Then the emperor tied one end of the thick strand to the heavy iron bar across the window and the other end stretched all the way down to Djeow Seow's tiny hands.

The emperor stepped to the window sill, slipped under the iron bar, saluted the gods, and slid down the rope. His robes billowed out around him like the wings of a bright kite. **15** **16** **17**

188

## ENGLISH-LANGUAGE LEARNERS

Point out the sentence *His robes billowed out around him like the wings of a bright kite* on page 188. Explain that this phrase means that the emperor's brightly colored robes were spread out in the wind. Then help students compare the wings of a bird to the wings of a kite. (both are used to fly)

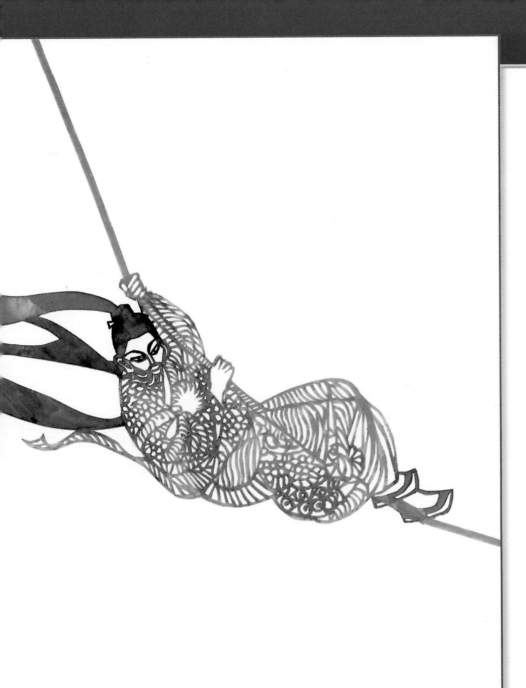

189

Monitor Progress

# Use Context to Confirm Meaning

What does the word *billowed* mean in the sentence, "His robes *billowed* out around him like the wings of a bright kite"? (to spread out)

If students are unable to answer the question, model the strategy:

**MODEL** At first, I do not know what the word *billowed* means. Then I see that the author compares the emperor's robes to the wings of a kite. I think about how the wings of a large, colorful kite move in the wind. They spread out in the air. That makes me think *billowed* means "spread out."

# Guided Comprehension

**18** **USE PRIOR KNOWLEDGE/DRAW CONCLUSIONS** **Why does the emperor kiss the ground after he escapes?** (Possible answers: He kisses the ground to show he is glad to be free again; he kisses the ground to show respect for Djeow Seow.)

**19** **AUTHOR'S PURPOSE** **Why do you think the author chooses to have the emperor carry Djeow Seow back to the palace?** (Possible answer: She wants us to see how much the emperor cherishes his clever daughter.)

When his feet reached the ground, he knelt before his tiny daughter. And he touched the ground before her with his lips. **18** Then he rose and embraced her, and she almost disappeared in his arms.

190

**BELOW-LEVEL**

Work with students to summarize how the emperor escapes from the tower.

- The monk's poem helps Djeow Seow figure out how to help her father.

- Djeow Seow makes a rope and attaches it to her kite.

- The emperor grabs the rope, ties it to an iron bar, and slides down the rope.

Tell students to keep reading to find out what happens now that the emperor has escaped.

With his arm encircling her, the emperor said, "Come to thy home with me, loyal child." He lifted the tiny princess to his shoulders and carried her all the way back to the palace. **19**

191

## Monitor Progress

 **Self-Question**

(Focus Strategy)

**How do you think the emperor will treat Djeow Seow in the future?** (Possible answer: He will show her gratitude and love. They will be very close.)

**Have students model using Self-Questioning to find the answer.**

**MODEL** To answer this question, I ask myself, *How would I feel about someone who saved my life? How would I treat that person?* I think I would be very grateful and would treat that person with kindness, love, and respect. I think that is how the emperor will treat Djeow Seow.

## SOCIAL STUDIES

**Cultural Gestures** Remind students that when the emperor reaches the ground, he kneels in front of his daughter and kisses the ground in front of her. Explain that in many cultures, kissing the ground is a way of showing gratitude, or saying thank you. Some people kiss the ground when they arrive in their home country after a long journey. Ask students the following questions:

What gesture do you use to show gratitude? (Possible responses: hand shakes, hugs, kisses, pats on the back)

In what other ways does the emperor show his gratitude toward Djeow Seow? (He gives her a hug.)

*The Emperor and the Kite* **191**

# Guided Comprehension

**20** **SUMMARIZE** **How do the people respond when the emperor arrives at the palace?** (The people are very happy to see the emperor. They are no longer afraid of the men who took over the kingdom. They help throw the men into prison.)

**21** **SPECULATE** **Why do you think the emperor's return gives the people the courage to put the plotters in prison?** (Possible response: The people know that the emperor is a good, strong leader who will support them. This knowledge gives them the courage to act bravely and do the right thing.)

192

**REACHING ALL LEARNERS**

## Diagnostic Check: Comprehension and Skills

**If** . . . students are having difficulty identifying the plot of the story . . .

**Then** . . . have them draw or write what happened in the beginning, the middle, and the end of the story.

### ADDITIONAL SUPPORT ACTIVITIES

| BELOW-LEVEL | Reteach, p. S42 |
| ADVANCED | Extend, p. S43 |
| ENGLISH-LANGUAGE LEARNERS | Reteach, p. S43 |

At the palace, the emperor was greeted by wild and cheering crowds. The people were tired of the evil men, but they had been afraid to act. With the emperor once again to guide them, they threw the plotters into prison. **20** **21**

193

**Monitor Progress**

 **Focus Strategy** **Self-Question**

**Why do the people greet the emperor with wild cheering?** (Possible response: because they are excited that he is alive and is going to be their ruler again)

**Have students model Self-Questioning to find the answer.**

**MODEL** To answer this question, I ask myself *When do I cheer about something?* I cheer when I am excited about something, so I conclude that the people must be cheering because they are excited that the emperor has returned.

# REREADING FOR FLUENCY

**Choral Reading** Have pairs of students prepare choral readings of "The Emperor and the Kite." Each pair should divide the text into speaking parts. Ask them to practice their readings and then perform. Encourage them to focus on reading with appropriate pacing, intonation, and expression.

LISTENING/SPEAKING/READING

**Note:** For assessment of oral reading accuracy and fluency, see pages T44–T46.

*The Emperor and the Kite* **193**

# Guided Comprehension

## RETURN TO THE PREDICTIONS/PURPOSE

**Were you able to determine what lesson the emperor learned?** Discuss with students whether their purposes for reading were met.

# Think and Respond

### Answers:

**1** Possible responses: She flies her kite to send food to him when he is locked in the tower. She makes a rope he can use to escape. **SUMMARIZE**

**2** When he changes his poem, it gives Djeow Seow the idea of using her kite to help her father escape from the tower. **IMPORTANT DETAILS**

**3** Possible responses: She was very tiny. Her older brothers and sisters all had important jobs, but no one paid attention to her. **DRAW CONCLUSIONS**

**4** Yes; they can learn that everyone is special and valuable, regardless of their size or appearance. **PERSONAL OPINION**

**5** Accept reasonable responses. **READING STRATEGIES**

### OPEN-ENDED RESPONSE

Is "The Emperor and the Kite" believable or unbelievable? Write a paragraph that tells which parts could have happened and which parts are fantasy. Support your response with specific reasons and details.

And when the other sons and daughters of the emperor heard of his return, they left off their sobbing and sighing, and they hurried home to welcome their father. But when they arrived, they were surprised to find Djeow Seow on a tiny throne by their father's side.

To the end of his day, the emperor ruled with Princess Djeow Seow close by. She never wanted for anything, especially love. And the emperor never again neglected a person—whether great or small. And, too, it is said that Djeow Seow ruled after him, as gentle as the wind and, in her loyalty, as unyielding.

194

## COMPREHENSION

**End-of-Selection Test**
To evaluate comprehension, see *Practice Book*, pages A25–A28.

# Think and Respond

**1** How does Djeow Seow save her father, the emperor?

**2** Why is the character of the monk important to the story?

**3** Why did people think of Djeow Seow as **insignificant**?

**4** Do you think people can learn something important from this folktale? Explain your answer.

**5** How did using a reading strategy help you as you read this selection?

195

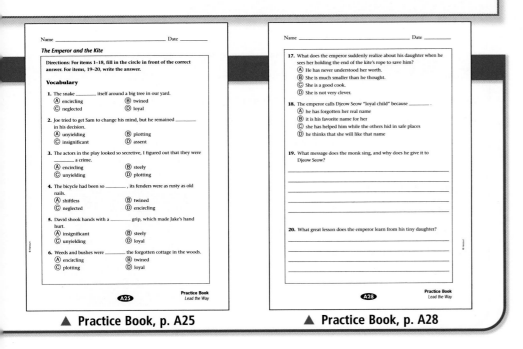
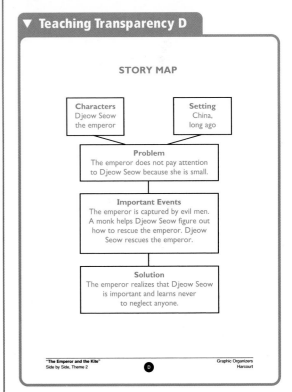

### RETELL

Use these questions to guide students as they retell "The Emperor and the Kite."

• Where does the selection take place?
• Who is Djeow Seow?
• What happens to the emperor?
• How does the emperor reward Djeow Seow?

### SUMMARIZE

Encourage students to summarize the selection, using their completed story maps. See Transparency D on Page T53.

▼ **Teaching Transparency D**

**STORY MAP**

| Characters | Setting |
|---|---|
| Djeow Seow | China, |
| the emperor | long ago |

**Problem**
The emperor does not pay attention to Djeow Seow because she is small.

**Important Events**
The emperor is captured by evil men. A monk helps Djeow Seow figure out how to rescue the emperor. Djeow Seow rescues the emperor.

**Solution**
The emperor realizes that Djeow Seow is important and learns never to neglect anyone.

"The Emperor and the Kite"        Graphic Organizers
Side by Side, Theme 2        Ⓓ        Harcourt

### ✏ WRITTEN SUMMARY

Have students use their completed story maps to write a summary telling how the emperor changes. PERFORMANCE ASSESSMENT

Meet the Author

# Jane Yolen

Jane Yolen began her writing career as a journalist and poet before turning to children's literature. She has written over 150 children's books, including the Piggins mystery series, and has won many literary awards. She says she comes from a family of storytellers, so writing children's tales continues the family tradition. Family is very important to Jane Yolen. She often includes family in her stories, having fashioned several characters after her husband and children.

## ABOUT THE AUTHOR

Books and stories have always been an important part of **Jane Yolen's** life. Her father was a journalist, and her mother wrote short stories. Her three children have collaborated with her on books, as well.

Jane Yolen says that her ideas for stories "come from all over"—from paintings, her family, dreams, newspaper articles, and song lyrics. Discuss what Yolen means when she says that "it is what one does with ideas that makes the difference."

Meet the Illustrator

# Ed Young

Ed Young has been illustrating children's books for more than 20 years. He says that when he worked as an advertising designer, he used to spend his lunch breaks at the zoo sketching the animals.

Young uses different techniques in the books he illustrates. For *The Emperor and the Kite*, he used an Oriental paper cutting technique. Besides being a gifted illustrator, he is also a talented writer. In fact, his book *Lon Po Po* won the Caldecott Medal.

Ed Young was born in Tientsin, China, and grew up in Shanghai. He now lives in Hastings-on-Hudson, New York, with his wife, Filomena.

**Visit *The Learning Site!***
**www.harcourtschool.com**

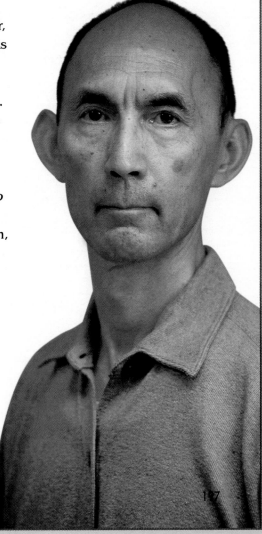

## ABOUT THE ILLUSTRATOR

**Ed Young**   In addition to having over twenty years of experience illustrating children's books, Ed Young has distinguished himself as a writer as well. As an artist, Ed Young uses techniques, such as Oriental paper cutting, to complement and enhance the stories he illustrates.

# Reading Across Texts

**Genre Study**  Have students read the title and headings. Tell students that this is a nonfiction article. Then have students predict how "Kite Festivals" will be similar to and different from "The Emperor and the Kite." (It will also be about kites; it will give real information about kites instead of telling a story.)

Have students read the selection silently, paying attention to the way information is organized. Then ask:

**1** **DRAW CONCLUSIONS**  **Why do you think most kite festivals take place in the spring?** (Possible response: because the weather during spring is best-suited to flying kites)

**2** **TEXT STRUCTURE AND FORMAT If you wanted to find information about stunt kites, under which heading would you look?** (Pretty Tricky)

**3** **SUMMARIZE**  **What is a kite battle?** (A kite battle is when two people fly their kites so that their lines cross. Then each person tries to saw through the other one's line.)

Genre
Magazine Article

# KITE FESTIVALS

**A**ll around the world, people get together to have fun with their kites at festivals. One is held every spring at the Washington Monument in Washington, D.C. People enter their special kites in flying competitions. You can see breathtaking flights of animal kites like the ones shown here. There are kite festivals year round, but most happen in spring. **1**

198

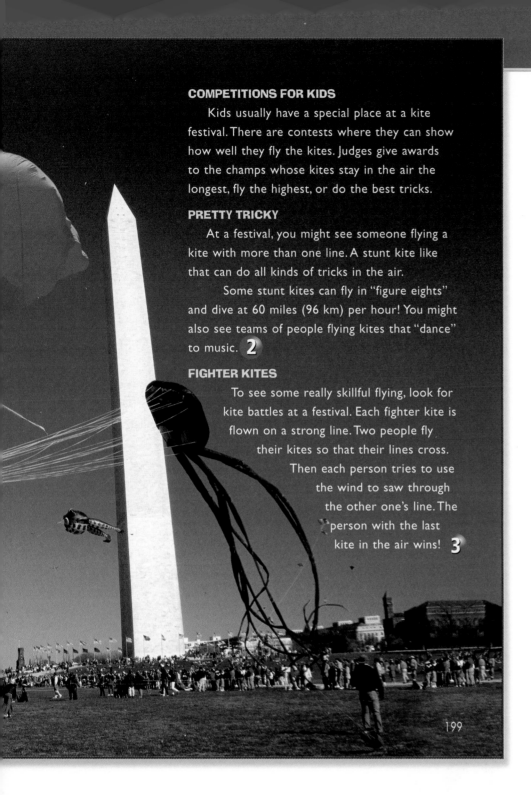

### COMPETITIONS FOR KIDS

Kids usually have a special place at a kite festival. There are contests where they can show how well they fly the kites. Judges give awards to the champs whose kites stay in the air the longest, fly the highest, or do the best tricks.

### PRETTY TRICKY

At a festival, you might see someone flying a kite with more than one line. A stunt kite like that can do all kinds of tricks in the air.

Some stunt kites can fly in "figure eights" and dive at 60 miles (96 km) per hour! You might also see teams of people flying kites that "dance" to music. **2**

### FIGHTER KITES

To see some really skillful flying, look for kite battles at a festival. Each fighter kite is flown on a strong line. Two people fly their kites so that their lines cross. Then each person tries to use the wind to saw through the other one's line. The person with the last kite in the air wins! **3**

199

# Reading Across Texts

**4 FOLLOW DIRECTIONS/SEQUENCE**
When making the paper fold kite, how should you fold your paper?
(from top to bottom)

**5 AUTHOR'S PURPOSE** Why do you think the author wrote this selection?
(to give people interesting information about kites; to teach people how to make a kite)

**6 EXPRESS PERSONAL OPINIONS**
Which part of the selection did you find most interesting? Why?
(Responses will vary.)

## REREADING FOR A PURPOSE

**Understanding Text Structure and Format** Have students write questions using the headings on pages 199 and 200. For example, students might write *What do Competitions for Kids Involve?* Then have students reread the page to find answers to their questions. When students are finished, discuss how the text format helped them locate specific information within the selection.

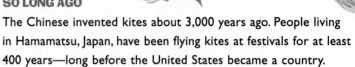

# KITE TALES

**SO LONG AGO**
The Chinese invented kites about 3,000 years ago. People living in Hamamatsu, Japan, have been flying kites at festivals for at least 400 years—long before the United States became a country.

**RECORD-SETTING KITES**
In 1919, some people in Germany flew a train of kites more than five miles (8 km) above the Earth. A group in Japan flew more than 11,000 kites on a single line in 1990. A bunch of college students in Long Beach, Washington, kept a kite in the air for more than a week!

**NOT JUST A TOY**
Did you know that the Wright brothers' first airplane was a lot like a kind of kite called a box kite? Imagine how brave they were to fly off in a kite with a motor and a propeller.

**WHOA, KITES, WHOA!**
About 150 years ago, a teacher in England built a carriage that was pulled by a train of kites. With a good wind, it could go about as fast as a carriage pulled by horses, and the teacher didn't have to feed his kites anything!

**HELP-ME KITES**
People sometimes carry a small kite on wilderness hikes. Then, if they need to be rescued, they can fly the kite to help show rescuers where they are.

**THE BEST KITE OF ALL?**
The very best kite is one you make and fly yourself. Many kinds of kites can be made with materials found around your house. Libraries have books on making and flying kites.

200

## BELOW-LEVEL

As students complete the steps for the paper fold kite, they may need help understanding the terms that describe the parts of a kite. Draw on the board a diagram like the one below, and use it to point out the parts of a kite.

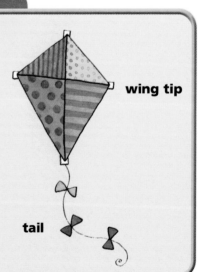

**wing tip**

**tail**

# PAPER FOLD KITE

This kite can be flown in light winds or indoors in a large space.

**What you need:**

- Typing, copier, or computer paper (8 by 11 inches)
- Clear tape
- Drinking straw
- Sewing thread or light string for the flying line
- Crepe paper for the tail

**What you do:**

1. Fold sheet of paper in half, top to bottom.

folded edge

2. Mark a diagonal on the folded paper. Offset the diagonal by 3/8 of an inch.

3. Fold the top leaf forward along the diagonal line and the bottom leaf backward.

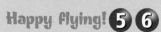
tape

4. Tape the keel together (see diagram 4) by putting tape across the wings.

hole

5. Make a hole 3 inches from the top of the keel.

6. Tape the drinking straw from wingtip to wingtip.

7. Make a tail the length of the kite. Tape the tail at bottom of kite point.

8. Attach the flying line through the hole (see diagram 5).

9. To fly indoors: Use a three-foot flying line attached to a ruler or a balloon stick.

**Happy Flying!** 5 6

**SAFETY TIP:**

Fly your kite in an open area at a park, field, or beach. Never use wire for your line. Stay away from electrical wires, and don't fly a kite during a thunderstorm. Also, if you fly a big kite, be sure to wear gloves. That will keep your hands from getting burned by a fast-moving line.

201

## related books

You may want to recommend to students interested in kites or family relationships that they locate these titles.

### LIBRARY BOOKS COLLECTION

*The Canada Geese Quilt* by Natalie Kinsey-Warnock. 1989.

### ADDITIONAL READING

- *Shibumi and the Kitemaker* by Mercer Mayer. Marshall Cavendish, 1987. **EASY**

- *Kites: Magic Wishes That Fly Up to the Sky* by Demi. Crown, 1999. **AVERAGE**

- *Dragonwings* by Laurence Yep. HarperCollins, 1975. **CHALLENGING**

# Making Connections

## COMPARE TEXTS

**Answers:**

**1** Possible response: The story shows that all people, from a mighty emperor to a tiny little girl, can work together to help one another. **THEME**

**2** Possible response: He changes *My soul goes on wings* to *My emperor goes on wings*. He is trying to tell Djeow Seow that she can use her kite to rescue her father. **IMPORTANT DETAILS/ CHARACTERS' MOTIVATIONS**

**3** Possible response: Yes, even though one selection is fiction and one is non-fiction, both authors show that kites are fun and can be useful. **AUTHOR'S VIEWPOINT**

**4** Responses will vary. **COMPARE AND CONTRAST**

**5** Possible responses: library card catalog, folktale collections, or anthologies **INQUIRY**

▲ The Emperor and the Kite

# Making Connections

## Compare Texts

**1** How does "The Emperor and the Kite" fit into the theme Side by Side?

**2** On page 184, what small change does the monk make to the poem? What is he trying to tell Djeow Seow?

**3** Do the author of "The Emperor and the Kite" and the author of "Kite Festivals" have the same viewpoint about kites? Explain.

**4** Think about another folktale you have read. In what ways is it like "The Emperor and the Kite"?

**5** If you wanted to read more folktales from Asia, where might you look for them?

### Write to Explain

**S**uppose the emperor decides to put Djeow Seow's kite on display. Write a paragraph to be displayed with the kite. Explain how Djeow Seow used the kite to rescue her father. Make a chart like this one to organize your ideas.

Writing CONNECTION

| What Is on Display? | |
| --- | --- |
| Why Is It on Display? | |
| How Was It Used? | |

202

## Making Connections

### Create a Display

**Social Studies CONNECTION**

Kites were invented in China about 3,000 years ago. Research a more recent invention, such as the electric light or the automobile. Make or use drawings, diagrams, or other graphic aids to create a visual display about this invention. Write captions for each graphic you include.

*Electric Light*

### Measure Perimeter and Area

**Math CONNECTION**

Kites are made in many different shapes and sizes, including squares and rectangles. Cut several square and rectangular miniature kites of different sizes from construction paper. Then find the perimeter and area of each shape, and write the measurements on it.

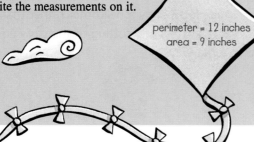

perimeter = 12 inches
area = 9 inches

203

### HOMEWORK FOR THE WEEK

Students and family members can work together to complete the activities on page T63. You may want to assign some or all of the activities as homework for each day of the week.

**TECHNOLOGY**
**Visit** *The Learning Site:*
**www.harcourtschool.com**
See Resources for Parents and Teachers:
Homework Helper.
**Teacher's Edition p. T63 ▶**

#### School–Home Connection

**Your child is reading "The Emperor and the Kite,"** a Chinese folktale by Jane Yolen. In this folktale, the tiny daughter of an emperor gets no attention or love because she is so small. When the emperor is captured by bad men and imprisoned in a tower, it is the tiny girl, and not her bigger and stronger brothers and sisters, who manages to save her father and finally win his everlasting love.

**Make a Kite**
Visit a library and learn how to make a homemade kite. Find books on Chinese art, and use them to get ideas for ways to paint your kite. Help your child fly the kite, and discuss how the wind works to keep the kite up in the air.

**VOCABULARY**
**Word of the Day**
The following words are new vocabulary your child has learned while reading "The Emperor and the Kite":

insignificant    plotting
twined           steely
encircling       loyal
neglected        unyielding

Play a vocabulary-building game with your child. Have your child arrange the words in alphabetical order, and then assign a word to each of the coming eight days. For example, on the first day, you and your child can try finding things you think are insignificant. Make a list of what you find for each word.

**More Folktales**
You and your child might enjoy searching for more international folktales at your local library. Choose character and narrative parts, and read each folktale aloud. Discuss the message of the folktale.

**Chinese Recipes**
Look in cookbooks for easy recipes for Chinese food. Help your child plan a simple meal and work together to prepare the meal and serve it. If possible, use chopsticks to eat the food you have prepared.

**TIME TO READ** Encourage your child to read for at least 30 minutes outside of class each day.

---

**Write to Explain**   Have students brainstorm a list of reasons why Djeow Seow's kite is on display. Then have them explain how the kite was used to rescue her father.

**PORTFOLIO OPPORTUNITY**
Students may choose to place their paragraphs in their working portfolios.

**SOCIAL STUDIES**

**Create a Display**   Students may use photos to help them draw conclusions about recent inventions. They may also use other references and resources to find information for their displays.

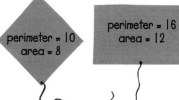

*The Automobile*
*Model T Ford*

**MATH**

**Measure Perimeter and Area**
Provide resources such as rulers, construction paper, and scissors. Review with students the formulas for finding the perimeter and the area of a quadrilateral.

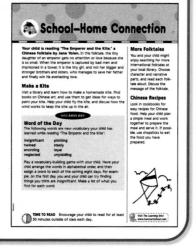

perimeter = 10
area = 8

perimeter = 16
area = 12

---

# Narrative Elements

Focus Skill

### SKILL TRACE
#### NARRATIVE ELEMENTS

| Introduce | p. 20I |
|-----------|--------|
| Reteach | pp. S4, S16, S40, T2 |
| Review | pp. 48, 78I, 100 |
| Test | Theme I |
| **Maintain** | **pp. 174I, 204** |

### RETURN TO THE SKILL

Have students read page 204 in the *Pupil Edition*. Point out that the diagram illustrates how the narrative elements are related. You may wish to use this model:

**MODEL** **I know the setting of "The Emperor and the Kite" is ancient China. I know that the main character is Djeow Seow, who saves her father, the emperor, by flying her kite. If any of these elements were to change, the story would be different.**

### PRACTICE/APPLY

Have students work in pairs to retell a popular folktale or fairy tale. Then have them rewrite the tale, changing one or two narrative elements. Discuss how changing narrative elements impacted the story.

**PERFORMANCE ASSESSMENT**

**TECHNOLOGY** ■ *Mission: Comprehension™ Skills Practice CD-ROM* provides additional practice with reading comprehension and focus skills.

**Visit** *The Learning Site*: www.harcourtschool.com
See Skill Activities and Test Tutors: Narrative Elements.

---

▲ The Emperor and the Kite

## Narrative Elements

**R**emember that narrative elements of a story include **characters**, **setting**, and **plot**. These elements combine to create a particular story. Changing any one of the elements would cause changes in the others as well, resulting in a different story.

The diagram shows how all of the elements are related.

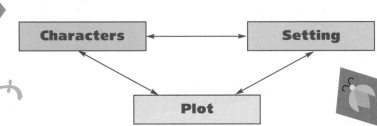

For example, if "The Emperor and the Kite" was set in the United States in the present, there would be no emperor. As a result, the plot of the story would also change.

Think about these questions:

• If the character Djeow Seow was not so tiny and insignificant, how might that change the plot of the story?

• If the rescue in the plot was by a helicopter rather than by a kite, would the characters and setting of the story also be different? In what ways?

**Visit** *The Learning Site!*
www.harcourtschool.com
See *Skills and Activities*

204

---

### REACHING ALL LEARNERS

## Diagnostic Check: Comprehension and Skills

**If** ... students are having difficulty understanding narrative elements ...

**Then** ... draw a story map on the board. Guide students in completing it by listing the characters, the setting, and the main plot events.

### ADDITIONAL SUPPORT ACTIVITIES

| BELOW-LEVEL | Reteach, p. S42 |
| ADVANCED | Extend, p. S43 |
| ENGLISH-LANGUAGE LEARNERS | Reteach, p. S43 |

## Test Prep
### Narrative Elements

▶ Read the passage. Then answer the questions.

> Harlan was the biggest boy in town. Some people said he was the biggest, strongest boy on the whole western frontier.
>
> One day Harlan's father was plowing the fields when his ox Bessie fell into a ditch and hurt her leg. Poor Bessie couldn't get up. Harlan's father ran to fetch him from the schoolhouse.
>
> Harlan lifted Bessie out of the ditch. Bessie's leg was sore, so Harlan carried her up and down the fields while his father steered the plow.

**Focus Skill**

1. How would the plot change if the character of Harlan was not so big and strong?

   A  Bessie would have to be rescued a different way.

   B  There would be a different plow.

   C  Bessie would not have fallen in the ditch.

   D  There would be no change.

**Tip** Identify an event that could not take place if the character was not so big and strong.

2. If the plot changed so that Harlan's father needed help reeling in a huge fish, how else would the story change?

   F  It would be set in a different place.

   G  It would be set in a different time.

   H  Harlan would not have to be so big and strong.

   J  There would be no change.

**Tip** Think about how the characters and the setting would have to change for this story to be about fishing.

205

## Test Prep

**Narrative Elements**  Have students read the passage carefully and look for details about the setting, plot, and characters. Use the Tips to reinforce good test-taking strategies. (I.A; 2.F)

**BELOW-LEVEL** ▲ Extra Support, p. 30

**ON-LEVEL** ▲ Practice Book, p. 30

**ADVANCED** ▲ Challenge, p. 30

**ENGLISH-LANGUAGE LEARNERS** ▲ ELL, p. 30

# Phonics

# Decoding/Phonics

## *Word Structure: Compound Words*

## OBJECTIVE

*To identify and decode compound words*

### SKILL TRACE

| COMPOUND WORDS | |
| --- | --- |
| Introduce | Grade 2 |
| **Maintain** | **p. 205A** |

### ONGOING ASSESSMENT

**If** students are not able to fluently read approximately 99 words per minute, **then** they require phonics instruction and will also benefit from fluency practice.

**NOTE:** For assessment of oral reading accuracy and fluency, see pages T44–T46.

### MAINTAIN THE SKILL

**Decode compound words.**   Write the word *poppyseed* on the board. Say the word, and ask students how many words make up the word *poppyseed*. (two) Ask a volunteer to identify the two words. Cover the second part of the word. Have students read the word *poppy*. Then cover the first part of the word, and have students read the word *seed.* Then have them read the entire word.

Tell students that there are different kinds of compound words. Some compound words are written as one word, such as *poppyseed*. Others are written as separate words, such as *swimming pool.* Hyphenated compound words are written with hyphens, such as *father-in-law*. Explain that the meaning of a compound word is usually related to the meanings of its parts. Ask students what the word *poppyseed* means. (seed of a poppy flower)

### PRACTICE/APPLY

**Decode other compound words.**   Draw on the board a chart like the one below. Ask students to copy it.

| Word | Meaning |
| --- | --- |
| snowstorm | a storm of or with snow |
| cowboy | a person who takes care of cows |
| doghouse | a house for a dog |
| sunset | the time when the sun dips below the horizon |
| backpack | a camping pack carried on a person's back |
| seashell | a shell from the sea |
| sandbox | a boxed play area filled with sand |

Ask students to read each word aloud by blending the root words. Then have them use the meanings of the root words to write a definition for the compound word. Have students work in teams to list other compound words. Have the teams share their compound words. PERFORMANCE ASSESSMENT

# Figurative Language

*Literary Response and Analysis*

## REVIEW THE SKILL

**Discuss figurative language.**   Remind students that writers sometimes use figurative language to help readers create a mental picture. Explain that similes and metaphors are types of figurative language that compare a person or thing to something else. Good readers keep an eye out for figurative language and pause to interpret its meaning before they continue reading.

Have students read page 179. Model how a reader can identify and interpret figurative language.

**MODEL**   The first sentence in the second paragraph says, "But Djeow Seow was like a tiny star in the emperor's sight." This is the author's way of saying that she is so small that her father doesn't notice her.

## PRACTICE/APPLY

**Explore figurative language.**   Ask students what mental image comes to mind when the author says that the emperor's sons "were like four rising suns in the eyes of their father." Then ask students what they think the author meant. (The sons are very important to the emperor; he has very high hopes for his sons.)

Have students use figurative language to describe a character from "The Emperor and the Kite." Then have them switch papers with a classmate and give the literal meaning of the figurative expression they receive. **PERFORMANCE ASSESSMENT**

**Summarize.**   Ask students to summarize what they know about figurative language. (Possible response: Understanding figurative language helps me picture the character or event the author is describing.)

**I'm all ears.**

| SKILL TRACE | |
| --- | --- |
| **FIGURATIVE LANGUAGE** | |
| Introduce | pp. 173A–173B |
| Reteach | p. T37 |
| **Review** | **pp. 205B, 251B** |
| Test | Theme 2 |
| Maintain | p. 589D |

### ADVANCED

Have students write a haiku about a topic of their choice. Tell them that one line of their haiku should be a metaphor.

# Writer's Craft

# Written Directions

## Writer's Craft: Effective Paragraphs

## TRAITS OF GOOD WRITING

| | INTRODUCE AND PRACTICE | APPLY TO LONGER WRITING FORMS |
|---|---|---|
| Focus/Ideas | 421E–F | 453E–F, 471C–D |
| Organization | 521E–F, 543E–F | 567C–D, 589E–F |
| Voice | 49E–F, 77E–F | 101C–D, 123C–D |
| Word Choice | 637E–F, 667E–F | 689C–D, 713C–D |
| Development | 421E–F, 437C–D | 453E–F, 471C–D |
| Effective Sentences | 299E–F, 325C–D | 349C–D, 371C–D |
| **Effective Paragraphs** | **173E–F, 205C–D** | **229E–F, 251C–D** |
| Conventions | (*See* Grammar and Spelling Lessons.) | (Applied to all writing lessons.) |

## technology

**Writing Express™ CD-ROM**

Visit *The Learning Site*:

www.harcourtschool.com

See Writing Detective:
Proofreading Makes Perfect.

## TRAITS OF GOOD WRITING

- **Focus/Ideas:** The writer focuses on the topic. Every sentence tells something about the steps for flying a kite.

- **Organization/Paragraphs:** There are no unnecessary sentences.

- **Development:** The writer provides the details to fly a kite successfully.

- **Voice:** The writer is enthusiastic about kite-flying.

- **Word Choice:** The writer uses sequence words, such as *first, then, when,* and *finally,* to help identify the order of the steps.

- **Effective Sentences:** The sequence words help the sentences flow together.

### DAY 1 — TEACH/MODEL

**CONNECT READING TO WRITING**
Review pages 185–188 of "The Emperor and the Kite." Point out the sequence words the author uses, and ask students where they could insert additional sequence words to make the steps clearer.

**EFFECTIVE PARAGRAPHS** Display Transparency 61. Guide students to analyze the structure of the paragraph: all the sentences are related to the topic; the paragraph begins with the first step and ends with the last step.

### DAY 2 — EXTEND THE CONCEPT

**EFFECTIVE PARAGRAPHS** Point out that when we give directions out loud or write them on paper, we use *sequence words* to show the order of the steps. Sequence words can also tie together the sentences in a paragraph of written directions.

Display Transparency 62. In Part A, have students choose sequence words from the box to connect the sentences to form a paragraph. Use Part B to extend the concept.

**APPLY TO WRITING** Have students write a list of steps and put them in paragraph form by adding transitions.

▼ **Teaching Transparency 61**

### WRITTEN DIRECTIONS

Written directions help people get places or do things correctly. Sequence words, or time-order words, make written directions easy to read and follow.

#### How to Fly a Kite

Flying a kite is easy and fun. First, take your kite out of the closet or garage where you keep it. Next, make sure there are no tears in the body of the kite or the tail. After you repair any tears, find a large ball of twine on a rod. Then, tie one end of the twine to the kite. When the twine is secure, take your kite to a large, open space. Hold the kite overhead, and run very fast into the wind. When the kite starts to fly, unroll the twine slowly. Finally, when the kite is flying high overhead, relax and admire its gentle motions through the air.

BEGINNING | END

"The Emperor and the Kite"
Side by Side, Theme 2 · 61 · Writing: Written Directions · Harcourt

▼ **Teaching Transparency 62**

### SEQUENCE WORDS

#### Part A

| finally | then | before |
|---|---|---|
| after | next | now |

Use words from the box above to fill in the blanks.

#### Directions to the Kite Festival at Shipe Park

To get to Shipe Park, <u>first</u> you must leave Williams Elementary School and walk three blocks west on Baton Rouge Drive. <u>Next</u>, make a left onto Arcadia Street and walk two blocks. <u>Finally</u>, make a right on Theriot Drive. The park is one block down on your right.

#### Part B

| At the end of the day | After a few minutes | When you finish registering |
|---|---|---|

Use the phrases in the box above to fill in the blanks.

When you get to the park, you will be eager to fly your kite. Before you do, go to the registration table and stand in line. <u>After a few minutes,</u> a volunteer will ask you to fill out a form. <u>When you finish registering,</u> you will be allowed to find a place to fly your kite. <u>At the end of the day,</u> prizes will be given for the prettiest kite and the kite that flies the longest.

"The Emperor and the Kite"
Side by Side, Theme 2 · 62 · Writing: Written Directions · Harcourt

# 5 Day Plan

## DAY 3 — PREWRITE

Have students use this prompt to brainstorm ideas for a paragraph that gives written directions:

**WRITING PROMPT:** *Imagine that you are having a party for a group of friends. Write one or two paragraphs, giving directions to your home from your school. Use time-order words to show the correct order of the steps.*

Tell students to state their focus (topic, audience, and purpose). Then have them list the steps of the process.

## DAY 4 — DRAFT

**DRAFT** Have students use the steps below to draft their essays:

> **1. Introduce** the topic in a catchy way. Include an announcement about the party.

> **2. Organize** ideas by putting steps in time order. Include **sequence words** as you move from step to step.

> **3. Develop** your ideas by giving the details the reader needs to get to the destination.

> **4. Conclude** by giving the street address of your home and a description of it.

## DAY 5 — REVISE AND REFLECT

**REVISION FOCUS: DELETING**
Explain that one part of revising is removing details or examples that do not develop the main point. For example, look at the directions below.

**Make a left on Main Street. Pass the library. I spend a lot of time there. Then make a right at the corner.**

Ask: *Which sentence does not help give the directions?* Work with students to remove the sentence that strays from the focus. (Delete "I spend a lot of time there.")

**PEER CONFERENCE CHECKLIST**
Have partners use these questions:

✓ **Does the essay name the destination in the introduction?**

✓ **Do sequence words make the order clear?**

✓ **What could we delete to make the writing clearer?**

**Language Handbook, pp. 30–33, 68, 111–113**

| SCORING RUBRIC | | | | |
|---|---|---|---|---|
| | **4** | **3** | **2** | **I** |
| **FOCUS/IDEAS** | Completely focused, purposeful. | Generally focused on task and purpose. | Somewhat focused on task and purpose. | Lacks focus and purpose. |
| **ORGANIZATION/ PARAGRAPHS** | Ideas progress logically; transitions make the relationships among ideas clear. | Organization mostly clear, but some lapses occur; some transitions are used. | Some sense of organization but inconsistent or unclear in places. | Little or no sense of organization. |
| **DEVELOPMENT** | Central idea supported by strong, specific details. | Central idea with adequate support, mostly relevant details. | Unclear central idea; limited supporting details. | Unclear central idea; little or no development. |
| **VOICE** | Viewpoint clear; original expressions used where appropriate. | Viewpoint somewhat clear; few original expressions. | Viewpoint unclear or inconsistent. | Writer seems detached and unconcerned. |
| **WORD CHOICE** | Clear, exact language; freshness of expression. | Clear language; some interesting word choices. | Word choice unclear or inappropriate in places. | Word choice often unclear or inappropriate. |
| **SENTENCES** | Variety of sentence structures; flows smoothly. | Some variety in sentence structures. | Little variety; choppy or run-on sentences. | Little or no variety; sentences unclear. |
| **CONVENTIONS** | Few, if any, errors. | Few errors. | Some errors. | Many errors. |

**REPRODUCIBLE STUDENT RUBRICS** for specific writing purposes and presentations are available on pages T56–T58.

# Grammar

## Compound Subjects and Predicates

### SKILL TRACE

**COMPOUND SUBJECTS AND PREDICATES**

| Introduce | p. 205E |
|---|---|
| Reteach | pp. S45, T40 |
| Review | pp. 205F, 229H |
| Test | Theme 2 |

### REACHING ALL LEARNERS

## Diagnostic Check: Grammar and Writing

**If** . . . students are unable to identify compound subjects and predicates . . .

**Then** . . . have them work in small groups. One student should choose a subject, another should add a subject, and other students should finish the sentence. Students can identify the compound subject. Repeat for compound predicates.

### ADDITIONAL SUPPORT ACTIVITIES

**BELOW-LEVEL** Reteach, p. S44

**ADVANCED** Extend, p. S45

**ENGLISH-LANGUAGE LEARNERS** Reteach, p. S45

## technology

**Grammar Jingles™ CD,**
Intermediate: Tracks 2 and 4
Visit *The Learning Site:*
**www.harcourtschool.com**
See Grammar Practice Park,
Go for Grammar Gold,
Multimedia Grammar Glossary.

---

### DAY 1 — TEACH/MODEL

**DAILY LANGUAGE PRACTICE**

1. **Do you have a kite fetsival at your school.** (festival; school?)
2. **Last year Marta made the prettyist kite** (prettiest; kite.)

**INTRODUCE THE CONCEPT** Refer to sentences 1–3 on Transparency 63 as you discuss these points:

• A **compound subject** is two or more subjects joined by the coordinating conjunctions *and* or *or*.

• If there are three or more subjects in a compound subject, use commas to separate them.

Ask students to complete sentences 4–5.

▼ **Teaching Transparency 63**

**COMPOUND SUBJECTS AND PREDICATES**

1. Marta and Kyle prepared for the big kite festival at Schamburg Elementary School.
2. Sara, Mike, and Taylor made kites for the big day.
3. Ms. Capshaw or Mr. Montero will announce the festival at the school assembly.
4. _____ and _____ will come to see their students fly their kites. Responses will vary.
5. _____ and _____ are popular colors for kites in the contest. Responses will vary.
6. Last year Principal Smythe announced the race and congratulated the winner. announced; congratulated
7. Contestants pay an entry fee and wear Kite Festival T-shirts. pay; wear
8. Therese entered the contest, flew her kite the longest, and won a prize. entered, flew, won

"The Emperor and the Kite"
Side by Side, Theme 2          63          Grammar
Harcourt

---

### DAY 2 — EXTEND THE CONCEPT

**DAILY LANGUAGE PRACTICE**

1. **Joel and Jenny. Want to enter a kite. Inn the festival.** (Jenny want; kite in)
2. **It is two late. the places are all taken.** (too; The)

**DEVELOP THE CONCEPT** Refer to sentences 6–8 on Transparency 63 as you discuss the following points:

• A **compound predicate** is two or more predicates joined by *and* or *or*. These predicates have the same subject.

• If there are three or more predicates in a compound predicate, use commas to separate them.

Have students identify the simple predicate in sentences 6–8. **PERFORMANCE ASSESSMENT**

Name _____

▶ Draw one line under each simple subject. Draw two lines under each simple predicate. Label each sentence *compound subject* or *compound predicate*.

1. Every year, Jake and Katie go to a kite-flying contest at school. _____ compound subject
2. The students and the teachers gather on the soccer field to watch the kites. _____ compound subject
3. Katie's kite dances and swirls through the air. _____ compound predicate
4. The principal chooses the best kite and gives the award. _____ compound predicate
5. Jake and his friend Kinuko fly their kites longer than anyone else. _____ compound subject
6. The winning kite is the biggest and soars the highest. _____ compound predicate

▶ Rewrite these sentences. Add commas where they are needed.

7. Last week, Katie made a kite attached some string to it and flew it in the park.
Last week, Katie made a kite, attached some string to it, and flew it in the park.

8. I think Katie Jaime and their friend Samir have the prettiest kites.
I think Katie, Jaime, and their friend Samir have the prettiest kites.

9. They have fun win prizes and show off their kites.
They have fun, win prizes, and show off their kites.

10. When they arrive home, their mother father and little brother cheer for them.
When they arrive home, their mother, father, and little brother cheer for them.

Practice Book

**Homework Option**

▲ **Practice Book, p. 31**

## DAILY LANGUAGE PRACTICE

1. **The Park is an open plase. Where people walk dogs?**
   (park; place where; dogs.)
2. **We shouldnt' fly. Our kites there.** (shouldn't; fly our)

**MAKE A COMPOUND**   Write on the board a list of subjects and predicates.

Have students take turns choosing simple subjects and predicates from the list and using them to create oral sentences with compound subjects or predicates.

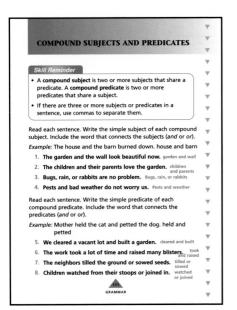

▲ Language Handbook, p. 111

## DAILY LANGUAGE PRACTICE

1. **Will kyle's kite fly for a long time.** (Kyle's; time?)
2. **He wonders if the whether will be good for flying?**
   (weather; flying.)

**ARTICLE**   Have students write a news article about a kite festival. Each article should contain several sentences with compound subjects or predicates.

### Test Prep Tip

"If there are three or more subjects or predicates, use a comma between each of them. Place the last comma before *and* or *or*."

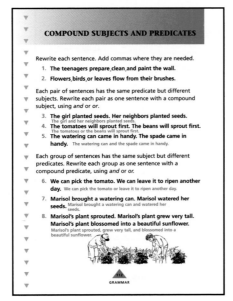

▲ Language Handbook, p. 112

## DAILY LANGUAGE PRACTICE

1. **Everyone liked Kyles kite last year** (Kyle's; year.)
2. **People on the street stopt, and smiled.** (stopped and)

**SUBJECTS AND PREDICATES**   Have students copy these sentences. Ask them to write *S* above each simple subject and *P* above each simple predicate. Then have them label each sentence *compound subject* or *compound predicate*.

1. **Marta made a kite and asked Carlos to fly it with her.**
   (s=Marta; p=made, asked; compound predicate)
2. **Becky and Yvonne cheered for the contestants.** (s=Becky, Yvonne; p=cheered; compound subject)

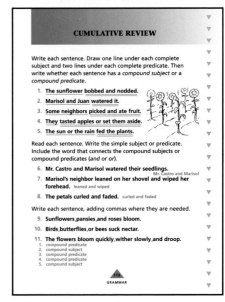

▲ Language Handbook, p. 113

*The Emperor and the Kite*   **205F**

## Spelling Words

1. pour
2. orbit
3. fourth*
4. source
5. sports
6. forward
7. force
8. order
9. wore
10. yourself
11. support
12. sore
13. orange
14. anymore
15. ignore
16. portrait
17. border
18. course
19. tornado
20. your

* Selection Words

### Challenge Words
21. emperor*
22. monarch
23. kingdom
24. palace*
25. noble

# Spelling

## Words with /ôr/

### DAY 1 — PRETEST/SELF-CHECK

**ADMINISTER THE PRETEST** Use the Dictation Sentences under Day 5. Help students self-check their pretests, using Transparency 64.

**ADVANCED**

Use the Challenge Words in these Dictation Sentences:

21. The **emperor** ruled for almost fifty years.
22. Queen Elizabeth was a powerful **monarch**.
23. The **kingdom** stretches from sea to sea.
24. A **palace** can be a very cold, drafty place to live.
25. Nursing is a **noble** profession.

### DAY 2 — TEACH/MODEL

**WORD SORT** Display Transparency 64. Discuss the meanings of the words. Ask students to copy the chart and write each Spelling Word where it belongs.

Point to and read the words *pour*, *orbit*, and *score*. Ask students how these three words are similar. (They have the same sound, /ôr/.) Have a volunteer circle the letters that stand for the /ôr/ sound. Ask students how this sound is spelled in the three words. (*our, or, ore*)

**HANDWRITING** Advise students to curve up and then down twice for the letter *r*. Otherwise, the letters *or* could look like *oi*.

*or oi*

### ▼ Teaching Transparency 64

**WORDS WITH THE /ôr/ SOUND**

**Spelling Words**

| | | | |
|---|---|---|---|
| 1. pour | 6. forward | 11. support | 16. portrait |
| 2. orbit | 7. force | 12. sore | 17. border |
| 3. fourth | 8. order | 13. orange | 18. course |
| 4. source | 9. wore | 14. anymore | 19. tornado |
| 5. sports | 10. yourself | 15. ignore | 20. your |

| our | or | ore |
|---|---|---|
| pour | orbit | wore |
| fourth | sports | sore |
| source | forward | anymore |
| yourself | force | ignore |
| course | order | |
| your | support | |
| | orange | |
| | portrait | |
| | border | |
| | tornado | |

The /ôr/ sound can be spelled *our, or,* or *ore.*

"The Emperor and the Kite"
Side by Side, Theme 2     64     Spelling
Harcourt

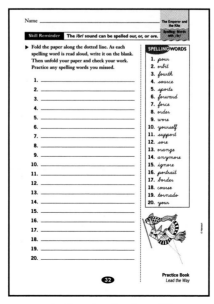

▲ Practice Book, p. 32

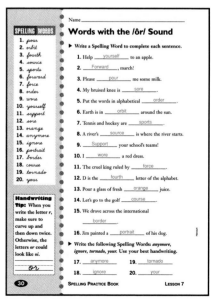

▲ Spelling Practice Book, p. 30

## DAY 3 — SPELLING STRATEGIES

**SMALLER WORDS** Write the word *forward* on the board. Explain to students that many words have smaller words within them. Tell students to look at the word *forward*. Ask a volunteer to find a smaller word in it. *(for)* Ask students how looking for smaller words within words can help their spelling. (Finding a smaller word in a larger word can help me remember how to spell the larger word.)

**Apply to Writing**

Remind students to look as they proofread for smaller words within larger words they have studied.

▲ Spelling Practice Book, p. 31

## DAY 4 — SPELLING ACTIVITIES

**MEMORY** Have students work in pairs. Ask each player to write each Spelling Word on a separate index card. Then have students turn the cards face down. Tell them to take turns turning up two cards. If the cards match, the player keeps them and gets an additional turn. If not, they are turned face down again. The winner is the player with more matches.

**WORD CONSTRUCTIONS** Write the chart below on the board.

| f | or | n |
|---|----|---|
| t | our | m |

Have students see how many words they can spell by combining the letters. (*form, torn, tour,* and *four.*)

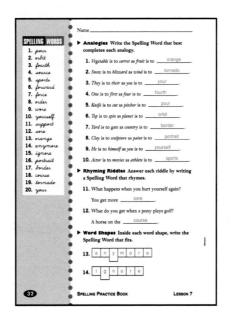

▲ Spelling Practice Book, p. 32

## DAY 5 — POSTTEST

**DICTATION SENTENCES**

1. **Pour** water in the glasses, Jill.
2. The rocket will **orbit** the Earth.
3. We came in **fourth** place in the art contest.
4. What is the **source** of the Colorado River?
5. My little sister is a real **sports** fan.
6. We moved **forward** in line.
7. The **force** of gravity makes things fall.
8. I'll put my notecards in **order**.
9. She **wore** her new bracelet.
10. You should be proud of **yourself**.
11. I need your **support** when I run for class president.
12. Are your legs **sore** from climbing?
13. The workers wore **orange** vests.
14. Maggie doesn't live here **anymore**.
15. My alarm clock is hard to **ignore**.
16. I have a **portrait** of my family.
17. Yesterday we crossed the **border** between California and Mexico.
18. We ran through an obstacle **course**.
19. The **tornado** caused great damage.
20. I really enjoyed **your** birthday party.

# Word Study

## ANALOGIES

## Word Relationships

**OBJECTIVE**

*To use knowledge of word relationships to determine analogies*

Write this analogy on the board: *Flying* is to a *kite* as *riding* is to a *bicycle*. Explain to students that this sentence is an analogy, a special kind of comparison. Read aloud the following analogies. Ask students to complete each one. (Possible responses are shown.)

1. *Remembered* is to *forgotten* as *neglected* is to _____. (*cherished*)

2. *Friendly* is to *warm* as *loyal* is to _____. (*faithful*)

3. *Tomato* is to *vegetable* as *steel* is to _____. (*metal*)

4. *Sunset* is to *daybreak* as *insignificant* is to _____. (*important*)

5. *Emperor* is to *empire* as *principal* is to _____. (*school*)

6. *Excited* is to *thrilled* as *shiftless* is to _____. (*lazy*)

***Flying*** is to a ***kite*** as ***riding*** is to a ***bicycle***.

## CONNOTATIONS

## Determine Meanings

**OBJECTIVE**

*To recognize and interpret the connotative meanings of words*

Explain that words can suggest feelings or ideas beyond their dictionary meanings. Tell students that the feeling a word creates is its connotation.

Write these sentences, including the underlines, on the board:

> The boys are <u>plotting</u> their next move.
>
> The boys are <u>planning</u> their next move.

Discuss the feeling each underlined word creates. (Possible responses: *Plotting* often involves something evil; *planning* sounds innocent or positive.) Point out that a word may have positive or negative connotations.

Have students discuss the connotations of the word pairs below and use them in sentences:

**call/shout** (*Shout* connotes loudness or anger.)

**ask/beg** (*Beg* connotes desperation.)

**pretty/stunning** (*Stunning* is a stronger word than *pretty*.)

### ADVANCED

Have students pick a paragraph from a selection they have read. Ask them to replace three or four words in the paragraph with words that have slightly different connotations. Then have them read aloud their revised paragraphs. Discuss how changing the words affects the meaning of the paragraph.

# Speaking and Listening

## Giving Directions

**OBJECTIVE**

*To use visual aids and sequence words to give directions*

Students may wish to publish their written works by giving directions orally to the class.

**Organization**   Share these **organizational tips** with students.

- Open with an explanation of where the directions will lead listeners.
- Draw a map to show the route to the location.
- Write your directions on a note card. Underline the sequence words and emphasize them as you read.
- Use specific details and examples to clarify information.

**Delivery**   Share the following **practice tips** with students.

- Practice speaking in front of a friend. Be sure to practice pointing to your map as you speak.
- Use your map to make your directions clear. With your hand, trace the route as you describe it.

Tell students to give directions to a small group of classmates. **PERFORMANCE ASSESSMENT**

## Audience Behavior

**OBJECTIVE**

*To understand and follow directions presented orally*

**Listening Tips**

- Pay attention when the speaker uses a visual aid.
- Listen for important details, such as the names of landmarks, and include them in your notes.

Have students take notes on the directions as the speaker gives them. Tell students to listen for time-order words. Share the Listening Tips above with students.

**A SHOE BOX SCENE**   Have students create a shoe box scene that shows them listening to directions. Encourage them to include captions or paper models that demonstrate one thing they do to listen actively.

## Evaluating Illustrations

**OBJECTIVE**

*To determine if illustrations reflect the events and theme of the story they support*

Tell students that the artist of "The Emperor and the Kite," Ed Young, won a Caldecott Medal for the story. Have students look again at the illustrations in "The Emperor and the Kite." Ask:

- **How does the style of art reflect the setting?**
- **Does each illustration clearly show the events in the story?**

# Books for All Learners

*Reinforcing Skills and Strategies*

## ■ BELOW-LEVEL

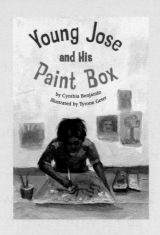

*Young Jose and His Paint Box*
by Cynthia Benjamin
illustrated by Tyrone Geter

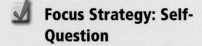

☑ **Focus Skill: Narrative Elements**

☑ **Focus Strategy: Self-Question**

☑ **Vocabulary: *insignificant, daily, plotting, twined, steely, encircling, neglected, unyielding***

**Genre:** Fiction
**Social Studies Connection:** Social Life of Other Cultures; Social Structure Within a Community

**SUMMARY** In a small country village, a young boy helps an old woman care for her garden when she becomes ill. He then sells her crops at the market. In return for his help, she buys him a paint box. With this gift he is able to enter an art contest and win first prize.

💻 For additional related activities, visit *The Learning Site* at **www.harcourtschool.com**

### BEFORE READING

**Preview/Set Purpose** Have students preview the book by reading the title and chapter titles. Ask them to set a purpose for reading.

**Reinforce Narrative Elements** Help students make a story map that they can fill in as they read. **NARRATIVE ELEMENTS/GRAPHIC AIDS**

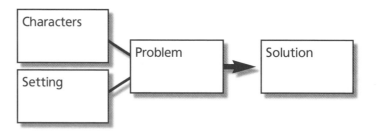

**Reinforce Vocabulary** Write sentence frames such as the following on the board: If you do the same thing every day, you do it _daily_. When a gardener does not take care of a plant, it is _neglected_.

### READING THE BOOK

**Page 2** What is the setting of this story? (a small village with simple houses.) **NARRATIVE ELEMENTS/IMPORTANT DETAILS**

**Pages 7–8** What happens when José goes to the market for the first time? (Very few people buy the vegetables and flowers.) **IMPORTANT DETAILS**

**Pages 15–16** What did Auntie María's gift allow José to do? (He won an art contest and became a famous artist.) **CAUSE/EFFECT**

**Reread for Fluency** Have students choose and reread aloud their favorite scenes in the book.

### RESPONDING

**Story Map** Students can complete the story map and use it to help them retell what happens in the story.

## ■ ON-LEVEL

 **Focus Skill: Narrative Elements**

 **Focus Strategy: Self-Question**

 **Vocabulary:** *insignificant, plotting, twined, steely, encircling, loyal, neglected, unyielding*

**Genre:** Realistic Fiction
**Science Connection:** Simple Machines Make Tasks Possible

**SUMMARY**   Kites transport a young boy safely home, help a boy and an engineer build a bridge, and serve as an antenna for an inventor.

For additional related activities, visit *The Learning Site* at
**www.harcourtschool.com**

### BEFORE READING

**Preview/Set Purpose**   Have students preview the illustrations and chapter titles to predict what the three stories have in common.

**Reinforce Narrative Elements**   Begin a story map for each story. Tell students to fill them in as they read. NARRATIVE ELEMENTS/GRAPHIC AIDS

### READING THE BOOK

**Pages 2–7**   How are  Djeow Seow and the boy similar? How are they different? (Possible responses: They are small but brave. At first, Djeow Seow is insignificant to her father, but the boy is always important to his father.) COMPARE AND CONTRAST

**Pages 8–12**   Why did the engineer have a kite contest? (He wanted a kite to carry a line across Niagara Falls Gorge.) CHARACTERS' MOTIVATIONS

**Pages 13–16**   Summarize "A Kite Antenna." A terrible storm broke an antenna during Guglielmo Marconi's test of his wireless telegraph. He used a long copper wire attached to a kite as an antenna and successfully sent a message.) SUMMARIZE

**Rereading for Fluency**   Have students reread aloud a section of one kite story, focusing on the speech of a character.

### RESPONDING

**Retell the Stories**   Have students use the story maps they started earlier to retell the three kite stories.

# Books for All Learners

*Reinforcing Skills and Strategies*

## ■ ADVANCED

THE CRYSTAL RADIO

by Max Winter
illustrated by Sandra Campbell

 **Focus Skill: Narrative Elements**

 **Focus Strategy: Self-Question**

☑ **Vocabulary:** *insignificant, plotting, twined, steely, encircling, loyal, neglected, unyielding, diode, galena*

**Genre:** Fiction
**Science Connection:** The Role of Electromagnets in the Construction of Simple Devices

**SUMMARY** Kevin's family doesn't understand his love of building things, but his crystal radio alerts the family to a tornado.

For additional related activities, visit *The Learning Site* at **www.harcourtschool.com**

### BEFORE READING

**Preview/Set Purpose** Have students preview the book's illustrations. Ask them to predict what this book will be about.

**Reinforce Narrative Elements** Have students create a character chart for the story characters. NARRATIVE ELEMENTS/GRAPHIC AIDS

| Character Chart | | |
|---|---|---|
| Character's Own Thoughts and Words | Character's Qualities and Traits | What Others Say and Think about the Character |
| | | |

**Expand Vocabulary** Discuss the meanings of *diode* and *galena*. (*diode*: an electronic device that allows current to flow in only one direction; *galena*: a dull gray mineral from which lead is extracted)

### READING THE BOOK

**Pages 2–4** How is Kevin different from his family? (They are fine musicians, but Kevin likes to build things.) IMPORTANT DETAILS

**Pages 5–8** Summarize the steps Kevin takes to build his radio. (He slipped copper wire through holes, in a cardboard tube. Next he attached the crystal and the earphone. Last, he attached a small clip to the copper wire.) SUMMARIZE

**Pages 14–16** How does Kevin's hobby save the family? (He hears a tornado warning on his radio and alerts his family.) STORY EVENTS

**Rereading for Fluency** Have students work in pairs to role-play a section of the story. Ask them to act out the dialogue.

### RESPONDING

**Animated Film** Ask students to use their character maps to create an animated film of the book.

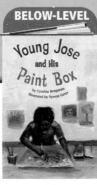
## Managing Small Groups

While you work with small groups have other students do the following:

- Self-Selected Reading
- Practice Pages
- Cross-Curricular Centers
- Journal Writing

▲ page 205K          ▲ page 205L

# ■ ENGLISH-LANGUAGE LEARNERS

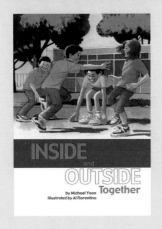

INSIDE and OUTSIDE Together
by Michael Yoon
illustrated by Al Fiorentino

 **Focus Skill: Narrative Elements**

 **Focus Strategy: Self-Question**

 **Concept Vocabulary:** *English, speak, idea, count, water, smiled*

**Genre:** Fiction
**Social Studies Connection:** Different Cultures Connect

**SUMMARY**   As a fourth-grade class learns to play a new game of shadow tag, a new student, Felipe, shows another student how to make shadow rabbits with her hands. The class then creates a play about shadow animals.

For additional related activities, visit *The Learning Site* at **www.harcourtschool.com**

## BEFORE READING

**Tap Prior Knowledge**   Write the words *inside and outside* on the board. Ask volunteers what these words have in common. (Both are adverbs that describe where.)

**Total Physical Response**   Draw a box on the board. Have volunteers draw something *inside*, *outside*, and *under* the box.

**Display Vocabulary Concept Words**   Use the illustrations in the book to discuss with students the meanings of the words.

**Preview the Book**   Read the title and point out the illustrations. Ask students what they think the book may be about.

## READING THE BOOK

**Page 4**   Where does this story take place? (on a school playground and in a classroom) **NARRATIVE ELEMENTS**

**Page 12**   What is this story mostly about? (A fourth-grade class learns to play a new game.) **MAIN IDEA**

**Page 15**   What happens after Felipe shows the students how to make shadow rabbits? (They create a shadow play.) **SUMMARIZE**

**Rereading**   Reread the book aloud with students. Have volunteers take turns being the characters in the book.

## RESPONDING

**Story Map**   Provide students with the following story map, and help them use it to retell the events in the story.

Beginning → Middle → End

## Teacher Notes

# Teacher Notes

**THEME CONNECTION:**
*Side by Side*

**GENRE:**
*Nonfiction*

ALA Notable Book

Outstanding Science Trade Book

SLJ Best Book

**Comparing Nonfiction and a Magazine Article**

▲ **READING ACROSS TEXTS:** "Caring for Crocs," by Lyle Prescott
**GENRE:** Magazine Article

## SUMMARY:

On Heimaey Island, near Iceland, a community works together to help young birds called pufflings return safely to the sea.

 Selections available on *Audiotext 2*

**206A** Side by Side

Below · On-Level · Advanced · ELL

# Books for
# All Learners

*Lesson Plans on pages 229M–229P*

| BELOW-LEVEL | ON-LEVEL | ADVANCED | ELL |
|---|---|---|---|
| • Lesson Vocabulary | • Lesson Vocabulary | • Challenge Vocabulary | • Concept Vocabulary |
| • Focus Skill: Summarize | • Focus Skill: Summarize | • Focus Skill: Summarize | • Focus Skill: Summarize |

## MULTI-LEVEL PRACTICE

**Extra Support,** pp. 33–35

**Practice Book,** pp. 33–37

**Challenge,** pp. 33–35

**English-Language Learners,** pp. 33–35

## ADDITIONAL RESOURCES

**Spelling Practice Book,** pp. 33–35

**Language Handbook,** pp. 64–65, 114–116

**Audiotext 2**

**Intervention Resource Kit,** Lesson 8
 • Intervention Reader, *Included in Intervention Resource Kit*

**English-Language Learners Resource Kit,**
 Lesson 8

## technology

• *Mission: Comprehension*™ *Skills Practice* **CD-ROM**

• *Media Literacy and Communication Skills Package* (Video)

• *Grammar Jingles*™ **CD**, Intermediate

• *Writing Express*™ **CD-ROM**

• *Reading and Language Skills Assessment* **CD-ROM**

• *The Learning Site:* **www.harcourtschool.com**

| | Day 1 | Day 2 |
|---|---|---|
| 5-15 Minutes<br>**ORAL LANGUAGE**<br>• Question of the Day<br>• Sharing Literature | **Question of the Day,** p. 206H<br>*What kinds of things does a bird do instinctively throughout its life?*<br>**Literature Read Aloud,** pp. 206G–H | **Question of the Day,** p. 206H<br>*What is life like for the children on Heimaey Island?*<br>**Think and Respond,** p. 216 |
| 15-30 Minutes<br>**SKILLS & STRATEGIES**<br>• Comprehension<br>• Vocabulary | **Comprehension:**<br>Skill Summarize, p. 206I T<br>Strategy Adjust Reading Rate, p. 206J<br>**Vocabulary,** p. 206L | **Comprehension:**<br>Skill Summarize, pp. 208–217 T<br>**Decoding/Phonics:**<br>Syllables: Open Syllables, p. 229C |
| 30-45 Minutes<br>**READING**<br>• Guided Comprehension<br>• Independent Reading<br>• Cross-Curricular Connections | **Read: Vocabulary Power,** pp. 206–207<br>Vocabulary Power Words:<br>*uninhabited, burrows, venture, stranded, nestles, instinctively*<br>**Independent Reading**<br>Books for All Learners<br>**SCIENCE** Volcanoes<br>**SOCIAL STUDIES** Comparing Locations<br>**INQUIRY PROJECT** Extending the Selection | **Reading the Selection,** pp. 208–217<br>GENRE: Nonfiction<br>**Independent Reading**<br>Books for All Learners<br>**LITERARY ANALYSIS** Figurative Language<br>**CULTURAL CONNECTIONS** Words from Other Languages |
| 45-90 Minutes<br>**LANGUAGE ARTS**<br>• Writing<br>*Daily Writing Prompt*<br>• Grammar<br>*Daily Language Practice*<br>• Spelling | **Writing:** Writing Process, p. 229E<br>**Writing Prompt:**<br>*Think about a time when you helped another person. Now write to describe how you felt about helping that person.*<br>**Grammar:**<br>Simple and Compound Sentences, p. 229G T<br>*Daily Language Practice*<br>1. What sorces could you use to learn about puffins. (sources; puffins?)<br>2. Our Library has oardered a book about puffins. (library; ordered)<br>**Spelling:**<br>Words with the /âr/ Sound, p. 229I T | **Writing:** Writing Process, p. 229E<br>**Writing Prompt:**<br>*Summer is a favorite time of year for many people. Think about your favorite season and what you like about it. Now write a poem about your favorite season.*<br>**Grammar:**<br>Extend the Concept, p. 229G<br>*Daily Language Practice*<br>1. Every summer the puffins. Come to iceland. (puffins come; Iceland.)<br>2. Wouldn't you like to sea them for you self. (see; yourself?)<br>**Spelling:**<br>Word Sort, p. 229I |

**Daily Routines**
- Question of the Day
- Daily Language Practice
- Daily Writing Prompt

T = tested skill

## Focus Skill

**Summarize**

**Objectives of the Week:**

- To summarize the most important information in a text
- To read and understand a nonfiction selection; to compare nonfiction with nonfiction narrative
- To use simple and compound sentences correctly
- To use the writing process in writing a summary

---

# Day 3

**Question of the Day,** p. 206H
*What do the puffins and crocodiles have in common?*

**Oral Grammar,** p. 229H

**Word Study:**
Synonyms and Antonyms, p. 229K

**Comprehension:**
 Summarize, pp. 228–229 **T**
Test Prep

**Rereading for Fluency,** p. 215
**Reading Across Texts,** pp. 221–225
GENRE: Magazine Article

 **Independent Reading**
Books for All Learners
**SCIENCE** Crocodile or Alligator?

**Writing:** Writing Process, p. 229F

**Writing Prompt:**
*Imagine that you visited Heimaey Island and that you have seen a puffin for the first time. Describe a puffin in a letter to your best friend who has never seen one.*

**Grammar:**
Compound-Sentence Summary, p. 229H

**Daily Language Practice**

1. The pufflings must make it to see or they will die.
   (sea, or)
2. Halla, and her friends help the pufflings. That go the wrong way. (Halla and; pufflings that)

**Spelling:**
Guessing and Checking, p. 229J

---

# Day 4

**Question of the Day,** p. 206H
*Where can you find information about Iceland?*

**Comprehension:**
 Summarize, pp. 229M–P **T**

**Search Techniques,** pp. 229A–B
**Locate Information,** p. 229D

**Self-Selected Reading,** p. 206F

 **Independent Reading**
Books for All Learners
**SCIENCE** Crocodile Family Tree
**TECHNOLOGY** Information Search

**Writing:** Writing Process, p. 229F

**Writing Prompt:**
*Write a thank-you letter to Halla and the children of Heimaey Island. Thank them for helping the pufflings.*

**Grammar:**
Bird's-Eye View, p. 229H

**Daily Language Practice**

1. The pufflings came out and the children starred.
   (out, and; stared.)
2. That tiny bird can bairly walk. but now it must fly.
   (barely walk, but)

**Spelling:**
Compound Concentration, p. 229J

---

# Day 5

**Question of the Day,** p. 206H
*Why do so few people live on Heimaey Island and the islands around it?*

**Speaking and Listening**
Giving a Descriptive Speech, p. 229L

**Comprehension:**
 Summarize, pp. 229M–P **T**

**Word Study:**
Analogies, p. 229K

**Self-Selected Reading,** pp. 255, T67

**Independent Reading**
Books for All Learners
**WRITING** Write a Project Description
**SOCIAL STUDIES** Make a Map
**SCIENCE** Make a Scientific Drawing

**Writing:** Writing Process, p. 229F

**Writing Prompt:**
*Write a description of the Everglades for a travel brochure. Be sure to include in your description the kinds of plants and animals that live in the Everglades.*

**Grammar:**
Compounds, p. 229H

**Daily Language Practice**

1. Waves, and wind carry the puffins forward.
   (Waves and; forward.)
2. The pufflings swam away and the children waved fairwell. (away, and; farewell.)

**Spelling:**
Posttest, p. 229J

**MANAGING THE CLASSROOM** While you provide direct instruction to individuals or small groups, other students can work on ongoing activities such as the ones below.

## Materials

- science book, encyclopedia, or nonfiction book about volcanoes
- paper
- markers
- pen or pencil

## Volcanoes

**OBJECTIVE: To understand how volcanoes form islands**

Many islands are formed by underwater volcanoes. Draw a diagram that shows how underwater volcanoes form islands.

- Research underwater volcanoes in your science textbook, an encyclopedia, or a nonfiction book.
- Draw diagrams that show how lava from the underwater volcano cools and hardens to form an island.
- Write a brief explanation of your diagrams.

A volcano erupts beneath the ocean's surface.

## Materials

- world map or globe
- self-stick notes
- reference sources, such as encyclopedias and almanacs
- pen or pencil
- paper

## Comparing Locations

**OBJECTIVE: To understand how one's state is similar to and different from other locations on Earth**

How is your state similar to Iceland? How is it different? Answer these questions to find out. Then make a Venn diagram to show how your state and Iceland are alike and different.

### Location

- Locate your state on the map and mark it with a self-stick note. Locate Iceland on the map and mark it with a self-stick note. To which ocean is your state closest? To which ocean is Iceland closest? In which hemisphere is your state located? In which hemisphere is Iceland located?

### Landscape

- What kinds of landforms does your state have? What kinds of landforms does Iceland have?

### Climate

- What is the weather like where you live? What is the weather like in Iceland?

### Industry

- What is the main industry in your state? What is the main industry in Iceland?

## LIBRARY CENTER

### Self-Selected Reading

**OBJECTIVES: To select and read books independently**

Look for these books about birds.

- *Wild Flamingos* by Bruce McMillan. Houghton Mifflin, 1997. **NONFICTION**
- *Puffins* by Susan E. Quinlan. Carolrhoda, 1999. **NONFICTION**
- *Song of the Swallows* by Leo Politi. Atheneum, 1987. **FICTION**

**Remember to**
- choose a book that interests you.
- note in your *Reading Log* what you have read each day.

**Materials**
- self-selected book
- *My Reading Log* copying master, p. R38

---

## INQUIRY PROJECT

### Extending the Selection

**OBJECTIVE: To select a focus for an inquiry project**

Use "Nights of the Pufflings" as a springboard to brainstorm topics you would like to know more about. Organize your ideas into a web. Use one of these books for your project.

- *The Bird on the Beach*
- *Summer Mystery*
- *Fire and Ice*
- *Beaks and Wings*

**Materials**
- research materials
- paper
- pencil

---

## TECHNOLOGY

### Information Search

**OBJECTIVE: To use technology resources to research seabirds**

Use the Internet to research a seabird.
- Use a search engine and keywords to search for facts. Write down the websites you use.
- Take notes about the bird you researched.

**Remember to**
- use specific keywords to narrow your search.
- use the rules for Internet safety.

**Materials**
- computer with Internet access
- printer
- paper

# Read Aloud

## What's a Puffin?

**by Susan E. Quinlan**

Imagine a bird that is more at home in water than in air. Imagine a bird for whom land is an unfamiliar place. Imagine a puffin.

A puffin is an unusual bird. You won't see one on the mainland or even along an ocean coast. To see a wild puffin, you would have to take a boat trip on the ocean. Puffins live almost their entire lives at sea, far from the sight of land. They sit on the water and fly over, and under, the sea in search of food. In winter they face storms in which rolling waves may tower 50 feet high (15 m).

Puffins must return to land to nest, but even then they rarely come near mainland shores. Instead, nesting puffins head to islands out in the ocean. When the birds are finished nesting, they return to the open sea.

Puffins are **seabirds**. A seabird is a kind of bird that lives most of its life on the ocean. Gulls, terns, shearwaters, pelicans, and certain ducks are seabirds, too. Yet puffins are different from all these kinds of birds. So what exactly is a puffin?

**MEET THE PUFFINS**

Because puffins have large, brightly colored bills, some people think of them as "sea parrots." Others think that puffins look like penguins because of their black and white feathers and the way they walk on land. Yet puffins are neither parrots nor penguins. They are members of an interesting family of seabirds called the Alcidae (AHL-sih-dee). Birds in this family are often called **auks** or **alcids**.

All of these are ocean-going birds with short, stubby wings, chunky bodies, and large, webbed feet. Most have black and white feathers, and all walk upright on land. All auks, including puffins, live only in the oceans of the Northern Hemisphere. And all **species**, or kinds, of auks alive today are able to fly.

- **Where do puffins live?** (mostly on the ocean, far from land)
  IMPORTANT DETAILS

- **Why do puffins come on land?** (to nest) CAUSE/EFFECT

- **What do puffins look like?** (They have black and white feathers and brightly colored bills.) IMPORTANT DETAILS

- **How are puffins different from other birds?** (They live most of their lives on the ocean, but they can also walk upright on land.)
  COMPARE AND CONTRAST

# Question of the Day

## DEVELOP ORAL LANGUAGE

- Display the first question on Teaching Transparency 67, or write it on the board. Have students read it silently.

- **Response Journal** Explain to students that they should think about the question throughout the day and write their responses in their journals. Tell students to be prepared to discuss their responses to the question by the end of the day or at another time you choose.

- You may want to repeat this process daily for each of the remaining discussion questions.

---

▼ **Teaching Transparency 67**

**QUESTION OF THE DAY**

**DAY 1:** What kinds of things does a bird do instinctively throughout its life? Possible responses: find food and shelter; nest; have young; migrate VOCABULARY AND CONCEPTS

**DAY 2:** What is life like for the children on Heimaey Island? Possible responses: They go to school; they swim in the cold ocean; they help care for the puffins by staying up late at night and sleeping during the day. SELECTION CONNECTION

**DAY 3:** What do the puffins and crocodiles have in common? Possible responses: Both hatch from eggs; both live in water and on land; both sometimes receive help from humans. READING ACROSS TEXTS

**DAY 4:** Where can you find information about Iceland? Possible responses: an atlas; the Internet; an encyclopedia LOCATE INFORMATION

**DAY 5:** Why do so few people live on Heimaey Island and the islands around it? Possible responses: It is very cold; it is difficult to get to the mainland; it is difficult to grow food there. CROSS-CURRICULAR CONNECTION

"Nights of the Pufflings"
Side by Side, Theme 2  **67** Question of the Day
Harcourt

## OBJECTIVE

*To summarize the most important information in a text*

### SKILL TRACE

| SUMMARIZE | |
|---|---|
| Introduce | p. 206I |
| Reteach | pp. S48, S60, S92, T39 |
| Review | pp. 228, 252I, 270 |
| Test | Theme 2 |
| Maintain | pp. 372I, 396 |

▼ **Teaching Transparency 68**

---

**SUMMARIZE**

When you **summarize**, you retell the most important ideas in your own words. A good summary tells the main ideas in a few words. As you summarize, ask yourself these questions:

• What are the main ideas or events in the selection?

• How can I describe these ideas or events in my own words?

**EXAMPLE**

Arctic foxes live in the tundra region near the Arctic where it is very cold. Their thick coats keep them warm. They can survive temperatures as low as 112 degrees below zero Fahrenheit.

Arctic foxes eat fruits, berries, and small animals. Small animals, such as voles and lemmings, are often part of their meals.

Arctic foxes are well-suited to their snowy environment. Their white coat helps them blend in with their surroundings during the winter. Their beautiful coats are the same color as the snow.

| Important Ideas to Include | Details Not to Include |
|---|---|
| • Arctic foxes live in the tundra.<br>• They can survive very cold temperatures.<br>• Arctic foxes eat fruit, berries, and small mammals.<br>• Arctic foxes have white coats that help them blend in with their environment. | • They can survive temperatures as low as 112 degrees below Fahrenheit.<br>• Voles and lemmings are often part of their meals.<br>• Their beautiful coats are the same color as the snow. |

"Nights of the Pufflings"  Side by Side, Theme 2  **68**  Focus Skill: Summarize  Harcourt

---

### BELOW-LEVEL

**Additional Support**

• *Intervention Teacher's Guide,* p. 80

### ENGLISH-LANGUAGE LEARNERS

**Additional Support**

• *English-Language Learners Teacher's Guide,* p. 45

---

## Focus Skill — Summarize

### INTRODUCE THE SKILL

**Access prior knowledge.** Ask a volunteer to tell about the plot of a book he or she has read. Explain that the student is summarizing, or retelling the story in his or her own words. Tell students that a good summary tells the most important ideas in a few words. It does not include opinions or descriptions.

### TEACH/MODEL

Tell students that when they read, they should summarize the most important ideas of the text. Explain that summarizing will help them better understand what they have read.

• **Ask a volunteer to read aloud the explanation of the skill.**

• **Read aloud the bulleted questions. Ask students to think about these questions as you read aloud the examples.**

• **Discuss with students which ideas they would and would not include in a summary of the passage. Then have them add one idea to each column of the chart.**

• **Model summarizing the passage. Tell students that summaries should be brief, include only the most important information, and be told in one's own words.**

### PRACTICE/APPLY

Have students begin a K-W-L chart about puffins to help them summarize what they learn as they read "Nights of the Pufflings."

| K-W-L Chart | | |
|---|---|---|
| What I Know | What I Want to Know | What I Learned |
| | | |

For opportunities to apply and reinforce the skill, see the following pages:

**During reading:** pages 210, 212, and 214
**After reading:** *Pupil Edition* pages 228–229

# Focus Strategy ★ Adjust Reading Rate

**OBJECTIVE**

*To monitor understanding by adjusting reading rate*

## INTRODUCE THE STRATEGY

Explain to students that good readers use different strategies to help them understand what they read. Tell them that they should read some texts, such as those with many facts and details, more slowly than other texts. Tell them they should **adjust their reading rate** according to the kind of text they are reading.

## TEACH/MODEL

Use the example on Transparency 68 to model the strategy.

> **MODEL** **When I read this passage, I see that there are many facts about Arctic foxes. I will read more slowly to make sure that I understand and remember the important information about the Arctic fox.**

### SKILL ←→ STRATEGY CONNECTION

Explain to students that if they are trying to **summarize** a nonfiction selection with many facts and details, they should **adjust their reading** rate by slowing down to make sure they understand what they are reading.

## PRACTICE/APPLY

Remind students to adjust their reading rate to help them understand facts and details as they read. For opportunities to apply and reinforce the strategy **during reading**, see pages 211 and 215.

## Strategies Good Readers Use

- Use Decoding/Phonics
- Make and Confirm Predictions
- Create Mental Images
- Self-Question
- Summarize
- Read Ahead
- Reread to Clarify
- Use Context to Confirm Meaning
- Use Text Structure and Format
- **Adjust Reading Rate** ★ Focus Strategy

# Building Background

## ACCESS PRIOR KNOWLEDGE

Tell students that in the next selection, children in Iceland save the lives of thousands of baby puffins. Discuss with students ways that people help animals. Guide them to make a web like the one below.

feed them

provide shelter for them

**Ways People Help Animals**

study them

care for them when they are sick

**technology**

**VIDEO** *Puffin Adventures,* ©1997, Library Video Company, 30 min.

## DEVELOP CONCEPTS

Help students use prior knowledge to develop concepts by asking the following questions:

- **When might animals need help from people?** (Possible responses: when they are young; when they are sick; when a storm or other natural disaster destroys their homes)

- **What might you learn from caring for an animal?** (Possible response: You might learn what the animal eats and where it lives; you might learn more about your environment.)

- **How should you act when you take care of an animal?** (Possible response: You should be responsible, careful, and kind.)

### REACHING ALL LEARNERS

## Diagnostic Check: Vocabulary

**If** . . . students do not understand at least 5 of the 6 words . . .

**Then** . . . have them use the glossary or a dictionary to find the definitions.

### ADDITIONAL SUPPORT ACTIVITIES

| BELOW-LEVEL | Reteach, p. S46 |
| ADVANCED | Extend, p. S47 |
| ENGLISH-LANGUAGE LEARNERS | Reteach, p. S47 |

# Vocabulary

**Vocabulary**

**uninhabited** having no people living there
**burrows** holes in the ground made by animals
**venture** go out into a dangerous place
**stranded** left behind or in a helpless situation
**nestles** moves snugly next to
**instinctively** without thinking; in a way that is natural

## TEACH VOCABULARY STRATEGIES

**Use affixes and root words.** Point out the word *uninhabited* on Transparency 69. Remind students that they can sometimes figure out the meaning of an unfamiliar word by looking for prefixes, suffixes, roots, and root words. Model using this strategy to determine the meaning of *uninhabited*.

**MODEL** When I look at *uninhabited*, I see a smaller word I know, *inhabit*. I also see the prefix *un-*. I know that *inhabit* means "to live in a place" and that *un-* means "not." I notice that *uninhabited* is used to describe an area. An uninhabited area must be a place that does not have people living in it.

Have students use this strategy as they encounter other unfamiliar words when they read.

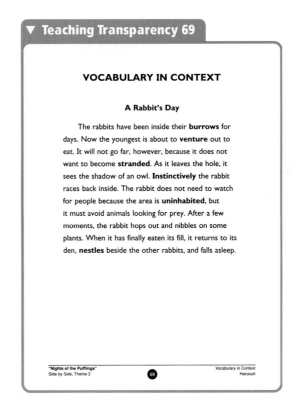

**▼ Teaching Transparency 69**

### VOCABULARY IN CONTEXT

#### A Rabbit's Day

The rabbits have been inside their **burrows** for days. Now the youngest is about to **venture** out to eat. It will not go far, however, because it does not want to become **stranded**. As it leaves the hole, it sees the shadow of an owl. **Instinctively** the rabbit races back inside. The rabbit does not need to watch for people because the area is **uninhabited**, but it must avoid animals looking for prey. After a few moments, the rabbit hops out and nibbles on some plants. When it has finally eaten its fill, it returns to its den, **nestles** beside the other rabbits, and falls asleep.

"Nights of the Pufflings"
Side by Side, Theme 2                69                Vocabulary in Context
                                                       Harcourt

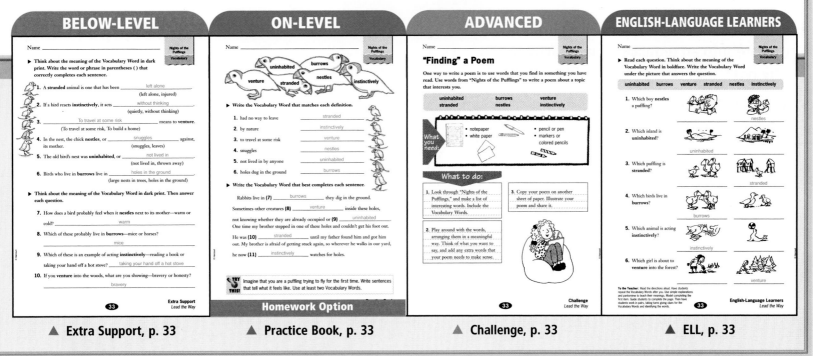

| BELOW-LEVEL | ON-LEVEL | ADVANCED | ENGLISH-LANGUAGE LEARNERS |
|---|---|---|---|
| ▲ Extra Support, p. 33 | ▲ Practice Book, p. 33 | ▲ Challenge, p. 33 | ▲ ELL, p. 33 |

# Vocabulary Power

## APPLY STRATEGIES

Read aloud the first two paragraphs on page 206. Then ask students to read the rest of the text silently. Remind them to use affixes and root words to help them determine the meaning of unfamiliar words.

## EXTEND WORD KNOWLEDGE

**Practice other vocabulary strategies.**
Ask students to answer questions with sentences that show what the vocabulary words mean. MEANINGFUL SENTENCES

• **What are some things you do** *instinctively*? **EXAMPLE**

• **Would you expect to find a restaurant on an** *uninhabited* **island? Why or why not? EXPLANATION**

• **What are some animals that make** *burrows*? **PRIOR KNOWLEDGE**

• **Which word is a synonym for** *snuggles*? **SYNONYMS**

• **Would a cautious person be likely to** *venture* **into an unfamiliar place? Why or why not? EXPLANATION**

• **How is being** *rescued* **different from being** *stranded*? **COMPARE/CONTRAST**

▲ Nights of the Pufflings

uninhabited

burrows

stranded

venture

instinctively

nestles

206

# Vocabulary Power

**I**t's interesting to read about different kinds of animals. Jack read an article about prairie dogs. Read his notebook to find out what he learned.

I just finished reading an article about prairie dogs. They live on plains and prairies. They aren't really dogs, but their cries sound like dogs barking.

Prairie dogs live mostly in uninhabited areas, where there are no people to bother them. They dig deep holes, or burrows, in the earth. During the day they come out of their burrows to find food and to spend time with other prairie dogs.

It would be unusual to find a prairie dog **stranded**, alone and helpless. Prairie dogs stay close to their burrows and don't **venture** out into dangerous places. They **instinctively** live together in large groups called towns. They don't think about it or plan to stay together. They do it because this kind of life is natural for them.

I like to imagine a little prairie dog deep down in its burrow at night. First it **nestles** close to its brothers and sisters. Then, when it is all snug and cozy, it closes its eyes and goes to sleep.

**Vocabulary–Writing**
**CONNECTION**

**B**irds **instinctively** build nests. What kinds of things do you do instinctively? Write a few sentences about each thing.

207

**QUICKWRITE**

**VOCABULARY–WRITING CONNECTION**

Ask students to prepare for writing by brainstorming a list of things they do instinctively. Then ask them to choose two or three ideas from their list to write about. Remind them to use vivid verbs in their writing. Have them add their vivid verbs and Vocabulary Power words to their Word Banks to use in future writing assignments.

# Prereading Strategies

## PREVIEW AND PREDICT

Have students read the **genre** information on page 208. Then have them preview the selection by reading the title and looking at the photographs. Ask them to predict what they will learn about puffins. They can begin a K-W-L chart like this. See Transparency G on page T54.

| K-W-L Chart | | |
|---|---|---|
| What I Know | What I Want to Know | What I Learned |
| Puffins are seabirds. | Where do puffins make their nests? | |

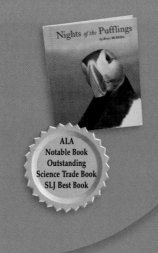

**Genre**

## Nonfiction

**Nonfiction tells about people, things, events, or places that are real.**

In this selection, look for

- **Characters who help out**
- **Information about a topic**

# NIGHTS —of the— PUFFLINGS

WRITTEN AND PHOTO-ILLUSTRATED
BY BRUCE McMILLAN

208

---

| **BELOW-LEVEL** | **ON-LEVEL** | **ADVANCED** | **ENGLISH-LANGUAGE LEARNERS** |
|---|---|---|---|
| Help students preview the selection. Discuss the meaning of words such as *cliffs, hatch, chicks,* and *release.* Help students set a purpose for reading through page 212. **SMALL GROUP** | Have students read the selection independently. Use the Guided Comprehension questions and Ongoing Assessments to check students' comprehension. **WHOLE GROUP/INDEPENDENT** | Pairs of students may enjoy reading silently and then sharing their comments. Encourage students to pause after several pages to discuss predictions and personal responses. **INDEPENDENT/ SMALL GROUP** | Read the selection aloud or have students listen to it on *Audiotext 2.* Have students read sections aloud to develop oral fluency. **SMALL GROUP** |

**ADDITIONAL SUPPORT**

*Intervention Reader: Moving Ahead Intervention Reader Teacher's Guide,* pp. 80–83

**ADDITIONAL SUPPORT**

See *English-Language Learners Resource Kit,* Lesson 8. *English-Language Learners Teacher's Guide,* p. 45

209

## SET PURPOSE

**Locate information.** Tell students that one purpose for reading is to locate information. Help students set a purpose for reading. Offer this suggestion:

**MODEL** I think this selection is about how some children help baby birds called pufflings. I will read to find out why the birds need help and how the children help them.

**★ Focus Strategy** **Adjust Reading Rate** Have students use this strategy to help them understand what they read.

## COMPREHENSION CARD 8

**Comparing Texts** Have students use Comprehension Card 8 to discuss *Comparing Texts* in "Nights of the Pufflings" and "Caring for Crocs."

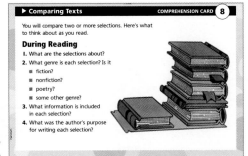

▶ **Comparing Texts**          COMPREHENSION CARD **8**

You will compare two or more selections. Here's what to think about as you read.

**During Reading**
1. What are the selections about?
2. What genre is each selection? Is it
   ▪ fiction?
   ▪ nonfiction?
   ▪ poetry?
   ▪ some other genre?
3. What information is included in each selection?
4. What was the author's purpose for writing each selection?

**Comprehension Card 8, page T49 ▶**

 "Nights of the Pufflings" and "Caring for Crocs" are available on *Audiotext 2.*

*Nights of the Pufflings*     **209**

# Guided Comprehension

**1** **IMPORTANT DETAILS** **Where do the events in the selection take place?** (on Heimaey Island, off the coast of Iceland)

**2** **DRAW CONCLUSIONS** **What time of year is it? How do you know?** (Spring; the second paragraph on page 211 mentions that the birds are returning from their winter at sea.)

**3** (Focus Skill) **SUMMARIZE** **What have you learned about puffins from reading this page?** (The puffins come to the island to lay their eggs and raise chicks.)

**4** **MAKE PREDICTIONS** **What do you think the "nights of the pufflings" will be?** (Possible response: the nights when the pufflings leave their nests and try to fly)

210

ENGLISH-LANGUAGE LEARNERS

Point out the words *the puffins continue to land*. Explain that *land* can be a noun or a verb. When it is a noun, it means "earth." When it is a verb, it means "to come to rest on a surface." Tell students that in this example, *land* is a verb. It tells what the puffins do when they come down from their flight.

land          land

Halla *(HATTL•lah)* searches the sky every day. As she watches from high on a cliff overlooking the sea, she spots her first puffin of the season. She whispers to herself, "Lundi" *(LOON•dah),* which means "puffin" in Icelandic.

Soon the sky is speckled with them—puffins, puffins everywhere. Millions of these birds are returning from their winter at sea. They are coming back to Halla's island and the nearby uninhabited islands to lay eggs and raise puffin chicks. It's the only time they come ashore. **1** **2**

While Halla and her friends are at school in the village beneath the cliffs, the puffins continue to land. These "clowns of the sea" return to the same burrows year after year. Once back, they busy themselves getting their underground nests ready. Halla and all the children of Heimaey *(HAY•mah•ay)* can only wait and dream of the nights of the pufflings yet to come. **3** **4**

211

## ONGOING ASSESSMENT

**Monitor Progress**

**Focus Strategy** **Adjust Reading Rate**

**What do the puffins do once they land?**

(Possible response: They get their nests ready.)

**Ask volunteers to model how they could use the Adjust Reading Rate strategy to answer the question. If students have difficulty, provide this model:**

**MODEL** I know that page 211 describes the return of the puffins. I will read these paragraphs more slowly to find out what the puffins do once they land.

## LITERARY ANALYSIS

**Figurative Language** Write the words *clowns of the sea* on the board. Work with students to identify who the clowns are. Then discuss with them what they think the words mean. Tell students that *clowns of the sea* is a metaphor. It compares the puffins to clowns. Metaphors compare two unlike things without using the words *like* or *as*. Explain that authors use metaphors to help readers understand something unfamiliar by comparing it to something familiar or to help readers think about something familiar in a new way. Have students brainstorm metaphors they might use to describe other kinds of birds.

# Guided Comprehension

**5** (Focus Skill) **SUMMARIZE   What do the children see and hear as they watch the puffins?** (Possible responses: the puffins flying back to Heimaey; the puffins splashing in the sea)

**6** **CAUSE-EFFECT   Why do the adult puffins have to catch lots of fish?** (They have to feed themselves and the chicks, too.)

**7** **IMPORTANT DETAILS   What season is it now? How do you know?** (Summer; the second paragraph on page 212 says that Halla splashes in the cold ocean water in the summer.)

**8** **MAKE PREDICTIONS   What do you think the children will see and hear next?** (Responses will vary.)

On the weekends, Halla and her friends climb over the cliffs to watch the birds. They see puffin pairs *tap-tap-tap* their beaks together. Each pair they see will soon tend an egg. Deep inside the cliffs that egg will hatch a chick. That chick will grow into a young puffling. That puffling will take its first flight. The nights of the pufflings will come.

In the summer, while Halla splashes in the cold ocean water, the puffins also splash. The sea below the cliffs is **5** dotted with puffins bobbing on the waves. Like Halla, many puffins that ride the waves close to shore are young. The older birds usually fly further out to sea where the fishing is better. The grown-up puffins have to catch lots of fish, because now that it's summer they are feeding more than just themselves. **6** **7**

Halla's friend, Arnar Ingi (*ATT•nar ING•ee*), spies a puffin overhead. "Fisk" (*FIHSK*), he whispers as he gazes at the returning puffin's bill full of fish. The puffin eggs have hatched, and the parents are bringing home fish to feed their chicks.

The nights of the pufflings are still long weeks away, but Arnar Ingi thinks about getting some cardboard boxes ready. **8**

212

## BELOW-LEVEL

Discuss with students why the puffins come ashore. (to lay their eggs) Then work with students to answer these questions to help them understand important story concepts and vocabulary:

• Why are the *cliffs* a good place for puffin nests? (It is safe there.)

• What will *hatch* from every egg? (a puffin chick)

• How do the adult puffins take care of the *chicks*? (They feed them fish.)

Help students set a purpose for reading to the end of the selection. Suggest that they read to find out what happens on the nights of the pufflings.

Halla and her friends never see the chicks—only the chicks' parents see them. The baby puffins never come out. They stay safely hidden in the long dark tunnels of their burrows. But Halla and her friends hear them calling out for food. "*Peep-peep-peep.*" The growing chicks are hungry. Their parents have to feed them—sometimes ten times a day—and carry many fish in their bills.

213

Monitor Progress

# Use Decoding/Phonics

**Have students reading below-level read aloud the paragraph on page 213. Listen for their pronunciation of *burrows*. If students have difficulty, model the strategy:**

**MODEL** I can say the first part of this word /bûr/, but I am not sure how to pronounce the ending. I know that the letters *ow* can be pronounced /ō/ or /ou/. When I say /bûr´ōz/, it sounds like a word I know.

## CULTURAL CONNECTIONS

**Words from Other Languages** Explain that the English word *geyser* comes from the name of Iceland's most famous hot spring, *Geysir,* which shoots hot water almost 200 feet into the air. Work with students to create a chart of some of the words that have come to English from other languages. Invite students whose first language is different from English to contribute words from their language which are now used in English.

| Word | Language It Came From |
|---|---|
| alphabet | Greek |
| volcano | Italian |
| tulip | Turkish |
| tea | Chinese |

# Guided
# Comprehension

**9** (Focus Skill) **SUMMARIZE  What are the nights of the pufflings?** (the nights when the young puffins leave their burrows to try to fly out to sea)

**10 DRAW CONCLUSIONS  What signs tell the children that the young pufflings' first flights are getting closer?** (Possible response: They see the adult puffins bring fish to feed their chicks; they hear the chicks calling out for food; the *baldusbrá* flowers are blossoming.)

**11 MAKE JUDGMENTS  Are the children doing a good thing by gathering the pufflings? Why or why not?** (Possible response: Yes; because the pufflings probably would die if the children did not gather them; no, because people should leave wild creatures alone.)

**A**ll summer long the adult puffins fish and tend to their feathers. By August, flowering baldusbrá (BAL•durs•broh) blanket the burrows. With the baldusbrá in full bloom, Halla knows that the wait is over. The hidden chicks have grown into young pufflings. The pufflings are ready to fly and will at last venture out into the night. Now it's time. **9 10**

It's time for Halla and her friends to get out their boxes and flashlights for the nights of the pufflings. Starting tonight, and for the next two weeks, the pufflings will be leaving for their winter at sea. Halla and her friends will spend each night searching for stranded pufflings that don't

make it to the water. But the village cats and dogs will be searching, too. It will be a race to see who finds the stray pufflings first. By ten o'clock the streets of Heimaey are alive with roaming children.

In the darkness of night, the pufflings leave their burrows for their first flight. It's a short, wing-flapping trip from the high cliffs. Most of the birds splash-land safely in the sea below. But some get confused by the village lights—perhaps they think the lights are moonbeams reflecting on the water. Hundreds of the pufflings crash-land in the village every night. Unable to take off from flat ground, they run around and try to hide.

214

## REACHING ALL LEARNERS

### Diagnostic Check:
### Comprehension and Skills

**If** . . . the students are unable to summarize the text . . .

**Then** . . . have them list the most important details about the events. Have students use their list to write a summary.

### ADDITIONAL SUPPORT ACTIVITIES

| BELOW-LEVEL | Reteach, p. S48 |
| ADVANCED | Extend, p. S49 |
| ENGLISH-LANGUAGE LEARNERS | Reteach, p. S49 |

Dangers await. Even if the cats and dogs don't get them, the pufflings might get run over by cars or trucks.

Halla and her friends race to the rescue. Armed with their flashlights, they wander through the village. They search dark places. Halla yells out "puffling" in Icelandic. "Lundi pysja!" *(LOON•dah PEESH•yar)*. She has spotted one. When the puffling runs down the street, she races after it, grabs it, and nestles it in her arms. Arnar Ingi catches one, too. No sooner are the pufflings safe in the cardboard boxes than more of them land nearby. "Lundi pysja! Lundi pysja!" **11**

215

**Monitor Progress**

**Focus Strategy** **Adjust Reading Rate**

**Why do some of the pufflings crash-land in the village?** (Possible response: They get confused by the village lights; they think the lights are moonbeams on the water.)

**Have students model adjusting their reading rate to find the answer. If they have difficulty, provide this model:**

 When I get to the sentence *In the darkness of night, the pufflings leave their burrows for their first flight,* I read more slowly because I know that I am going to read important information about what happens to the pufflings. By slowing my reading rate and carefully reading the paragraph, I find out that some pufflings crash-land because they think the village lights are moonbeams on the water.

## REREADING FOR FLUENCY

**Film Documentary**   Have students form small groups and read "Nights of the Pufflings" aloud as if they were reading the narrative for a film documentary about puffins. Tell them to use an appropriate tone and pace. Remind them that selections with many details need to be read more slowly so that listeners can absorb all the information.

LISTENING/SPEAKING/READING

**Note:** For assessment of oral reading accuracy and fluency, see pages T44–T46.

# Guided Comprehension

**RETURN TO THE PREDICTIONS/PURPOSE**

**What information did you locate about puffins?** Discuss with students whether their purposes for reading were met.

# Think and Respond

## Answers:

**1** Possible response: They pick them up, place them in cardboard boxes, and release them over the water. **SUMMARIZE**

**2** Possible response: by using vivid words and descriptions **AUTHOR'S CRAFT**

**3** Possible response: They probably make it safely to the sea because they don't get confused by the lights of the village. **CRITICAL THINKING**

**4** Responses will vary. **PERSONAL RESPONSE**

**5** Accept reasonable responses. **READING STRATEGIES**

### OPEN-ENDED RESPONSE

Choose your favorite photograph from the selection. Write a paragraph that describes the photograph and explains why it is your favorite. Support your response with specific details and reasons.

For two weeks all the children of Heimaey sleep late in the day so they can stay out at night. They rescue thousands of pufflings. There are pufflings, pufflings everywhere, and helping hands too—even though the pufflings instinctively nip at helping fingers. Every night Halla and her friends take the rescued pufflings home. The next day they send their guests on their way. Halla meets her friends and, with the boxes full of pufflings, they hike down to the beach.

It's time to set the pufflings free. Halla releases one first. She holds it up so that it will get used to flapping its wings.

Then, with the puffling held snugly in her hands, she counts "Einn–tveir–ÞRÍR!" (*EYN • TVAIR • THEER*) as she swings the puffling three times between her legs. The last swing is the highest, launching the bird up in the air and out over the water beyond the surf. It's only the second time this puffling has flown, so it flutters just a short distance before safely splash-landing.

216

**COMPREHENSION**

**End-of-Selection Test**
To evaluate comprehension, see *Practice Book*, pages A29–A32.

Day after day Halla's pufflings paddle away, until the nights of the pufflings are over for the year. As she watches the last of the pufflings and adult puffins leave for their winter at sea, Halla bids them farewell until next spring. She wishes them a safe journey as she calls out "goodbye, goodbye" in Icelandic. "Bless, bless!"

# Think and Respond

**1** What do Halla and the other children do to help the **stranded** pufflings?

**2** How does the author help readers understand what the children do and how they feel?

**3** What do you think happens to the pufflings that hatch on the **uninhabited** islands nearby?

**4** Would you like to help Halla and her friends rescue the **stranded** pufflings? What do you think you would like or dislike about the experience?

**5** What reading strategy did you use as you read "Nights of the Pufflings"? How was the strategy helpful to you?

217

## RETELL

Use these questions to guide students as they retell "Nights of the Pufflings."
• **What is the setting of the selection?**
• **What are the main events in the selection?**
• **How do the puffins care for their young?**

## SUMMARIZE

Encourage students to use their completed K-W-L charts to summarize the selection. See Transparency G on page T54.

### ▼ Teaching Transparency G

| | K-W-L Chart | |
| What I Know | What I Want to Know | What I Learned |
|---|---|---|
| Puffins are sea birds. | Why do they come ashore and what are pufflings? | Puffins come ashore to lay their eggs. Pufflings are baby puffins. |
| Many birds migrate. | Where do puffins make their nests? | They nest in underground burrows. |
| Puffins stay awake during the day. | What is going to happen to the pufflings at night? | When grown, they will try to fly to sea. |
| It is hard to see at night. | How can the pufflings be helped? | The children have flashlights and rescue the pufflings. They release the birds by the shore the next day. |

"Nights of the Pufflings"
Side by Side, Theme 2          **G**          Graphic Organizer
                                                Harcourt

## WRITTEN SUMMARY

Have students use their completed K-W-L charts to write a summary telling how the pufflings make it safely to sea. PERFORMANCE ASSESSMENT

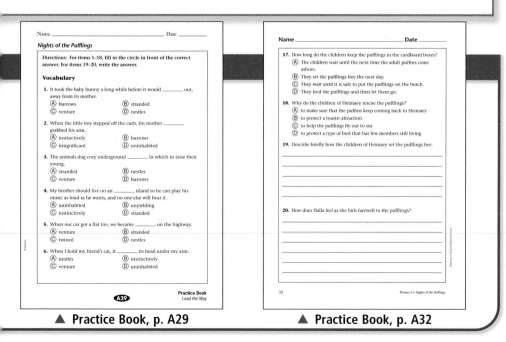

Name _____ Date _____
*Nights of the Pufflings*

Directions: For items 1–18, fill in the circle in front of the correct answer. For items 19–20, write the answer.

**Vocabulary**

1. It took the baby bunny a long while before it would _____ out, away from its mother.
   Ⓐ burrows        Ⓑ stranded
   Ⓒ venture         Ⓓ nestles

2. When the little boy stepped off the curb, his mother _____ grabbed his arm.
   Ⓐ instinctively    Ⓑ burrows
   Ⓒ insignificant    Ⓓ uninhabited

3. The animals dug cozy underground _____ in which to raise their young.
   Ⓐ stranded        Ⓑ nestles
   Ⓒ venture         Ⓓ burrows

4. My brother should live on an _____ island so he can play his music as loud as he wants, and no one else will hear it.
   Ⓐ uninhabited     Ⓑ unyielding
   Ⓒ instinctively    Ⓓ stranded

5. When our car got a flat tire, we became _____ on the highway.
   Ⓐ venture         Ⓑ stranded
   Ⓒ twined          Ⓓ nestles

6. When I hold my friend's cat, it _____ its head under my arm.
   Ⓐ nestles         Ⓑ instinctively
   Ⓒ venture         Ⓓ uninhabited

A29          Practice Book
              Lead the Way

17. How long do the children keep the pufflings in the cardboard boxes?
   Ⓐ The children wait until the next time the adult puffins come ashore.
   Ⓑ They set the pufflings free the next day.
   Ⓒ They wait until it is safe to put the pufflings on the beach.
   Ⓓ They feed the pufflings and then let them go.

18. Why do the children of Heimaey rescue the pufflings?
   Ⓐ to make sure that the puffins keep coming back to Heimaey
   Ⓑ to protect a tourist attraction
   Ⓒ to help the pufflings fly out to sea
   Ⓓ to protect a type of bird that has few members still living

19. Describe briefly how the children of Heimaey set the pufflings free.
   _____
   _____
   _____
   _____
   _____

20. How does Halla feel as she bids farewell to the pufflings?
   _____
   _____
   _____
   _____
   _____

32          Theme 2 • *Nights of the Pufflings*

▲ **Practice Book, p. A29**          ▲ **Practice Book, p. A32**

# TRAVEL

## Photo-illustrator Highlights Iceland
# Bruce McMillan

Author and photographer Bruce McMillan says he loves happy endings.

218

# NEWS

## Meet the Author

REYKJAVIK, ICELAND — Children's book author Bruce McMillan has traveled all over, from Alaska to the Caribbean, to create his popular books. Three of his recent works, *Nights of the Pufflings, Gletta the Foal*, and *My Horse of the North*, are set in Iceland.

McMillan has been taking photographs all his life, but he did not start writing until he spent two years living on an island off the coast of Maine. While he was there, he wrote a book about lobstering and took photographs for it. He decided to make it a children's book because he noticed not many children's books had photographs.

McMillan gets most of his ideas from his own interesting experiences and from things happening around him. For example, he tells about growing apples and making sneakers. He does more than just give information, though. He likes to tell a story with his books. "I love a happy ending," he says.

Bruce McMillan likes speaking to groups about his work—and they can tell that he likes being an author. His readers hope he will create many more colorful books for them to enjoy.

 **Visit *The Learning Site!*** www.harcourtschool.com

219

## ABOUT THE AUTHOR/PHOTO-ILLUSTRATOR

When **Bruce McMillan** turned five years old, he was given a camera as a present. He learned to use it so well, that when he was nine years old, his father gave him a professional camera. McMillan later became the photographer for his high school newspaper and then worked at a public television station while in college. After three years at the station, McMillan moved to an island off the coast of Maine. It was there that he wrote and photographed his first book, *Finest Kind O' Day: Lobstering in Maine*.

 **TECHNOLOGY** Additional author information can be found on *The Learning Site* at **www.harcourtschool.com**

# Reading Across Texts

## INTRODUCING THE MAGAZINE ARTICLE

**Genre Study** Have students preview by reading the title and looking at the photographs. Point out text features such as headings and captions. Ask them to predict how "Caring for Crocs" will be similar to "Nights of the Pufflings." (It has photographs of real animals; because the title contains the word *caring* it probably will be about people caring for animals.)

## READING NONFICTION

Have students read the magazine article, paying attention to the photographs, captions, and headings.

**1** **SUMMARIZE** **What happens in late July?** (Late July is crocodile nesting season. Frank Mazzotti and Laura Brandt begin looking for newly hatched American crocodiles.)

**2** **CAUSE-EFFECT** **What is one reason that crocodiles are endangered?** (People are building houses in the same places that crocodiles make their homes.)

**3** **IMPORTANT DETAILS** **What is the U.S. government doing to help the crocodiles?** (They are protecting a large area of the crocodiles' natural habitat.)

Genre
Magazine Article

## A toothy terror?

American crocodiles are gentler than they look— and endangered as well. But the good news is that scientists in Florida are working to save them.

Late July is an exciting time of year for scientists Frank Mazzotti and Laura Brandt. Every day they walk along certain beaches and inlets on Florida's southern coast, checking for clues.

What are they looking for? Dug-out nests in the sand. Broken eggshells. Tiny tracks at the water's edge. These are all clues that lead to newly hatched American crocodiles! **1**

220

### ENGLISH-LANGUAGE LEARNERS

Point out the word *Crocs* in the title of the selection. Explain that *croc* is a shortened form of *crocodile.* Tell students that authors often use abbreviations and less formal language when they want their writing to have a friendly tone. Provide these examples of other animals whose names are often abbreviated: *alligator–gator; rhinoceros–rhino; seagull–gull.*

Crocodile = Croc
Alligator = gator

Frank and Laura have been studying this endangered species since 1977. At that time, the number of crocodiles in southern Florida had dropped to about 300. One reason was that too much of the crocs' natural home area had been bulldozed to make way for houses. (Crocs like to live around beaches, lagoons, and bays—just as people do.) **2**

Luckily, by the early 1980s, the U.S. government started to help. It began to protect a big chunk of what remained of the crocs' natural area. And since then, the

This pop-up croc is a Nile crocodile. It's half-way hatched from its leathery egg.

number of crocs in southern Florida has grown to almost 500. **3**

But these huge reptiles are still endangered. To help save them, Frank and Laura have been studying the animals. Where do crocs go after they hatch? How

# CARING for CROCS

BY LYLE PRESCOTT

221

## SCIENCE

**Crocodile or Alligator?**   Discuss with students ways crocodiles and alligators are alike. (both live in the water, are reptiles, are greenish-brown) Then point out these differences: an alligator has a blunt snout and a crocodile has a narrow, pointed snout; alligators are much less aggressive than crocodiles; a crocodile's fourth tooth is visible when its mouth is closed.

**crocodile**                                                          **alligator**

# Reading Across Texts

**④ IMPORTANT DETAILS  How do the scientists recognize the crocs if they catch them later?** (They mark each croc by clipping different scales off its tail.)

**⑤ SUMMARIZE  What have the scientists learned about crocodiles from tracking them?** (They have learned that female crocodiles often make their nests in the exact same spot each year. They have also learned that each crocodile roams an area about the size of 250 football fields.)

Scientists Laura Brandt and Frank Mazzotti cruise up a Florida waterway in search of American crocodiles. They've studied these crocs for many years. And there's still a lot to learn.

much living space do they need? The two scientists have been trying to answer questions like these.

One thing they've learned is that these crocs aren't so scary. "American crocodiles are more scared of people than you need to be of them," says Laura.

## NESTING SEASON

The two scientists study the crocs year round. But the most important time is nesting season. It begins in late April when female crocs trudge ashore to make nests in the sand or soil. (A nest can be a hole a female digs in the ground or a mound of leaves and dirt she pushes together above the

222

### BELOW-LEVEL

Work with students to define the word *prey* by using the surrounding words: Read aloud this sentence: *The crocs eat crabs, birds, fish, turtles, snakes, and other* <u>*prey*</u>. Ask students what crabs, birds, fish, turtles, and snakes have in common. (They are all animals that crocs eat.) Explain to students that these animals are examples of *prey*. Then ask students what they think *prey* means. (Animals that are eaten by other animals.)

ground.) When a female has laid about 40 eggs in her nest, she kicks sand, dirt, or leaves over the eggs to bury them.

The female comes back often to check on her nest. After about 90 days, she hears little chirps coming out of it. She lays her head on the nest to listen closely. Her babies are finally hatching! She helps them dig their way out of the nest. Then she starts carrying them one by one in her mouth down to the water's edge.

The babies will hang out near the water's edge for a few weeks. While they're there, Frank and Laura get busy catching the little creatures to weigh and measure them. They also clip a few scales off each baby's tail (see photo at right).

Later, by looking at the different patterns of clipped scales, the scientists can tell the crocs apart. This helps them keep track of where each croc goes and what it does— even when it's grown up. For example, they've found that a female croc often makes her nest in the exact same spot each year. **4**

## HOME, SWEET HOME

The scientists have also learned that each crocodile roams an area about the size of 250 football fields. A croc may share most of this area with other crocs. But each croc needs this much space to find enough crabs, birds, fish, turtles, snakes, and other favorite prey. **5**

The scientists mark each croc by clipping different scales off its tail (above). That way they can recognize it if they catch it later.

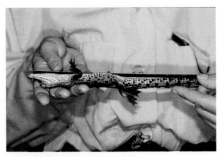

They also measure the length of each baby. This newly hatched croc is about 10 inches (25 cm) long.

223

# SCIENCE

## Crocodile Family Tree

Have students use an online or print encyclopedia to research the crocodile family tree. Ask students to name the dinosaurs that were crocodile ancestors and compare them to the existing species of crocodiles. Work with students to create a Venn diagram showing the similarities and differences between dinosaurs and crocodiles.

# Reading Across Texts

**6** **CAUSE-EFFECT** **Why do scientists weigh and measure crocodiles?** (to keep track of how fast they grow)

**7** **DRAW CONCLUSIONS** **Are the scientists doing a good thing? How do you know?** (Yes. The number of crocodiles in southern Florida has increased.)

# Think and Respond

**Answer:**

Possible response: It's important to study crocodiles because crocodiles are endangered. By studying them, scientists are better able to help them. **SYNTHESIZE**

## READING FOR A PURPOSE

**Understanding Text Structure** Have students read the captions under the photographs. Then ask them to tell what the captions add to the selection and why the author chose to use them. (The captions help explain the photographs and add important details and descriptions to the text.)

No, this is not a game of hang-croc. The rope is attached to a scale, which Frank is using to weigh a baby croc. By catching and weighing crocodiles often, the scientists keep track of how fast they grow.

Some people think that the way to save these endangered animals is to dig up their eggs and raise the babies in labs. But Frank says he has learned that's not the best idea. "The most important way we can help these animals is to make sure their habitat is protected," he explains. "If we protect their natural areas and then leave them alone, they do just fine."

Right now the two scientists are getting ready to weigh and mark a whole new batch of hatchlings. Keep up the **6** good work, Frank and Laura! **7**

## Think and Respond

Why is it important for the scientists to study American crocodiles?

224

**ENGLISH-LANGUAGE LEARNERS**

Students may be unfamiliar with some of the vocabulary in this selection. Point out the words *hatchling, habitat, prey, lagoon,* and *snatch.* Read each word aloud and ask students to repeat it after you. Use simple synonyms and demonstrations to explain each word. Guide students to use each concept word in an oral sentence. Write their sentences on the board as they say them aloud.

**We watched the hatchling.**

These baby crocs just hatched from a nest under a pile of leaves. Only a couple of the hatchlings in each nest will live to become adults. Big birds and fish will snatch up most of them before they're a year old.

225

## related books

You may want to recommend to students interested in this subject that they locate these titles.

### LIBRARY BOOKS COLLECTION

*Can We Be Friends?* by Alexandra Wright. 1994.

### ADDITIONAL READING

- *Song of the Swallows* by Leo Politi. Atheneum, 1987. **EASY**

- *Watching Water Birds* by Jim Arnosky. National Geographic Society, 1997. **AVERAGE**

- *Black Star, Bright Dawn* by Scott O'Dell. Houghton Mifflin, 1998. **CHALLENGING**

## ABOUT THE AUTHOR

**Lyle Prescott** grew up outdoors, climbing trees and mountains. She studied ecology in college to learn more about how nature works. Crocodiles used to scare her, but after learning more about them, she has a new respect and appreciation for them.

# Making Connections

**COMPARE TEXTS**

**Answers:**

**1** Possible response: It shows how the community of Heimaey works together to help the pufflings survive. **THEME**

**2** Possible response: The photograph of Halla at the beginning shows her smiling. She is happy because she sees the puffins returning to the island. In the photograph at the end of the selection, Halla has her arms raised as she watches a puffling fly away. She is excited and happy because the pufflings are safely on their way. **GRAPHIC AIDS**

**3** Possible response: The children and the scientists both care about wild creatures and work hard to help them. The children help by taking lost pufflings to the sea. The scientists help by studying crocodiles and working to protect their habitat. **COMPARE AND CONTRAST**

**4** Responses will vary. **EXPRESS PERSONAL OPINION**

**5** Responses will vary. **INQUIRY**

▲ Nights of the Pufflings

# Making Connections

## Compare Texts

**1** What does "Nights of the Pufflings" show about working together?

**2** How do the photographs help you understand Halla's emotions at the beginning and the end of the selection?

**3** How are the children in "Nights of the Pufflings" and the scientists in "Caring for Crocs" alike? How are they different?

**4** Would you find the story of the pufflings as interesting to read if it were written as fiction instead of nonfiction? Why or why not?

**5** What questions about puffins do you still have?

### Write a Project Description

Saving pufflings is an exciting project for the children of Heimaey. Think of an activity that would make a good project for a group of student volunteers where you live. Write a short description of the project. You may want to use a chart like the one below to help you organize your ideas.

Writing
CONNECTION

| Why Would This Be a Good Project? | How Many People Would Be Needed? | What Supplies Might Be Needed? | What Are the Main Steps of the Project? |
|---|---|---|---|
| | | | |

226

## Make a Map

The people in Iceland use their land to raise livestock, and they catch fish in the water off their coast. Find out how people in your state use their land and water. Then create a product map of your state to show how its land and water are used. You may want to look at an example of a product map in your social studies book before you draw your map.

**Social Studies CONNECTION**

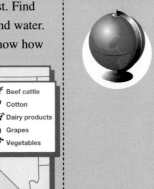

Beef cattle
Cotton
Dairy products
Grapes
Vegetables

San Francisco
Sacramento
Los Angeles
PACIFIC OCEAN
San Diego

## Make a Scientific Drawing

All birds have adaptations that help them live in their environments. Choose a bird to research. Draw a picture of the bird and its environment. Add captions that describe how this bird's wings, beak, feet, and other body parts are suited to where and how it lives.

**Science CONNECTION**

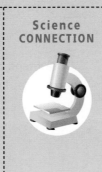

Penguin

227

**Making Connections**

### HOMEWORK FOR THE WEEK

Students and family members can work together to complete the activities on page T64. You may want to assign some or all of the activities as homework for each day of the week.

**TECHNOLOGY**
Visit *The Learning Site:*
**www.harcourtschool.com**
See Resources for Parents and Teachers: Homework Helper.

Teacher's Edition p. T64 ▶

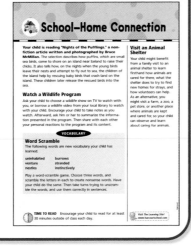

**School–Home Connection**

Your child is reading "Nights of the Pufflings," a nonfiction article written and photographed by Bruce McMillan. The selection describes how puffins, which are small sea birds, come to shore on an island near Iceland to raise their chicks. It also tells how, on the nights when the young birds leave their nests and attempt to fly out to sea, the children of the island help by rescuing baby birds that crash-land on the island. These children later release the rescued birds into the sea.

**Watch a Wildlife Program**
Ask your child to choose a wildlife show on TV to watch with you, or borrow a wildlife video from your local library to watch with your child. Encourage your child to take notes as you watch. Afterward, ask him or her to summarize the information presented in the program. Then share with each other your personal reactions to the program and its content.

**Visit an Animal Shelter**
Your child might benefit from a family visit to an animal shelter to learn firsthand how animals are cared for there, what the shelter does to try to find new homes for strays, and how volunteers can help. As an alternative, you might visit a farm, a zoo, a pet store, or another place where animals are kept and cared for, so your child can observe and learn about caring for animals.

**VOCABULARY**

**Word Scramble**
The following words are new vocabulary your child has learned.

| | |
|---|---|
| uninhabited | burrows |
| venture | stranded |
| nestles | instinctively |

Play a word-scramble game. Choose three words, and scramble the letters in each to create nonsense words. Have your child do the same. Then take turns trying to unscramble the words, and use them correctly in sentences.

**TIME TO READ** Encourage your child to read for at least 30 minutes outside of class each day.

Visit The Learning Site! www.harcourtschool.com

---

**Write a Project Description** To help students think of appropriate projects, write on the board: *recycling, cleanup, garden, art mural, fundraiser, food collection,* and *painting*. Have students share their finished proposals and vote on one project that they would like to carry through as a class.

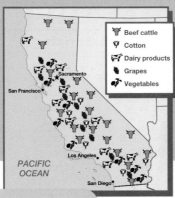

Save the Manatees

**SOCIAL STUDIES**

**Make a Map** Have students use the Internet or encyclopedias to research ways the land and water in their state is used.

**SCIENCE**

**Make a Scientific Drawing**
After students have finished the drawings and captions, have them display the drawings in the classroom.

Pelican

 **Summarize**

## SKILL TRACE

| SUMMARIZE | |
|---|---|
| Introduce | p. 206I |
| Reteach | pp. S48, S60, S92, T39 |
| **Review** | **pp. 228, 252I, 270** |
| Test | Theme 2 |
| Maintain | pp. 372I, 396 |

### RETURN TO THE SKILL

Have students read page 228 in the *Pupil Edition*. You may wish to use this model:

**MODEL** **To help me understand the events in the selection, I can summarize them. The chart shows me that to write a summary I need to retell the most important ideas from the selection, using my own words.**

Ask students how summarizing helped them understand and remember events from "Nights of the Pufflings."

### PRACTICE/APPLY

Students can work in pairs or in small groups to write a summary of a magazine article or a passage from another textbook. Tell them to make sure they include the important ideas from the passage, and retell the information in their own words. PERFORMANCE ASSESSMENT

 **TECHNOLOGY ■** *Mission: Comprehension™ Skills Practice CD-ROM* provides additional practice with reading comprehension and focus skills.

Visit *The Learning Site*: www.harcourtschool.com
See Skill Activities and Test Tutors: Summarize.

---

▲ **Nights of the Pufflings**

# Summarize

**W**hen you **summarize** a passage or selection, you tell about the most important parts in a few words.

The chart below provides tips for summarizing.

| Summarizing | |
|---|---|
| **Do** | **Do Not** |
| • tell about the most important ideas in the passage or selection<br>• follow the same order and pattern used by the author<br>• keep your summary short<br>• tell the information in your own words<br>• summarize to help you understand and remember what you read | • include information that is not important<br>• change the author's meaning<br>• include your own ideas or opinions<br>• include information from other sources |

If a friend asked you what "Nights of the Pufflings" is about, what information would you include? What would you leave out?

**Visit** *The Learning Site!*
www.harcourtschool.com
See *Skills* and *Activities*

228

### REACHING ALL LEARNERS

## Diagnostic Check: Comprehension and Skills

**If** . . . students are having difficulty summarizing . . .

**Then** . . . help them list the key events in the selection. Ask students to discuss those events. Then have them provide an oral summary.

### ADDITIONAL SUPPORT ACTIVITIES

| BELOW-LEVEL | Reteach, p. S48 |
| ADVANCED | Extend, p. S49 |
| ENGLISH-LANGUAGE LEARNERS | Reteach, p. S49 |

# Test Prep

**Summarize**

▶ Read the passage. Then answer the questions.

> Children who live in parts of Florida or the Caribbean, along the Amazon River system in South America, or near the rivers and coasts of West Africa may have manatees for neighbors. Manatees are large water mammals, also called sea cows. Three different species live in these three different parts of the world. They all have skin that is light to dark gray in color, eat large amounts of water plants, have front legs shaped like paddles, and have no hind legs.
>
> All three species are threatened or endangered, but efforts are being made to protect them. The United States government is among those that have taken steps to save the manatees. One reason for protecting them is their usefulness in eating weeds that might otherwise block waterways.

1. **What is the most important information to include in a summary of this article?**

   **A** Manatees have no hind legs.

   **B** Manatees are threatened or endangered.

   **C** Manatees are found along the Amazon River system.

   **D** Manatees' front legs are shaped like paddles.

   **Tip** Decide which of the sentences states the most important idea. Which of these sentences is the subject of a paragraph?

2. **On another sheet of paper, write a brief summary of the article.**

   **Tip** Express the most important ideas from the article in your own words.

229

# Test Prep

**Summarize** Have students read the passage carefully looking for the most important ideas. Use the Tips to reinforce good test-taking strategies. (I.B; 2. Responses will vary.)

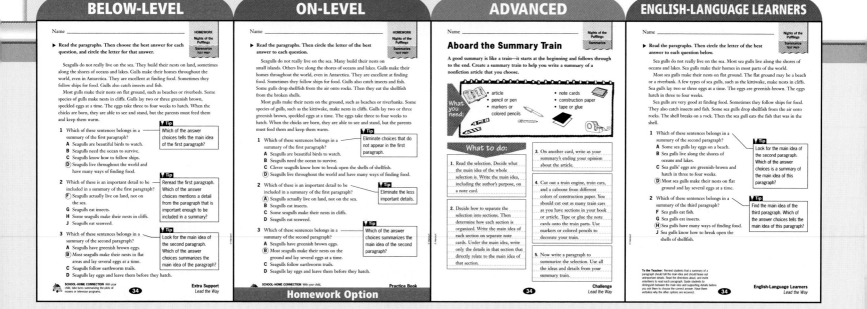

| BELOW-LEVEL | ON-LEVEL | ADVANCED | ENGLISH-LANGUAGE LEARNERS |
|---|---|---|---|

▲ Extra Support, p. 34   ▲ Practice Book, p. 34   ▲ Challenge, p. 34   ▲ ELL, p. 34

# Search Techniques

## Research and Technology

**OBJECTIVE**

*To understand how to use print and electronic resources available for research*

### INTRODUCE THE SKILL

**Discuss locating information on the Internet.** Have students identify the steps they would take to find information about puffins in an encyclopedia. (Use the keyword *puffin* to find the information alphabetically.) Have students name other sources they could use to look for this information.

| REFERENCE SOURCES | |
|---|---|
| **Print Reference Sources** | **Computer Reference Sources** |
| encyclopedia | CD-ROM encyclopedia |
| books about birds | Internet |
| nature magazines | online magazines |

Explain that the Internet is a system of connections that links information on computers all over the world. Tell students that to find information on the Internet, they should type keywords into a search engine. Point out that the correct spelling of the keywords is very important. Review with students the rules for Internet safety.

### TEACH/MODEL

**Model how to choose a search method.** Help students compare the different search techniques used in print and computer resources. Point out that one advantage of computer resources is that the information can be more current. For example, some Internet news services update information every few hours.

**MODEL** I want to find out which country won the most gold medals in the last Olympic Games. I could look in volume *O* of an encyclopedia, but the encyclopedia might not include the latest Olympic Games. I could type the keywords *Olympic Games* and *gold medals* into an Internet search engine. After reading the website summaries, I could visit the websites that seem to have the information I need.

## GUIDED PRACTICE

**Display Transparency 70.** Use the Transparency to make sure students understand the following points:

- Use specific keywords to help you narrow your search. A keyword is a word that best describes the topic. The more specific it is, the better.
- **The word AND** makes a search more specific.
- Information on a topic can often be found in both **print resources and computer resources.**

Discuss with students what print resources or computer resources they might use to look up information about puffins. Have them describe how they would find information in each resource.

## PRACTICE/APPLY

**Write directions for conducting a search.** Ask students to write directions that would help someone search for information on the Internet. Tell them to imagine that the person wants to find information on Arctic birds. Have students exchange lists and use each other's directions. PERFORMANCE ASSESSMENT

### SEARCH TECHNIQUES

**Choosing Key Words for Searching the Internet**

| My Question | Keywords | Better Keywords |
|---|---|---|
| Which country won the most gold medals at the last Olympic Games? | Olympic Games | Olympic Games AND gold medals |
| In which parts of Europe could I find puffins? | puffins | puffins AND Europe |
| Where is the nearest animal rescue shelter? | animal rescue shelters | animal rescue shelter AND (name of state) |

**Comparing Search Techniques**

| | Print Resources | Computer Resources |
|---|---|---|
| What you want to find | information on puffins | information on puffins |
| How you find it | Use alphabetical order and guide words to find an entry. Use the table of contents or index to find page numbers. | Use the find tool or an online table of contents to find entries. Type keywords into a search engine on the Internet. |
| Kind of information you get | General information that is easy to read; some information might be out of date. | General information that you may want to print out; some information might contain opinions rather than facts. |

"Nights of the Pufflings"
Side by Side, Theme 2
**70**
Search Techniques
Harcourt

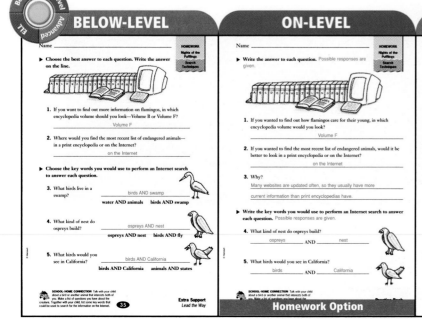

▲ Extra Support, p. 35   ▲ Practice Book, p. 35

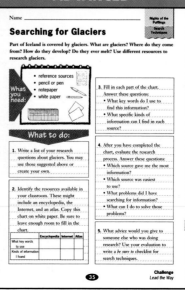

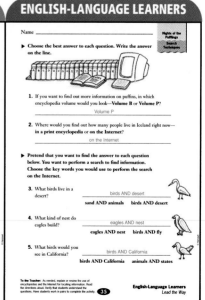

▲ Challenge, p. 35   ▲ ELL, p. 35

*Nights of the Pufflings* **229B**

![Phonics]

# Decoding/Phonics

## Syllables: Open Syllables

### OBJECTIVE

*To use knowledge of open sylla-bles to pronounce and read words.*

| SKILL TRACE | |
|---|---|
| SYLLABLES: OPEN SYLLABLES | |
| Introduce | Grade 2 |
| **Maintain** | **p. 229C** |

### ONGOING ASSESSMENT

**If** students are not able to fluently read approximately 99 words per minute, **then** they require phonics instruction and will also benefit from fluency practice.

**Note:** For assessment of oral reading accuracy and fluency, see pages T44–T46.

### MAINTAIN THE SKILL

**Decode words with open syllables.**   Write the word *paper* on the board, and read it aloud slowly. Ask students to divide the word into syllables (pa • per) and to identify the vowel sound in the first syllable. /ā/ Review with students that the first syllable is an open syllable—it ends with a vowel. Tell them that in an open sylla-ble, the vowel sound is usually long. Have students blend the sylla-bles to read the word *paper*. Write the word *pat* on the board and have a volunteer read it aloud. Ask students to identify the /a/ vowel sound. Tell students this is an example of a closed syllable—it ends with a consonant, and the vowel sound is usually short. Repeat the procedure with the word *table*. Encourage students to use what they know about open syllables to pronounce difficult or unfamiliar words.

### PRACTICE/APPLY

**Decode longer words.**   Write on the board the following words: *fever, music, label, final, motor, silent,* and *student*. Ask students to write the words on a sheet of paper. Have them identify the open syllable in each word. Then ask volunteers to blend the syllables to pronounce each word.

| fever | fe-ver |
| music | mu-sic |
| label | la-bel |
| final | fi-nal |
| motor | mo-tor |
| silent | si-lent |
| student | stu-dent |

Have students revisit "Nights of the Pufflings" and look for words with open syllables. **PERFORMANCE ASSESSMENT**

# Locate Information

*Research and Information Skills*

## REVIEW THE SKILL

**Discuss locating information.** Ask students what unanswered questions they may have about Iceland. Then ask what sources they could use to find the answers. (Possible responses: encyclopedias and nonfiction books on Iceland, the Internet, an atlas) Tell students that if they want to find specific information about a topic in a nonfiction book, they should use the index. Explain that an index is located in the back of the book and lists specific topics and the pages in the book where they can be found. Model using an index to find specific information about fishing in Iceland.

**MODEL** To find information about fishing in Iceland, I would turn to the index in the back of the book. Topics are listed alphabetically, so I would use alphabetical order to find the word *fishing*. Then I would see what pages in the book are about fishing. I would turn to those pages to find the information for which I am looking.

## PRACTICE/APPLY

**Answer questions about locating information.** Provide groups of students with nonfiction books that include tables of contents, indexes, and glossaries. Have each group choose a book, answer each question below, and name the part of the book that contained the answer. **PERFORMANCE ASSESSMENT**

• What is the title?

• In what year was this book published?

• Who is the publisher?

• How many chapters are in the book?

• What subjects does it cover?

**BELOW-LEVEL**

To help students determine where to look for information in a book, provide these guidelines:

• Look for general information about the book, such as the title or the chapter titles, in the front of the book.

• Look for specific information, such as definitions or what can be found on each page, in the back of the book.

# Writing Process

# Summary

## Writing Process: Informative Writing

## TRAITS OF GOOD WRITING

| | INTRODUCE AND PRACTICE | APPLY TO LONGER WRITING FORMS |
|---|---|---|
| Focus/Ideas | 421E–F | 453E–F, 471C–D |
| Organization | 521E–F, 543E–F | 567C–D, 589E–F |
| Voice | 49E–F, 77E–F | 101C–D, 123C–D |
| Word Choice | 637E–F, 667E–F | 689C–D, 713C–D |
| Development | 421E–F, 437C–D | 453E–F, 471C–D |
| Effective Sentences | 299E–F, 325C–D | 349C–D, 371C–D |
| **Effective Paragraphs** | **173E–F, 205C–D** | **229E–F, 251C–D** |
| Conventions | (*See* Grammar and Spelling Lessons.) | (Applied to all writing lessons.) |

## technology

**Writing Express™ CD-ROM**
Visit *The Learning Site*:
**www.harcourtschool.com**
See Writing Detective:
Proofreading Makes Perfect.

## TRAITS OF GOOD WRITING

- **Focus ideas:** The writer summarizes "Nights of the Pufflings."

- **Organization/Effective Paragraphs:** The beginning states the topic. The summary then retells the main events and important details of the book, following the order of events in the selection.

- **Voice:** The writer does not express personal opinions.

- **Development:** The writer uses his or her own words to summarize the ideas and adds transitions to help the reader move from one idea to the next idea.

- **Word Choice:** The writer uses clear, exact words.

- **Effective Sentences:** The writer varies sentence structures.

---

### DAY 1 — TEACH/MODEL

**CONNECT READING TO WRITING**
Explain that summarizing is a way to share information about a selection with people who have not read it. Tell students that they will learn to write a summary.

**REVIEW WRITER'S CRAFT** As students analyze the model on Transparency 71, discuss the effectiveness of the paragraphs. Point out that the summary begins with general information about the book and then includes the most important facts and events. Have students find the sequence words that help tie the sentences together.

▼ **Teaching Transparency 71**

**STUDENT MODEL: SUMMARY**

In a summary, the writer tells the main idea and important details of a selection in his or her own words. Here is a student summary of "Nights of the Pufflings."

**Introduction states the main idea of the book** — The book "Nights of the Pufflings" is about birds called puffins who return each year to an island near Iceland. There they lay eggs and have their young.

**Paragraph summarizes pages 211–213** — A young girl named Halla and her friends are waiting and watching for the puffins. They watch the birds dig burrows to lay eggs.

**Important details support the main idea** — They watch the birds swim in the ocean and catch fish to feed their young. The children cannot see the baby chicks because they are hidden in the burrows.

**Paragraph 9 summarizes pages 214–216** — At the end of summer, the "nights of the pufflings" arrive. The pufflings are ready to leave the nest and fly. The children stay up late at night to search for pufflings who become confused and stranded in the village.

**Important details support the main idea** — The children rescue thousands of pufflings by gathering them into cardboard boxes and taking them to the beach. Then they help the birds fly out to sea. For two weeks the children help the pufflings.

**Concluding sentence summarizes p. 217** — Next spring the puffins will come again to have their young and the children will rescue the pufflings.

"Nights of the Pufflings"
Side by Side, Theme 2
71
Writing: Summary
Harcourt

---

### DAY 2 — ANALYZE AND PREWRITE

**ANALYZE THE WRITING PROMPT**
Have students use the following prompt or choose another nonfiction selection to summarize.

**WRITING PROMPT:** *A written summary tells readers the main ideas and important details of a selection. Write a summary of "Nights of the Pufflings" in your own words.*

## ASK THE FOLLOWING QUESTIONS:

- What is the main event in the selection?

- How is the selection organized?

- What important details support the main event?

▼ **Teaching Transparency 72**

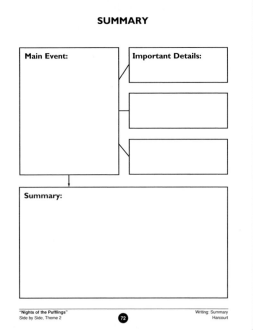

**SUMMARY**

Main Event:

Important Details:

Summary:

"Nights of the Pufflings"
Side by Side, Theme 2
72
Writing: Summary
Harcourt

# 5 Day Plan

## DAY 3 — DRAFT

Have students use the steps below to draft their summaries:

1. **Introduce** the summary by giving the title of the selection and telling what the selection is mainly about.

2. **Organize** ideas by summarizing the main idea and important details in each section.

3. **Develop** ideas by including the most important details. Use your own words. Add transitions between paragraphs.

4. **CONCLUDE** by retelling the main idea of the selection.

## DAY 4 — EDIT

**REVISE** Have students work in pairs or small groups to discuss their summaries. Encourage them to focus on whether they have included the most important ideas and whether the ideas flow smoothly.

Students may use the rubric on page T56 or T57 as they revise.

**PROOFREAD** Have students use these questions as they proofread:

- Did I use capital letters and punctuation marks correctly?
- Did I use the correct conjunctions to connect compound sentences?
- Are all my sentences complete?

## DAY 5 — PUBLISH AND ASSESS

**PUBLISH** Students may wish to publish their summaries by

- reading them aloud to class-mates
- illustrating them and displaying them on the walls of the class-room
- sharing them with family members

**ASSESS** Have students use the student rubric to evaluate their work.

Students may keep their revised summaries in their portfolios.

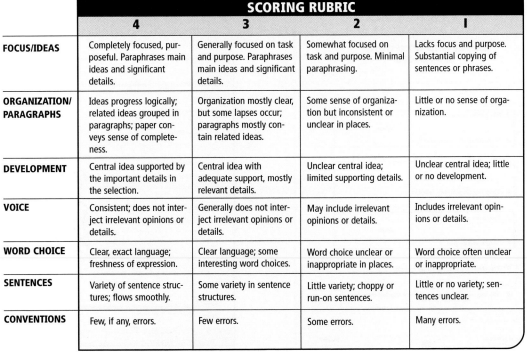

| SCORING RUBRIC | | | |
|---|---|---|---|
| | **4** | **3** | **2** | **1** |
| **FOCUS/IDEAS** | Completely focused, purposeful. Paraphrases main ideas and significant details. | Generally focused on task and purpose. Paraphrases main ideas and significant details. | Somewhat focused on task and purpose. Minimal paraphrasing. | Lacks focus and purpose. Substantial copying of sentences or phrases. |
| **ORGANIZATION/ PARAGRAPHS** | Ideas progress logically; related ideas grouped in paragraphs; paper conveys sense of completeness. | Organization mostly clear, but some lapses occur; paragraphs mostly contain related ideas. | Some sense of organization but inconsistent or unclear in places. | Little or no sense of organization. |
| **DEVELOPMENT** | Central idea supported by the important details in the selection. | Central idea with adequate support, mostly relevant details. | Unclear central idea; limited supporting details. | Unclear central idea; little or no development. |
| **VOICE** | Consistent; does not interject irrelevant opinions or details. | Generally does not interject irrelevant opinions or details. | May include irrelevant opinions or details. | Includes irrelevant opinions or details. |
| **WORD CHOICE** | Clear, exact language; freshness of expression. | Clear language; some interesting word choices. | Word choice unclear or inappropriate in places. | Word choice often unclear or inappropriate. |
| **SENTENCES** | Variety of sentence structures; flows smoothly. | Some variety in sentence structures. | Little variety; choppy or run-on sentences. | Little or no variety; sentences unclear. |
| **CONVENTIONS** | Few, if any, errors. | Few errors. | Some errors. | Many errors. |

**REPRODUCIBLE STUDENT RUBRICS** for specific writing purposes and presentations are available on pages T56–T58.

**Language Handbook,**
**pp. 64–65, 114–116,**
**190–191**

# Grammar

## Simple and Compound Sentences

## SKILL TRACE

| SIMPLE AND COMPOUND SENTENCES | |
|---|---|
| Introduce | p. 229G |
| Reteach | pp. S51, T41 |
| Review | pp. 229H, 251F |
| Test | Theme 2 |

### REACHING ALL LEARNERS

## Diagnostic Check: Grammar and Writing

**If** . . . students have difficulty forming compound sentences . . .

**Then** . . . write several related simple sentences on sentence strips. Include a word card for "and." Have students form compound sentences and rewrite them correctly.

### ADDITIONAL SUPPORT ACTIVITIES

| BELOW-LEVEL | Reteach, p. S50 |
| ADVANCED | Extend, p. S51 |
| ENGLISH-LANGUAGE LEARNERS | Reteach, p. S51 |

## technology

**Grammar Jingles™ CD,**
Intermediate: Track 4
Visit *The Learning Site:*
www.harcourtschool.com
See Grammar Practice Park,
Go for Grammar Gold,
Multimedia Grammar Glossary.

---

### DAY 1 — TEACH/MODEL

**DAILY LANGUAGE PRACTICE**

1. What sorces could you use to learn about puffins. (sources; puffins?)
2. Our Library has oardered a book about puffins. (library; ordered)

**INTRODUCE THE CONCEPT** Use Transparency 73 for discussion:

- A **simple sentence** expresses only one complete thought.
- A **compound sentence** is two or more simple sentences joined by a comma and a conjunction.

Ask students to write the compound sentences in items 3–8.

#### ▼ Teaching Transparency 73

**SIMPLE AND COMPOUND SENTENCES**

1. The puffins arrive.
2. The puffins arrive, and the children cheer.
3. The puffins come ashore.

   AND

4. They return to their old burrows.

   The puffins come ashore, and they return to their old burrows.

5. The pufflings peep for food.

   AND

6. They stay silent in their burrows.

   The pufflings peep for food, or they stay silent in their burrows.

7. Puffins are seabirds.

   AND

8. They breed on land.

   Puffins are seabirds, but they breed on land.

9. The chicks try to fly, some get stranded.

   comma splice; The chicks try to fly, but some get stranded.

10. The cats may find them the children may find them first.

    run-on sentence; Possible response: The cats may find them, or the children may find them first.

"Nights of the Pufflings"
Side by Side, Theme 2          73          Grammar
Harcourt

---

### DAY 2 — EXTEND THE CONCEPT

**DAILY LANGUAGE PRACTICE**

1. Every summer the puffins. Come to iceland. (puffins come; Iceland.)
2. Wouldn't you like to sea them for you self. (see; yourself?)

**DEVELOP THE CONCEPT** Refer to sentences 9–10 on Transparency 73 as you discuss these points:

- One error is to use only a comma to join two sentences. That is called a **comma splice**.
- Another error is to join two sentences with nothing between them. This is called a **run-on sentence**.

Ask students to suggest corrections to items 9 and 10. PERFORMANCE ASSESSMENT

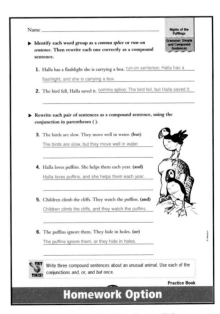

▲ Practice Book, p. 36

**Homework Option**

---

# 5
## Day Plan

---

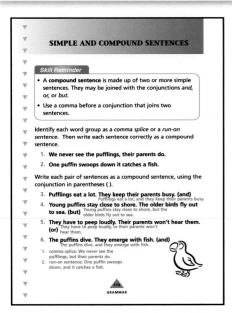

## DAY 3 — ORAL REVIEW/PRACTICE

### DAILY LANGUAGE PRACTICE

1. The pufflings must make it to see or they will die. (sea, or)
2. Halla, and her friends help the pufflings. That go the wrong way. (Halla and; pufflings that)

### COMPOUND-SENTENCE SUMMARY

Ask students to write six simple sentences summarizing the life of the pufflings. Then ask the students to form compound sentences as appropriate. Have volunteers place commas and conjunctions.

### Test Prep Tip

"Place a comma before the conjunction in a compound sentence. Use *but* if the compound sentence shows a contrast, or difference. Use *or* if it shows a choice."

**SIMPLE AND COMPOUND SENTENCES**

**Skill Reminder**

- A compound sentence is made up of two or more simple sentences. They may be joined with the conjunctions *and, or,* or *but.*
- Use a comma before a conjunction that joins two sentences.

Identify each word group as a *comma splice* or a *run-on sentence.* Then write each sentence correctly as a compound sentence.

1. We never see the pufflings, their parents do.
2. One puffin swoops down it catches a fish.

Write each pair of sentences as a compound sentence, using the conjunction in parentheses ( ).

3. Pufflings eat a lot. They keep their parents busy. (and)
   Pufflings eat a lot, and they keep their parents busy.
4. Young puffins stay close to shore. The older birds fly out to sea. (but)
   Young puffins stay close to shore, but the older birds fly out to sea.
5. They have to peep loudly. Their parents won't hear them. (or)
   They have to peep loudly, or their parents won't hear them.
6. The puffins dive. They emerge with fish. (and)
   The puffins dive, and they emerge with fish.

1. comma splice; We never see the pufflings, but their parents do.
2. run-on sentence; One puffin swoops down, and it catches a fish.

GRAMMAR

▲ **Language Handbook, p. 114**

---

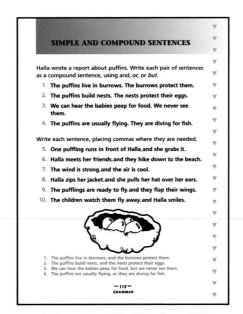

## DAY 4 — APPLY TO WRITING

### DAILY LANGUAGE PRACTICE

1. The pufflings came out and the children starred. (out, and; stared.)
2. That tiny bird can bairly walk. but now it must fly. (barely walk, but)

### BIRD'S-EYE VIEW

Invite students to write a story from a puffling's point of view about its rescue. The puffling could describe what it sees, hears, and feels as it is being rescued. Tell students to include at least three compound sentences, one with each of the conjunctions in the lesson.

**SIMPLE AND COMPOUND SENTENCES**

Halla wrote a report about puffins. Write each pair of sentences as a compound sentence, using *and, or,* or *but.*

1. The puffins live in burrows. The burrows protect them.
2. The puffins build nests. The nests protect their eggs.
3. We can hear the babies peep for food. We never see them.
4. The puffins are usually flying. They are diving for fish.

Write each sentence, placing commas where they are needed.

5. One puffling runs in front of Halla, and she grabs it.
6. Halla meets her friends, and they hike down to the beach.
7. The wind is strong, and the air is cool.
8. Halla zips her jacket, and she pulls her hat over her ears.
9. The pufflings are ready to fly, and they flap their wings.
10. The children watch them fly away, and Halla smiles.

1. The puffins live in burrows, and the burrows protect them.
2. The puffins build nests, and the nests protect their eggs.
3. We can hear the babies peep for food, but we never see them.
4. The puffins are usually flying, or they are diving for fish.

— 115 —
GRAMMAR

▲ **Language Handbook, p. 115**

---

## DAY 5 — CUMULATIVE REVIEW

### DAILY LANGUAGE PRACTICE

1. Waves, and wind carry the puffins foreward. (Waves and; forward.)
2. The pufflings swam away and the children waved fairwell. (away, and; farewell.)

### COMPOUNDS

Have students copy these sentences and label each as a *compound subject, compound predicate,* or *compound sentence.* Have them circle each conjunction.

1. Janine (and) I saw puffins at the zoo.
2. The puffins splashed (and) swam in the water.
3. The man threw fish, (but) the puffins weren't hungry.

(1. compound subject; 2. compound predicate; 3. compound sentence)

**CUMULATIVE REVIEW**

Tell whether each sentence has a *compound subject,* has a *compound predicate,* or is a *compound sentence.* Then write the conjunction.

1. Puffins and gulls are sea birds. — compound subject; and
2. They swim and dive well. — compound predicate; and
3. They eat fish, or they eat scraps. — compound sentence; or
4. Gulls fly well, but puffins do not. — compound sentence; but
5. They wobble or drop like a stone. — compound predicate; or
6. Halla and her friends rescue the pufflings. — compound subject; and

Write each pair of sentences as a compound sentence, using the conjunction in parentheses ( ).

7. Puffins look like penguins. They are quite different. (but)
8. Both live in cold water. Both eat fish. (and)
9. Penguins can swim. They can walk awkwardly. (or)
10. Puffins spend the winter at sea. They come ashore to lay their eggs. (but)

7. Puffins look like penguins, but they are quite different.
8. Both live in cold water, and both eat fish.
9. Penguins can swim, or they can walk awkwardly.
10. Puffins spend the winter at sea, but they come ashore to lay their eggs.

GRAMMAR

▲ **Language Handbook, p. 116**

*Nights of the Pufflings* **229H**

## Spelling Words

1. cared
2. dairy
3. unfair
4. rarely
5. stared
6. dared
7. glare
8. airplanes
9. barely
10. farewell*
11. software
12. staircase
13. everywhere*
14. declare
15. square
16. therefore
17. despair
18. prepared
19. beware
20. repair

* Selection Words

### Challenge Words

21. puffins*
22. geyser
23. volcanic
24. boulder
25. island*

# Spelling

## Words with the /âr/ Sound

DAY 1

### PRETEST/SELF-CHECK

**ADMINISTER THE PRETEST** Use the Dictation Sentences under Day 5. Have students self-check their pretests using Transparency 74.

### ADVANCED

Use the Challenge Words in these Dictation Sentences:

21. **Puffins** are birds that live on the sea.
22. A natural hot spring can be called a **geyser**.
23. Rock produced by a volcano is **volcanic** rock.
24. A very large rock is called a **boulder**.
25. An **island** is completely surrounded by water.

DAY 2

### TEACH/MODEL

**WORD SORT** Display Transparency 74. Briefly discuss the meaning of each word. Then ask students to copy the chart and write each Spelling Word where it belongs.

Point to and read the words *cared* and *dairy*. Ask students what vowel sound is the same in both words. (/âr/) Have a volunteer circle the letters that stand for this sound. Have students read the generalization to confirm their conclusions.

**HANDWRITING** Remind students to be sure the downstroke of the letter *a* touches the bottom line so it will not be mistaken for *o*.

*fare*

### ▼ Teaching Transparency 74

**WORDS WITH THE /âr/ SOUND**

**Spelling Words**

| | | | |
|---|---|---|---|
| 1. cared | 6. dared | 11. software | 16. therefore |
| 2. dairy | 7. glare | 12. staircase | 17. despair |
| 3. unfair | 8. airplanes | 13. everywhere | 18. prepared |
| 4. rarely | 9. barely | 14. declare | 19. beware |
| 5. stared | 10. farewell | 15. square | 20. repair |

| are | air | ere |
|---|---|---|
| cared | dairy | everywhere |
| rarely | unfair | therefore |
| stared | airplanes | |
| dared | staircase | |
| glare | despair | |
| barely | repair | |
| farewell | | |
| software | | |
| declare | | |
| square | | |
| prepared | | |
| beware | | |

"Nights of the Pufflings"
Side by Side, Theme 2 · 74 · Spelling Harcourt

Name _____

**Skill Reminder** The /âr/ sound can be spelled are, air, or ere.

► Fold the paper along the dotted line. As each spelling word is read aloud, write it in the blank. Then unfold your paper, and check your work. Practice any spelling words you missed.

1. _____
2. _____
3. _____
4. _____
5. _____
6. _____
7. _____
8. _____
9. _____
10. _____
11. _____
12. _____
13. _____
14. _____
15. _____
16. _____
17. _____
18. _____
19. _____
20. _____

**SPELLING WORDS**
1. cared
2. dairy
3. unfair
4. rarely
5. stared
6. dared
7. glare
8. airplanes
9. barely
10. farewell
11. software
12. staircase
13. everywhere
14. declare
15. square
16. therefore
17. despair
18. prepared
19. beware
20. repair

37

Practice Book
Lead the Way

▲ Practice Book, p. 37

Name _____

**Words with the /âr/ Sound**

► Write the Spelling Word that fits each clue.

1. not often — rarely
2. looked at without blinking — stared
3. flying vehicles — airplanes
4. hardly at all — barely
5. goodbye — farewell
6. computer programs — software
7. all places — everywhere
8. to say or state — declare
9. a set of steps — staircase
10. deep sorrow; depression — despair
11. ready — prepared
12. to fix — repair

► Write these Spelling Words in alphabetical order.

| square | glare | beware | therefore |
|---|---|---|---|

13. beware    15. square
14. glare    16. therefore

► Write the following Spelling Words: *cared, dairy, dared, unfair.* Use your best handwriting.

17. cared    19. dared
18. dairy    20. unfair

**SPELLING WORDS**
1. cared
2. dairy
3. unfair
4. rarely
5. stared
6. dared
7. glare
8. airplanes
9. barely
10. farewell
11. software
12. staircase
13. everywhere
14. declare
15. square
16. therefore
17. despair
18. prepared
19. beware
20. repair

**Handwriting Tip:** When you write the letter *a*, make sure that the downstroke touches the bottom line, or it might look like an *o*.

*glare*

LESSON 8    SPELLING PRACTICE BOOK    33

▲ Spelling Practice Book, p. 33

## 5 Day Plan

### GUESSING AND CHECKING   Write the following on the board:

*steres  airea  mair*

Suggest to students that when they are unsure how to spell a word they can first guess. Ask students to write the correct spelling of each word. (stairs, area, mare) Ask students to explain what they should do if a word still does not look right. (Check a dictionary.)

#### Apply to Writing

Have students use the guessing-and-checking strategy when they are proofreading. Have them look for words with /âr/ to be sure they have spelled them correctly.

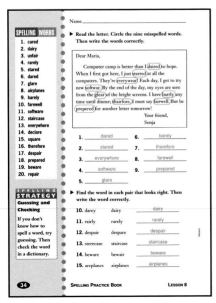

▲ **Spelling Practice Book, p. 34**

### COMPOUND CONCENTRATION

Have pairs of students write the five compound spelling words and ten more compound words, drawing a line between the two parts. On 30 index cards, students should write the smaller words from each compound.

Have students place the cards facedown into two decks. Students take turns turning over two cards, one from each deck. If the two cards form a compound, the student spells the word, keeps the pair, and continues. If the two words do not form a compound, the cards are put back in the deck. The game ends when all the cards are gone.

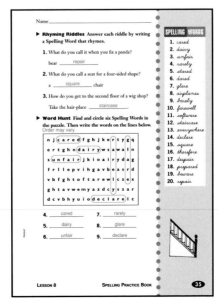

▲ **Spelling Practice Book, p. 35**

### DICTATION SENTENCES

1. Bev **cared** deeply about her cat.
2. Our class visited a **dairy** farm.
3. Our board game seemed **unfair**, so we changed the rules.
4. She **rarely** plays video games.
5. He **stared** at the purple truck.
6. I **dared** Kim to enter the contest.
7. Sunglasses will block out the sun's **glare**.
8. The **airplanes** at the air show flew in a V-shape.
9. We **barely** made it to the train on time.
10. George said **farewell** to his aunt and returned home.
11. The library received new **software** for its computer.
12. The **staircase** leads to the attic.
13. The feathers from the pillow flew **everywhere**.
14. To **declare** means "to state firmly."
15. Maria cut a **square** piece of cake.
16. It was **therefore** necessary for us to leave the game.
17. Do not **despair** if you cannot understand the directions.
18. We **prepared** a special breakfast for our guests.
19. The sign warned us to **beware** of high water.
20. The roof was in need of much **repair**.

# Word Study

## SYNONYMS AND ANTONYMS

## Word Relationships

**OBJECTIVE**
*To identify synonyms and antonyms*

Remind students that a synonym is a word that has a similar meaning to another word. An antonym is a word that means the opposite of another word. Write the following pairs of words on the board. Ask students to identify each pair of words as synonyms or antonyms.

uninhabited — crowded (antonyms)

holes — burrows (synonyms)

venture — attempt (synonyms)

stranded — rescued (antonyms)

nestles — cuddles (synonyms)

naturally — instinctively (synonyms)

Then ask students to think of three more pairs of synonyms and three more pairs of antonyms, and add them to the list.

### ENGLISH-LANGUAGE LEARNERS

If students have difficulty determining whether the word pairs are synonyms or antonyms, you may want to provide simple definitions for each word in the pair. Then ask students if the definitions have similiar or different meanings. Explain that if the definitions for the words are almost the same, then the words are synonyms. If the definitions are different, then the words are antonyms.

## ANALOGIES

## Make Comparisons

**OBJECTIVE**
*To use knowledge of word relationships to complete analogies*

Write this analogy on the board:

> Puffling is to puffin as kitten is to cat.

Explain that an analogy states a special kind of comparison. Ask volunteers to explain the relationship in the analogy above. (Possible response: The second word is the name of a kind of animal and the first word is the name of a young animal of the same kind.) Ask volunteers to replace the second half of the analogy with another appropriate phrase. (Possible response: *puppy* is to *dog*)

Ask students to complete these analogies:

1. *Fish* is to *puffling* as _____.
   (Possible response: *milk* is to *kitten*)

2. *Puffin* is to *Iceland* as _____.
   (Possible response: *polar bear* is to *Alaska*)

3. *Fox* is to *den* as _____.
   (Possible response: *rabbit* is to *burrow*)

# Speaking and Listening

## Giving a Descriptive Speech

**OBJECTIVE**

*To describe important events using sensory details*

Ask students to prepare a description of what happens to the puffins in spring and summer. Remind them to use vivid words.

**Organization**   Share these **organizational tips** with students.

- Begin with a short description of the setting.
- Tell about events in time order.
- List important events and details on note cards.

**Delivery**   Share the following **practice tips** with students.

- Practice reading the description with a partner before speaking in front of the whole class.
- Emphasize important details by using gestures or by changing the pitch of your voice.
- Make eye contact with your audience.
- Add visual interest to your speech by using pictures or drawings.

Have students give their descriptive speeches to a small group. Ask audience members to give a "thumbs up" each time they hear a vivid description.

**PERFORMANCE ASSESSMENT**

## Listening to a Descriptive Speech

**OBJECTIVES**

- *To identify important facts and details*
- *To listen attentively to a speaker*

**Listening Tips**

- Face the speaker, and make eye contact with him or her.
- Show interest by your posture and your body language.
- Keep your attention focused on the description.
- Give positive feedback.

Remind students to listen for words that appeal to their senses. Suggest that they try to visualize the scene that is being described. Ask them to keep track of the important events in the lives of the puffins during the spring and summer. Share the Listening Tips with students.

**LISTENING CHECKLIST**   Have students create their own checklists of things that good listeners should do. Suggest that students illustrate their checklists with pictures of a person showing good listening behavior.

# Books for All Learners

*Reinforcing Skills and Strategies*

## ■ BELOW-LEVEL

 **Focus Skill: Summarize**

 **Focus Strategy: Adjust Reading Rate**

 **Vocabulary: *uninhabited, burrows, venture, stranded, nestles, instinctively***

**Genre:** Nonfiction
**Science Connection:** Living Things Interact

**SUMMARY**   A blind boy on Heimaey Island recalls his first adventure rescuing a puffling.

For additional related activities, visit *The Learning Site* at **www.harcourtschool.com**

### BEFORE READING

**Preview/Set Purpose**   Have students read the title and look at the illustrations to preview the book. Ask them to tell what they think it is about and why they might want to read it.

**Reinforce Summarize**   Help students make a story map to retell the story events. SUMMARIZE/GRAPHIC AIDS

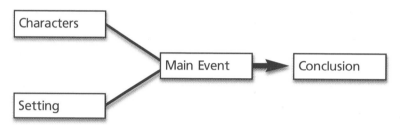

**Reinforce Vocabulary**   Use the illustrations to review key vocabulary. Ask questions such as, "What does this illustration show about *burrows*?"

### READING THE BOOK

**Pages 3–8**   What does this book tell you about puffins? (What they look like, where they nest, and how they leave the nest.) SUMMARIZE

**Pages 12–16**   What senses does Lars use to help him on his adventure? (touch and hearing) DRAW CONCLUSIONS

**Reread for Fluency**   Have students choose and reread aloud favorite parts of the book to you.

### RESPONDING

**Story Map**   Students can complete the story map and use it to help them summarize the events in the book.

**Managing Small Groups**

While you work with small groups have other students do the following:

• Self-selected Reading
• Practice Pages
• Cross-Curricular Centers
• Journal Writing

## ■ ON-LEVEL

 **Focus Skill: Summarize**

 **Focus Strategy: Adjust Reading Rate**

 **Vocabulary:** *uninhabited, burrows, venture, stranded, nestles, instinctively*

**Genre:** Mystery
**Science Connection:** People and Animals Interact

**SUMMARY**   On a trip to Iceland, Sarah makes new friends and helps the puffins find their way.

🖥 For additional related activities, visit *The Learning Site* at **www.harcourtschool.com**

### BEFORE READING

**Preview/Set Purpose**   Have students use the chapter headings and illustrations to preview the book. Ask them to tell why they might want to read this book.

**Reinforce Summarize**   Have students make a K-W-L chart like the following to help them record key events as they read.
SUMMARIZE/GRAPHIC SOURCES

| K-W-L Chart | | |
|---|---|---|
| What I Know | What I Want to Know | What I Learned |
| | | |

### READING THE BOOK

**Page 5**   What has happened in the story so far? (Sarah is lonely during her visit to Iceland. While Sarah is on a walk with her grandfather, a secret pal leaves a mysterious note for her.) SUMMARIZE

**Pages 5–7**   Who do you think left the note for Sarah? Do you think Sarah's grandparents know who left the note? Why do you think this? (Accept reasonable responses; Yes; Sarah's grandparents know who left the note; Grandpa winked at Grandma.) SPECULATE

**Pages 15–16**   Why do the children help the pufflings? How do they help them? (As the pufflings learn to fly, they get confused. The children take them to the ocean.) SUMMARIZE

**Rereading for Fluency**   Have students reread aloud pages 14–16 of this book. Remind them to read the dialogue with expression.

### RESPONDING

**Sequence Chart**   Have students complete their sequence charts to determine ten important sentences in the story.

# Books for All Learners

*Reinforcing Skills and Strategies*

## ■ ADVANCED

 **Focus Skill: Summarize**

 **Focus Strategy: Adjust Reading Rate**

☑ **Vocabulary:** *uninhabited, burrows, venture, stranded, nestles, instinctively, chieftain, serpents*

**Genre:** Nonfiction
**Social Studies Connection:** The Impact of Geographic Features on Early Settlements

**SUMMARY** This book describes Iceland's geographical features, discusses the settlement of the island by Vikings, and explores how the early settlers used the island's features to survive.

💻 For additional related activities, visit *The Learning Site* at **www.harcourtschool.com**

### BEFORE READING

**Preview/Set Purpose** Have students preview the book's illustrations and maps. Ask them to tell when they think the events in this book took place and what they might learn from this book.

**Reinforce Summarize** Begin a sequence chart. Ask students to complete the chart as they read to help them track events.

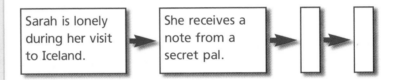

**Expand Vocabulary** Write *chieftain* and *serpents* on the board, and discuss prior knowledge of these words. (chieftain: the head of a clan or tribe; serpent: a snake, especially a large one)

### READING THE BOOK

**Pages 2–5** What is the author's purpose for writing this book? (to provide factual information about Iceland) What reading strategy can you use to better understand informational books? (adjust reading rate) **AUTHOR'S PURPOSE/ADJUST READING RATE**

**Pages 7–12** What information does the author provide about how Iceland was settled? (Ingolfur Arnarson lost a battle with another chieftain. He and his family traveled with others to the island.) **SUMMARIZE**

**Rereading for Fluency** Have students select their favorite sections and reread them aloud.

### RESPONDING

**Dramatic Interpretation** Have students write a short play depicting the Vikings' journey to Iceland.

BELOW-LEVEL

ON-LEVEL

ADVANCED

ELL

▲ page 229M     ▲ page 229N

## ■ ENGLISH-LANGUAGE LEARNERS

 Focus Skill: Summarize

 Focus Strategy: Adjust Reading Rate

 Concept Vocabulary: *eggs, eyes, hungry, food, fly, nest*

**Genre:** Nonfiction

**Science Connection:** Animals' Unique Features Enable Them to Survive

**SUMMARY** The text begins by discussing the similarities among birds, and then it highlights different birds and gives specific information about their appearances, nesting habits, and food preferences. Photographs show the birds in action.

For additional related activities, visit *The Learning Site* at **www.harcourtschool.com** See Language Support.

### BEFORE READING

**Tap Prior Knowledge** Write *birds* on the board, and ask students to tell what they know about birds. Write their responses in a web with the word *birds* in the center.

**Total Physical Response** Invite volunteers to pantomime: flying, pecking, singing or cawing, and nesting.

**Display Vocabulary/Concept Words** Use the photographs in the book to discuss with students the meanings of the words.

**Preview the Book** Help students preview the book. Read the title aloud. Then discuss the photographs and captions.

### READING THE BOOK

**Page 3** How are all birds alike? (They have two wings, two legs, and a beak. They have feathers, and they lay eggs.) **MAKE COMPARISONS**

**Pages 2–16** Choose one bird and summarize what you learned about it. (Responses will vary.) **SUMMARIZE**

**Rereading** Reread the book aloud with students.

### RESPONDING

**Chart** Use a chart like the following to help students retell what they read.

|  | Food | Nest | Behavior |
|---|---|---|---|
| Bald Eagle |  |  |  |
| Barn Owl |  |  |  |
| Crow |  |  |  |
| Woodpecker |  |  |  |

**THEME CONNECTION:**
*Side by Side*

**GENRE:**
*Realistic Fiction*

ERIKA TAMAR
*The Garden of Happiness*

Illustrated by Barbara Lambase

Notable Social Studies Trade Book

Comparing Realistic Fiction and Poetry

▲ **READING ACROSS TEXTS:** "I do not plant my garden," by Lynne Cherry, and "The City," by David Ignatow
**GENRE:** Poetry

**SUMMARY:**

Marisol plants a sunflower seed in a new neighborhood garden. When autumn comes and her flower dies, Marisol gets discouraged. Her happiness returns, however, when she discovers that a group of teenagers has painted a mural of sunflowers on a brick wall nearby.

 Selections available on *Audiotext 2*

# Books for All Learners

*Lesson Plans on pages 25IK–25IN*

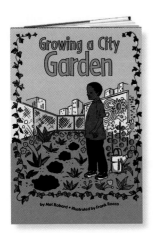  

| BELOW-LEVEL | ON-LEVEL | ADVANCED | ELL |
|---|---|---|---|
| • Lesson Vocabulary<br>• Focus Skill: Cause and Effect | • Lesson Vocabulary<br>• Focus Skill: Cause and Effect | • Challenge Vocabulary<br>• Focus Skill: Cause and Effect | • Concept Vocabulary<br>• Focus Skill: Cause and Effect |

## MULTI-LEVEL PRACTICE

**Extra Support,** pp. 38–39

**Practice Book,** pp. 38–41

**Challenge,** pp. 38–39

**English-Language Learners,** pp. 38–39

## ADDITIONAL RESOURCES

**Spelling Practice Book,** pp. 36–38

**Language Handbook,** pp. 69, 117–119

**Audiotext 2**

**Intervention Resource Kit,** Lesson 9
• Intervention Reader, *Included in Intervention Resource Kit*

**English-Language Learners Resource Kit,** Lesson 9

 ## technology

• *Mission: Comprehension™ Skills Practice* **CD-ROM**

• *Media Literacy and Communication Skills Package* (Video)

• *Grammar Jingles™* **CD,** Intermediate

• *Writing Express™* **CD-ROM**

• *Reading and Language Skills Assessment* **CD-ROM**

• *The Learning Site:* **www.harcourtschool.com**

# The Garden of Happiness    pp. 230–251

## ORAL LANGUAGE
5-15 Minutes

• **Question of the Day**

• **Sharing Literature**

15-30 Minutes

## SKILLS & STRATEGIES

• **Comprehension**

• **Vocabulary**

30-45 Minutes

## READING

• **Guided Comprehension**

**Independent Reading**

• **Cross-Curricular Connections**

45-90 Minutes

## LANGUAGE ARTS

• **Writing**

  *Daily Writing Prompt*

• **Grammar**

  *Daily Language Practice*

• **Spelling**

**Daily Routines**
• Question of the Day
• Daily Language Practice
• Daily Writing Prompt

---

## Day 1

**Question of the Day,** p. 230H
*Imagine that you walked past a garden on a spring day and inhaled. What did you smell?*

**Literature Read-Aloud,** pp. 230G–H

**Comprehension:**
 **Skill** Cause and Effect, p. 230I **T**
**Strategy** Make and Confirm Predictions, p. 230J

**Vocabulary,** p. 230L

**Read: Vocabulary Power,** pp. 230–231
Vocabulary Power Words:
*inhaled, lavender, mural, skidded, haze*

 **Independent Reading**
Books for All Learners

**WRITING** A Plant's Perspective
**SCIENCE** Growth Journal
**INQUIRY PROJECT** Extending the Selection

**Writing:** Writing Process, p. 251C

✏ **Writing Prompt:**
*Imagine that you have been asked to draw a mural for your town. Think about what people, places, or things should be on the mural. Explain what you will draw on the mural.*

**Grammar:**
Independent and Dependent Clauses, p. 251E **T**

*Daily Language Practice*
1. Do you have a gardin in your neighborhood. (garden; neighborhood?)
2. Planting flowers was the smartist thing we could have done (smartest, done.)

**Spelling:**
Words with the /ûr/ Sound, p. 251G **T**

---

## Day 2

**Question of the Day,** p. 230H
*What are some reasons that people work together in communities?*

**Think and Respond,** p. 242

**Comprehension:**
 **Skill** Cause and Effect, pp. 232–243 **T**

**Decoding/Phonics:**
Syllables: Closed Syllables, p. 251A

**Reading the Selection,** pp. 232–243
GENRE: Realistic Fiction

 **Independent Reading**
Books for All Learners

**CULTURAL CONNECTIONS** Punctuation, Alphabets, and Pronunciation
**SCIENCE** Plants in the Food Chain

**Writing:** Writing Process, p. 251C

✏ **Writing Prompt:**
*Imagine that your town has planted a Garden of Happiness. Write a paragraph describing what is planted in your town's garden.*

**Grammar:**
Extend the Concept, p. 251E

*Daily Language Practice*
1. Marisol wants to plant something. Inn the garden. (something in)
2. It is to late, the plots are all taken. (too late. The)

**Spelling:**
Word Sort, p. 251G

---

**Objectives of the Week:**

• To use cause-and-effect relationships to understand a character's motivations and actions

• To read and understand a realistic fiction selection; to compare realistic fiction with poetry

• To use clauses correctly

• To use the writing process in writing a how-to essay

## Day 3

**Question of the Day,** p. 230H
*Think about plants you have seen growing in unusual places. How do you think they survive in these difficult conditions?*

**Oral Grammar,** p. 251F

**Comprehension:**
 Cause and Effect, pp. 250–251
Test Prep

**Word Study:**
Synonyms, p. 251I

**Rereading for Fluency,** p. 241

**Reading Across Texts,** pp. 246–247
GENRE: Poetry

 **Independent Reading**
Books for All Learners

**LITERARY ANALYSIS** Similes

**Writing:** Writing Process, p. 251D

 **Writing Prompt:**
*Write a shape poem about a plant in the Garden of Happiness. Describe what kind of plant it is and what it looks like.*

**Grammar:**
Dependent or Independent? p. 251F

***Daily Language Practice***
1. Marisol found some soil. Where the sidewalk had cracked? (soil where; cracked.)
2. Shee found a seed. To plant there. (She; seed to)

**Spelling:**
Use a Dictionary, p. 251H

## Day 4

**Question of the Day,** p. 230H
*"It's raining cats and dogs" is an example of figurative language. What are some other examples?*

**Comprehension:**
 Cause and Effect, pp. 251K–N

**Figurative Language,** p. 251B **T**

**Self-Selected Reading,** p. 230F

**Independent Reading**
Books for All Learners

**TECHNOLOGY** Plan a Garden

**Writing:** Writing Process, p. 251D

 **Writing Prompt:**
*Think about the foods in your favorite meal. Then write a paragraph telling a classmate what foods would be in your favorite meal.*

**Grammar:**
Order of Events, p. 251F

***Daily Language Practice***
1. Will marisol's seed sprout. (Marisol's; sprout?)
2. She wanders what her seedling will be come. (wonders; become)

**Spelling:**
Think and Spell, Write Haiku, p. 251H

## Day 5

**Question of the Day,** p. 230H
*How would a community garden in a city with a cold climate differ from a community garden in a city with a warm climate?*

**Speaking and Listening**
Give a Demonstration, p. 251J

**Comprehension:**
 Cause and Effect, pp. 251K–N **T**

**Word Study:**
Foreign Words, p. 251I

**Self-Selected Reading,** pp. 247, T67

**Independent Reading**
Books for All Learners

**WRITING** Write to Explain
**SCIENCE** Make a Booklet
**ART** Paint a Mural

**Writing:** Writing Process, p. 251D

**Writing Prompt:**
*Imagine that you are going to clean up a vacant lot. Think about the steps that would be involved. Write to explain how you would clean up the lot.*

**Grammar:**
Clauses and Compound Sentences, p. 251F

***Daily Language Practice***
1. Everyone enjoyed Marisols sunflower (Marisol's sunflower.)
2. people on the street stopt and smiled. (People; stopped)

**Spelling:**
Posttest, p. 251H

# Cross-Curricular Stations

**MANAGING THE CLASSROOM** While you provide direct instruction to individuals or small groups, other students can work on ongoing activities such as the ones below.

## WRITING

### A Plant's Perspective

**OBJECTIVE: To write a narrative from the perspective of a plant**

Imagine that you are a plant or a flower. Write a story about your life. Answer the following questions as you write:

- Where do you grow? How did you get there?
- What do you look like?
- What do you need to survive?
- Who takes care of you?

**Materials**
- paper
- pen or pencil

*A Plant's Life*

*When Mrs. Anderson's class planted their spring garden, I was lucky enough to be planted by a girl named Angela. She carefully read the directions on my packet.*

## SCIENCE

### Growth Journal

**OBJECTIVE: To observe how different environments affect plant growth**

See whether a plant grows better in a sunny environment or a shady environment.

- Choose two seeds from the same seed packet.
- Follow the planting instructions on the seed packet. Plant each seed in its own paper cup.
- Place one cup in a sunny spot in the room and the other cup in a shady spot in the room. Make a prediction about which plant will grow better.
- Care for both plants as directed in the growing instructions.
- Observe the changes in each plant, and measure each one at the end of the week for three weeks. Keep track of your results in a chart and record your observations.
- Determine which plant grew more over the three-week period, and draw a conclusion about the effects of sunlight on plant growth.

**Materials**
- packet of seeds
- paper cups
- soil or growing medium
- water
- paper
- pen or pencil

|  | Week 1 | Week 2 | Week 3 |
|---|---|---|---|
| Plant in the Sun |  |  |  |
| Plant in the Shade |  |  |  |

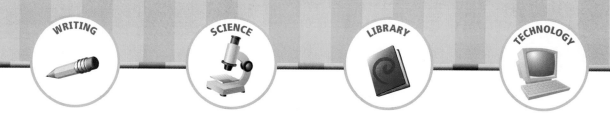

## LIBRARY CENTER

### Self-Selected Reading

**OBJECTIVE: To select and read books independently**

Look for these books about gardens and communities.

- *Market!* by Ted Lewin. Routledge, 1998. NONFICTION
- *June 29, 1999* by David Wiesner. Clarion, 1992. FICTION
- *City Green* by DyAnne DiSalvo-Ryan. William Morrow, 1994. FICTION

**Remember to**

- select a book that interests you.
- recommend books that you like to your friends.
- keep track in your Reading Log of what you read each day.

### Materials

- self-selected book
- *My Reading Log* copying master, p. R38

---

## INQUIRY PROJECT

### Extending the Selection

**OBJECTIVE: To select a focus for an inquiry project**

With a partner, use the ideas in "The Garden of Happiness" to brainstorm related topics to explore. Organize your ideas into a web. Choose a topic, and use one of these books for your project.

- *Growing a City Garden*
- *Faces to the Sun*
- *Home Grown*
- *Sunshine Place*

### Materials

- research materials
- paper
- pencils

---

## TECHNOLOGY

### Plan a Garden

**OBJECTIVE: To use a computer to plan a garden**

Use a computer's word processing software to plan a garden. List the plants you would like to grow, and tell what you would do with them.

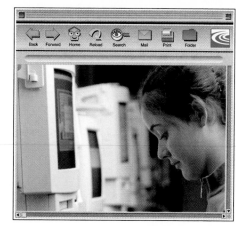

**Remember to**

- open and name a new file.
- print and save your work when you are done.

### Materials

- computer with word processing software and printer
- computer printer and paper

---

# Read Aloud

## SET A PURPOSE
### Listen for Enjoyment
Point out that people often read and listen to poetry for enjoyment. Explain that poets often use lively language and interesting details to engage their audience. Read this poem aloud with expression, using voice cues to signal rising action. Have volunteers tell which part of the poem they thought was the most exciting.

## LISTENING STRATEGY
### Keep an Open Mind
Explain that many authors include personal experiences in their writing. When people listen to poetry, the way they think about a poem is often affected by their own experiences. Tell students that to fully appreciate a poem, they should keep an open mind as they listen to the poet's experience. It may help them think about their own experiences in a new way.

## Apple Picking
**by Erich Hoyt**

From the age of seven, I wanted
my own apple orchard. I collected seeds
from the tastiest apples, planting them around the yard.
But every two years we moved. I never got to pick an apple.

Later we bought a small farm in the mountains of western Canada.
Outside my window were fifteen apple trees—my dream orchard.
Apple blossoms filled the spring air. In the short, hot summer,
the green fruit soon showed red.

In autumn, as the evenings turned cooler, a mother black bear appeared
with twin cubs. The cubs climbed each tree to shake the apples down.
My precious apples! The bears ate until they were full—a loud crunching—
and kept coming back for more.

One dusky evening, walking out my back door, I almost bumped into the bears.
They looked up, crunching my apples all the while. I knew that bears might
either attack or retreat. They ran. But I ran faster—back into the house.

Thereafter the bears and I made a deal. They gathered apples
every evening. I picked by day. I put the perfect apples in crates
for winter. Bruised apples were made into juice, cider, or pies.
There were enough apples for bears and people.

- **What do you learn about the poet's childhood?**
  (Possible response: He lived on a farm in Canada. He moved around a lot.) IMPORTANT DETAILS

- **Why do you think the author wrote this piece?**
  (Responses will vary. Possible response: to share information about his childhood) POET'S PURPOSE

- **What details make it easy to picture the bear's actions?**
  (Possible response: details such as "climbed each tree to shake the apples down," and "They looked up, crunching my apples all the while.") POET'S CRAFT

# Question of the Day

## DEVELOP ORAL LANGUAGE

- Display the first question on Teaching Transparency 77, or write it on the board. Ask a volunteer to read it aloud.

- **Response Journal**  Explain to students that they should think about the question throughout the day and write their responses in their journals. Tell students to be prepared to discuss their responses to it by the end of the day or at another time you choose.

- You may want to repeat this process daily for each of the remaining discussion questions.

## OBJECTIVE

*To use cause-and-effect relation-ships to understand a character's motivations and actions*

### SKILL TRACE

**CAUSE AND EFFECT**

| Introduce | p. 150I |
|---|---|
| Reteach | pp. S36, S54, T36 |
| **Review** | **pp. 172, 230I, 250** |
| Test | Theme 2 |
| Maintain | p. 397B |

▼ **Teaching Transparency 78**

**CAUSE AND EFFECT**

- Identifying cause-and-effect relationships can help you better understand a character's feelings, actions, or motivations.
- To find an effect, ask *What happened?* To find a cause, ask *Why did this happen?*
- Sometimes an effect can cause something else to happen. Events often have more than one cause or effect.

**EXAMPLE**

When Leo woke up, it was raining. He felt frustrated because he could not go outside and work on the tree house he was building with his father. He sulked around the house all morning. Soon he got tired of feeling sorry for himself and decided to make the best of a rainy day. He gathered some board games and invited his brother and sister to play with him. They all had a good time. They knew there would be plenty of time for outdoor activities when the sun came out again.

| CAUSE | EFFECT |
|---|---|
| It was raining. | Leo could not go outside and work on his tree house. |
| Leo could not go outside and work on his tree house. | He felt frustrated. |
| Leo got tired of feeling sorry for himself. | He invited his sister and brother to play board games. |
| He invited his sister and brother to play board games. | They all had a good time. |

"The Garden of Happiness"
Side by Side, Theme 2          78          Focus Skill: Cause and Effect
                                            Harcourt

### BELOW-LEVEL

**Additional Support**
- *Intervention Teacher's Guide,* p. 90

### ENGLISH-LANGUAGE LEARNERS

**Additional Support**
- *English-Language Learners Teacher's Guide,* p. 51

# Focus Skill — Cause and Effect

### REVIEW THE SKILL

**Access prior knowledge.** Ask students what they would do if they wanted to do well on a test. (Possible response: pay close attention in class, study every night before the test) Explain that this is an example of a cause-and-effect relationship. The desire to do well on the test is the *cause*. Preparing for the test is the *effect*.

### TEACH/MODEL

Tell students that identifying the cause of a story character's actions will help them figure out why he or she behaves in a certain way.

- **Have a volunteer read aloud the bulleted items.**

- **Read the passage aloud. Point out that signal words such as *because* and *so* can reveal a cause-and-effect relationship.**

- **Explain to students that identifying cause-and-effect relation-ships will help them understand the reasons for a character's feelings or actions. Ask: Why does Leo feel frustrated?** (He can't go outside to work on his tree house because it is raining.)

**Text Structure** Explain that authors often use a cause-and-effect organization to clearly show how events in the plot are related.

### PRACTICE/APPLY

Students can use a cause-and-effect chart to map the cause-and-effect relationships in "The Garden of Happiness."

| Cause | Effect |
|---|---|
|  |  |

For opportunities to apply and reinforce the skill, see these pages:

**During reading:** pages 236, 238, and 240
**After reading:** *Pupil Edition* pages 250–251

 **Focus Strategy**

# Make and Confirm Predictions

## REVIEW THE STRATEGY

Remind students that good readers use strategies, such as **making and confirming predictions**, to help them understand a story. Good readers are active readers, and they use what they know and what they read to make predictions. Then they confirm or revise their predictions as they read.

## TEACH/MODEL

Use the example on Transparency 78 to model the strategy.

> **MODEL** What will Leo probably do when it stops raining? In the beginning of the passage, Leo is frustrated because he cannot work on his tree house. I predict that he will go outside and work on his tree house when the rain stops.

### SKILL ⟷ STRATEGY CONNECTION

Explain to students that as they read, they can use **cause-and-effect relationships** to help them **make predictions** about the characters and events in a story. Then they can try to confirm their predictions as they continue reading.

## PRACTICE/APPLY

Remind students to use the Make and Confirm Predictions strategy to help them be active readers. For opportunities to apply and reinforce the strategy **during reading**, see pages 237 and 241.

## Strategies Good Readers Use

- Use Decoding/Phonics
- **Make and Confirm Predictions**  *Focus Strategy*
- Create Mental Images
- Self-Question
- Summarize
- Read Ahead
- Reread to Clarify
- Use Context to Confirm Meaning
- Use Text Structure and Format
- Adjust Reading Rate

# Building Background

## ACCESS PRIOR KNOWLEDGE

Tell students that "The Garden of Happiness" is a story about how a girl and her neighbors improve their neighborhood by turning an empty lot into a community garden.

Discuss with students what they already know about helping others and about community projects. Then guide them to develop a chart like the one below.

| Helping Neighbors | Helping the Community |
|---|---|
| Take food to someone who is sick. | Take part in community activities. |
| Help elderly people with chores. | Clean up the streets. |
| Share tools. | Help build a community playground. |

technology

Visit *The Learning Site:*
**www.harcourtschool.com**
See Building Background.

## DEVELOP CONCEPTS

Help students use prior knowledge to develop concepts by asking the following questions:

- **How can picking up litter improve a community?** (Possible response: It can help clean up a neighborhood and make it safer.)

- **How can working in a community garden bring people together?** (Possible response: Working in a community garden can promote friendship among community members.)

- **How can working in a community garden benefit individuals?** (Possible response: Working in a garden can provide exercise and fresh food.)

### REACHING ALL LEARNERS

## Diagnostic Check: Vocabulary

**If** . . . students do not understand at least 4 of the 5 words . . .

**Then** . . . have them play a matching game with a partner using the word cards on page T60 and cards on which the definitions are written.

### ADDITIONAL SUPPORT ACTIVITIES

| BELOW-LEVEL | Reteach, p. S52 |
| ADVANCED | Extend, p. S53 |
| ENGLISH-LANGUAGE LEARNERS | Reteach, p. S53 |

# Vocabulary

## Vocabulary

**lavender** a light purple color
**haze** mist; fog
**inhaled** breathed in
**mural** a large painting on a wall
**skidded** slid or slipped across

## TEACH VOCABULARY STRATEGIES

**Use sentence and word context.** Point to the word lavender on Transparency 79. Remind students that they can sometimes confirm the meaning of an unfamiliar word by looking at surrounding words and sentences. Model using context to confirm the meaning of the word *lavender*.

**MODEL** I'm not sure what *lavender* means. The story says that the sky is changing from purple to *lavender*, so *lavender* must be a color. The sun is rising, which would make the sky lighter. I think *lavender* is a light purple color.

Have students use this strategy when they encounter other unfamiliar words as they read.

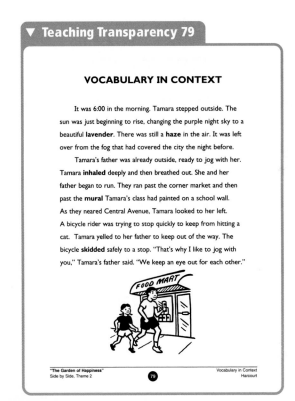

**▼ Teaching Transparency 79**

### VOCABULARY IN CONTEXT

It was 6:00 in the morning. Tamara stepped outside. The sun was just beginning to rise, changing the purple night sky to a beautiful **lavender**. There was still a **haze** in the air. It was left over from the fog that had covered the city the night before.

Tamara's father was already outside, ready to jog with her. Tamara **inhaled** deeply and then breathed out. She and her father began to run. They ran past the corner market and then past the **mural** Tamara's class had painted on a school wall. As they neared Central Avenue, Tamara looked to her left. A bicycle rider was trying to stop quickly to keep from hitting a cat. Tamara yelled to her father to keep out of the way. The bicycle **skidded** safely to a stop. "That's why I like to jog with you," Tamara's father said. "We keep an eye out for each other."

"The Garden of Happiness"
Side by Side, Theme 2

79

Vocabulary in Context
Harcourt

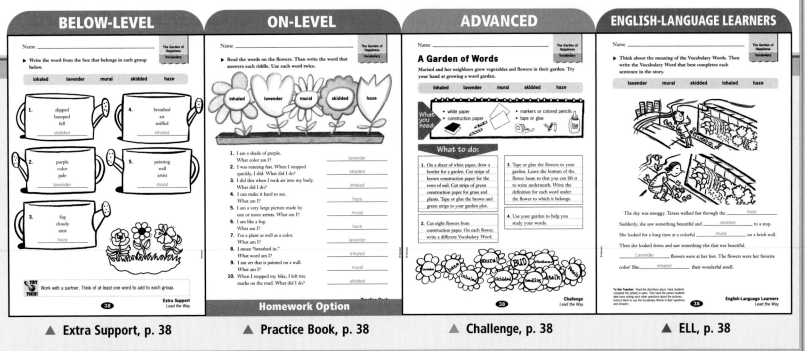

| BELOW-LEVEL | ON-LEVEL | ADVANCED | ENGLISH-LANGUAGE LEARNERS |
|---|---|---|---|

▲ Extra Support, p. 38   ▲ Practice Book, p. 38   ▲ Challenge, p. 38   ▲ ELL, p. 38

# Vocabulary Power

# Vocabulary Power

## APPLY STRATEGIES

Read aloud the first paragraph on page 230. Then ask students to read the remaining text silently. Remind them to apply the strategy of using sentence and word context to determine or confirm the meanings of unfamiliar words.

## EXTEND WORD KNOWLEDGE

**Practice other vocabulary strategies.** Ask students to answer questions with sentences that show what the vocabulary words mean. MEANINGFUL SENTENCES

- **If someone liked to only wear dark-colored clothing, would they wear a *lavender* shirt? Why or why not? EXPLANATION/COMPARE/CONTRAST**

- **Can you see clearly through *haze*? Why or why not? PRIOR KNOWLEDGE**

- **What is another word for *slid*? SYNONYMS**

- **How would you describe a *mural*? DESCRIPTION**

- **If you *inhaled*, did you breathe in or breathe out? How do you know? EXPLANATION**

▲ The Garden of Happiness

mural

lavender

inhaled

haze

skidded

You can plant many things in a garden. Herbs, flowers, and vegetables are just a few of the possibilities. These students are painting a picture of a flower garden.

The students' picture is a **mural** on a wall. Their mural shows a flower garden in bloom.

One part of the mural shows a girl smelling some flowers. The flowers are **lavender**, or light purple, in color. The girl has **inhaled**, or breathed in, to enjoy their sweet scent.

230

The flowers at the right side of the mural are partly hidden by **haze**, or fog. The students want to show that it is early morning and the sun hasn't reached that part of the garden yet.

Do you see the paintbrush on the floor? Maggie gave it a push, and it **skidded**, or slid, across the floor to Anthony.

### Vocabulary–Writing CONNECTION

**T**hink about a **mural** you would like to paint. Write a paragraph describing what it would look like.

231

 **QUICKWRITE**

**VOCABULARY–WRITING CONNECTION**

Tell students to use vivid, colorful words to describe their murals. Students should add their vivid words and the Vocabulary Power words to their Word Banks to use in future writing assignments.

# Prereading Strategies

## PREVIEW AND PREDICT

Have students read the **genre** information on page 232. Then have them preview the selection. Ask them to predict what will grow in "The Garden of Happiness." Have students begin a cause-and-effect chart. See Transparency F.

| Cause | Effect |
|---|---|
| Marisol watches her neighbors clean the empty lot. | Marisol wants a plot in the garden. |

Notable
Social Studies
Trade Book

### Genre

## Realistic Fiction

Realistic fiction has characters and events that are like people and events in real life.

In this selection, look for

● A setting that could be a real place

● Realistic characters and events

232

---

| **BELOW-LEVEL** | **ON-LEVEL** | **ADVANCED** | **ENGLISH-LANGUAGE LEARNERS** |
|---|---|---|---|
| Guide students as they preview the selection. Discuss the meanings of these words: *block*, *lot*, *funky*, and *plot*. Help students visualize the city scene. **SMALL GROUP** | Students can read the selection with a partner. Use the Guided Comprehension questions and Ongoing Assessments to gauge students' understanding. **WHOLE GROUP/PARTNER** | Students may read independently at their own pace. Encourage students to write their reactions to the story in their Reading Journals. **INDIVIDUAL/WHOLE CLASS** | Read aloud the selection or have students listen to it on *Audiotext 2*. Then have students read aloud selected pages as a group to develop oral fluency. **SMALL GROUP** |
| **ADDITIONAL SUPPORT**  *Intervention Reader: Moving Ahead Intervention Reader Teacher's Guide, pp. 90–93* | | | **ADDITIONAL SUPPORT** See *English-Language Learners Resource Kit*, Lesson 9. *English-Language Learners Teacher's Guide*, p. 51 |

# The Garden of Happiness

by Erika Tamar
illustrated by Barbara Lambase

On Marisol's block near East Houston Street, there was an empty lot that was filled with garbage and broken, tired things. It had a funky smell that made Marisol wrinkle her nose whenever she passed by.

One April morning, Marisol was surprised to see many grown-ups busy in the lot. Mr. Ortiz carried a rusty refrigerator door. Mrs. Willie Mae Washington picked up newspapers. Mr. Singh rolled a tire away.

The next afternoon, Marisol saw people digging up stones. Mr. Ortiz worked with a pickax.

233

## SET PURPOSE

**Read for enjoyment.** Remind students that one purpose for reading is for enjoyment. Ask students to set their own purposes for reading. Offer this suggestion:

**MODEL** **People seem to be working hard to clean up the empty lot. I'll read to find out how it turns out.**

**(Focus Strategy)** **Make and Confirm Predictions** Have students use this strategy to help them understand and enjoy what they read.

---

## COMPREHENSION CARD 9

**Think-Along** Use the Think-Along strategy to help students understand the key points of the text.

**Comprehension Card 9, page T50 ▶**

---

"The Garden of Happiness," "I do not plant my garden," and "The City" are available on *Audiotext 2.*

# Guided Comprehension

**1** **DRAW CONCLUSIONS** Why is Marisol surprised to see grown-ups busy in the empty lot? (Possible response: The empty lot has been ugly and dirty. People don't usually go there.)

**2** **CLASSIFY** What do the crops Mrs. Washington and Mr. Singh are planting have in common? (Possible response: The crops are the kinds of vegetables that grow in the places from which the people who are planting them came.)

**3** **FIGURATIVE LANGUAGE** Can a brick wall feel sad or have eyes? Why do you think the author describes the wall the way she does? (Possible response: no; to help readers picture it)

"*¿Qué pasa?*" Marisol asked.

Mrs. Willie Mae Washington leaned on her shovel and wiped her forehead. "I'm gonna grow black-eyed peas and greens and sweet potatoes, too," she said. "Like on my daddy's farm in Alabama. No more store-bought collard greens for me."

"We will call it The Garden of Happiness," Mr. Singh said. "I am planting *valore*—such a beautiful vine of lavender and red. Yes, everyone is happy when they see this bean from Bangladesh." **2**

On another day, Marisol watched Mr. Castro preparing the ground. Mrs. Rodriguez rolled a wheelbarrow full of peat moss. Marisol inhaled the fresh-soil smell of spring.

"Oh, I want to plant something in The Garden of Happiness!" Marisol said.

"Too late, *niña*," Mr. Ortiz said. "All the plots are already taken."

Marisol looked everywhere for a leftover spot, but the ground was crisscrossed by markers of sticks and string. She looked and looked. Just outside the chain-link fence, she found a bit of earth where the sidewalk had cracked.

"*¡Mira!* Here's my patch!" Marisol called. It was no bigger than her hand, but it was her very own. She picked out the pebbles and scraped the soil with a stick.

Marisol noticed a crowd of teenagers across the street from the lot. They were staring at a brick wall. It was sad and closed

## BELOW-LEVEL

Guide students in summarizing what they have read. Ask the following questions:

- How do Marisol's neighbors clean up the empty lot? (They carry the trash away, dig up stones, and prepare the ground for plants.)

- What do the neighbors plan to plant? (foods from their homelands or cultures)

- Does Marisol get her own plot? Why or why not? (No, all the plots are taken.)

Then have students read on to find out what Marisol plants.

up, without windows for eyes. Marisol crossed over to ask what they were doing.

"City Arts is giving us paint to make a mural on the wall," a girl told her. ❸

"What will it be?" Marisol asked.

"Don't know yet," one of the big boys said. "We haven't decided."

"I'm making a garden," Marisol said. "I haven't decided, either, about what to plant."

235

Monitor Progress

# Read Ahead

**Mr. Ortiz tells Marisol that all of the plots are taken. What is a plot?** (Possible response: a piece of land)

**If students were unable to answer, use this model:**

**MODEL** **When I first read the sentence, "All the plots are already taken," I am not sure what *plot* means. I read ahead to the next sentence. This sentence tells me that Marisol looks for a leftover spot, but all the ground is marked off with sticks and strings. *Plot* must mean "a small section of land."**

## CULTURAL CONNECTIONS

**Punctuation, Alphabets, and Pronunciation** Tell students that many languages have punctuation marks, alphabets, and pronunciations that are different from those used in English. Explain that in Spanish, for example, question marks are used at both the beginning and the end of a question. The mark at the beginning is upside-down. Help students pronounce these words: *habichuelas* (a•bē•chwe'las), *muy grande* (mwē gran'de), *apúrate* (a•poo'ra•te). Ask students to list other words they know from other languages.

Hello! ¡Hola!

# Guided Comprehension

**④** **(Focus Skill)** **CAUSE AND EFFECT** **When Marisol takes the flat seed, what effect does this have on the birds?** (It makes them angry.)

**⑤** **SEQUENCE** **After Marisol finds her patch in the Garden of Happiness, what does she do?** (She finds a seed, and then plants and waters it.)

**⑥** **CHARACTERS' EMOTIONS** **Is Marisol anxious to find out what her seed will turn into? How do you know?** (Possible response: Yes. She keeps asking her neighbors whether they know what it is. Also, she checks on it every day.)

**⑦** **DRAW CONCLUSIONS** **How is the teenagers' mural coming along? How can you tell?** (Possible response: They are not making very much progress. They are still measuring the wall and talking about what to paint.)

In The Garden of Happiness, the ground had become soft and dark. Mr. Castro talked to his seedlings as he placed them in straight rows. "Come on now, little baby things, grow nice and big for me."

Marisol had no seedlings or even small cuttings or roots. *What can I do*, she thought, *where can I find something to plant?*

She went to the corner where old Mrs. Garcia was feeding the pigeons. Marisol helped herself to a big flat seed. The birds fluttered about angrily. "Only one," she told them, "for my garden." **④**

Marisol skipped back to her patch. She poked a hole with her finger, dropped in the seed, and patted the soil all around. And every single day that spring, Marisol carried a watering can to the lot and gave her seed a cool drink. **⑤**

Before long, a green shoot broke through in Marisol's patch. Even on rainy days, she hurried to the lot to see. Soon there were two leaves on a strong, straight stalk, and then there were four. It became as high as Marisol's knee! **⑥**

236

**ENGLISH-LANGUAGE LEARNERS**

Draw students' attention to the words *dunno* and *gonna* on page 237. Write the words on the board, and write *don't know* and *going to* beneath them. Point out that *dunno* is a shortened version of *don't know* and that *gonna* is a shortened version of *going to*. Tell students that the author uses shorter slang forms of these words to give readers a sense of how people sometimes speak. Then ask students to identify other words on the page that are spelled as they are spoken. (somethin', lookin', thinkin')

| dunno |
| don't know |
| gonna |
| going to |

Green things were growing all around in The Garden of Happiness. Mr. Castro's tiny seedlings became big bushy things with ripe tomatoes shining like rubies.

"What's *my* plant?" Marisol asked. Now it reached to her shoulder. "What's it going to be?"

"Dunno," Mrs. Willie Mae Washington answered. "But it sure is *somethin'!*"

Marisol pulled out the weeds in the late afternoons, when it wasn't so summer-hot.

Sometimes she watched the teenagers across the street. They measured the wall. They talked and argued about what they would paint. **7**

Often Marisol saw Mr. Ortiz in his plot, resting in a chair.

"I come back from the factory and breathe the fresh air," he said. "And I sit among my *habichuelas,* my little piece of Puerto Rico."

"Is *my* plant from Puerto Rico? Do you know what it is?" Marisol asked.

Mr. Ortiz shook his head and laughed. "*¡Muy grande!* Maybe it's Jack's beanstalk from the fairy tale."

By the end of July, Marisol's plant had grown way over her head. And then, at the very top, Marisol saw a bud! It became fatter every day. She couldn't wait for it to open.

"Now don't be lookin' so hard," Mrs. Willie Mae Washington chuckled. "It's gonna open up behind your back, just when you're thinkin' about somethin' else."

237

## Monitor Progress

### Make and Confirm Predictions

**Will Marisol continue to take good care of her plant? Why do you think so?** (Possible response: Yes. She seems interested in the garden and spends time watering the plant.)

**Ask volunteers to model how they could use the Make and Confirm Predictions strategy to answer the question. If students have difficulty, provide this model:**

**MODEL** So far, Marisol has watered her plant every day and watched its growth carefully. I predict that she will continue to take good care of her plant. I will keep reading to confirm my predictions.

## SCIENCE

**Plants in the Food Chain** Explain to students that plants, or producers, play an essential role in every ecosystem. Plants are at the base of the food chain. They are the most basic source of energy for animals, or consumers, and decomposers, such as mushrooms, bacteria, and some insects. Ask students to illustrate the role of plants in a food chain. Have them show both a consumer and a decomposer getting energy from a plant.

# Guided Comprehension

**8** ⑧ (Focus Skill) **CAUSE AND EFFECT** **How do Mrs. Anderson and Mrs. Majewska react when they see the sunflower? What causes them to act this way?**
(Possible response: They both stop what they are doing and comment on the flower because it is so beautiful.)

**9** ⑨ **DRAW CONCLUSIONS** **Did Marisol plant a sunflower, a *słoneczniki* /swän•nek′•nēk/, or a *girasol*?**
(Possible response: The three words name the same flower in different languages.)

**10** ⑩ **DRAW CONCLUSIONS** **Are sunflowers popular? How do you know?**
(Possible response: Yes. All the neighbors recognize sunflowers or have some memory of them.)

238

## REACHING ALL LEARNERS

### Diagnostic Check: Comprehension and Skills

**If** . . . students are having difficulty understanding characters' actions . . .

**Then** . . . ask them to write a series of "why" questions about the characters' actions. Have students answer the questions to create cause-and-effect statements.

#### ADDITIONAL SUPPORT ACTIVITIES

| BELOW-LEVEL | Reteach, p. S54 |
| ADVANCED | Extend, p. S55 |
| ENGLISH-LANGUAGE LEARNERS | Reteach, p. S55 |

One morning, Marisol saw an amazing sight from halfway down the block. She ran the rest of the way. Standing higher than all the plants and vines in the garden was a flower as big as a plate! Her bud had turned into petals of yellow and gold.

"A sunflower!" Mrs. Anderson exclaimed as she pushed her shopping cart by. "Reminds me of when I was a girl in Kansas."

Mrs. Majewska was rushing on her way to the subway, but she skidded to a stop. "Ah, słoneczniki! So pretty in the fields of Poland!" **8**

Old Mrs. Garcia shook her head. "No, no, los girasoles from Mexico, where they bring joy to the roadside." **9 10**

239

**ONGOING ASSESSMENT**

Monitor Progress

# Use Decoding/ Phonics

Have students reading below-level read aloud the second paragraph on page 239. Listen for their reading of the word *sunflower*. If students have difficulty, model the strategy.

**MODEL** When I come to a longer word, such as *sunflower*, I can try breaking the word into smaller parts. I see the root words *sun* and *flower*. When I blend these parts together, I read the word as /sun′flou•ər/.

## LITERARY ANALYSIS

**Similes** Explain to students that a simile is a comparison that uses *like* or *as*. Sometimes authors use this type of figurative language to help the reader picture something in the story. Read aloud the following example from the selection: *Standing higher than all the plants and vines in the garden was a flower as big as a plate!*

The author has compared the flower to a plate to help the reader get an idea of how big the flower is. Ask students to write other similes about sunflowers. (Possible responses: The sunflower was as yellow as a banana.)

**The sunflower was as yellow as a banana.**

# Guided Comprehension

**11** **UNDERSTAND FIGURATIVE LANGUAGE** Can Marisol's sunflower feel happy or sad? What do you think the author means by *the happiest plant in the Garden of Happiness*? (Possible response: No; its bright color gives a feeling of happiness, more than other plants do.)

**12** **SUMMARIZE** What happens to the Garden of Happiness in autumn? (Possible response: The vegetables get ripe; people pick the vegetables and dig the sweet potatoes; Marisol's sunflower starts to die.)

**13** (Focus Skill) **CAUSE AND EFFECT** What effect does water have on Marisol's dying plant? (None; the plant's leaves continue to dry up and drop off.)

"I guess sunflowers make themselves right at home in every sun-kissed place on earth," Mrs. Willie Mae Washington said.

"Even right here in New York City," Marisol said proudly. The flower was a glowing circle, brighter than a yellow taxi. *A flower of sunshine*, Marisol thought, *the happiest plant in The Garden of Happiness.* **11**

All summer long, it made the people on the street stop and smile.

Soon the air became cool and crisp with autumn. Mr. Castro picked the last of his tomatoes. Mr. Singh carried away a basket full of beans. Mrs. Rodriguez picked her *tomatillos*. "To dry and cut up for *salsa*," she said.

Mrs. Willie Mae Washington dug up orange potatoes. "I can almost smell my sweet potato pie." She winked at Marisol. "I'm gonna save an extra big slice for a good little gardener I know."

But something terrible was happening to Marisol's flower. Its leaves were turning brown and dry. **12**

240

## ADVANCED

Ask students to use an online language dictionary to find the spellings, pronunciations, and meanings of five words from a language other than English. Challenge students to write a dialogue between two speakers that uses these words. When they have finished, students can work in pairs to act out their dialogues.

¿Qué pasa?

Marisol watered and watered until a stream ran down the sidewalk. But her flower's leaves began to fall.

"Please get well again," Marisol whispered.

Every day, more golden petals curled and faded.

"My flower of sunshine is sick," Marisol cried. "What should I do?" **13**

241

ONGOING ASSESSMENT

## Monitor Progress

### (Focus Strategy) Make and Confirm Predictions

Did you expect Marisol's seed to grow into a sunflower? (Responses will vary.)

Have students model how they could use the Make and Confirm Predictions strategy to answer the question.

**MODEL** The story didn't give me much information on which to base a prediction. However, I know that sunflower seeds are often fed to birds, so I wasn't surprised that this is what Marisol grew.

## REREADING FOR FLUENCY

**Readers Theatre**   Have students work in small groups to prepare a Readers Theatre performance of part of "The Garden of Happiness." Group members can select roles, with one person reading the narrator's line. To present the performance, have students face the audience and read aloud their lines. **LISTENING/ SPEAKING/READING**

**Note:** For assessment of oral reading accuracy and fluency, see pages T44–T46.

*The Garden of Happiness*     **241**

# Guided Comprehension

**Did "The Garden of Happiness" turn out as you thought it would? What did you like best about it?** Discuss with students whether their purposes for reading were met.

# Think and Respond

**Answers:**

**1** Possible response: She is happy watching her sunflower grow. At the end of summer, she is sad because her sunflower is dying. **SUMMARIZE**

**2** Possible response: The teenagers have painted a mural of Marisol's sunflower. Readers see what Marisol sees. **AUTHOR'S CRAFT/IMAGERY**

**3** Possible response: Everyone can see her sunflower. **DRAW CONCLUSIONS**

**4** Possible response: Yes; Marisol's neighbors are cooperative and respectful. **PERSONAL RESPONSE**

**5** Responses will vary. **READING STRATEGIES**

## OPEN-ENDED RESPONSE

Have students write a paragraph that describes how the garden made Marisol's neighborhood a better place.

---

"Oh, child," Mrs. Willie Mae Washington said. "Its season is over. There's a time to bloom and a time to die."

"No! I don't want my flower to die!"

"*Mi cariño,* don't cry," Mrs. Rodriguez said. "That's the way of a garden. You must save the seeds and plant again next spring."

Marisol's flower drooped to the ground. The Garden of Happiness wasn't happy for her anymore. The vines had tumbled down. The bushy green plants were gone. She

collected the seeds and put them in her pocket, but spring was much too far away.

Marisol was too sad to go to the empty lot anymore. For a whole week, she couldn't even look down the block where her beautiful flower used to be.

Then one day she heard people calling her name.

"Marisol! Come quick!"

"Marisol! *¡Apúrate!* Hurry!"

A golden haze shone on the street. There was a big crowd, like on a holiday. Music from the *bodega* was loud and bright. And what she saw made Marisol laugh and dance and clap her hands.

242

---

**COMPREHENSION**

**End-of-Selection Test**
To evaluate comprehension, see *Practice Book*, pages A33–A36.

# Think and Respond

**1** How do Marisol's feelings about the garden change from the spring to the end of summer?

**2** At the end of the story, what information do you get from a picture rather than from words? Why do you think the author chose to end the story this way?

**3** Why does the **mural** make Marisol so happy?

**4** Do you think Marisol's neighborhood is a good example of how people should get along? Explain your answer.

**5** What reading strategies did you use as you read this story? How were they helpful?

243

---

**Name** _____ **Date** _____

*The Garden of Happiness*

**Directions: For items 1–18, fill in the circle in front of the correct answer. For items 19–20, write the answer.**

**Vocabulary**

**1.** Our car _____ on the ice, but luckily, we were able to stop safely.
Ⓐ mural Ⓑ skidded
Ⓒ haze Ⓓ inhaled

**2.** I _____ deeply when my mother took a freshly baked loaf of bread from the oven.
Ⓐ haze Ⓑ inhaled
Ⓒ venture Ⓓ lavender

**3.** The color _____ is a light shade of purple.
Ⓐ mural Ⓑ yellow
Ⓒ red Ⓓ lavender

**4.** The _____ that filled the sky made it hard to see the mountains.
Ⓐ haze Ⓑ lavender
Ⓒ mural Ⓓ burrows

**5.** In our city, each school painted a _____ on the side of a tall building.
Ⓐ lavender Ⓑ skidded
Ⓒ mural Ⓓ inhaled

**Comprehension**

**6.** Most of the story takes place in _____.
Ⓐ an empty lot Ⓑ a garage
Ⓒ an apartment building Ⓓ Marisol's home

**A33**
Practice Book
*Lead the Way*

▲ **Practice Book, p. A33**

---

**Name** _____ **Date** _____

**18.** Why is the garden called The Garden of Happiness?
Ⓐ It makes everyone happy to grow and raise vegetables there.
Ⓑ No one can be sad in such a pretty place.
Ⓒ It is a good name for an empty lot.
Ⓓ Everyone thinks that a happy garden name will make the vegetables grow well.

**19.** What does Mrs. Rodriguez explain to Marisol about the sunflower?

_____
_____
_____
_____
_____
_____
_____

**20.** Why does everyone call Marisol to the street?

_____
_____
_____
_____
_____
_____
_____
_____

36

Theme 2 • *The Garden of Happiness*

▲ **Practice Book, p. A36**

---

### RETELL

Use these questions to guide students as they retell "The Garden of Happiness."
• **Where does the selection take place?**
• **What happens to the seed that Marisol plants?**
• **What is the main idea of this selection?**

### SUMMARIZE

Encourage students to summarize the selection using their completed cause-and-effect charts. See Transparency F on page T52.

▼ **Teaching Transparency F**

#### CAUSE-AND-EFFECT CHART

| Cause | Effect |
|---|---|
| Marisol watches her neighbors clean the empty lot. | Marisol wants a plot in the garden. |
| Marisol sees Mrs. Garcia feeding seeds to the birds. | She takes a seed and plants it in the garden. |
| Marisol takes good care of her seed. | Her seed grows into a sunflower. |
| Autumn comes. | Marisol's sunflower dies. |
| Marisol's sunflower dies. | Marisol is sad. |
| Marisol sees the mural with the sunflower. | Marisol feels better. |

"The Garden of Happiness"
Side by Side, Theme 2
**F**
Graphic Organizers
Harcourt

### WRITTEN SUMMARY

Have students use their completed cause-and-effect charts to write a summary telling how the neighbors worked to make the neighborhood a better place. PERFORMANCE ASSESSMENT

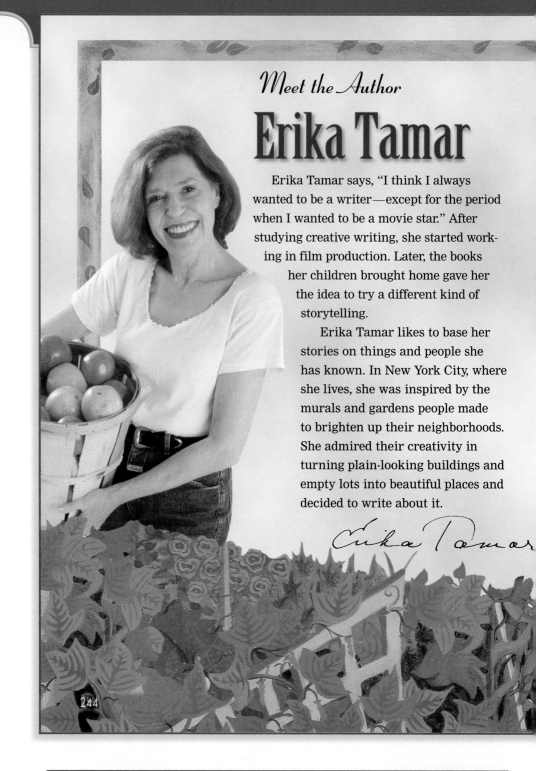

## Meet the Author

# Erika Tamar

Erika Tamar says, "I think I always wanted to be a writer—except for the period when I wanted to be a movie star." After studying creative writing, she started working in film production. Later, the books her children brought home gave her the idea to try a different kind of storytelling.

Erika Tamar likes to base her stories on things and people she has known. In New York City, where she lives, she was inspired by the murals and gardens people made to brighten up their neighborhoods. She admired their creativity in turning plain-looking buildings and empty lots into beautiful places and decided to write about it.

244

## ABOUT THE AUTHOR

**Erica Tamar** believes that movies and television offer good ways to tell stories, but her favorite way to tell stories is by writing them. "The Garden of Happiness" was inspired by sights in her hometown; she would also like to write about her experiences as a child actress and about helping to produce a live television show for five years.

Invite students to talk about experiences of their own that they think would make good stories and to tell why these would interest readers.

**TECHNOLOGY**
**Visit** *The Learning Site:*
**www.harcourtschool.com**

## *Meet the Illustrator*
# Barbara Lambase

Barbara Lambase loves gardens and thinks they are a perfect way of bringing people together. She wanted to illustrate *The Garden of Happiness* because it showed people from different cultures working together and caring about their neighborhood. From her parents, Barbara Lambase learned to respect all cultures. She enjoys visiting other countries and tries not to miss a museum.

Barbara Lambase has won many awards for her artwork. When she is not painting or thinking about painting, she enjoys animals, gardening, good conversation, reading, and the radio. Her dog, her cat, and the radio are her painting companions. She lives in California.

*Barbara Lambase*

**Visit** *The Learning Site!*
**www.harcourtschool.com**

245

## ABOUT THE ILLUSTRATOR

**Barbara Lambase** says that her work as a painter and illustrator is her passion and that everything else is a hobby. One of her favorite hobbies is traveling. Ms. Lambase has said that she and her husband "both hope to see much of this world in our lives." They have already seen Greece, Italy, France, and Switzerland.

# Reading Across Texts

## INTRODUCING THE POEMS

**Genre Study**   Draw students' attention to the first line of the poem on page 246. Guide students to see that the first line acts as the title. Have volunteers read aloud the titles of both poems. Then have students predict what the poems will be about. (Possible responses: The first poem might be about a wild garden; the second poem might be about a city garden.)

## APPRECIATING THE POEMS

Ask students to read both poems silently, paying attention to the way the words are laid out. Then read both poems aloud. Ask:

1 **MAIN IDEA**   In "I do not plant my garden," what garden does the poet write about? (nature)

2 **IMPORTANT DETAILS**   What is unusual about the flowers in the poem "The City"? (They grow out of cracks in the sidewalk.)

## REREADING FOR A PURPOSE

**Understanding Mood**   Have one group of students read aloud "I do not plant my garden" and "The City" while a second group acts them out, pantomiming, as appropriate. Then discuss whether the mood of the poems is happy or sad. (happy)

Genre
Poetry

*I do not plant my garden,*
but every year it appears.
On summer days I go out hunting
for those ripe wild raspberries
that glow so red against the leafy green
along the forest's edge. And then I watch as
catbirds! thrushes! bluebirds!
gobble berries, too.
On summer days I go out
hunting the tart and sweet blueberries
that lie hidden under clusters of leaves
down low, or high, in trees. And then I watch
as cedar waxwings eat the ones I've left.
This garden is for all of us—
for me and for the birds,
for all the hunters and the gatherers,
for the turtles, the chipmunks, and the slugs,
for the bees, the butterflies,
and the bugs. 1

*written and illustrated by Lynne Cherry*

Award-Winning Author

## TEXT STRUCTURE AND FORMAT

**Unusual Punctuation**   Direct students' attention to line 7 of the poem on page 246. Point out that the poet places exclamation points after the names of birds in the middle of a sentence. Explain that poets sometimes use punctuation in unusual ways to emphasize certain words or to change the rhythm of the poem. In this poem, the exclamation points signal the reader to emphasize the name of each bird.

catbirds!     thrushes!     bluebirds!

# The City

If flowers want to grow
right out of the concrete sidewalk cracks
I'm going to bend down to smell them. 2

*written by David Ignatow*
*illustrated by Erika LeBarre*

247

## related books

You may want to recommend these titles to students interested in this subject.

### LIBRARY BOOKS COLLECTION

**Under the Lemon Moon**
by Edith Hope Fine.
1999.

### ADDITIONAL READING

• *Wanda's Roses*
by Pat Brisson. Boyds Mills, 2000. **EASY**

• *June 29, 1999*
by David Wiesner. Houghton Mifflin, 1992.
**AVERAGE**

• *Brooklyn Doesn't Rhyme*
by Joan W. Blos. Scribner, 1994. **CHALLENGING**

## ABOUT THE POETS

**Lynne Cherry** has written and illustrated numerous children's books, including *The Great Kapok Tree*, which was a Teachers' Choice for 1991 and an Outstanding Science Trade Book for Children. Ms. Cherry is a lover of nature and the outdoors.

**David Ignatow** has published more than fifteen volumes of poetry and three prose collections, including *Whisper to the Earth* and *Shadowing the Ground*. Mr. Ignatow has received many honors, including an award for a lifetime of creative effort from the National Institute of Arts and Letters, and the Poetry Society of America's Shelley Memorial Award.

# Making Connections

## COMPARE TEXTS

**Answers:**

**1** Possible response: The neighbors work together to create a community garden. The teenagers work together to paint a mural for everyone to enjoy. **THEME**

**2** Possible response: They are from different cultures, and they grow different kinds of plants. They all love gardening and respect their neighbors. **COMPARE AND CONTRAST**

**3** Possible responses: The garden in "I do not plant my garden" is not planted by people, as the one in the story is. The poet thinks of plants growing wild in nature as a kind of garden. **MAKE COMPARISONS**

**4** Responses will vary. **EXPRESS PERSONAL OPINION**

**5** Possible responses: attend community meetings; check the community website; listen for announcements on local television or radio stations. **INQUIRY**

▲ The Garden of Happiness

# Making Connections

## Compare Texts

**1** How do the characters in "The Garden of Happiness" work together?

**2** How are the neighbors who plant the garden different from each other? How are they alike?

**3** How is the garden in the poem "I do not plant my garden" different from the garden in the story?

**4** Think of another realistic fiction story that has a surprise ending. Which ending did you like better, and why?

**5** How could you find out more about community projects where you live?

### Write to Explain

**M**arisol's fellow gardeners talk about the special dishes they plan to make. Think about something you know how to make, such as a favorite sandwich. Write a paragraph that explains the steps involved. Use a graphic organizer like this to organize your steps.

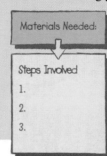

Materials Needed:

Steps Involved
1.
2.
3.

Writing
CONNECTION

248

## Make a Booklet

Did you know that sunflowers are also an important farm crop? Research where and how sunflowers are grown and how they are used for foods and other products. Look for information in an encyclopedia or in nonfiction books on farm crops and gardening. Create a booklet of information about sunflowers.

**Science CONNECTION**

## Paint a Mural

Work with a group to create a mural to display on a wall in your classroom or school. Brainstorm ideas for an interesting mural. Choose the idea you like best, or combine several ideas that work well together. Sketch the mural lightly in pencil on a long strip of paper. Use markers or paints and brushes to complete it.

**Art CONNECTION**

249

---

## HOMEWORK FOR THE WEEK

Students and family members can work together to complete the activities on page T65. You may want to assign some or all of the activities as homework for each day of the week.

**TECHNOLOGY**
**Visit** *The Learning Site:*
**www.harcourtschool.com**
See Resources for Parents and Teachers: Homework Helper.

**Teacher's Edition p. T65** ▶

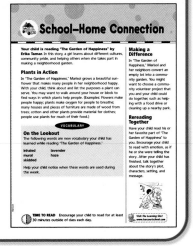

### School–Home Connection

**Your child is reading "The Garden of Happiness" by Erika Tamar.** In this story, a girl learns about different cultures, community pride, and helping others when she takes part in making a neighborhood garden.

**Plants in Action**
In "The Garden of Happiness," Marisol grows a beautiful sunflower that makes many people in her neighborhood happy. With your child, think about and list the purposes a plant can serve. You may want to walk around your house or block to find ways in which plants help people. (Examples: Flowers make people happy; plants make oxygen for people to breathe; many houses and pieces of furniture are made of wood from trees; cotton and other plants provide material for clothes; people use plants for much of their food.)

**VOCABULARY**

**On the Lookout**
The following words are new vocabulary your child has learned while reading "The Garden of Happiness."

inhaled        lavender
mural          haze
skidded

Help your child notice when these words are used during the week.

**Making a Difference**
In "The Garden of Happiness," Marisol and her neighbors convert an empty lot into a community garden. You might want to choose a community volunteer project that you and your child could do together, such as helping with a food drive or cleaning up a nearby park.

**Rereading Together**
Have your child read his or her favorite part of "The Garden of Happiness" to you. Encourage your child to read with emotion, as if he or she were telling the story. After your child has finished, talk together about the story's plot, characters, setting, and message.

**TIME TO READ** Encourage your child to read for at least 30 minutes outside of class each day.

*Visit The Learning Site!* www.harcourtschool.com

---

### WRITING

**Write to Explain** Have students write a paragraph that explains how to make or do something. Ask students to use a graphic organizer like the one below to plan their steps.

**PORTFOLIO OPPORTUNITY**
Students may choose to place their how-to paragraphs in their working portfolios.

### SCIENCE

**Make a Booklet** Have students research where and how sunflowers grow and how they are used for food and other products. Ask students to use the information they find to create an informational booklet on sunflowers.

### ART

**Paint a Mural** Have students work in groups to brainstorm subjects for a mural. Ask students to choose the idea they like best or combine several ideas that work well together.

# Cause and Effect

| SKILL TRACE | |
|---|---|
| **CAUSE AND EFFECT** | |
| Introduce | p. 150I |
| Reteach | pp. S36, S54, T36 |
| **Review** | **pp. 172, 230I, 250** |
| Test | Theme 2 |
| Maintain | p. 397B |

## RETURN TO THE SKILL

Have students read page 250 in the *Pupil Edition*. You may want to use this model:

**MODEL** Recognizing causes and effects can help me understand why characters in a story act and feel as they do. This chart shows several causes and effects related to Marisol's behavior.

Ask students how recognizing causes and effects helped them understand "The Garden of Happiness."

## PRACTICE/APPLY

Students can work individually to complete a cause-and-effects web. Ask students to think of three effects of doing something nice for someone. Then have them complete their webs. Students can present their webs to the class. PERFORMANCE ASSESSMENT

**TECHNOLOGY** ■ *Mission: Comprehension™ Skills Practice CD-ROM* provides additional practice with reading comprehension and focus skills.

**Visit** *The Learning Site:* **www.harcourtschool.com**
See Skill Activities and Test Tutors: Cause and Effect.

▲ **The Garden of Happiness**

# Cause and Effect ( Focus Skill )

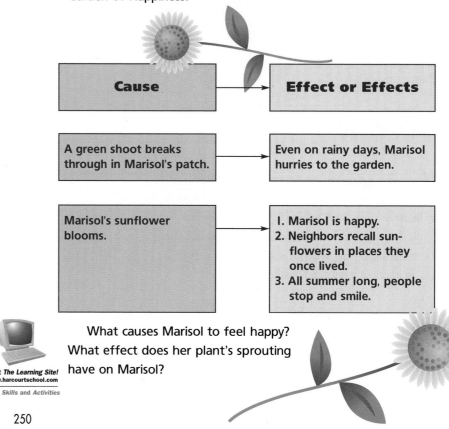

**R**emember that a **cause** is an action or event that makes something happen. An **effect** is what happens as a result of an action or event. An event may have more than one cause or effect. Understanding causes and effects can help you understand why characters in a story feel or act as they do. Look at this chart, which shows causes and effects in "The Garden of Happiness."

| Cause | Effect or Effects |
|---|---|
| A green shoot breaks through in Marisol's patch. | Even on rainy days, Marisol hurries to the garden. |
| Marisol's sunflower blooms. | 1. Marisol is happy.<br>2. Neighbors recall sunflowers in places they once lived.<br>3. All summer long, people stop and smile. |

What causes Marisol to feel happy? What effect does her plant's sprouting have on Marisol?

**Visit** *The Learning Site!*
**www.harcourtschool.com**
*See Skills and Activities*

250

---

**REACHING ALL LEARNERS**

## Diagnostic Check: Comprehension and Skills

**If** . . . students are having difficulty understanding a character's motivation . . .

**Then** . . . ask them to write a series of "why" questions about the character's actions. Have students use them to write cause-and-effect statements.

### ADDITIONAL SUPPORT ACTIVITIES

| BELOW-LEVEL | Reteach, p. S54 |
| ADVANCED | Extend, p. S55 |
| ENGLISH-LANGUAGE LEARNERS | Reteach, p. S55 |

**Focus Skill**

## Test Prep
### Cause and Effect

▶ **Read the passage. Then answer the questions.**

> Juan liked his new home, but he missed the flower garden he had at his house in Puerto Rico. One day, Juan found an old bucket with a small hole in it. Juan had an idea. He filled the bucket with soil, planted some seeds, and set it by the front steps of his apartment house. No one passing in the street noticed the old bucket until at last the flowers bloomed. Then Juan saw people pointing to the bright red and yellow flowers. Their frowns turned to smiles at the beautiful sight.

**1. Why does Juan plant seeds in the bucket?**

  **A**  to make people smile

  **B**  so people will point at his flowers

  **C**  so people will bring him more containers

  **D**  because he misses his flower garden

**Tip**

Two of the choices tell what happens after Juan plants his garden. Only one answer tells why he planted it.

**2. What happens as a result of the flowers' blooming?**

  **F**  People frown.

  **G**  People smile.

  **H**  People start buying old buckets.

  **J**  No one notices the flowers.

**Tip**

The words *as a result* in the question tell you that you need to identify the effect of the event described in the question.

251

## Test Prep

**Cause and Effect** Have students read the passage carefully, looking for the actions or events that make things happen and the results of these actions or events. Remind them that an event may have more than one cause or effect. Use the Tips to reinforce good test-taking strategies. (I.D; 2.G)

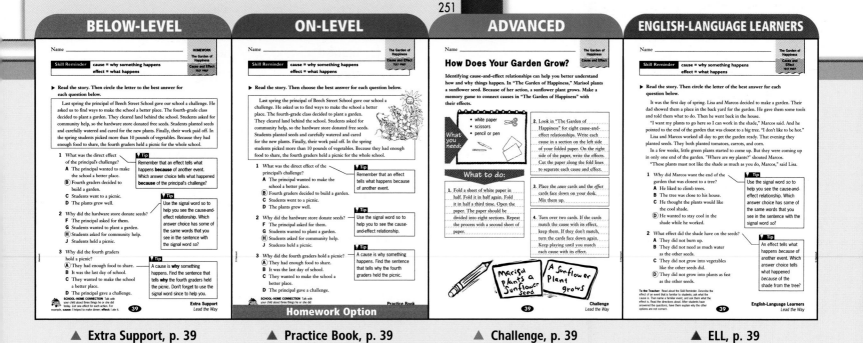

▲ **Extra Support, p. 39**    ▲ **Practice Book, p. 39**    ▲ **Challenge, p. 39**    ▲ **ELL, p. 39**

## OBJECTIVE

*To use knowledge of closed syllables to pronounce and read words*

### SKILL TRACE

**SYLLABLES: CLOSED SYLLABLES**

| Introduce | Grade 2 |
|---|---|
| **Maintain** | **p. 251A** |

### ONGOING ASSESSMENT

**If** students are not able to fluently read approximately 99 words per minute, **then** they require phonics instruction and will also benefit from fluency practice.

**NOTE:** For assessment of oral reading accuracy and fluency, see pages T44–T46.

# Decoding/Phonics

*Syllables: Closed Syllables*

### MAINTAIN THE SKILL

**Decode words with closed syllables.** Write the word *picnic* on the board, and say it aloud. Model breaking the word into syllables. Slide your hand under *pic* as students say /pik/. Then slide your hand under *nic* as students say /nik/. Ask students what vowel sound they hear in the first syllable. (the /i/ sound) Tell students that a closed syllable is one in which the single vowel sound is followed by a consonant. Closed syllables have a short vowel sound.

Write the word *napkin* on the board. Ask students to find the pattern of vowel and consonant letters and tell whether each syllable is open or closed. (closed) Cover the second syllable, and ask students to pronounce the first. Uncover the second syllable, and ask students why it is a closed syllable. (because the single vowel *i* is closed in by the consonants *k* and *n*) Have students blend the syllables to say the word *napkin*.

### PRACTICE/APPLY

**Decode longer words.** Write on the board the words in this chart.

| | |
|---|---|
| ribbon | mitten |
| pencil | basket |
| biggest | hundred |
| tunnel | cotton |

Ask a volunteer to read the first word aloud and use it in a short sentence. Then work with students to divide the words into syllables and to blend the syllables to read the words. Have students identify the vowel sound they hear in the first syllable of each word. Revisit the selection with students and ask them to identify and pronounce words with closed syllables. **PERFORMANCE ASSESSMENT**

# Figurative Language

## Literary Response and Analysis

### REVIEW THE SKILL

**Discuss figurative language.** Remind students that figurative language includes expressions that mean something different from the exact meaning of the individual words. Point out that in "The Garden of Happiness," the author describes some objects and plants as though they have feelings or can do things that people can do. Explain that this is called **personification**. Write on the board the following sentence from the story:

**I guess sunflowers make themselves right at home in every sun-kissed place on earth.**

Draw attention to the expressions *make themselves right at home* and *every sun-kissed place on earth*. Model interpreting personification.

> **MODEL** **I know that sunflowers can't actually go somewhere or make themselves at home. I also know that the sun can't kiss the earth. I think the sentence means that sunflowers can grow anywhere the sun is shining.**

### PRACTICE/APPLY

**Hunt for figurative language.** Have students look for examples of figurative language in other stories. Have them use a dictionary to find literal meanings. Then have small groups talk about what they think each expression means. Have students fill in a chart like the one below. **PERFORMANCE ASSESSMENT**

| Figurative Language | What Each Word Means by Itself | What the Words Mean Together |
|---|---|---|
|  |  |  |
|  |  |  |

**Summarize.** Have a volunteer summarize what he or she knows about figurative language and personification. (Possible response: Figurative language expressions mean something different from the exact meanings of the words. Personification is giving objects human qualities.)

**SKILL TRACE**

**FIGURATIVE LANGUAGE**

| Introduce | pp. 173A–173B |
|---|---|
| Reteach | p. T37 |
| **Review** | **pp. 205B, 251B** |
| Test | Theme 2 |
| Maintain | p. 589D |

**ENGLISH-LANGUAGE LEARNERS**

You may want to work with students to create a glossary of the figurative language expressions they have learned so far. Encourage them to add expressions to the glossary as they come across more examples.

# Writing Process

# How-to Essay

## Writing Process: Expository Writing

### TRAITS OF GOOD WRITING

| | INTRODUCE AND PRACTICE | APPLY TO LONGER WRITING FORMS |
|---|---|---|
| Focus/Ideas | 421E–F | 453E–F, 471C–D |
| Organization | 521E–F, 543E–F | 567C–D, 589E–F |
| Voice | 49E–F, 77E–F | 101C–D, 123C–D |
| Word Choice | 637E–F, 667E–F | 689C–D, 713C–D |
| Development | 421E–F, 437C–D | 453E–F, 471C–D |
| Effective Sentences | 299E–F, 325C–D | 349C–D, 371C–D |
| **Effective Paragraphs** | 173E–F, 205C–D | 229E–F, 251C–D |
| Conventions | (See Grammar and Spelling Lessons.) | (Applied to all writing lessons.) |

## technology

Writing Express™ CD-ROM
Visit *The Learning Site*:
www.harcourtschool.com
See Writing Detective:
Proofreading Makes Perfect.

### TRAITS OF GOOD WRITING

- **Focus/Ideas:** The writer clearly states in the introduction the process the reader will learn about. The writer gives details and elaborates on important ideas.

- **Organization/Effective Paragraphs:** The materials are listed. The steps are clearly presented in the correct order, with a paragraph for each step.

- **Voice:** The writer speaks directly to the reader, and the tone is friendly.

- **Development:** The writer uses interesting details.

- **Word Choice:** The writer uses specific verbs such as *slice*, *beat*, and *dip*, and time-order words.

- **Effective Sentences:** The writer varies the length and complexity of the sentences to hold the reader's attention.

**251C  Side by Side**

## DAY 1  TEACH/MODEL

### CONNECT READING TO WRITING

Remind students that in "The Garden of Happiness," Marisol had to follow certain steps to grow and care for her plant. Ask students to name the steps Marisol followed to help her plant grow.

Tell students that they will be writing an essay to explain how to make or do something.

### REVIEW WRITER'S CRAFT  Display Transparency 80, and read the model with students. Ask students to analyze how the writer creates effective paragraphs. Explain to students that ordering ideas and using sequence words will help them write effective paragraphs.

### ▼ Teaching Transparency 80

**STUDENT MODEL: HOW-TO ESSAY**

A how-to essay tells others how to do or make something. A student wrote the following how-to essay to tell a friend how to prepare breaded eggplant.

| | |
|---|---|
| **introduction** | How to Make Breaded Eggplant
My favorite dish is breaded eggplant. My mother and I have a great recipe for this delicious food! |
| **materials needed** | Before you start, set out bread crumbs, an egg, an eggplant, two large plates, and a bowl. |
| **steps in order** | The first step is to have an adult slice the eggplant. Each slice should be half an inch thick. At the same time, you can put some bread crumbs on one of the plates. |
| **time-order words** | Next, beat the egg in the bowl. After that, dip the eggplant into the egg and then into the bread crumbs. Put the breaded slices on the other plate.
Finally, have the adult fry the slices. They turn golden brown in just a few minutes.
Now that you know the steps, you can make this wonderful dish anytime! |

"The Garden of Happiness"
Side by Side, Theme 2 — 80 — Writing: How-to Essay
Harcourt

## DAY 2  ANALYZE AND PREWRITE

### ANALYZE THE WRITING PROMPT

Have students use this prompt or brainstorm their own ideas.

**WRITING PROMPT:** *Most students have a special food or craft they know how to make. Before you begin writing, think about how you make the food or craft. Now explain to a classmate how to make your food or craft.*

### ASK THE FOLLOWING QUESTIONS:

- **What are you explaining?**
- **What materials are needed?**
- **What are the steps in the process?**
- **What details should you add?**

### ▼ Teaching Transparency 81

**HOW-TO ESSAY**

| Topic: | Audience: |
|---|---|

Materials needed:

First Step/Details:

Second Step/Details:

Third Step/Details:

Final Step/Details:

"The Garden of Happiness"
Side by Side, Theme 2 — 81 — Writing: How-to Essay
Harcourt

# 5 Day Plan

## DAY 3 — DRAFT

Have students use the steps below to draft their essays:

1. **Introduce** the topic in an interesting way. List all materials needed.

2. **Organize** ideas. Put the steps of the process in order.

3. **Provide** details the reader needs to perform the process. Use descriptive words.

4. **Create** a strong conclusion. Tell the result or outcome of the process.

## DAY 4 — EDIT

**REVISE** Have students work in pairs or small groups to discuss their how-to essays. Encourage them to focus on whether the steps are in the correct order and whether they are described in enough detail to allow the reader to perform the process.

Have students use the rubric on page T56 or T57 to revise their essays.

**PROOFREAD** Have students use these questions as they proofread:

- **Does each sentence begin with a capital letter and end with the correct punctuation mark?**
- **Are words spelled correctly?**
- **Are paragraphs indented?**

## DAY 5 — PUBLISH AND ASSESS

**PUBLISH** Students may publish their how-to paragraphs in a class recipe book or a class craft book. Place the books in the Library Center. Students may also want to take turns demonstrating their processes to classmates.

**ASSESS** Have students use the student rubric on page T56 or T57 to evaluate their own and one another's work. They should add their paragraphs and their evaluations to their portfolios.

### SCORING RUBRIC

| | 4 | 3 | 2 | 1 |
|---|---|---|---|---|
| **FOCUS/IDEAS** | Completely focused, purposeful. | Generally focused on task and purpose. | Somewhat focused on task and purpose. | Lacks focus and purpose. |
| **ORGANIZATION/ PARAGRAPHS** | Ideas progress logically; transitions make the relationships among ideas clear. | Organization mostly clear, but some lapses occur; some transitions are used. | Some sense of organization but inconsistent or unclear in places. | Little or no sense of organization. |
| **DEVELOPMENT** | Central idea supported by strong, specific details. | Central idea with adequate support, mostly relevant details. | Unclear central idea; limited supporting details. | Unclear central idea; little or no development. |
| **VOICE** | Viewpoint clear; original expressions used where appropriate. | Viewpoint somewhat clear; few original expressions. | Viewpoint unclear or inconsistent. | Writer seems detached and unconcerned. |
| **WORD CHOICE** | Clear, exact language; freshness of expression. | Clear language; some interesting word choices. | Word choice unclear or inappropriate in places. | Word choice often unclear or inappropriate. |
| **SENTENCES** | Variety of sentence structures; flows smoothly. | Some variety in sentence structures. | Little variety; choppy or run-on sentences. | Little or no variety; sentences unclear. |
| **CONVENTIONS** | Few, if any, errors. | Few errors. | Some errors. | Many errors. |

**REPRODUCIBLE STUDENT RUBRICS** for specific writing purposes and presentations are available on pages T56–T58.

**Language Handbook,** pp. 69, 117–119

# Grammar

## Independent and Dependent Clauses

### SKILL TRACE

**INDEPENDENT AND DEPENDENT CLAUSES**

| Introduce | p. 251E |
|---|---|
| Reteach | pp. S57, T42 |
| Review | pp. 251F, 271F |
| Test | Theme 2 |

### REACHING ALL LEARNERS

## Diagnostic Check: Grammar and Writing

**If** . . . students are unable to distinguish between independent and dependent clauses . . .

**Then** . . . have them find connecting words such as *after, because, while, before, it, since,* or *when* to help them identify the dependent clauses.

### ADDITIONAL SUPPORT ACTIVITIES

**BELOW-LEVEL** Reteach, p. S56

**ADVANCED** Extend, p. S57

**ENGLISH-LANGUAGE LEARNERS** Reteach, p. S57

## technology

**Grammar Jingles™ CD,**
Intermediate: Track 27
See Grammar Practice Park,
Go for Grammar Gold,
Multimedia Grammar Glossary.
Visit *The Learning Site:*
www.harcourtschool.com

---

### DAY 1 — TEACH/MODEL

**DAILY LANGUAGE PRACTICE**

1. **Do you have a gardin in your neighborhood.** (garden; neighborhood?)

2. **Planting flowers was the smartist thing we could have done** (smartest; done.)

**INTRODUCE THE CONCEPT**   Use Transparency 82 to discuss:

- A **clause** has both a subject and a predicate.

- **Independent clauses** can stand alone as sentences.

- **Dependent clauses** cannot stand alone as sentences.

Have students add dependent clauses to items 3–6.

▼ **Teaching Transparency 82**

**CLAUSES**

**Examples:**

| Independent Clause |
|---|
| 1. Marisol planted a seed. |

| Dependent Clause |
|---|
| 2. after Marisol planted a seed |

SOME WORDS THAT CAN BEGIN DEPENDENT CLAUSES

| after | before | because | since | when |
|---|---|---|---|---|

3. Marisol watered the plant _____.
4. Mr. Castro picked the last of the tomatoes _____.
5. _____, Marisol's flower began to die.
6. The mural of sunflowers was finished _____.

3–6. Responses will vary.

"The Garden of Happiness"
Side by Side, Theme 2          82          Grammar Harcourt

---

### DAY 2 — EXTEND THE CONCEPT

**DAILY LANGUAGE PRACTICE**

1. **Marisol wants to plant something. Inn the garden.** (something in)

2. **It is to late, the plots are all taken.** (too late. The)

**DEVELOP THE CONCEPT**   Refer to sentences 3–6 on Transparency 82 as you discuss these points:

- A **dependent clause** can come at the beginning or the end of a sentence.

- When a **dependent clause** comes at the beginning of a sentence, it is followed by a comma.

Have students identify the dependent clause in each sentence.

**PERFORMANCE ASSESSMENT**

Name _____                                  The Garden of Happiness
                                              Grammar: Clauses

▶ Find the independent and dependent clauses in these sentences. Draw one line under each independent clause. Draw two lines under each dependent clause.

1. After Mrs. Willie Mae Washington and Mr. Singh told her about The Garden of Happiness, Marisol decided to plant something, too.

2. When Marisol planted a seed, it grew into a tall plant.

3. Marisol was happy because her sunflower was so beautiful.

4. Because she loved sweet potato pie, Mrs. Willie Mae Washington planted sweet potatoes.

▶ Rewrite each sentence. Add the kind of clause shown in parentheses ( ). Remember to add commas as needed.
Responses will vary.

5. The teenagers painted a mural _____ (dependent)

6. After the neighbors prepared the ground, _____ (independent)

7. _____ because Marisol wanted to plant something in The Garden of Happiness. (independent)

8. _____ Mr. Singh planted beans. (dependent)

**TRY THIS!** Identify sentences in "The Garden of Happiness" with dependent clauses. Change them into independent clauses. Then identify sentences with independent clauses, and change them into dependent clauses.

Practice Book

**Homework Option**

▲ **Practice Book, p. 40**

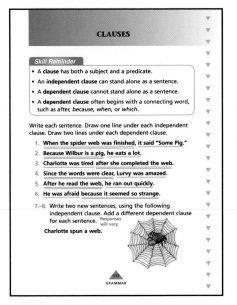

**DAY 3 — ORAL REVIEW/PRACTICE**

## DAILY LANGUAGE PRACTICE

1. Marisol found some soil. Where the sidewalk had cracked? (soil where; cracked.)
2. Shee found a seed. To plant there. (She; seed to)

## DEPENDENT OR INDEPENDENT?

Have students form two teams—the Dependents and the Independents. Say a clause. If the clause is dependent, the Dependents clap. If the clause is independent, the Independents clap.

### Test Prep Tip

"A clause that begins with *after, since,* or *because* is usually dependent. It cannot stand alone as a sentence."

---

**CLAUSES**

**Skill Reminder**

- A **clause** has both a subject and a predicate.
- An **independent clause** can stand alone as a sentence.
- A **dependent clause** cannot stand alone as a sentence.
- A **dependent clause** often begins with a connecting word, such as *after, because, when,* or *which.*

Write each sentence. Draw one line under each independent clause. Draw two lines under each dependent clause.

1. When the spider web was finished, it said "Some Pig."
2. Because Wilbur is a pig, he eats a lot.
3. Charlotte was tired after she completed the web.
4. Since the words were clear, Lurvy was amazed.
5. After he read the web, he ran out quickly.
6. He was afraid because it seemed so strange.
7.–8. Write two new sentences, using the following independent clause. Add a different dependent clause for each sentence. Responses will vary.

Charlotte spun a web.

GRAMMAR

▲ Language Handbook, p. 117

---

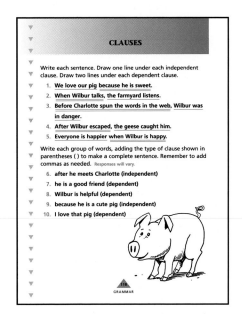

**DAY 4 — APPLY TO WRITING**

## DAILY LANGUAGE PRACTICE

1. Will marisol's seed sprout. (Marisol's; sprout?)
2. She wanders what her seedling will be come. (wonders; become.)

## ORDER OF EVENTS
Have students jot down several steps in a simple process, such as making a sandwich. Then have them write five sentences about the process, using dependent clauses to tell when or why certain steps should be performed—for example, *Before you begin, assemble all the ingredients.*

---

**CLAUSES**

Write each sentence. Draw one line under each independent clause. Draw two lines under each dependent clause.

1. We love our pig because he is sweet.
2. When Wilbur talks, the farmyard listens.
3. Before Charlotte spun the words in the web, Wilbur was in danger.
4. After Wilbur escaped, the geese caught him.
5. Everyone is happier when Wilbur is happy.

Write each group of words, adding the type of clause shown in parentheses ( ) to make a complete sentence. Remember to add commas as needed. Responses will vary.

6. after he meets Charlotte (independent)
7. he is a good friend (dependent)
8. Wilbur is helpful (dependent)
9. because he is a cute pig (independent)
10. I love that pig (dependent)

GRAMMAR

▲ Language Handbook, p. 118

---

**DAY 5 — CUMULATIVE REVIEW**

## DAILY LANGUAGE PRACTICE

1. Everyone enjoyed Marisols sunflower (Marisol's sunflower.)
2. people on the street stopt and smiled. (People; stopped)

## CLAUSES AND COMPOUND SENTENCES
Have students copy these sentences, underlining independent clauses once and dependent clauses twice. Then ask which one is a compound sentence. (2)

1. After Marisol planted a seed, it began to sprout.
2. Marisol loved her plant, and she tended to it daily.

(1. After Marisol planted a seed, it began to spout.
2. Marisol loved her plant, and she tended to it daily.)

---

**CUMULATIVE REVIEW**

Write each sentence. Underline the independent clauses, and circle the conjunction that connects them.

1. Charlotte is a spider, and Wilbur is a pig.
2. They live peacefully, but they are in danger.
3. Avery wants Charlotte, but Fern saves her.
4. Wilbur will be killed, or Charlotte will rescue him.
5. The two are friends, and they like each other.

Write each group of words, adding the type of clause shown in parentheses ( ) to make a complete sentence. Remember to add commas as needed. Responses will vary.

6. because Wilbur is frightened (independent)
7. Wilbur may be eaten (dependent)
8. Charlotte has an idea (dependent)
9. since Charlotte is very smart (independent)
10. Wilbur is saved (dependent)

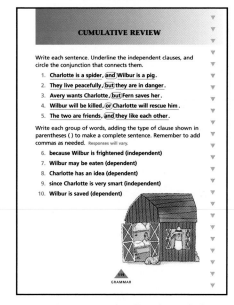

GRAMMAR

▲ Language Handbook, p. 119

## Spelling Words

1. curve
2. learned
3. curly
4. pearl
5. purse
6. further
7. turtle
8. urgent
9. burning
10. hurried*
11. earth*
12. earned
13. purpose
14. surface
15. overheard
16. rehearse
17. current
18. disturb
19. furniture
20. research

\* Selection Words

### Challenge Words

21. pickax*
22. crisscrossed*
23. cultivate
24. raspberries
25. irrigate

# Spelling

## Words with /ûr/

DAY 1

### PRETEST/SELF-CHECK

**ADMINISTER THE PRETEST** Use the Dictation Sentences under Day 5. Help students self-check their pretests using Transparency 83.

### ADVANCED

Use the Challenge Words in these Dictation Sentences.

21. The worker used a **pickax** to break up the rocks.
22. The farmer **crisscrossed** the garden, checking each row.
23. The vegetables will grow better if you **cultivate** the soil before planting the seeds.
24. Juicy red **raspberries** make a great dessert.
25. In dry areas, farmers may **irrigate** the land to provide water.

DAY 2

### TEACH/MODEL

**WORD SORT** Display Transparency 83. Briefly discuss the meaning of each word. Then ask students to copy the chart and to write each Spelling Word where it belongs.

Point to and say *curve* and *learned*. Ask what sound is heard in both. (/ûr/) Have a volunteer circle the letters in each word that stand for this sound. Have them read the generalization on Transparency 83 to confirm their conclusions.

**HANDWRITING** Remind students to bring the last downstroke of *u* to the bottom writing line to prevent it from resembling *v*.

*curve*

### ▼ Teaching Transparency 83

**WORDS WITH /ûr/**

**Spelling Words**

| 1. curve | 6. further | 11. earth | 16. rehearse |
| 2. learned | 7. turtle | 12. earned | 17. current |
| 3. curly | 8. urgent | 13. purpose | 18. disturb |
| 4. pearl | 9. burning | 14. surface | 19. furniture |
| 5. purse | 10. hurried | 15. overheard | 20. research |

| ur | | ear |
|---|---|---|
| curve | hurried | learned |
| curly | purpose | pearl |
| purse | surface | earth |
| further | current | earned |
| turtle | disturb | overheard |
| urgent | furniture | rehearse |
| burning | | research |

**The /ûr/ sound can be spelled *ur* or *ear*.**

"The Garden of Happiness"
Side by Side, Theme 2          83          Spelling
Harcourt

▲ Practice Book, p. 41

▲ Spelling Practice Book, p. 36

# 5 Day Plan

## DAY 3 — SPELLING STRATEGIES

**USE A DICTIONARY** Remind students that when checking spelling, they should first look under the spelling that seems correct. Put these rhyming pairs on the board:

*turn/learn    nurse/rehearse*

Ask a volunteer to circle the letters that stand for the /ûr/ sound. Point out that words may rhyme but be spelled differently. Ask students to explain why using a dictionary to spell these words is helpful.

### Apply to Writing

Have students use the dictionary when they proofread their writing. Have them look for words with the /ûr/ sound that do not follow a spelling rule or pattern.

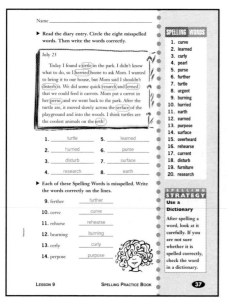

▲ Spelling Practice Book, p. 37

## DAY 4 — SPELLING ACTIVITIES

**THINK AND SPELL** Divide the class into small groups. Have one group member think of a Spelling Word and write it on a slip of paper. The other students in the group have to guess the word by spelling it within a given number of turns. They start by guessing the first letter, the second, and so on. The student who is "It" records the correct letters on a piece of paper. The student who completes the word becomes "It."

| e | a | r | t | h |   |   |
|---|---|---|---|---|---|---|
| e | a | r | n | e | d |   |
| b | u | r | n | i | n | g |

**WRITE HAIKU** Have students write a haiku on a topic of their own choosing, using Spelling Words and Challenge Words.

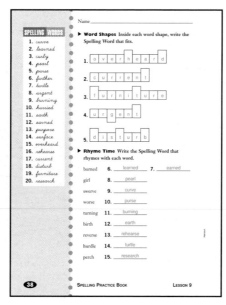

▲ Spelling Practice Book, p. 38

## DAY 5 — POSTTEST

### DICTATION SENTENCES

1. That player throws a great **curve** ball.
2. I **learned** to skate today.
3. My puppy's fur is **curly**.
4. I would love to find a **pearl** in an oyster.
5. Where did I leave my **purse**?
6. She didn't say anything **further** about the picnic.
7. I have a pet **turtle**.
8. Is the message **urgent**?
9. I smell something **burning**.
10. We **hurried** to meet the train on time.
11. The **earth** looks deep blue from outer space.
12. Jeff **earned** ten dollars by baby-sitting.
13. What is the **purpose** of the meeting?
14. The water's **surface** is covered with bubbles.
15. I **overheard** their conversation.
16. We will **rehearse** our play tonight.
17. What is the **current** temperature?
18. Please do not **disturb** the baby.
19. Keep your shoes off the **furniture**.
20. Do your **research** in the library.

*The Garden of Happiness*   **251H**

# Word Study

## Say It in Spanish

**OBJECTIVE**

*To use context and other strategies to determine the meanings of foreign words*

Point out the question *"¿Qué pasa?"* on page 234. Explain that writers sometimes include foreign words in a story to show the way people speak.

When this happens, readers can often understand what the words mean by using the context of the surrounding words. Say each Spanish word or phrase below, and ask students to use the context of the surrounding sentences in the selection to "translate" the word or words. Ask any Spanish-speaking students to confirm the meaning and to suggest other common words and phrases with similar meanings.

- page 234: *¿Qué pasa?* (What's going on?)
- page 234: *¡Mira!* (Look!)
- page 237: *¡Muy grande!* (very big)

**ENGLISH-LANGUAGE LEARNERS**

You may want to invite students who speak other languages to share common words and phrases in their first language. Suggest that they share with the class how to say *hello*, *thank-you*, and *How are you?* in their first language.

*¿Qué pasa?*

*¡Muy grande!*

## Word Relationships

**OBJECTIVE**

*To apply knowledge of synonyms to determine word relationships*

Remind students that a **synonym** is a word that means the same or almost the same as another word. Ask students to name a synonym for *mural*. (painting) Remind students that they can use a thesaurus to find synonyms for a word. Write the following sentences on the board, and ask students to give a synonym for each underlined word. Possible responses are shown.

1. Darren <u>skidded</u> on the wet pavement. (slid)
2. Elena is kind and <u>modest</u>. (humble)
3. We <u>yelled</u> as we rode the roller coaster. (screamed)
4. Joe and Sam <u>disagreed</u> about whose turn it was. (argued)

Then have students use a thesaurus to find synonyms for the word *haze*. They may use some of these synonyms in a paragraph describing a wet, gray day.

# Speaking and Listening

## Give a Demonstration

**OBJECTIVE**

*To present directions in an organized manner*

Students may publish their how-to essays by giving a demonstration.

**Organization**   Share these **organizational tips:**

- Use note cards to help you plan your demonstration. List each step on a different note card.
- Open by describing what you are going to teach your classmates how to do or make.
- Show the materials needed for the process.

**Delivery**   Share the following **practice tips:**

- Practice your demonstration before presenting it to the class. Ask friends for feedback.
- Speak clearly and use a tone and pace appropriate for the topic and your audience.
- Use gestures to clarify information for listeners.
- Make eye contact with your audience. If they look confused, repeat your instructions.

Have students present their demonstrations. Remind them that the most important part of giving a demonstration is making sure the audience is able to follow the steps. PERFORMANCE ASSESSMENT

## Listening to a Demonstration

**OBJECTIVE**

*To ask questions to clarify the understanding of directions*

**Listening Tips**

- Look at the speaker.
- Identify the sequence of steps.
- After the speaker has finished, ask questions.

Have students listen for the steps in each demonstration and pay attention to the order in which they are presented. Share the Listening Tips with students.

**STEPS TO GOOD LISTENING**   Have students write a list of steps for listening to a demonstration. Tell students to write a brief description of each step and number the steps.

## Viewing an Illustration

**OBJECTIVE**

*To analyze the visual elements of an illustration*

Discuss with students the picture on pages 238–239. Ask:

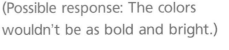

**Why does the sunflower appear so large?** (Possible response: to give it attention)

**How would the illustration be different if it were realistic?** (Possible response: The colors wouldn't be as bold and bright.)

# Books for
# All Learners
*Reinforcing Skills and Strategies*

Guided Reading OPTIONS

## ■ BELOW-LEVEL

Growing a City Garden

*by Mel Robard • illustrated by Frank Rocco*

 **Focus Skill: Cause and Effect**

 **Focus Strategy: Make and Confirm Predictions**

 **Vocabulary: *inhaled, lavender, mural, skidded, haze***

**Genre:** Nonfiction
**Science Connection:** Plants provide a primary source of energy in food chains.

**SUMMARY** This book explains how a city community garden can be developed. Illustrations show the process, from choosing an appropriate location to planting and enjoying the results.

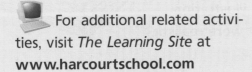 For additional related activities, visit *The Learning Site* at
**www.harcourtschool.com**

### BEFORE READING

**Preview/Set Purpose** Have students preview the book by reading the title and looking at the illustrations. Have them tell why they might want to read this book.

**Reinforce Cause/Effect** Have students begin a flowchart that they can fill in as they read. CAUSE/EFFECT/GRAPHIC AIDS

**Reinforce Vocabulary** Review key vocabulary by having students act out words such as *inhaled* and *skidded*. Have them pantomime painting a *mural*.

### READING THE BOOK

**Pages 5–7** What benefits can community gardens provide? (They can provide flowers and vegetables for the gardeners. The gardens also allow community members to work and play together.) CAUSE/EFFECT

**Pages 14–16** What will probably happen if you do not weed your garden? (The weeds will take food and water away from the other plants. The plants will not grow as well.) MAKE PREDICTIONS

**Reread for Fluency** Have students reread aloud the steps involved in creating a community garden.

### RESPONDING

**Flowchart** Students can complete the flowchart and use it to help them retell the important ideas in the book.

**BELOW-LEVEL**

Growing a City Garden

**ON-LEVEL**

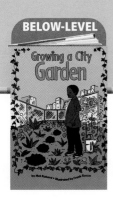
Faces to the Sun

**ADVANCED**

Home Grown

**ELL**

Sunshine Place

▲ page 251M          ▲ page 251N

## ■ ON-LEVEL

Faces to the Sun

 **Focus Skill: Cause and Effect**

 **Focus Strategy: Make and Confirm Predictions**

 **Vocabulary:** *inhaled, lavender, mural, skidded, haze*

**Genre:** Realistic Fiction
**Science Connection:** All organisms need matter and energy to live and grow.

**SUMMARY** This book describes how Melinda's new friend helps her choose the topic for a report. Preparing and giving the report deepens Melinda's appreciation for her family's way of life.

For additional related activities, visit *The Learning Site* at **www.harcourtschool.com**

### BEFORE READING

**Preview/Set Purpose** Have students look at the chart on page 13. Have them predict what the story is about, and check their predictions after they finish reading.

**Reinforce Cause and Effect** Have students make a cause-and-effect chart such as the one below to help them record key events as they read. CAUSE AND EFFECT/GRAPHIC SOURCES

| Cause | Effect |
|-------|--------|
|       |        |
|       |        |
|       |        |

### READING THE BOOK

**Pages 4–10** What were some of the things Melinda did that caused Sarah to give her a painting of sunflowers? (Melinda made Sarah feel welcome at her new school by sitting with her on the bus, telling her about their teacher, introducing her to their teacher.) CAUSE AND EFFECT

**Pages 9–12** Summarize how Melinda learned more about sunflowers. (Melinda read books about sunflowers, helped her father in the field, and asked him questions.) SUMMARIZE

**Page 13** Look at the chart on page 13. Why do you think Melinda made a chart of this information instead of just telling the class? (Possible response: She wanted students to be able to see it during the whole report.) USE GRAPHIC AIDS

**Rereading for Fluency** Have students reread aloud pages 12–15 of this book.

### RESPONDING

**Chart** Students can complete the cause-and-effect chart they started earlier and use it to help them summarize the events in the story.

*The Garden of Happiness* **251L**

# Books for All Learners

*Reinforcing Skills and Strategies*

## ■ ADVANCED

 **Focus Skill: Cause and Effect**

 **Focus Strategy: Make and Confirm Predictions**

 **Vocabulary: *inhaled, lavender, mural, skidded, haze, predators, compost***

**Genre:** Realistic Fiction
**Science Connection:** All organisms need energy and matter to live and grow.

**SUMMARY** With the help of his neighbor Mrs. Salter, Eric plants his first vegetable garden, tends the garden, and harvests the vegetables.

For additional related activities, visit *The Learning Site* at **www.harcourtschool.com**

### BEFORE READING

**Preview/Set Purpose** Have students read the title of the book. Ask them to predict what the book will be about.

**Reinforce Cause and Effect** Begin a flowchart. Invite students to fill it in as they read to help them understand that effects can become causes.

**Expand Vocabulary** Write *predators* and *compost* on the board, and discuss prior knowledge of these words. (*predators*: animals that kill and eat other animals; *compost*: a mixture of decayed organic matter and is used for fertilizing and conditioning land)

### READING THE BOOK

**Pages 2–4** What happens in Chapter 1? (Eric meets his new neighbor and thinks about planting a vegetable garden.) **SUMMARIZE**

**Pages 5–6** What do you think caused Eric to decide to grow a vegetable garden? (Possible response: The radishes from Mrs. Salter's garden tasted good.) **CAUSE AND EFFECT**

**Pages 13–15** Who are the hidden heroes? (the bats, praying mantises, ladybugs, and other predators who eat insects that damage the plants in the garden) **DRAW CONCLUSIONS**

**Rereading for Fluency** Have students reread aloud a section as they believe the writer might have wanted it read.

### RESPONDING

**Illustrations** Have students draw story frames to illustrate their flowcharts.

**Managing Small Groups**

While you work with small groups have
other students do the following:
- **Self-selected Reading**
- **Practice Pages**
- **Cross-Curricular Centers**
- **Journal Writing**

▲ page 251K    ▲ page 251L

# ■ ENGLISH-LANGUAGE LEARNERS

 **Focus Skill: Cause and Effect**

 **Focus Strategy: Make and Confirm Predictions**

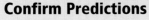 **Concept Vocabulary:** *green, red, orange, yellow, brown, blue*

**Genre:** Fiction
**Social Studies Connection:** Community members work together.

**SUMMARY**   A group of students work together to paint a mural on a drab downtown building. The whole town watches the process take place, and in the end they all celebrate the completion of the mural with a big party.

 For additional related activities, visit *The Learning Site* at **www.harcourtschool.com** See Language Support.

## BEFORE READING

**Tap Prior Knowledge**   Have students look at page 15 of the book. Ask students to describe murals they have seen.

**Total Physical Response**   Have students follow these directions: Draw a yellow sun. Make the sky blue around the sun. Draw green grass. Draw a brown dog with a red ball.

**Display Vocabulary Concept Words**   Write the words on the board and illustrate their meanings.

**Preview the Book**   Read the title, and ask students what they think it means. Then discuss the illustrations.

## READING THE BOOK

**Pages 2–3**   What is downtown Milford like at the beginning of the book? (It is empty and quiet.) **IMPORTANT DETAILS**

**Pages 3–4**   What do you think caused Alberto to paint the sign? (Possible response: He wanted to brighten up his town.) **CAUSE AND EFFECT**

**Page 16**   How do the townspeople feel about the mural? (They like it and celebrate when it is finished.) **CHARACTERS' EMOTIONS**

**Rereading**   Reread the book aloud with students. Ask volunteers to read the dialogue of different characters.

## RESPONDING

**Story Map**   Have students complete a story map like the following to retell the events of the book.

| Characters | Setting |
|---|---|

| Problem |
|---|

| Important Events |
|---|

| Solution |
|---|

# Teacher Notes

## Teacher Notes

**THEME CONNECTION:**

*Side by Side*

**GENRE:**

*Nonfiction*

Award-Winning Author

How to Babysit an **Orangutan**

Story and Photographs by
Tara Darling and Kathy Darling

**SUMMARY:**

Camp Leakey, on the island of Borneo, provides a home for orphaned baby orangutans. Human caretakers raise the young orangs, teach them survival skills, and eventually return them to the forest.

 Selections available on *Audiotext 2*

# Books for All Learners

*Lesson Plans on pages 271K–271N*

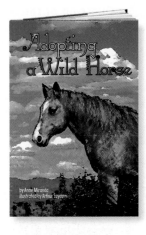

| BELOW-LEVEL | ON-LEVEL | ADVANCED | ELL |
|---|---|---|---|
| • Lesson Vocabulary | • Lesson Vocabulary | • Challenge Vocabulary | • Concept Vocabulary |
| • Focus Skill: Summarize | • Focus Skill: Summarize | • Focus Skill: Summarize | • Focus Skill: Summarize |

## MULTI-LEVEL PRACTICE

**Extra Support,** pp. 42–43

**Practice Book,** pp. 42–45

**Challenge,** pp. 42–43

**English-Language Learners,** pp. 42–43

## ADDITIONAL RESOURCES

**Spelling Practice Book,** pp. 39–41

**Language Handbook,** pp. 52–54, 120–122

**Audiotext 2**

**Intervention Resource Kit,** Lesson 10
• Intervention Reader, *Included in Intervention Resource Kit*

**English-Language Learners Resource Kit,** Lesson 10

## technology

- *Mission: Comprehension™ Skills Practice* **CD-ROM**
- *Media Literacy and Communication Skills Package* (Video)

- *Grammar Jingles™* **CD**, Intermediate
- *Writing Express™* **CD-ROM**
- *Reading and Language Skills Assessment* **CD-ROM**

- *The Learning Site:* **www.harcourtschool.com**

# How to Babysit an Orangutan
pp. 252–271

## Day 1

## Day 2

5–15 Minutes

### ORAL LANGUAGE

• **Question of the Day**

• **Sharing Literature**

**Question of the Day,** p. 252H
*When you are listening, why is it important to pay attention to the speaker's facial expressions?*

**Literature Read-Aloud,** pp. 252G–H

**Question of the Day,** p. 252H
*The orangutan orphans learn skills from their babysitters? What are some important skills you have learned from your parents or other adults?*

**Think and Respond,** p. 264

15–30 Minutes

### SKILLS & STRATEGIES

• **Comprehension**

• **Vocabulary**

**Comprehension:**
 Summarize, p. 252I  **T**
 Use Text Structure and Format, p. 252J
**Vocabulary,** p. 252K

**Comprehension:**
 Summarize, pp. 254–266  **T**

**Decoding/Phonics:**
Syllables: VV Syllable Pattern, p. 271A

30–45 Minutes

### READING

• **Guided Comprehension**

• **Independent Reading**

• **Cross-Curricular Connections**

**Read: Vocabulary Power,** pp. 252–253
Vocabulary Power Words:
*displeasure, jealous, endangered, smuggled, facial, coordination*

 **Independent Reading**
Books for All Learners

**SOCIAL SCIENCE** Where in the World?
**MATH** Solve a Problem
**INQUIRY PROJECT** Extending the Selection

**Reading the Selection,** pp. 254–266
GENRE: Nonfiction

 **Independent Reading**
Books for All Learners

**SOCIAL STUDIES** Borneo
**SCIENCE** Rainforest

45–90 Minutes

### LANGUAGE ARTS

• **Writing**

*Daily Writing Prompt*

• **Grammar**

*Daily Language Practice*

• **Spelling**

**Writing:** Timed or Tested Writing, p. 271C

✎ **Writing Prompt:**
*Imagine that you are a babysitter at Camp Leakey. Think about what you would do and what you would see in a typical day. Write an entry in your diary, telling what a typical day is like.*

**Grammar:**
Complex Sentences, p. 271E  **T**

*Daily Language Practice*
1. When I visited the zoo I learnt a lot about animals. (zoo, I; learned)
2. Many wild animal are becoming very rair. (animals; rare)

**Spelling:**
Words with /ou/, p. 271G  **T**

**Writing:** Timed or Tested Writing, p. 271C

✎ **Writing Prompt:**
*Write a poem about an animal that fascinates you. Include details to support your choice. Use vivid language to make your poem interesting to read.*

**Grammar:**
Extend the Concept, p. 271E

*Daily Language Practice*
1. I especially enjoyd the orangutans they are playful animals. (enjoyed; orangutans. They)
2. Orangutans come from the Islands of Borneo, and Sumatra. (islands of Borneo and)

**Spelling:**
Word Sort, p. 271G

**Daily Routines**
• Question of the Day
• Daily Language Practice
• Daily Writing Prompt

**T** = tested skill

**Focus Skill**

**Summarize**

- To use important ideas and details to summarize a text
- To read and understand a nonfiction selection
- To use complex sentences correctly
- To practice writing a summary in a timed or tested situation

## Day 3

**Question of the Day,** p. 252H
*Would you prefer a career working with animals or a career working with people? Explain.*

**Oral Grammar,** p. 271F

**Comprehension:**
 Summarize, pp. 270–271
Test Prep
**Word Study:**
Structural Analysis, p. 271I

**Rereading for Fluency,** p. 263

 **Independent Reading**
Books for All Learners
**COMPARING TEXTS** Informational Texts

**Writing:** Timed or Tested Writing, p. 271D

 **Writing Prompt:**
*Write a description of Camp Leakey for a nature program on your local public television station.*

**Grammar:**
Add a Clause, p. 271F

***Daily Language Practice***
1. Most monkeys have tales apes do not. (tails, but apes)
2. Baby orangutans need help. When their Mothers have been killed. (help when; mothers)

**Spelling:**
Checking Twice, p. 271H

## Day 4

**Question of the Day,** p. 252H
*How would you start a search on the Internet for organizations that help endangered animals?*

**Comprehension:**
 Summarize, pp. 271K–N **T**

**Search Techniques,** p. 271B

**Self-Selected Reading,** p. 252F

 **Independent Reading**
Books for All Learners
**TECHNOLOGY** Endangered Species

**Writing:** Timed or Tested Writing, p. 271D

 **Writing Prompt:**
*Imagine that your job is to write the classified ads for your local newspaper. There is an opening for a babysitter at Camp Leakey. Think about what an orangutan babysitter does, and then write a classified ad.*

**Grammar:**
Sentences, p. 271F

***Daily Language Practice***
1. Would you like, to babysit an orangutan. (like to; orangutan?)
2. The orphans need help. Until they are seven or eight year old. (help until; years)

**Spelling:**
Build a Word, p. 271H

## Day 5

**Question of the Day,** p. 252H
*Why are rain forests a valuable natural resource?*

**Speaking and Listening**
Giving a Speech, p. 271J

**Comprehension:**
 Summarize, pp. 271K–N **T**

**Word Study:**
Prefixes, p. 271I

**Self-Selected Reading,** pp. 261, T67

 **Independent Reading**
Books for All Learners
**WRITING** Writing Instructions
**SCIENCE** Make a Diagram
**SOCIAL STUDIES** Give an Oral Report

**Writing:** Timed or Tested Writing, p. 271D

**Writing Prompt:**
*Imagine that you have been asked to build a new zoo in your city. Think about the kinds of animals that would be in your zoo. Write a paragraph describing the zoo you would build.*

**Grammar:**
Clauses in Sentences, p. 271F

***Daily Language Practice***
1. The babys make nests on the grownd. (babies; ground)
2. Someday they will, make nests, in the trees. (will make nests in)

**Spelling:**
Posttest, p. 271H

**MANAGING THE CLASSROOM** While you provide direct instruction to individuals or small groups, other students can work on ongoing activities such as the ones below.

## SOCIAL STUDIES

### Where in the World?

**OBJECTIVE: To use the coordinate grid system of latitude and longitude to determine absolute locations**

Work with a partner to locate the latitude and longitude of these places. Write your answers on an index card.

- Borneo
- The North Pole and the South Pole
- The equator
- The capital of your state

Share your findings with another set of partners.

20 Minutes

**Materials**

- world map, showing latitude and longitude
- index cards
- pen or pencil

## MATH

### Solve a Problem

**OBJECTIVE: To apply problem-solving strategies to real-life problems**

Imagine that you have an older sister who has started her own babysitting business. She charges $4 an hour. Here are the hours she babysat each week in August. Figure out how much money she earned each week. Then figure out how much she earned for the entire month.

WEEK 1:   2 hours on Friday and 3 hours on Saturday

WEEK 2:   4 hours on Monday, 2 hours on Wednesday, and 1 hour on Friday

WEEK 3:   2 1/2 hours on Wednesday

WEEK 4:   3 hours each on Monday, Tuesday, and Friday

**Remember to**

- read the problem carefully.
- determine the steps necessary to solve each part of the problem.
- check your work.

20 Minutes a day

**Materials**

- pen or pencil
- paper

## LIBRARY CENTER

### Self-Selected Reading

**OBJECTIVE: To select and read books independently**

Look for these books about wild animals:

- *Desert Babies* by Kathy Darling. Walker, 1997. NONFICTION
- *Snakes Are Hunters* by Patricia Lauber. HarperCollins, 1988. NONFICTION
- *Dick King-Smith's Animal Friends* by Dick King-Smith. Candlewick, 1996. NONFICTION

**Remember to**

- use appropriate reading strategies.
- keep track in your Reading Log of what you read each day.

**Materials**

- self-selected book
- pen or pencil
- *My Reading Log* copying master, p. R38

---

## INQUIRY PROJECT

### Extending the Selection

**OBJECTIVE: To select a focus for an inquiry project**

Use the ideas in the selection to brainstorm related topics to explore. Organize your thoughts into a K-W-L chart. Choose a topic to research, and use one of these books for your inquiry project.

- *The Rain Forest Is Their Home*
- *Bravo!*
- *Adopting a Wild Horse*
- *Kid Care*

**Materials**

- research materials
- pen or pencil
- paper

---

## TECHNOLOGY

### Endangered Species

**OBJECTIVE: To use technology resources to research an endangered species**

Use the Internet or a CD-ROM encyclopedia to research an endangered species. Take notes, and restate the important ideas in your own words. Then prepare an oral report.

**Remember to**

- use search engines to find information.
- follow the rules for Internet safety.

**Materials**

- computer with Internet access or CD-ROM encyclopedia
- pen or pencil
- paper

# Read Aloud

SET A PURPOSE

## SET A PURPOSE
### Listen for Enjoyment

Remind students that people often read and listen to poetry for enjoyment. Explain that poets sometimes use rhymes and alliteration, the repetition of initial sounds of words, to make the poem more appealing to listen to. Read the poem and riddles aloud. Ask students to point out passages from the poem they think are appealing or humorous.

## LISTENING STRATEGY
### Create Mental Images

Tell students that one way to understand a poem better is to form in their minds pictures of what is happening. Ask students to imagine what might happen if they pulled a tiger's tail. Explain to students that imagining the effects of the actions described will help them understand the poem better.

## My Uncle Looked Me in the Eye
**by Jack Prelutsky**

My uncle looked me in the eye
about an hour ago
he said: "There are some things I think
that you had better know—
do not throw bricks at bumblebees
or grab a grizzly bear,
and never tug a tiger's tail
or pull a panther's hair.

"Don't wrestle with a rattlesnake
or ask a skunk to fight,
don't irritate an elephant
or tempt a lion to bite,
don't scuffle with a buffalo
or tease electric eels,
don't interrupt piranhas
at their underwater meals.

"Don't tickle a gorilla
or invite a shark to smile,
don't ridicule a rhino
or provoke a porcupine."
I've followed his advice so far,
and I am doing fine.

## Riddles

What's a bird's favorite vegetable?
A tweet-potato

What do you call a dog that likes to take bubble baths? A shampoodle

What does it take to make an octopus laugh? Ten-tickles

What is another name for a wolf pack? Fang gang

Which animal has the "highest" intelligence? The giraffe

How much food does a crab eat? Just a pinch

Which animals are karate experts? Zebras, because they have so many black belts

What is a termite's favorite cereal? Oakmeal

What would the world be like without pandas? Unbear-able

Why don't ants mind lots of phone calls? Because they have ants-ering machines

Who is in charge of cow school? The princi-bull

What is the monkey's national anthem? "The Star-Spangled Banana"

What makes a frog jump for joy? Finding a fly in its soup

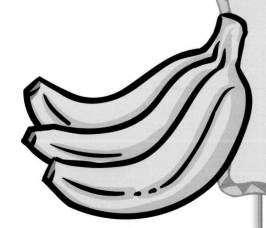

- **What mental images did you create as the poem was read aloud?** (Possible responses: throwing a brick at a bee, tickling a gorilla, smiling at a shark) POET'S CRAFT/IMAGERY

- **What do you think the poet's purpose was for writing this poem?** (The poet wanted to make us laugh; the poet wanted to entertain.) POET'S PURPOSE

- **Name an example of alliteration that is used in the poem.** (Possible response: tug a tiger's tail; grab a grizzly bear) FIGURATIVE LANGUAGE

# Question of the Day

## DEVELOP ORAL LANGUAGE

- Display the first question on Teaching Transparency 86, or write it on the board. Ask a volunteer to read it aloud.

- **Response Journal** Explain to students that they should think about the question throughout the day and write their responses in their journals. Tell students to be prepared to discuss their responses to it by the end of the day or at another time you choose.

- You may want to repeat this process daily for each of the remaining discussion questions.

orangutan

## OBJECTIVE

*To use important ideas and details to summarize a text*

### SKILL TRACE

| SUMMARIZE | |
|---|---|
| Introduce | page 206I |
| Reteach | pp. S48, S60, S92, T39 |
| **Review** | **pp. 228, 252I, 270** |
| Test | Theme 2 |
| Maintain | pp. 372I, 396 |

### ▼ Teaching Transparency 87

---

#### SUMMARIZE

When you summarize, you restate the most important events of a selection in the correct sequence. A summary contains only the most important ideas.

| DO | DO NOT |
|---|---|
| • tell only the most important ideas. | • include very specific details. |
| • briefly retell the information in your own words. | • change the author's meaning. |
| • retell events or ideas in the correct order. | |

#### EXAMPLE

Orangutans begin their adult lives at approximately eight years old. Mother orangutans spend up to eight years caring for and teaching their young. After that time, the young males go off to the treetops and the young females prepare to raise more baby orangutans. An orangutan can live forty-five or fifty years in the rain forest.

"How to Babysit an Orangutan"
Side by Side, Theme 2          ⑧⑦          Focus Skill
                                              Harcourt

---

### BELOW-LEVEL

**Additional Support**
• *Intervention Teacher's Guide*, p. 100

### ENGLISH-LANGUAGE LEARNERS

**Additional Support**
• *English-Language Learners Teacher's Guide*, p. 57

---

# ★ Focus Skill Summarize

## REVIEW THE SKILL

**Access prior knowledge.** Have students tell about the most important event of the previous day. Explain that restating the important parts of an event or a story is called summarizing. Tell students that when they summarize a story, they should restate the most important events in the order in which they occurred. Point out that good readers take a moment after reading each section to summarize it.

## TEACH/MODEL

Remind students that when they read, they should summarize the most important ideas in their own words.

• **Ask a volunteer to read aloud the explanation of the skill.**

• **Review with students the information in the chart.**

• **Read aloud the example paragraph to students. Ask students to use the information in the chart and what they know about summarizing to summarize the paragraph in two or three sentences.** (Possible response: At around age 8, orangutans begin their adult life. The average life span of an orangutan is 50 years.)

## PRACTICE/APPLY

Have students use a K-W-L chart like the one below to summarize the information they learn about orangutans.

| K-W-L Chart | | |
|---|---|---|
| What I Know | What I Want to Know | What I Learned |
| | | |

To apply and reinforce the skill, see the following pages:

**During reading:** pages 258 and 260
**After reading:** *Pupil Edition* pages 270–271

---

**252I      Side by Side**

# Use Text Structure and Format

**OBJECTIVE**
*To use text features and text structure to locate information and to monitor comprehension*

## Strategies Good Readers Use

- Use Decoding/Phonics
- Make and Confirm Predictions
- Create Mental Images
- Self-Question
- Summarize
- Read Ahead
- Reread to Clarify
- Use Context to Confirm Meaning
- **Use Text Structure and Format**  **Focus Strategy**
- Adjust Reading Rate

### INTRODUCE THE STRATEGY

Point out that authors organize their writing in a logical way. Tell students that identifying the **text structure** of a selection will help them locate and understand information. Paying attention to the **format**, or text features, of a selection will also help them locate important information. Tell students that text features they should look for include headings, subheadings, photographs, captions, and graphic aids.

### TEACH/MODEL

Use the example paragraph on Transparency 87 to model the strategy.

> **MODEL** The first sentence of this paragraph tells me that this paragraph is about the adult life of orangutans. The details are about male and female adult orangutans. Identifying the text structure, or how information is organized, helps me to understand that the purpose of this paragraph is to give information about adult orangutans.

#### SKILL ←→ STRATEGY CONNECTION

Tell students that knowing how a selection is organized can help them locate and understand information. Remind them to **use text structure and format** to help them as they **summarize** information from a selection.

### PRACTICE/APPLY

Remind students to use the Use Text Structure and Format strategy to help them understand and locate information as they read. For opportunities to apply and reinforce the strategy **during reading**, see pages 257 and 259.

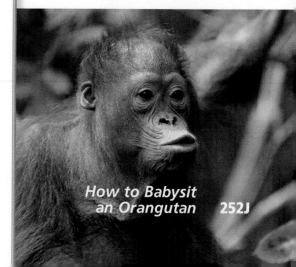

*How to Babysit an Orangutan* **252J**

# Building Background

## ACCESS PRIOR KNOWLEDGE

Discuss with students what they already know about the needs of babies and young children. Ask them to make predictions, based on their answers, about the needs of baby orangutans. Work with students to create a Venn diagram to compare and contrast the needs of baby humans with the needs of baby orangutans.

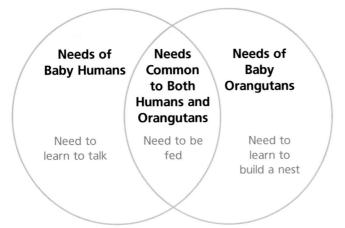

**Needs of Baby Humans**

Need to learn to talk

**Needs Common to Both Humans and Orangutans**

Need to be fed

**Needs of Baby Orangutans**

Need to learn to build a nest

## DEVELOP CONCEPTS

Help students use prior knowledge to develop concepts by asking the following questions:

- **Why are some animals at risk of dying out?** (Possible responses: food shortages, disease, destruction of habitat, hunters)

- **What can people do to help animals that are at risk?** (Possible responses: provide food, protect their habitats, provide medical care for them)

- **Why might some baby orangutans need to be cared for by humans?** (Possible response: They might not have parents, and baby orangutans are unable to care for themselves.)

## technology

Visit *The Learning Site:*
**www.harcourtschool.com**
See Building Background.

### REACHING ALL LEARNERS

## Diagnostic Check: Vocabulary

**If** . . . students do not understand at least 5 of 6 vocabulary words . . .

**Then** . . . duplicate the word cards on page T61, and have pairs of students take turns giving definition clues and holding up corresponding word cards.

### ADDITIONAL SUPPORT ACTIVITIES

| BELOW-LEVEL | Reteach, p. S58 |
| ADVANCED | Extend, p. S59 |
| ENGLISH-LANGUAGE LEARNERS | Reteach, p. S59 |

# Vocabulary

## TEACH VOCABULARY STRATEGIES

**Use affixes and root words.** Display Transparency 88. Read the first paragraph aloud. Then point to the word *displeasure*. Ask students what they think this word means. Remind them that they can sometimes figure out unfamiliar words by looking for word parts they know, such as prefixes, suffixes, or root words. Model using affixes and root words to determine the meaning of the word *displeasure*:

> **MODEL** I have seen the prefix *dis-* in other words such as *dishonest* and *disappear*. I know that it usually means "the opposite of." *Displeasure* has this prefix plus a word I know, *pleasure*. *Displeasure* must mean "the opposite of being pleased."

Encourage students to use this strategy as they encounter other unfamiliar words when they read.

### Vocabulary

**displeasure** the feeling of being displeased; dissatisfaction

**jealous** full of envy

**endangered** in danger of dying out

**smuggled** taken out of a place illegally

**facial** having to do with the face

**coordination** the ability to make the parts of the body work together smoothly

### ▼ Teaching Transparency 88

#### VOCABULARY IN CONTEXT

Jennie is unhappy. She shows her **displeasure** by squealing. She has had one banana, but she became **jealous** when Ben gave Maria a banana. Jennie wants another banana.

Jennie and Maria are golden lion tamarins, a very rare kind of monkey. There are fewer than 400 of these **endangered** animals left in the wild. It is against the law to take them out of Brazil. They are so small, however, that they are easily **smuggled** out to other countries.

Some people want tamarins as pets because they are cute. Baby tamarins look lost. Their **facial** expressions seem to ask, "Where am I?" Their parents are often killed by smugglers, and these babies must be cared for by humans until they are old enough to live on their own.

Jennie and Marie are young and still clumsy. As they grow older, they will learn to climb tall trees. They will develop the **coordination** they need to make their home in the rain forest canopy.

"How to Babysit an Orangutan"
Side by Side, Theme 2

88

Vocabulary in Context
Harcourt

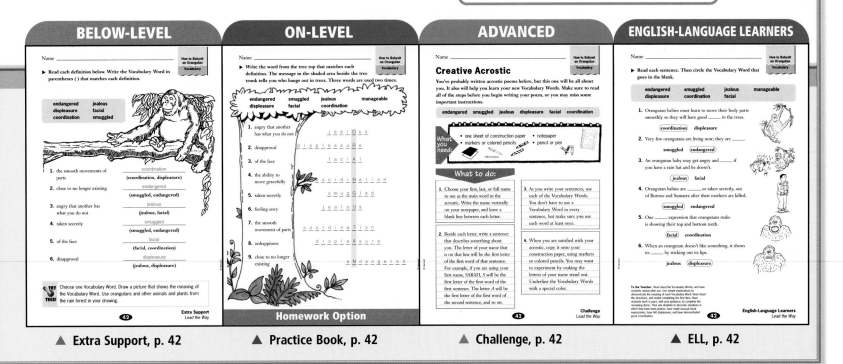

**BELOW-LEVEL**

▲ Extra Support, p. 42

**ON-LEVEL**

▲ Practice Book, p. 42

**ADVANCED**

▲ Challenge, p. 42

**ENGLISH-LANGUAGE LEARNERS**

▲ ELL, p. 42

# Vocabulary Power

## APPLY STRATEGIES

Read aloud the first paragraph on page 252. Then ask students to read the remaining text silently. Remind them to apply the strategies of using context and affixes and root words to determine or confirm the meanings of unfamiliar words.

## EXTEND WORD KNOWLEDGE

### Practice other vocabulary strategies.

Ask students to answer questions with sentences that show what the vocabulary words mean. MEANINGFUL SENTENCES

- What does it mean to say that a species is *endangered*? DEFINITION

- What might cause someone to show *displeasure*? EXAMPLE

- How might a person's *facial* expression change if the person became angry? EXAMPLE

- What does it mean to say that someone *smuggled* something out of a country? EXPLANATION

- What might make a small child *jealous*? EXAMPLE

- If someone has good *coordination*, what might he or she be good at? PRIOR KNOWLEDGE

▲ How to Babysit an Orangutan

| endangered |
| jealous |
| smuggled |
| displeasure |
| facial |
| coordination |

252

# Vocabulary Power

**I**n "How to Babysit an Orangutan," you will read about a woman who learns how to care for orphaned orangutans. People who own a pet must also learn how to care for their animal friends.

For my tenth birthday, I asked my parents if I could have a chimpanzee. I had seen a television show about a scientist who worked with one, and it looked like so much fun. My parents explained that chimpanzees are **endangered**. Animals that are in danger of dying out cannot be kept as pets. Instead, I got Bronco, my border collie puppy.

My friends were all **jealous** that I had my own dog, but they weren't filled with envy for long. They soon saw that caring for a puppy is a big responsibility.

I trained Bronco myself. Every time he did something good, I smiled and scratched behind his ears. I taught him that some things were wrong, such as stealing food from the table. When he **smuggled** my socks, I showed my **displeasure** by putting on a big frown. Using **facial** expressions works well because Bronco really understands smiles and frowns!

Bronco needs a lot of exercise. He loves to run, and he can jump and catch at the same time, because of his good **coordination**. Plenty of activity outdoors makes him more manageable in the house. He is easy to control after a lot of exercise because he is usually ready for a nap!

**Vocabulary–Writing CONNECTION**

**T**hink of two games or other activities you enjoy. One should require your eyes and hands to work in **coordination**. The other should not. Write a paragraph to compare and contrast the two games or activities.

253

 **QUICKWRITE**

**VOCABULARY–WRITING CONNECTION**

Remind students to use vivid verbs to describe the two activities that they are comparing and contrasting. Students should add the Vocabulary Power words and their vivid verbs to their Word Banks to use in future writing assignments.

# Prereading Strategies

## PREVIEW AND PREDICT

Have students read the **genre** information on page 254. Then have them preview the selection by looking at the photographs and captions. Ask them what they think this selection is about, based on their preview and the characteristics of nonfiction. Then have them make predictions about what they might learn about orangutans. They can begin a K-W-L chart like this. See Transparency G.

| K-W-L Chart | | |
|---|---|---|
| What I Know | What I Want to Know | What I Learned |
| Orangutans are wild animals. | Why do humans babysit orangutans? | |

**Award-Winning Author**

Genre

## Nonfiction

Nonfiction tells about people, things, events, or places that are real.

In this selection, look for

● Facts and details about orangutans

● Text features such as photographs and captions

254

| BELOW-LEVEL | ON-LEVEL | ADVANCED | ENGLISH-LANGUAGE LEARNERS |
|---|---|---|---|
| Guide students as they preview the selection. Discuss the meaning of these words: *orphan, orphanage,* and *starvation.* Help students set a purpose for reading through page 258. **SMALL GROUP** | Students can read the selection in small groups. Use the Guided Comprehension questions and Ongoing Assessments to gauge students' understanding. **WHOLE GROUP/SMALL GROUP** | Students reading above-level may read independently and add questions and facts to their K-W-L charts. Students might join with a partner after reading and compare their charts. **INDEPENDENT/PARTNER** | Read aloud the selection, or have students listen to it on *Audiotext 2.* Then have students as a group read aloud selected pages to develop oral fluency. **SMALL GROUP** |
| **ADDITIONAL SUPPORT**  *Intervention Reader: Moving Ahead Intervention Reader Teacher's Guide,* pp. 100–103 | | | **ADDITIONAL SUPPORT** See *English-Language Learners Resource Kit,* Lesson 10. *English-Language Learners Teacher's Guide,* p. 57 |

How to
Babysit an
Orangutan

story and photographs by
**Tara Darling and Kathy Darling**

255

**SET PURPOSE**

**Locate information.** Remind students that one purpose for reading is to locate information. Ask students to think about the questions they wrote in the K-W-L chart, and have them set a purpose for reading "How to Babysit an Orangutan" based on their questions. Offer this suggestion:

**MODEL** **I want to find out what the babysitter's job is and whether it is fun to babysit an orangutan.**

**Focus Strategy** **Use Text Structure and Format** Tell students that determining how the text is organized and using text features, such as photographs and captions, can help them locate information more easily. Encourage students to use this strategy as they read "How to Babysit an Orangutan."

"How to Babysit an Orangutan" is available on *Audiotext 2.*

## COMPREHENSION CARD 10

**Questioning the Author** Use the Questioning the Author strategy to help students understand the key points of the text.

> ▶ **Questioning the Author** COMPREHENSION CARD 10
>
> **How to Babysit an Orangutan**
> **Key Understanding:** Camp Leakey is an orangutan orphanage. The babysitters there care and teach the baby orangutans skills they will need to be released back into the wild.
>
> 1. p. 257, line 3: To establish the concept that Camp Leakey is an animal protection camp: **What is going on at Camp Leakey?** (Possible response: Humans are taking care of young, orphaned orangutans so the orphans don't die.)
> 2. p. 257, line 15: To establish the babysitters' objective: The author says that a "good babysitter's" job is done when **the baby grows up and goes off to live on its own. What does that mean?** (Possible response: The babysitters want the baby orangutans to live normal lives like the other wild apes in the rain forest.)
> 3. p. 258, line 11: To establish that the author is saying the animal-smuggling business is detrimental to the survival of orangutans: **The author says that there are only 5,000 wild orangutans remaining. If eight orangutans must die for every baby who survives the smuggling, it means that smuggling is not good for the total orangutan population.**
> 4. p. 258, line 15: To clarify the concept that the rain forest environment is in danger: **What is the author trying to tell us here?** (Possible response: The rain forest environment and the animals that live there are in danger of extinction.)
> 5. p. 259, line 12: To establish the relationship between the babysitters and the orangutans: **What is the relationship**
>
> between the babysitters and the baby orangutans? (Possible response: The babysitters must try to give the babies the same things that the wild orangutan mothers give their babies, such as attention and milk.)
> 6. p. 260, line 8: To establish that wild orangutans eat a variety of foods: **What does the author want us to know about orangutans' food?** (Possible response: Babysitters want the babies to eat the same variety of foods that wild orangutans eat, such as fruit, nuts, flowers, leaves, termites, and ants.)
> 7. p. 261, line 6: To establish that baby orangutans are playful. **What is Nanang doing when he steals the author's hat?** (Possible response: Nanang is jealous and wants the hat for himself. He is also being playful.)
> 8. p. 261, line 12: To establish that the babysitters must do unpleasant things in order to care for the babies: The author has told us of unpleasant things babysitters must **do like eat leaves and give orangutans baths. Why do the babysitters do these unpleasant things?** (Possible response: To make sure that the babies eat properly and do not get sick.)
> 9. p. 262, line 14: To establish that orangutans have a variety of emotions and a babysitter needs to be able to identify

**Comprehension Card 10,
page T51 ▶**

# Guided Comprehension

**1** **MAIN IDEA** **What is Camp Leakey?** (a place in Borneo where orphaned orangutans are cared for)

**2** **IMPORTANT DETAILS** **Why is an orangutan orphanage necessary?** (The orangutans' mothers have been killed, and the babies are helpless.)

**3** **DRAW CONCLUSIONS** **Why do the babysitters want the orangutans to go off on their own when they are grown up?** (Possible response: They want to put wild animals back in their natural homes.)

256

ow do you babysit an orangutan? Well, first you have to find an orangutan that needs babysitting.

That's easy here at Camp Leakey. Located in the middle of a rain forest on the island of Borneo, Camp Leakey is not your average camp. It's really an orangutan orphanage. **1**

Ordinarily, orangutan babies don't need human babysitters, but the mothers

**ENGLISH-LANGUAGE LEARNERS**

Point out the words *babysit, babysitting,* and *babysitter.* If necessary, explain that a babysitter takes care of a baby or a child while the parents are away. Pantomime rocking an infant in your arms. Then explain that an *orphan* is someone without a mother or father and that an *orphanage* is a place where orphans live together and are taken care of.

babysit

babysitting

babysitter

of these little red apes have been killed and the orphans are too young to survive alone in the jungle. Without babysitters, all the babies would die from disease, starvation, or injuries. **2**

My friend Birute Galdikas is teaching me how to be an orangutan sitter. For more than twenty years she has been taking care of orangutan babies and training babysitters at Camp Leakey.

The first thing she told me was that babysitting an orangutan is not a "forever" job. A good babysitter's job is done when the baby grows up and can go off into the rain forest and live as a wild ape.

Our job is to teach the orphans the skills they need to get along on their own. That usually takes until they are seven or eight years old, the age when they would leave their natural mother. Then we must say good-bye. **3**

Orangutans at Camp Leakey like to hug.

257

**ONGOING ASSESSMENT**

**Monitor Progress**

(Focus Strategy) **Use Text Structure and Format**

**What is something that the orangutans at Camp Leakey like to do?** (The orangutans at Camp Leakey like to hug. )

Ask volunteers to model how they could use text structure and format to answer the question. If students have difficulty, provide this model:

**MODEL** I notice that the photographs in the selection show young orangutans doing different activities. I look at the caption for the photograph on page 257. It tells me that orangutans like to hug. As I read the selection, I will look at the photographs and read the captions to find out more about what the orangutans at Camp Leakey enjoy doing.

## SOCIAL STUDIES

**Borneo**  Have students use the maps on page 266 to locate Camp Leakey in Borneo and to locate Borneo's position in relation to the rest of the world. Explain that Borneo is the third-largest island in the world. Small boats can travel up rivers to the interior of the island, but many remote areas are still unexplored. Borneo was once covered with rain forests, but today only a few remain.

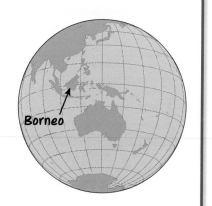

Borneo

# Guided Comprehension

**4 IMPORTANT DETAILS** Why are some orangutan babies smuggled out of their homelands? (Possible response: They are cute, and some people think they would make good pets.)

**5 (Focus Skill) SUMMARIZE** Why is it important to rescue the baby orangutans and return them to the rain forest? (Orangutans are endangered, and they need tropical rain forests to find food.)

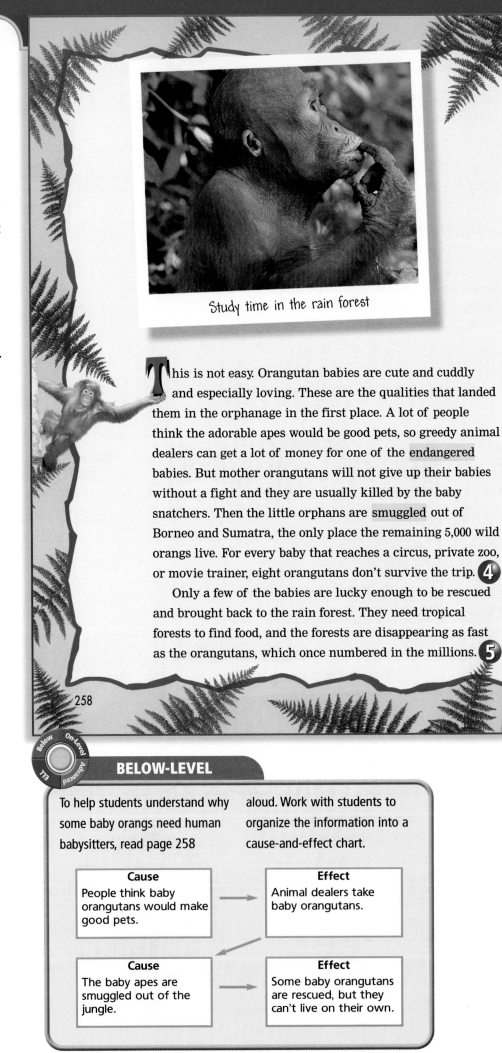

Study time in the rain forest

This is not easy. Orangutan babies are cute and cuddly and especially loving. These are the qualities that landed them in the orphanage in the first place. A lot of people think the adorable apes would be good pets, so greedy animal dealers can get a lot of money for one of the endangered babies. But mother orangutans will not give up their babies without a fight and they are usually killed by the baby snatchers. Then the little orphans are smuggled out of Borneo and Sumatra, the only place the remaining 5,000 wild orangs live. For every baby that reaches a circus, private zoo, or movie trainer, eight orangutans don't survive the trip. **4**

Only a few of the babies are lucky enough to be rescued and brought back to the rain forest. They need tropical forests to find food, and the forests are disappearing as fast as the orangutans, which once numbered in the millions. **5**

258

## BELOW-LEVEL

To help students understand why some baby orangs need human babysitters, read page 258 aloud. Work with students to organize the information into a cause-and-effect chart.

| Cause | | Effect |
|---|---|---|
| People think baby orangutans would make good pets. | → | Animal dealers take baby orangutans. |

| Cause | | Effect |
|---|---|---|
| The baby apes are smuggled out of the jungle. | → | Some baby orangutans are rescued, but they can't live on their own. |

ive-year-old Nanang is my special favorite, but I am also helping with other orphans. Those under two years old take a lot of time, so all the babysitters help with them. The infants are pretty helpless for the first couple of years, much like human children.

Wild orangutan mothers nurse their babies for five or six years. So, if babies under this age come to camp, we must give them milk. Twice a day we mix up a big bucket of powdered cow's milk. Infants get the milk in a bottle. Three- and four-year-olds prefer to drink from a cup, and the wise-guy five- and six-year-olds think it is cool to slurp right from the bucket.

Milk is good for orangutan babies.

**Monitor Progress**

**Focus Strategy Use Text Structure and Format**

**Why do the babysitters give milk to the young orangutans?** (Possible response: because milk is good for orangutan babies)

**Ask volunteers to model using text structure and format to find the answer to the question.**

**MODEL** I see a picture of a baby orangutan drinking milk. I look under the photograph for more information. The caption tells me that the milk is good for orangutan babies.

## SCIENCE

**Rain Forest** The rain forest is a valuable natural resource. It is home to between 50 and 90 percent of the world's species. Almost one quarter of all modern medicine originally came from the rain forest. Many of the fruits, nuts, grains, and spices that are part of our everyday diets come from the rain forest, too. Discuss with students how changes to the rain forest might affect the plants and animals that are part of the rain forest ecosystem.

# Guided Comprehension

**6** **COMPARE AND CONTRAST** **How are orangutans like human babies? How are they different?** (Possible response: Both depend on their care-takers for food, are messy eaters, grab at things they want, and need baths. But orangutans eat leaves and insects, and they hate getting wet.)

**7** (Focus Skill) **SUMMARIZE** **What are some ways in which the humans help the baby orangs?** (Possible responses: They feed them. They help them learn what foods to eat. They give them baths so the babies won't get skin dis-eases.)

**8** **AUTHOR'S VIEWPOINT** **How can you tell that the babysitters think their work is important?** (Possible responses: They do the job even though it isn't all fun; they probably wouldn't be there if they didn't think the job is important.)

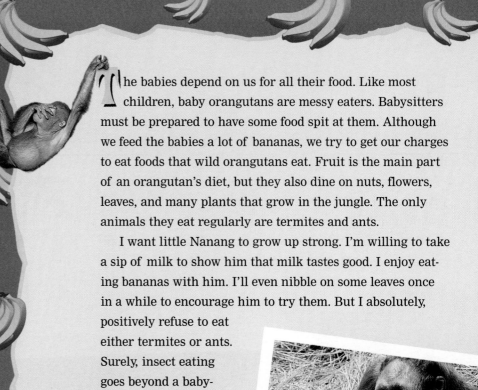

The babies depend on us for all their food. Like most children, baby orangutans are messy eaters. Babysitters must be prepared to have some food spit at them. Although we feed the babies a lot of bananas, we try to get our charges to eat foods that wild orangutans eat. Fruit is the main part of an orangutan's diet, but they also dine on nuts, flowers, leaves, and many plants that grow in the jungle. The only animals they eat regularly are termites and ants.

I want little Nanang to grow up strong. I'm willing to take a sip of milk to show him that milk tastes good. I enjoy eating bananas with him. I'll even nibble on some leaves once in a while to encourage him to try them. But I absolutely, positively refuse to eat either termites or ants. Surely, insect eating goes beyond a baby-sitter's duty!

Tom loves to slurp soap lather.

Bananas are the babies' favorite food.

## REACHING ALL LEARNERS

### Diagnostic Check: Comprehension and Skills

**If** . . . students are having difficulty summarizing . . .

**Then** . . . help them list key events. Ask small groups to act out those events. Other students can provide an oral summary of the scene.

### ADDITIONAL SUPPORT ACTIVITIES

| BELOW-LEVEL | Reteach, p. S60 |
| ADVANCED | Extend, p. S61 |
| ENGLISH-LANGUAGE LEARNERS | Reteach, p. S61 |

This baby is jealous that Nanang has my hat and has made himself a hat out of a leaf.

In the rain forest it rains a lot. (I am sure this does not come as much of a surprise to you.) To make sure a downpour doesn't take me by surprise, I wear a rain hat. Nanang is very jealous. He snatches my hat and plops it onto his own head whenever he can. He loves wearing it even though it is so big he can't see anything with it on.

In a heavy rain, wild orangutans often hold leaf umbrellas over their heads. Orangutans don't like to get wet. That's why bath time is not fun for a babysitter. The littlest orangs get skin diseases and lose their hair in the hot months. It is the babysitter's unlucky chore to give medicine baths. There is a lot of screaming and biting during the bath.

Orangutans don't like baths, but they do love soap. When I do my wash, Tom always begs for a bar. He has rather un-usual ideas about what to do with soap. He thinks of it as food, soaping his arm and sucking the lather off with great slurps of delight. I guess he never heard that washing your mouth out with soap was supposed to be a punishment. **6 7 8**

261

## COMPARING TEXTS

**Informational Texts**  Point out that this selection and "Nights of the Pufflings" are both informational selections about people helping animals. Work with students to compare the two selections. Draw on the board a chart like this one and record students' responses in it.

| "How to Babysit an Orangutan" | "Nights of the Pufflings" |
| --- | --- |
| Author uses first person. | Author uses third person. |
| Author really experienced what she describes. | Author visited Heimaey but did not take part in what he describes. |
| Selection tells about real events. | Selection tells about real events. |
| | |

# Guided Comprehension

**9** **MAIN IDEA** **How does a babysitter tell what an orangutan is feeling?** (Possible response: The orangutan's facial expressions show whether it is happy or angry. Babysitters must not confuse an orangutan's expression with one a human might use.)

**10** **MAKE COMPARISONS** **How are the older baby orangs like human children?** (Possible responses: They get lonesome. They play in groups. Friends stick together.)

**11** **DRAW CONCLUSIONS** **How can you tell that baby orangs need climbing experience?** (Possible response: The humans have to teach them to climb.)

**12** **CAUSE/EFFECT** **Why do the babysitters teach the orangutans to climb?** (Possible response: to prepare them for life in the rain forest canopy)

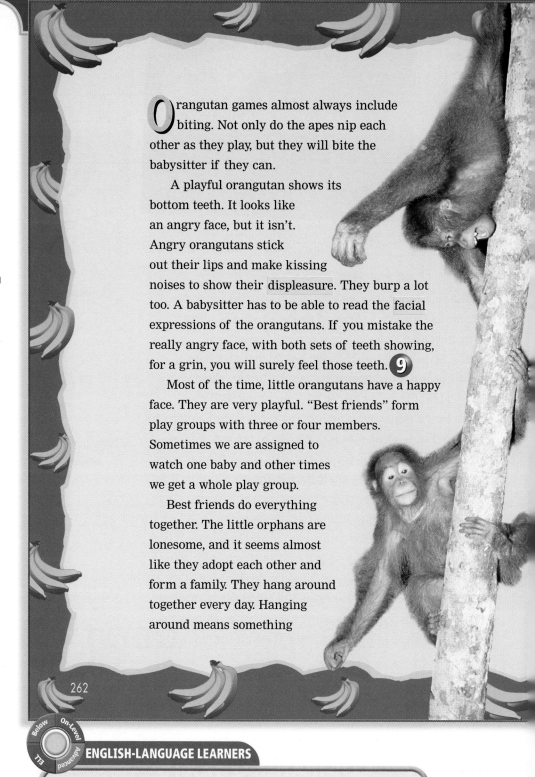

Orangutan games almost always include biting. Not only do the apes nip each other as they play, but they will bite the babysitter if they can.

A playful orangutan shows its bottom teeth. It looks like an angry face, but it isn't. Angry orangutans stick out their lips and make kissing noises to show their displeasure. They burp a lot too. A babysitter has to be able to read the facial expressions of the orangutans. If you mistake the really angry face, with both sets of teeth showing, for a grin, you will surely feel those teeth. **9**

Most of the time, little orangutans have a happy face. They are very playful. "Best friends" form play groups with three or four members. Sometimes we are assigned to watch one baby and other times we get a whole play group.

Best friends do everything together. The little orphans are lonesome, and it seems almost like they adopt each other and form a family. They hang around together every day. Hanging around means something

262

**ENGLISH-LANGUAGE LEARNERS**

Ask students to reread the last paragraph on page 262. Discuss the meaning of *hanging around*: "spending time somewhere doing nothing in particular." Tell students that *hanging around* is an example of an idiom. Point out that the authors are making a play on words by using the idiom to talk about orangutans actually hanging from the trees.

Ask volunteers to think of other idioms that contain *hang*. (*get the hang of, hang out, hang up, hang together, hang on*)

**hang on**

Tara is teaching Nanang to feel at home in the trees.

different to an orangutan. Any game that is fun on the ground is more fun when hanging in the trees. ⑩

One of the most important lessons we teach to the orphan orangutans is that they belong in the trees. Every day we go to the forest so they can build muscles, practice balancing, and get the judgment and coordination necessary for life in the rain forest canopy. Thank goodness the babysitter is not required to climb into the trees with her charges. I couldn't begin to go where Nanang goes with ease. He can hang on with his feet as well as his hands. His wrists allow him to swivel around without changing grip. Even so, he falls once in a while. It takes a few years to get the hang of hanging around. ⑪ ⑫

Nanang knows I can't climb very well. When it is bed-time, he climbs right to the very top of a tree. He hangs up there sucking his thumb till I lure him down with a banana snack.

263

## ONGOING ASSESSMENT

Monitor Progress

# Use Decoding/Phonics

Have students reading below-level read aloud the third paragraph on page 262. Listen for their pronunciation of *assigned.* If students have difficulty, model the strategy.

**MODEL** When I come to an unfamiliar word, such as *assigned,* I try breaking the word into smaller parts. When I read this word, I see the smaller words *a* and *sign.* I also see the ending *-ed.* When I blend the parts together, I read the word /ə•sīnd′/.

## REREADING FOR FLUENCY

**Film Narration** Students may take turns reading aloud all or parts of "How to Babysit an Orangutan" as if they were providing the background narrative for a film about orangutans. Tell them to focus on using volume and phrasing appropriately. **LISTENING/SPEAKING/READING**

**Note:** For assessment of oral reading accuracy and fluency, see pages T44–T45.

# Guided Comprehension

**Were you able to locate information that told you what an orangutan babysitter's job is like?** Ask students whether their purposes for reading were met.

# Think and Respond

**Answers:**

**1** They need babysitters to feed them and get them ready to live on their own. **SUMMARIZE**

**2** The captions explain the photographs and give information that is not in the text. **AUTHOR'S CRAFT**

**3** Possible response: to explain why it is important to rescue the orangutans **AUTHOR'S CRAFT**

**4** Responses will vary. **PERSONAL RESPONSE**

**5** Responses will vary. **READING STRATEGIES**

**OPEN-ENDED RESPONSE**

Which part of the orangutan babysitting job sounds like the most fun? Write a paragraph explaining which part would be the most fun. Include reasons and details.

 **TIMED WRITING OPTION** Allow 15 minutes for students to write their paragraphs.

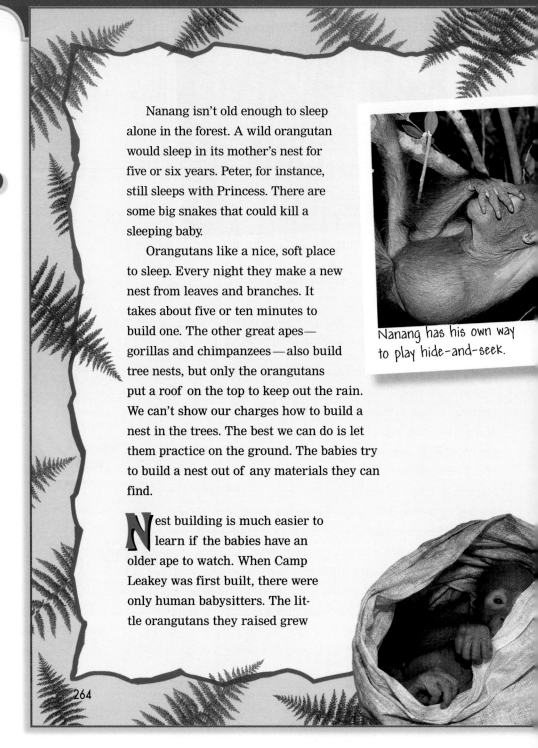

Nanang isn't old enough to sleep alone in the forest. A wild orangutan would sleep in its mother's nest for five or six years. Peter, for instance, still sleeps with Princess. There are some big snakes that could kill a sleeping baby.

Orangutans like a nice, soft place to sleep. Every night they make a new nest from leaves and branches. It takes about five or ten minutes to build one. The other great apes—gorillas and chimpanzees—also build tree nests, but only the orangutans put a roof on the top to keep out the rain. We can't show our charges how to build a nest in the trees. The best we can do is let them practice on the ground. The babies try to build a nest out of any materials they can find.

Nest building is much easier to learn if the babies have an older ape to watch. When Camp Leakey was first built, there were only human babysitters. The little orangutans they raised grew

Nanang has his own way to play hide-and-seek.

264

**COMPREHENSION**

**End-of-Selection Test**
To evaluate comprehension, see *Practice Book*, pages A37–A40.

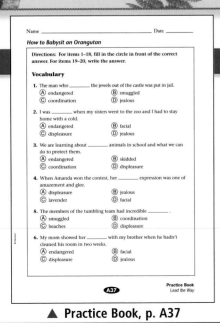

up and went out into the forest. But not for good. Many live nearby and come often to visit. Some come with babies of their own. They are wonderful role models. Adult orangutans can teach the orphans things that human babysitters can't.

Every evening when I see Princess and Peter go walking off into the forest, it makes me happy. They are free. Free to climb in the canopy and free to come and visit when they want to.

The babysitters at Camp Leakey have happily said good-bye to more than 100 orphans. These ex-captives have become wild again.

Although I love him very much, I hope someday I will be able to say good-bye to Nanang too.

## Think and Respond

**1** Why do orangutan orphans need babysitters?

**2** Why do the authors include captions under the photographs?

**3** Why do you think the authors mention that orangutans are **endangered**?

**4** Would you like to babysit an orangutan? Why or why not?

**5** What reading strategy did you use as you read this selection? How was it helpful?

265

▲ Practice Book, p. A37          ▲ Practice Book, p. A40

## ONGOING ASSESSMENT

### RETELL

Use these questions to guide students as they retell "How to Babysit an Orangutan."

• Where does this selection take place?

• Why do some orangutans need human babysitters?

• What are the duties of the babysitters?

### SUMMARIZE

Encourage students to summarize the selection by using their completed K-W-L charts. See Transparency G on page T54.

▼ **Teaching Transparency G**

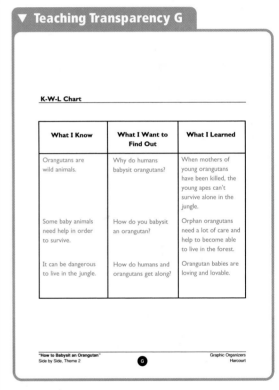

**K-W-L Chart** _____

| What I Know | What I Want to Find Out | What I Learned |
|---|---|---|
| Orangutans are wild animals. | Why do humans babysit orangutans? | When mothers of young orangutans have been killed, the young apes can't survive alone in the jungle. |
| Some baby animals need help in order to survive. | How do you babysit an orangutan? | Orphan orangutans need a lot of care and help to become able to live in the forest. |
| It can be dangerous to live in the jungle. | How do humans and orangutans get along? | Orangutan babies are loving and lovable. |

"How to Babysit an Orangutan"
Side by Side, Theme 2          **G**          Graphic Organizers
Harcourt

### ✏ WRITTEN SUMMARY

Have students use their completed K-W-L charts to write a summary telling what human babysitters must do for orphaned orangutans. PERFORMANCE ASSESSMENT

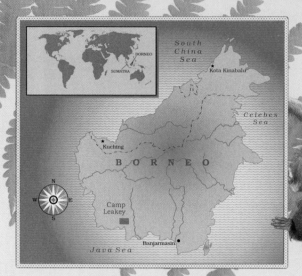

# Orangutan Facts

### Asian Ape

The orangutan is one of the three "great apes." The others are the gorilla and the chimpanzee of Africa.

### Rain Forest Animal

Great apes are found only in tropical rain forests. Orangutans live on the islands of Borneo and Sumatra.

### No Tail

A quick way to tell apes from monkeys is to look for a tail. Most monkeys have tails but none of the apes do.

### Males and Females Very Different in Size

Male orangutans are two or three times bigger than the 100-pound females.

### Babies Stay with Mother for Six or Seven Years

Father never babysits. All adult male orangutans live alone in the treetops.

### Treetop Singers

Orangutans rarely come to the ground. Males call out in search of mates in a loud voice that can be heard for miles.

266

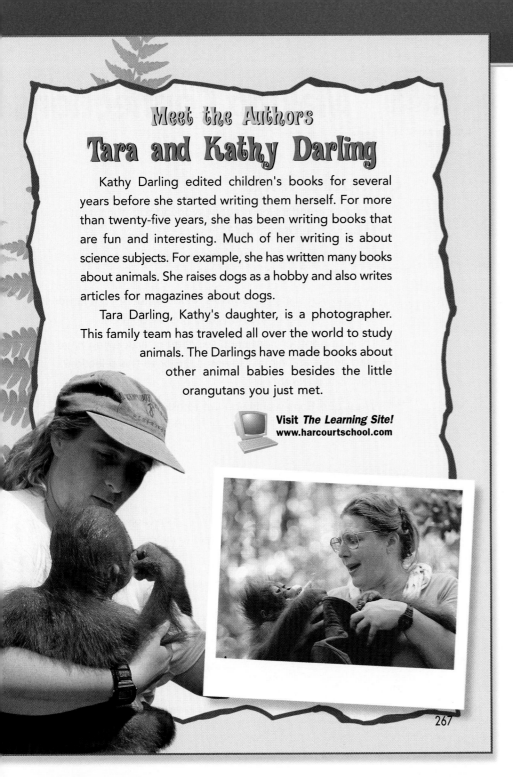

## Meet the Authors
# Tara and Kathy Darling

Kathy Darling edited children's books for several years before she started writing them herself. For more than twenty-five years, she has been writing books that are fun and interesting. Much of her writing is about science subjects. For example, she has written many books about animals. She raises dogs as a hobby and also writes articles for magazines about dogs.

Tara Darling, Kathy's daughter, is a photographer. This family team has traveled all over the world to study animals. The Darlings have made books about other animal babies besides the little orangutans you just met.

Visit *The Learning Site!*
www.harcourtschool.com

267

## related books

You may want to recommend these titles to students interested in this subject.

### LIBRARY BOOKS COLLECTION

*Can We Be Friends?*
by Alexandra Wright.
1994.

### ADDITIONAL READING

- *Animal Fact/Animal Fable*
  by Seymour Simon. Crown, 1987. **EASY**

- *Tornado*
  by Betsy Byars.
  HarperCollins, 1996. **AVERAGE**

- *Komodo Dragon: On Location*
  by Kathy Darling.
  Lothrop, Lee, and Shepard, 1997. **CHALLENGING**

## ABOUT THE AUTHORS

**Kathy Darling** and her daughter **Tara Darling** have traveled all over the world to learn about and photograph rare animals.

Discuss the differences betweeen reading books based on personal experience like the Darlings' and books based on research. (Possible responses: The books based on personal experience tell livelier stories; the books based on research gather facts from the personal experiences or studies of many people.)

*How to Babysit an Orangutan*    **267**

# Making Connections

## COMPARE TEXTS

**Answers:**

**1** Possible response: Readers learn how the people at Camp Leakey work together to take care of the baby orangutans and teach them the skills they need to survive in the wild. **THEME**

**2** Possible response: Looking at the photos and captions helps you picture what the author is describing in the text. **GRAPHIC AIDS**

**3** Possible responses: Most readers are probably not familiar with orangutans' habits and behavior. Comparing orangutans to something familiar gives readers a better understanding of what they are like. **AUTHOR'S CRAFT**

**4** Responses will vary. **COMPARE AND CONTRAST**

**5** Responses will vary. **INQUIRY**

---

▲ How to Babysit an Orangutan

# Making Connections

## Compare Texts

**1** What can readers learn about working together from "How to Babysit an Orangutan"?

**2** How do the photos and captions help you better understand the selection?

**3** Why do you think the authors make frequent comparisons between young orangutans and human children?

**4** Think of another nonfiction selection or article you have read about an animal. How is it similar to this selection? How is it different?

**5** What questions would you like to ask the authors about orangutans?

### Write Instructions

**N**anang's babysitter has a day off. Write instructions to help the new sitter know what to do for the day. Use details from the selection to describe daily activities. Clearly explain each part of the day. Use a sequence chart like this one to organize your ideas.

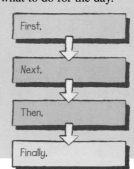

First,

Next,

Then,

Finally,

Writing CONNECTION

268

**Making Connections**

## Give an Oral Report

Find out about a group of people who help animals. Many organizations have websites. You might do a telephone interview with someone in your community who works for this kind of organization. Take notes, and report on your findings.

**Social Studies CONNECTION**

## Make a Diagram

Camp Leakey is located on the island of Borneo. Use the Internet, encyclopedia articles, and nonfiction books to learn about rain forests in Borneo or another part of the world. Use your information to create a diagram that shows how some of the plants and animals are connected.

**Science CONNECTION**

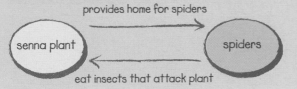

provides home for spiders

senna plant → spiders

eat insects that attack plant

269

## HOMEWORK FOR THE WEEK

Students and family members can work together to complete the activities on page T66. You may want to assign some or all of the activities as homework for each day of the week.

**TECHNOLOGY** Visit
*The Learning Site:*
**www.harcourtschool.com**
See Resources for Parents and Teachers:
Homework Helper.
**Teacher's Edition p. T66 ▶**

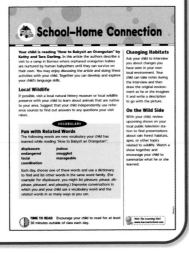

### School–Home Connection

**Your child is reading "How to Babysit an Orangutan" by Kathy and Tara Darling.** In this article the authors describe a visit to a camp in Borneo where orphaned orangutan babies are nurtured by human babysitters until they can survive on their own. You may enjoy discussing the article and doing these activities with your child. Together you can develop and explore your child's language skills.

**Local Wildlife**
If possible, visit a local natural history museum or local wildlife preserve with your child to learn about animals that are native to your area. Suggest that your child independently use reference sources to find out answers to any questions your visit raises.

**Changing Habitats**
Ask your child to interview you about changes you have seen in your own local environment. Your child can take notes during the interview and then draw the original environment as he or she imagines it and write a description to go with the picture.

**On the Wild Side**
With your child, review upcoming shows on your local public television station to find presentations about rain forest habitats, apes, or other topics related to wildlife. Watch a show together, and encourage your child to summarize what he or she learned.

**VOCABULARY**

**Fun with Related Words**
The following words are new vocabulary your child has learned while reading "How to Babysit an Orangutan":

displeasure      jealous
endangered      smuggled
facial            manageable
coordination

Each day, choose one of these words and use a dictionary to find and list other words in the same word family. (For example for displeasure, you might list pleasure, please, displease, pleasant, and pleasing.) Improvise conversations in which you and your child use a vocabulary word and the related words in as many ways as you can.

**TIME TO READ** Encourage your child to read for at least 30 minutes outside of class each day.

*Visit The Learning Site!*
*www.harcourtschool.com*

---

**Writing Instructions** Encourage students to list the tasks first, add the helpful hints next, and then produce a final version of the instructions.

**PORTFOLIO OPPORTUNITY**
Students may choose to place their written instructions in their working portfolios.

### SCIENCE

**Make a Diagram** Remind students that a Web directory may have special sections for science topics. They may also use online search engines to find information about their topic. As students take notes, remind them to restate important ideas in their own words.

Provides home for spiders

Senna Plant      Spiders

Eats insects that attack plants

### SOCIAL STUDIES

**Give an Oral Report** Tell students that a librarian or a science teacher could help them develop a list of organizations that help wild animals. Students may also need help arranging telephone interviews. Tell them to think of some questions and to be prepared to change or add to them during the interview.

# Focus Skill ★ Summarize

## SKILL TRACE

| SUMMARIZE | |
|---|---|
| Introduce | p. 206I |
| Reteach | pp. S48, S60, S92, T39 |
| **Review** | **pp. 228, 252I, 270** |
| Test | Theme 2 |
| Maintain | pp. 372I, 396 |

### RETURN TO THE SKILL

Have students read page 270 in the *Pupil Edition*. You may wish to use this model:

**MODEL** **To help me understand the events in the selection, I can summarize them. This chart shows me what information to include and what information not to include when I write a summary.**

Ask students how deciding what to include in a summary helped them summarize events from "How to Babysit an Orangutan."

### PRACTICE/APPLY

Students can work in small groups to choose a magazine article or a passage from a book. Have them create a chart like the one on page 270, listing information from the article or passage they would include and information they would not include in a summary. **PERFORMANCE ASSESSMENT**

**TECHNOLOGY** ■ *Mission: Comprehension™ Skills Practice CD-ROM* provides additional practice with reading comprehension and focus skills.

**Visit** *The Learning Site*: www.harcourtschool.com
See Skill Activities and Test Tutors: Summarize.

---

▲ How to Babysit an Orangutan

# Summarize

Focus Skill

**T**o **summarize** a passage or a selection, you should briefly retell the most important information.

Turn back to page 260 of "How to Babysit an Orangutan" and reread the information on that page. How would you summarize it? What would you include or not include?

Now look at the chart for some ideas about summarizing this information.

| Include in Summary | | Do Not Include in Summary |
|---|---|---|
| **The Most Important Idea** | **Other Important Information That Supports the Most Important Idea** | **Information That Is Not as Important** |
| Babysitters feed the baby orangutans. | • The babysitters encourage the orangutans to eat the same foods as wild orangutans.<br>• Orangutans mainly eat fruit, but they also need to learn to eat other foods. | • Orangutans are messy eaters who spit food.<br>• The author drinks milk and eats bananas with Nanang, but she does not eat termites or ants. |

**Visit** *The Learning Site!*
www.harcourtschool.com
See *Skills* and *Activities*

270

---

### REACHING ALL LEARNERS

## Diagnostic Check: Comprehension and Skills

**If** . . . students are unable to identify the most important information in a text . . .

**Then** . . . work with them to list the important events. Ask groups to write summary statements for each event.

### ADDITIONAL SUPPORT ACTIVITIES

| BELOW-LEVEL | Reteach, p. S60 |
| ADVANCED | Extend, p. S61 |
| ENGLISH-LANGUAGE LEARNERS | Reteach, p. S61 |

---

# Test Prep
Summarize

▶ **Read the passage. Then answer the questions.**

> **Monkey Tails**
>
> Monkeys, lively and playful, are a favorite attraction in zoos. Many people think that orangutans and other apes are types of monkeys, but monkeys and apes are actually different kinds of animals.
>
> There are more than 200 species of monkeys in the world, ranging in size from about 6 inches to about 32 inches long, not including the length of the tail. A monkey's tail is very useful. Monkeys use their tails to help them balance as they run or jump, or to slow them down as they soar from branch to branch. Some monkeys can swing by their tails and hold objects with them.

1. **Which of these ideas is most important to include in a summary of this passage?**

   **A** Some monkeys are only 6 inches long.

   **B** An orangutan is a kind of ape.

   **C** Monkeys are favorite attractions in zoos.

   **D** Monkeys' tails are very useful.

Choose the sentence that states the most important idea. The title of the passage provides a clue.

2. **On a separate sheet of paper, write a brief summary of the passage.**

State the most important ideas from the passage in your own words.

271

**Focus Skill**

# Test Prep

**Summarize** Have students read the passage carefully, looking for information that should be included in a summary. Use the Tips to reinforce good test-taking strategies. (1ID; 2. Monkeys use their tails for many purposes.)

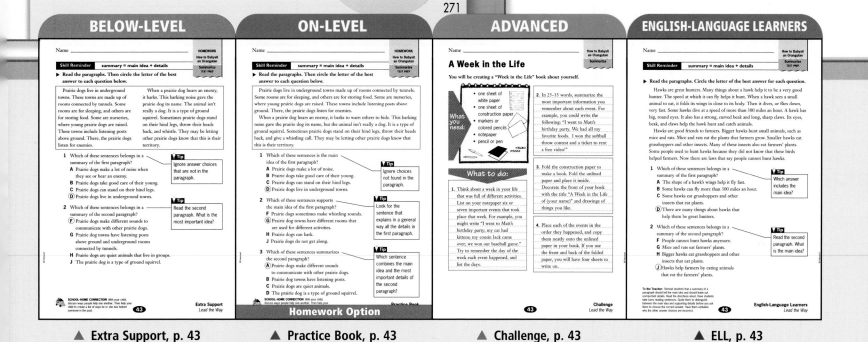

▲ Extra Support, p. 43  ▲ Practice Book, p. 43  ▲ Challenge, p. 43  ▲ ELL, p. 43

*How to Babysit an Orangutan* **271**

# Phonics

## OBJECTIVE:

*To decode words with the VV syllable pattern*

### SKILL TRACE

**SYLLABLE PATTERNS: VV**

| Introduce | Grade 2 |
|-----------|---------|
| **Maintain** | **p. 271A** |

### ONGOING ASSESSMENT

**If** students are not able to fluently read approximately 99 words per minute, **then** they require phonics instruction and will also benefit from fluency practice.

NOTE: For assessment of oral reading accuracy and fluency, see pages T44–T45.

# Decoding/Phonics

*Syllables: VV Syllable Pattern*

### MAINTAIN THE SKILL

**Decode words with the VV pattern.** Write the words *piece* and *flier* on the board. Remind students that when they see a word with two vowels that often act as a team, they should first try pronouncing the two vowels as one vowel sound. Explain that if the word does not sound familiar, they should divide the word into syllables between the vowels and say the first syllable with the long vowel sound. Have students read *piece* and *flier*.

### PRACTICE/APPLY

**Decode VV words.** Write these words on the board: *duet, toast, float, oasis, influenza, peer, fierce,* and *reenter*. For each word, have students tell how they would divide it into syllables and why. Record their responses in a chart like the one below.

| One Syllable | More Than One Syllable |
|--------------|------------------------|
| toast | duet |
| float | oasis |
| peer | influenza |
| fierce | reenter |

Have students pronounce each word in the chart and use it in an oral sentence. Then ask students to read aloud the following longer words: *diagram, reappear.* PERFORMANCE ASSESSMENT

# Search Techniques

*Research and Information Skills*

## REVIEW THE SKILL

**Discuss search engines and keywords.** Remind students that a search engine is a computer service that will locate websites containing the specified keywords. A keyword is a word that describes a topic; the more specific it is, the better. Tell students that they can use keywords in a search engine to narrow their search.

Ask students: **How can I find information about the habits of orangutans?** Then model how keywords can be used in a search engine to narrow a search.

> **MODEL** To narrow my search of orangutans' habits, I can add keywords such as *social* or *eating* to *orangutan* and *habits*. These keywords will help me find more specific information about my topic.

## PRACTICE/APPLY

**Create a keyword web.** Ask students to choose a topic they would like to research. Have them create a word web of keywords that would narrow a search of their topic. Encourage students to make their keywords as specific as possible. **PERFORMANCE ASSESSMENT**

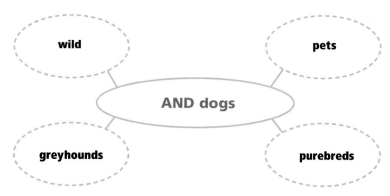

**Summarize.** Ask a volunteer to summarize what he or she knows about search techniques. (Possible response: Keywords can be used in a search engine to make a search more specific.)

**BELOW-LEVEL**

You may want to help students narrow their topics before they begin their keyword web.

# Tested & Timed Writing

## TRAITS OF GOOD WRITING

| | INTRODUCE AND PRACTICE | APPLY TO LONGER WRITING FORMS |
|---|---|---|
| Focus/Ideas | 421E–F | 453E–F, 471C–D |
| Organization | 521E–F, 543E–F | 567C–D, 589E–F |
| Voice | 49E–F, 77E–F | 101C–D, 123C–D |
| Word Choice | 637E–F, 667E–F | 689C–D, 713C–D |
| Development | 421E–F, 437C–D | 453E–F, 471C–D |
| Effective Sentences | 299E–F, 325C–D | 349C–D, 371C–D |
| Effective Paragraphs | 173E–F, 205C–D | 229E–F, 251C–D |
| Conventions | (See Grammar and Spelling Lessons.) | (Applied to all writing lessons.) |

## technology

**Writing Express™ CD-ROM**
Visit *The Learning Site*:
**www.harcourtschool.com**
See Writing Detective:
Proofreading Makes Perfect.

# Summary

## Expository Writing

### DAY 1 — ANALYZE A PROMPT

**DISCUSS TESTS OF WRITING** Review with students that a summary is a retelling of the most important ideas or events in a selection. Explain that they may sometimes be tested on their ability to write a summary.

**ANALYZE THE PROMPT** Display Transparency 89, and read the prompt aloud. Ask students to identify the elements of the prompt they would need to address on a test. Emphasize to students that they will succeed at writing a summary for a test if they address the prompt, include only the most important ideas and details, and use their time wisely.

#### ▼ Teaching Transparency 89

**TIMED OR TESTED WRITING: SUMMARY**

In timed or tested writing, a writer responds to a prompt in a limited amount of time. The prompt tells the writer what to write about.

**Sample Prompt**
Write a summary of your favorite book or of an article you enjoyed. Restate in your own words the main events of the book or article.

**STRATEGIES**

**Analyze the Prompt**

1. What is the writing form? (a summary)

2. Who is the audience? (Possible responses: teacher, classmates, parents)

3. What kind of graphic organizer might be helpful in planning the summary? (Possible response: a story map)

**Budget the Time**

| prewrite | draft | revise and proofread |
|---|---|---|
| 10 | 25 | 10 |

Total Time: 45 minutes

"How to Babysit an Orangutan"
Side by Side, Theme 2          89          Writing Harcourt

### DAY 2 — DISCUSS STRATEGIES

**DISCUSS TIME USE** Display Transparency 89, and have students focus on the time allotment section. Show students how budgeting their time will allow them to finish in the time frame given.

**PREWRITING STRATEGY** Tell students that before they begin writing, they need to organize their ideas. Suggest graphic organizers that they might use, such as a story map or an idea web.

**SELF-ASSESSMENT CHECKLIST** Display Transparency 90, and discuss each item on the checklist. Tell students that they will return to this checklist after their test.

#### ▼ Teaching Transparency 90

**SELF-ASSESSMENT CHECKLIST**

When answering a writing prompt for a summary, use the following guidelines:

- My summary focuses on a topic related to the prompt.  Yes ☐  No ☐

- My summary gives the most important ideas and details.  Yes ☐  No ☐

- My ideas are in a sequence that makes sense.  Yes ☐  No ☐

- My sentence types and lengths are varied.  Yes ☐  No ☐

- My punctuation, capitalization, grammar, and spelling are correct.  Yes ☐  No ☐

"How to Babysit an Orangutan"
Side by Side, Theme 2          90          Writing Harcourt

# 5 Day Plan

## DAY 3 — PRACTICE TEST

Give students practice in taking a timed test. Write the prompt and the allotted time on the board and, below them, the starting time of the test.

**WRITING PROMPT:** *Summarize "How to Babysit an Orangutan." Remember to include only the most important information and details in the selection.* (45 minutes)

Help students identify the writing form, an appropriate audience, and the topic. Remind them to organize their time to allow for prewriting, drafting, and revising. Tell them that you will announce when the first 20 minutes have passed.

## DAY 4 — EVALUATE

### DISCUSS THE PRACTICE TEST

Have students reflect upon their experience with the practice test. Ask questions such as these:

- Did you understand what the prompt required you to do? If not, what could you have done?

- What kind of graphic organizer did you use? How did it help you?

- What kinds of things did you look for as you revised?

Display the Self-Assessment Checklist on Transparency 90, and have students evaluate their summaries. You may also want to give students the scoring rubric on page T88 or T89.

## DAY 5 — REVISE

Give students a chance to revise their summaries. Have them look for and correct errors in punctuation, grammar, spelling, and capitalization. Remind them to delete any details that are not essential to their summaries. Have students make a clean copy of their summaries.

Tell students to keep their practice tests in their portfolios so that they may monitor their writing progress.

| SCORING RUBRIC | | | |
|---|---|---|---|
| | **4** | **3** | **2** | **I** |
| **FOCUS/IDEAS** | Completely focused, purposeful. Paraphrases main ideas and significant details. | Generally focused on task and purpose. Paraphrases main ideas and significant details. | Somewhat focused on task and purpose. Minimal paraphrasing. | Lacks focus and purpose. Substantial copying of sentences or phrases. |
| **ORGANIZATION/ PARAGRAPHS** | Ideas progress logically; related ideas grouped in paragraphs; paper conveys sense of completeness. | Organization mostly clear, but some lapses occur; paragraphs mostly contain related ideas. | Some sense of organization but inconsistent or unclear in places. | Little or no sense of organization. |
| **DEVELOPMENT** | Central idea supported by the important details in the selection. | Central idea with adequate support, mostly relevant details. | Unclear central idea; limited supporting details. | Unclear central idea; little or no development. |
| **VOICE** | Consistent; does not interject irrelevant opinions or details. | Generally does not interject irrelevant opinions or details. | May include irrelevant opinions or details. | Includes irrelevant opinions or details. |
| **WORD CHOICE** | Clear, exact language; freshness of expression. | Clear language; some interesting word choices. | Word choice unclear or inappropriate in places. | Word choice often unclear or inappropriate. |
| **SENTENCES** | Variety of sentence structures; flows smoothly. | Some variety in sentence structures. | Little variety; choppy or run-on sentences. | Little or no variety; sentences unclear. |
| **CONVENTIONS** | Few, if any, errors. | Few errors. | Some errors. | Many errors. |

**REPRODUCIBLE STUDENT RUBRICS** for specific writing purposes and presentations are available on pages T88–T90.

**Language Handbook,** pp. 52–53, 64–65, 120–121

# Grammar

## Complex Sentences

## SKILL TRACE

### COMPLEX SENTENCES

| Introduce | p. 271E |
| --- | --- |
| Reteach | pp. S63, T43 |
| Review | p. 271F |
| Test | Theme 2 |

## REACHING ALL LEARNERS

## Diagnostic Check: Grammar and Writing

**If** . . . students have difficulty with complex sentences . . .

**Then** . . . ask them to write two simple sentences about a favorite activity. Have them combine the sentences, using at least one independent clause and one dependent clause.

### ADDITIONAL SUPPORT ACTIVITIES

**BELOW-LEVEL** Reteach, p. S62

**ADVANCED** Extend, p. S63

**ENGLISH-LANGUAGE LEARNERS** Reteach, p. S63

## technology

**Grammar Jingles™ CD,**
Intermediate: Track 4
See Grammar Practice Park,
Go for Grammar Gold,
Multimedia Grammar Glossary.
Visit *The Learning Site:*
www.harcourtschool.com

---

### DAY 1 — TEACH/MODEL

#### DAILY LANGUAGE PRACTICE

1. When I visited the zoo I learnt a lot about animals. (zoo, I; learned)

2. Many wild animal are becoming very rair. (animals; rare)

**INTRODUCE THE CONCEPT** Refer to Transparency 91 as you discuss these points:

- A **complex sentence** is made up of an independent clause and at least one dependent clause.

- A dependent clause often begins with a connecting word.

Have students rewrite the sentence pairs in items 4–6 as complex sentences.

#### ▼ Teaching Transparency 91

##### COMPLEX SENTENCES

1. The babies are cute. simple sentence
2. The babies are cute, but they are helpless. compound sentence
3. Although the babies are cute, they are helpless. complex sentence

**Some Connecting Words That Can Begin Dependent Clauses**

| after | because | since | when |
| --- | --- | --- | --- |
| although | before | if | while |

4. Orangutans are born. They are helpless.
5. There is a lot of screaming. The babysitter gives the bath.
6. Orangutans can live as wild apes. The babysitters did a good job.

Responses will vary. Possible responses:
4. When orangutans are born, they are helpless.
5. There is a lot of screaming (while or when) the babysitter gives the bath.
6. If orangutans can live as wild apes, the babysitters did a good job.

"How to Babysit an Orangutan"
Side by Side, Theme 2
**91**
Grammar
Harcourt

---

### DAY 2 — EXTEND THE CONCEPT

#### DAILY LANGUAGE PRACTICE

1. I especially enjoyd the orangutans they are playful animals. (enjoyed; orangutans. They)

2. Orangutans come from the Islands of Borneo, and Sumatra. (islands of Borneo and)

**BUILD ORAL LANGUAGE** Display the chart of connecting words on Transparency 91. Ask students to take turns choosing connecting words and adding dependent clauses to the following independent clauses, creating complex sentences:

Our class went to the zoo.

Our class will go to the zoo.

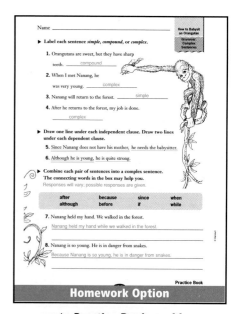

▲ Practice Book, p. 44

<table>
<tr><td>

**DAY 3** ORAL REVIEW/PRACTICE

**DAILY LANGUAGE PRACTICE**

1. **Most monkeys have tales apes do not.** (tails, but apes)
2. **Baby orangutans need help. When their Mothers have been killed.** (help when; mothers)

**ADD A CLAUSE** Write on the board several independent clauses. Ask volunteers to add a dependent clause to each independent clause to form a complex sentence.

**Test Prep Tip**

"Remember that a dependent clause begins with a connecting word such as *after* or *because* and is followed by a comma."

</td><td>

**DAY 4** APPLY TO WRITING

**DAILY LANGUAGE PRACTICE**

1. **Would you like, to babysit an orangutan.** (like to; orangutan?)
2. **The orphans need help. Until they are seven or eight year old.** (help until; years)

**SENTENCES** Ask students to skim "How to Babysit an Orangutan" to find and copy one of each kind of sentence: simple, compound, and complex. Then have them make up one of each kind of sentence, telling something about orangutans.

</td><td>

**DAY 5** CUMULATIVE REVIEW

**DAILY LANGUAGE PRACTICE**

1. **The babys make nests on the grownd.** (babies; ground)
2. **Someday they will, make nests, in the trees.** (will make nests in)

**CLAUSES IN SENTENCES** Have students tell whether each sentence below is simple, compound, or complex. Have them draw one line under each independent clause and two lines under each dependent clause.

1. Babysitters must be prepared to have some food spit at them. (simple)
2. If you like animals, you will like babysitting orangs. (complex)
3. Orangutans don't like baths, but they do love soap. (compound)

</td></tr>
</table>

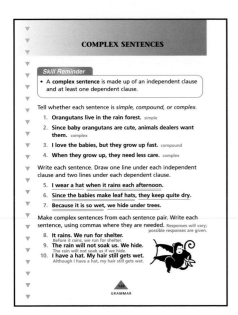

▲ Language Handbook, p. 120

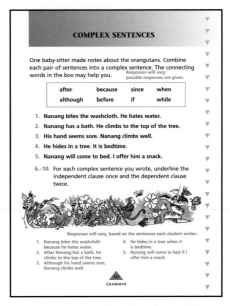

▲ Language Handbook, p. 121

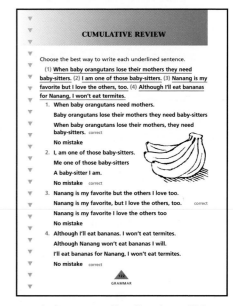

▲ Language Handbook, p. 122

## Spelling Words

1. ground*
2. frown
3. downtown
4. bounced
5. council
6. about
7. scout
8. counter
9. background
10. amount
11. bound
12. shower
13. mountain
14. county
15. thousand
16. allowance
17. counselor
18. discount
19. countless
20. rebound

* Selection Words

### Challenge Words

21. orangutan*
22. primate
23. rain forest*
24. banana*
25. species

# Spelling

## Words with /ou/

### DAY 1 — PRETEST/SELF-CHECK

**ADMINISTER THE PRETEST** Use the Dictation Sentences under Day 5. Help students self-check their pretests by using Transparency 92.

### ADVANCED

Use the Challenge Words in these Dictation Sentences:

21. An **orangutan** is one of the great apes.
22. Orangutans belong to the order called **primate**.
23. Many animals make their homes in the **rain forest**.
24. A **banana** is a tropical fruit.
25. Some animal **species** are endangered.

### DAY 2 — TEACH/MODEL

**WORD SORT** Display Transparency 92. Discuss the meanings of the words. Then ask students to copy the chart and to write each Spelling Word where it belongs.

Write on the board the words *ground* and *frown*, and read them aloud. Ask students what vowel sound they hear in both words. (/ou/) Have a volunteer circle the letters that represent this sound. (*ou* and *ow*)

**HANDWRITING** Remind students that each letter and letter part should be the same size in relation to the other letters.

*frown*

### ▼ Teaching Transparency 92

**WORDS WITH THE /ou/ SOUND**

**Spelling Words**

| | | | |
|---|---|---|---|
| 1. ground | 6. about | 11. bound | 16. allowance |
| 2. frown | 7. scout | 12. shower | 17. counselor |
| 3. downtown | 8. counter | 13. mountain | 18. discount |
| 4. bounced | 9. background | 14. county | 19. countless |
| 5. council | 10. amount | 15. thousand | 20. rebound |

| ou proud | | ow plow |
|---|---|---|
| ground | bound | frown |
| bounced | mountain | downtown |
| council | county | shower |
| about | thousand | allowance |
| scout | counselor | |
| counter | discount | |
| background | countless | |
| amount | rebound | |

The letters ou or ow can stand for the *ou* sound.

"How to Babysit an Orangutan"
Side by Side, Theme 2        92        Spelling Harcourt

▲ Practice Book, p. 45

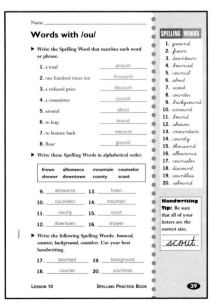

▲ Spelling Practice Book, p. 39

## 5 Day Plan

**CHECKING TWICE** Write the following on the board:

*abowt  frown  bound  shouer*

Tell students to proofread the words and then check them again. Have a volunteer circle any misspelled words and write them correctly. *(about, shower)* Ask students to explain why checking twice might reveal a mistake that they missed the first time.

### Apply to Writing

Have students think of the two possible ways to spell /ou/. Then have them check their writing twice to make sure the words are spelled correctly.

▲ Spelling Practice Book, p. 40

**BUILD A WORD** Have students create Build-a-Word puzzles. Tell students to list words that contain the letters *ou* or *ow*. Then have them reorder the list so that the first word adds three letters to the *ou* or *ow*; the second, four letters; and so on. Encourage students to use Spelling Words.

Have students copy the puzzle on a sheet of paper, inserting blanks for all letters other than *ou* or *ow*. Then have them add a definition beside each word. Students can then exchange puzzles.

Display this model:

to show displeasure
on the face          _ _ ow _
a light rainfall        _ _ ow _ _

▲ Spelling Practice Book, p. 41

**DICTATION SENTENCES**

1. The **ground** is frozen.
2. Draw a **frown** on the clown's face.
3. Let's meet **downtown** for lunch.
4. He **bounced** up and down on the bed.
5. When will the **council** vote?
6. Tell me **about** your trip.
7. I'll go **scout** for water.
8. Who is that behind the **counter**?
9. Tell me about your **background**.
10. What **amount** of sugar do you need?
11. The package is **bound** with tape.
12. Do you think the **shower** will last long?
13. We watched the sun rise over the **mountain**.
14. What **county** do you live in?
15. They raised one **thousand** dollars for the project.
16. Some people receive a weekly **allowance**.
17. Our school has a wonderful **counselor**.
18. Did you receive a **discount** when you bought that shirt?
19. You can find **countless** ways to be helpful.
20. The basketball player grabbed the **rebound**.

*How to Babysit an Orangutan*  **271H**

# Word Study

## STRUCTURAL ANALYSIS

## Word Parts

**OBJECTIVE**

*To use word parts to determine the meaning of longer words*

Write the word *starvation* on the board, and have students identify and discuss the meanings of its familiar word parts. (*starve-tion*; the word *starve* means "to suffer because of a lack of food," and the *-tion* ending means "the condition of.") Help students figure out the meaning of *starvation*. ("the condition of suffering because of a lack of food") Then write the following words on the board, and have students identify the word parts and discuss their meanings.

| Word | Parts |
| --- | --- |
| wasteful | waste + ful |
| argument | argue + ment |
| expression | express + ion |

Have students look in materials from other content areas to find five long words that can be decoded by breaking them into parts. Ask students to use in sentences the words they found.

### ADVANCED

Have students brainstorm five long words they might use in a writing assignment. Have them use a dictionary and write one definition for each word on their list. Then tell them to exchange lists with a partner and write a sentence for each word on their partner's list.

## PREFIXES

## Prefix *dis–*

**OBJECTIVE**

*To use knowledge of prefixes to analyze the meaning of longer words*

Tell students that the prefix *dis-* can mean "the opposite of." Point out that adding the prefix *dis-* to a word turns the word into its antonym.

Demonstrate by using the word *pleasure* and the vocabulary word *displeasure*. Ask students to write the antonym suggested by each of these definitions:

- not connected (disconnected)
- not to allow (disallow)
- not to appear (disappear)
- not organized (disorganized)
- without trust (distrust)

Then have students brainstorm a list of other words that begin with the prefix *dis-*.

**connected**

**disconnected**

# Speaking and Listening

## Informational Speech

**OBJECTIVE**

*To present a speech, using clear diction, correct pacing, and appropriate volume*

Ask students to prepare a speech about a group of people who help animals. Tell students that most major cities have organizations that provide shelter for homeless dogs and cats.

**Organization**   Share these **organizational tips** with students.

• Write a beginning for your speech that introduces the topic and your main idea.

• Write the main ideas for your speech on separate note cards. Be sure to include facts to help listeners focus. Keep notes short and easy to read. Number your note cards.

**Delivery**   Share the following **practice tips** with students.

• Take a deep breath to help you relax. Smile. Talk directly to your classmates. Make eye contact.

Have students give their speeches to a small group of classmates.

**PERFORMANCE ASSESSMENT**

## Audience Behavior

**OBJECTIVE**

*To identify important facts and details in a speech*

**Listening Tips**

• Show respect by making eye contact and paying attention.

• Listen for a beginning, a middle, and an ending.

Remind students that good listeners pay close attention and don't interrupt. Have students identify the most important ideas in their classmates' speeches.

Share the Listening Tips with students.

**LISTENING CHECKLIST**   Have students create their own checklist of things that good listeners should do. Suggest that students illustrate the checklist with a picture of a person showing good listening behavior.

## Identifying Main Ideas

**OBJECTIVE**

*To understand the main concept and supporting details in a video*

Borrow a wildlife video from the library to watch as a class. Afterward, summarize the video by using these prompts:

• **What was the main concept of the video?**

• **Name one detail that you remember from the video.**

## Books for All Learners

*Reinforcing Skills and Strategies*

### ■ BELOW-LEVEL

 **Focus Skill: Summarize**

 **Focus Strategy: Use Text Structure and Format**

 **Vocabulary:** *displeasure, jealous, endangered, smuggled, facial, coordination*

**Genre:** Nonfiction
**Science Connection:** Interdependence of Living Things

**SUMMARY** The text and illustrations describe Jane Goodall's work with chimpanzees in East Africa. It explains how she patiently observed them and eventually gained their trust. Her observations show that chimpanzees are intelligent creatures that express various emotions.

 **Visit *The Learning Site:* www.harcourtschool.com**
Resources for Parents and Teachers: Books for All Learners.

### BEFORE READING

**Preview/Set Purpose**   Have students preview the book title and illustrations. Help them set a purpose for reading.

**Reinforce Summarize**   Help students make a K-W-L chart to summarize the main ideas in the book. **SUMMARIZE/GRAPHIC AIDS**

| K-W-L Chart | | |
|---|---|---|
| What I Know | What I Want to Know | What I Learned |
| | | |

**Reinforce Vocabulary**   Write on the board sentence frames such as these to review vocabulary: An angry person shows displeasure. Gymnasts must have physical coordination.

### READING THE BOOK

**Pages 6–10**   In what order is this information given? (in the order of events in Jane Goodall's life) **TEXT STRUCTURE**

**Pages 11–14**   What is Jane Goodall like? (Possible responses: patient, observant, caring, curious) **CHARACTER TRAITS**

**Page 16**   What did you learn about chimpanzees? (They live in groups and depend on one another. **MAIN IDEA**

**Reread for Fluency**   Have students choose and reread aloud favorite parts of the book to you.

### RESPONDING

**K-W-L Chart**   Have students complete the K-W-L chart and use it to help them summarize the main ideas in the book.

**BELOW-LEVEL**

**ON-LEVEL**

**ADVANCED**

**ELL**

▲ page 271M     ▲ page 271N

## ■ ON-LEVEL

 **Focus Skill: Summarize**

 **Focus Strategy: Use Text Structure and Format**

 **Vocabulary: *displeasure, jealous, endangered, smuggled, facial, coordination***

**Genre:** Realistic Fiction
**Social Studies Connection:** Importance of Personal and Civic Responsibility

**SUMMARY** Carmen and her family take in a two-month-old puppy and train it for about a year to get it ready for guide dog school.

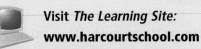 **Visit *The Learning Site:*
www.harcourtschool.com**
Resources for Parents and Teachers:
Books for All Learners.

### BEFORE READING

**Preview/Set Purpose** Have students preview the book by noting the dates of the diary entries. Ask them how much time passes.

**Reinforce Summarize** Have students create a flowchart. Tell them to summarize the events in the story, using one square for each diary entry. **SUMMARIZE/GRAPHIC SOURCES**

### READING THE BOOK

**Pages 2–3** What are Carmen's parents talking about? (becoming puppy-raisers) Why don't they want her to understand? (They don't want her to be disappointed if their application is not accepted.) **CAUSE AND EFFECT**

**Pages 7–11** What does Carmen learn between January 28 and February 18 about how to train Bravo? (Be honest; don't tease; use short commands; say "no" to show displeasure, say "yes" or "good boy" when Bravo does the right thing; give rewards right away.) **SUMMARIZE**

**Page 13–14** What do you think happened between Carmen's March 3rd diary entry and her entry on the following January 1? (Bravo learned how to behave in public in more and more difficult situations.) **DRAW CONCLUSIONS**

**Rereading for Fluency** Have students choose several days of diary entries to read aloud. Ask them to read so that they express Carmen's feelings as she wrote.

### RESPONDING

**Chart** Students can complete the flowchart of diary entries and use it to summarize the selection.

## Books for
# All Learners
*Reinforcing Skills and Strategies*

---

### ■ ADVANCED

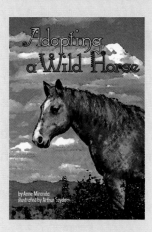

 **Focus Skill: Summarize**

 **Focus Strategy: Use Text Structure and Format**

 **Vocabulary:** *displeasure, jealous, endangered, smuggled, facial, coordination, bureau, skittered*

**Genre:** Realistic Fiction
**Science Connection:** Patterns of Interdependency in Ecological Systems

**SUMMARY**   Alice convinces her parents to adopt a wild horse from the Bureau of Land Management. Alice cares for the horse, working patiently to gain the horse's trust so she can ride it.

 **Visit *The Learning Site:*
www.harcourtschool.com**
Resources for Parents and Teachers:
Books for All Learners.

---

### BEFORE READING

**Preview/Set Purpose**   Have students use the chapter titles to determine the setting and what they might learn from this book.

**Reinforce Summarize**   Ask students to create a time line showing the steps Alice took to ride Curiosity. **SUMMARIZE/GRAPHIC SOURCES**

**Expand Vocabulary**   Discuss with students two meanings of *bureau*. (a government department; a low chest of drawers) Tell them to find the meaning of *bureau* used in this story.

### READING THE BOOK

**Pages 2–3**   What does Chapter I say about wild horses in North America? (They lived 10,000 years ago and disappeared. Some horses that Spanish explorers brought formed wild herds. Their descendants still live as wild horses today.) **SUMMARIZE**

**Pages 4–16**   Why do you think this book has many short chapters instead of a few long ones? (to show the steps Alice took to get and tame her horse) **USE TEXT STRUCTURE AND FORMAT**

**Page 10**   What does the author mean by "Alice has good horse sense"? (She knows how to treat the horse properly.) **AUTHOR'S PURPOSE**

**Rereading for Fluency**   Have students reread a chapter.

### RESPONDING

**Illustrate Events**   Have students draw pictures illustrating how Alice and Curiosity interact at different times in the story.

While you work with small groups have other students do the following:
- Self-Selected Reading
- Practice Pages
- Cross-Curricular Centers
- Journal Writing

▲ page 271K     ▲ page 271L

## ■ ENGLISH-LANGUAGE LEARNERS

 **Focus Skill: Summarize**

 **Focus Strategy: Use Text Structure and Format**

 **Concept Vocabulary:** *jobs, protect, healthy, work, smile, remember*

**Genre:** Nonfiction
**Science Connection:** Structures and Functions of Human Body Systems

**SUMMARY** This book describes and explains different systems of the human body and how they support its functions. The book concludes with recommendations for maintaining a healthy body through diet, exercise, and sleep.

 **Visit** *The Learning Site:*
**www.harcourtschool.com**
Resources for Parents and Teachers: Books for All Learners. See Language Support.

### BEFORE READING

**Tap Prior Knowledge** Point to the illustration on page 3. Ask students to tell what they see.

**Total Physical Response** Read the names of the body systems in the book. Have students respond by pointing to the correct body parts. (eyes, ears, nose, teeth, tongue, bones, hair, nails, and skin)

**Display Vocabulary Concept Words** Write the words on the board. Use the words in sentences such as these: The skin's *job* is to protect the body. You are *growing* taller every day.

**Preview the Book** Help students preview the book by pointing out and discussing the title, illustrations, and captions.

### READING THE BOOK

**Pages 2–16** What does this book tell you about your body? (It describes parts of the body and shows how they work together.) SUMMARIZE

**Page 6** How does the nose help take care of the body? (The nose brings in air to breathe. It keeps dust from entering the body. It can help you smell danger, such as smoke from a fire.) IMPORTANT DETAILS

**Rereading** Reread the book aloud with students. Have volunteers point out the body parts that are discussed in each section.

### RESPONDING

**Chart** Have students complete a chart like the following to help them organize and retell the information in the book.

| Body Part | Function |
|-----------|----------|
| eyes | |

# Theme Wrap-Up & Review

## Discuss the Literature

- **What are some of the ways in which the selections in this theme are alike?** (Possible responses: The selections contain stories about people in communities or groups that work together. All show characters who help others in some way.)

- **Name another story, poem, or article that you think might fit this theme. Explain why you think it would be a good fit.** (Responses will vary.)

- **Why do you think this theme is called "Side by Side"?** (Responses will vary but should mention that the stories deal with ways that people affect each other or work together, side by side.)

## Return to the Theme Connections

Ask students to review and revise their chart to include information about all the selections they have read and listened to.

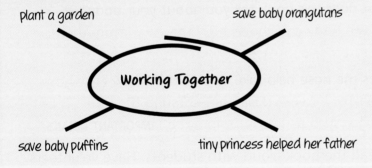

plant a garden

save baby orangutans

**Working Together**

save baby puffins

tiny princess helped her father

## Response Options

 **REFLECT** Have students reflect on what they have learned about meeting challenges or overcoming obstacles. Students can write their reflections in their journals.

 **SELF-ASSESSMENT** Students can reflect on their own progress using the **Thinking About My Reading** and the **My Reading Log** blackline masters on pp. R38–R39.

> THEME PROJECT

## Project Presentations

### Save a Species

Students who have completed their inquiry projects can present their work to an audience. Encourage students to demonstrate what they have learned in a creative way. Here is an idea you may suggest:

Presenters may choose to share posters to convince the audience to take a stand to protect endangered animals. Posters could show pictures of the species and its habitat, maps that pinpoint the location of the habitat, reasons why protection is necessary, and things people can do to help protect the species.

Direct students to the Presenting Your Writing section of the *Writer's Handbook* pages R3–R13.

See also the Rubric for Presentations on p. T58 of this *Teacher's Edition.*

# Review

## Comprehension

You may want to use the Read Aloud selection for **"The Baker's Neighbor"** to review the tested focus skills for this theme. Reread the selection to students, and ask questions like the following:

 **SUMMARIZE**

**What is this poem about?** (Possible response: It is about the speaker's experiences picking apples from his orchard.)

 **CAUSE AND EFFECT**

**Why does the boy decide to pick apples only in the daytime?** (Bears come to eat apples at night. The speaker wants to avoid the bears.)

## Grammar

Have students revisit a writing assignment or choose a piece from their portfolios. Have them edit that piece of writing according to the following directions:

- check all subjects and predicates for spelling and agreement
- use connecting words such as *and, but,* and *or* to combine short choppy sentences into compound sentences
- use a comma to set off a clause that is not necessary to the meaning of a sentence
- make sure each sentence expresses a complete thought

 Visit *The Learning Site:*
www.harcourtschool.com
See Go for Grammar Gold.

## Vocabulary

Students can use vocabulary from the theme to play an alphabetizing game. Write each word on an index card, and have students divide the cards among a group of players. Tell students to add extra words if needed so that each group has the same number of cards. Players must arrange their cards in alphabetical order and then use the first and last of their words in oral sentences.

| | | |
|---|---|---|
| ad lib | insignificant | shiftless |
| assent | instinctively | skidded |
| burrows | jealous | smuggled |
| coordination | lavender | steely |
| displeasure | loyal | stranded |
| elated | luxury | twined |
| encircling | mural | uninhabited |
| endangered | neglected | unyielding |
| facial | nestles | venture |
| haze | plotting | |
| indignantly | privilege | |
| inhaled | shamefacedly | |

## Spelling

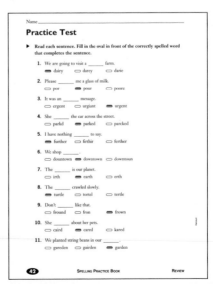

▲ Spelling Practice Book, pages 42–43

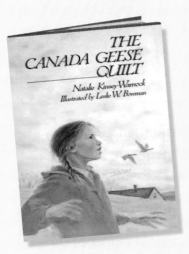

▲ *The Canada Geese Quilt*
by Natalie Kinsey-Warnock

## THEME: Side by Side

As students read *The Canada Geese Quilt*, they will learn about a young girl's relationship with her grandmother and how the girl's love of nature helps her grandmother recover from an illness.

## GENRE: Realistic Fiction

**Summary**: Ten-year-old Ariel's comfortable life on her family's Vermont farm begins to change when her mother announces a baby is on the way and her beloved grandmother has a serious stroke. Despite all the changes, Ariel feels reassured once her recovering grandmother gives her a special token of her love.

## ABOUT THE AUTHOR

**Natalie Kinsey-Warnock** was raised on a dairy farm in Vermont. The experience of helping her grandmother make a special quilt depicting Canada geese inspired her first children's book.

# Library Book Lesson

## Access Prior Knowledge

Preview the book title and cover with students. Tell them that the novel takes place on a Vermont farm near the Canadian border. Then draw their attention to the geese. Ask students to tell anything they know about Canada geese. Use students' responses to create a web.

| Canada geese |
|---|
| I) large birds |
| 2) fly south during the winter |
| 3) travel in large groups |
| 4) fly in V formation |
| 5) often choose mates for life |
| 6) make honking noises |
| 7) intelligent and cautious |

## Set Purpose/Predict

Have students read the first chapter of *The Canada Geese Quilt.* Then have them predict what might happen between Ariel and Grandma. They may write their predictions in their journals to check after reading. Then have them set a purpose for reading the rest of the book. (Possible response: to find out why Canada geese are important to the story.)

### DEVELOP VOCABULARY

Have students provide as many definitions as they can for the following multiple-meaning words: *legend, design, protest, stroke, and pace.* Have students set up their definitions to look like dictionary definitions, with illustrations. For example: *design 1. (noun) A plan or sketch used as a pattern. 2. (verb) to draw plans and sketches for something.*

# Options for Reading

## Guided Comprehension

 **STRATEGY REMINDER**
Remind students that good readers *self-question,* or ask themselves silent questions, as they read. Tell students that this book is told from Ariel's point of view, and since it is not always possible for Ariel to understand why the other characters behave as they do, it is helpful for students to ask themselves questions about what is really going on in the story. During reading, ask the questions at the upper right to help students monitor their own comprehension.
WHOLE CLASS/INDEPENDENT

## Cooperative Reading

Have groups of three to four students use Comprehension Card 7 (Setting) to guide their discussion.
INDEPENDENT/SMALL GROUP

## Independent Reading

Students can write questions they have about characters' actions or anything that seems confusing in their journals. After reading, have students complete the self-assessment forms found on pages R38–R39 and add them to their reading portfolios. INDEPENDENT

## Teacher Read-Aloud

Read aloud through page 12 and display the illustrations. Ask volunteers to describe people in their lives who are easy to talk to and with whom they can share secrets or ideas. Students may then read the book independently.
WHOLE CLASS/INDEPENDENT

# Options for Responding

## Personal Response

Have students answer the responding questions at the right to demonstrate understanding and share their interpretations.
INDEPENDENT/WHOLE CLASS

## Compare Selections

Have students compare this book to another realistic fiction story about a family by answering questions about each story:
• How do the family members feel about each other?
• Does the family have a conflict?
• How is the conflict solved?
INDEPENDENT/SMALL GROUP

## Discuss Setting

Have students find places in the story in which the setting affects the characters' feelings and actions. Have students work in small groups to answer these questions:
• Why do you think the author points out on the first page that Ariel does not shiver from the cold, but from the way the geese "stirred her?"
• How would this story change if it took place in a different setting?
• How do the illustrations add to the idea that the setting of the story is very important to the story's plot? INDEPENDENT/SMALL GROUP

## Improv Theater

Have small groups look through the book for a scene that has more than one character. Invite groups to discuss how each character is feeling in the scene, then to improvise appropriate dialogue as they act out the scene. SMALL GROUP

---

## OPTIONS FOR READING

**1** **Ariel's mother is away for four days, but it seems like months to Ariel. Why do you think she feels this way?** (Possible response: Ariel is very worried about Grandma's illness.)
INFERENTIAL: DETERMINE CHARACTER'S EMOTIONS

**2** **Why do you think Grandma improved when Ariel took her outside?** (Possible response: Nature was very important and inspiring to Grandma.)
INFERENTIAL: CAUSE-EFFECT

**3** **Why do you think Grandma made Ariel her own quilt?** (Possible response: Grandma wanted Ariel to know that Grandma loved her for being a special, unique person.) CRITICAL: INTERPRET CHARACTERS' MOTIVATIONS

## OPTIONS FOR RESPONDING

**1** **How do you think Ariel has changed at the end of the story?** (Responses will vary.)
METACOGNITIVE: INTERPRET DETAILS

**2** **Why does the author want us to know that the geese are so important to Ariel?** (Responses will vary.) CRITICAL: RECOGNIZE AUTHOR'S PURPOSE

## ENGLISH-LANGUAGE LEARNERS

Have students discuss what they see in the illustrations. Invite them to take notes about each picture to help them as they read the story independently.

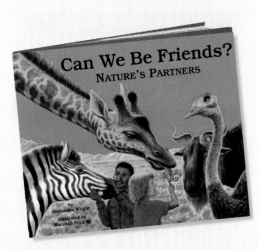

▲ *Can We Be Friends? Nature's Partners*
**by Alexandra Wright**

## THEME: Side by Side

As students read *Can We Be Friends? Nature's Partners,* they will meet a variety of animals who have developed helpful "friendships" with other creatures.

## GENRE: Nonfiction

**Summary:** Readers are introduced to thirteen different animal pairs, including birds, fish, reptiles, mammals, and insects, that have symbiotic relationships. The animal partners work cooperatively to find food, watch for predators, rid the partner of parasites, or share home duties. Students are encouraged to think about how humans can use animal partnerships as models for working cooperatively.

## ABOUT THE AUTHOR

**Alexandra Wright** has written several nature books for young readers. These include *Will We Miss Them? Endangered Species* and *At Home in the Tide Pool.*

# Library Book Lesson

## Access Prior Knowledge

Display the book cover and have students read the title aloud. Ask students what a *partner* is. (someone who shares something) Explain that animals, like people, sometimes rely on partners for help. Begin a web with students by asking: **When do you find it helpful to have a partner?**

Then challenge students to brainstorm ways in which different kinds of animals might help each other as partners.

## Set Purpose/Predict

Have students read the first page of the book and then flip through the rest of it to view the illustrations. Ask students whether this seems to be a fiction or a nonfiction book, and what helped them decide. Have students use their prior knowledge and their preview to guess how the two animals on the first page might be helping each other. (The bird is getting food by cleaning the crocodile's teeth.) Then have them predict what they might learn and set a purpose for reading the book. (to learn about how these and other animal partners help each other)

### DEVELOP VOCABULARY

Ask students to list unfamiliar words in their journals as they read. These might include unusual animal names and features (such as *anemone* and *tentacles*) and science words (such as *symbiosis*). Encourage students to use the phonetic respellings in a dictionary to help them pronounce these words.

# Options for Reading

## Guided Comprehension

**Focus Strategy** **STRATEGY REMINDER** As students read, remind them that they can **use reference sources** such as atlases and encyclopedias to help them understand what they read or find more information about topics they encounter while reading. Offer these examples:

- **An encyclopedia could help you find additional facts about the animals described in the book.**
- **An atlas could help you locate where these animals live.**

WHOLE CLASS/SMALL GROUP

## Cooperative Reading

Have groups of three or four students use Comprehension Card 6 (Theme and Mood) to guide their discussions. INDEPENDENT/SMALL GROUP

## Independent Reading

Students can write in their journals about whether their purpose for reading was met, whether they would recommend this book to a friend, and why they would or would not do this. After reading, have students complete the self-assessment forms found on pages R38–R39 and add them to their reading portfolios.

INDEPENDENT/WHOLE CLASS

## Teacher Read-Aloud

Read aloud the first three pages as students listen responsively. Then display the picture of the ants and aphids on the fourth page, and have students guess how these insects help each other. Encourage students to make similar guesses about each new pair of animal partners as they read. INDEPENDENT/WHOLE CLASS

# Options for Responding

## Personal Response

Have students answer the responding questions at the right to demonstrate their understanding and share their interpretations.
INDEPENDENT/WHOLE CLASS

## Compare Selections

Have students compare this book to *Nights of the Pufflings* by completing a Venn diagram. Write the following diagram on the board to get them started.
INDEPENDENT/WHOLE CLASS

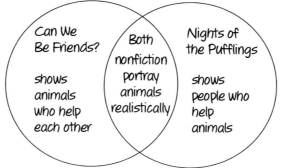

## Write a Dialogue

Have students work in pairs to create imaginary dialogues between one set of animal partners described in the book. Students might have their animal characters tell what they like and dislike about working with their partner. Have student pairs present their dialogues to the class.
SMALL GROUP/WHOLE CLASS

## Create Animal Fact Sheets

Ask students to find out more about one of the animals described in the book, or about another symbiotic relationship in nature, and to create an illustrated fact sheet to show what they learned.
INDEPENDENT/WHOLE CLASS

## OPTIONS FOR READING

1. **What are some ways animals help each other?**
(Possible responses: finding food, protection, and shelter; providing cleaning and companionship.)
INFERENTIAL: SUMMARIZE

2. **Based on what you read, what makes a human or an animal partnership successful?** (Possible response: Both members give something and receive something in return.)
INFERENTIAL: DRAW CONCLUSIONS

## OPTIONS FOR RESPONDING

1. **Do you agree that humans can learn from animal partnerships? Explain.** (Possible response: Yes, people can learn to help each other even though, like animals, people are different from each other.) CRITICAL: EXPRESS PERSONAL OPINIONS

2. **How do the illustrations add to your understanding of the information in the book?** (Possible response: They show how the animals help each other.) CRITICAL: EXPRESS PERSONAL OPINIONS

## ENGLISH-LANGUAGE LEARNERS

Have students acquiring English read with English-proficient partners who can help with pronunciation. Encourage partners to discuss the animals described.

# Assessing Student Progress
## to Modify Instruction

- End of Selection Test (in Practice Book)

- Oral Reading Fluency Assessment

- Reading and Language Skills Assessment: Posttest
- Holistic Assessment

### Monitoring of Progress

| END-OF-SELECTION TESTS<br><br>**IF** you want to monitor student progress in **selection vocabulary** and **comprehension,** | **THEN** administer the multiple-choice and short answer diagnostic **End-of-Selection Tests.** |
| --- | --- |
| ORAL READING FLUENCY ASSESSMENT<br><br>**IF** you want to know how your students' fluency skills are progressing, | **THEN** use the **Oral Reading Fluency Assessment.** |

### Multiple Measures

**Anecdotal Records** To track the progress of each student's literacy development, establish procedures for keeping anecdotal records. Consider setting aside several pages in a spiral notebook for each student. Focus on one to three behaviors or understandings during each week.

**Checklists** Use the checklists on pages R35–R37 to track students' progress in listening, speaking, reading, and writing.

**Portfolios** Have students keep copies of their works-in-progress and final drafts of writing assignments in a Working Portfolio. Encourage them to choose their best work and keep it in a Show Portfolio. Use teacher-student conferences to review student progress in writing.

**Reading Notebooks** To learn about students' independent or self-selected reading, have students keep a log of their reading in a Reading Notebook, or use the My Reading Log copying master (page R38). Encourage them to keep lists of titles, authors, and genres that they enjoy.

### Summative Assessment

| READING AND LANGUAGE SKILLS<br>ASSESSMENT: Posttest<br><br>**IF** you want to evaluate a student's mastery of the skills in this theme, | **THEN** administer the **Reading and Language Skills Assessment.** |
| --- | --- |
| HOLISTIC ASSESSMENT<br><br>**IF** you want to know more about a student's ability to read a passage and apply literal, inferential, and critical thinking skills in a global and holistic manner, revising and editing skills in writing, and how he or she responds to multiple-choice and short and extended open-ended questions, | **THEN** administer the **Holistic Assessment.** |

# Additional Support Activities

# Side by Side
## Additional Support Activities

# Additional Support Activities
# Vocabulary

## ■ BELOW-LEVEL

### Reteach: Vocabulary

**See the Words**

Display Transparency 56. Discuss each picture. Then point to each word and pronounce it.

**Hear the Words**

Say these sentences to reteach vocabulary.

- Tanya was **elated** to become a new member.

- It was a **privilege** and an honor.

- Everyone had given their **assent**.

- The new vase they gave her was a **luxury** item.

- After the announcement, people began to **ad lib** a song.

- Some **shiftless** people did not want to sing.

- When someone spoke to them **indignantly**, they looked down **shamefacedly**.

**Say the Words**

Have students read aloud the vocabulary words from the transparency.

**Need More Intensive Instruction?**

**See Intervention Resource Kit, Lesson 6** for additional **preteach** and **reteach** activities.

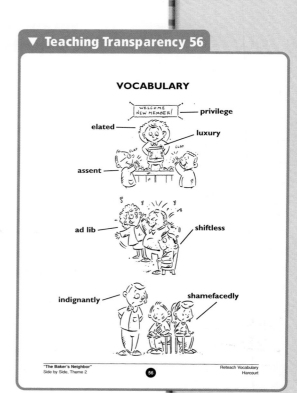

▼ **Teaching Transparency 56**

VOCABULARY

"The Baker's Neighbor"
Side by Side, Theme 2

56

Reteach Vocabulary
Harcourt

## ■ ADVANCED

### Bonus Words

- **sullenly**—silently; out of anger
- **saunters**—walks about in a relaxed way
- **sneering**—showing or saying with scorn
- **taunt**—to tease
- **vigorously**— with healthy strength

### Extend: Bonus Words

Display Transparency 57. Read the sentences aloud, and challenge students to suggest a definition for each word, based on context clues and the illustrations. Then have students classify the words by part of speech. Conclude by having student pairs act out the meanings of the words. The rest of the class may guess the words.

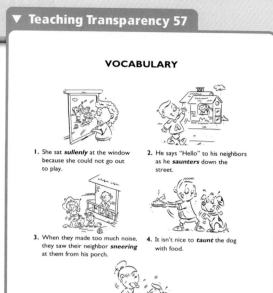

VOCABULARY

1. She sat **sullenly** at the window because she could not go out to play.

2. He says "Hello" to his neighbors as he **saunters** down the street.

3. When they made too much noise, they saw their neighbor **sneering** at them from his porch.

4. It isn't nice to **taunt** the dog with food.

5. Her new neighbor shook her hand **vigorously**.

"The Baker's Neighbor"
Side by Side, Theme 2
57
Bonus Words
Harcourt

## ■ ENGLISH-LANGUAGE LEARNERS

### Reteach: Background and Vocabulary

Revisit Transparency 56. As you describe each scene, point to and read aloud each vocabulary word, and have students repeat it after you. You may want to pantomime words such as *elated*, *assent*, *indignantly*, and *shamefacedly* to ensure student understanding.

Prompt discussion by asking questions about the illustrations. Encourage students to use vocabulary words as they respond. Provide question-and-response frames such as the ones below to help students begin.

| Question | Response |
|---|---|
| How did Tanya feel about becoming a new member? | She felt ___elated___. |
| What kind of item was the vase? | The vase was a ___luxury___ item. |
| What kind of people did not want to sing? | The ___shiftless___ people did not want to sing. |

### Need More Language Development?

See **English-Language Learners Resource Kit, Lesson 6** for additional **preteach** and **reteach** activities.

# Additional Support Activities
# Comprehension and Skills

### ■ BELOW-LEVEL

## Reteach: Cause and Effect

Remind students that a **cause** is an action or event that makes something happen. An **effect** is what happens as the result of an action or event. Tell students that to find an effect, they should ask, *What happened?* To find a cause, they should ask, *Why did this happen?* Work with students to make a list of effects, or events that happen, in the selection. Then help them identify causes by guiding them to ask *why* the events happened.

| Cause | Effect |
|---|---|
| Pablo smells Manuel's pastries but does not pay for them. | Manuel gets upset. |
| The Judge orders Pablo to bring his money to the court. | Pablo brings his money to the court. |
| Manuel enjoys counting Pablo's money. | The Judge declares the case settled. |

Have each student draw a picture showing one of the cause-and-effect relationships listed. Students should include a caption for the picture that uses a signal word to explain the relationship, such as *Pablo brought his money to the court because the Judge ordered him to do so.*

 **TECHNOLOGY ■** *Mission: Comprehension™ Skills Practice* **CD-ROM**

**Need More Intensive Instruction?**

**See Intervention Resource Kit, Lesson 6** for additional **preteach** and **reteach** activities.

## ■ ADVANCED

### Extend: Cause and Effect

Have students work in pairs to create a cause-and-effect chart that shows multiple causes and/or effects. Tell students to choose a natural phenomenon, such as an earthquake or a tornado, or a historic event, such as the Civil War or the Great Depression, and research its causes and effects. Then have students represent their findings in a diagram such as the following:

| Cause | | Effect |
|-------|---|--------|
| | → | |

| Cause | | Effect |
|-------|---|--------|
| | → | |

## ■ ENGLISH-LANGUAGE LEARNERS

### Reteach: Cause and Effect/Selection Summary

Walk students through the selection page by page. Discuss each page and illustration. Work with students to compose a cause-and-effect sentence that describes what is happening on the page or in the illustration. As students say the sentence aloud, write it on the board. You may want to point out signal words such as *because* and *so*. Use students' completed sentences to help them develop an oral summary of the selection. Provide sentence frames such as these:

- Manuel is the richest man in town because
  he keeps all the money from his bakery for himself .

- Manuel the baker is angry at Pablo because
  he always sniffs the pastries but never buys any .

- Manuel thinks Pablo is a thief so  he goes to see the Judge  .

- The Judge orders Pablo to bring his money to the courtroom so
  Pablo brings the money .

- The Judge says the case is settled because
  Manuel enjoyed counting Pablo's money .

**Need More Language Development?**

**See English-Language Learners Resource Kit, Lesson 6** for additional **preteach** and **reteach** activities.

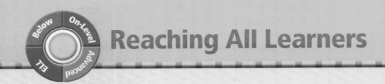

# Additional Support Activities
# Grammar and Writing

## ■ BELOW-LEVEL

### Reteach: Ordering Ideas

**BUILD ON PRIOR KNOWLEDGE**   Recall with students that when they write a paragraph of information, it is important for them to order their ideas in a logical way. Remind students that two ways to order their ideas are by time order and by order of importance. Use this topic to model ordering ideas: Planning a Party

Brainstorm with students a list of steps for planning a party.

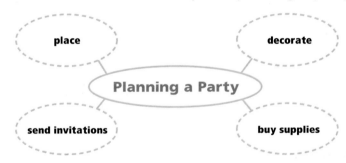

**CONSTRUCT THE TEXT**   Tell students that because this topic is about the steps for doing something, they should order their ideas in time order. "Share the pen" with students by having them arrange the steps from the web in time order and write sentences.

**REVISIT THE TEXT**   Reread the draft aloud and prompt them to think about how it could be improved.  Are the ideas in time order or order of importance?  Do all the sentences have a complete subject and predicate?  Guide students to make revisions as necessary.

**Need More
Intensive Instruction?**

**See Intervention
Resource Kit, Lesson 6**
for additional **preteach**
and **reteach** activities.

## ■ ADVANCED

### Extend: Writing

**INFORMATIVE WRITING** Tell students that
the purpose of pamphlets and brochures is to
give information. Ask students to write a paragraph of information about a topic they are
interested in, such as being a good pet owner
or being a good brother or sister. Challenge
them to turn their paragraph of information
into an informational pamphlet. Tell them to
include illustrations or photos with captions to make their pamphlets
visually appealing. You may want to show students models of pamphlets before they begin.

## ■ ENGLISH-LANGUAGE LEARNERS

### Reteach: Grammar and Writing

**PREDICATE PRACTICE** Explain to students that most simple predicates are words that tell about actions. (action verbs) Have volunteers demonstrate actions such as *hop, sit, stretch,* and *jump,* and
have other students name the action.

Then write these sentences on the board.

- I ___hop___ on one foot.
- I ___sit___ in a chair.
- I ___stretch___ before running.

Work with students to identify and circle the simple predicate in
each sentence. Then tell students that the complete predicate is
made up of the action verb and all the words that tell more about
the action, such as *how, where,* or *when.*

**WRITING PRACTICE** Revisit the interactive writing steps on page
S38. Work with students to effectively order their ideas.

**Need More Language
Development?**

**See English-Language
Learners Resource Kit,
Lesson 6** for additional
**preteach** and **reteach**
activities.

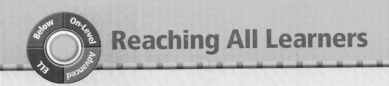
# Additional Support Activities
# Vocabulary

### ■ BELOW-LEVEL

## Reteach: Vocabulary

**See the Words**

Display Transparency 65. Discuss the scenes, pointing to each word as you say it.

**Hear the Words**

Say these sentences aloud to reteach vocabulary.

- Kara and Marisa are **loyal** friends. Today they worked together to make a kite.

- Marisa thought that the kite's tail seemed **insignificant**, but Kara was **unyielding** in her belief that it was important.

- Kara **twined** the kite's string around a stick. She made sure it was **encircling** her wrist.

- The string wasn't very thick, but it was **steely** strong.

- The kite flew well until Marisa **neglected** her job of telling Kara when the kite was getting close to a tree.

- They spent a long time **plotting** how to get the kite out of the tree.

**Say the Words**

Have students read aloud the vocabulary words from the transparency.

insignificant      twined      neglected

▼ Teaching Transparency 65

**VOCABULARY**

loyal friends

unyielding in her belief

encircling her wrist

insignificant kite tail

steely strong string

twined around a stick

neglected her job

plotting how to get the kite out of the tree

"The Emperor and the Kite"
Side by Side, Theme 2          65          Reteach Vocabulary
Harcourt

**Need More Intensive Instruction?**

**See Intervention Resource Kit, Lesson 7** for additional **preteach** and **reteach** activities.

The Emperor
and the Kite
*by JANE YOLEN illustrated by ED YOUNG*

## ■ ADVANCED

### Bonus Words

- **poppyseed cakes**—a snack spiced with poppy seeds
- **water chestnuts**—nutlike fruits
- **green tea**—a hot drink that is brewed from leaves
- **rice cakes**—a snack made of puffed rice

## Extend: Bonus Words

Display Transparency 66. Ask students to look at the picture as you read the menu aloud. Then ask students to use their own experience and the pictures to write definitions for the Bonus Words. When they are finished, have students confirm the meanings of the words in a dictionary.

**BONUS WORDS**

**MENU**

Hao Hao's Lunch Special:
Lunch begins with an appetizer of crunchy **rice cakes**, soothing **green tea**, and wonton soup. Then, for your main dish, choose between Beef and Broccoli or Sesame Chicken with **water chestnuts**. Finish off with two tasty **poppyseed cakes**.

"The Emperor and the Kite"
Side by Side, Theme 2　　　　**66**　　　　Bonus Words
　　　　　　　　　　　　　　　　　　　　　　　Harcourt

## ■ ENGLISH-LANGUAGE LEARNERS

### Reteach: Background and Vocabulary

Revisit Transparency 65. Point to and read aloud each vocabulary word, and have students repeat the words after you. Use questions and response frames such as these to monitor students' understanding. Work with students to complete each sentence about the story with a vocabulary word. Have students read the completed sentences aloud.

| Question | Response Frame |
|---|---|
| What kind of friends are Kara and Marisa? | Kara and Marisa are ___loyal___ friends. |
| Did Marisa think the kite tail was important? | ___No___ , she thought it was ___insignificant___ . |
| Did Kara agree with Marisa about the kite tail? | ___No___ , she was ___unyielding___ in her belief that it was important. |
| How strong was the kite string? | It was ___steely___ strong. |
| What did Kara do with the kite string? | She ___twined___ it around a stick. Then she ___encircled___ her wrist with it. |
| Why did the kite get stuck in a tree? | Marisa ___neglected___ her job. |
| What were Marisa and Kara doing after the kite got stuck in a tree? | They were ___plotting___ a way to get it down. |

### Need More Language Development?

**See English-Language Learners Resource Kit, Lesson 7** for additional **preteach** and **reteach** activities.

# Additional Support Activities
# Comprehension and Skills

## ■ BELOW-LEVEL

### Reteach: Narrative Elements

Review with students that every story is made up of the setting, the characters, and the plot. Each of these elements works together to create a particular story. Draw on the board a 3-column chart like the one below. Have students reread the story and work together to fill in the chart. Remind students that they can use the self-questioning strategy to fill in the chart by asking themselves questions such as *Who is in the story? Where does it take place?* and *What happens?*

| Characters | Setting | Important Plot Events |
|---|---|---|
|  |  |  |

Then discuss with students how Djeow Seow's size is an important part of her character and the plot. Ask: **How would this story be different if Djeow Seow was the same size as her sisters?** (The plotters probably would have noticed her when they kidnapped the emperor. She wouldn't have been able to rescue him.)

 **TECHNOLOGY** ■ *Mission: Comprehension™ Skills Practice CD-ROM*

**Need More Intensive Instruction?**

**See Intervention Resource Kit, Lesson 7** for additional **preteach** and **reteach** activities.

The Emperor
and the Kite
by JANE YOLEN    illustrated by ED YOUNG

## ■ ADVANCED

### Extend: Narrative Elements

Ask students to imagine a new setting for "The Emperor and the Kite." Encourage them to think of a setting that is very different from ancient China. Have them consider how the story would be different if it took place in a different time and place. Then ask them to rewrite the story with the new setting. Have them exchange stories with a partner and discuss how a change in setting affects the plot and the characters.

## ■ ENGLISH-LANGUAGE LEARNERS

### Reteach: Narrative Elements/Selection Summary

Display "The Emperor and the Kite" and walk students through the selection, page by page. Discuss the illustrations and important events on each page.

Then have students make a comic strip that shows the narrative elements of "The Emperor and the Kite." Ask them to draw the following:

- **Frame 1:** the main characters (Emphasize their differences.)
- **Frame 2:** the setting (according to what they have learned from the text)
- **Frame 3:** the problem or problems (They may wish to split this frame into two smaller frames.)
- **Frame 4:** the solution

When students have finished their drawings, work with them to develop an **oral summary** of the selection. Encourage them to refer to their comic strips for ideas about what to include in their summaries.

**Need More Language Development?**

See English-Language Learners Resource Kit, **Lesson 7** for additional **preteach** and **reteach** activities.

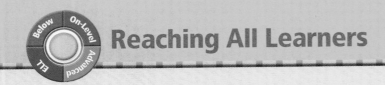

# Additional Support Activities
# Grammar and Writing

## ■ BELOW-LEVEL

### Reteach: Writer's Craft

**BUILD ON PRIOR KNOWLEDGE**   Ask students when they read directions. (when they want to know how to do something) Explain that directions should be clear and easy to follow. Tell students that an appropriate audience for their directions is someone who does not know how to do the thing that they are describing. Work with students to choose a topic and an audience. Then brainstorm with them a list of sequence words to use in their directions.

| Sequence Words | |
|---|---|
| first | after |
| second | during |
| third | finally |
| then | last |

**CONSTRUCT THE TEXT**   "Share the pen" with students by working with them to create a draft. Use these steps to think aloud the process:

- Tell where your directions will lead someone.
- On scrap paper, list the steps of the directions.
- Make sure the steps are in order and that what is to be done in each step is clear.
- Choose sequence words from the list. Add them to your steps.
- Rewrite your steps in paragraph form.

**REVISIT THE TEXT**   As you work with students to revise their directions, **reread** frequently with them to help them identify and add any missing steps. Then work with them to revise any steps that are unclear and to rearrange any steps that are out of order.

**Need More Intensive Instruction?**

**See Intervention Resource Kit, Lesson 7** for additional **preteach** and **reteach** activities.

The Emperor
and the Kite
by JANE YOLEN illustrated by ED YOUNG

## ■ ADVANCED

### Extend: Writing

**TREASURE HUNT**   Have students work in pairs to write a story about a treasure hidden on the school playground. In their stories students should provide written directions to the hidden treasure.
Encourage students to exchange stories and to determine the location of the treasure in the story they receive.

## ■ ENGLISH-LANGUAGE LEARNERS

### Reteach: Grammar and Writing

**COMPOUND SUBJECTS AND PREDICATES**   Point to and name a person in the room. Then make up a complete sentence that describes something about that person. For example, say:

> **Maria has brown hair.**

Then work with students to revise the sentence, giving it a compound subject or a compound predicate. For example:

> **Maria and Jonah have brown hair.**
>
> **Maria has brown hair and rides the bus.**

Have students repeat the process. Guide them to create sentences with compound subjects and predicates. Then have them complete sentence frames such as these:

> Linda and _____ fly kites.
>
> Roberto reads and _____ everyday.
>
> John or _____ will walk the dog.

**WRITING PRACTICE**   Revisit the writer's craft activity on page S44. Work with students to develop their written directions. Remind students to connect ideas with compound subjects and predicates.

**Need More Language Development?**

See English-Language Learners Resource Kit, **Lesson 7** for additional **preteach** and **reteach** activities.

# Additional Support Activities
## Vocabulary

### ■ BELOW-LEVEL

## Reteach: Vocabulary

### See the Words
Display Transparency 75. Discuss each word, using the illustrations for clarification.

### Hear the Words
Read these sentences aloud to reteach vocabulary.

- The island has many animals but is **uninhabited** by people.

- Many small animals live here in **burrows** under the ground.

- A field mouse waits until the storm has passed to **venture** out for food.

- The storm has left some baby birds **stranded** on the island.

- The birds **instinctively** begin to look for shelter.

- A young rabbit sees the birds and **nestles** close to its mother.

### Say the Words
Have students read aloud the vocabulary words from the transparency.

**Need More Intensive Instruction?**

**See Intervention Resource Kit, Lesson 8** for additional **preteach** and **reteach** activities.

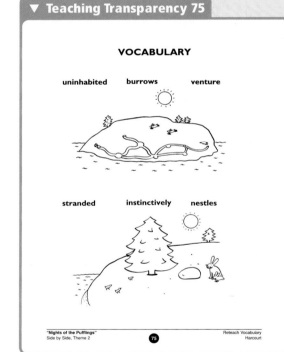

▼ **Teaching Transparency 75**

VOCABULARY

uninhabited    burrows    venture

stranded    instinctively    nestles

"Nights of the Pufflings"
Side by Side, Theme 2    75    Reteach Vocabulary
Harcourt

### ■ ADVANCED

**Bonus Words**

- **lundi**—puffin
- **fisk**—fish
- **baldusbrá**—flowers
- **Heimaey Island**—a small island off the southwestern coast of Iceland

### Extend: **Bonus Words**

Display Transparency 76. Have students look at each illustration as you read the sentences aloud. Then have students classify the words into categories (*lundi* and *fisk* are animals; *baldusbrá* is a flower; Heimaey Island is a place.) Have students substitute an English word for each Icelandic word in the first three sentences.

▼ Teaching Transparency 76

**BONUS WORDS**

The *lundi* comes ashore to lay eggs.

The puffins eat many *fisk*.

In the spring the *baldusbrá* bloom on the island.

Heimaey Island is a small island off the southwestern coast of Iceland.

"Nights of the Pufflings"
Side by Side, Theme 2    76    Bonus Words
Harcourt

### ■ ENGLISH-LANGUAGE LEARNERS

### Reteach: **Vocabulary**

Revisit Transparency 75. Describe the scenes, using the bulleted sentences on page S46. As you read aloud each vocabulary word, point it out on the transparency and ask students to repeat it after you. Use simple synonyms as necessary to ensure student understanding.

You may also want to use the photographs in "Nights of the Pufflings" to illustrate the meanings of words such as *uninhabited*, *nestles*, and *stranded*. Work with students to use the vocabulary words in sentences by providing question and sentence frames such as the ones below.

**Need More Language Development?**

See **English-Language Learners Resource Kit, Lesson 8** for additional **preteach** and **reteach** activities.

| Question | Response Frame |
|---|---|
| Do people live on the island? | No, it is _uninhabited_ . |
| Where do small animals live? | Many small animals live in _burrows_ . |
| What does the mouse do after the storm? | It _ventures_ out for food. |

# Additional Support Activities
# Comprehension and Skills

## ■ BELOW-LEVEL

### Reteach: Summarize

Remind students that **summarizing** is retelling the main events or main ideas of a selection. Explain that they should use their own words and retell the events in the order in which they happened.

Revisit the selection with students. Work with them to summarize each page in one or two sentences. For example, students might summarize page 211 in this way: "Every year, many puffins return to an island in Iceland to have their young." As students summarize each page, write their sentences on the board. Then have students answer these questions:

- **Do these sentences accurately summarize the main events?**
- **Do these sentences include only the most important ideas from the selection?**
- **Are the events told in your own words?**
- **Are the events retold in the same order as in the selection?**

Help students arrange the sentences into a paragraph that summarizes the whole selection.

 **TECHNOLOGY** ■ *Mission: Comprehension™ Skills Practice CD-ROM*

**Need More
Intensive Instruction?**

**See Intervention
Resource Kit, Lesson 8**
for additional **preteach**
and **reteach** activities.

## ■ ADVANCED

### Extend: Summarize

Have students work in groups to summarize other nonfiction texts, such as a newspaper article or a section from a textbook. Remind them to use their own words as they summarize and to focus on main ideas or events. Challenge students to summarize a fiction selection as well. Ask students to compare summarizing nonfiction to summarizing fiction, and to discuss the similarities and differences.

**Summarizing Nonfiction**
Look for important facts.

**Both**
Include only the most important information.

**Summarizing Fiction**
Look for important plot events.

## ■ ENGLISH-LANGUAGE LEARNERS

### Reteach: Summarize

Display "Nights of the Pufflings" and walk students through the selection, page by page. Discuss with students what they see on each page. Guide them to use the accompanying photographs along with the text to develop an **oral summary** of the selection.

- **Pages 210–211:** Many seabirds called puffins return to an island each year to have their young.

- **Pages 212–213:** Halla and her friends watch the puffins catch fish to feed their young.

- **Pages 214–215:** The children catch the pufflings that accidentally land in the village. Then they put them in boxes.

- **Pages 216–217:** The children help the pufflings fly safely out to sea.

**Need More Language Development?**

**See English-Language Learners Resource Kit, Lesson 8** for additional **preteach** and **reteach** activities.

# Additional Support Activities
# Grammar and Writing

## ■ BELOW-LEVEL

### Reteach: Summary/Interactive Writing

Work with students to complete Teaching Transparency 72. Tell students that you will develop a summary of "Nights of the Pufflings" together.

Ask volunteers to identify the main event of the selection. Then have students identify several important details to support the main event.

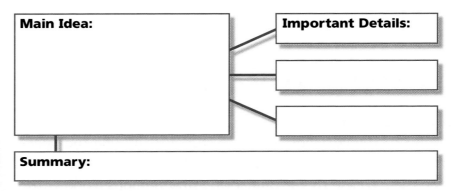

| Main Idea: | Important Details: |
| --- | --- |
| | |
| | |
| Summary: | |

Work with students to write the summary on the board. As you write the words, ask students to think about how to use sequence words to connect ideas.

Then ask students to read aloud the summary on the board. Have them suggest ways to revise the summary to make its meaning clearer.

As you work with students to revise the summary, remind them of the importance of proofreading to avoid mistakes and to make sure text is legible.

**Need More Intensive Instruction?**

**See Intervention Resource Kit, Lesson 8** for additional **preteach** and **reteach** activities.

## ■ ADVANCED

### Extend: **Summary**

**PUFFIN NEWS STORY**   Challenge students to write a news story about one of the nights when the children help the pufflings. Remind them that news writers summarize the most important information first and then give details. Tell students that the first paragraph should answer *who, what, when, where, why,* and *how*. Have students read aloud their news stories.

☆☆☆**NEWS**☆ ☆☆
WORLDWIDE          LATE EDITION
Three Children Save
Pufflings in Iceland

## ■ ENGLISH-LANGUAGE LEARNERS

### Reteach: **Grammar/Writing**

**JOINING SENTENCES**   Tell students that a longer sentence that is made up of two shorter ones is called a **compound sentence**. Explain that sentences are joined with a comma followed by the word *and, or* or *but*. Write on the board the sentence pairs below. Guide students to choose the correct conjunction to join each pair. Read aloud the compound sentence and ask students to repeat it after you. Model correctly punctuating each sentence.

- **I searched. I found no puffins.** (but) (I searched, but I found no puffins.)

- **The puffins land. Then they build nests.** (and) (The puffins land, and then they build nests.)

- **The pufflings may fly out to sea. They may land in the village.** (or) (The pufflings may fly out to sea, or they may land in the village.)

**WRITING PRACTICE**   Revisit the interactive writing steps on page S50 and work with students to draft their summaries.

**Need More Language Development?**

See **English-Language Learners Resource Kit, Lesson 8** for additional **preteach** and **reteach** activities.

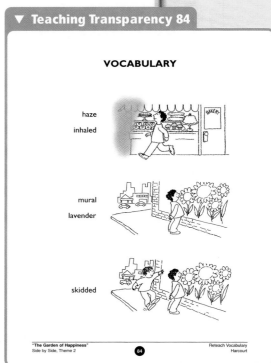
# Additional Support Activities
# Vocabulary

## ■ BELOW-LEVEL

### Reteach: Vocabulary

**See the Words**

Display Transparency 84. Discuss the picture, pointing to each word as you say it.

**Hear the Words**

Say these sentences to reteach vocabulary.

- Luis walked through the thick, gray, morning **haze**.

- He passed Destefano's bakery and **inhaled** the sweet smell of pastries.

- Then he passed the **mural** on First Street.

- He paused to admire the life-like **lavender** flowers on the painting.

- When Tony saw Luis, he **skidded** to a stop so that they could walk the rest of the way to the bus stop together.

**Say the Words**

Have students read aloud the vocabulary words from the Transparency.

### Need More Intensive Instruction?

**See Intervention Resource Kit, Lesson 9** for additional **preteach** and **reteach** activities.

haze

inhaled

lavender

skidded

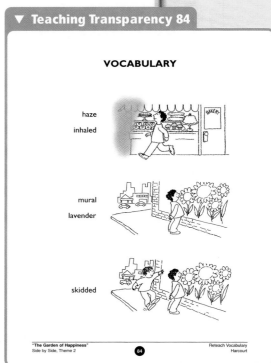

▼ **Teaching Transparency 84**

**VOCABULARY**

haze
inhaled

mural
lavender

skidded

"The Garden of Happiness"
Side by Side, Theme 2
84
Reteach Vocabulary
Harcourt

## ■ ADVANCED

### Bonus Words

- **bud**—the first growth of a flower, branch or leaf
- **seedling**—a young tree or plant grown from a seed
- **wheelbarrow**—a vehicle with one wheel and two handles
- **stalk**—a stem of a plant
- **petals**—bright-colored leaflike flower parts

### Extend: **Bonus Words**

Display Transparency 85. Ask students to read each sentence and look at the illustrations. Then have students write an approximate definition for each word. When they have finished, have them confirm the meanings of the words in a dictionary. Then ask them to draw a diagram of a plant and use Bonus Words such as *bud*, *petals*, and *stalk* to label the parts.

▼ Teaching Transparency 85

**BONUS WORDS**

The flower **bud** was just beginning to open.

The tiny **seedling** poked its way through the dirt.

Jason filled the **wheelbarrow** with dirt and pushed it to the garden.

Tomiko tied the **stalk** to the pole to keep the plant from falling over.

The sunflower has bright yellow **petals**.

"The Garden of Happiness"
Side by Side, Theme 2

85

Bonus Words
Harcourt

## ■ ENGLISH-LANGUAGE LEARNERS

### Reteach: **Background and Vocabulary**

Revisit Transparency 84. Describe each scene, using the bulleted sentences on page S52. As you read aloud each vocabulary word, point it out on the Transparency and ask students to repeat it after you. Use simple demonstrations, as necessary, to ensure student understanding of the vocabulary. Then ask students to take turns describing the scenes. Encourage them to use vocabulary words in their oral descriptions. You may wish to model a question-and-answer format like the one below. Possible reponses are shown.

**Need More Language Development?**

See **English-Language Learners Resource Kit, Lesson 9** for additional **preteach** and **reteach** activities.

| Question | Response Frame |
|---|---|
| Is *lavender* a color or a painting? | Lavender is a _____color_____ . |
| What does *haze* look like? | Haze looks like _____fog_____ . |

 **Visit** *The Learning Site:*
**www.harcourtschool.com**
See Language Support.

# Additional Support Activities
# Comprehension and Skills

**Need More Intensive Instruction?**

**See Intervention Resource Kit, Lesson 9** for additional **preteach** and **reteach** activities.

### ■ BELOW-LEVEL

## Reteach: Cause and Effect

Remind students that a **cause** is an action or event that makes something happen. An **effect** is what happens as the result of an action or event. Tell students that to identify an effect, they should ask *What happened?* To identify a cause, they should ask *Why did this happen?*

On the board begin a chart like the one below. Model using the question *What happened?* to help students identify the effect of the first event. Then point out the effect on the second line of the chart. Model using the question *Why did this happen?* to help students identify the cause.

Work with students to complete the chart with causes and effects from "The Garden of Happiness." Have students use the questions to think aloud as they complete the chart.

| Cause | Effect |
|---|---|
| Marisol sees her neighbors cleaning an empty lot. | Marisol wants to plant a garden. |
| Marisol waters her plant. | Marisol's plant grows well. |

## ■ ADVANCED

### Extend: **Cause and Effect**

Ask students to locate information about caring for one of the flowers or vegetables mentioned in the selection. Challenge them to write cause-and-effect sentences about their findings. Encourage students to focus on the relationships among sunlight, water, temperature, plant nutrients, and the plant's growth.

*If you plant a sunflower seed too deep, it will not grow properly.*

## ■ ENGLISH-LANGUAGE LEARNERS

### Reteach: **Cause and Effect/Selection Summary**

Walk students through "The Garden of Happiness" page by page. Work with students to compose a cause-and-effect sentence that describes what is happening on each page or in each illustration. As students say the sentence aloud, write it on the board. Point out signal words such as *because* and *since*. Use the completed cause-and-effect sentences to help students develop an oral summary of the selection. Provide sentence starters such as these:

- **Marisol's neighbors clean up the lot since** they want to plant a garden .

- **Because Marisol sees her neighbors planting things,** she wants to plant something .

- **Marisol is watering the plant because** plants need water to grow .

- **Because Marisol's plant dies,** she is very sad .

- **Marisol dances and sings because** she sees the mural .

**Need More Language Development?**

**See English-Language Learners Resource Kit, Lesson 9** for additional **preteach** and **reteach** activities.

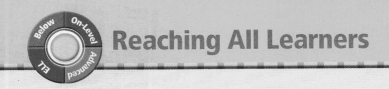
# Additional Support Activities
# Grammar and Writing

**Need More Intensive Instruction?**

**See Intervention Resource Kit, Lesson 9** for additional **preteach** and **reteach** activities.

### ■ BELOW-LEVEL

## Reteach: Interactive Writing

**BUILD ON PRIOR KNOWLEDGE**   Work with students to determine the purpose and audience for a how-to essay. Help them choose a topic and make a flowchart to list three key steps in the process.

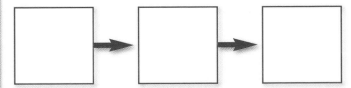

**CONSTRUCT THE TEXT**   "Share the pen" with students by writing the draft together. Discuss these steps as you write:

- **Clearly introduce the process.**
- **Tell what materials are needed.**
- **Use the flowchart to write the steps in order.**
- **Conclude with a sentence about what has been done or made.**

**REVISIT THE TEXT**   As you work with students to revise their essays, **reread** with them frequently to check the text meaning and to plan what to write next.

## ■ ADVANCED

### Extend: Writing

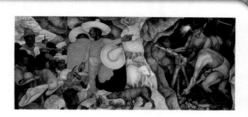

**HOW TO PAINT A MURAL**
Students may work in pairs to research techniques used by a famous muralist such as Diego Rivera, José Clemente Orozco, David Alfaro Siqueiros, Stuart Davis, or Ben Shahn. Have students investigate the artist's style, methods, and materials, and write a paragraph that explains how to paint a mural from the perspective of the artist they chose.

## ■ ENGLISH-LANGUAGE LEARNERS

### Reteach: Grammar and Writing

**DEPENDENT AND INDEPENDENT CLAUSES**   Write on the board the sentence *Anna went to the store.* Ask: **Who went to the store?** (Anna); **What did Anna do?** (She went to the store.) Explain that this is an independent clause because it tells a complete thought.

Now write on the board this dependent clause: *After she came home from school.* Ask: **Do these words tell a complete thought?** Explain that this is a dependent clause because it does not express a complete thought. Model joining the dependent clause and the independent clause from above to form a sentence: *After she came home from school, Anna went to the store.* Then work with students to add an independent clause to each dependent clause below.

- **When** I got up this morning, I _____.
- **After** I eat lunch, I _____.

**WRITING PRACTICE**   Revisit the interactive Writing steps on page S56. Work with students to choose a topic and write a draft of a how-to essay.

**Need More Language Development?**

See English-Language Learners Resource Kit, Lesson 9 for additional preteach and reteach activities.

# Additional Support Activities
# Vocabulary

## ■ BELOW-LEVEL

### Reteach: Vocabulary

**See the Words**

Display Transparency 93. Discuss each picture, pointing to the related words as you say them.

**Hear the Words**

Say these sentences aloud to reteach vocabulary.

- I hid the kitten under a blanket and **smuggled** it into the house.

- My mother's **facial** expression showed her disapproval.

- There was a look of **displeasure** on her face.

- She didn't believe me when I jokingly said the kitten was an **endangered** species.

- The kitten leapt from my arms to the counter with surprising **coordination**.

- My dog looked **jealous** as I stroked the kitten's fur.

**Say the Words**

Have students read aloud the vocabulary words from the transparency.

**Need More Intensive Instruction?**

See Intervention Resource Kit, Lesson **10** for additional **preteach** and **reteach** activities.

▼ **Teaching Transparency 93**

VOCABULARY

smuggled    facial displeasure

coordination    endangered

jealous

"How to Babysit an Orangutan"
Side by Side, Theme 2        93        Vocabulary
Harcourt

smuggled    facial    coordination    jealous

## ■ ADVANCED

### Bonus Words

- **canopy**—rooflike covering made by trees and leaves
- **termite**—a pale-colored insect that destroys wood
- **gorilla**—largest of the great apes
- **chimpanzee**—a small ape known for its intelligence

### Extend: Bonus Words

Display Transparency 94. Ask students to use context clues and to look at the illustrations to write a definition for each word. When students have finished, ask them to use a dictionary to confirm their definitions.

### ▼ Teaching Transparency 94

**BONUS WORDS**

The thick, green **canopy** of the rain forest provides the apes with protection and a place to play.

**Gorillas** love to eat **termites** and other small insects.

The **chimpanzee**, also a member of the ape family, often uses sticks and leaves as tools.

"How to Babysit an Orangutan"
Side by Side, Theme 2     94     Vocabulary Harcourt

## ■ ENGLISH-LANGUAGE LEARNERS

### Reteach: Background and Vocabulary

Revisit Transparency 93. Describe the scenes, using the bulleted sentences on page S58. Point to and read aloud each vocabulary word and have students repeat after you.

Then use the photographs in "How to Babysit an Orangutan" to illustrate the vocabulary words such as *facial*, *displeasure*, *jealous*. Have students complete sentences such as these with a vocabulary word. Then have them read aloud the completed sentences.

- A smile is a kind of __facial__ expression.
- You need good __coordination__ to play baseball.
- I felt __displeasure__ when I didn't do well on the test.
- An orangutan is an __endangered__ animal.
- The dog __smuggled__ food from the table.
- Don't be __jealous__ of other people's success.

### Need More Language Development?

**See English-Language Learners Resource Kit, Lesson 10** for additional **preteach** and **reteach** activities.

*How to Babysit an Orangutan*    **S59**

# Additional Support Activities
# Comprehension and Skills

## ■ BELOW-LEVEL

### Reteach: Summarize

Review with students that to **summarize** is to tell the main events or main ideas of the selection. Remind them that when they summarize, they should use their own words and retell the events in the order in which they happened.

Work with students to write a one- or two-sentence summary of each page. For example, for page 257, students might write: "Most of the captured baby orangutans die. The rest go to buyers for circuses, private zoos, or movie trainers." Write the summary sentences on the board. Then have students answer these questions:

- **Do the sentences accurately summarize the main events?**
- **Are the events told in your own words?**
- **Are the events retold in the same order as in the selection?**

Help students arrange their sentences in a paragraph that summarizes the whole selection.

 **TECHNOLOGY ■** *Mission: Comprehension™ Skills Practice CD-ROM*

**Need More Intensive Instruction?**

**See Intervention Resource Kit, Lesson 10** for additional **preteach** and **reteach** activities.

## ■ ADVANCED

### Extend: Summarize

Ask students to locate short nonfiction articles in magazines or newspapers. After they have read their articles, have them present an oral summary of information to a partner. Then ask students to create a poster with captions to summarize the article.

Koalas eat eucalyptus leaves.

## ■ ENGLISH-LANGUAGE LEARNERS

### Reteach: Summarize/Selection Summary

Remind students that nonfiction writing often uses photographs to help readers understand information. Walk students through the selection, page by page. Have them use the photographs with the text to develop an oral summary of the selection.

- **Pages 254–257:** At Camp Leakey in Borneo, orangutan orphans are cared for by human babysitters, who teach the orphans the skills they need to live in the wild.

- **Pages 258–260:** Many orangutan babies are stolen from their mothers. A few are rescued and taken to Camp Leakey, where human babysitters care for them and prepare them for a life in the rain forest.

- **Pages 261–265:** The babysitters teach the babies that orangutans belong in trees and help them learn to build nests. When the baby has enough skills, it goes to live on its own in the rain forest.

**Need More Language Development?**

**See English-Language Learners Resource Kit, Lesson 10** for additional **preteach** and **reteach** activities.

# Additional Support Activities
## Grammar and Writing

### ■ BELOW-LEVEL

### Reteach: Writing

**BUILD ON PRIOR KNOWLEDGE**   Ask students what they learned about babysitting an orangutan. Tell them that next they will work together to summarize "How to Babysit an Orangutan." Then work with students to create a story map. Remind students that during a timed writing, they should budget the amount of time they spend on each part of the writing process.

| Beginning |
| --- |
| ↓ |
| Middle |
| ↓ |
| Ending |

**CONSTRUCT THE TEXT**   Ask students to identify the main ideas in three parts of the selection: the beginning, the middle, and the ending. Record their ideas in the story map. Then work with students to turn their main ideas into complete sentences.

**REVISIT THE TEXT**   Reread the draft aloud with students, and prompt them to think about how it could be improved:

- **Have you identified the main ideas of the story?**
- **Are the main ideas in the order in which they happened?**
- **Did you briefly describe the events in your own words?**

Guide students to rearrange any text that is not in the correct sequence and to make revisions and corrections as necessary.

**Need More Intensive Instruction?**

**See Intervention Resource Kit, Lesson 10** for additional **preteach** and **reteach** activities.

## ■ ADVANCED

### Extend: Summarize Search Techniques

**SEARCH SUMMARY** Ask students to work in pairs. Have them review techniques for using keywords to search for information on the Internet. Ask them to summarize the main steps for doing a search and to write a "Search Engine Manual" for a younger student. Have them illustrate their summaries.

## ■ ENGLISH-LANGUAGE LEARNERS

### Reteach: Grammar and Writing

**COMPLEX SENTENCES** Review with students that a complex sentence is made up of a dependent clause and an independent clause. An independent clause can stand alone. A dependent clause must be attached to an independent clause. Remind students that these connecting words often begin a dependent clause: *after, although, as, because, before, if, since, though, unless, when, where, while.*

Work with students to combine these sentences into complex sentences.

1. Orangutans don't like baths. They do like soap. (Although orangutans don't like baths, they do like soap.)

2. Our class went to the zoo. I saw an orangutan. (When our class went to the zoo, I saw an orangutan.)

**WRITING PRACTICE** Revisit the interactive writing steps on page S62. Work with students to complete the story map and to write a draft of a summary. Remind them to vary their sentences by using complex sentences.

### Need More Language Development?

**See English-Language Learners Resource Kit, Lesson 10** for additional **preteach** and **reteach** activities.

# Teacher Notes

# Theme Resources

# Side by Side
## *Theme Resources*

#  Cause and Effect

## OBJECTIVE

*To identify cause-and-effect relationships in a literary text and use them to understand plot development*

## Focus

Share the following information with students:

**A *cause* is an event that makes another event happen. An *effect* is what happens as a result of an action or event. An event may have more than one cause, and a single cause can have more than one effect. Authors sometimes use signal words such as *because* to show a cause. Sometimes readers must figure out causes and effects on their own. Understanding what happens and why it happens is important to following a story.**

## Reteach the Skill

**Visual Model**   Display the following story on the board:

> **Last winter, the weather in northern California was terrible. Heavy snow fell in the mountains. There was a constant dense fog over San Francisco Bay, and freezing rain fell on many nights. Often, pilots could not land their planes at San Francisco International Airport. Many roads were closed due to icy conditions. The ships in the bay were always sounding their fog horns. In the spring, the creeks that carried water down the mountains overflowed.**

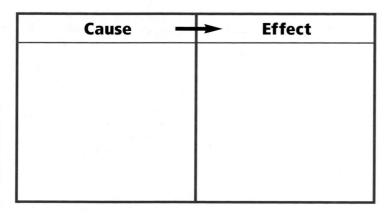

| Cause | → | Effect |
|-------|---|--------|
|       |   |        |

Have students read the story. Ask them to copy and complete the chart. Then follow the suggestions in **Summarize/Assess**.

**Kinesthetic Model**   Have students draw a three-panel comic strip that shows cause-and-effect relationships. For example, they might draw a cartoon of a child standing near a large mud puddle. When the child jumps in the puddle, it splatters all over, making a mess. Students can use speech balloons to show dialogue. Invite students to act out their cartoons and have the audience name all causes and effects. Then follow the suggestions in **Summarize/Assess**.

**Auditory Model**   Have partners play a cause-and-effect game. The student who begins should tell the partner a made-up event. For example: *I tripped over the curb*. That student should expand the sentence by making up a cause for the event. Example: *because I was looking at the sky*. The partner then restates the cause as an event. Example: *I was looking at the sky.* The partner then finishes the sentence with a new cause. Example: *because I saw a cloud of smoke*. The back-and-forth process continues until each partner has had five turns. Then follow the suggestions in **Summarize/Assess**.

## Summarize/Assess

Ask students to summarize what they have learned. (An effect is something that happens because of another event, which is called a cause. Effects can have more than one cause, and causes can have more than one effect.) To assess students' understanding, have them write about two recent events and their causes.

# Figurative Language

## OBJECTIVE

*To identify figurative language, such as metaphor, simile, hyperbole, and personification, and interpret its meaning*

## Focus

Share the following information with students:

*Figurative Language*, **or phrases whose meanings are different from the exact meanings of the words, creates vivid descriptions in writing. Some types of figurative language are** *personification, simile, metaphor,* **and** *hyperbole.* *Personification* **describes an object as if it were human. A** *simile* **is a comparison using** *like* **or** *as.* **A** *metaphor* **compares two different things by saying that one thing is another. A** *hyperbole* **is an extreme exaggeration. Understanding the meaning of figurative language helps readers more fully enjoy and comprehend what they read.**

## Reteach the Skill

**Visual Model**   Write these sentences on the board, omitting the underlining and the words in parentheses:

> The alarm clock <u>opened its metal mouth</u> at dawn. (rang)

> I always <u>cry my eyes out</u> during a sad movie. (cry a lot)

> The first light of <u>dawn tiptoed into the room silently</u> and woke all the children. (daybreak came)

> Tonight I will <u>sleep like a baby</u>. (sleep really well)

Have students underline the part of each sentence that is an example of figurative language. Work with them to identify why the first statement is a metaphor, the second is hyperbole, the third is personification, and the fourth is simile. Then have students draw pictures depicting the literal and figurative meanings of the sentences. Invite students to discuss their drawings. Then follow the suggestions in **Summarize/Assess**.

**Kinesthetic Model**   Write the sentences from the Visual Model on the board. Read each aloud as you underline the figurative phrase in it. Have pairs or small groups act out the literal meaning of the figurative phrase. Ask other students to tell what they think each phrase really means. Then follow the suggestions in **Summarize/Assess**.

**Auditory Model**   Write the following expressions on the board: *opened its metal mouth, cry my eyes out, dawn tiptoed into the room silently, sleep like a baby.* Then read aloud the first sentence below:

> The alarm clock <u>rang</u> at dawn.
> I always <u>cry a lot</u> during a sad movie.
> <u>Daybreak came</u> and woke all the children.
> Tonight I will <u>sleep really well</u>.

Ask: *What phrase could take the place of rang in this sentence?* (opened its metal mouth) Reread the sentence with the figurative phrase in place. Repeat the process with the remaining sentences. Then follow the suggestions in **Summarize/Assess**.

## Summarize/Assess

Ask students to summarize what they have learned. (Expressions that say one thing but mean another are called figurative language. Four types of figurative language are personification, hyperbole, metaphor, and simile.) To reinforce the lesson, have students write poems that include some of the types of figurative language mentioned above.

# Complete and Simple Predicates

## OBJECTIVE
*To identify a complete predicate and a simple predicate*

## Focus
Share the following information with students:

**A *complete predicate* is all the words in a sentence that tell what a subject is or does. A *simple predicate* is the main word or words in the complete predicate.**

## Reteach the Skill
**Visual Model**   Write these sentences on the board, omitting the underlines and words in parentheses.

**Miss Lovett smiles easily**. (smiles)
**The class was excited about the play**. (was)
**Consuela could build sets for the play**.
(could build)
**She prefers artistic jobs**. (prefers)

Have volunteers underline the complete predicate in each sentence. Then have them identify each simple predicate. Ask students to copy the sentences on chart paper, writing the complete predicate in one color, and circling the simple predicate in another color. Have students find four more examples of complete and simple predicates in their own writing and add them to their charts. Then follow the suggestions in **Summarize/Assess**.

**Kinesthetic Model**   Write the sentences from the Visual Model on the board. Underline the complete predicate in each sentence, and circle the simple predicate. Then have partners copy the sentences on four sentence strips. Students can cut the sentence strips apart, dividing the subject from the complete predicate. Students can then further cut the simple predicate from the complete predicate. Then follow the suggestions in **Summarize/Assess**.

**Auditory Model**   Read aloud the sentences from the Visual Model. As you slowly reread the sentences, have students identify the complete predicates and write them on the board, circling the simple predicate. Read the sentences aloud again, and have students say aloud the complete and simple predicates. Students can then take turns creating oral sentences. Have them use these sentences to repeat the above process. Then follow the suggestions in **Summarize/Assess**.

## Summarize/Assess
Ask students to summarize what they have learned. (The word or words that tell what the subject of a sentence is or does is called the complete predicate. The main word or words in the complete predicate is called the simple predicate.) To assess students' understanding, ask them to identify the complete and simple predicates in a favorite story.

 **Summarize**

## OBJECTIVE

*To use main idea and details to summarize the most important information in a text*

## Focus

Share the following information with students:

**When you *summarize*, you restate the most important ideas and details of a selection in the correct sequence in a shorter way. A summary contains only the most important ideas and details. Knowing how to summarize can help you quickly obtain and remember the key facts of a text.**

## Reteach the Skill

**Visual Model**   Draw the following chart on the board:

| Main Idea | Important Details |
|-----------|-------------------|
|           | First             |
|           | Second            |
|           | Third             |
|           | Fourth            |

Help students work together to fill in the chart using a nonfiction selection they have read recently. Once the chart is complete, have students use it to summarize the most important information from the selection. Then follow the suggestions in **Summarize/Assess**.

**Kinesthetic Model**   Have students complete the chart from the Visual Model. Encourage them to choose a nonfiction selection that can be dramatized. Then have groups act out a summary of the text while a narrator uses the chart to tell the most important information from the selection. Have audience members decide if everything in the scene was important to the summary. Then follow the suggestions in **Summarize/Assess**.

**Auditory Model**   Read aloud a few pages from a nonfiction selection that students have studied recently. Ask them to tell you the main idea and some important details from the passage in the order in which they occur. Discuss whether their responses can be used to accurately summarize the passage. Continue this procedure for a few more pages from the same selection. Then follow the suggestions in **Summarize/Assess**.

## Summarize/Assess

Ask students to summarize what they have learned. (When you *summarize*, you restate the most important ideas and details of a selection in the correct sequence in a shorter way. A summary contains only the most important ideas and details.) To check understanding, have students summarize a short science or social studies article.

# Compound Subjects and Predicates

## OBJECTIVE
*To recognize and understand compound subjects and predicates*

## Focus
Share the following information with students:

**A *compound subject* consists of two or more subjects that share the same predicate. These subjects are joined by *and* or *or*. A *compound predicate* is two or more predicates that have the same subject and are connected by *and* or *or*. If there are three or more subjects in a compound subject, or three or more predicates in a compound predicate, use commas to separate them.**

## Reteach the Skill
**Visual Model**   Write the following sentences on the board omitting the underlining and the words in parentheses:

**Maria, Juan, and Pat like to run.** (and)
**Did Sal or Julia have a party?** (or)
**Kate sings and writes very well.** (and)
**Max paints, sculpts, or draws in art class.** (or)

Have students copy the sentences. Ask them to write any compound subjects in one color, and circle the word that joins them. Then have students write any compound predicates in another color, and circle the word that joins them. Challenge students to find two compound subjects and two compound predicates in a favorite story and add them to their charts, repeating the coloring process. Then follow the suggestions in **Summarize/Assess**.

**Kinesthetic Model**   Divide students into pairs. Using the sentences from the Visual Model as an example, each student should write four similar sentences on sentence strips, then cut their sentence strips apart and mix up the pieces. Students can trade sentence strip pieces and put them in the correct order. Ask them to explain the difference between a compound subject and a compound predicate. Then follow the suggestions in **Summarize/Assess**.

**Auditory Model**   Give students two index cards each. Have them write a large *S* for *subject* on one card, and a large *P* for *predicate* on the other. Then read aloud the sentences from the Visual Model. Slowly reread them again, and have students hold up one of their index cards whenever they hear a subject or a predicate. Then ask them to tell which sentences have compound subjects and which have compound predicates. Ask them to explain how they know. Then follow the suggestions in **Summarize/Assess**.

## Summarize/Assess
Ask students to summarize what they have learned. (A compound subject consists of two or more subjects that share the same predicate. These subjects are joined by *and* or *or*. A compound predicate is two or more predicates that have the same subject and are connected by *and* or *or*. Three or more subjects or predicates are separated by commas.) To reinforce ideas, have students write two sentences with a compound subject and two with a compound predicate.

**Grammar Skill**

# Simple and Compound Sentences

## OBJECTIVE

*To recognize simple and compound sentences; to join two simple sentences to make a compound sentence*

## Focus

Share the following information with students:

**A *simple sentence* has only one subject and one predicate. A *compound sentence* may be made by joining two simple sentences with a conjunction (*and, or,* or *but*) preceded by a comma. Recognizing simple and compound sentences can help readers better understand what they read.**

## Reteach the Skill

**Visual Model**   Display this sentence and the three conjunctions in parentheses below:

**Lee jumped over the hurdle**
**(and)**
**(or)**
**(but)**

Have students recognize and explain why the sentence is simple. Then have them work with a partner to create another simple sentence and use each conjunction to join the two. Instruct them to make any minor adjustments that would make each sentence make sense. Next, have partners write their compound sentences on the board under the conjunctions *and, or,* and *but.* Discuss the difference in meaning created by each conjunction. Then follow the suggestions in **Summarize/Assess.**

**Kinesthetic Model**   Have students work in groups of four. Ask each group member to write two sentences on separate index cards, using the following format: First card—*I like _____,* Second card—*I don't like _____.* Have the group members combine and shuffle their cards. Ask each member to select two cards. Group members should take turns reading the two cards aloud and combining

the two simple sentences to form a compound sentence that uses the conjunction *and* or *but.* Have students display their new sentences, including correct comma placement. For the conjunction *or,* have students create sentences that are questions, such as *Do you like _____, or do you like _____?* Then follow the suggestions in **Summarize/Assess.**

**Auditory Model**   Seat students in a circle. Clap or use a metronome to provide rhythm. Start a chant that uses the names of members of the group, in order, following a pattern like this:

**Suzy has a green shirt. J.J. has a blue shirt.**
**Suzy has a green shirt, and J.J. has a blue shirt.**
**J.J. has a blue shirt. Howard has a red shirt.**
**J.J. has a blue shirt, and Howard has a red shirt.**

As you go around the circle, have each student build on the old sentence by adding one new line to the chant. Continue the chant with other articles of clothing and the conjunction *but.* For the conjunction *or,* you might use a similar chant in a question format, such as *Does Suzy have a blue shirt or does Suzy have a green shirt?* Next, ask students where the comma should go in each compound sentence. Finally, follow the suggestions in **Summarize/Reinforce.**

## Summarize/Assess

Check students' understanding of the lesson by having them summarize what they learned. (A simple sentence expresses one complete thought and has one subject and one predicate. A compound sentence joins two simple sentences and uses the conjunction *and, or,* or *but* preceded by a comma.) As reinforcement, you might have students search their own writing for simple sentences that could be combined to make the writing flow more smoothly.

 # Clauses

## OBJECTIVE

*To distinguish between independent and dependent clauses*

## Focus

Share the following information with students:

> A *clause* is a group of words that has both a subject and a predicate. Some clauses can stand alone as sentences. These are called *independent clauses*. *Dependent clauses* cannot stand alone as sentences. They begin with connecting words, such as *after, before, because, since*, and *when*. Understanding how to use the two types of clauses will help you be a better writer.

## Reteach the Skill

**Visual Model** Write the following sentences on the board:

> Because Sam was sick, he couldn't go to school.
> Fred ate the cookies after they were baked.
> Since Jose's mother works, he has to babysit his sister.

Display the following clause chart and help students use the above sentences to complete it:

| Dependent | Independent |
|---|---|
| Because Sam was sick | he couldn't go to school |
| after they were baked | Fred ate the cookies |
| Since Jose's mother works | he has to babysit his sister |

Have students explain their decisions. Then follow the suggestions in **Summarize/Assess**.

**Kinesthetic Model** Write the sentences from the Visual Model on sentence strips. Have volunteers cut the strips apart, dividing the dependent clause from the independent clause. Mix up the cut strips and ask other students to choose one and tell if it is a dependent or an independent clause and why. Then follow the suggestions in **Summarize/Assess**.

**Auditory Model** Read aloud the sentences from the Visual Model, one at a time. For each sentence, ask students to identify and repeat the dependent clause and do the same for the independent clause. Have them explain the rationale for their decisions. Then follow the suggestions in **Summarize/Assess**.

## Summarize/Assess

Ask students to summarize what they have learned. (A clause is a group of words that has both a subject and a predicate. Some clauses can stand alone as sentences. These are called independent clauses. Dependent clauses cannot stand alone as sentences. They begin with connecting words, such as *after, before, because, since,* and *when*.) To reinforce the lesson, have students write three sentences that consist of an independent clause and a dependent clause. Ask them to explain the clauses that they wrote.

# Complex Sentences

## OBJECTIVE

*To recognize and understand complex sentences*

## Focus

Share the following information with students:

**A *complex sentence* is made up of an independent clause and at least one dependent clause. A dependent clause often begins with a connecting word such as *after, because,* or *if*. Understanding how to identify and use complex sentences will help you to be a better reader and writer.**

## Reteach the Skill

**Visual Model** Write the following chart on the board. Use a different color for each column:

| Dependent | Independent | Complex Sentence |
|---|---|---|
| because I am smart | I can help others learn | Because I am smart, I can help others learn. |

Have students explain how the two clauses make a complex sentence. Invite students to suggest other dependent and independent clauses and the complex sentences they create to add to the chart. Challenge students to create a complex sentence from two related independent clauses. Guide them to use a connecting word. Then follow the suggestions in **Summarize/Assess**.

**Kinesthetic Model** Have students brainstorm a list of independent clauses about one topic. For example: **Our school is large. There are a lot of students.** Write their responses on the board. Then have partners work together to create a booklet about the topic, using the list of independent clauses and connecting words to make complex sentences. They can add other complex sentences and illustrations to their booklet. Then follow the suggestions in **Summarize/Assess**.

**Auditory Model** Read aloud this passage several times:

> **Bill's party was fun. Everyone loved playing together. The food was great. Everyone ate a lot. People were tired at the end. The guests went home.**

Have students use connecting words to create complex sentences from the independent clauses (simple sentences) in the passage. Write their responses on the board. Have a volunteer read aloud the new passage. Ask students to name the new dependent clauses in the passage. Then follow the suggestions in **Summarize/Assess**.

## Summarize/Assess

Ask students to summarize what they have learned. (A complex sentence is made up of an independent clause and at least one dependent clause. A dependent clause often begins with a connecting word such as *after, because,* or *if*.) To reinforce ideas, have students find examples in their writing in which they can make a complex sentence from two independent clauses.

# Oral Reading Fluency

## What Is Oral Reading Fluency?

Research recognizes fluency as a strong indicator of efficient and proficient reading. A fluent reader reads orally with accuracy and expression, at a speech-like pace. Oral reading fluency is an assessment of accuracy and rate. It is expressed as the number of words read correctly per minute (WCPM).

Oral reading fluency is an important goal of reading instruction in the elementary grades. If a reader devotes most of his or her attention to pronouncing words, comprehension and meaning will suffer. Students who read fluently can devote more attention to meaning and thus increase comprehension.

The oral reading passage and recording form that follow provide a tool for gathering quantitative information about an individual's oral reading. Use the passages provided in each Teacher's Edition to collect a one-minute sample of a student's oral reading periodically throughout the school year. Track the student's progress and development on the Oral Reading Recording Forms completed and collected throughout the school year.

The passages provided were written with controlled vocabulary and progressive levels of difficulty. The originality of the passages ensures that students will not already be familiar with the content.

## Administering the Oral Reading Passage

For administering the assessment you will need
- a stopwatch or a watch with a second hand
- a clean copy of the passage for the student to read
- a copy of the Recording Form version of the same passage to mark as the student reads

1. Explain the task. The student is to read the passage aloud, beginning and ending with your signals.

2. Use a stopwatch to time a one-minute interval inconspicuously. Tell the student when to begin and when to end reading. Put a slash mark on the Recording Form after the last word the student reads.

3. As the student reads, record reading errors unobtrusively on the Recording Form. Mark mispronunciations, substitutions, omissions of a sound or word, and other errors. Do not count repetitions or self-corrections as reading errors.

## Scoring the Oral Reading Fluency Rate

Complete the Oral Reading Fluency Form and save it. Use the completed forms to track growth and progress throughout the school year and to share the results with parents or guardians.

### To Compute the Fluency Rate

1. Total the number of words the student read in one minute.

2. Total the number of reading errors the student made.

3. Subtract the number of reading errors from the number of words read to get the total words read correctly per minute (WCPM).

Total Words Read Per Minute          _____

Number of Errors          _____

Number of Words Read Correctly (WCPM)          _____

## Interpreting the Oral Reading Fluency Rate

See the tables of norms provided in the *Oral Reading Fluency Assessment* to make a normative interpretation of a student's oral reading fluency score. Students who read significantly below the oral reading fluency norms will need additional word recognition instruction, more frequent monitoring of performance, and building fluency strategies such as repeated reading, echo reading, tape-assisted reading, and partner reading.

# Oral Reading Passage

Kay's father had been jogging for many years. Every morning before breakfast, Mr. Benson left the house wearing his sneakers and jogging shorts. Lucky, the Benson's dog, usually ran with him.

Now Kay was ten years old and wanted to start running. Her father told her that if she did all her homework each night, and got to bed on time, she could run with him for part of his route each day. Kay saved her allowance and got some neat running shoes. The first week, Kay was tired in the afternoon in school, but she didn't tell anyone. She didn't want her parents to make her stop running. After a few weeks, Kay felt wonderful, and looked forward to running with her father each day. It was a special time for them to be together. Kay began to train to run in the town's three-mile race. She felt confident that she would do well, because she enjoyed running and was getting better each day.

# Oral Reading Fluency Recording Form

Student _____     Date _____

Word Count 166

|   |   |
|---|---|
| Kay's father had been jogging for many years. Every | 9 |
| morning before breakfast, Mr. Benson left the house | 17 |
| wearing his sneakers and jogging shorts. Lucky, the Benson's dog, | 27 |
| usually ran with him. | 31 |
|     Now Kay was ten years old and wanted to start running. | 42 |
| Her father told her that if she did all her homework each | 54 |
| night, and got to bed on time, she could run with him for | 67 |
| part of his route each day. Kay saved her allowance and | 78 |
| got some neat running shoes. The first week, Kay was tired | 89 |
| in the afternoon in school, but she didn't tell anyone. She didn't | 101 |
| want her parents to make her stop running. After a few weeks, | 113 |
| Kay felt wonderful, and looked forward to running with her | 123 |
| father each day. It was a special time for them to be together. | 136 |
| Kay began to train to run in the town's three-mile race. She | 149 |
| felt confident that she would do well, because she enjoyed | 159 |
| running and was getting better each day. | 166 |

**Fluency Score**

Total Words Read Per Minute _____

Number of Errors _____

Number of Words Read Correctly (WCPM) _____

## After Reading

4. What was the author's message? Which story events helped you get the message?

5. What part was
   - ■ the funniest?
   - ■ the saddest?
   - ■ the most exciting?

6. Think of another story you have read. How are the themes the same? How are they different?

------------------------------------------------ FOLD ------------------------------------------------

## During Reading

1. From what you have read so far, what do you think the story is mostly about?

2. What point is the author trying to make? Why do you think that?

3. What do you remember most about the story so far?

Harcourt

or in a different time?
if it were set in a different place
5. How would the story be different

in what way?
4. Was the setting important to the story? If so,

## After Reading

------------------------------------FOLD------------------------------------

# During Reading

**1.** Describe where the story takes place.

**2.** When does this story take place—long ago, in the present, or in the future? What clues helped you decide?

**3.** Have you ever been to a place like this? If you have, how was it like the place in the story?

Harcourt

the author helped you understand.
Which one? Give examples from the selection of
ways the author helped you understand.

**7.** Was one of the selections easier to understand?

**6.** How is the information in the selections alike?
How is it different?

**5.** Is there information included in one selection
that is not in the other? If so, what kind?

## After Reading

◄ **Comparing Texts**          **COMPREHENSION CARD** (8)

-------------------------------FOLD-------------------------------

▶ **Comparing Texts**          **COMPREHENSION CARD** (8)

You will compare two or more selections. Here's what
to think about as you read.

## During Reading

**1.** What are the selections about?

**2.** What genre is each selection? Is it

- ■ fiction?
- ■ nonfiction?
- ■ poetry?
- ■ some other genre?

**3.** What information is included
in each selection?

**4.** What was the author's purpose
for writing each selection?

Harcourt

**12. Why might the leaves be turning brown?** (Possible response: The plant can't live when the weather gets cold.)

**13. What are you thinking about now?** (Possible response: Marisol is giving the plant too much water; the sunflower may not survive.)

▶ **Think Along** ◀        **COMPREHENSION CARD** (6)

--------------------------------------------------FOLD--------------------------------------------------

▶ **Think Along**        **COMPREHENSION CARD** (9)

# The Garden of Happiness

You may wish to have students respond to the Think-Along questions in writing in their Response Journals.

1. **What do you think the people are planning to do in the empty lot?** (Possible response: I think that they are going to make a garden.)

2. **Why do you think they are planting things in the lot?** (Possible response: To get better food; to make the neighborhood beautiful.)

3. **What do you think the teenagers might tell her?** (Possible response: They are planning to knock over the wall and turn the area where it used to be into more garden space.)

4. **Why is Marisol talking to the birds?** (Possible response: She feels bad about taking one of their seeds away and wants to explain why she did it.)

5. **What are you thinking about right now?** (Possible response: I'm wondering if and when the plant will begin to sprout.)

6. **What kind of plant do you think Marisol might have?** (Possible response: She might have a small tree or a bush, because it is big and it hasn't even started to bud.)

7. **What ideas do you think the teenagers might have for their painting?** (Possible response: I think they might paint what they see on the street, or use colors to show how they are feeling.)

8. **What words might describe Marisol's feelings right now?** (Possible response: happy, proud, excited)

9, 10. **What does this scene tell you about sunflowers?** (Possible response: Lots of people like sunflowers; they grow in many different places.)

11. **What are some of the good things about Marisol's flower?** (Possible response: It makes people feel happy; it is bright and pretty.)

Harcourt

10. p. 262, line 25: To help students understand that baby orangutans need other orangutans and not just babysitters to survive: **What is the author telling us when she says that the orphans are lonesome even though they have babysitters?** (Possible response: The babies need to be with one of their own kind so they feel that they are part of a real orangutan family.)

11. p. 263, line 12: To clarify that the author is stating the importance of trees to orangutans: **Why do orangutans need to know how to climb and hang in trees?** (Possible response: The rain forest canopy is made of trees, and this is the orangutan's natural home; orangutans must know how to climb trees to survive in the wild.)

12. p. 263, line 16: To further develop the relationship between Nanang and the author: **Why does Nanang climb to the top of the tree at bedtime? What is he doing to the author?** (Possible response: He's being a little naughty and teasing her because he knows she can't climb up and get him down. He's trying to get a snack out of her.)

13. p. 264, line 7: To clarify the identities of Peter and Princess: **Why does Peter still sleep with Princess?** (Possible response: Princess is Peter's mother; and Peter is an orangutan under the age of six years.)

14. p. 264, line 15: To reinforce the fact that orangutans do not like to get wet: **What is the author trying to tell us about the nests that orangutans build?** (Possible response: Unlike the other great apes, orangutans put roofs on their nests because they don't like to get wet.)

15. p. 264, line 19: To further clarify that the babysitters are not able to do everything that the wild orangutan mothers can do: **What is the author telling us about the limitations of the babysitters?** (Possible response: They are not able to do everything that wild orangutan mothers can do for the babies.)

16. p. 265, line 2: To establish that the previous inhabitants of Camp Leakey still have an attachment to the camp: **The author says that many of the freed baby orangutans that grew up in Camp Leakey come to visit often. What does this say about the type of place Camp Leakey is?** (Possible response: Camp Leakey must be a safe and comfortable place for the orangutans.)

17. p. 265, line 14: To draw attention to the feelings the author has for Nanang: **The author says that she hopes she will be able to say good-bye to Nanang. What does this tell us?** (Possible response: She loves him and wants him to have a normal life in the wild as he would have had if he hadn't been captured.)

---FOLD---

▶ **Questioning the Author**     COMPREHENSION CARD (10)

# How to Babysit an Orangutan

**Key Understanding:** Camp Leaky is an orangutan orphanage. The babysitters there care and teach the baby orangutans skills they will need to be released back into the wild.

1. p. 257, line 3: To establish the concept that Camp Leakey is an animal protection camp: **What is going on at Camp Leaky?** (Possible response: Humans are taking care of young, orphaned orangutans so the orphans don't die.)

2. p. 257, lines 9–11: To establish the babysitters' objective: **The author says that a "good babysitter's" job is done when the baby grows up and goes off to live on its own. What does that mean?** (Possible response: The babysitters want the baby orangutans to live normal lives like the other wild apes in the rain forest.)

3. p. 258, line 11: To establish that the author is saying the animal-smuggling business is detrimental to the survival of orangutans: **The author says that there are only 5,000 wild orangutans remaining. If eight orangutans must die for every baby who survives the smuggling, it means that smuggling is not good for the total orangutan population.**

4. p. 258, line 15: To clarify the concept that the rain forest environment is in danger: **What is the author trying to tell us here?** (Possible response: The rain forest environment and the animals that live there are in danger of extinction.)

5. p. 259, line 12: To establish the relationship between the babysitters and the orangutans: **What is the relationship between the babysitters and the baby orangutans?** (Possible response: The babysitters must try to give the babies the same things that the wild orangutan mothers give their babies, such as attention and milk.)

6. p. 260, line 8: To establish that wild orangutans eat a variety of foods: **What does the author want us to know about orangutans' food?** (Possible response: Babysitters want the babies to eat the same variety of foods that wild orangutans eat, such as fruit, nuts, flowers, leaves, termites, and ants.)

7. p. 261, line 6: To establish that baby orangutans are playful: **What is Nanang doing when he steals the author's hat?** (Possible response: Nanang is jealous and wants the hat for himself. He is also being playful.)

8. p. 261, line 12: To establish that the babysitters must do unpleasant things in order to care for the babies: **The author has told us of unpleasant things babysitters must do like eat leaves and give orangutans baths. Why do the babysitters do these unpleasant things?** (Possible response: To make sure that the babies eat properly and do not get sick.)

9. p. 262, line 14: To establish that orangutans have a variety of emotions and a babysitter needs to be able to identify

Harcourt

| | |
|---|---|
| | |
| | |

**Transparency F**

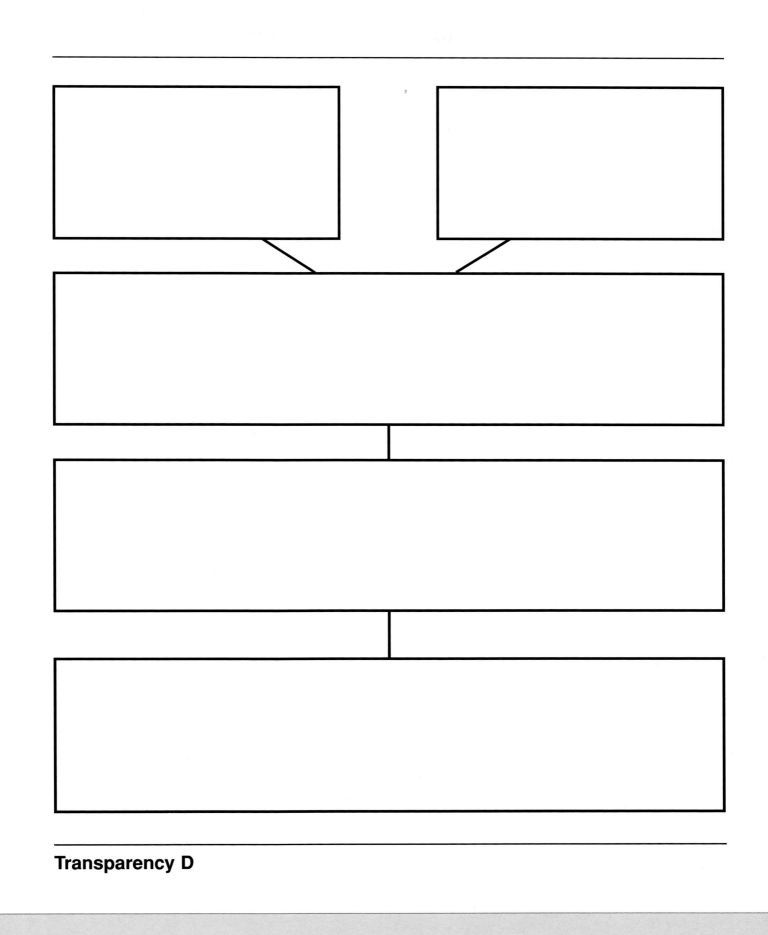

**Transparency D**

Harcourt

| | | |
|---|---|---|
| | | |

Harcourt

# Using Student Rubrics

**A rubric is a tool a teacher can use to score a student's work. A rubric lists the criteria for evaluating the work, and it describes different levels of success in meeting those criteria. Rubrics are useful assessment tools for teachers, but they can be just as useful for students. In fact, rubrics can be powerful teaching tools.**

## Before Writing

- When you **introduce** students to **a new kind of writing** through a writing model, discuss the criteria listed on the rubric, and ask students to decide how well the model meets each criterion. Have students add to the rubric other criteria they think are important.

- Before students attempt a new kind of writing, have them focus on the **criteria for excellence** listed on the rubric so that they have specific goals to aim for.

## During Writing and Editing

- As students are **prewriting** and **drafting**, have them refer to the rubric for important aspects of organization and elaboration that they need to include in their writing.

- When students are ready to **revise**, have them check their writing against the rubric to determine if there are any aspects of organization and elaboration that they can improve.

- As students **proofread**, the rubric will remind them to pay attention to grammar, usage, punctuation, and sentence variety. You may wish to have individual students add to their rubrics, depending on particular language problems they have demonstrated.

## After Writing

- The rubric can be used by individuals to **score their own writing** or by pairs or small groups for peer assessment. Students can highlight the parts of the rubric that they believe apply to a piece of writing.

- Students can keep the marked rubric in their portfolios with the piece of writing it refers to. The marked rubrics will help students **see their progress** through the school year. In conferences with students and family members, you can refer to the rubrics to point out both strengths and weaknesses.

| | Score of 4 | Score of 3 | Score of 2 | Score of 1 |
|---|---|---|---|---|
| **FOCUS/IDEAS** | The paper is completely focused on the task and has a clear purpose. The writer summarizes main ides and important details. | The paper is generally focused on the task and the purpose. The writing shows understanding of the topic. | The paper is somewhat focused on the task and purpose. The writing shows some understanding of the topic. | The paper does not have a clear focus or a purpose. The writing shows little understanding of the topic. |
| **ORGANIZATION/PARAGRAPHS** | The paper has a clear beginning, middle, and ending. The ideas and details are presented in logical order. The writer groups related ideas in paragraphs. | The writing seems complete. The ideas and details are mostly presented in logical order. The writer usually groups related ideas in paragraphs. | The organization is not clear in some places. | The paper has little or no organization. |
| **DEVELOPMENT** | The paper has a clear central idea that is supported by strong, specific details. | The paper has a central idea and is supported by details. | The paper does not have a clear central idea and has few supporting details. | The central idea is not clear and there are few or no supporting details. |
| **VOICE** | The writer's voice is consistent throughout the paper. The writer does not include unnecessary opinions or details. | The writer does not usually include unnecessary opinions or details. | The writer includes some opinions and unnecessary details. | The writer includes many opinions and unnecessary details. |
| **WORD CHOICE** | The writer uses clear, exact words and phrases. The writing is interesting to read. | The word choices are clear. The writer uses some interesting words and phrases. | The writer does not use words or phrases that make the writing clear to the reader. | The writer uses word choices that are unclear or inappropriate. |
| **SENTENCES** | The writer uses a variety of sentences. The writing flows smoothly. | The writer uses some variety in sentences. | The writer does not use much variety in his or her sentences. | There is little or no variety in sentences. Some of the sentences are unclear. |
| **CONVENTIONS** | There are few or no errors in grammar, punctuation, capitalization, and spelling. | There are a few errors in grammar, punctuation, capitalization, and spelling. | There are some errors in grammar, punctuation, capitalization, and spelling. | There are many errors in grammar, punctuation, capitalization, and spelling. |

Harcourt

# SCORING RUBRIC FOR WRITING

| | FOCUS | ORGANIZATION | SUPPORT | CONVENTIONS |
|---|---|---|---|---|
| **Score of 6** ☆☆☆☆☆☆ | The writing is completely focused on the topic and has a clear purpose. | The ideas in the paper are well-organized and presented in logical order. The paper seems complete to the reader. | The writing has strong, specific details. The word choices are clear and fresh. | The writer uses a variety of sentences. There are few or no errors in grammar, spelling, punctuation, and capitalization. |
| **Score of 5** ☆☆☆☆☆ | The writing is focused on the topic and purpose. | The organization of the paper is mostly clear. The paper seems complete. | The writing has strong, specific details and clear word choices. | The writer uses a variety of sentences. There are few errors in grammar, spelling, punctuation, and capitalization. |
| **Score of 4** ☆☆☆☆ | The writing is generally focused on the topic and purpose. | The organization is mostly clear, but the paper may seem unfinished. | The writing has supporting details and some variety in word choice. | The writer uses some variety in sentences. There are a few errors in grammar, spelling, punctuation, and capitalization. |
| **Score of 3** ☆☆☆ | The writing is somewhat focused on the topic and purpose. | The organization is somewhat organized, but seems unfinished. | The writing has few supporting details. It needs more variety in word choice. | The writer uses simple sentences. There are some errors in grammar, spelling, punctuation, and capitalization. |
| **Score of 2** ☆☆ | The writing is related to the topic but does not have a clear focus. | There is little organization to the paper. | The writing uses few supporting details and very little variety in word choice. | The writer uses simple sentences. There are many errors in grammar, spelling, punctuation, and capitalization. |
| **Score of 1** ☆ | The writing is not focused on the topic and purpose. | There is no organization to the paper. | The writing uses few or no supporting details. The word choices are unclear. | The writer uses unclear sentences. There are many errors in grammar, spelling, punctuation, and capitalization. |

Harcourt

| | Score of 6 | Score of 5 | Score of 4 | Score of 3 | Score of 2 | Score of 1 |
|---|---|---|---|---|---|---|
| **HANDWRITING** | The slant of the letters is the same throughout the whole paper. The letters are clearly formed and the spacing between words is equal, which makes the text very easy to read. | The slant of the letters is almost the same through most of the paper. The letters are clearly formed. The spacing between words is usually equal. | The slant of the letters is usually the same. The letters are clearly formed most of the time. The spacing between words is usually equal. | The handwriting is readable. There are some differences in letter shape and form, slant, and spacing that make some words easier to read than others. | The handwriting is somewhat readable. There are many differences in letter shape and form, slant, and spacing that make some words hard to read. | The letters are not formed correctly. The slant spacing is not the same throughout the paper, or there is no regular space between words. The paper is very difficult to read. |
| **WORD PROCESSING** | Fonts and sizes are used very well, which helps the reader enjoy reading the text. | Fonts and sizes are used well. | Fonts and sizes are used fairly well, but could be improved upon. | Fonts and sizes are used well in some places, but make the paper look cluttered in others. | Fonts and sizes are not used well. The paper looks cluttered. | The writer has used too many different fonts and sizes. It is a very distracting to the reader. |
| **MARKERS** | The title, side heads, page numbers, and bullets are used very well. They make it easy for the reader to find information in the text. These markers clearly show how the writer organized the information. | The title, side heads, page numbers and bullets are used well. They help the reader find information. | The title, side heads, page numbers and bullets are used fairly well. They usually help the reader find information. | The writer uses some markers such as a title, page numbers, or bullets. However, the use of markers could be improved upon to help the reader get more meaning from the text. | The writer uses very few markers. This makes it hard for the reader to find and understand the information in the text. | There are no markers such as a title, page numbers, bullets, or side heads. |
| **VISUALS** | The writer uses visuals such as illustrations, charts, graphs, maps, and tables very well. The text and visuals clearly relate to each other. | The writer uses visuals well. The text and visuals relate to each other. | The writer uses visuals fairly well. | The writer uses visuals with the text, but the reader may not understand how they are related. | The writer tries to use visuals with the text, but the reader is confused by them. | The visuals do not make sense with the text. |
| **SPEAKING** | The speaker uses very effective pacing, volume, intonation, and expression. | The speaker uses effective pacing, volume, intonation, and expression. | The speaker uses mostly effective pacing, volume, intonation, and expression. | The speaker uses somewhat effective pacing, volume, intonation, and expression. | The speaker needs to work on pacing, volume, intonation, and expression. | The speaker's techniques are unclear or distracting to the listener. |

Harcourt

| The Baker's Neighbor | The Emperor and the Kite |
|---|---|
| ad lib | insignificant |
| shiftless | plotting |
| luxury | twined |
| privilege | steely |
| elated | encircling |
| shamefacedly | loyal |
| indignantly | neglected |
| assent | unyielding |
|  |  |

Harcourt

| Nights of the Pufflings | The Garden of Happiness |
|---|---|
| uninhabited | inhaled |
| burrows | lavender |
| venture | mural |
| stranded | skidded |
| nestles | haze |
| instinctively | |
| | |
| | |
| | |

Harcourt

| How to Babysit an Orangutan | |
|---|---|
| displeasure | |
| jealous | |
| endangered | |
| smuggled | |
| facial | |
| coordination | |
| | |
| | |
| | |

Harcourt

# School–Home Connection

**Your child is reading "The Baker's Neighbor," a play adapted by Adele Thane.** In this play, the neighbor of a baker enjoys the smells of the baked goods but never buys anything. The greedy baker employs a judge to make his neighbor pay for smelling his pastries, but the judge's idea of payment is to let the greedy baker enjoy touching the neighbor's golden coins. In the end, the judge claims free pies for all the villagers as his fee.

## What If Game

The children in the story play a game in which they ask each other what they would like to be if they were not people— what color, what sight, what sound, and what smell. Play this game with your child, using such prompts as this one: "If you could be a beautiful smell instead of a child, what smell would you be?"

### VOCABULARY

### Say It, Guess It

The following words are new vocabulary your child has learned while reading "The Baker's Neighbor":

| | |
|---|---|
| ad lib | shiftless |
| luxury | privilege |
| elated | shamefacedly |
| indignantly | assent |

To reinforce the meanings, play a game in which you say a word's dictionary definition and your child tries to guess the word.

## Bakery Math

Bake muffins, a pie, or a cake with your child, and use the experience to practice math. Have your child divide each pastry into enough equal parts to feed the number of people in your family.

## Catch That Thief

Arrange for your child to talk with a store security guard to learn about the procedure for catching shoplifters. Visit banks or automated tellers to show your child surveillance cameras.

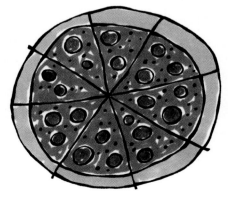

Harcourt

 **TIME TO READ** Encourage your child to read for at least 30 minutes outside of class each day.

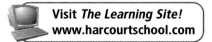 Visit *The Learning Site!* www.harcourtschool.com

# School-Home Connection

**Your child is reading "The Emperor and the Kite," a Chinese folktale by Jane Yolen.** In this folktale, the tiny daughter of an emperor gets no attention or love because she is so small. When the emperor is captured by bad men and imprisoned in a tower, it is the tiny girl, and not her bigger and stronger brothers and sisters, who manages to save her father and finally win his everlasting love.

## Make a Kite

Visit a library and learn how to make a homemade kite. Find books on Chinese art, and use them to get ideas for ways to paint your kite. Help your child fly the kite, and discuss how the wind works to keep the kite up in the air.

### VOCABULARY

## Word of the Day
The following words are new vocabulary your child has learned while reading "The Emperor and the Kite":

| | |
|---|---|
| insignificant | plotting |
| twined | steely |
| encircling | loyal |
| neglected | unyielding |

Play a vocabulary-building game with your child. Have your child arrange the words in alphabetical order, and then assign a word to each of the coming eight days. For example, on the first day, you and your child can try finding things you think are *insignificant*. Make a list of what you find for each word.

## More Folktales
You and your child might enjoy searching for more international folktales at your local library. Choose character and narrative parts, and read each folktale aloud. Discuss the message of the folktale.

## Chinese Recipes
Look in cookbooks for easy recipes for Chinese food. Help your child plan a simple meal and work together to prepare the meal and serve it. If possible, use chopsticks to eat the food you have prepared.

Harcourt

 **TIME TO READ** Encourage your child to read for at least 30 minutes outside of class each day.

**Visit *The Learning Site!*
www.harcourtschool.com**

 # School-Home Connection

**Your child is reading "Nights of the Pufflings," a non-fiction article written and photographed by Bruce McMillan.** The selection describes how puffins, which are small sea birds, come to shore on an island near Iceland to raise their chicks. It also tells how, on the nights when the young birds leave their nests and attempt to fly out to sea, the children of the island help by rescuing baby birds that crash-land on the island. These children later release the rescued birds into the sea.

## Watch a Wildlife Program

Ask your child to choose a wildlife show on TV to watch with you, or borrow a wildlife video from your local library to watch with your child. Encourage your child to take notes as you watch. Afterward, ask him or her to summarize the information presented in the program. Then share with each other your personal reactions to the program and its content.

**VOCABULARY**

## Word Scramble

The following words are new vocabulary your child has learned:

| | |
|---|---|
| uninhabited | burrows |
| venture | stranded |
| nestles | instinctively |

Play a word-scramble game. Choose three words, and scramble the letters in each to create nonsense words. Have your child do the same. Then take turns trying to unscramble the words, and use them correctly in sentences.

## Visit an Animal Shelter

Your child might benefit from a family visit to an animal shelter to learn firsthand how animals are cared for there, what the shelter does to try to find new homes for strays, and how volunteers can help. As an alternative, you might visit a farm, a zoo, a pet store, or another place where animals are kept and cared for, so your child can observe and learn about caring for animals.

 **TIME TO READ** Encourage your child to read for at least 30 minutes outside of class each day.

 Visit *The Learning Site!*
www.harcourtschool.com

Harcourt

 # School–Home Connection

**Your child is reading "The Garden of Happiness" by Erika Tamar.** In this story, a girl learns about different cultures, community pride, and helping others when she takes part in making a neighborhood garden.

## Plants in Action

In "The Garden of Happiness," Marisol grows a beautiful sunflower that makes many people in her neighborhood happy. With your child, think about and list the purposes a plant can serve. You may want to walk around your house or block to find ways in which plants help people. (Examples: Flowers make people happy; plants make oxygen for people to breathe; many houses and pieces of furniture are made of wood from trees; cotton and other plants provide material for clothes; people use plants for much of their food.)

### VOCABULARY

### On the Lookout

The following words are new vocabulary your child has learned while reading "The Garden of Happiness."

| | |
|---|---|
| inhaled | lavender |
| mural | haze |
| skidded | |

Help your child notice when these words are used during the week.

## Making a Difference

In "The Garden of Happiness," Marisol and her neighbors convert an empty lot into a community garden. You might want to choose a community volunteer project that you and your child could do together, such as helping with a food drive or cleaning up a nearby park.

## Rereading Together

Have your child read his or her favorite part of "The Garden of Happiness" to you. Encourage your child to read with emotion, as if he or she were telling the story. After your child has finished, talk together about the story's plot, characters, setting, and message.

 **TIME TO READ** Encourage your child to read for at least 30 minutes outside of class each day.

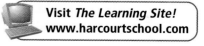 Visit *The Learning Site!* www.harcourtschool.com

Harcourt

# School-Home Connection

**Your child is reading "How to Babysit an Orangutan" by Kathy and Tara Darling.** In this article the authors describe a visit to a camp in Borneo where orphaned orangutan babies are nurtured by human babysitters until they can survive on their own. You may enjoy discussing the article and doing these activities with your child. Together you can develop and explore your child's language skills.

## Local Wildlife

If possible, visit a local natural history museum or local wildlife preserve with your child to learn about animals that are native to your area. Suggest that your child independently use reference sources to find out answers to any questions your visit raises.

## VOCABULARY

### Fun with Related Words

The following words are new vocabulary your child has learned while reading "How to Babysit an Orangutan":

| | |
|---|---|
| displeasure | jealous |
| endangered | smuggled |
| facial | manageable |
| coordination | |

Each day, choose one of these words and use a dictionary to find and list other words in the same word family. (For example: for *displeasure*, you might list *pleasure, please, displease, pleasant,* and *pleasing*.) Improvise conversations in which you and your child use a vocabulary word and the related words in as many ways as you can.

## Changing Habitats

Ask your child to interview you about changes you have seen in your own local environment. Your child can take notes during the interview and then draw the original environment as he or she imagines it and write a description to go with the picture.

## On the Wild Side

With your child, review upcoming shows on your local public television station to find presentations about rain forest habitats, apes, or other topics related to wildlife. Watch a show together, and encourage your child to summarize what he or she learned.

Harcourt

**TIME TO READ** Encourage your child to read for at least 30 minutes outside of class each day.

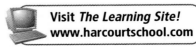
**Visit *The Learning Site!*** www.harcourtschool.com

# Additional Reading
## Lead the Way

This list is a compilation of the additional theme- and topic-related books cited in the lesson plans. You may wish to use this list to provide students with opportunities to read at least thirty minutes a day outside of class.

## THEME 2: SIDE BY SIDE

**Ada, Alma Flor.** *The Malachite Palace.* Atheneum, 1998. A tiny yellow bird helps a lonely princess learn the truth about songs, freedom, and the children who are playing beyond the palace gates. AVERAGE

**Arnosky, Jim.** *Watching Water Birds.* National Geographic Society, 1997. The author shares, in text and illustrations, his feelings and knowledge of water birds such as ducks, gulls, and herons. ⚐*SLJ Best Book; Outstanding Science Trade Book.* AVERAGE

**Blos, Joan W.** *Brooklyn Doesn't Rhyme.* Scribner's, 1994. Rosie struggles to complete a school writing assignment about her life in early twentieth-century Brooklyn. CHALLENGING

**Brisson, Pat.** *Wanda's Roses.* Boyds Mills, 1994. Wanda nurtures a bare thornbush in an empty lot hoping it will produce roses. EASY

**Byars, Betsy.** *Tornado.* HarperCollins, 1996. A family makes room in their hearts and home for a very special pet after a tornado lands a doghouse, with a dog inside, in their backyard. ⚐*Children's Choice; Teachers' Choice.* AVERAGE

**Dakos, Kalli.** *Don't Read This Book, Whatever You Do! More Poems About School.* Aladdin, 1998. Poems reflect life in lively classrooms and are based on the author's experiences as an elementary school teacher. ⚐*Children's Choice.* CHALLENGING

**Darling, Kathy.** *Desert Babies.* Walker, 1997. Colorful portraits of fourteen desert animals, including unusual facts about each. AVERAGE

**Darling, Kathy.** *Komodo Dragon: On Location.* Lothrop, Lee & Shepard, 1997. A detailed description of the physical characteristics and habitat of this endangered lizard, from its hunting habits to its size. CHALLENGING

**Demi.** *Kites: Magic Wishes That Fly Up to the Sky.* Crown, 1999. A mother has a kite made to fly to the heavens to make her son strong and wise. AVERAGE

**DiSalvo-Ryan, Dyanne.** *City Green.* William Morrow, 1994. Shows the delights that can be gained from a communal garden as Marcy, tired of a littered vacant lot on her block, decides to start planting things there. EASY

**King-Smith, Dick.** *Dick King-Smith's Animal Friends.* Candlewick, 1996. A personal account of one man's experience with animals, from his first elephant ride at the zoo to his job working on a dairy farm. CHALLENGING

**Lauber, Patricia.** *Snakes Are Hunters.* HarperCollins, 1988. Describes the physical characteristics of a variety of snakes and how they hunt, catch, and eat their prey. EASY

**Lewin, Ted.** *Market!* Lothrop, Lee & Shepard, 1996. Six markets from around the world, including ones in New York City, Morocco, and the jungles of central Africa, are described in this book. ⚐*SLJ Best Book;* New York Times *Best Illustrated Book; Notable Social Studies Trade Book.* CHALLENGING

**Mayer, Mercer.** *Shibumi and the Kitemaker.* Cavendish, 1987. Shibumi, daughter of the Emperor of Japan, lives a sheltered life within the palace walls. Curious about what's on the other side she peeks over the wall to find poverty surrounding her. She seeks out change. EASY

**McMillan, Bruce.** *Wild Flamingos.* Houghton Mifflin, 1997. A photo essay describing the physical characteristics, natural habitat, and behavior of the flamingos of Bonaire, Netherlands Antilles. ⚐*Outstanding Science Trade Book.* AVERAGE

**Nolen, Jerdine.** *In My Momma's Kitchen.* Lothrop, Lee & Shepard, 1999. A child describes family events that center around Mamma's kitchen. AVERAGE

**O'Dell, Scott.** *Black Star, Bright Dawn.* Houghton Mifflin, 1998. Bright Dawn must face the challenge of the Iditarod dog sled race alone when her father is injured. ⚐*Notable Social Studies Trade Book.* CHALLENGING

**Paterson, Katherine.** *The King's Equal.* HarperCollins, 1992. A King must fulfill his father's last wish of finding a wife that is his equal. In his search, he is taught a lesson and becomes a better King. ⚐*Irma Simonton Black Award.* AVERAGE

**Politi, Leo.** *Song of the Swallows.* Atheneum, 1987. Sad when the swallows leave for the winter, young Juan prepares to welcome them back to the old California Mission at Capistrano on St. Joseph's Day the following spring. ⚐*Caldecott Medal.* EASY

**Quinlan, Susan E.** *Puffins.* Carolrhoda, 1999. Discusses the physical characteristics, life cycle, and ecology of Atlantic puffins, tufted puffins, and horned puffins. ⚐*Teachers' Choice.* CHALLENGING

**Simon, Seymour.** *Animal Fact/Animal Fable.* Crown, 1987. Humorous illustrations reveal the truth about common beliefs about animals, such as a cat having nine lives, a bull getting angry when he sees red, or a raccoon washing. EASY

**Wiesner, David.** *June 29, 1999.* Clarion, 1992. While her third-grade classmates are sprouting seeds in paper cups, Becky has a more ambitious, innovative science project in mind. ⚐*ALA Notable Book; SLJ Best Book; Parents' Choice.* AVERAGE

**Yep, Laurence.** *Dragonwings.* HarperCollins, 1975. Moonshadow, an eight-year-old boy, sails from China to America to join his father, who he has never met. ⚐*ALA Notable;* Boston Globe - Horn Book *Honor; Children's Choice; Newbery Honor; Notable Social Studies Trade Book.* CHALLENGING

**Zelinsky, Paul O.** *Rapunzel.* Dutton, 1997. A beautiful girl with long golden hair is taken by a sorceress and forced to live in a lonely tower. ⚐*Caldecott Medal; ALA Notable Book; SLJ Best Book.* CHALLENGING

## Teacher Notes

# Additional Resources

# Side by Side
## *Additional Resources*

## Writer's Handbook

Contents

739

*Writer's Handbook*

# Introducing the Handbook

## Teach/Model

Tell students that the Writer's Handbook will help them with their writing. Have students find the Table of Contents on *Pupil Edition* page 739. Then model as follows:

**Model**   Begin by saying: **The Table of Contents shows the topics that will be covered. You may be familiar with some of these areas, and some may provide new information that will be useful to you in your writing.**

## Practice/Apply

Provide students with a **KWL** chart. In the **K** column, direct them to record what they already know about the topics to be covered. In the **W** column, have them record what they want to learn. Tell students that as they work through the handbook, they will write what they've learned in the **L** column.

Planning Your Writing

## Purposes for Writing

Each time you write, you have a reason. You may want to give information, respond to something you read, share an experience, or persuade someone to agree with you. The reason you write is called the **purpose for writing.** What you write depends on your purpose and on the people who will read your writing. These people are called the **audience.**

- **Expository writing** gives information. Expository writing includes how-to essays, literary responses, research reports, comparison and contrast essays, and explanatory essays.

    **Sample prompt:** *Compare and contrast dogs and wolves.* **Think about** *the ways dogs and wolves are alike and different.* **Now write** *about how dogs and wolves are alike and different.*

    ### Tips for Expository Writing
    - Write a topic sentence that tells the main idea.
    - Organize your details or steps in a logical order.
    - Use transition words or sequence words, such as *first* and *finally.*
    - Summarize the main idea in your conclusion.

When you **respond to literature,** your purpose is to demonstrate an understanding of what you have read.

    **Sample Prompt:** *Explain the theme of "The Emperor and the Kite." Use details from the selection to support your ideas.*

### Tips for Literary Response
- Write a topic sentence that tells your main idea.
- Use details from the literature and your prior knowledge to support your topic sentence.
- Summarize the main idea in your conclusion.

- **Expressive writing** tells a story or entertains. Stories and personal narratives are both examples of expressive writing.

    **Sample prompt:** *Imagine you are going to visit the Amazon rainforest.* **Think about** *what you might do there.* **Now write a** *story about visiting the Amazon rainforest.*

- **Persuasive writing** gives an opinion. When you write to persuade, you try to convince your audience to agree with your opinion and to take action.

    **Sample prompt:** *Is it better to live in the city or the country? Why? Try to persuade other students to agree with you.*

### Tips for Persuasive Writing
- Begin by getting your audience's attention and telling your opinion.
- Explain at least three supporting reasons.
- Give your strongest reason last.
- Support each reason with facts and details.
- Use emotional words to persuade your reader.
- Write a conclusion that restates your opinion and calls readers to take action.

### Try This
Identify the audience and purpose for each of these writing tasks: tell a younger child how to play a new game; tell why you think your school should have a book fair; tell why you like mysteries better than science fiction books; present an oral report about tigers.

740

741

# Purposes for Writing

## Teach/Model

Remind students that there are several purposes for writing. Read *Pupil Edition* pages 740–741 with them and discuss the distinct characteristics of each purpose and type of writing. Then model as follows:

**Model**   Begin by saying: **Before you write, examine your topic and identify the purpose for which you are writing. Decide which category of writing it best fits and follow the tips for that specific type of writing.**

## Practice/Apply

Have students make a three-column chart of the main categories of writing: expository, expressive, persuasive. Challenge them to brainstorm as many topics as they can and place each in the column that best fits the purpose for writing.

## The Writing Process

A finished piece of writing does not simply happen. Writers go through a series of steps to complete their work and present a finished product. The amount of writing time spent on each step can vary. Here are the five basic steps in the **writing process:**

### Prewriting

Before you begin to write, think about your purpose and audience. Decide what form your writing will take. Do research, and collect the information you need. Then **prewrite** by organizing your notes in an outline or another type of graphic organizer.

### Drafting

Once you have a plan, you are ready to write. A **draft** is your first try at the finished story, essay, or other piece of writing. After you have finished your draft, you will still have to change parts of it to better fit your purpose and your audience.

### Revising

**Revising** is the first step in the editing process. In this step, go over your draft to make sure that it fits your purpose and audience. Here are some things to do when you revise:

- Use an interesting opening sentence and a clear introduction.
- Add, delete, combine, or rearrange the text in your draft to make your writing more understandable to your audience.

- Make sure your writing follows a logical order from beginning to end.
- Use sequence words to help your audience follow your thoughts.
- Use words and ideas that your audience can understand.

It is often helpful to discuss your writing with a partner or in a small group. You can use what others say about your writing to revise it.

### Proofreading

**Proofreading** is the second step in editing. When you proofread, you correct mistakes and polish your writing. Look for and correct errors in grammar, punctuation, capitalization, and spelling.

### Publishing

After you have completed the first four steps, you are ready to **publish** your work, or to present it in its final, polished state. Depending on your purpose and audience, you may publish your writing as a speech, a video, or part of a class book. You may want to add pictures or other visual aids to enhance your work.

### Try This

Write a paragraph to describe a person you know well. Follow the five steps in the writing process. On which step did you spend the most time?

742

743

# The Writing Process

## Teach/Model

Review the five steps of the writing process with students. Have students read *Pupil Edition* pages 742–743 and discuss each step with them.
Then model as follows:

**Model**  Begin by saying: **When I write, I think of my composition as a sandwich. If one of the steps is missing, the sandwich isn't complete.**

## Practice/Apply

Have each student make a mobile of a three-ingredient sandwich. Tell students to label the top slice of bread *Prewriting*. On each layer, working down, have students provide the following labels: *Drafting, Revising, Proofreading*. Label the bottom slice *Publishing*. Hang the mobiles for students to use for reference as they write.

## How to Get Ideas

All writers must find ideas and topics. Writers think about everyday experiences and events and look for ways to write about them. They might ask themselves why an event made them feel a certain way. They might ask what they learned from an important or unusual experience. They might ask what they would like to learn more about or what they would like to teach others.

Writers use prewriting strategies like these to get ideas and to decide what to include in their writing.

### Keep a Journal

You may want to carry a small notebook to write down interesting things you see or hear, unusual or meaningful things people say, and descriptions of people or places. You can refer to your notebook for writing topics later.

### Search

If the topic you must write about is unfamiliar to you, **search** first on the Internet or in an encyclopedia. Newspapers and magazines may also have information on your topic. If you don't know how to begin your research, ask a librarian to help you find information on your topic.

### Brainstorm

When you **brainstorm,** you write down everything you can think of about your idea or topic. Give yourself about ten minutes to do this. Then read what you wrote and look for only those ideas you think you can really use. Sometimes it helps to brainstorm with a group and to share ideas.

744

### Make a Web Diagram

In a **web diagram** you write your topic in a circle. Then you draw spokes around the circle and write words or phrases about your topic at the end of each spoke.

### Ask Questions

Ask questions to guide your thinking and writing about your topic. If you were writing a personal narrative, you could use questions like these as your guide.

- **Who** are the characters, besides yourself?
- **Where** and **when** does the narrative take place?
- **What** happens first? Next? Last?

### Interview

Other people are often good sources of information and ideas. Talk with your teacher or your family about who you could interview and how you could contact that person. Always arrive on time for an interview, have questions prepared, and take careful notes.

**Try This**

Choose strategies you would use to get ideas for an essay about an important job in your community. How would you use each of the strategies you chose?

745

# How to Get Ideas

## Teach/Model

Ask students to share ways in which they choose what topics to write about. Invite students to read *Pupil Edition* pages 744–745 to see if their methods are among those suggested, and to learn about new ways to get ideas. Then model as follows:

**Model**   Begin by saying: **Writers sometimes have difficulty deciding on a topic for their writing. Many writers turn to their experiences to find ideas. Others keep track of ideas as they come to them and always have an idea bank ready when they need a new topic.**

## Practice/Apply

On a large piece of poster board, make a class Idea Web in the shape of a light bulb. Label the center of the web "Idea Sources." As students share idea-gathering methods, write their ideas on beams of light radiating from the center of the web. Display the poster in class for reference.

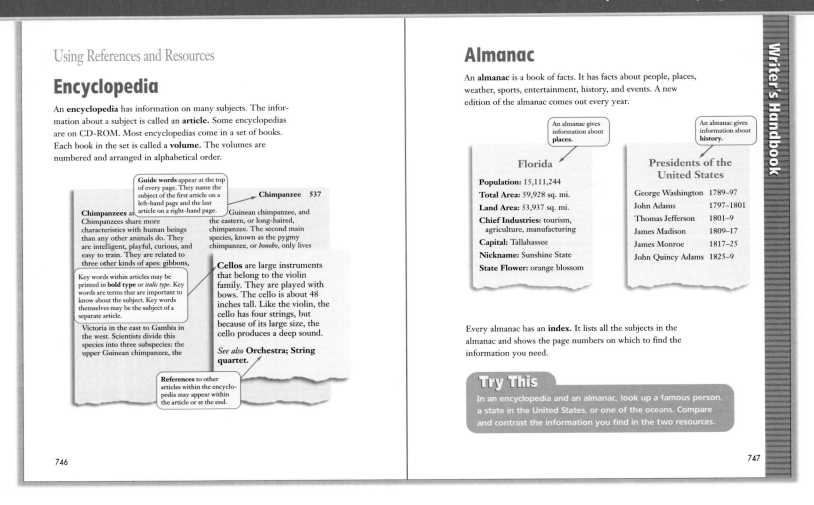

## Encyclopedia

### Teach/Model

Use *Pupil Edition* page 746 to review what an encyclopedia is and how it is used. Then model as follows:

**Model**   Begin by saying: **Information in an encyclopedia is organized alphabetically by the topic.**

### Practice/Apply

Give students topics to look up in an encyclopedia.

## Almanac

### Teach/Model

Use *Pupil Edition* page 747 to discuss the function of an almanac. Then model as follows:

**Model**   Begin by saying: **An almanac lists current facts about many topics. The index at the back will help you locate the page on which information can be found.**

### Practice/Apply

Provide teams of students with almanacs, and have a Fact Race. Name a topic, such as *Chicago,* and challenge teams to be the quickest to locate and state a fact about that topic.

## CD-ROM Resources

Encyclopedias and other reference works are available on **CD-ROM**. This is a compact disk that is read by a computer.

After you open a CD-ROM, you will see the **home screen** first. It will tell you how to get to the instructions for using the reference work.

The home screen for this CD-ROM encyclopedia shows the major resources available through it. Click on the section that you want to use.

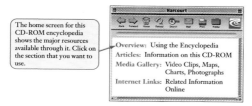

Overview: Using the Encyclopedia
Articles: Information on this CD-ROM
Media Gallery: Video Clips, Maps, Charts, Photographs
Internet Links: Related Information Online

Use the articles section to research a topic. It should have guide words to help you. Use keywords as you would on the Internet. Your search will result in a list of articles that contain your keywords. Click on an article title to display the article. Move between articles by clicking the Back button.

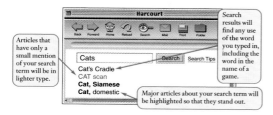

Articles that have only a small mention of your search term will be in lighter type.

Cats

Cat's Cradle
CAT scan
**Cat, Siamese**
**Cat,** domestic

Search results will find any use of the word you typed in, including the word in the name of a game.

Major articles about your search term will be highlighted so that they stand out.

748

## The Internet

The **Internet**—often called the Net—is a network that connects computers all over the world. A **network** is a group of computers that are linked electronically. The Internet is the largest computer network of all.

The Internet is an especially good resource for finding recent information about a topic. You can find specific information by using a **search engine**. A search engine matches your request for information with relevant websites. Follow these steps to get information from the Internet.

- Choose a search engine on the Internet.

- Type in a **keyword** about your topic. The more specific you are, the more exact your information will be. If your keyword is *cats*, you will find a variety of websites on cats. You might get websites about lions or tigers, about adopting kittens, or about the musical *Cats*.

- If you need to narrow your search, enter a more specific keyword or phrase such as *domestic cats*. Look through the list of websites and decide which will be useful. Click twice on each website to open it and to read the information it contains.

- To exit a website and return to the list, click on **Back** at the top of the screen.

**Try This**
At the library, do an Internet search for information about a pet you would like to have. Then check a CD-ROM encyclopedia. Which source gives you more information?

749

**Writer's Handbook**

# CD-ROM Resources

## Teach/Model

Discuss *Pupil Edition* page 749 with students. Model as follows:
**Model**  Begin by saying: **Information can be found on a CD-ROM by entering your topic word in the appropriate place. Then review the matches that are found.**

## Practice/Apply

Have students locate information using the keyword "dog."

# Internet

## Teach/Model

Use *Pupil Edition* page 748 to review and present the topic. Then model as follows:
**Model**  Begin by saying: **The Internet can be a direct link to the most current information on a topic.**

## Practice/Apply

Give students a topic. Have them practice selecting a search engine, choosing a keyword, and linking to a web site to locate information on the topic.

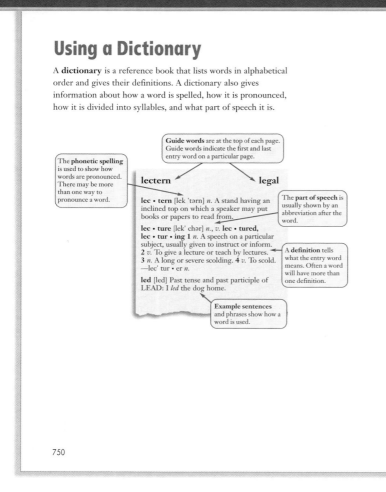

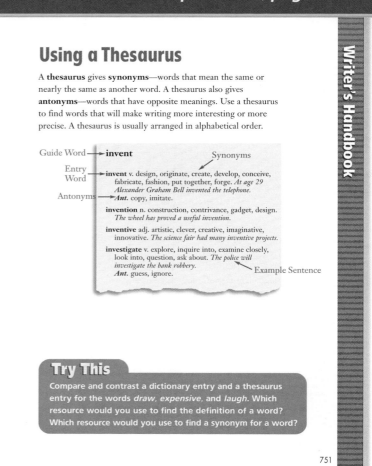

# Using a Dictionary

## Teach/Model

Use *Pupil Edition* page 750 to discuss the dictionary. Then model as follows:

**Model**    Begin by saying: **To check the meaning, pronunciation, or spelling of a word, look it up in the dictionary. The words are arranged in alphabetical order.**

## Practice/Apply

Have students locate the meanings of the following words: *conifer, odoriferous, containment.*

# Using a Thesaurus

## Teach/Model

Use *Pupil Edition* page 751 to discuss the thesaurus.

**Model**    Begin by saying: **To make your writing more interesting, vary the wording. The thesaurus gives synonyms and antonyms to help with word choice.**

## Practice/Apply

Provide students with a writing sample containing an overly used word. Challenge them to use the thesaurus to vary the wording to make it more interesting.

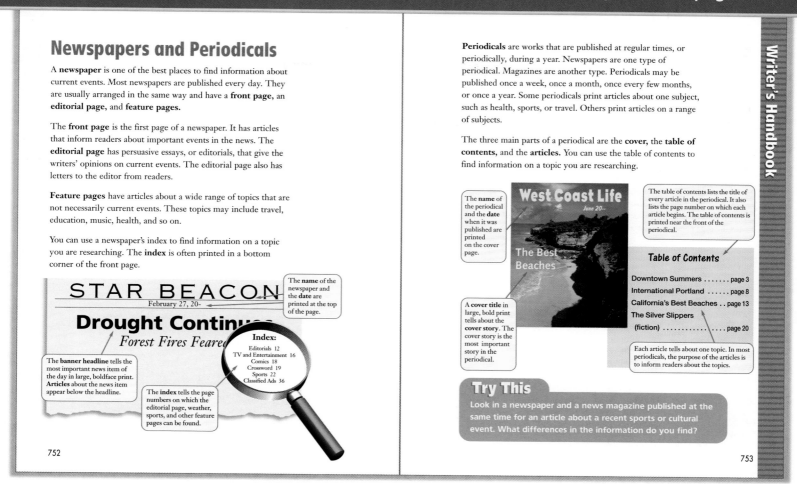

Writer's Handbook

**Newspapers and Periodicals**

A **newspaper** is one of the best places to find information about current events. Most newspapers are published every day. They are usually arranged in the same way and have a **front page,** an **editorial page,** and **feature pages.**

The **front page** is the first page of a newspaper. It has articles that inform readers about important events in the news. The **editorial page** has persuasive essays, or editorials, that give the writers' opinions on current events. The editorial page also has letters to the editor from readers.

**Feature pages** have articles about a wide range of topics that are not necessarily current events. These topics may include travel, education, music, health, and so on.

You can use a newspaper's index to find information on a topic you are researching. The **index** is often printed in a bottom corner of the front page.

The **name** of the newspaper and the **date** are printed at the top of the page.

## STAR BEACON
February 27, 20-

## Drought Continues
*Forest Fires Feared*

The **banner headline** tells the most important news item of the day in large, boldface print. **Articles** about the news item appear below the headline.

**Index:**
Editorials 12
TV and Entertainment 16
Comics 18
Crossword 19
Sports 22
Classified Ads 36

The **index** tells the page numbers on which the editorial page, weather, sports, and other feature pages can be found.

752

**Periodicals** are works that are published at regular times, or periodically, during a year. Newspapers are one type of periodical. Magazines are another type. Periodicals may be published once a week, once a month, once every few months, or once a year. Some periodicals print articles about one subject, such as health, sports, or travel. Others print articles on a range of subjects.

The three main parts of a periodical are the **cover,** the **table of contents,** and the **articles.** You can use the table of contents to find information on a topic you are researching.

The **name** of the periodical and the **date** when it was published are printed on the cover page.

## West Coast Life
June 20-

The Best Beaches

A **cover title** in large, bold print tells about the **cover story.** The cover story is the most important story in the periodical.

The table of contents lists the title of every article in the periodical. It also lists the page number on which each article begins. The table of contents is printed near the front of the periodical.

### Table of Contents

Downtown Summers . . . . . . . page 3
International Portland . . . . . . page 8
California's Best Beaches . . page 13
The Silver Slippers
(fiction) . . . . . . . . . . . . . . . page 20

Each article tells about one topic. In most periodicals, the purpose of the articles is to inform readers about the topics.

**Try This**

Look in a newspaper and a news magazine published at the same time for an article about a recent sports or cultural event. What differences in the information do you find?

753

# Newspapers and Periodicals

## Teach/Model

Ask students to describe any newspapers or periodicals they know are read in their homes or the homes of friends. Read *Pupil Edition* pages 752–753 with them to learn about the kinds of information found in both resources. Then model as follows:

**Model** Begin by saying: **When I want to learn about things happening locally or in the world each day, I read the newspaper. To learn about specific topics, I find a magazine dealing with that topic. Then I check to see if there are any articles in it that interest me.**

## Practice/Apply

Give students a topic to research, and ask them to decide which source, newspapers or periodicals, would be most useful for them. Repeat with various other topics.

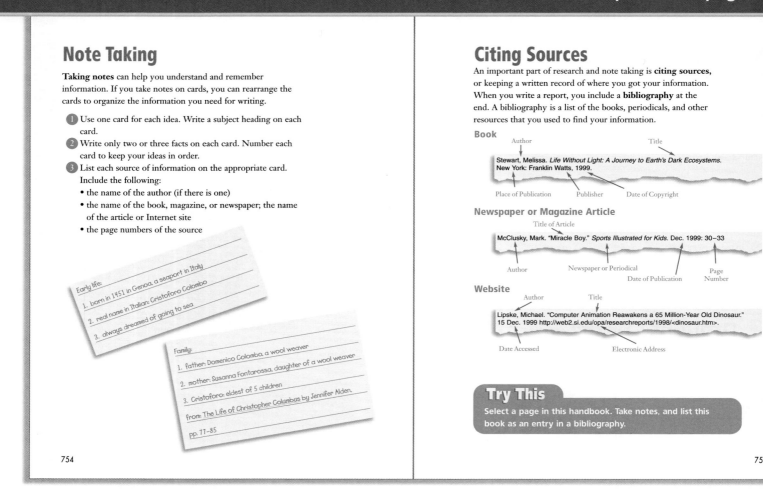

# Note Taking

## Teach/Model

Use *Pupil Edition* page 754 to present and review the topic. Model as follows:

**Model**  Begin by saying: **When I read a specific fact or detail and want to include it in my writing, I record it on a note card. This helps me organize my information later when it is time to write.**

## Practice/Apply

Have students practice taking notes on a specific topic. Discuss what information they choose to record.

# Citing Sources

## Teach/Model

Use *Pupil Edition* page 755 to discuss the importance and proper methods of citing sources. Then model as follows:

**Model**  Begin by saying: **It is important to show where you have found the information you use in your writing. A bibliography is one place in which you list the sources of your information.**

## Practice/Apply

Provide students with a list of sources. Have students arrange them in the correct order using the proper format for each entry.

Polishing Your Writing

## Traits of Good Writing

All good writing has certain characteristics, or **traits**. Use these strategies to make your writing the best it can be.

- **Make your focus and ideas clear.** Select a focus for your writing, based on your purpose and audience. Make sure that you present your ideas clearly. As you write, imagine your audience reading your work.
- **Organize your writing in a logical way.** You may organize your writing in one of several ways. Unless a pattern for organization has been assigned by your teacher, you should select one that best suits your topic and your purpose for writing. For example, a story is organized by a sequence of events. A how-to essay is organized by a sequence of steps. A research report is organized by topics and subtopics.
- **Express your personal voice.** Your interest in your topic should be clear in your writing. Personal voice is shown in your tone, or attitude, and in the words and expressions you use. Your writing should sound as though you wrote it and no one else.
- **Develop your writing with supporting details.** After you have introduced your main idea, support it with simple facts, details, and explanations. If you are writing a persuasive essay, provide details and reasons to support your opinion.

- **Think about vivid word choice.** Vivid words will make your writing interesting for your readers. Precise verbs and strong adjectives help readers picture in their minds what you have written about. A thesaurus is an excellent resource for vivid and exact words.
- **Use effective and varied sentences.** Using a variety of sentence structures will hold your audience's attention much better than using the same kinds of sentences over and over. Short sentences are effective when you want to make important points. Long sentences are effective for providing descriptions and details. Try to use a variety of declarative, imperative, interrogative, and exclamatory sentences.
- **Check your writing for errors.** Make your best effort to fix any errors in your writing. Proofread for errors in grammar, spelling, punctuation, and capitalization. If you pay attention to these details, your writing will be easier to read.

### Try This

Choose a magazine article or a newspaper article on any topic. As you read the article, look for as many traits of good writing as you can find.

Writer's Handbook

756

757

# Traits of Good Writing

## Teach/Model

Discuss with students the necessary components of a piece of writing. Then have students read *Pupil Edition* pages 756–757 to learn what traits make writing interesting and effective. Model as follows:

**Model** Begin by saying: **When I write, first I make a chart or outline to organize my thoughts. Next, I write a simple draft to get all my ideas down on paper. Then I go back and add details, vivid words, and other sentences. I check for clarity as well. I also ask myself if my writing would appeal to another reader.**

## Practice/Apply

Give students a simple paragraph. Have them practice editing the selection to include all traits of good writing. Allow them to compare their final drafts with each other.

## Using a Rubric

A **rubric** is a checklist or a set of guidelines that you can use to evaluate your writing. Your teacher may give you a special rubric for a writing assignment. That rubric may tell you what you need to include in your writing. It also will tell you what you can do to get your best score. Use the rubric **before, during,** and **after** writing.

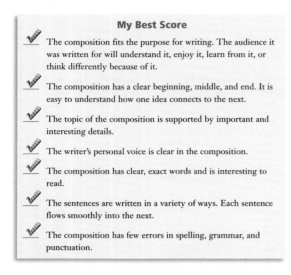

### My Best Score

✓ The composition fits the purpose for writing. The audience it was written for will understand it, enjoy it, learn from it, or think differently because of it.

✓ The composition has a clear beginning, middle, and end. It is easy to understand how one idea connects to the next.

✓ The topic of the composition is supported by important and interesting details.

✓ The writer's personal voice is clear in the composition.

✓ The composition has clear, exact words and is interesting to read.

✓ The sentences are written in a variety of ways. Each sentence flows smoothly into the next.

✓ The composition has few errors in spelling, grammar, and punctuation.

758

## Peer Conferences

When you participate in a **peer conference,** you meet with a partner or in a small group to read and discuss one another's writing. Getting feedback on your work will help you become a better writer.

Use these tips when you participate in peer conferences:

* Bring a clean copy of your composition for each group member including yourself.

* Use the feedback you get from your partner or group members to revise or proofread your composition. You can also use a rubric to check your work.

* When you look at the work of others, read carefully to find the main ideas. Then read to see whether you can follow the organization easily. Next, look at the sentence variety and word choice. Finally, check for errors.

* Tell your partner or group members what you liked about their work first. Then discuss with them any problems you noticed.

* Be helpful and polite. Work together to suggest ways you can all improve your writing.

**Try This**

Exchange compositions with a partner. Check your partner's work against the rubric on page 758.

759

# Using a Rubric

## Teach/Model

Use *Pupil Edition* page 758 to discuss what a rubric is and how it is used. Then model as follows:
**Model**   Begin by saying: **When I evaluate writing, I use a rubric. The rubric helps me to be fair and accurate in my judgment.**

## Practice/Apply

Distribute a writing sample and provide students with a scoring rubric. Have students use the rubric to evaluate the piece. Discuss their evaluations as a class.

# Peer Conferences

## Teach/Model

Use *Pupil Edition* page 759 to discuss peer conferencing techniques. Model as follows:
**Model**   Begin by saying: **Peer conferencing helps you get a clear perspective of your writing. A peer can tell you if your writing is easy to understand. He or she can tell you if there is anything to do to make your writing clearer or more interesting.**

## Practice/Apply

Allow students to free-write for 15 minutes. Have students make suggestions to improve each other's writing. Have them also give positive feedback and praise.

### Oral Presentations

One way of publishing your writing is to present it orally. Follow these steps to publish your composition as a speech.

- Write your main ideas or topic sentences on note cards. Keep the notes short and neat so they are easy to read. Add short notes to remind you about details so that you can talk about them without having to read directly from your notes.

- Number your note cards to keep them in order.

- Think about visual media that would make your speech more interesting and clear. You might use pictures, charts, graphs, diagrams, maps, or other media such as music or film. Remember to write on your note cards when to use your visual media.

- Underline or highlight your most important points in your notes. As you speak, emphasize those points. Remember to speak slower, louder, and with expression.

- Practice your speech before you present it. Speak slowly, clearly, and loud enough for everyone to hear. Remember to make eye contact with your audience during your speech.

760

### Multimedia Presentations and Graphics

Multimedia presentations are oral presentations in which you use visual or auditory aids.

- Think about your audience and your purpose. Would photographs, drawings, diagrams, videotapes, or music help the audience understand your information or make it more interesting?

- Ask your teacher about using equipment such as a videocassette player, a CD player, or an audiotape player.

- Design appropriate visual aids by hand, or use a computer to create graphics such as charts, tables, or graphs.

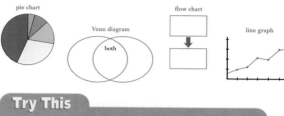

pie chart    Venn diagram    flow chart    line graph    both

**Try This**

Think of all the subjects about which you have written compositions or given presentations. Use information on these subjects to complete one of the four graphic organizers on this page. Make sure the information you use is appropriate for the graphic organizer you choose.

761

# Oral Presentations

## Teach/Model

Use *Pupil Edition* page 760 to discuss oral presentations. Then model as follows:
**Model**   Begin by saying: **When you present information orally, it is important to be organized and well prepared. This will also help you be less nervous during your presentation.**

## Practice/Apply

Have students record basic information about their childhood on note cards. Invite them to give oral presentations about their childhoods.

# Multimedia Presentations and Graphics

## Teach/Model

Discuss the use of multimedia presentations after students read *Pupil Edition* page 761. Model as follows:
**Model**   Begin by saying: **Including things for the audience to look at and listen to can make a presentation more interesting and effective.**

## Practice/Apply

Give a short speech on a topic such as a recent trip you have taken. Have students list the presentation aids that would make your speech more interesting.

# Introducing the Glossary

Explain to students that a glossary often is included in a book so that readers can find the meanings of words used in the book. Read aloud the introductory pages. Then model looking up one or more words, pointing out how you rely on alphabetical order and the guide words at the top of the Glossary pages to help you locate the entry word. You may also want to demonstrate how to use the pronunciation key to confirm the correct pronunciation.

■ As students look over the Glossary, point out that illustrations accompany some definitions. Have students read a Word Origins note and a Fact Finder note, and discuss the type of information in each.

■ Encourage students to look up several words in the Glossary, identifying the correct page and the guide words. Then have them explain how using alphabetical order and the guide words at the top of each page helps them locate the words.

■ Tell students to use the Glossary to confirm the pronunciations of vocabulary words during reading and to help them better understand the meanings of unfamiliar words.

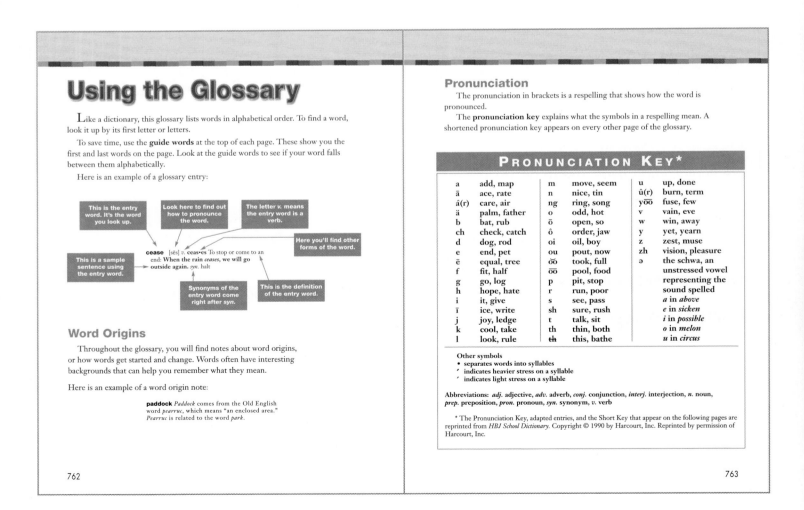

## Using the Glossary

Like a dictionary, this glossary lists words in alphabetical order. To find a word, look it up by its first letter or letters.

To save time, use the **guide words** at the top of each page. These show you the first and last words on the page. Look at the guide words to see if your word falls between them alphabetically.

Here is an example of a glossary entry:

- This is the entry word. It's the word you look up.
- Look here to find out how to pronounce the word.
- The letter *v.* means the entry word is a verb.
- Here you'll find other forms of the word.
- This is a sample sentence using the entry word.
- Synonyms of the entry word come right after *syn.*
- This is the definition of the entry word.

**cease** [sēs] *v.* **ceas·es** To stop or come to an end: When the rain *ceases*, we will go outside again. *syn.* halt.

### Word Origins

Throughout the glossary, you will find notes about word origins, or how words get started and change. Words often have interesting backgrounds that can help you remember what they mean.

Here is an example of a word origin note:

**paddock** *Paddock* comes from the Old English word *pearruc*, which means "an enclosed area." *Pearruc* is related to the word *park*.

### Pronunciation

The pronunciation in brackets is a respelling that shows how the word is pronounced.

The **pronunciation key** explains what the symbols in a respelling mean. A shortened pronunciation key appears on every other page of the glossary.

### PRONUNCIATION KEY*

| | | | | | |
|---|---|---|---|---|---|
| a | add, map | m | move, seem | u | up, done |
| ā | ace, rate | n | nice, tin | û(r) | burn, term |
| â(r) | care, air | ng | ring, song | yōō | fuse, few |
| ä | palm, father | o | odd, hot | v | vain, eve |
| b | bat, rub | ō | open, so | w | win, away |
| ch | check, catch | ô | order, jaw | y | yet, yearn |
| d | dog, rod | oi | oil, boy | z | zest, muse |
| e | end, pet | ou | pout, now | zh | vision, pleasure |
| ē | equal, tree | ŏŏ | took, full | ə | the schwa, an |
| f | fit, half | ōō | pool, food | | unstressed vowel |
| g | go, log | p | pit, stop | | representing the |
| h | hope, hate | r | run, poor | | sound spelled |
| i | it, give | s | see, pass | | *a* in *above* |
| ī | ice, write | sh | sure, rush | | *e* in *sicken* |
| j | joy, ledge | t | talk, sit | | *i* in *possible* |
| k | cool, take | th | thin, both | | *o* in *melon* |
| l | look, rule | th | this, bathe | | *u* in *circus* |

Other symbols
• separates words into syllables
´ indicates heavier stress on a syllable
ʹ indicates light stress on a syllable

Abbreviations: *adj.* adjective, *adv.* adverb, *conj.* conjunction, *interj.* interjection, *n.* noun, *prep.* preposition, *pron.* pronoun, *syn.* synonym, *v.* verb

* The Pronunciation Key, adapted entries, and the Short Key that appear on the following pages are reprinted from *HBJ School Dictionary.* Copyright © 1990 by Harcourt, Inc. Reprinted by permission of Harcourt, Inc.

762

763

## A

**a·ban·doned** [ə·ban′dənd] *adj.* Deserted or left behind: **The empty house seemed** *abandoned.* *syns.* discarded, cast aside

**a·bun·dant** [ə·bun′dənt] *adj.* More than enough: **The garage has** *abundant* **room for the many boxes we store there.** *syn.* plentiful

**ac·cept·a·ble** [ak·sep′tə·bəl] *adj.* Permitted, as an action that is allowed: **Blue jeans are not** *acceptable* **clothes for a wedding.**

**ac·ci·den·tal·ly** [ak·sə·dent′lē] *adv.* By mistake; without meaning to: **I** *accidentally* **let Josh know about his surprise party.** *syn.* mistakenly

**ac·cor·di·on** [ə·kôr′dē·ən] *n.* A musical instrument that sounds like a small organ: **Kaitlyn plays tunes on the** *accordion* **without looking at the keyboard.**

**accordion**

**Fact File**
**accordion** The word *accordion* came into use in the 1820s. It comes from the Italian word *accordare,* which means "to be in tune." A related word is *accord,* which means "to agree" or "to harmonize." *Accord* comes from the Latin word *cordis,* which means "heart." The harmony of music and feeling is related to the heart.

**ac·quaint·ance** [ə·kwānt′əns] *n.* Knowledge of someone or something: **I made the** *acquaintance* **of Mikaila's mother on the class trip.**

**ad·lib** [ad′lib′] *v.* To make up lines or music on the spot: **The actor had to** *ad-lib* **when she forgot her lines.** *ants.* rehearsed, planned

**a·dore** [ə·dôr′] *v.* To love something or someone dearly: **The puppies** *adore* **their owner.**

**a·larm** [ə·lärm′] *v.* **a·larmed** To frighten suddenly: **The noise** *alarmed* **the ducks and they flew away.** *syn.* startle

**Word Origins**
**alarm** The word *alarm* comes from the Italian word *all'arme,* which means "to arm" as in battle. This call to arms is a call to defend oneself.

**al·i·bi** [al′ə·bī′] *n.* A reason or an excuse for not doing something or not being in a certain place: **Dan's** *alibi* **was that he was in his room when the window was broken.** *syn.* explanation, defense

**anx·ious** [angk′shəs] *adj.* Eager: **Dan was** *anxious* **to find out if he had been chosen for the school play.**

**a·pol·o·gize** [ə·päl′ə·jīz] *v.* **a·pol·o·gized** To express regret over doing something wrong; to say one is sorry: **Ann** *apologized* **to her mother for coming home late.**

**ap·par·ent·ly** [ə·pâr′ənt·lē] *adv.* Seemingly easy to observe and understand: **You are** *apparently* **too big to ride a tricycle anymore.** *syn.* clearly

**ap·pe·tiz·ing** [ap′ə·tī′zing] *adj.* Delicious-looking: **The fresh fruit salad plate looked** *appetizing.* *syn.* appealing

**ap·pre·ci·a·tion** [ə·prē′shē·ā′shən] *n.* Recognition for good qualities; gratitude for something good: **He received an award in** *appreciation* **of his work.** *syn.* gratefulness

**ar·bor** [är′bər] *n.* A place that is shaded by trees or shrubs: **We rested on a bench in the cool, shady** *arbor.*

**as·sent** [ə·sent′] *v.* To agree or approve: **I will** *assent* **to the plan.** *syn.* consent

**at·ten·tive·ly** [ə·ten′tiv·lē] *adv.* With great interest and with careful attention: **Juan listened** *attentively* **to the directions.** *syn.* intently

## B

**bar·be·cue** [bär′bə·kyōō] *n.* A party or picnic where meat is cooked outdoors over coals: **Our family's** *barbecue* **is held every July 4.** *syn.* cookout

**barbecue**

**beck·ons** [bek′ənz] *v.* Attracts or lures by tempting with something desirable: **The ocean** *beckons* **scientists to explore its mysteries.** *syns.* entices, summons

764

**bel·low·ing** [bel′ō·ing] *n.* A loud sound made by an animal; an animal call: **The farm was full of the animals'** *bellowing* **as feeding time drew near.** *syn.* roar

**bick·er** [bik′ər] *v.* To have a minor argument: **Phillip and his sister often** *bicker* **over where to sit at the dinner table.** *syn.* squabble

**bil·low** [bil′ō] *v.* **bil·low·ing** To rise like a wave and push outward: **The sound of the orchestra was** *billowing* **through the halls and out into the street.** *syn.* swell

**bog·gy** [bäg′ē] *adj.* **bog·gi·est** Soggy or swampy: **We wore boots to hike through the** *boggiest* **part of the trail.** *syn.* marshy

**Word Origins**
**bog** *Bog* is an old Gaelic word meaning "soft and moist," like the wet spongy ground in a bog or swamp. To get bogged down in something is to become stuck in it, as one's feet would become stuck in mud.

**bond** [bänd] *v.* **bond·ing** To form a close relationship: **The mother and baby are** *bonding* **whenever they spend time together.** *syn.* link

**bri·gade** [bri·gād′] *n.* A group of people who work together to accomplish a task: **The volunteers formed a window-cleaning** *brigade* **and got the job done quickly.** *syn.* squad

**brisk** [brisk] *adj.* Cool and stimulating, as weather can be: **I wore a jacket when I went outside in the** *brisk,* **cool weather.** *syn.* chilly

**brush** [brush] *n.* Low bushes and shrubs that grow close together: **The young deer leaped over rocks and** *brush* **as it ran.** *syn.* undergrowth

**bur·rows** [bûr′ōz] *n.* Holes or tunnels that an animal digs in the ground to live in: **Snakes shelter in their** *burrows* **to protect themselves from the hot sun.** *syn.* nests

## C

**car·niv·o·rous** [kär·niv′ə·rəs] *adj.* Meat-eating, or, in the case of certain plants, insect-eating: **To survive,** *carnivorous* **plants need insects.**

**cease** [sēs] *v.* **ceas·es** To stop or come to an end: **When the rain** *ceases,* **we will go outside again.** *syn.* halt

**conch**

**cer·tain·ty** [sûr′tən·tē] *n.* The state of being sure about something: **I know with** *certainty* **that the book is good.**

**cer·tif·i·cate** [sûr·tif′ə·kit] *n.* An official piece of paper that shows one has met certain requirements: **Arthur got a** *certificate* **showing that he had completed a first-aid course.** *syn.* document

**chem·i·cal** [kem′i·kəl] *n.* **chem·i·cals** A substance that has certain properties: **The students wear safety glasses when mixing** *chemicals* **in science class.**

**chil·e** [chil′ē] *n.* A kind of stew that includes beans, chile peppers, and other ingredients: *Chile* **and salad make a tasty meal.**

**chor·tle** [chôr′təl] *v.* To laugh heartily: **Grandpa would grin and** *chortle* **whenever Connie told a joke.** *syn.* chuckle

**Fact File**
**chortle** The word *chortle* was coined in the 1800s by Lewis Carroll, the author of *Alice's Adventures in Wonderland* and *Through the Looking Glass.* *Chortle* is probably a combination of the words *chuckle* and *snort.*

**cir·cu·lar** [sûr′kyə·lər] *adj.* In the shape of a circle: **The wheel turned with a** *circular* **motion.** *syn.* round

**cir·cum·stance** [sûr′kəm·stans] *n.* **cir·cum·stanc·es** Any fact or event, especially as it relates to a larger event: **The** *circumstances* **of the accident were very unusual.**

**com·pro·mise** [käm′prə·mīz′] *v.* To settle a disagreement by having each party give in on certain points: **Sam and Bob agreed to** *compromise* **on how much they would spend.**

**conch** [känk] *n.* A sea animal of the mollusk family and the shell in which it lives: **We found a large pink** *conch* **during our vacation at the beach.**

765

**con·fet·ti** [kən·fet′ē] *n.* Bits of colorful paper that are thrown during celebrations to make them more festive: **The guests tossed** *confetti* **as the bride and groom passed by.**

**Fact File**
**confetti** The first *confetti* was actually small candies, which people would throw during carnivals and other celebrations. Then plaster candies were used. Finally, bits of paper took the place of plaster. The word *confetti* comes from the Italian word *confetto,* which means "candy." The English word *confection* also means "candy."

**co·or·di·na·tion** [kō·ôr′də·nā′shən] *n.* The act of working together smoothly for a purpose: **The movements of the dancer's arms and legs showed graceful** *coordination.*

**cor·ri·dor** [kôr′ə·dər] *n.* A long passageway or hall: **Our classroom door opens onto the** *corridor.* *syn.* hallway

**cou·ra·geous** [kə·rā′jəs] *adj.* Brave: **The** *courageous* **firefighter saved a child from the smoky room.** *syn.* fearless

**cul·ture** [kul′chər] *n.* The customs and way of life of a group of people: **Music, food, and literature are some of the ways a** *culture* **expresses itself.** *syn.* civilization

**cur·few** [kûr′fyōō] *n.* A time, usually in the evening or at night, after which people must be home or may not gather publicly: **During the emergency, no one was allowed outside after** *curfew.*

## D

**de·com·pose** [dē′kəm·pōz′] *v.* **de·com·pos·es** To decay: **A pile of fallen leaves** *decomposes* **and becomes part of the soil.** *syn.* rot

**de·cor** [dā·kôr′] *n.* The way a room is decorated: **The room was done in Early American** *decor.* *syn.* design

**de·cree** [di·krē′] *v.* **de·creed** To make an official order, such as from a ruler or a government: **The queen** *decreed* **a holiday in honor of her birthday.** *syn.* commitment

**ded·i·ca·tion** [ded′ə·kā′shən] *n.* Great loyalty or devotion: **The cellist feels great** *dedication* **to his music, so he practices four hours every day.** *syn.* commitment

**des·per·ate·ly** [des′pər·ət·lē] *adv.* With great need for help; with almost no hope: **The swimmer held on** *desperately* **to his rescuer.**

**de·vice** [di·vīs′] *n.* A piece of equipment that was designed to do a certain task: **The telephone is a communication** *device.* *syn.* tool

**dis·a·bil·i·ty** [dis′ə·bil′ə·tē] *n.* **dis·a·bil·i·ties** A condition, such as an illness or injury, that interferes with normal activity: **The Special Olympics is a sports event for athletes with** *disabilities.* *syn.* handicap

**dis·ap·point·ment** [dis′ə·point′mənt] *n.* The feeling that something did not meet expectations: **After I had seen the toy again and again in ads, actually owning it was a** *disappointment.* *syn.* letdown

**dis·card** [dis·kärd′] *v.* **dis·cards** To toss away as something without value: **Valerie** *discards* **the gift wrap after she opens a present, but Kayla saves it.**

**dis·pleas·ure** [dis·plezh′ər] *n.* The feeling of being annoyed: **The librarian showed his** *displeasure* **when he saw that the book cover was torn.** *syn.* irritation

**dis·po·si·tion** [dis′pə·zish′ən] *n.* The character of a person; the way an individual usually acts: **He has a pleasant** *disposition.* *syn.* nature

**dis·solve** [di·zälv′] *v.* To break up into tiny parts and become part of a liquid: *Dissolve* **some sugar into the lemonade so it will taste sweet.** *syn.* melt

**doc·u·ment** [däk′yə·mənt] *n.* A printed or written record that contains information: **A passport is a** *document* **that allows you to travel from one country to another.**

## E

**eaves·drop** [ēvz′dräp] *v.* **eaves·drop·ping** To listen secretly to someone else's private conversation: **Shana was** *eavesdropping* **to find out what her birthday present would be.**

**Word Origins**
**eavesdrop** *Eavesdrop* is an old term for the water that drips from the eaves, which are the edges of a roof. An eavesdropper may have been a person who would sit under the eaves of a roof in order to listen to someone else's conversation.

**e·lat·ed** [i·lā′tid] *adj.* Filled with joy or pride, as over success or good fortune: **Mark was** *elated* **when his soccer team won the championship.** *syns.* thrilled, overjoyed

**el·e·gant** [el′ə·gənt] *adj.* tasteful, stylish, and beautiful: **Grandma's lace tablecloth and fine china made her dining room table look** *elegant.* *syns.* lovely, appealing

766

**el·e·va·tions** [el′ə·vā′shənz] *n.* Heights above the ground or sea level: **The helicopter rose to higher** *elevations* **on its trip up the mountain.** *syn.* altitudes

**en·cir·cling** [in·sûr′kling] *v.* Forming a circle around; surrounding: *Encircling* **the farm was a white picket fence.** *syns.* enclosing, surrounding

**en·dan·gered** [in·dān′jərd] *adj.* Being in danger of no longer existing as a species: **The bald eagle is no longer an** *endangered* **species, as its numbers have increased.**

**en·rich** [in·rich′] *v.* To improve something by increasing its value, importance, or effectiveness: **Marsha will** *enrich* **her vocabulary if she looks up the words she doesn't know.** *syn.* enhance

**en·thu·si·as·ti·cal·ly** [in·thōō′zē·as′tik·lē] *adv.* In a way that shows intense or eager interest: **The audience clapped** *enthusiastically* **when the conductor walked onstage.** *syn.* spiritedly

**e·quiv·a·lent** [i·kwiv′ə·lənt] *n.* Having the same meaning or worth: **One hundred pennies is the** *equivalent* **of a dollar.** *syn.* counterpart

**ex·am·in·er** [ig·zam′ə·nər] *n.* Someone whose job is to give official tests: **The** *examiner* **gave Sarah her driver's test.**

**ex·cit·a·ble** [ik·sīt′ə·bəl] *adj.* Easily stirred up or provoked: **Paul has an** *excitable* **nature, so break the bad news gently.**

## F

**fa·cial** [fā′shəl] *n.* Having to do with the face: **Her** *facial* **features are almost the same as her mother's.**

**fam·ine** [fam′ən] *n.* A period of time when there is not enough food, such as during a crop failure: **The lack of rain caused many crops to die, which resulted in a** *famine.* *syn.* hunger

**fares** [fârz] *n.* Money paid for rides in a ship, bus, train, or airplane: **Bus** *fares* **cost more today than they did twenty years ago.** *syns.* fees, charges

**fas·ci·nate** [fas′ə·nāt′] *v.* **fas·ci·nat·ed** To interest very much: **The baby was** *fascinated* **by bright colors.** *syns.* captivate, attract

**fate·ful** [fāt′fəl] *adj.* Leading to an important outcome, often by chance: **Marta's** *fateful* **meeting with the program director led to a career change.**

**fer·tile** [fûr′təl] *adj.* Able to support growth of plants: **Crops grew well in the** *fertile* **soil.** *syn.* fruitful

**fer·til·iz·er** [fûr′təl·ī′zər] *n.* Something spread on the soil, such as chemicals, to make it richer and able to produce better crops: **After we added** *fertilizer,* **the plants grew better.**

**flam·ma·ble** [flam′ə·bəl] *adj.* Able to catch on fire: **Tamara made sure there were no** *flammable* **objects near the stove before she turned it on.** *syn.* burnable

**flammable**

## G

**gadg·et** [gaj′it] *n.* **gadg·ets** A small instrument or tool: **The** *gadgets* **Sue took camping included a hand-held can opener.**

**gadget**

**gen·er·ous** [jen′ər·əs] *adj.* Large, more than enough: **The restaurant gives** *generous* **portions of dessert.** *syn.* plentiful

**Word Origins**
**generous** *Generous* is related to the Latin word *genus,* meaning "origin" or "birth," and refers to people born into the aristocracy. Such people were expected to have a high standard of behavior. Being *generous* was one of the character traits they were expected to display.

**glum·ly** [glum′lē] *adv.* With a gloomy feeling or expression: **The cat gazed** *glumly* **at its empty bowl.** *syn.* sadly

**grudge** [gruj] *n.* Long-lasting bitterness or anger that one feels as a result of another's action: **Carlos held a** *grudge* **against Neil because Neil had never chosen him for the team.** *syn.* resentment

767

**hab·i·tat** [hab′ə·tat′] *n.* The place where something or someone lives: *A pond is a* habitat *for many kinds of plants, animals, and insects.* *syn.* environment

**har·mo·ny** [här′mə·nē] *n.* Two or more musical tones sung or played at the same time as a chord; pleasant musical sounds: *The choir sang in* harmony.

**haze** [hāz] *n.* Air that appears foggy because it contains small particles of dust, water, or pollutants: *This morning you can barely see the skyline through the* haze. *syn.* mist

haze

**heart·i·ly** [härt′əl·ē] *adv.* With much enthusiasm and energy: *The food was delicious and we were hungry, so we ate* heartily.

**hys·ter·i·cal·ly** [his·ter′ik·lē] *adv.* With uncontrolled emotion: *The sad news caused the children to weep* hysterically. *syn.* wildly

**im·mi·grant** [im′ə·grant] *n.* **im·mi·grants** A person who comes to live in a new country: *In our school are* immigrants *from Spain, Russia, and Haiti.* *syn.* newcomer

**im·plore** [im·plôr′] *v.* **im·plored** To ask in a pleading way: *Joan* implored *Coach Ames to let her run the race.* *syn.* beg

**im·pose** [im·pōz′] *v.* To force on someone: *We don't want to* impose *our opinions on you.* *syn.* force

**in·dif·fer·ent** [in·dif′ər·ənt] *adj.* Showing no interest: *Simon walked calmly,* indifferent *to the activity around him.*

**in·dig·nant·ly** [in·dig′nənt·lē] *adv.* Being angry about something that does not seem right or fair: *Susan reacted* indignantly *when her sister received a bigger dessert than she did.* *syn.* angrily

**in·hale** [in·hāl′] *v.* **in·haled** To take a deep breath in order to smell something: *Madison* inhaled *the fresh morning air.*

**in·jus·tice** [in·jus′tis] *n.* An unfair act: *It was an* injustice *when the innocent man was punished.*

**in·sig·nif·i·cant** [in′sig·nif′ə·kənt] *adj.* Lacking in importance, meaning, size, or worth: *The minor detail seemed* insignificant *compared to the larger problem.* *syns.* trivial, unimportant

**in·stinc·tive·ly** [in·stingk′tiv·lē] *adv.* With an action that is automatic and not thought out in advance: *While training, the athlete knew* instinctively *when to run and when to rest.* *syn.* naturally

**in·ter·pret·er** [in·tûr′prə·tər] *n.* A person whose job is to translate spoken words from one language to another: *Someone who enjoys learning languages may choose a career as an* interpreter. *syn.* translator

**in·ves·ti·gate** [in·ves′tə·gāt′] *v.* To search out and study the facts in order to find the truth about something: *Joel's doctor had to* investigate *the cause of his rash.* *syn.* examine

**ir·ri·ga·tion** [ir′ə·gā′shən] *n.* An artificial way to water the soil so that plants will grow: Irrigation *allows farmers to grow crops when there isn't enough rain.*

irrigation

**ir·ri·ta·bly** [ir′i·tə·blē] *adv.* With annoyance or anger: *The boy answered his friend* irritably *but later was sorry.* *syn.* crossly

**jeal·ous** [jel′əs] *adj.* Resentful of someone's relationship with another person: *Lloyd was* jealous *of his brother for having so many friends.* *syn.* envious

**lav·en·der** [lav′ən·dər] *n.* A pale shade of purple: *The sunset colored the sky orange, pink, and* lavender. *syn.* orchid

lavender

**lei·sure** [lē′zhər] *n.* Time free from work or other duties: *Summer vacation is a time of* leisure. *syn.* relaxation

**Word Origins**
**leisure** The word *leisure* comes from an Old French word meaning "something that is permitted, or freedom to do something." Now its meaning has changed to "free time."

**loathe** [lōth] *v.* To dislike very much: *On the playing field, the teams act as if they* loathe *each other.* *syn.* despise

**log·i·cal** [läj′i·kəl] *adj.* Naturally expected based on what has already happened: *A good math grade is the* logical *result of studying.* *syn.* reasonable

**loy·al** [loi′əl] *adj.* Constant and faithful to people or ideals: *The* loyal *dog stayed with the family and never ran away.* *syn.* devoted

**loy·al·ty** [loi′əl·tē] *n.* Faithfulness to a person or thing: *The citizens showed their* loyalty *to the mayor by reelecting her.*

**lux·u·ry** [luk′shər·ē] *n.* Anything of value that gives comfort or pleasure but is not necessary for life or health: *A diamond ring is a* luxury, *not a necessity.* *syns.* extravagance, frill

**mar·veled** [mär′vəld] *v.* Became filled with awe or wonder: *We* marveled *at the sight of the magnificent waterfall.* *syn.* stood in awe

**mes·quite** [mes·kēt′] *n.* A thorny tree or shrub common in the southwestern United States and Mexico: *The ranch was surrounded by* mesquite *bushes.*

**Fact File:**
**mesquite** *Mesquite* wood has a pleasant aroma that is used to add flavor to barbecued meat. Some commercially made barbecue sauces use it.

mesquite

**min·i·a·tures** [min′ē·ə·chərz] *n.* small-scale models of larger things: *Scott kept his collection of airplane* miniatures *in a shoebox.* *syns.* replicas, models

**mod·est** [mäd′ist] *adj.* Not showy; proper and quiet in manner: *Pat is* modest *about his art ability, but he is actually very talented.* *syns.* unassuming, humble

**mod·i·fy** [mäd′ə·fī] *v.* To change slightly: *Since it is raining, we will have to* modify *our plans for the class picnic.* *syn.* alter

**mul·ti·cul·tur·al** [mul′ti·kul′chər·əl] *adj.* Showing the varied customs, religions, or beliefs of different people: *The* multicultural *feast had food from many countries.* *syn.* diverse

**mu·ral** [myoor′əl] *n.* A large picture painted on a wall: *The artist painted a* mural *in the lobby of the office building.*

mural

**mut·ter** [mut′ər] *v.* **mut·tered** To speak in an unclear way and in a low voice, usually in anger: *Debbie* muttered *a complaint that her sister did not hear.* *syn.* grumble

| a add | e end | o odd | ōō pool | oi oil | th this | ə = { a in above |
|---|---|---|---|---|---|---|
| ā ace | ē equal | ō open | u up | ou pout | zh vision | e in sicken |
| â care | i it | ô order | û burn | ng ring | | i in possible |
| ä palm | ī ice | ōō took | yōō fuse | th thin | | o in melon |
| | | | | | | u in circus |

**nec·tar** [nek′tar] *n.* A sweet liquid found in flowers: *The bee drank* nectar *from the flower.*

**neg·lect·ed** [ni·glek′tid] *v.* Failed to care for or attend to: *The lawn is overgrown because Jason* neglected *to mow it.*

**nes·tle** [nes′əl] *v.* **nes·tles** To hug or pull close to give affection: *The child* nestles *her puppy in her arms.* *syn.* snuggle

**o·blige** [ə·blīj′] *v.* **o·bliged** To do a favor for someone: *Sal* obliged *his fans and played another song.*

**oc·ca·sion·al·ly** [ə·kā′zhən·əl·ē] *adv.* Happening now and then: *Walter* occasionally *plays ball after school, but usually he practices chess.* *syn.* sometimes

**out·spo·ken** [out′spō′kən] *adj.* Bold or honest in speech: *The* outspoken *man firmly stated his opinion.* *syns.* blunt, straightforward

**o·ver·whelm** [ō′vər·hwelm′] *v.* To overpower: *Don't* overwhelm *a new puppy with too many commands or you will confuse it.* *syn.* overburden

**pad·dock** [pad′ək] *n.* A small, fenced field next to a stable, where horses can exercise: *The horse and the pony grazed together in the* paddock.

**Word Origins:**
**paddock** *Paddock* comes from the Old English word *pearruc,* which means "an enclosed area." *Pearruc* is related to the word *park.*

paddock

**pag·eant** [paj′ənt] *n.* A performance in honor of an important event or holiday: *Tina played the part of a general in the town's history* pageant. *syn.* show

**pas·time** [pas′tīm′] *n.* **pas·times** An enjoyable activity one does in one's free time: *Reading and hiking are Raul's favorite* pastimes. *syn.* entertainment

**perch** [pûrch] *v.* To sit or settle on a high or dangerous spot: *The bird was about to* perch *on the tree branch.*

perch

**per·se·ver·ance** [pûr′sə·vir′əns] *n.* Trying to do something no matter what difficulties arise: *Through his* perseverance, *he earned a place on the baseball team.* *syns.* steadfastness, determination

**pe·ti·tion·er** [pə·tish′ən·ər] *n.* **pe·ti·tion·ers** One who makes a written request of those who are in charge: *The* petitioners *asked the king to lower their taxes.*

**pi·o·neer** [pī′ə·nir′] *n.* A person who explores and settles new land in a faraway area: *A* pioneer *had to struggle to survive on the frontier.*

**Fact File**
**pioneer** The idea of a *pioneer* has come to mean someone who explores the unknown, not only on land. We refer to *pioneers* as leading the way in fields such as science, medicine, and space.

**pit·e·ous·ly** [pit′ē·əs·lē] *adv.* Causing feelings of sadness: *The puppy howled* piteously *the first night, so Sheila sat up with it.* *syn.* touchingly

**plen·ti·ful·ly** [plen′ti·fəl·ē] *adv.* With nothing lacking; with more than enough: *The art supplies closet was* plentifully *stocked with brushes, paper, paints, and clay.* *syn.* abundantly

**plot·ting** [plot′ing] *v.* Planning in secret to do something, often something evil: *The bank robber was* plotting *his next crime.* *syn.* scheming

**pos·si·bil·i·ty** [päs′ə·bil′ə·tē] *n.* **pos·si·bil·i·ties** Something that has a chance of happening: *There are many job* possibilities *for an educated person.* *syn.* likelihood

**prac·ti·cal** [prak′ti·kəl] *adj.* Useful or sensible: *It is* practical *to have a spare set of house keys.* *syns.* reasonable, wise

**priv·i·lege** [priv′ə·lij] *n.* A special benefit, favor, or right enjoyed only under special circumstances: *It is a* privilege *to vote in this country.* *syn.* advantage

**prof·it·a·ble** [prof′it·ə·bəl] *adj.* Bringing advantage or monetary gain: *The artist's business was so* profitable *that she became a millionaire.* *syns.* beneficial, rewarding

**pros·thet·ic** [präs·thet′ik] *adj.* Having to do with a replacement body part, such as a tooth, an eye, or a limb: *With her* prosthetic *hand, Hilda could draw.*

**pro·trude** [prō·trood′] *v.* **pro·trud·ed** To stick out: *The dock* protruded *thirty yards into the water.* *syns.* extend, bulge

**ras·cal·ly** [ras′kəl·ē] *adj.* Mischievous, dishonest: *The* rascally *hamster escaped from its cage and hid in the house for two days.* *syn.* impish

**ra·tion** [rash′ən] *n.* A limited amount; a part of the whole: *Each soldier got a small daily* ration *of food and water.* *syns.* measure, share

**rec·og·nize** [rek′əg·nīz′] *v.* **rec·og·niz·ing** To know someone or something by details such as appearance or sound: *My dog is capable of* recognizing *the sound of my footsteps.* *syn.* identify

**re·hears·al** [ri·hûr′səl] **re·hears·als** *n.* Preparation and practice before an actual performance: *The actors read their lines during* rehearsals. *syn.* drill

**re·pent·ant** [ri·pent′ənt] *adj.* Showing sorrow and regret for past actions: *Noreen's* repentant *letter about the broken window led her neighbor to forgive her.* *syn.* remorseful

**re·sound** [ri·zound′] *v.* **re·sound·ed** To echo or to fill a place with sound: *The last notes of the symphony* resounded *in the hall.*

**rest·less** [rest′ləs] *adj.* Unable to rest or relax: *The cattle were* restless *as they sensed the coming storm.* *syns.* nervous, uneasy

**re·tire** [ri·tīr′] *v.* To leave a job because one has reached one's goals or has reached an advanced age: *The star athlete's decision to* retire *from basketball shocked his fans.* *syn.* withdraw

**re·tort** [ri·tôrt′] *v.* **re·tort·ed** To answer in an arguing way: *Jane* retorted *angrily when I said the mistake was her fault.*

**ro·guish** [rō′gish] *adj.* Full of mischief; likely to stir up trouble: *The child's* roguish *smile led his mother to suspect that he had made the mess.* *syn.* sneaky

**rug·ged** [rug′id] *adj.* Having a rough, uneven, or broken surface: *The farmer had to smooth out the* rugged *strip of land.* *syn.* irregular

**rus·tle** [rus′əl] *n.* A swishing sound: *The* rustle *of leaves in the trees means the wind is getting stronger.* *syn.* whisper

**sal·a·ry** [sal′ə·rē] *n.* The amount of money that a person gets for doing a job: *Josh receives his* salary *every Friday.* *syn.* pay

**Fact File**
Salt is necessary for life. Because it keeps food from spoiling, it was considered very valuable in times and places where there was no refrigeration. In ancient Rome, soldiers were paid in salt! The Latin word *salarium* means "salt money" and is the root of the word *salary* that we use today.

**schol·ar·ship** [skäl′ər·ship] *n.* The quality and character of a serious student: *Ray's high grades showed good* scholarship. *syn.* studiousness

**script** [skript] *n.* The words of a play, including stage directions: *Each actor got a copy of the* script.

**scrounge** [skrounj] *v.* **scroung·ing** To hunt around for what is needed: *We saw a raccoon* scrounging *around in the trash.* *syn.* search

**sculp·tor** [skulp′tər] *n.* An artist who carves wood or stone or who shapes clay: *The* sculptor *makes drawings before she carves.*

**shame·fa·ced·ly** [shām′fā′səd·lē] *adv.* In a way that shows shame for having done something bad: *Robert* shamefacedly *told his mother that he broke her favorite vase.* *syns.* guiltily, sorrowfully

sculptor

**shift·less** [shift′lis] *adj.* Showing lack of ambition or energy: *The* shiftless *hare slept under the tree while the tortoise won the race.* *syn.* lazy

| a add | e end | o odd | ōō pool | oi oil | th this | ə = { a in above |
|---|---|---|---|---|---|---|
| ā ace | ē equal | ō open | u up | ou pout | zh vision | e in sicken |
| â care | i it | ô order | û burn | ng ring | | i in possible |
| ä palm | ī ice | ōō took | yōō fuse | th thin | | o in melon |
| | | | | | | u in circus |

**skid** [skid] *v.* **skid•ded** To slide in an unexpected direction: **The car *skidded* on the icy road before it stopped.**

**smug•gle** [smug′əl] *v.* **smug•gled** To take something secretly: **The diamond was *smuggled* out in an empty soda can.** *syn.* sneak

**soft•heart•ed** [sôft′härt′id] *adj.* Kind; full of mercy: **Paul is so *softhearted* that he kept the stray kittens.**

**spin•y** [spī′nē] *adj.* Covered with thorns or needles: **A porcupine's *spiny* quills keep enemies away.** *syn.* sharp

**spiny**

**sports•man•ship** [spôrts′mən•ship′] *n.* Conduct, such as fair play, expected of an athlete: **The losing team showed good *sportsmanship* by cheering for the winning team.**

**spruce** [sproōs] *v.* **spruc•ing** To fix something up: **The scouts are *sprucing* up the campsites as part of their community service.**

**star•struck** [stär′struk] *adj.* Full of stars: **She looked up at the *starstruck* sky.**

**starstruck**

**steel•y** [stē′lē] *adj.* Like steel, as in strength, hardness, or coldness: **The athlete lifted the heavy weight with a *steely* grip.** *syns.* strong, vise-like

**straight•a•way** [strāt′ə•wā′] *adv.* Without delay: **The ambulance came *straightaway*.** *syn.* immediately

**strand** [strand] *v.* **strand•ed** To leave behind without help: **The tourist was *stranded* when his plane took off without him.** *syn.* abandon

**strength•en•ing** [streng(k)th′ən•ing] *adj.* Adding more force and growing in power: **The darkening skies and *strengthening* wind meant a storm was on the way.** *syn.* increasing

**sulk•i•ly** [sulk′ə•lē] *adv.* With a withdrawn, unpleasant attitude: **The small child sat *sulkily* on the rug after her crayons were taken away.** *syn.* gloomily

**sur•ren•der** [sə•ren′dər] *n.* The act of giving up: **Generals from both sides met to work out the terms of the *surrender*.**

**sym•pa•thet•i•cal•ly** [sim′pə•thet′ik•lē] *adv.* With the same feelings as another person has: **The coach talked *sympathetically* after the player sprained his ankle.** *syn.* understandingly

 **T**

**teem** [tēm] *v.* **teem•ing** To be very full: **The rain forest is *teeming* with animals.** *syn.* overflowing

**thrift•y** [thrift′ē] *adj.* Careful about saving money, or doing things to make it last longer: **The *thrifty* family found ways to use all the leftovers from meals.**

**top•ple** [täp′əl] *v.* To make fall over: **Rahaili liked to make a big block pile and then *topple* it with the tiniest push.** *syn.* collapse

**trag•e•dy** [traj′ə•dē] *n.* A very sad event that brings suffering: **The fire was a *tragedy* for the families who lost their homes.** *syn.* disaster

**trans•form** [trans•fôrm′] *v.* **trans•formed** To undergo a change, either in appearance or in character: **The schoolyard was *transformed* into fairgrounds for Family Appreciation Day.**

**tre•men•dous** [tri•men′dəs] *adj.* Very large: **The diver in the shark cage saw only the shark's *tremendous* open mouth.** *syn.* enormous

**trick•le** [trik′əl] *n.* A thin, slow stream of something, such as water or sand: **A *trickle* of raindrops slid down the windowpane.**

**trickle**

**tri•um•phant•ly** [trī′um′fant•lē] *adv.* In a way that indicates success or victory: **We sang *triumphantly* all the way home after winning the championship game.**

**trop•i•cal** [träp′i•kəl] *adj.* Having to do with the hot area of the earth: **A *tropical* storm can develop into a hurricane.**

**Fact File**

**tropical** The area known as the *Tropics* extends from 23.5 degrees north latitude to 23.5 degrees south latitude. Within these boundaries, the sun's rays shine directly on earth. Because the area receives so much direct light, it is warm all year.

**tropical**

**trou•ble•some** [trub′əl•səm] *adj.* Causing difficulty and worry: **Carl's odd behavior was *troublesome* to his parents.** *syn.* bothersome

**tun•dra** [tun′drə] *n.* A flat, treeless region near the Arctic Circle: **Summer in the *tundra* is brief and cool.**

**tundra**

**tu•tor** [tōō′tər] *v.* To teach privately: **Luis is home with his leg in a cast, so his mother and father *tutor* him every day.** *syn.* instruct

**twined** [twīnd] *v.* Twisted around: **The machine *twined* the wires around each other to make a cable.** *syns.* twisted, wound

**U**

**un•doubt•ed•ly** [un•dout′id•lē] *adv.* Surely; proven beyond question: **Science was *undoubtedly* her best subject.** *syn.* definitely

**un•eas•y** [un•ē′zē] *adj.* Nervous or troubled: **Jan was *uneasy* every time she had to go down into the dark basement.** *syn.* worried

**un•in•hab•it•ed** [un′in•hab′it•id] *adj.* Unoccupied; empty: **The old cottage stood *uninhabited* for years.**

**un•yield•ing** [un•yēl′ding] *adj.* Constant and never-ending, not giving way: **Her desire to become an astronaut was *unyielding* throughout her life.** *syn.* uncompromising

 **V**

**va•cant** [vā′kənt] *adj.* Empty, having nothing in it: **A new family has rented the *vacant* apartment.**

**val•u•a•ble** [val′yōō•ə•bəl] *adj.* Having great worth and meaning, either in terms of money or in personal terms: **A good education is a *valuable* tool for reaching one's goals.** *syn.* precious

**ven•ti•late** [ven′təl•āt′] *v.* To bring fresh air into a place: **In order to *ventilate* the house, open all the windows.** *syn.* freshen

**Word Origins**

**ventilate** The word *ventilate* comes from the Latin word *ventus*, meaning "wind." Another related meaning of *ventilate* has to do with "airing" feelings or points of view — discussing things in an open way.

**ven•ture** [ven′chər] *v.* To risk moving from a safe place: **The mouse sniffs the air before it will *venture* from its nest.**

**vic•tim** [vik′təm] *n.* A living thing that is harmed: **The mouse was the *victim* that became the snake's lunch.**

 **W**

**wind•break** [wind′brāk] *n.* A fence or line of trees that breaks the force of the wind: **The farmer planted a *windbreak* to protect his crops.** *syn.* barrier

**wist•ful•ly** [wist′fəl•ē] *adv.* With a thoughtful, wishful feeling for something: **Papa sighed *wistfully* as he shared his childhood memories.** *syn.* longingly

| a add | e end | o odd | ōō pool | oi oil | th this | ə = { a in above |
|---|---|---|---|---|---|---|
| â ace | ē equal | ō open | u up | ou pout | zh vision | e in sicken |
| â care | i it | ô order | û burn | ng ring | | i in possible |
| ä palm | ī ice | ōō took | yōō fuse | th thin | | o in melon |
| | | | | | | u in circus |

**GLOSSARY**

**Lead the Way**    **R17**

# Index *of* Titles *and* Authors

774

775

# Managing the Classroom
# Setting the Stage

## Designing a Space

One of the keys to productive learning is the physical arrangement of your classroom. Each classroom has unique characteristics, but the following areas should be considered in your floor plan.

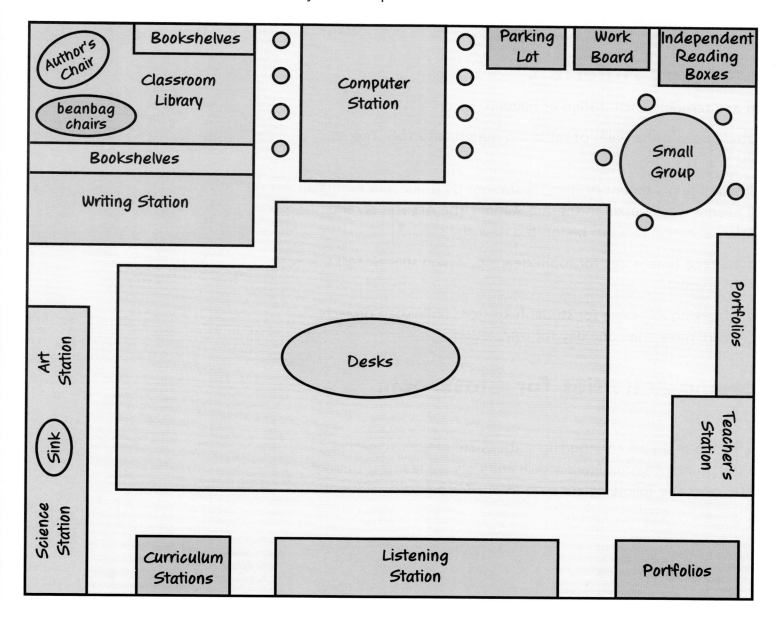

When arranging your classroom, consider traffic patterns and usage of areas. Place quiet stations near small group and independent work areas. Provide some private spaces for students to work.

A three-sided cardboard divider can instantly become a "private office" or a portable learning station.

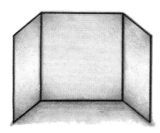

## Introducing the Stations

Before beginning a routine, acquaint students with procedures for and use of each area. All station activities should involve literacy with a balance of reading and writing tasks.

Help students understand how much time they will spend in a station. For example, they can read several chapters in a book from the Classroom Library, listen to one tape recording in the Listening Station, and play one game in the Technology Station.

Show students how to use the computer, tape recorder, and headphones. Demonstrate proper usage of art supplies.

## Organizing Materials

Clean and resupply each station as needed.

Get students into the habit of returning materials to their proper places.

Determine the placement of items in stations by usage. For example, you'll need a wastebasket in the Art Station. The Art Station and the Science Station need to be located near the sink.

Set aside time once a day for room cleaning. Assign specific tasks for each student.

Have a "parking lot" table for students to store unfinished projects that require more than one day for completion.

## Planning Activities for Classroom Stations

Many of the materials for ongoing stations are at your fingertips. Base station activities on literacy skills students are learning throughout the year. The following are suggestions for particular stations.

# Classroom Library

One corner of your room can house books students can freely choose and enjoy reading on their own. Include books of all kinds: reference books, chapter books, and books students have made themselves.

# Independent Reading Boxes

Provide boxes of books for each small guided reading group. Use color-coded boxes or bins to hold fifteen or more books. Provide multiple copies if possible. Books can include those that have been shared during group sessions and books that are appropriate for independent reading.

# Listening Station

Include tape recorder and headsets. Provide audiotexts and a variety of commercial tapes and tapes recorded by volunteers and students. If you are providing text with a tape, make multiple copies and store the tape and books in a plastic bag. Suggest an extension activity following listening.

# Technology Station

Students can write on the computer using word processing software, such as ClarisWorks for Kids, or interact with literature software, such as Instant Readers and Living Books™. See technology references throughout the lessons.

# Writing Station

This should be a clearly defined space where writing materials are stored. Possible materials include:

| | | |
|---|---|---|
| blank books | a variety of paper | stationery and envelopes |
| stickers | poster board | staples and staple remover |
| pencils | markers | hole punch and yarn |

# Curriculum Stations

Ideas for cross-curricular activities are provided before each lesson in the Teacher's Edition. Supply materials as needed for students to:

■ create graphs in a math activity

■ perform an experiment and keep a log in a science activity

■ make a map in a social studies activity

■ create new verses to perform a song in a music activity

■ create artwork in response to stories

# Establishing Flexible Work Groups

In order for the teacher to work with small groups without interruption, the other class members must clearly understand what they are to do. To plan a series of tasks these students can do independently, establish small work groups. These are heterogeneous groups of students who are scheduled for the same station activities on a daily basis. You can change these groups as often as you like.

# The Value of Flexible Grouping

Flexible grouping is a way to ensure that all students will achieve instructional standards. Grouping should be a fluid process—changing on a daily, weekly, or monthly basis—based upon your assessment of individual students' progress.

**Whole-Class Instruction**   Students can be grouped all together for activities, such as reading and discussing literature, writing compositions, and creating art.

**Small-Group Instruction**   You may wish to use small-group instruction for

- a group of students who do not understand a skill and need another approach to learning it;

- a group of students who have already mastered a skill and need an additional challenge.

**The Teacher's Role**   With some groups, the teacher may establish the group's goal and then step aside, letting the group decide how to achieve that goal. With other groups, the teacher may remain close by, monitoring the group as needed to achieve the goal. With still others, the teacher may provide direct instruction and assistance to help group members achieve the goal.

# Introducing a Work Board

One way to schedule classroom activity is with a Work Board. A typical Work Board includes the names of small-group members and icons that represent independent tasks. For example, you may wish to use an atom to represent the Science Station or headphones to represent the Listening Station. The Work Board can also be a cork board, a peg board with hooks, or a magnetic board. Its design should be flexible, enabling you to move cards on a daily basis.

| Carrie   Josh | Maritza   Dan |
| Derek   Amy | Jenny   Ty |
| Art Station | Science Station |
| Science Station | Art Station |

# Handwriting

**Individual students have various levels of handwriting skills,** but they all have the desire to communicate effectively. To write correctly, they must be familiar with concepts of

- **size (tall, short).**
- **open and closed.**
- **capital and lowercase letters.**
- **manuscript vs. cursive letters.**
- **letter and word spacing.**
- **punctuation.**

To assess students' handwriting skills, review samples of their written work. Note whether they use correct letter formation and appropriate size and spacing. Note whether students follow the conventions of print such as correct capitalization and punctuation. Encourage students to edit and proofread their work and to use editing marks. When writing messages, notes, and letters, or when publishing their writing, students should leave adequate margins and indent new paragraphs to help make their work more readable for their audience.

## Stroke and Letter Formation

Most manuscript letters are formed with a continuous stroke, so students do not often pick up their pencils when writing a single letter. When students begin to use cursive handwriting, they will have to lift their pencils from the paper less frequently and will be able to write more fluently. Models for Harcourt and D'Nealian handwriting are provided on pages R25–R28.

## Position for Writing

Establishing the correct posture, pen or pencil grip, and paper position for writing will help prevent handwriting problems.

**Posture**   Students should sit with both feet on the floor and with hips to the back of the chair. They can lean forward slightly but should not slouch. The writing surface should be smooth and flat and at a height that allows the upper arms to be perpendicular to the surface and the elbows to be under the shoulders.

**Writing Instrument**   An adult-sized number-two lead pencil is a satisfactory writing tool for most students. As students become proficient in the use of cursive handwriting, have them use pens for writing final drafts. Use your judgment in determining what type of instrument is most suitable.

**Paper Position And Pencil Grip**   The paper is slanted along the line of the student's writing arm, and the student uses his or her nonwriting hand to hold the paper in place. The student holds the pencil or pen slightly above the paint line—about one inch from the lead tip.

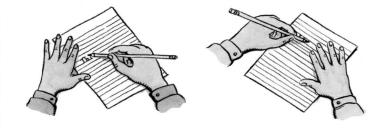

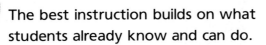

## Reaching All Learners

The best instruction builds on what students already know and can do. Given the wide range in students' handwriting abilities, a variety of approaches may be needed.

**Extra Support**   For students who need more practice keeping their handwriting legible, one of the most important understandings is that legible writing is important for clear communication. Provide many opportunities for writing that communicates among students. For example, students can

- make a class directory listing names and phone numbers of their classmates.
- record observations in science.
- draw and label maps, pictures, graphs, and picture dictionaries.
- write and post messages about class assignments or group activities.

**ELL**   English Language Learners can participate in meaningful print experiences. They can

- write signs, labels for centers, and messages.
- label drawings.
- contribute in group writing activities.
- write independently in journals.

You may also want to have students practice handwriting skills in their first language.

**Challenge**   To ensure continued rapid advancement of students who come to fourth grade writing fluently, provide

- a wide range of writing assignments.
- opportunities for independent writing on self-selected and assigned topics.

# Handwriting
## Manuscript Alphabet

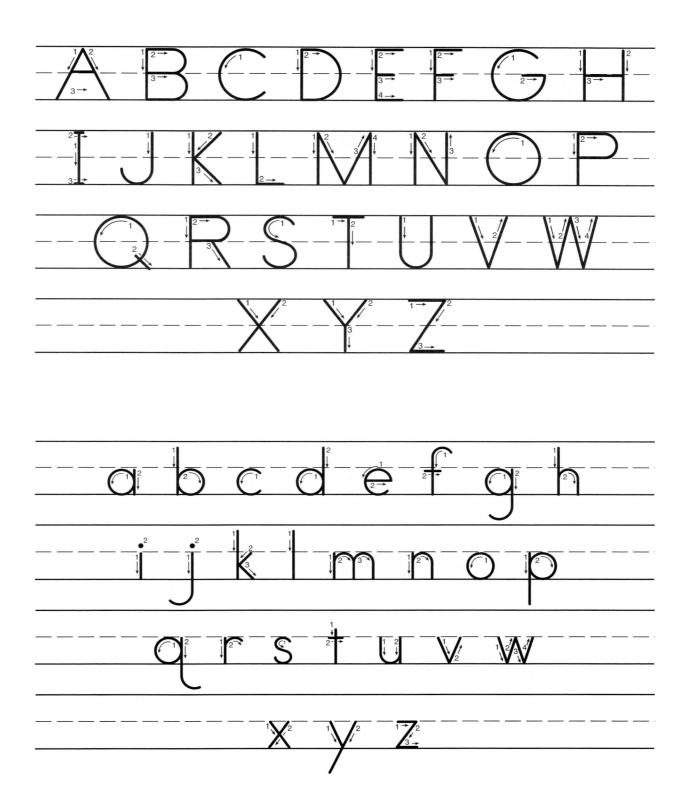

# Handwriting
## Cursive Alphabet

$A$ $B$ $C$ $D$ $E$ $F$ $G$ $H$
$I$ $J$ $K$ $L$ $M$ $N$ $O$ $P$
$Q$ $R$ $S$ $T$ $U$ $V$ $W$
$X$ $Y$ $Z$

$a$ $b$ $c$ $d$ $e$ $f$ $g$ $h$
$i$ $j$ $k$ $l$ $m$ $n$ $o$ $p$
$q$ $r$ $s$ $t$ $u$ $v$ $w$
$x$ $y$ $z$

# D'Nealian
# **Handwriting**
## Manuscript Alphabet

A B C D E F G H
I J K L M N O P
Q R S T U V W
X Y Z

a b c d e f g h
i j k l m n o p
q r s t u v w
x y z

# D'Nealian
# Handwriting
## Cursive Alphabet

*A B C D E F G H*

*I J K L M N O P*

*Q R S T U V W*

*X Y Z*

*a b c d e f g h*

*i j k l m n o p*

*q r s t u v w*

*x y z*

# Hands-on Grammar Activities

Photocopy the page, cut apart the strips, and distribute them to students. One or more sentences can be distributed at a time. You may also need to distribute blanks and punctuation marks. Students can cut the strips apart into cards and can write replacement words on the backs of the cards for some activities. Depending on the needs of your students, have them use the cards to practice and reinforce word order and other grammatical concepts with activities such as the following:

## Hands-on Diagramming

- separate subjects and predicates with extra space
- place modifiers below the word they modify
- attach parts of compounds with conjunctions placed vertically between them
- create oversized diagrams with cards and lines on chart paper
- make a Diagramming Wall with larger cards and butcher paper

## Sentences

- rearrange words to change a statement to a question
- change the sentence type by adding, replacing, or rearranging words
- combine sentences using conjunctions

## Subjects/Nouns

- replace common nouns with proper nouns, and vice versa
- identify the simple and complete subject
- combine sentences using compound subjects
- replace general nouns with specific nouns

## Predicates/Verbs

- identify complete and simple predicates
- combine sentences using compound predicates
- replace common verbs with more interesting verbs
- change the subject and then change the verb to agree
- change present-tense verbs to past-tense verbs

## Pronouns

- replace nouns with pronouns
- replace possessive nouns with possessive pronouns
- change the pronoun and then change the verb to agree

## Adjectives, Adverbs, and Prepositions

- add or remove adjectives or adverbs
- change the order of the two adjectives or the placement of adverbs
- move prepositional phrases to different positions in the sentence

Megan    filled    a    tin    with    cookies    .

How    well    you    danced    !

Dad    is    a    very    good    driver    .

Snow    piled    up    quickly    .

Many    loaves    filled    the    bread    box    .

The    oldest    girl    in    my    family    is    Sara    .

Wow    ,    she    joined    every    club    in    school    !

Do    you    know    his    name    ,    Rachel    ?

I    did    ride    the    short    gray    horse    .

Did    Julian    meet    a    friend    at    the    store    ?

| | | | |
|---|---|---|---|
| . | ? | ! | , | " | " | ' | . |

The garden and the wall look beautiful now .

Pink , blue , and purple are my favorite colors .

Would you like to dig the soil or

plant the seeds ?

Before it rains , we run for shelter .

Thomas saw a leaf fall from the tree .

The cat ' s whiskers were white .

Jacob will see Dr . Cortin on

Monday , August 12 .

Marie likes this restaurant better .

. ? ! , " " , .

Harcourt

Elephants are the largest land animals .

Firefighters have responded quickly .

When you ' re using the telephone ,

you must speak clearly .

Have you worn that dress before ?

Grandma brought out platefuls of food .

One hundred children would not fit in

this room .

Uncle Jed hitched the oxen expertly .

Tammy likes to play on the swing .

. ? ! , " " , .

Harcourt

That was my nose !

Mary , Lin , and I signed the card .

Lester wrapped and tied the package .

Who is the friend of the fox ?

You taught me a valuable lesson .

Which would be worse , rain or no rain ?

The plumber ' s truck rode slowly down

the street .

Mother dressed more warmly than the

others did .

| | | | |
|---|---|---|---|
| . | ? | ! | , | " | " | , | . |

Penguins can swim , or they can walk on land .

Laura ' s hands nearly froze .

Almost everything costs more at this store .

A strong wind blew fiercely .

We can hear the crickets , but we never

see them .

First , she gathered sticks for kindling .

She carefully places some books on the

table .

Finally , the men finished the work .

| | | | |
|---|---|---|---|
| . | ? | ! | , | " | " | , | . |

# Using the Student Record Form

## Using the Student Record Form

The record form on the following pages is a tool for tracking each student's progress toward grade-level standards. In addition to formal records on assessment results and instructional plans, you may also wish to complete this form several times yearly for each student. Make one copy of the form for each student. Record the date at the top of the column, and use the codes provided to record student progress. You may wish to add comments at the bottom or on the back of the form.

## Sharing Student Progress with Family Members

The record form can be one vehicle for communicating with families about how students are making progress toward grade-level standards. Explain that students are expected to master the standards toward the end of the school year. Therefore, a code of B, or Beginning, at the start of the year is expected for most students. After that time, most students should be receiving a P for Making Progress, and by the end of the year they should meet or exceed each standard.

Students who are not making progress, of course, require intervention and frequent assessment to monitor progress and adapt instruction. Explain to family members the levels of support offered by *Trophies* and how you are using these tools to help their students succeed. On the other hand, some students may begin to meet or exceed the standards early in the year. For these families, you can explain how you are using *Trophies* to extend and accelerate progress. (For more information about levels of support in *Trophies*, see Theme Assessment to Plan Instruction at the beginning of each theme.)

## Encouraging Family Involvement

Besides explaining student progress, there are several things you can do to encourage parents and guardians to support their students' achievement:

- Use the School-Home Connections pages in the Theme Resources section to suggest activities and reading materials on a weekly basis.
- Copy the Additional Homework Ideas pages at the beginning of each theme, and send them home with students. Encourage family members to use at least one activity per day.
- Have students use My Reading Log (provided in this tabbed section) daily, to record their reading outside of class. Stress repeatedly that sustained daily reading is essential to student growth. Request that parents or guardians sign off on the My Reading Log form, to encourage them to monitor students' reading.
- Above all, offer praise and recognition for all efforts that family members make to support students' literacy.

# Student Record Form

Student _____ Teacher _____ Grade _____

| | Date____ | Date____ | Date____ | Date____ | Date____ | Date____ |
|---|---|---|---|---|---|---|
| **WORD ANALYSIS, FLUENCY, AND SYSTEMATIC VOCABULARY DEVELOPMENT** | | | | | | |
| Read narrative and expository text aloud with grade-appropriate fluency and accuracy and with appropriate pacing, intonation, and expression. | | | | | | |
| Apply knowledge of word origins, derivations, synonyms, antonyms, and idioms to determine the meaning of words and phrases. | | | | | | |
| Use knowledge of root words to determine the meaning of unknown words within a passage. | | | | | | |
| Know common roots and affixes derived from Greek and Latin and use this knowledge to analyze the meaning of complex words. | | | | | | |
| Use a thesaurus to determine related words and concepts. | | | | | | |
| Distinguish and interpret words with multiple meanings. | | | | | | |
| **READING COMPREHENSION** | | | | | | |
| Identify structural patterns found in informational text to strengthen comprehension. | | | | | | |
| Use appropriate strategies when reading for different purposes. | | | | | | |
| Make and confirm predictions about text by using prior knowledge and ideas presented in the text itself, including illustrations, titles, topic sentences, important words, and foreshadowing clues. | | | | | | |
| Evaluate new information and hypotheses by testing them against known information and ideas. | | | | | | |
| Compare and contrast information on the same topic after reading several passages or articles. | | | | | | |
| Distinguish between cause and effect and between fact and opinion in expository text. | | | | | | |
| Follow multiple-step instructions in a basic technical manual. | | | | | | |
| **LITERARY RESPONSE AND ANALYSIS** | | | | | | |
| Describe the structural differences of various imaginative forms of literature, including fantasies, fables, myths, legends, and fairy tales. | | | | | | |
| Identify the main events of the plot, their causes, and the influence of each event on future actions. | | | | | | |
| Use knowledge of the situation and setting and of a character's traits and motivations to determine the causes for that character's actions. | | | | | | |
| Compare and contrast tales from different cultures by tracing the exploits of one character type and develop theories to account for similar tales in diverse cultures. | | | | | | |
| Define figurative language and identify its use in literary works. | | | | | | |
| **WRITING STRATEGIES** | | | | | | |
| Select a focus, an organizational structure, and a point of view based upon purpose, audience, length, and format requirements. | | | | | | |
| Create multiple-paragraph compositions (provide an introductory paragraph; establish and support a central idea with a topic sentence at or near the beginning of the first paragraph; include supporting paragraphs with simple facts, details, and explanations; conclude with a paragraph that summarizes the points; use correct indention). | | | | | | |
| Use traditional structures for conveying information. | | | | | | |
| Write fluidly and legibly in cursive or joined italic. | | | | | | |
| Quote or paraphrase information sources, citing them appropriately. | | | | | | |
| Locate information in reference texts by using organizational features. | | | | | | |
| Use various reference materials as an aid to writing. | | | | | | |
| Understand the organization of almanacs, newspapers, and periodicals and how to use those print materials. | | | | | | |
| Demonstrate basic keyboarding skills and familiarity with computer terminology. | | | | | | |
| Edit and revise selected drafts to improve coherence and progression by adding, deleting, consolidating, and rearranging text. | | | | | | |

Harcourt

## WRITING APPLICATIONS
## (Genres and Their Characteristics)

| | | | | | | |
|---|---|---|---|---|---|---|
| Write narratives (relate ideas, observations, or recollections of an event or experience; provide a context to enable the reader to imagine the world of the event or experience; use concrete sensory details; provide insight into why the selected event or experience is memorable). | | | | | | |
| Write responses to literature (demonstrate an understanding of the literary work; support judgments through references to both the text and prior knowledge). | | | | | | |
| Write information reports (frame a central question about an issue or situation; include facts and details for focus; draw from more than one source of information). | | | | | | |
| Write summaries that contain the main ideas of the reading selection and the most significant details. | | | | | | |

## WRITTEN AND ORAL ENGLISH LANGUAGE CONVENTIONS

| | | | | | | |
|---|---|---|---|---|---|---|
| Use simple and compound sentences in writing and speaking. | | | | | | |
| Combine short, related sentences with appositives, participial phrases, adjectives, adverbs, and prepositional phrases. | | | | | | |
| Identify and use regular and irregular verbs, adverbs, prepositions, and coordinating conjunctions in writing and speaking. | | | | | | |
| Use parentheses, commas in direct quotations, and apostrophes in the possessive case of nouns and in contractions. | | | | | | |
| Use underlining, quotation marks, or italics to identify titles of documents. | | | | | | |
| Capitalize names of magazines, newspapers, works of art, musical compositions, organizations, and the first word in quotations when appropriate. | | | | | | |
| Spell correctly roots, inflections, suffixes and prefixes, and syllable constructions. | | | | | | |

## LISTENING AND SPEAKING STRATEGIES

| | | | | | | |
|---|---|---|---|---|---|---|
| Ask thoughtful questions and respond to relevant questions with appropriate elaboration in oral settings. | | | | | | |
| Summarize major ideas and supporting evidence presented in spoken messages and formal presentations. | | | | | | |
| Identify how language usages reflect regions and cultures. | | | | | | |
| Give precise directions and instructions. | | | | | | |
| Present effective introductions and conclusions that guide and inform the listener's understanding of important ideas and evidence. | | | | | | |
| Use traditional structures for conveying information. | | | | | | |
| Emphasize points in ways that help the listener or viewer to follow important ideas and concepts. | | | | | | |
| Use details, examples, anecdotes, or experiences to explain or clarify information. | | | | | | |
| Use volume, pitch, phrasing, pace, modulation, and gestures appropriately to enhance meaning. | | | | | | |
| Evaluate the role of the media in focusing attention on events and in forming opinions on issues. | | | | | | |

## SPEAKING APPLICATIONS
## (Genres and Their Characteristics)

| | | | | | | |
|---|---|---|---|---|---|---|
| Make narrative presentations (relate ideas, observations, or recollections about an event or experience; provide a context that enables the listener to imagine the circumstances of the event or experience; provide insight into why the selected event or experience is memorable). | | | | | | |
| Make informational presentations (frame a key question; include facts and details that help listeners to focus; incorporate more than one source of information). | | | | | | |
| Deliver oral summaries of articles and books that contain the main ideas of the event or article and the most significant details. | | | | | | |
| Recite brief poems, soliloquies, or dramatic dialogues, using clear diction, tempo, volume, and phrasing. | | | | | | |

**Comments:**

Harcourt

**Key:**

B = Beginning

P = Making Progress

M = Meets Standard

E = Exceeds Standard

# My Reading Log

Student: _____   Date: _____   Grade: _____

Teacher: _____   School: _____

Book Title: _____   Book Author: _____

Total number of pages: _____

Date I started the book: _____   Date I finished the book: _____

I read:

    (date/time) _____ (pages) _____   (date/time) _____ (pages) _____

    (date/time) _____ (pages) _____   (date/time) _____ (pages) _____

    (date/time) _____ (pages) _____   (date/time) _____ (pages) _____

I am spending   more time/less time   reading because _____
_____.

I chose this book to read because _____
_____.

My favorite part of the book was _____
_____.

This book was   easy/difficult   to read because:

   ❑ I could figure out _____ of the words.   (all, most, some, a few)

   ❑ I   understood/didn't understand   the topic.

   ❑ I   liked/disliked   the author.

    Other: _____

I   would/would not   choose another book like this because _____
_____.

Harcourt

# Thinking About My Reading and Writing

Student: _____     Date: _____     Grade: _____

Teacher: _____     School: _____

## When I read,

| | | | |
|---|---|---|---|
| I think about why I am reading something. | **Always** | **Sometimes** | **Need to work on this** |
| I think about what I already know about the topic. | **Always** | **Sometimes** | **Need to work on this** |
| I think about what might happen in the story. | **Always** | **Sometimes** | **Need to work on this** |
| I picture in my mind what I am reading. | **Always** | **Sometimes** | **Need to work on this** |
| I ask myself if what I'm reading makes sense. | **Always** | **Sometimes** | **Need to work on this** |
| I think about what kind of story it might be. | **Always** | **Sometimes** | **Need to work on this** |

## When I write,

| | | | |
|---|---|---|---|
| I think about my purpose and my reader. | **Always** | **Sometimes** | **Need to work on this** |
| I list or draw my main ideas. | **Always** | **Sometimes** | **Need to work on this** |
| I use an organization that makes sense. | **Always** | **Sometimes** | **Need to work on this** |
| I use my own words and ideas. | **Always** | **Sometimes** | **Need to work on this** |
| I choose exact, vivid words. | **Always** | **Sometimes** | **Need to work on this** |
| I use a variety of sentences. | **Always** | **Sometimes** | **Need to work on this** |
| My writing sounds smooth when I read it aloud. | **Always** | **Sometimes** | **Need to work on this** |
| I add facts and details when they are needed. | **Always** | **Sometimes** | **Need to work on this** |
| I group my ideas in paragraphs. | **Always** | **Sometimes** | **Need to work on this** |
| I proofread to check for errors. | **Always** | **Sometimes** | **Need to work on this** |

Harcourt

# Listening and Speaking Checklist

Student _____  Teacher _____  Grade _____

| | Date____ | Date____ | Date____ | Date____ | Date____ | Date____ |
|---|---|---|---|---|---|---|
| **LISTENING AND SPEAKING STRATEGIES** | | | | | | |
| Ask thoughtful questions and respond to relevant questions with appropriate elaboration in oral settings. | | | | | | |
| Summarize major ideas and supporting evidence presented in spoken messages and formal presentations. | | | | | | |
| Identify how language usages (e.g., sayings, expressions) reflect regions and cultures. | | | | | | |
| Give precise directions and instructions. | | | | | | |
| Present effective introductions and conclusions that guide and inform the listener's understanding of important ideas and evidence. | | | | | | |
| Use traditional structures for conveying information (e.g., cause and effect, similarity and difference, and posing and answering a question). | | | | | | |
| Emphasize points in ways that help the listener or viewer to follow important ideas and concepts. | | | | | | |
| Use details, examples, anecdotes, or experiences to explain or clarify information. | | | | | | |
| Use volume, pitch, phrasing, pace, modulation, and gestures appropriately to enhance meaning. | | | | | | |
| Evaluate the role of the media in focusing attention on events and in forming opinions on issues. | | | | | | |
| **SPEAKING APPLICATIONS** | | | | | | |
| Make narrative presentations: Relate ideas, observations, or recollections about an event or experience. | | | | | | |
| Provide a context that enables the listener to imagine the circumstances of the event or experience. | | | | | | |
| Provide insight into why the selected event or experience is memorable. | | | | | | |
| Make informational presentations: Frame a key question. | | | | | | |
| Include facts and details that help listeners to focus. | | | | | | |
| Incorporate more than one source of information (e.g., speakers, books, newspapers, television or radio reports). | | | | | | |
| Deliver oral summaries of articles and books that contain the main ideas of the event or article and the most significant details. | | | | | | |
| Recite brief poems (i.e., two or three stanzas), soliloquies, or dramatic dialogues, using clear diction, tempo, volume, and phrasing. | | | | | | |

**Comments:**

**Key:**

N = Not Observed

O = Observed Occasionally

R = Observed Regularly

Harcourt

# Traveling on the Internet

There are so many things to see and do on the Internet that new users may wish they had a "tour guide" to help them see the most interesting sites and make sure they don't miss anything. There are many ways to become a savvy Web traveler—one is by learning the language. Here are some common terms.

**bookmark** A function that lets you return to your favorite Web sites quickly.

**browser** Application software that allows you to navigate the Internet and view a Web site.

**bulletin board/newsgroup** Places to leave an electronic message or to share news that anyone can read and respond to.

**chat room** A place for people to converse online by typing messages to each other. Once you're in a chat room, others can contact you by e-mail. Some online services monitor their chat rooms and encourage participants to report offensive chatter. Some allow teachers and parents to deny children access to chat rooms altogether.

**cookie** When you visit a site, a notation known as a "cookie" may be fed to a file in your computer. If you revisit the site, the cookie file allows the Web site to identify you as a return guest—and offer you products tailored to your interests or tastes. You can set your online preferences to limit or let you know about cookies that a Web site places on your computer.

**cyberspace** Another name for the Internet.

**download** To move files or software from a remote computer to your computer.

**e-mail** Messages sent to one or more individuals via the Internet.

**filter** Software that lets you block access to Web sites and content that you may find unsuitable.

**ISP** (Internet Service Provider) A service that allows you to connect to the Internet.

**junk e-mail** Unsolicited commercial e-mail; also known as "spam."

**keyword** A word you enter into a search engine to begin the search for specific information or Web sites.

**links** Highlighted words on a Web site that allow you to connect to other parts of the same Web site or to other Web sites.

**listserv** An online mailing list that allows individuals or organizations to send e-mail to groups of people at one time.

**modem** An internal or external device that connects your computer to a phone line that can link you to the Internet.

**password** A personal code that you use to access your Internet account with your ISP.

**privacy policy** A statement on a Web site describing what information about you is collected by the site and how this information is used.

**search engine** A function that helps you find information and Web sites. Accessing a search engine is like using the catalog in a library.

**URL** (Uniform Resource Locator) The address that lets you locate a particular site. For example, **http://www.ed.gov** is the URL for the U.S. Department of Education. All government URLs end in **.gov**. Nonprofit organizations and trade associations end in **.org**. Commercial companies now end in **.com**, and non-commercial educational sites end in **.edu**. Countries other than the United States use different endings.

**virus** A file maliciously planted in your computer that can damage files and disrupt your system. Antivirus software is available.

**Web site** An Internet destination where you can look at and retrieve data. All the Web sites in the world, linked together, make up the World Wide Web or the "Web."

 **Visit *The Learning Site!*** www.harcourtschool.com

Harcourt

**My Rules for Internet Safety**

I agree that

- **I will never give out private information,** such as my last name, my address, my telephone number, or my parents' work addresses or telephone numbers on the Internet.

- **I will never give out the address or telephone number** of my school on the Internet without first asking an adult's permission.

- **I understand which sites I can visit** and which ones are off-limits.

- **I will tell an adult right away** if something comes up on the screen that makes me feel uncomfortable.

- **I will never agree to meet in person** with anyone I meet online.

- **I will never e-mail a person any pictures** of myself or my classmates without an adult's permission.

- **I will tell an adult** if I get an inappropriate e-mail message from anyone.

- **I will remember that going online** on the Internet is like going out in public, so all the safety rules I already know apply here as well.

- **I know the Internet is a useful tool,** and I will always use it responsibly.

- **I will follow these same rules when I am at home,** in school, at the library, or at a friend's.

X _____    _____
(Student signs here)                              (Parent/Guardian signs here)

Visit *The Learning Site!*
www.harcourtschool.com

Harcourt

# Professional Bibliography

**Adams, M. J.** 1990. *Beginning to Read: Thinking and Learning About Print.* Cambridge: Massachusetts Institute of Technology Press.

**Adams, M. J., et al.** 1998. "The Elusive Phoneme: Why Phonemic Awareness Is So Important and How to Help Children Develop It," *American Educator: The Unique Power of Reading and How to Unleash It,* Vol. 22, Nos. 1 and 2, 18–29.

**Adams, M. J.; R. Treiman; and M. Pressley.** 1998. "Reading, Writing, and Literacy," in *Handbook of Child Psychology: Child Psychology in Practice* (Fifth edition). Vol. 4. Edited by I. E. Sigel and K. A. Renninger. New York: Wiley.

**Allen, L.** 1998. "An Integrated Strategies Approach: Making Word Identification Instruction Work for Beginning Readers," *The Reading Teacher,* Vol. 52, No. 3, 254–68.

**American Association of School Librarians and the Association of Educational Communications and Technology.** 1998. *Information Power: Building Partnerships for Learning.* Chicago: American Library Association.

**Anderson, R. C., et al.** 1985. *Becoming a Nation of Readers: The Report of the Commission on Reading.* Washington, D.C.: National Academy of Education, Commission on Education and Public Policy.

**Anderson, R. C.; P. T. Wilson; and L. G. Fielding.** 1988. "Growth in Reading and How Children Spend Their Time Outside of School," *Reading Research Quarterly,* Vol. 23, No. 3, 285–303.

**Anderson, R. C., and W. E. Nagy.** 1991. "Word Meanings," in *Handbook of Reading Research.* Vol. 2. Edited by R. Barr, et al. New York: Longman.

**Ball, E. W., and B. A. Blachman.** 1991. "Does Phoneme Awareness Training in Kindergarten Make a Difference in Early Word Recognition and Developmental Spelling?" *Reading Research Quarterly,* Vol. 26, No. 1, 49–66.

**Barinaga, M.** 1996. "Giving Language Skills a Boost," *Science,* Vol. 271, 27–28.

**Baumann, J. F., and E. J. Kame'enui.** 1991. "Research on Vocabulary Instruction: Ode to Voltaire," in *Handbook of Research on Teaching the English Language Arts.* Edited by J. Flood, J. J. D. Lapp, and J. R. Squire. New York: Macmillan.

**Beck, I., et al.** 1996. "Questioning the Author: A Year-Long Classroom Implementation to Engage Students with Text," *The Elementary School Journal,* Vol. 96, 385–414.

**Beck, I., et al.** 1998. "Getting at the Meaning: How to Help Students Unpack Difficult Text," *American Educator: The Unique Power of Reading and How to Unleash It,* Vol. 22, Nos. 1 and 2, 66–71, 85.

**Beck, I., et al.** 1997. *Questioning the Author: An Approach for Enhancing Student Engagement with Text.* Newark, Del.: International Reading Association.

**Berninger, V. W., et al.** 1994. "Developmental Skills Related to Writing and Reading Acquisition in the Intermediate Grades," *Reading and Writing: An Interdisciplinary Journal,* Vol. 6, 161–96.

**Berthoff, A. E.** 1984. "Recognition, Representation, and Revision," in *Rhetoric and Composition: A Sourcebook for Teachers and Writers.* Edited by R. Graves. Portsmouth, N.H.: Boynton Cook.

**Blachman, B. A., et al.** 1994. "Kindergarten Teachers Develop Phoneme Awareness in Low-Income, Inner-City Classrooms," *Reading and Writing: An Interdisciplinary Journal,* Vol. 6, 1–18.

**Blachowicz, C. L. Z., and P. Fisher.** 1996. *Teaching Vocabulary in All Classrooms.* Englewood Cliffs, N.J.: Merrill/Prentice Hall.

**Bloom, B. S., ed.** 1985. *Developing Talent in Young People.* New York: Ballantine Books.

**Bus, A. G.; M. H. vanIJzendoorn; and A. D. Pellegrini.** 1995. "Joint Book Reading Makes for Success in Learning to Read: A Meta-Analysis on Inter-generational Transmission of Literacy," *Review of Educational Research,* Vol. 65, 1–21.

**Byrne, B., and R. Fielding-Barnsley.** 1995. "Evaluation of a Program to Teach Phonemic Awareness to Young Children: A One- and Three-Year Follow-Up and a New Preschool Trial," *Journal of Educational Psychology,* Vol. 87, No. 3, 488–503.

**California Department of Education.** 1996. *Connect, Compute, and Compete: The Report of the California Education Technology Task Force.* Sacramento: California Department of Education.

**California Department of Education.** 1994. *Differentiating the Core Curriculum and Instruction to Provide Advanced Learning Opportunities.* Sacramento: California Department of Education.

**California Department of Education.** 1998. *English-Language Arts Content Standards for California Public Schools, Kindergarten Through Grade Twelve.* Sacramento: California Department of Education.

**California Department of Education.** 1995. *Every Child a Reader: The Report of the California Reading Task Force.* Sacramento: California Department of Education.

**California Department of Education.** 1998. *Fostering the Development of a First and a Second Language in Early Childhood.* Sacramento: California Department of Education.

**California Department of Education.** 1999. *Reading/Language Arts Framework for California Public Schools: Kindergarten Through Grade Twelve.* Sacramento: California Department of Education.

**California Department of Education.** 1996. *Recommended Readings in Literature, Kindergarten Through Grade Eight* (Revised annotated edition). Sacramento: California Department of Education.

**Calkins, L.** 1996. "Motivating Readers," ERIC Clearinghouse on Assessment and Evaluation (No. SP525606), *Instructor,* Vol. 106, No. l, 32–33.

**Campbell, F. A., and C. T. Ramsey.** 1995. "Cognitive and Social Outcomes for High-Risk African American Students at Middle Adolescence: Positive Effects of Early Intervention," *American Educational Research Journal*, Vol. 32, 743–72.

**Carlisle, J. F., and D. M. Nomanbhoy.** 1993. "Phonological and Morphological Awareness in First-Graders," *Applied Psycholinguistics,* Vol. 14, 177–95.

**Carnine, D.; J. Silbert; and E. J. Kame'enui.** 1990. *Direct Instruction Reading.* Columbus, Ohio: Merrill Publishing Company.

**Chall, J.; V. Jacobs; and L. Baldwin.** 1990. *The Reading Crisis: Why Poor Children Fall Behind.* Cambridge: Harvard University Press.

**Cornwall, A., and H. Bawden.** 1992. "Reading Disabilities and Aggression: A Critical Review," *Journal of Learning Disabilities,* Vol. 25, 281–88.

**Corson, D.** 1995. *Using English Words.* Dordrecht, Netherlands: Kluwer.

**Cunningham, A. E., and K. E. Stanovich.** 1993. "Children's Literacy Environments and Early Word Recognition Subskills," *Reading and Writing: An Interdisciplinary Journal,* Vol. 5, 193–204.

**Cunningham, A. E., and K. E. Stanovich.** 1998. "What Reading Does for the Mind," *American Educator: The Unique Power of Reading and How to Unleash It,* Vol. 22, Nos. 1 and 2, 8–15.

**Cunningham, P. M.** 1998. "The Multisyllabic Word Dilemma: Helping Students Build Meaning, Spell, and Read 'Big' Words," *Reading and Writing Quarterly,* Vol. 14, 189–218.

**Daneman, M.** 1991. "Individual Differences in Reading Skills," in *Handbook of Reading Research* (Vol. 2). Edited by R. Barr, M. L. Kamil, P. B. Mosenthal, and P. D. Pearson. New York: Longman.

**Defior, S., and P. Tudela.** 1994. "Effect of Phonological Training on Reading and Writing Acquisition," *Reading and Writing,* Vol. 6, 299–320.

**Delpit, L. D.** 1986. "Skills and Other Dilemmas of a Progressive Black Educator," *Harvard Educational Review,* Vol. 56, 379–85.

**Dickinson, D. K., and M. W. Smith.** 1994. "Long-Term Effects of Preschool Teachers' Book Readings on Low-Income Children's Vocabulary and Story Comprehension," *Reading Research Quarterly,* Vol. 29, No. 2, 104–22.

**Dillard, A.** 1998. "What Reading Does for the Soul: A Girl and Her Books," *American Educator: The Unique Power of Reading and How to Unleash It,* Vol. 22, Nos. 1 and 2, 88–93.

**Ediger, M.** 1988. "Motivation in the Reading Curriculum," ERIC Clearinghouse on Assessment and Evaluation (No. CS009424).

**Ehri, L.** 1994. "Development of the Ability to Read Words: Update," in *Theoretical Models and Processes of Reading.* Edited by R. Ruddell, M. Ruddell, and H. Singer. Newark, Del.: International Reading Association.

**Ehri, L. C., and S. McCormick.** 1998. "Phases of Word Learning: Implications for Instruction with Delayed and Disabled Readers," *Reading and Writing Quarterly,* Vol. 14, 135–63.

**Ehri, L. C.** 1991. "Development of the Ability to Read Words," in *Handbook of Reading Research* (Vol. 2). Edited by R. Barr, et al. New York: Longman.

**Ehrlich, M. F.; B. Kurtz-Costess; and C. Loridant.** 1993. "Cognitive and Motivational Determinants of Reading Comprehension in Good and Poor Readers," *Journal of Reading Behavior,* Vol. 25, No. 4, 365–81.

**Eisenberg, M., and R. Berkowitz.** 1990. *Information Problem Solving: The Big Six Skills Approach to Library and Information Skills Instruction.* Norwood, N.J.: Ablex.

**Englert, C. S., et al.** 1995. "The Early Literacy Project: Connecting Across the Literacy Curriculum," *Learning Disability Quarterly,* Vol. 18, 253–75.

**Epstein, J. L.** 1995. "School-Family-Community Partnerships: Caring for Children We Share," *Phi Delta Kappan,* Vol. 76, No. 9, 701–2.

**Felton, R. H., and P. P. Pepper.** 1995. "Early Identification and Intervention of Phonological Deficits in Kindergarten and Early Elementary Children at Risk for Reading Disability," *School Psychology Review,* Vol. 24, 405–14.

**Fielding, L. G., and Pearson, P. D.** 1994. "Synthesis of Research—Reading Comprehension: What Works," *Educational Leadership,* Vol. 51, No. 5, 62–7.

**Fielding-Barnsley, R.** 1997. "Explicit Instruction in Decoding Benefits Children High in Phonemic Awareness and Alphabet Knowledge," *Scientific Studies of Reading,* Vol. 1, No. 1, 85–98.

**Fitzgerald, J.** 1995. "English-as-a-Second-Language Learners' Cognitive Reading Processes: A Review of Research in the U.S.," *Review of Educational Research,* Vol. 65, 145–90.

**Flower, L.** 1985. *Problem-Solving Strategies for Writing.* New York: Harcourt Brace Jovanovich.

**Foorman, B., et al.** 1998. "The Role of Instruction in Learning to Read: Preventing Reading Failure in At-Risk Children," *Journal of Educational Psychology,* Vol. 90, 37–55.

**Foster, K. C., et al.** 1994. "Computer-Assisted Instruction in Phonological Awareness: Evaluation of the DaisyQuest Program," *Journal of Research and Development in Education,* Vol. 27, 126–37.

**Fuchs, L. S., et al.** 1993. "Formative Evaluation of Academic Progress: How Much Growth Can We Expect?" *School Psychology Review,* Vol. 22, No. 1, 27–48.

**Gambrell, L. B., et al.** 1996. *Elementary Students' Motivation to Read.* Reading Research Report No. 52. Athens, Ga.: National Reading Research Center.

**Gardner, H.** 1983. *Frames of Mind: The Theory of Multiple Intelligences.* New York: Basic Books.

**Gersten, R., and J. Woodward.** 1995. "A Longitudinal Study of Transitional and Immersion Bilingual Education Programs in One District," *Elementary School Journal,* Vol. 95, 223–39.

**Giles, H. C.** 1997. "Parent Engagement as a School Reform Strategy," ERIC Clearinghouse on Urban Education (Digest 135).

**Goldenberg, C. N., and R. Gallimore.** 1991. "Local Knowledge, Research Knowledge, and Educational Change: A Case Study of Early [First-Grade] Spanish Reading Improvement," *Educational Researcher,* Vol. 20, No. 8, 2–14.

**Goldenberg, C.** 1992–93. "Instructional Conversations: Promoting Comprehension Through Discussion," *The Reading Teacher,* Vol. 46, 316–26.

**Good, R. III; D. C. Simmons; and S. Smith.** 1998. "Effective Academic Interventions in the United States: Evaluating and Enhancing the Acquisition of Early Reading Skills," *School Psychology Review,* Vol. 27, No. 1, 45–56.

**Greene, J. F.** 1998. "Another Chance: Help for Older Students with Limited Literacy," *American Educator: The Unique Power of Reading and How to Unleash It,* Vol. 22, Nos. 1 and 2, 74–79.

**Guthrie, J. T., et al.** 1996. "Growth of Literacy Engagement: Changes in Motivations and Strategies During Concept-Oriented Reading Instruction," *Reading Research Quarterly,* Vol. 31, 306–25.

**Hanson, R. A., and D. Farrell.** 1995. "The Long-Term Effects on High School Seniors of Learning to Read in Kindergarten," *Reading Research Quarterly,* Vol. 30, No. 4, 908–33.

**Hart, B., and T. R. Risley.** 1995. *Meaningful Differences in the Everyday Experience of Young American Children.* Baltimore: Paul H. Brookes Publishing Co.

**Hasbrouck, J. E., and G. Tindal.** 1992. "Curriculum-Based Oral Reading Fluency Norms for Students in Grades 2 Through 5," *Teaching Exceptional Children,* Vol. 24, 41–44.

**Hiebert, E. H., et al.** 1992. "Reading and Writing of First-Grade Students in a Restructured Chapter I Program," *American Educational Research Journal,* Vol. 29, 545–72.

**Hillocks, G., Jr.** 1986. *Research on Written Composition: New Directions for Teaching.* Urbana, Ill.: National Council for Teachers of English.

**Honig, B.; L. Diamond; and L. Gutlohn.** 2000. *Teaching Reading Sourcebook for Kindergarten Through Eighth Grade.* Emeryville, CA: CORE, Consortium on Reading Excellence.

**Honig, B.; L. Diamond; and R. Nathan.** 1999. *Assessing Reading: Multiple Measures for Kindergarten Through Eighth Grade.* Emeryville, CA: CORE, Consortium on Reading Excellence.

**Hoover-Dempsey, K. V., and H. M. Sandler.** 1997. "Why Do Parents Become Involved in Their Children's Education?" *Review of Educational Research,* Vol. 67, No. 1, 3–42.

**Hunter, M., and G. Barker.** 1987. "If at First . . . : Attribution Theory in the Classroom," *Educational Leadership,* Vol. 45, No. 2, 50–53.

**Jimenez, R. T.; G. E. Garcia; and P. D. Pearson.** 1996. "The Reading Strategies of Latina/o Students Who Are Successful Readers: Opportunities and Obstacles," *Reading Research Quarterly,* Vol. 31, 90–112.

**Juel, C.** 1991. "Beginning Reading," in *Handbook of Reading Research* (Vol. 2). Edited by R. Barr, M. L. Kamil, P. B. Mosenthal, and P. D. Pearson. New York: Longman.

**Juel, C.** 1988. "Learning to Read and Write: A Longitudinal Study of 54 Children from First Through Fourth Grades," *Journal of Educational Psychology,* Vol. 80, 437–447.

**Kame'enui, E. J.** 1996. "Shakespeare and Beginning Reading: 'The Readiness Is All,'" *Teaching Exceptional Children,* Vol. 28, No. 2, 77–81.

**Kuhn, M. R., and S. A. Stahl.** 1998. "Teaching Children to Learn Word Meanings from Context: A Synthesis and Some Questions," *Journal of Literacy Research,* Vol. 30, No. 1, 119–38.

**Lance, K. C.; L. Welborn; and C. Hamilton-Pennell.** 1993. *The Impact of School Library Media Centers on Academic Achievement.* San Jose, Calif.: Hi Willow Research and Publishing.

**Leather, C. V., and L. A. Henry.** 1994. "Working Memory Span and Phonological Awareness Tasks as Predictors of Early Reading Ability," *Journal of Experimental Child Psychology,* Vol. 58, 88–111.

**Levy, B. A.; A. Nicholls; and D. Kohen.** 1993. "Repeated Readings: Process Benefits for Good and Poor Readers," *Journal of Experimental Child Psychology,* Vol. 56, 303–27.

**Liberman, I. Y.; D. Shankweiler; and A. M. Liberman.** 1991. "The Alphabetic Principle and Learning to Read," in *Phonology and Reading Disability: Solving the Reading Puzzle.* Edited by D. Shankweiler and I. Y. Liberman. Ann Arbor: University of Michigan Press.

**Lie, A. 1991.** "Effects of a Training Program for Stimulating Skills in Word Analysis in First-Grade Children," *Reading Research Quarterly,* Vol. 26, No. 3, 234–50.

**Lipson, M. Y., and K. K. Wixson.** 1986. "Reading Disability Research: An Interactionist Perspective," *Review of Educational Research,* Vol. 56, 111–36.

**Louis, K. S.; H. M. Marks; and S. Kruse.** 1996. "Teachers' Professional Community in Restructuring Schools," *American Educational Research Journal* (Vol. 33).

**Lundberg, I.; J. Frost; and O. P. Petersen.** 1988. "Effects of an Extensive Program for Stimulating Phonological Awareness in Preschool Children," *Reading Research Quarterly,* Vol. 23, 263–284.

**Lyon, G. R.** 1995. "Toward a Definition of Dyslexia," *Annals of Dyslexia,* Vol. 45, 3–27.

**Lyon, G. R., and V. Chhabra.** 1996. "The Current State of Science and the Future of Specific Reading Disability," *Mental Retardation and Developmental Disabilities Research Reviews,* Vol. 2, 2–9.

**Markell, M. A., and S. L. Deno.** 1997. "Effects of Increasing Oral Reading: Generalization Across Reading Tasks," *The Journal of Special Education,* Vol. 31, No. 2, 233–50.

**McCollum, H., and A. Russo.** 1993. *Model Strategies in Bilingual Education: Family Literacy and Parent Involvement.* Washington, D.C.: United States Department of Education.

**McGuinness, D.; C. McGuinness; and J. Donahue.** 1996. "Phonological Training and the Alphabetic Principle: Evidence for Reciprocal Causality," *Reading Research Quarterly,* Vol. 30, 830–52.

**McWhorter, J.** 1998. *The Word on the Street: Fact and Fable about American English.* New York: Plenum.

**Moats, L. C.** 1995. *Spelling: Development, Disability, and Instruction.* Baltimore: York Press.

**Moats, L. C.** 1998. "Teaching Decoding," *American Educator: The Unique Power of Reading and How to Unleash It,* Vol. 22, Nos. 1 and 2, 42–49, 95–96.

**Moffett, J., and B. J. Wagner.** 1991. *Student-Centered Language Arts, K-12.* Portsmouth, N.H.: Boynton Cook.

**Morrow, L. M.** 1992. "The Impact of a Literature-Based Program on Literacy, Achievement, Use of Literature, and Attitudes of Children from Minority Backgrounds," *Reading Research Quarterly,* Vol. 27, 250–75.

**Mosenthal, P.** 1984. "The Problem of Partial Specification in Translating Reading Research into Practice," *The Elementary School Journal,* Vol. 85, No. 2, 199–227.

**Mosenthal, P.** 1985. "Defining Progress in Educational Research," *Educational Researcher,* Vol. 14, No. 9, 3–9.

**Mosteller, F.; R. Light; and J. Sachs.** 1996. "Sustained Inquiry in Education: Lessons from Skill Grouping and Class Size," *Harvard Educational Review,* Vol. 66, No. 4, 797–842.

**National Center to Improve the Tools of Educators.** 1997. *Learning to Read, Reading to Learn—Helping Children to Succeed: A Resource Guide.* Washington, D.C.: American Federation of Teachers.

**National Research Council.** 1998. *Preventing Reading Difficulties in Young Children.* Edited by M. S. Burns, P. Griffin, and C. E. Snow. Washington, D.C.: National Academy Press.

**National Research Council.** 1999. *Starting Out Right: A Guide to Promoting Children's Reading Success.* Edited by M. S. Burns, P. Griffin, and C. E. Snow. Washington, D.C.: National Academy Press.

**Neuman, S. B.** 1996. "Children Engaging in Storybook Reading: The Influence of Access to Print Resources, Opportunity, and Parental Interaction," *Early Childhood Research Quarterly,* Vol. 11, 495–513.

**O'Connor, R. E.; J. R. Jenkins; and T. A. Slocum.** 1995. "Transfer Among Phonological Tasks in Kindergarten: Essential Instructional Content," *Journal of Educational Psychology,* Vol. 87, 202–17.

**Pearson, P. D., et al.** 1992. "Developing Expertise in Reading Comprehension," in *What Research Says to the Teacher.* Edited by S. J. Samuels and A. E. Farstrup. Newark, Del.: International Reading Association.

**Pearson, P. D., and K. Camperell.** 1985. "Comprehension in Text Structures," in *Theoretical Models and Processes of Reading.* Edited by H. Singer and R. B. Ruddell. Newark, Del.: International Reading Association.

**Perfetti, C. A., and S. Zhang.** 1995. "The Universal Word Identification Reflex," in *The Psychology of Learning and Motivation* (Vol. 33). Edited by D. L. Medlin. San Diego: Academic Press.

**Phillips, L. M.; S. P. Norris; and J. M. Mason.** 1996. "Longitudinal Effects of Early Literacy Concepts on Reading Achievement: A Kindergarten Intervention and Five-Year Follow-Up," *Journal of Literacy Research,* Vol. 28, 173–95.

**Pinnell, G. S., and L C. Fountas.** 1997. *Help America Read: A Handbook for Volunteers.* Portsmouth, N.H.: Heinemann.

**Pressley, M.; J. Rankin; and L. Yokoi.** 1996. "A Survey of Instructional Practices of Primary Teachers Nominated as Effective in Promoting Literacy," *The Elementary School Journal,* Vol. 96, 363–84.

**Purcell-Gates, V.; E. McIntyre; and P. Freppon.** 1995. "Learning Written Storybook Language in School: A Comparison of Low-SES Children in Skills-Based and Whole-Language Classrooms," *American Educational Research Journal,* Vol. 32, 659–85.

**Robbins, C., and L. C. Ehri.** 1994. "Reading Storybooks to Kindergartners Helps Them Learn New Vocabulary Words," *Journal of Educational Psychology,* Vol. 86, No. 1, 54–64.

**Rosenshine, B., and C. Meister.** 1994. "Reciprocal Teaching: A Review of the Research," *Review of Educational Research,* Vol. 64, No. 4, 479–530.

**Ross, S. M., et al.** 1995. "Increasing the Academic Success of Disadvantaged Children: An Examination of Alternative Early Intervention Programs," *American Educational Research Journal,* Vol. 32, 773–800.

**Ruddell, R.; M. Rapp Ruddell; and H. Singer, eds.** 1994. *Theoretical Models and Processes of Reading* (Fourth edition). Newark, Del.: International Reading Association.

**Ryder, R. J., and M. F. Graves.** 1994. "Vocabulary Instruction Presented Prior to Reading in Two Basal Readers," *Elementary School Journal,* Vol. 95, No. 2, 139–53.

**Sacks, C. H., and J. R. Mergendoller.** 1997. "The Relationship Between Teachers' Theoretical Orientation Toward Reading and Student Outcomes in Kindergarten Children with Different Initial Reading Abilities," *American Educational Research Journal,* Vol. 34, 721–39.

**Samuels, S. J.** 1979. "The Method of Repeated Reading," *The Reading Teacher,* Vol. 32, 403–08.

**Sanacore, J.** 1988. "Linking Vocabulary and Comprehension Through Independent Reading," ERIC Clearinghouse on Assessment and Evaluation (No. CS009409).

**Shefelbine, J.** 1991. *Encouraging Your Junior High Student to Read.* Bloomington, Ind.: ERIC Clearinghouse on Reading, English, and Communication.

**Shefelbine, J. L.** 1990. "Student Factors Related to Variability in Learning Word Meanings from Context," *Journal of Reading Behavior,* Vol. 22, No. 1, 71–97.

**Shore, B. M., et al.** 1991. *Recommended Practices in Gifted Education: A Critical Analysis.* New York: Teachers College Press.

**Shore, W. J., and F. T. Durso.** 1990. "Partial Knowledge in Vocabulary Acquisition: General Constraints and Specific Detail," *Journal of Educational Psychology,* Vol. 82, 315–18.

**Simmons, D. C., and E. J. Kame'enui.** 1996. "A Focus on Curriculum Design: When Children Fail," in *Strategies for Teaching Children in Inclusive Settings.* Edited by E. Meyen, G. Vergason, and R. Whelan. Denver: Love Publishing.

**Simmons, D. C., and E. J. Kame'enui, eds.** 1998. *What Reading Research Tells Us About Children with Diverse Learning Needs: Bases and Basics.* Mahwah, N.J.: Lawrence Erlbaum Associates.

**Sindelar, P. T.; L. Monda; and L. O'Shea.** 1990. "Effects of Repeated Readings on Instructional- and Mastery-Level Readers," *Journal of Educational Research,* Vol. 83, 220–26.

**Slavin, R. E.; N. L. Karweit; and B. A. Wasik, eds.** 1993. *Preventing Early School Failure: Research, Policy, and Practice.* 1993. Boston: Allyn and Bacon.

**Snider, V. E.** 1995. "A Primer on Phonological Awareness: What It Is, Why It's Important, and How to Teach It," *School Psychology Review,* Vol. 24, 443–55.

**Spear-Swerling, L., and R. J. Sternberg.** 1998. "Curing Our 'Epidemic' of Learning Disabilities," *Phi Delta Kappan,* Vol. 79, No. 5, 397–401.

**Spear-Swerling, L., and R. J. Sternberg.** 1996. *Off Track: When Poor Readers Become Learning Disabled.* Boulder, Colo.: Westview Press.

**Stanovich, K. E.** 1986. "Matthew Effects in Reading: Some Consequences of Individual Differences in the Acquisition of Literacy," *Reading Research Quarterly,* Vol. 21, 360–407.

**Stanovich, K. E.** 1994. "Constructivism in Reading Education," *The Journal of Special Education,* Vol. 28, 259–74.

**Stanovich, K. E.** 1993–94. "Romance and Reality," *The Reading Teacher,* Vol. 47, 280–90.

**Sulzby, E., and W. Teale.** 1991. "Emergent Literacy," in *Handbook of Reading Research* (Vol. 2). Edited by R. Barr, M. L. Kamil, P. B. Mosenthal, and P. D. Pearson. New York: Longman.

**Topping, K.** 1998. "Effective Tutoring in America Reads: A Reply to Wasik," *The Reading Teacher,* Vol. 52, No. 1, 42–50.

**Torgesen, J. K.** 1998. "Catch Them Before They Fall: Identification and Assessment to Prevent Reading Failure in Young Children," *American Educator: The Unique Power of Reading and How to Unleash It,* Vol. 22, Nos. 1 and 2, 32–39.

**Treiman, R.** 1985. "Onsets and Rimes as Units of Spoken Syllables: Evidence from Children," *Journal of Experimental Child Psychology,* Vol. 39, 161–81.

**Treiman, R.; S. Weatherston; and D. Berch.** 1994. "The Role of Letter Names in Children's Learning of Phoneme-Grapheme Relations," *Applied Psycholinguistics,* Vol. 15, 97–122.

**Vandervelden, M. C., and L. S. Siegel.** 1995. "Phonological Recoding and Phoneme Awareness in Early Literacy: A Developmental Approach," *Reading Research Quarterly,* Vol. 30, 854–73.

**Vellutino, F. R., et al.** 1996. "Cognitive Profiles of Difficult-to-Remediate and Readily Remediated Poor Readers: Early Intervention as a Vehicle for Distinguishing Between Cognitive and Experiential Deficits as Basic Causes of Specific Reading Disability," *Journal of Educational Psychology,* Vol. 88, 601–38.

**Wagner, R. K., et al.** 1993. "Development of Young Readers' Phonological Processing Abilities," *Journal of Educational Psychology,* Vol. 85, 83–103.

**Walberg, H. J.** 1984. "Families as Partners in Educational Productivity," *Phi Delta Kappan,* Vol. 65, No. 6, 397–400.

**Wasik, B. A., and R. E. Slavin.** 1993. "Preventing Early Reading Failure with One-to-One Tutoring: A Review of Five Programs," *Reading Research Quarterly,* Vol. 28, 178–200.

**Wells, G.** 1986. *The Meaning Makers: Children Learning Language and Using Language to Learn.* Portsmouth, N.H.: Heinemann.

**White, T. G.; M. F. Graves; and W. H. Slater.** 1990. "Growth of Reading Vocabulary in Diverse Elementary Schools: Decoding and Word Meaning," *Journal of Educational Psychology,* Vol. 82, 281–90.

**Whitehurst, G. J., et al.** 1994. "Outcomes of an Emergent Literacy Intervention in Head Start," *Journal of Educational Psychology,* Vol. 86, 542–55.

**Yopp, H. K.** 1988. "The Validity and Reliability of Phonemic Awareness Tests," *Reading Research Quarterly,* Vol. 23, No. 2, 159–77.

**PROFESSIONAL BIBLIOGRAPHY**

# Program Reviewers

**Dr. Judylynn Baily-Mitchell**
Principal
West Salisbury
Elementary School
Salisbury, Maryland

**Dr. Judith F. Barry**
Coordinator of Reading/
Language Arts
Taunton Public Schools
Taunton, Massachusetts

**Carol Berman**
Lead Teacher
Crestview Elementary School
Miami, Florida

**Angela Berner**
Language Arts Staff Developer
Huntington Unified
School District
Administration Offices
Huntington Station, New York

**Susan Birch**
Teacher
Dunns Corners
Elementary School
Westerly, Rhode Island

**Candace Bouchard**
Teacher
Sandburg Elementary School
San Diego, California

**Sandra Carron**
Teacher
Moreno Valley Unified
School District
Moreno Valley, California

**Loretta Cudney**
Teacher
Riverside Unified School District
Riverside, California

**Justyne Davis**
Teacher
Wallbridge Community
Education Center
St. Louis, Missouri

**Dr. Ann Dugger**
Reading Teacher/Title I
Will Rogers Elementary School
Stillwater, Oklahoma

**Rosemary Forsythe**
Reading Specialist
West Pottsgrove
Elementary School
Pottstown, Pennsylvania

**Stanley Foster**
Teacher
Magnolia Avenue School
Los Angeles, California

**Kimberly Griffeth**
Teacher
Fulton Elementary
Aurora, Colorado

**Jeffrey Guerra**
Teacher
Westchase Elementary School
Tampa, Florida

**Anne Henry**
Teacher
Northern Hills
Elementary School
Edmond, Oklahoma

**Carol Hookway**
Teacher
Memorial Elementary School
Natick, Massachusetts

**Arlene Horkey**
Curriculum/Technology
Specialist
Belleair Elementary School
Clearwater, Florida

**Carolyn M. Horton**
District Reading Facilitator
Cedar Rapids Community
School District,
Educational Service Center
Cedar Rapids, Iowa

**Patty Jacox**
Teacher
Lansing Elementary School
Aurora, Colorado

**Beverly Keeley**
Teacher
Grant Foreman
Elementary School
Muskogee, Oklahoma

**Rebecca L. Kelly**
Teacher
Wekiva Elementary School
Longwood, Florida

**Lisa Leslie**
Teacher
Costello Elementary School,
Troy Public Schools
Troy, Michigan

**Arlene D. Loughlin**
Student Achievement Specialist
Curlew Creek
Elementary School
Palm Harbor, Florida

**Christin Machado**
Teacher
Jefferson Elementary School
Burbank, California

**Alicia L. Marsh**
Teacher
Pearl Sample
Elementary School
Culpeper, Virginia

**K. Gale Martin**
Teacher
JEB Stuart Elementary School
Richmond, Virginia

**Anne M. Merritt**
Teacher
Citrus Glen Elementary School
Ventura, California

**Joan Miller**
Teacher
Carlton Hills Elementary School
Santee, California

**Bobbie A. Overbey**
Teacher
Carillon Elementary School
Oviedo, Florida

**Katherin Pagakis**
English Teacher
Washington Elementary School
Waukegan, Illinois

**Barbara Pitts**
Administrator
Joy Middle School
Detroit, Michigan

**Sundee Preedy**
Teacher
Aloma Elementary School
Winter Park, Florida

**Dr. Carolyn Reedom**
Principal
Vanderberg Elementary School
Henderson, Nevada

**Dorina Rocas**
Teacher
Corono-Norco Unified
School District
Corona, California

**Josephine Scott**
Language Arts
Curriculum Director
Columbus City School District,
Northgate Center
Columbus, Ohio

**Renee Seifert**
Teacher
Serrano Elementary School
Moreno Valley, California

**Gayle E. Sitter**
Mathematics Resource
Teacher
Educational Leadership Center
Orlando, Florida

**Linda Smolen**
Director of Reading
Buffalo City School District
Buffalo, New York

**Gail Soft**
Teacher
Vermillion Primary School
Maize, Kansas

**Alejandro Soria**
Teacher
Leo Politi Elementary
Los Angeles, California

**Jan Strege**
Vice-Principal
Schlegel Road
Elementary School
Webster, New York

**Dahna Taylor**
Teacher
Chavez Elementary School
San Diego, California

**Dr. Sandra Telfort**
Teacher
Palmetto Elementary School
Miami, Florida

**Dana Thurm**
Teacher
Olivenhain Pioneer
Elementary School
Carlsbad, California

**Geralyn Wilson**
Literacy Coordinator
James McCosh Intermediate
Chicago, Illinois

**John L. York**
Teacher
Cedar Heights
Elementary School
Cedar Falls, Iowa

**Maureen A. Zoda**
Reading Specialist Coordinator
Meadow Brook
Elementary School
East Longmeadow,
Massachusetts

## KINDERGARTEN REVIEWERS

**Janice Allocco**
Teacher
Klem Road South
Elementary School
Webster, New York

**Irma A. Barr**
Teacher
Embassy Creek
Elementary School
Cooper City, Florida

**Dikki Cie Chanski**
Teacher
Martell Elementary School
Troy, Michigan

**Rosemary Gaskin**
Reading Specialist
Broad Rock Elementary School
Richmond, Virginia

**Carol Grenfell**
District Language
Arts Specialist
Ventura Unified School District
Ventura, California

**Cathleen Hunter**
Teacher
Peterson Elementary
Huntington Beach, California

**Karen A. Kuritar**
Teacher
Allen Elementary School
Dayton, Ohio

**Charlotte Otterbacher**
Teacher
Hamilton Elementary
Troy, Michigan

**Gwendolyn Perkins**
Teacher
Ginter Park Elementary School
Richmond, Virginia

**Kelly Schmitt**
Teacher
Public School #225 Seaside
Rockaway Parkway, New York

**Corene Selman**
Teacher
Westwood Early
Childhood Center
Woodward, Oklahoma

**Laureen B. Stephens**
Teacher
Mountainview
Elementary School
Saycus, California

**Pam Styles**
Teacher
World of Wonder
Community School
Dayton, Ohio

# Scope and Sequence

| | GR K | GR I | GR 2 | GR 3 | GR 4 | GR 5 | GR 6 |
|---|---|---|---|---|---|---|---|
| **Reading** | | | | | | | |
| **Concepts about Print** | | | | | | | |
| Understand that print provides information | ▨ | | | | | | |
| Understand how print is organized and read | ▨ | | | | | | |
| Know left-to-right and top-to-bottom directionality | ▨ | | | | | | |
| Distinguish letters from words | ▨ | | | | | | |
| Recognize name | ▨ | | | | | | |
| Name and match all uppercase and lowercase letter forms | ▨ | | | | | | |
| Understand the concept of word and construct meaning from shared text, illustrations, graphics, and charts | ▨ | | | | | | |
| Identify letters, words, and sentences | ▨ | ▨ | | | | | |
| Recognize that sentences in print are made up of words | ▨ | ▨ | | | | | |
| Identify the front cover, back cover, title page, title, and author of a book | ▨ | ▨ | | | | | |
| Match oral words to printed words | ▨ | ▨ | | | | | |
| **Phonemic Awareness** | | | | | | | |
| Understand that spoken words and syllables are made up of sequences of sounds | ▨ | | | | | | |
| Count and track sounds in a syllable, syllables in words, and words in sentences | ▨ | | ▨ | ▨ | | | |
| Know the sounds of letters | ▨ | ▨ | | | | | |
| Track and represent the number, sameness, difference, and order of two or more isolated phonemes | ▨ | | | | | | |
| Match, identify, distinguish, and segment sounds in initial, final, and medial position in single-syllable spoken words | ▨ | | | | | | |
| Blend sounds (phonemes) to make words or syllables | ▨ | ▨ | ▨ | | | | |
| Track and represent changes in syllables and words as target sound is added, substituted, omitted, shifted, or repeated | ▨ | ▨ | ▨ | ▨ | | | |
| Distinguish long- and short-vowel sounds in orally stated words | | ▨ | ▨ | | | | |
| Identify and produce rhyming words | ▨ | | | | | | |
| **Decoding: Phonic Analysis** | | | | | | | |
| Understand and apply the alphabetic principle | ▨ | ▨ | | | | | |
| Consonants: single, blends, digraphs in initial, final, medial positions | • | • | • | | | | |
| Vowels: short, long, digraphs, r-controlled, variant, schwa | | • | • | | | | |
| Match all consonant and short-vowel sounds to appropriate letters | • | • | | | | | |
| Understand that as letters in words change, so do the sounds | • | • | | | | | |
| Blend vowel-consonant sounds orally to make words or syllables | • | • | ▨ | | | | |
| Blend sounds from letters and letter patterns into recognizable words | ▨ | ▨ | ▨ | | | | |
| **Decoding: Structural Analysis** | | | | | | | |
| Inflectional endings, with and without spelling changes: plurals, verb tenses, possessives, comparatives-superlatives | | • | • | | | | |
| Contractions, abbreviations, and compound words | | • | • | | | | |
| Prefixes, suffixes, derivations, and root words | | | • | • | • | • | • |
| Greek and Latin roots | | | | | • | • | • |
| Letter, spelling, and syllable patterns | | ▨ | ▨ | ▨ | ▨ | ▨ | ▨ |
| Phonograms/word families/onset-rimes | ▨ | ▨ | | | | | |
| Syllable rules and patterns | | | ▨ | • | | | |

**Key**

Shaded area   Explicit Instruction / Modeling / Practice and Application

•   Tested

Assessment resources include: Kindergarten Assessment Handbook; Placement and Diagnostic Assessments, Grades 1, 2, and 3–6; Reading and Language Skills Assessments, Grades 1–6; Holistic Assessments, Grades 1–6; End-of-Selection Tests, Grades 1–6; and Oral Reading Fluency Assessment, Grades 1–6

| | GR K | GR I | GR 2 | GR 3 | GR 4 | GR 5 | GR 6 |
|---|---|---|---|---|---|---|---|
| **Decoding: Strategies** | | | | | | | |
| Visual cues: sound/symbol relationships, letter patterns, and spelling patterns | | ▨ | ▨ | ▨ | ▨ | ▨ | ▨ |
| Structural cues: compound words, contractions, inflectional endings, prefixes, suffixes, Greek and Latin roots, root words, spelling patterns, and word families | | ▨ | ▨ | ▨ | ▨ | ▨ | ▨ |
| Cross check visual and structural cues to confirm meaning | | | ▨ | ▨ | ▨ | ▨ | ▨ |
| Syllabication rules and patterns | | | ▨ | ▨ | ▨ | ▨ | ▨ |
| **Word Recognition** | | | | | | | |
| One-syllable and high-frequency words | • | • | • | | | | |
| Common, irregular sight words | • | • | • | | | | |
| Common abbreviations | | | • | | | | |
| Lesson vocabulary | | • | • | • | • | • | • |
| **Fluency** | | | | | | | |
| Read aloud in a manner that sounds like natural speech | | • | • | | | | |
| Read aloud accurately and with appropriate intonation and expression | | | • | • | | | |
| Read aloud narrative and expository text with appropriate pacing, intonation, and expression | | | | • | • | • | • |
| Read aloud prose and poetry with rhythm and pace, appropriate intonation, and vocal patterns | | | | ▨ | ▨ | ▨ | ▨ |
| **Vocabulary and Concept Development** | | | | | | | |
| Academic language | ▨ | ▨ | ▨ | ▨ | ▨ | ▨ | ▨ |
| Classify-categorize | | • | | • | | • | |
| Antonyms | | | • | • | • | | |
| Synonyms | | | • | • | • | | |
| Homographs | | | | • | • | | |
| Homophones | | | • | • | • | • | |
| Multiple-meaning words | | | • | • | | • | |
| Figurative and idiomatic language | | | | | | | • |
| Context/context clues | | | • | • | • | • | |
| Content-area words | | | | ▨ | ▨ | ▨ | ▨ |
| Dictionary, glossary, thesaurus | | | | • | • | | |
| Foreign words | | | | ▨ | ▨ | ▨ | ▨ |
| Connotation-denotation | | | | | | • | • |
| Word origins (acronyms, clipped and coined words, regional variations, etymologies, jargon, slang) | | | | | ▨ | ▨ | ▨ |
| Analogies | | | | | ▨ | ▨ | ▨ |
| Word structure clues to determine meaning | | | • | • | • | • | • |
| Inflected nouns and verbs, comparatives-superlatives, possessives, compound words, prefixes, suffixes, root words | | | • | • | • | • | • |
| Greek and Latin roots, prefixes, suffixes, derivations, and root words | | | | | • | • | • |
| Develop vocabulary | | | | | | | |
| Listen to and discuss text read aloud | ▨ | ▨ | ▨ | ▨ | ▨ | ▨ | ▨ |
| Read independently | ▨ | ▨ | ▨ | ▨ | ▨ | ▨ | ▨ |
| Use reference books | | | ▨ | ▨ | ▨ | ▨ | ▨ |
| **Comprehension and Analysis of Text** | | | | | | | |
| Ask/answer questions | ▨ | ▨ | ▨ | ▨ | ▨ | ▨ | ▨ |
| Author's purpose | | | | • | • | • | • |
| Author's perspective | | | | | | • | • |
| Propaganda/bias | | | | | | | • |

**Key**

Shaded area   Explicit Instruction/Modeling/Practice and Application

•      Tested

    Assessment resources include: Kindergarten Assessment Handbook; Placement and Diagnostic Assessments, Grades 1, 2, and 3–6; Reading and Language Skills Assessments, Grades 1–6; Holistic Assessments, Grades 1–6; End-of-Selection Tests, Grades 1–6; and Oral Reading Fluency Assessment, Grades 1–6

| | GR K | GR 1 | GR 2 | GR 3 | GR 4 | GR 5 | GR 6 |
|---|---|---|---|---|---|---|---|
| Background knowledge: prior knowledge and experiences | | | | | | | |
| Cause-effect | | | • | • | • | • | • |
| Compare-contrast | | | • | • | • | • | • |
| Details | | • | • | • | • | • | • |
| Directions: one-, two-, multi-step | • | • | • | • | • | | |
| Draw conclusions | | | | • | • | • | • |
| Fact-fiction | | | | | | | |
| Fact-opinion | | | | • | • | • | • |
| Higher order thinking | | | | | | | |
|     Analyze, critique and evaluate, synthesize, and visualize text and information | | | | | | | |
| Interpret information from graphic aids | | | • | • | • | • | • |
| Locate information | | • | • | • | • | • | • |
|     Book parts | | | | • | | | • |
|     Text features | | | | • | | • | |
|     Alphabetical order | | • | | | | | |
| Main idea: stated/unstated | | • | • | • | • | • | • |
| Main idea and supporting details | | | | • | • | • | • |
| Make generalizations | | | | | | | |
| Make inferences | | | • | • | • | • | • |
| Make judgments | | | | | | | |
| Make predictions/predict outcomes | | | | | | | |
| Monitor comprehension | | | | | | | |
|     Adjust reading rate, create mental images, reread, read ahead, set/adjust purpose, self-question, summarize/paraphrase, use graphic aids, text features, and text adjuncts | | | | | | | |
| Paraphrase/restate facts and details | | | • | • | • | • | • |
| Preview | | | | | | | |
| Purpose for reading | | | | | | | |
| Organize information | | | | | | | |
|     Alphabetical order | | | | | | | |
|     Numerical systems/outlines | | | | | | | |
|     Graphic organizers | | | | | | | |
| Referents | | | | | | | |
| Retell stories and ideas | | | | | | | |
| Sequence | | • | • | • | • | • | • |
| Summarize | | | • | • | • | • | • |
| Text structure | | | | | | | |
|     Narrative text | | | • | • | • | • | • |
|     Informational text (compare and contrast, cause and effect, sequence/chronological order, proposition and support, problem and solution) | | | | | • | • | • |
| **Study Skills** | | | | | | | |
| Follow and give directions | | | • | • | • | | |
| Apply plans and strategies: KWL, question-answer-relationships, skim and scan, note taking, outline, questioning the author, reciprocal teaching | | | | | | | |
| Practice test-taking strategies | | | | | | | |

**Key**

Shaded area   Explicit Instruction / Modeling / Practice and Application

-   Tested
  Assessment resources include: Kindergarten Assessment Handbook; Placement and Diagnostic Assessments, Grades 1, 2, and 3–6; Reading and Language Skills Assessments, Grades 1–6; Holistic Assessments, Grades 1–6; End-of-Selection Tests, Grades 1–6; and Oral Reading Fluency Assessment, Grades 1–6

| | GR K | GR 1 | GR 2 | GR 3 | GR 4 | GR 5 | GR 6 |
|---|---|---|---|---|---|---|---|
| **Research and Information** | | | | | | | |
| Use resources and references | | ▓ | ▓ | ▓ | ▓ | ▓ | ▓ |
| Understand the purpose, structure, and organization of various reference materials | | | | | | | |
|    Title page, table of contents, chapter titles, chapter headings, index, glossary, guide words, citations, end notes, bibliography | ▓ | ▓ | ▓ | • | ▓ | ▓ | • |
|    Picture dictionary, software, dictionary, thesaurus, atlas, globe, encyclopedia, telephone directory, on-line information, card catalog, electronic search engines and data bases, almanac, newspaper, journals, periodicals | ▓ | ▓ | • | • | • | • | • |
|    Charts, maps, diagrams, timelines, schedules, calendar, graphs, photos | ▓ | ▓ | • | • | ▓ | ▓ | • |
| Choose reference materials appropriate to research purpose | | | | | | | • |
| **Viewing/Media** | | | | | | | |
| Interpret information from visuals (graphics, media, including illustrations, tables, maps, charts, graphs, diagrams, timelines) | ▓ | ▓ | • | • | • | • | • |
| Analyze the ways visuals, graphics, and media represent, contribute to, and support meaning of text | | | | ▓ | ▓ | ▓ | ▓ |
| Select, organize, and produce visuals to complement and extend meaning | | | | ▓ | ▓ | ▓ | ▓ |
| Use technology or appropriate media to communicate information and ideas | | ▓ | ▓ | ▓ | ▓ | ▓ | ▓ |
| Use technology or appropriate media to compare ideas, information, and viewpoints | | | ▓ | ▓ | ▓ | ▓ | ▓ |
| Compare, contrast, and evaluate print and broadcast media | | | | ▓ | ▓ | ▓ | ▓ |
|    Distinguish between fact and opinion | | | | ▓ | ▓ | ▓ | ▓ |
|    Evaluate the role of media | | | | ▓ | | ▓ | ▓ |
| Analyze media as sources for information, entertainment, persuasion, interpretation of events, and transmission of culture | | | | | ▓ | ▓ | ▓ |
| Identify persuasive and propaganda techniques used in television and identify false and misleading information | | | | | | ▓ | ▓ |
| Summarize main concept and list supporting details and identify biases, stereotypes, and persuasive techniques in a nonprint message | | | | | | | ▓ |
| Support opinions with detailed evidence and with visual or media displays that use appropriate technology | | | | | | | ▓ |
| **Literary Response and Analysis** | | | | | | | |
| **Genre Characteristics** | | | | | | | |
| Know a variety of literary genres and their basic characteristics | ▓ | ▓ | • | • | • | • | • |
| Distinguish between fantasy and realistic text | ▓ | ▓ | ▓ | | | | |
| Distinguish between informational and persuasive texts | | | | ▓ | ▓ | ▓ | ▓ |
| Understand the distinguishing features of literary and nonfiction texts: everyday print materials, poetry, drama, fantasies, fables, myths, legends, and fairy tales | ▓ | ▓ | • | • | • | • | • |
| Explain the appropriateness of the literary forms chosen by an author for a specific purpose | | | | | ▓ | ▓ | ▓ |
| **Literary Elements** | | | | | | | |
| Plot/Plot Development | | | | | | | |
|    Important events | ▓ | • | • | • | • | • | • |
|    Beginning, middle, end of story | ▓ | • | • | | | | |
|    Problem/solution | ▓ | ▓ | • | | | | |
|    Conflict | | | | • | | | |
|    Conflict and resolution/causes and effects | | | | | • | • | • |
|    Compare and contrast | | ▓ | ▓ | ▓ | | | |
| Character | | | | | | | |
|    Identify | ▓ | • | | | | | |
|    Identify, describe, compare and contrast | | | • | • | • | • | • |
|    Relate characters and events | | | | | • | • | • |

Key

Shaded area   Explicit Instruction/Modeling/Practice and Application

•     Tested

      Assessment resources include: Kindergarten Assessment Handbook; Placement and Diagnostic Assessments, Grades 1, 2, and 3–6; Reading and Language Skills Assessments, Grades 1–6; Holistic Assessments, Grades 1–6; End-of-Selection Tests, Grades 1–6; and Oral Reading Fluency Assessment, Grades 1–6

| | GR K | GR 1 | GR 2 | GR 3 | GR 4 | GR 5 | GR 6 |
|---|---|---|---|---|---|---|---|
| Traits, actions, motives | | | | • | • | • | • |
| Cause for character's actions | | | | | • | | |
| Character's qualities and effect on plot | | | | | | | • |
| **Setting** | | | | | | | |
| Identify and describe | | • | • | • | • | • | • |
| Compare and contrast | | | • | • | • | • | • |
| Relate to problem/resolution | | | | | | | |
| **Theme** | | | | | | | |
| Theme/essential message | | | | • | • | • | • |
| Universal themes | | | | | | | |
| **Mood/Tone** | | | | | | | |
| Identify | | | | | | | • |
| Compare and contrast | | | | | | | • |

## Literary Devices/Author's Craft

| | GR K | GR 1 | GR 2 | GR 3 | GR 4 | GR 5 | GR 6 |
|---|---|---|---|---|---|---|---|
| Rhythm, rhyme, pattern, and repetition | | | | | | | |
| Alliteration, onomatopoeia, assonance, imagery | | | | | | | |
| Figurative language (similes, metaphors, idioms, personification, hyperbole) | | | | • | • | • | • |
| Characterization/character development | | | | • | | • | |
| Dialogue | | | | • | • | • | • |
| Narrator/narration | | | | | • | • | • |
| Point of view (first-person, third-person, omniscient) | | | | | • | • | • |
| Informal language (idioms, slang, jargon, dialect) | | | | | | | |

## Response to Text

| | GR K | GR 1 | GR 2 | GR 3 | GR 4 | GR 5 | GR 6 |
|---|---|---|---|---|---|---|---|
| Relate characters and events to own life | | | | | | | |
| Read to perform a task or learn a new task | | | | | | | |
| Recollect, talk, and write about books read | | | | | | | |
| Describe the roles and contributions of authors and illustrators | | | | | | | |
| Generate alternative endings and identify the reason and impact of the alternatives | | | | | | | |
| Compare and contrast versions of the same stories that reflect different cultures | | | | | | | |
| Make connections between information in texts and stories and historical events | | | | | | | |
| Form ideas about what had been read and use specific information from the text to support these ideas | | | | | | | |
| Know that the attitudes and values that exist in a time period or culture affect stories and informational articles written during that time period | | | | | | | |
| Explore origin and historical development of words and changes in sentence patterns over the years | | | | | | | |

## Self-Selected Reading

| | GR K | GR 1 | GR 2 | GR 3 | GR 4 | GR 5 | GR 6 |
|---|---|---|---|---|---|---|---|
| Select material to read for pleasure | | | | | | | |
| Read a variety of self-selected and assigned literary and informational texts | | | | | | | |
| Use knowledge of authors' styles, themes, and genres to choose own reading | | | | | | | |
| Read literature by authors from various cultural and historical backgrounds | | | | | | | |

## Cultural Awareness

| | GR K | GR 1 | GR 2 | GR 3 | GR 4 | GR 5 | GR 6 |
|---|---|---|---|---|---|---|---|
| Connect information and events in texts to life and life to text experiences | | | | | | | |
| Compare language, oral traditions, and literature that reflect customs, regions, and cultures | | | | | | | |
| Identify how language reflects regions and cultures | | | | | | | |
| View concepts and issues from diverse perspectives | | | | | | | |
| Recognize the universality of literary themes across cultures and language | | | | | | | |

**Key**

Shaded area   Explicit Instruction/Modeling/Practice and Application

•        Tested

Assessment resources include: Kindergarten Assessment Handbook; Placement and Diagnostic Assessments, Grades 1, 2, and 3–6;
Reading and Language Skills Assessments, Grades 1–6; Holistic Assessments, Grades 1–6; End-of-Selection Tests, Grades 1–6; and
Oral Reading Fluency Assessment, Grades 1–6

| Writing | GR K | GR 1 | GR 2 | GR 3 | GR 4 | GR 5 | GR 6 |
|---|---|---|---|---|---|---|---|
| **Writing Strategies** | | | | | | | |
| Writing process: prewriting, drafting, revising, proofreading, publishing | | | | | | | |
| Collaborative, shared, timed writing, writing to prompts | | • | • | • | • | • | • |
| Evaluate own and others' writing | | | | | | | |
| Proofread writing to correct convention errors in mechanics, usage, punctuation, using handbooks and references as appropriate | | | | • | • | • | • |
| **Organization and Focus** | | | | | | | |
| Use models and traditional structures for writing | | | | | | | |
| Select a focus, structure, and viewpoint | | | | | | | |
| Address purpose, audience, length, and format requirements | | | | | | | |
| Write single- and multiple-paragraph compositions | | | • | • | • | • | • |
| **Revision Skills** | | | | | | | |
| Correct sentence fragments and run-ons | | | | | • | • | • |
| Vary sentence structure, word order, and sentence length | | | | | | | |
| Combine sentences | | | | | • | • | • |
| Improve coherence, unity, consistency, and progression of ideas | | | | | | | |
| Add, delete, consolidate, clarify, rearrange text | | | | | | | |
| Choose appropriate and effective words: exact/precise words, vivid words, trite/overused words | | | | | | • | • |
| Elaborate: details, examples, dialogue, quotations | | | | | | | |
| Revise using a rubric | | | | | | | |
| **Penmanship/Handwriting** | | | | | | | |
| Write uppercase and lowercase letters | | | | | | | |
| Write legibly, using appropriate word and letter spacing | | | | | | | |
| Write legibly, using spacing, margins, and indention | | | | | | | |
| **Writing Applications** | | | | | | | |
| Narrative writing (stories, paragraphs, personal narratives, journal, plays, poetry) | | • | • | • | • | • | • |
| Descriptive writing (titles, captions, ads, posters, paragraphs, stories, poems) | | • | • | • | • | • | • |
| Expository writing (comparison-contrast, explanation, directions, speech, how-to article, friendly/business letter, news story, essay, report, invitation) | | | | • | • | • | • |
| Persuasive writing (paragraph, essay, letter, ad, poster) | | | | | | • | • |
| Cross-curricular writing (paragraph, report, poster, list, chart) | | | | | | | |
| Everyday writing (journal, message, forms, notes, summary, label, caption) | | | | | | | |
| **Written and Oral English Language Conventions** | | | | | | | |
| **Sentence Structure** | | | | | | | |
| Types (declarative, interrogative, exclamatory, imperative, interjection) | | • | • | • | • | • | • |
| Structure (simple, compound, complex, compound-complex) | | • | • | • | • | • | • |
| Parts (subjects/predicates: complete, simple, compound; clauses: independent, dependent, subordinate; phrase) | | • | • | • | • | • | • |
| Direct/indirect object | | | | | | | |
| Word order | | • | | | | | |
| **Grammar** | | | | | | | |
| Nouns (singular, plural, common, proper, possessive, collective, abstract, concrete, abbreviations, appositives) | | • | • | • | • | • | • |
| Verbs (action, helping, linking, transitive, intransitive, regular, irregular; subject-verb agreement) | | • | • | • | • | • | • |
| Verb tenses (present, past, future; present, past, and future perfect) | | • | • | • | • | • | • |
| Participles; infinitives | | | | | | | |

**Key**

Shaded area  Explicit Instruction/Modeling/Practice and Application

• Tested

Assessment resources include: Kindergarten Assessment Handbook; Placement and Diagnostic Assessments, Grades 1, 2, and 3–6; Reading and Language Skills Assessments, Grades 1–6; Holistic Assessments, Grades 1–6; End-of-Selection Tests, Grades 1–6; and Oral Reading Fluency Assessment, Grades 1–6

| | GR K | GR 1 | GR 2 | GR 3 | GR 4 | GR 5 | GR 6 |
|---|---|---|---|---|---|---|---|
| Adjectives (common, proper; articles; comparative, superlative) | | • | • | • | • | • | • |
| Adverbs (place, time, manner, degree) | | | | • | • | • | • |
| Pronouns (subject, object, possessive, reflexive, demonstrative, antecedents) | | • | • | • | • | • | • |
| Prepositions; prepositional phrases | | | | | • | • | • |
| Conjunctions | | | | | | | |
| Abbreviations, contractions | | | | • | • | • | • |

## Punctuation

| | GR K | GR 1 | GR 2 | GR 3 | GR 4 | GR 5 | GR 6 |
|---|---|---|---|---|---|---|---|
| Period, exclamation point, or question mark at end of sentences | | • | • | • | • | • | • |
| Comma | | | • | • | • | • | • |
|    Greeting and closure of a letter | | | • | • | • | • | • |
|    Dates, locations, and addresses | | | • | • | • | • | • |
|    For items in a series | | | • | • | • | • | • |
|    Direct quotations | | | | | | | |
|    Link two clauses with a conjunction in compound sentences | | | | | • | • | • |
| Quotation marks | | | • | • | • | • | • |
|    Dialogue, exact words of a speaker | | | | • | • | • | • |
|    Titles of books, stories, poems, magazines | | | | | | • | • |
| Parentheses/dash/hyphen | | | | | • | • | • |
| Apostrophes in possessive case of nouns and in contractions | | | | • | • | • | • |
| Underlining or italics to identify title of documents | | | | | • | • | • |
| Colon | | | | | • | • | • |
|    Separate hours and minutes | | | | | • | • | • |
|    Introduce a list | | | | | • | • | • |
|    After the salutation in business letters | | | | | | • | • |
| Semicolons to connect independent clauses | | | | | | | |

## Capitalization

| | GR K | GR 1 | GR 2 | GR 3 | GR 4 | GR 5 | GR 6 |
|---|---|---|---|---|---|---|---|
| First word of a sentence, names of people, and the pronoun *I* | • | • | • | • | • | • | • |
| Proper nouns, words at the beginning of sentences and greetings, months and days of the week, and titles and initials of people | | • | • | • | • | • | • |
| Geographical names, holidays, historical periods, and special events | | | | | | | • |
| Names of magazines, newspapers, works of art, musical compositions, organizations, and the first word in quotations when appropriate | | | | | | | • |
| Use conventions of punctuation and capitalization | | | | | | | |

## Spelling

| | GR K | GR 1 | GR 2 | GR 3 | GR 4 | GR 5 | GR 6 |
|---|---|---|---|---|---|---|---|
| Spell independently by using pre-phonetic knowledge, sounds of the alphabet, and knowledge of letter names | | | | | | | |
| Use spelling approximations and some conventional spelling | | | | | | | |
| Common, phonetically regular words | | | • | • | • | • | • |
| Frequently used, irregular words | | • | • | • | • | • | • |
| One-syllable words with consonant blends | | | | • | • | • | • |
| Contractions, compounds, orthographic patterns, and common homophones | | | | | • | • | • |
| Greek and Latin roots, inflections, suffixes, prefixes, and syllable constructions | | | | | | • | • |
| Use a variety of strategies and resources to spell words | | | | | | | |

## Listening and Speaking

## Listening Skills and Strategies

| | GR K | GR 1 | GR 2 | GR 3 | GR 4 | GR 5 | GR 6 |
|---|---|---|---|---|---|---|---|
| Listen to a variety of oral presentations such as stories, poems, skits, songs, personal accounts, or informational speeches | | | | | | | |
| Listen attentively to the speaker (make eye contact and demonstrate appropriate body language) | | | | | | | |

**Key**

Shaded area   Explicit Instruction / Modeling / Practice and Application

•     Tested

     Assessment resources include: Kindergarten Assessment Handbook; Placement and Diagnostic Assessments, Grades 1, 2, and 3–6; Reading and Language Skills Assessments, Grades 1–6; Holistic Assessments, Grades 1–6; End-of-Selection Tests, Grades 1–6; and Oral Reading Fluency Assessment, Grades 1–6

| | GR K | GR 1 | GR 2 | GR 3 | GR 4 | GR 5 | GR 6 |
|---|---|---|---|---|---|---|---|
| **Listen for a purpose** | | | | | | | |
| Follow oral directions (one-, two-, three-, and multi-step) | ▪ | ▪ | ▪ | ▪ | ▪ | ▪ | ▪ |
| For specific information | ▪ | ▪ | ▪ | ▪ | ▪ | ▪ | ▪ |
| For enjoyment | ▪ | ▪ | ▪ | ▪ | ▪ | ▪ | ▪ |
| To distinguish between the speaker's opinions and verifiable facts | | | | ▪ | ▪ | ▪ | ▪ |
| To actively participate in class discussions | | | | ▪ | ▪ | ▪ | ▪ |
| To expand and enhance personal interest and personal preferences | | | | | ▪ | ▪ | ▪ |
| To identify, analyze, and critique persuasive techniques | | | | | | | ▪ |
| To identify logical fallacies used in oral presentations and media messages | | | | | | ▪ | ▪ |
| To make inferences or draw conclusions | | | | | | | ▪ |
| To interpret a speaker's verbal and nonverbal messages, purposes, and perspectives | | | | | | | ▪ |
| To identify the tone, mood, and emotion | | | | | | | ▪ |
| To analyze the use of rhetorical devices for intent and effect | | | | | | | ▪ |
| To evaluate classroom presentations | | | | | | | ▪ |
| To respond to a variety of media and speakers | ▪ | ▪ | ▪ | ▪ | ▪ | ▪ | ▪ |
| To paraphrase/summarize directions and information | | | ▪ | ▪ | ▪ | ▪ | ▪ |
| For language reflecting regions and cultures | | | | | | | ▪ |
| To recognize emotional and logical arguments | | | | | | | ▪ |
| To identify the musical elements of language | | | | ▪ | | | |
| Listen critically to relate the speaker's verbal communication to the nonverbal message | | | | | | | ▪ |
| **Speaking Skills and Strategies** | | | | | | | |
| Speak clearly and audibly and use appropriate volume and pace in different settings | ▪ | ▪ | ▪ | ▪ | ▪ | ▪ | ▪ |
| Use formal and informal English appropriately | ▪ | ▪ | ▪ | ▪ | ▪ | ▪ | ▪ |
| Follow rules of conversation | ▪ | ▪ | ▪ | ▪ | ▪ | ▪ | ▪ |
| Stay on the topic when speaking | ▪ | ▪ | ▪ | ▪ | ▪ | ▪ | ▪ |
| Use descriptive words | ▪ | ▪ | ▪ | ▪ | ▪ | ▪ | ▪ |
| Recount experiences in a logical sequence | | | | ▪ | ▪ | ▪ | ▪ |
| Clarify and support spoken ideas with evidence and examples | | | | ▪ | ▪ | ▪ | ▪ |
| Use eye contact, appropriate gestures, and props to enhance oral presentations and engage the audience | | | | ▪ | ▪ | ▪ | ▪ |
| Give and follow two-, three-, and four-step directions | | | | ▪ | ▪ | ▪ | ▪ |
| Recite poems, rhymes, songs, stories, soliloquies, or dramatic dialogues | ▪ | ▪ | ▪ | ▪ | ▪ | ▪ | ▪ |
| Plan and present dramatic interpretations with clear diction, pitch, tempo, and tone | | | ▪ | ▪ | ▪ | ▪ | ▪ |
| Organize presentations to maintain a clear focus | | | | ▪ | ▪ | ▪ | ▪ |
| Use language appropriate to situation, purpose, and audience | ▪ | ▪ | ▪ | ▪ | ▪ | ▪ | ▪ |
| **Make/deliver** | | | | | | | |
| Oral narrative, descriptive, informational, and persuasive presentations | | | | ▪ | ▪ | ▪ | ▪ |
| Oral summaries of articles and books | | | | ▪ | ▪ | ▪ | ▪ |
| Oral responses to literature | | | | ▪ | ▪ | ▪ | ▪ |
| Presentations on problems and solutions | | | | | ▪ | ▪ | ▪ |
| Presentation or speech for specific occasions, audiences, and purposes | | | | | ▪ | ▪ | ▪ |
| Vary language according to situation, audience, and purpose | | | | | ▪ | ▪ | ▪ |
| Select a focus, organizational structure, and point of view for an oral presentation | | | | | ▪ | ▪ | ▪ |
| Participate in classroom activities and discussions | ▪ | ▪ | ▪ | ▪ | ▪ | ▪ | ▪ |

**Key**

Shaded area  Explicit Instruction / Modeling / Practice and Application

• Tested

Assessment resources include: Kindergarten Assessment Handbook; Placement and Diagnostic Assessments, Grades 1, 2, and 3–6; Reading and Language Skills Assessments, Grades 1–6; Holistic Assessments, Grades 1–6; End-of-Selection Tests, Grades 1–6; and Oral Reading Fluency Assessment, Grades 1–6

# Index

## A

**Abbreviations.**
> *See* **Grammar.**

**Academic Language:** xxxiv, 20I, 25, 35, 39, 61, 65, 78I, 87, 91, 111, 124I, 133, 155, 173A–B, 174I, 179, 181, 205B, 211, 224, 229D, 251B, 315, 333, 339, 355, 405, 421D, 443, 453A, 463, 477, 490, 499B, 502I, 509, 511, 522I, 529, 544I, 568I, 589D, 637D, 714I, S4–S5, S16–S17, S28–S29, S42–S43, S132–S133, S144–S145, R14

**Active Reading Strategies.**
> *See* **Strategies Good Readers Use.**

**Activity Cards**
> comprehension cards: 23, 53, 81, 105, 127, 153, 177, 209, 233, 255, 277, 303, 329, 353, 375, 403, 425, 441, 457, 475, 505, 525, 547, 571, 593, 615, 641, 671, 693, 717, T12–T16, T47–T51, T80–T84, T115–T119, T149–T153, T185–T189

> word cards: 20L, 50L, 78L, 102L, 124L, 150L, 174L, 206L, 230L, 252L, 274L, 300L, 326L, 350L, 372L, 400L, 422L, 438L, 522L, 568L, 714L, T25–T28, T59–T61, T91–T93, T127–T129, T161–T163, T196–T198

**Additional Reading:** 45, 73, 93, 119, 143, 201, 225, 247, 295, 321, 343, 393, 415, 433, 495, 539, 563, 585, 605, 631, 663, 685, 709, 733, T33, T67, T99, T135, T169, T204

**Additional Support Activites:** S2–S31, S34–S63, S66–S95, S98–S127, S132–S159, S162–S191

**Adjectives.**
> *See* **Grammar.**

**Adjust Reading Rate.**
> *See* **Strategies Good Readers Use.**

**Advanced Students, Activities for:** 20B, 22, 32, 49B, 49I, 50B, 52, 60, 77I, 78B, 80, 84, 101G, 102B, 104, 112, 123G, 124B, 147G, 158, 173D, 173I, 184, 192, 229I, 240, 251G, 260, 271G, 271I, 299I, 306, 325G, 338, 342, 349I, 371G, 397G,

404, 421I, 437G, 453I, 462, 471G, 471I, 486, 499G, 514, 521K, 522K, 534, 542, 567G, 576, 589I, 609G, 626, 637I, 648, 667I, 676, 689G, 704, 713G, 713I, 737B, 737I
> *See also* **Reaching All Learners.**

**Adverbs.**
> *See* **Grammar.**

**Affixes.**
> *See* **Decoding/Phonics; Prefixes and Suffixes; Vocabulary and Concepts; Word Study.**

**Alliteration.**
> *See* **Author's Craft.**

**Almanac.**
> *See* **Reference Sources.**

**Alternative Teaching Strategies:** T2–T8, T36–T43, T70–T76, T104–T111, T138–T145, T174–T181

**Analogies.**
> *See* **Word Study.**

**Antonyms.**
> *See* **Word Study.**

**Apostrophe.**
> *See* **Mechanics.**

**Art Activities.**
> *See* **Content Areas; Cross-Curricular Connections.**

**Articles.**
> *See* **Grammar.**

**Assessment**
> entry-level: 18F, 148F, 272F, 398F, 500F, 610F

> formal
>> *End-of-Selection Tests:* 42, 70, 94, 114, 138, 168, 194, 216, 242, 286, 318, 344, 366, 388, 416, 448, 466, 492, 516, 536, 558, 582, 600, 632, 660, 680, 706, 728

>> *Holistic Assessment:* 147U, 271U, 397U, 499U, 609U, 737U

>> *Oral Reading Fluency Assessment:* T9–T11, T44–T46, T77–T79, T112–T114, T146–T148, T182–T184

>> *Placement and Diagnostic Assessments:* 18F–G, 148F–G, 272F–G, 398F–G, 500F–G, 610F–G

> *Reading and Language Skills Assessment:* 18F–G, 147U, 148F–G, 271U, 272F–G, 397U, 398F–G, 499U, 500F–G, 609U, 610F–G, 737U

> informal
>> anecdotal records: 147U, 271U, 397U, 499U, 609U, 737U

>> benchmarks: R36–R37

>> checklists for evaluation
>>> listening: R37, R40
>>> reading: R36, R39
>>> speaking: R37, R40
>>> writing: R36–R37, R39

>> comprehension skills: 18F, 42, 70, 94, 114, 138, 147U, 148F, 168, 194, 216, 242, 271U, 272F, 286, 318, 344, 366, 388, 397U, 398F, 416, 448, 466, 492, 499U, 500F, 516, 536, 558, 600, 609U, 632, 660, 680, 706, 728, 737U

>> conferences: 49F, 77F, 173F, 205D, 299F, 325D, 421F, 437D, 543F, 667F

>> literary response and analysis: 18F–G, 147U, 148F–G, 271U, 272F–G, 397U, 398F–G, 499U, 500F–G, 609U, 610F–G, 737U

>> ongoing oral reading fluency: 18F–G, 41, 49C, 77C, 93, 101A, 113, 123A, 137, 147A, 147U, 148F–G, 167, 173C, 193, 205A, 241, 251A, 271U, 272F–G, 365, 397U, 398F–G, 415, 429, 447, 491, 499U, 500F–G, 609U, 610F–G, 631, 653, 679, 705, 727, 737U, T9–T11, T44–T46, T77–T79, T112–T114, T146–T148, T182–T183

>> peer assessment: 49F, 77F, 173F, 205D, 251D, 299F, 325D, 371D, 421F, 437D, 609D, 637F, 667F

>> portfolio assessment: 147U, 271U, 397U, 499U, 609U, 737U

>> record forms, student: R35–R37

>> retell and summarize: 43, 71, 95, 115, 139, 169, 217, 243, 265, 287, 319, 345, 367, 389, 417, 431, 449, 467, 493, 517, 537, 559, 583, 601, 633, 661, 681, 707, 729

499C, 499K, 499L, 521P, 604, 607, 698, 731L, 733

*See also* **Thinking, organizing and connecting ideas.**

text structure, compare and contrast.

*See* **compare and contrast.**

text structure, main idea and details.

*See* **main idea and details.**

text structure, sequence.

*See* **sequence.**

visual images, draw or discuss based on text: 18J, 135, 147O, 148, 271O, 272, 272K, 369, 397O, 398, 438E, 454E, 499O, 500K, 522E, 544E, 595, 609O, 620, 714E, 737O

*See also* **Selection Comprehension; Strategies Good Readers Use.**

word relationships

introduce: 638I

reteach: S170–S171, S182–S183, T176

review: 666, 690I, 712

**Comprehension Cards:** 23, 53, 81, 105, 127, 153, 177, 209, 233, 255, 277, 303, 329, 353, 375, 403, 425, 441, 457, 475, 505, 525, 547, 571, 593, 615, 641, 671, 693, 717, T12–T15, T48–T51, T80–T84, T115–T119, T149–T153, T185–T189

*See also* **Literary Response and Analysis.**

**Computer Skills.**

*See* **Writing.**

**Computer Station:** 20F, 50F, 78F, 102F, 124F, 150F, 174F, 206F, 230F, 252F, 274F, 300F, 326F, 350F, 372F, 400F, 422F, 438F, 454F, 472F, 502F, 522F, 544F, 568F, 590F, 612F, 638F, 668F, 690F, 714F

*See also* **Technology, Internet/*The Learning Site.***

**Computers, Using.**

*See* **Technology.**

**Conclusions, Drawing.**

*See* **Comprehension, draw conclusions.**

**Conferences.**

*See* **Assessment, informal.**

**Conjunctions.**

*See* **Grammar, simple and compound sentences.**

**Connotation and Denotation.**

*See* **Vocabulary and Concepts.**

**Consonant Blends.**

*See* **Decoding/Phonics.**

**Content-Area Reading**

additional reading: 45, 73, 93, 119, 143, 201, 225, 247, 295, 321, 343, 393, 415, 433, 495, 539, 563, 585, 605, 631, 663, 685, 709, 733

selections in *Pupil Edition*

health

"Donavan's Word Jar": 52–70

"In the Days of King Adobe": 440–448

language arts

"Red Writing Hood": 456–467

math

"One Grain of Rice": 474–492

"Stealing Home": 302–318

physical education

"Lou Gehrig: The Luckiest Man": 104–115

science

"Amelia and Eleanor Go for a Ride": 126–139

"The Case of Pablo's Nose": 424–430

"The Cricket in Times Square": 328–344

"The Down and Up Fall": 714–737

"Fly Traps! Plants That Bite Back": 690–713

"The Gardener": 22–43

"The Gold Rush": 612–637

"How to Babysit an Orangutan": 254–265

"I Have Heard of a Land": 638–667

"The Kids' Invention Book": 402–416

"Look to the North": 374–389

"Nights of the Pufflings": 208–217

"Paul Bunyan and Babe the Blue Ox": 668–689

"Saguaro Cactus": 544–567

social studies

"The Baker's Neighbor": 152–168

"Blue Willow": 568–589

"The Emperor and the Kite": 176–195

"Fire!": 502–521

"The Garden of Happiness": 232–243

"In My Family": 590–609

"My Name Is María Isabel": 80–95

"Sarah, Plain and Tall": 276–287

"Two Lands, One Heart": 352–366

"A Very Important Day": 522–543

*See also* **Books for All Learners; Cross-Curricular Stations; Genre; Independent Reading.**

**Content-Area Vocabulary.**

*See* **Vocabulary and Concepts.**

**Content Areas**

art

activities: 57, 135, 249, 435, 465, 469, 607

information/discussions: 193, 465

health

activities: 50E

information/discussions: 511

math

activities: 27, 33, 50E, 57, 75, 78E, 102E, 109, 174E, 252E, 300E, 347, 350E, 472E, 497, 565, 575

information/discussions: 57, 109, 407, 549

music

activities: 665

information/discussions: 55, 85

physical education

information/discussions: 107

science

activities: 20E, 37, 47, 59, 89, 99, 121, 131, 145, 150E, 171, 206E, 223, 227, 230E, 237, 249, 259, 297, 300E, 323, 331, 347, 361, 369, 385, 395, 419, 451, 461, 469, 519, 541, 551, 553, 560, 565, 587, 595, 607, 635, 687, 695, 697, 711, 719, 735

information/discussions: 37, 59, 89, 221, 307, 357, 381, 383, 409, 411, 427, 485, 531, 595, 623, 645, 673, 695, 703

social studies

activities: 31, 75, 99, 121, 129, 145, 150E, 171, 206E, 227, 252E, 257, 269, 283, 297, 323, 335, 369, 395, 419, 451, 469, 497, 513, 519, 527, 541, 577, 587, 635, 649, 657, 665, 687, 711, 735

information/discussions: 47, 63, 83, 107, 183, 187, 291, 309, 311, 313, 413, 445, 459, 477, 481, 487, 513, 533, 579, 597, 617, 621, 627, 651, 655, 675, 699, 721, 731

long vowel /ā/ *ai, ay ei(gh)*: 37

long vowel /ō/ *o, oa, ow, oe*: 213

prefixes and suffixes

introduce: 50I

reteach: S10–S11, S22–S23, T4

review 76, 102I, 122

maintain: 173D

related words: 147I, 638, 666, 690I, 712

silent letters: 609A

structural analysis

compound words: 123A, 205A, 371A

inflected endings: 349A, 589C

prefixes and suffixes: 437A, 499A, 737A

roots: 637C

root words: 349A, 437A, 499A, 589C, 737A

syllables

accent marks: 299C

*Cle* syllable pattern: 543C

closed syllables: 251A, 453C

CVC spelling pattern: 49C, 77C

CVC*e* spelling pattern: 77C

CVVC spelling pattern: 271A, 471A

open syllables: 229C, 453C

schwa: 325A, 521C

unaccented syllables: 567A

VCCV syllable pattern: 421C, 689A

VCV syllable pattern: 713A

word structure.

*See* **Decoding Multisyllabic Words.**

*See also* **Spelling.**

**Decoding Strategies.**

*See* **Decoding Multisyllabic Words; Decoding/Phonics; Strategies Good Readers Use; Word Identification Strategies.**

**Denotation.**

*See* **Word Study, connotation/ denotation.**

**Description.**

*See* **Author's Craft, descriptive images; Writing, student writing models, analyze, paragraphs that describe; Writing, writing activities; Writing Forms, expressive.**

**Details, Noting Important.**

*See* **Comprehension, details; Thinking.**

**Diagrams, Use and Interpret.**

*See* **Research and Information Skills, graphic sources.**

**Dialogue:** 133, 315, 491, 725

**Dictionary.**

*See* **Reference Sources; Research and Information Skills.**

**Differentiated Instruction:** 18H–I, 22, 49M–P, 52, 77M–P, 80, 101K–N, 104, 123K–N, 126, 147K–N, 148H–I, 152, 173M–P, 176, 205K–N, 208, 229M–P, 232, 251K–N, 254, 271K–N, 272H–I, 276, 299M–P, 302, 325K–N, 328, 349K–N, 352, 371K–N, 374, 397K–N, 398H–I, 402, 421M–P, 424, 437K–N, 440, 453M–P, 456, 471K–N, 474, 499K–N, 500H–I, 504, 521M–P, 524, 543M–P, 546, 567K–N, 570, 589M–P, 592, 609K–N, 610H–I, 614, 637M–P, 640, 670, 689K–N, 692, 713K–N, 716, 737K–N

**Digraphs.**

*See* **Decoding/Phonics.**

**Diphthongs.**

*See* **Decoding/Phonics.**

**Directions, Following.**

*See* **Research and Information Skills, follow written directions; Writing, writing activities.**

**Domains of Writing.**

*See* **Writing, purposes.**

**Drama.**

*See* **Genre, play; Literary Forms.**

**Drama Activities.**

*See* **Content Areas; Cross-Curricular Connections.**

**Draw Conclusions:** 274I, 326I, 471B

*See also* **Comprehension, draw conclusions; Research and Information Skills.**

**Easy Readers.**

*See* **Additional Reading; Books for All Learners; Intervention Resource Kit.**

**Editing.**

*See* **Writing, editing skills.**

**Elements of Nonfiction:** 502I, 544I, 637D, S132–S133, S144–S145

*See also* **Comprehension, elements of nonfiction; Expository Nonfiction; Literary Response and Analysis.**

**Encyclopedia:** 102F, 121, 131, 145, 150E, 174E, 206E, 223, 229A, 252F, 265, 274F,

300E, 326F, 331, 350F, 354, 395, 400E, 427, 451, 471I, 489, 497, 521A–B, 544F, 567B, 568F, 587, 609B, 638F, 668E, 690F, 714F

*See also* **Reference Sources; Research and Information Skills, multiple resources, use to locate information.**

**End Marks.**

*See* **Grammar, sentences; Mechanics, punctuation, sentence.**

**End-of-Selection Tests.**

*See* **Assessment, formal.**

**English as a Second Language (ESL).**

*See* **English-Language Learners, Activities for; Reaching All Learners.**

**English for Speakers of Other Languages.**

*See* **English-Language Learners, Activities for.**

**English-Language Learners, Activities For:** 22, 24, 26 28, 30, 36, 38, 49G, 49P, 52, 54, 56, 64, 66, 77, 77B, 77P, 78L, 80, 82, 90, 101N, 102L, 104, 106, 108, 123B, 123E, 128, 136, 150L, 152, 156, 173, 173B, 173G, 173P, 206L, 208, 210, 224, 230L, 232, 236, 251B, 252L, 256, 271E, 284, 299, 299B, 299P, 304, 314, 316, 325N, 340, 356, 358, 364, 371, 371E, 371N, 374, 376, 382, 397, 397E, 397N, 408, 412, 414, 421, 421B, 421G, 422L, 424, 426, 437, 437B, 437E, 437N, 438L, 440, 442, 444, 453, 453B, 453G, 453L, 453P, 454L, 456, 460, 462, 464, 471, 471E, 471N, 476, 478, 480, 484, 486, 499, 499B, 499E, 499N, 502L, 506, 512, 521D, 522L, 528, 534, 543G, 544L, 550, 554, 556, 568L, 589D, 596, 610F–G, 616, 618, 620, 624, 628, 637D, 642, 644, 652, 658, 667D, 672, 689B, 689I, 690L, 694, 696, 700, 702, 714K, 720, 722, 724, 726, 737E; S3, S5, S7, S9, S11, S13, S15, S17, S19, S21, S23, S25, S27, S29, S31, S35, S37, S39, S41, S43, S45, S47, S49, S51, S53, S55, S57, S59, S61, S67, S69, S71, S73, S75, S77, S79, S81, S83, S85, S87, S89, S91, S93, S95, S99, S101, S103, S105, S107, S109, S111, S113, S115, S117, S119, S121, S123, S125, S127, S131, S133, S135, S137, S139, S141, S143, S145, S147, S149, S151, S153, S155, S157, S159, S163, S165, S167,

**Grammar**

abbreviations
  introduce: 371E–F
  reteach: S89

action and linking verbs
  introduce: 543G–H
  reteach: S141, T142

activities, hands-on: R29–R34

adjectives and articles
  introduce: 453G–H
  reteach: S115, T109

adjectives that compare
  introduce: 471E–F
  reteach: S121, T110

adverbs
  introduce: 667G–H
  reteach: S173, S179, T178

clauses
  introduce: 251E–F
  reteach: S57, T42

common and proper nouns
  introduce: 299G–H
  reteach: S71, T71

comparing with adverbs
  introduce: 689E–F
  reteach: S179, T179

complete and simple predicates
  introduce: 173G–H
  reteach: S39, T38

complete and simple subjects
  introduce: 147E–F
  reteach: S31, T8

complex sentences
  introduce: 271E–F
  reteach: S63, T43

compound subjects and predicates
  introduce: 205E–F
  reteach: S45, T40

contractions and negatives
  introduce: 637G–H
  reteach: S167, T175

declarative and interrogative sentences
  introduce: 77G–H
  reteach: S13, T5

imperative and exclamatory sentences
  introduce: 101E–F
  reteach: S19, T6

independent and dependent clauses
  introduce: 251E–F
  reteach: S57, T42

irregular verbs
  introduce: 609E–F
  reteach: S159, T145

main and helping verbs

introduce: 521G–H
  reteach: S135, T140

past and future tense verbs
  introduce: 589G–H
  reteach: S153, T144

possessive nouns
  introduce: 349E–F
  reteach: S83, T74

possessive pronouns
  introduce: 437E–F
  reteach: S109, T108

prepositional phrases
  introduce: 737E–F
  reteach: S191, T181

prepositions
  introduce: 713E–F
  reteach: S185, T180

present tense
  introduce: 567E–F
  reteach: S147, T143

pronouns and antecedents
  introduce: 397E–F
  reteach: S95, T76

sentences
  introduce: 49G–H
  reteach: S7, T3

simple and compound sentences
  introduce: 229G–H
  reteach: S51, T41

singular and plural nouns
  introduce: 325E–F
  reteach: S77, T73

subject and object pronouns
  introduce: 421G–H
  reteach: S103, T106

subjects and predicates
  introduce: 123E–F
  reteach: S25, T7

verbs
  introduce: 499E–F
  reteach: S127, T111

*See also* **Daily Language Practice;**
**Listening and Speaking, speaking;**
**Usage.**

**Graphic Aids.**
  *See* **Comprehension, graphic aids;**
**Research and Information Skills;**
**Strategies Good Readers Use.**

**Graphic Sources:** 49L, 77L, 101J, 123B,
299A–B, 325J, 371B
  *See also* **Comprehension, graphic aids;**
**Research and Information Skills,**
**graphic aids.**

**Graphs:** 27, 75, 78E, 109, 299A–B, 371B,
502E, 521E, 522E, 690E
  *See also* **Research and Information**
**Skills, graphic aids; Thinking,**
**organizing and connecting ideas.**

**Greek and Latin Roots.**
  *See* **Decoding/Phonics.**

**Guided Comprehension**

modeling: 25, 27, 33, 35, 37, 57, 59, 61,
63, 65, 67, 69, 83, 85, 87, 89, 91, 107,
109, 111, 113, 131, 133, 135, 137,
155, 157, 159, 161, 163, 165, 179,
181, 183, 185, 187, 189, 191, 193,
211, 213, 215, 235, 237, 239, 241,
257, 259, 261, 263, 265, 279, 281,
283, 285, 305, 307, 309, 311, 313,
315, 331, 333, 335, 337, 339, 341,
355, 357, 359, 361, 363, 377, 379,
381, 383, 385, 387, 405, 407, 409,
411, 413, 415, 417, 427, 429, 443,
445, 447, 459, 461, 463, 465, 477,
479, 481, 483, 485, 487, 489, 507,
509, 511, 513, 515, 527, 529, 531,
533, 535, 549, 551, 553, 555, 557,
559, 561, 573, 575, 579, 581, 595,
596, 597, 617, 619, 621, 623, 625,
629, 643, 645, 647, 649, 651, 653,
655, 657, 659, 667, 673, 675, 679,
695, 697, 699, 701, 703, 705, 719,
721, 723, 725, 727

questions: 24, 26, 28, 30, 32, 34, 36, 38,
40, 43, 54, 56, 58, 60, 62, 64, 66, 68,
70, 82, 84, 86, 88, 90, 92, 95, 106,
108, 110, 112, 115, 128, 130, 132,
134, 136, 139, 154, 156, 158, 160,
162, 164, 166, 168, 178, 180, 182,
184, 186, 188, 190, 192, 195, 210,
212, 214, 217, 222, 224, 234, 236,
238, 240, 243, 256, 258, 260, 262,
265, 278, 280, 282, 284, 287, 304,
306, 308, 310, 312, 314, 316, 318,
330, 332, 334, 336, 338, 340, 342,
344, 354, 356, 358, 360, 362, 364,
366, 376, 378, 380, 382, 384, 386,
389, 404, 406, 408, 410, 412, 414,
416, 426, 428, 430, 442, 444, 446,
448, 458, 460, 462, 464, 467, 476,
478, 480, 482, 484, 486, 488, 490,
492, 506, 508, 510, 512, 514, 526,
528, 530, 532, 534, 548, 550, 552,
554, 556, 558, 572, 574, 576, 578,
580, 594, 596, 598, 616, 618, 620,
622, 624, 628, 630, 642, 646, 648,

650, 652, 654, 656, 658, 672, 674,
676, 678, 694, 696, 698, 700, 702,
704, 718, 720, 722, 724, 726

*See also* **Comprehension; Strategies
Good Readers Use.**

**Handbook, Writer's:** R2–R13

**Handwriting:** 49I, 77I, 101G, 123G, 147G,
173I, 205G, 229I, 251G, 271G, 299I,
325G, 349G, 371G, 397G, 421I, 437G,
453I, 471G, 499G, 521I, 543I, 567G,
589I, 609G, 637I, 667I, 689G, 713G,
737G, R23–R28

**Health/Safety Activities.**

*See* **Content Areas; Cross-Curricular
Connections.**

**Higher-Order Thinking Skills.**

*See* **Thinking.**

**Historical Fiction:** 124–147, 274–299,
638–667

*See also* **Genre.**

**Holistic Assessment.**

*See* **Assessment, formal.**

**Homework:** 18K, 21, 43, 47, 49, 49B, 51,
71, 75, 77, 77B, 79, 95, 99, 101, 103, 115,
117, 121, 123, 125, 139, 145, 147, 148K,
151, 169, 171, 173, 173B, 175, 195, 203,
205, 206D, 207, 217, 227, 229, 229B, 231,
243, 249, 251, 253, 265, 269, 271, 272K,
275, 287, 297, 299, 299B, 301, 319, 323,
325, 325E, 345, 347, 349, 350L, 367, 369,
371, 371E, 373, 389, 395, 397, 398K, 401,
417, 419, 421, 421B, 423, 431, 435, 437,
439, 449, 451, 453, 454L, 469, 471, 472L,
493, 497, 499, 500K, 502L, 519, 521, 541,
543, 544L, 565, 567, 587, 589, 590L, 601,
607, 609, 610K, 612L, 635, 637, 638L,
665, 667, 667G, 667I, 668L, 681, 687,
689, 689E, 689G, 690L, 711, 713, 729,
735, 737, 737E, 737G, T28–T32,
T62–T66, T94–T98, T130–T134,
T164–T168, T199–T203

**Homographs and Homophones.**

*See* **Vocabulary and Concepts; Word
Study.**

**Idioms.**

*See* **Vocabulary and Concepts.**

**Illustrations, Discussing.**

*See* **Viewing.**

**Imagery.**

*See* **Author's Craft.**

**Imaginative Literature.**

*See* **Comprehension, imaginative
literature.**

**Imperative Sentences.**

*See* **Author's Craft; Grammar.**

**Independent Reading**

Books for All Learners: 20B, 49M–P,
50B, 77M–P, 78B, 101K–N, 102B,
123K–N, 124B, 147K–N, 150B,
173M–P, 174B, 205K–N, 206B,
229M–P, 230B, 251K–N, 252B,
271K–N, 274B, 299M–P, 300B,
325K–N, 326B, 349K–N, 350B,
371K–N, 372B, 397K–N, 400B,
421M–P, 422B, 437K–N, 438B,
453M–P, 454B, 471K–N, 472B,
499K–N, 502B, 521M–P, 522B,
543M–P, 544B, 567K–N, 568B,
589M–P, 590B, 609K–N, 612B,
637M–P, 638B, 667M–P, 668B,
689K–N, 690B, 713K–N, 714B,
737K–N

*My Reading Log:* 20F, 50F, 78F, 102F,
124F, 147O, 150F, 174F, 206F, 230F,
252F, 271O, 274F, 300F, 326F, 350F,
372F, 397O, 400F, 422F, 438F, 454F,
472F, 499O, 502F, 522F, 544F, 568F,
590F, 609O, 612F, 638F, 668F, 690F,
714F, 737O, R38

Theme Resources: 18B–C, 148B–C,
272B–C, 398B–C, 500B–C, 610B–C,
T2–T34, T36–T67, T70–T101,
T104–T136

**Independent Reading Books:** 18C, 45,
49M–P, 50B, 50F, 73, 77M–P, 93,
101K–N, 119, 123M–P, 143, 147K–N,
148C, 150B, 150F, 167, 173M–P, 199,
201, 205K–N, 206B, 206F, 225, 229M–P,
230B, 230F, 247, 251K–N, 252B, 252F,
267, 271K–N, 272C, 274B, 274F, 295,
299M–P, 321, 325K–N, 326B, 326F, 343,
349K–N, 350B, 350F, 365, 371K–N,
372B, 372F, 393, 397K–N, 398C, 400B,
400F, 415, 421M–P, 422B, 422F, 433,

437K–N, 438B, 438F, 453M–P, 454B,
454F, 471K–N, 472B, 472F, 495,
499K–N, 500C, 521M–P, 539, 543M–P,
563, 567K–N, 585, 589M–P, 605,
609K–N, 610C, 631, 637M–P, 663,
667M–P, 685, 689K–N, 709, 713K–N,
733, 737K–N

**Index.**

*See* **Research and Information Skills,
book parts, locate information.**

**Inferences, Make and Explain.**

*See* **Comprehension, make
inferences.**

**Inferential Thinking.**

*See* **Comprehension, make inferences; Thinking.**

**Inflected Forms.**

*See* **Decoding/Phonics; Grammar;
Word Study, related words.**

**Informal Assessment.**

*See* **Assessment.**

**Informational Narrative:** 372–397,
522–543, 690–713

*See also* **Genre.**

**Informative Writing.**

*See* **Writing Purposes.**

**Inquiry and Research**

inquiry projects: 20F, 50F, 78F, 102F,
124F, 150F, 174F, 206F, 230F, 252F,
274F, 300F, 326F, 350F, 372F, 400F,
422F, 438F, 454F, 472F, 502F, 522F,
544F, 568F, 590F, 612F, 638F, 668F,
690F, 714F

questions, write or dictate: 20C–D,
20H, 50C–D, 50H, 78C–D, 78H,
102C–D, 102H, 124C–D, 124H,
150C–D, 150H, 174C–D, 174H,
206C–D, 206H, 230C–D, 230H,
252C–D, 252H, 274C–D, 274H,
300C–D, 300H, 326C–D, 326H,
350C–D, 350H, 372C–D, 372H,
400C–D, 400H, 422C–D, 422H,
438C–D, 438H, 454C–D, 454H,
472C–D, 472H, 502C–D, 502H,
522C–D, 522H, 544C–D, 544H,
568C–D, 568H, 590C–D, 590H,
612C–D, 612H, 638C–D, 638H,
668C–D, 668H, 690C–D, 690H,
714C–D, 714H

theme projects: 18J, 147O, 148J, 271O,
272J, 397O, 398J, 499O, 500J, 609O,
610J, 737O

**Process Writing.**

See **Writing Process.**

**Professional Development:** vi–xxix,
R43–R47

**Program Reviewers:** R48–R49

**Pronouns.**

See **Grammar.**

**Proofreading:** 49F, 77F, 101D, 123D,
147D, 173F, 229F, 251D, 265D, 271D,
299F, 325D, 349D, 371D, 397D, 421F,
437D, 453F, 471D, 499D, 521F, 543F,
567D, 589F, 609D, 637F, 667F, 689D,
713D, 737D, S152–S153

See also **Mechanics; Writing Process.**

**Proper Nouns.**

See **Grammar, common and proper
nouns.**

**Punctuation.**

See **Mechanics.**

**Purpose for Listening:** 20G, 50G, 78G,
102G, 124G, 150G, 174G, 206G, 230G,
252G, 274G, 300G, 326G, 350G, 372G,
400G, 422G, 438G, 454G, 472G, 502G,
522G, 544G, 568G, 590G, 612G, 638G,
668G, 690G, 714G

See also **Listening Strategies; Oral
Language.**

**Purpose for Reading, Setting.**

See **Prereading Strategies, Preview
and Predict/Set Purpose.**

**Purpose for Writing.**

See **Writing.**

**Question of the Day:** 20C–D, 20H,
50C–D, 50H, 78C–D, 78H, 102C–D,
102H, 124C–D, 124H, 150C–D, 150H,
174C–D, 174H, 206C–D, 206H,
230C–D, 230H, 252C–D, 252H,
274C–D, 274H, 300C–D, 300H,
326C–D, 326H, 350C–D, 350H,
372C–D, 372H, 400C–D, 400H,
422C–D, 422H, 438C–D, 438H,
454C–D, 454H, 472C–D, 472H,
502C–D, 502H, 522C–D, 522H,
544C–D, 544H, 568C–D, 568H,
590C–D, 590H, 612C–D, 612H,
638C–D, 638H, 668C–D, 668H,
690C–D, 690H, 714C–D, 714H

**Questions for Inquiry.**

See **Inquiry and Research.**

**Quickwrite:** 19, 21, 51, 79, 103, 125, 149,
151, 175, 207, 231, 253, 273, 275, 301,
327, 351, 373, 399, 401, 423, 439, 455,
473, 501, 503, 523, 545, 569, 591, 611,
613, 639, 669, 691, 715

See also **Writing, writing activities,
conversation.**

**Reaching All Learners**

advanced: 18I, 20B, 22, 32, 49B, 49I,
49K, 49O, 50B, 52, 60, 77I, 77O,
78B, 78L, 80, 84, 101G, 101M, 102B,
104, 106, 112, 123G, 123M, 124B,
124L, 126, 134, 136, 147, 147E,
147G, 147I, 148I, 150B, 150L, 152,
156, 158, 166, 173, 173D, 173G,
173I, 173O, 184, 192, 205, 205B,
205E, 205G, 205M, 206B, 206L, 208,
214, 229, 229B, 229G, 229I, 229O,
230L, 232, 238, 240, 251, 251E,
251G, 251M, 252B, 252L, 254, 260,
271, 271E, 271G, 271I, 271M, 272I,
274B, 274L, 276, 282, 299, 299B,
299G, 299I, 299K, 299O, 300B,
300L, 302, 306, 312, 314, 325, 325E,
325G, 325I, 325M, 326B, 326L, 328,
334, 338, 342, 349, 349B, 349E,
349G, 349I, 349M, 350B, 350L, 352,
358, 362, 371, 371B, 371E, 371G,
371I, 371M, 372B, 372L, 374, 382,
384, 386, 397, 397B, 397E, 397G,
397M, 398I, 400B, 400L, 402, 404,
410, 412, 421, 421B, 421G, 421I,
421K, 421O, 422B, 422L, 424, 426,
437, 437E, 437G, 437M, 438B, 438L,
440, 442, 453, 453B, 453G, 453I,
454B, 454L, 456, 462, 471, 471E,
471G, 471I, 471M, 472B, 472L, 474,
480, 486, 490, 499, 499E, 499G,
499M

below-level: 18H, 20B, 20L, 22, 28, 34,
38, 40, 49, 49B, 49D, 49G, 49M, 50B,
50L, 52, 60, 64, 77, 77B, 77G, 77M,
78B, 78L, 80, 82, 88, 90, 92, 101,
101E, 101K, 102B, 102L, 104, 106,
110, 123, 123E, 123K, 124B, 124L,
126, 132, 136, 147, 147B, 147E,
148H, 150B, 150L, 152, 154, 156,
160, 166, 173, 173B, 173G, 173K,

173M, 174B, 174L, 176, 178, 182,
184, 190, 192, 200, 205, 205E, 205K,
206B, 206L, 208, 212, 214, 222, 229,
229B, 299D, 229G, 229M, 230B,
230L, 232, 234, 238, 251, 251E,
251K, 252B, 252L, 254, 258, 260,
271, 271B, 271E, 271K, 272H, 274B,
274L, 276, 278, 280, 282, 299, 299B,
299D, 299G, 299M, 300B, 300L, 302,
308, 312, 314, 325, 325B, 325E,
325K, 326B, 326L, 328, 330, 334,
336, 342, 349, 349E, 349K, 350B,
350L, 352, 354, 358, 360, 362, 371,
371E, 371K, 372B, 372L, 374, 378,
380, 382, 384, 386, 397, 397B, 397E,
397K, 398H, 400B, 400L, 402, 406,
410, 412, 421, 421B, 421D, 421G,
421M, 422B, 422L, 424, 426, 428,
437, 437E, 437K, 438B, 438L, 440,
442, 446, 453, 453B, 453D, 453G,
453M, 454B, 454L, 456, 458, 462,
471, 471B, 471E, 471K, 472B, 472L,
473, 478, 480, 482, 486, 488, 499,
499E, 499K

English-language learners: 18H, 20B,
20L, 22, 24, 26, 28, 30, 36, 38, 49,
49B, 49G, 49P, 50B, 50L, 52, 56, 60,
64, 66, 77, 77B, 77G, 77K, 77P, 78B,
78L, 80, 82, 90, 92, 101, 101E, 101I,
101N, 102B, 102L, 104, 106, 108,
123, 123B, 123E, 123I, 123N, 124B,
124L, 126, 128, 130, 136, 147, 147E,
147R, 147T, 148H, 150B, 150L, 152,
156, 162, 164, 166, 173, 173B, 173G,
173P, 174B, 174L, 176, 180, 184, 186,
188, 192, 205, 205E, 205N, 206B,
206L, 208, 210, 214, 220, 224, 229,
229B, 229G, 229K, 229P, 230B,
230L, 232, 236, 238, 251, 251B,
251E, 251I, 251N, 252B, 252L, 254,
256, 260, 262, 271, 271E, 271N,
271R, 271T, 272H, 274B, 274L, 276,
282, 284, 299, 299B, 299G, 299P,
300B, 300L, 302, 304, 310, 312, 314,
316, 325, 325E, 325N, 326B, 326L,
328, 332, 334, 340, 342, 349, 349E,
349N, 350B, 350L, 352, 356, 358,
362, 364, 371, 371E, 371N, 372B,
372L, 374, 376, 382, 384, 397, 397E,
397I, 397N, 397R, 397T, 398H,
400B, 400L, 402, 408, 410, 412, 414,
421, 421B, 421G, 421P, 422B, 422L,
424, 426, 437, 437B, 437I, 437N,

synonym finder/thesaurus: 50F, 102L, 300L, 521B, 609B, 687, R8

*See also* **Comprehension, reference sources; Research and Information Skills, locate information; Research and Information Skills, multiple resources, use to locate; Research and Information Skills, reference sources; Stategies Good Readers Use.**

**Representing.**

*See* **Viewing.**

**Reread.**

*See* **Strategies Good Readers Use.**

**Rereading for Fluency:** 41, 69, 93, 113, 137, 167, 193, 215, 241, 263, 285, 317, 343, 365, 387, 415, 429, 447, 465, 491, 515, 535, 557, 581, 631, 679, 705, 727

*See also* **Assessment, formal,** *Oral Reading Fluency Assessment.*

**Research.**

*See* **Research and Information Skills.**

**Research and Information Skills**

additional questions, raising: 274F, 300F, 326F, 350F, 372F, 612F, 638F, 668F, 690F, 714F

alphabetical order, use to locate information: 229D, 269

book parts: 124I, 146, 229D, 269, 472E, S28–S29

charts, use and interpret: 20E, 20I, 20K, 47, 49D, 71, 75, 77N, 78I, 78K, 80, 99, 101G, 102I, 150E, 150I, 155, 206I, 208, 230K, 252F, 252I, 254, 299A–B, 300K, 323, 324, 325B, 349B, 395, 397B, 421A, 421L, 471B, 451, 541, 565, 568I, 576, 587, 590E, 638I, 704, 711

demonstrate learning

displays: 145, 203, 451, 737O

murals: 57, 249, 369, 500K

oral reports: 99, 121, 269, 347, 461, 541

written reports: 419, 435, 451, 469, 497, 500J, 521E–F, 541, 543E–F, 567E–F, 589E–F, 609C–D

draw conclusions from information gathered: 274I, 326I, 471B

follow written directions

introduce: 421A–B

maintain: 521D

reteach: T105

review: 437B, 453D

graphic aids

introduce: 299A–B

review: 371B

library/media center

introduce: 124I

review: 229D, 371B, 421D

locate information

introduce: 124I

maintain: 421D

reteach: S28–S29

review: 146, 229D

multiple resources, use to locate information

encyclopedia (print/online/CD–ROM): 102F, 121, 124E–F, 131, 145, 150E, 174F, 206E, 223, 229A, 252F, 274F, 300E, 326F, 350E, 395, 400E, 451, 471I, 497, 521A, 521F, 544F, 567B, 568F, 587, 590E, 607, 609B, 638E, R6

experts: 47

technology: 20F, 78E, 102F, 124F, 129, 150E, 174F, 206F, 229A, 244, 252F, 269, 271B, 274F, 299D, 326E, 326F, 350F, 372F, 395, 454F, 497, 502F, 521A, 521F, 567B, 590E, 609B, 668F, 690F, 714F, 721

textbooks, nonfiction books: 47, 206E, 229A, 300E, 469, 521F, 567B, 607, 638E

organizing information graphically.

*See* **Comprehension, text information, represent in different ways; Thinking, organizing and connecting ideas.**

outlining

introduce: 637A–B

review: 713B

reference sources

introduce: 521A–B

reteach: T139

review: 567B, 609B

search techniques

introduce: 229A–B

review: 271B, 299D

test-taking skills

maintain : 543A–B

*See also* **Test Prep, test tutor.**

**Research Base:** vi–xxiv, R43–R47

**Research Report:** 521E–F, 543E–F, 567C–D, 589E–F, 609C–D

*See also* **Writing, purposes.**

**Resources, Additional.**

*See* **Teacher Resources.**

**Responding to Literature.**

*See* **Literary Response and Analysis.**

**Response Activities:** 18K, 20H, 42, 47, 49M–P, 50H, 70, 75, 77M–P, 78H, 94, 99, 101K–N, 102H, 114, 121, 123K–N, 124H, 138, 145, 147K–N, 148K, 150H, 171, 173M–P, 174H, 194, 203, 205K–N, 206H, 216, 227, 229M–P, 230H, 242, 249, 251K–N, 252H, 269, 271K–N, 272K, 274H, 286, 297, 299M–P, 300H, 318, 323, 325K–N, 326H, 344, 347, 349K–N, 350H, 366, 369, 371K–N, 372H, 388, 395, 397K–N, 398K, 400H, 416, 419, 421M–P, 422H, 430, 435, 437K–N, 438H, 448, 451, 453M–P, 454H, 466, 469, 471K–N, 472H, 492, 497, 499K–N, 500K, 502H, 516, 519, 521M–P, 522H, 522L, 536, 541, 543M–P, 544H, 558, 565, 567K–N, 568H, 568L, 582, 587, 589M–P, 590H, 600, 607, 609K–N, 610K, 612H, 632, 635, 637M–P, 638H, 660, 665, 667M–P, 668H, 680, 687, 689K–N, 690H, 706, 711, 713K–N, 714H, 728, 735, 737K–N

*See also* **Literary Response and Analysis.**

**Response to Literature, Writing:** 18J, 42, 47, 70, 75, 94, 99, 114, 121, 138, 148J, 168, 171, 194, 203, 216, 227, 242, 249, 269, 272J, 286, 297, 318, 323, 344, 347, 366, 369, 388, 395, 398J, 416, 419, 430, 435, 448, 451, 453E–F, 466, 469, 492, 497, 500J, 516, 519, 536, 541, 558, 565, 582, 587, 600, 607, 610J, 632, 635, 660, 665, 680, 687, 706, 711, 728, 735

**Restate:** 43, 71, 95, 115, 139, 169, 195, 217, 243, 265, 287, 319, 345, 367, 389, 417, 431, 449, 467, 493, 517, 537, 559, 583, 601, 633, 661, 681, 707, 729

**Reteach Lessons:**

*See* **Additional Support Activities; Alternative Teaching Strategies.**

**Retelling.**

*See* **Listening and Speaking, speaking.**

**Retellings, Evaluate.**

*See* **Assessment, informal.**

**Rhyme.**

*See* **Author's Craft; Listening and Speaking, musical elements of literary language.**

**Rhythm.**

> See **Author's Craft; Listening and Speaking,** purposes for listening/speaking, musical elements of literary language, identify.

**Rubrics, Writing:** 49F, 77F, 101D, 123D, 147D, 173F, 205D, 229F, 251D, 271D, 349D, 371D, 453F, 471D, 499D, 567D, 589F, 609D, 637F, 713D, 737D, T21–T24, T55–T58, T87–T90, T123–T126, T157–T160, T192–T195

> See also **Assessment,** informal; **Writing,** evaluation.

**School-Home Connection.**

> See **Homework.**

**Science Activities.**

> See **Content Areas; Cross-Curricular Connections; Cross-Curricular Stations.**

**Scope and Sequence:** R50–R57

**Search Techniques:** 229A–B, 299D

> See also **Comprehension,** search techniques; **Research and Information Skills.**

**Second-Language Support.**

> See **English-Language Learners, Activities for; Reaching All Learners.**

**Selection Comprehension**

> guided comprehension questions: 24–40, 54–68, 82–94, 106–114, 128–138, 154–168, 178–194, 210–216, 234–242, 256–264, 278–286, 304–318, 330–344, 354–366, 376–388, 404–416, 426–430, 442–448, 458–466, 476–492, 506–514, 526–534, 548–559, 572–580, 594–599, 616–630, 642–658, 672–679, 718–729, 732

> response activities: 42, 70, 94, 114, 138, 168, 194, 216, 242, 286, 318, 344, 366, 388, 416, 430, 448, 466, 492, 516, 536, 558, 582, 600, 632, 660, 680, 706, 728

> retell and summarize: 43, 71, 95, 115, 139, 169, 195, 217, 243, 265, 287,

319, 345, 367, 389, 417, 431, 449, 467, 493, 517, 537, 559, 583, 601, 633, 661, 681, 707, 729

> think and respond questions: 42, 70, 94, 114, 138, 168, 194, 216, 242, 264, 286, 318, 344, 366, 388, 416, 430, 448, 466, 492, 516, 536, 558, 582, 600, 632, 660, 680, 706, 728

**Selection Information:** 18B, 20A, 50A, 78A, 102A, 124A, 148B, 150A, 174A, 206A, 230A, 252A, 274A, 300A, 326A, 350A, 372A, 400A, 422A, 438A, 454A, 472A, 502A, 522A, 544A, 568A, 590A, 612A, 638A, 668A, 690A, 714A

**Selections in** *Pupil Edition*

> "Amelia and Eleanor Go for a Ride": 126–139

> "The Baker's Neighbor": 152–168

> "Blue Willow": 568–589

> "The Case of Pablo's Nose": 424–430

> "The Cricket in Times Square": 328–344

> "Donavan's Word Jar": 52–70

> "The Down and Up Fall": 714–737

> "The Emperor and the Kite": 176–195

> "Fire!": 502–521

> "Fly Traps! Plants That Bite Back": 690–713

> "The Garden of Happiness": 232–243

> "The Gardener": 22–43

> "The Gold Rush": 612–637

> "How to Babysit an Orangutan": 254–265

> "I Have Heard of a Land": 638–667

> "In My Family": 590–609

> "In the Days of King Adobe": 440–448

> "The Kids' Invention Book": 402–416

> "Look to the North": 374–389

> "Lou Gehrig: The Luckiest Man": 104–115

> "My Name Is María Isabel": 80–95

> "Nights of the Pufflings: 208–217

> "One Grain of Rice": 472–492

> "Paul Bunyan and Babe the Blue Ox": 668–689

> "Red Writing Hood": 456–467

> "Saguaro Cactus": 544–567

> "Sarah, Plain and Tall": 276–287

> "Stealing Home": 302–318

> "Two Lands, One Heart": 352–366

> "A Very Important Day": 522–543

**Self-Question.**

> See **Strategies Good Readers Use.**

**Self-Selected Reading.**

> See **Trade Books.**

**Sentences.**

> See **Grammar; Writing,** writing activities.

**Sequence:** 422I, 454I, 590I

> See also **Comprehension,** sequence; **Text Structure.**

**Set Purpose.**

> See **Prereading Strategies, Preview and Predict/Set Purpose.**

**Setting.**

> See **Literary Response and Analysis,** narrative elements.

**Shared Writing:** 78E, 124F, 205D, 206F, 229F, 230E, 251D, 271D, 300E, 419, 421F, 437D, 438E, 453F, 454E, 469, 471D, 497, 499D, 502E, 590E, 609C–D, 637F, 667F, 668F, 689D, 690F, 713F, 714F, 737D, S6, S18, S24, S38, S44, S50, S56, S70, S82, S88, S108, S114, S126, S140, S146, S166, S172, S178, S184, S190

**Silent Reading:** 20F, 50F, 78F, 102F, 124F, 150F, 174F, 206F, 230F, 252F, 274F, 300F, 326F, 350F, 359, 372F, 400F, 422F, 438F, 472F, 502F, 522F, 544F, 568F, 590F, 612F, 638F, 668F, 690F, 714F

**Simile.**

> See **Author's Craft.**

**Skills.**

> See **Comprehension; Decoding/Phonics; Literary Response and Analysis; Research and Information Skills; Vocabulary and Concepts.**

**Skills Assessment.**

> See **Assessment,** formal; **Assessment,** informal.

**Skills in** *Pupil Edition*

> author's purpose: 522I, 542, 568I, 588, 714I, 736, S138–S139, S150–S151, S182–S183, T141

> cause and effect: 150I, 172, 230I, 250, 397B, S36–S37, S54–S55, T36

> compare and contrast: 300I, 324, 350I, 370, 472I, 498, S74–S75, S86–S87, S124–S125, T72

> draw conclusions: 274I, 298, 326I, 348, 471B, S68–S69, S80–S81, T70

> elements of nonfiction: 502I, 520, 544I, 566, 637D, S132–S133, S144–S145, T138

**Text Structure**

expository text: 502I, 520, 544I, 566, S132–S133, S144–S145

cause and effect: 397B, 502I, 520, 544I, S132

compare and contrast: 350I, 370, 502I, 544I, S124, S132

main idea and details: 400I, 420, 438I, 452, 502I, 520, 544I, S100–S101, S112–S113

sequence: 111, 502I, 520, 544I, 566, S106–S107, S118–S119, S156–S157

*See also* **Comprehension; Strategies Good Readers Use.**

**Text Structure and Format, Use:** 25, 111, 355, 372J, 377, 405, 422I, 502J, 590I, 612J, 627

**Texts, Read a Variety of.**

*See* **Literary Forms.**

**Theme Projects:** 18J, 147O, 148J, 271O, 272J, 397O, 398J, 499O, 500J, 609O, 610J, 737O

**Theme Review:** 147P, 271P, 397P, 499P, 609P, 737P

**Theme Wrap-Up:** 147O, 271O, 397O, 499O, 609O, 737O

**Themes:** 18–19, 18A–K, 147O–U, 148–149, 148A–K, 271O–U, 272–273, 272A–K, 397O–U, 398A–J, 398–399, 399O–Q, 499O–U, 500–501, 500A–K, 609O–P, 610–611, 610A–K, 737O–P

**Thesaurus.**

*See* **Reference Sources.**

**Think and Respond.**

*See* **Selection Comprehension, think and Respond questions.**

**Think-Aloud.**

*See* **Modeling.**

**Thinking**

classifying: 698

*See also* **Comprehension, classify/categorize.**

critical thinking: 42, 46, 70, 74, 94, 98, 114, 120, 138, 144, 168, 170, 194, 202, 216, 226, 242, 248, 264, 268, 286, 296, 318, 322, 344, 346, 366, 368, 388, 394, 416, 418, 430, 434, 448, 450, 466, 468, 492, 496, 516, 518, 536, 540, 558, 564, 582, 586, 600, 604, 632, 634, 660, 664, 680, 686, 706, 710, 728

*See also* **Comprehension.**

distinguishing between fact and opinion: 426, 508, 610K, 612I, 616, 618, 622, 636, 668I, 672, 678, 688

*See also* **Comprehension, fact and opinion.**

expressing personal opinions/personal responses: 20H, 42, 50H, 70, 94, 114, 124H, 138, 168, 194, 216, 242, 264, 286, 310, 318, 344, 366, 372H, 388, 400H, 412, 416, 418, 430, 438H, 448, 450, 466, 488, 490, 492, 496, 502H, 516, 518, 536, 558, 582, 590H, 600, 626, 632, 638H, 646, 660, 674, 680, 684, 690H, 706, 728

inferential thinking: 24, 26, 28, 30, 32, 34, 49A–B, 77D, 101B, 256, 262, 280, 282, 284, 349B, 556

inquiry: 46, 74, 98, 120, 144, 170, 202, 226, 248, 268, 296, 322, 346, 368, 394, 418, 434, 450, 468, 496, 518, 540, 564, 586, 606, 634, 664, 686, 710, 734

literal thinking: 26, 30, 36, 44, 256, 278, 280

making comparisons: 46, 47, 56, 66, 74, 98, 120, 144, 170, 202, 206H, 226, 248, 260, 262, 268, 282, 296, 306, 308, 314, 320, 322, 326H, 340, 346, 356, 358, 362, 368, 394, 418, 434, 450, 468, 482, 484, 496, 528, 540, 564, 584, 586, 594, 606, 634, 664, 686, 710, 734

*See also* **Comprehension, compare and contrast.**

making judgments: 54, 64, 78H, 82, 108, 112, 168, 214, 334, 350H, 366, 414, 418, 454H, 476, 488, 510, 568H, 578, 616, 704

noting important details: 56, 62, 82, 92, 108, 112, 150H, 206H, 210, 212, 220, 222, 230H, 246, 256, 258, 278, 280, 292, 330, 360, 362, 366, 372H, 380, 388, 400H, 404, 460, 478, 482, 508, 514, 530, 532, 550, 552, 556, 618, 630, 632, 644, 650, 654, 678, 680, 694, 708, 722, 730, 732

organizing and connecting ideas

bar graph: 109, 299B, 371B, 610J, 690E

chart: 20E, 20I, 20K, 47, 49D, 71, 77N, 78K, 80, 99, 101G, 102E, 102I, 150E, 150I, 155, 206I, 208, 230K, 252F, 252I, 254, 299A,

300K, 323, 324, 325B, 349B, 371A, 395, 397B, 421A, 421L, 471B, 519, 541, 568I, 576, 587, 609I, 612E, 638E, 638I, 668I, 704, 711, 714K, S166, S176

diagram: 77K, 150E, 163, 269, 274I, 369, 400E, 419, 519, 541, 612E, 638E, 690F, 735

flowchart: 150E, 422I, 474, S56

graphic organizers: 19, 20I, 49A–B, 50I, 77D, 78I, 101B, 102I, 124I, 136, 150I, 173E, 174E, 174I, 206I, 230I, 248, 251C, 252I, 273, 274I, 300I, 326I, 350I, 399, 434, 435, 450, 451, 496, 497, 501, 521E, 567C, 609B, 611, 612I, 638I, 668I, 690I, 714O, 737O, T17–T20, T52–T54, T85–T86, T120–T122, T154–T156, T190–T191

K–W–L chart: 104, 206I, 208, 252F, 252I, 254, 323, 372I, 389, 395, 454F, 502I, 504, 517, 522F, 543A, 568F, 614, 633, 638I, 640, 661, 707, 730, 732, T19

line graph: 75, 575

list: 18K, 148J–K, 251J, 272J–K, 372E, 398J–K, 399, 420, 422E, 490, 610K

outline: 543E–F, 637A–B, 690E, 713B, S144

predict-o-gram: 78I, 80

prediction chart/diagram: 78I, 80, 522I, 670, 681, 692

sequence chart/diagram: 78K, 99, 422I, 454I, 456, 474, 544I, 546, 559, 590I, 592, 601, S144

SQ3R chart: 402, 543A

story map: 48, 50I, 52, 77P, 173N, 174I, 205K, 205L, 205N, 229M, 251N, 325N, 437N, 453M, 567N, 589M, 667P, 524, T18

time line: 145, 435, 612F

Venn diagram: 124I, 206E, 252K, 300I, 350I, 352, 362, 367, 469, 472I, 498, 499, 499C, 499K, 499L, 521P, 604, 607, 698, 713L, 733, S144

web: 50K, 88, 124F, 124K, 149, 206F, 206K, 230F, 271B, 274F, 350F, 350K, 385, 400K, 422F, 422K, 438I, 440, 472F, 472K, 502K, 521A, 522K, 544F, 590F, 590K, 638F, 668F, 668K, 690K, 714F

**Vocabulary and Concepts**

bonus words: 49K, 77K, 101I, 147I, 173I, 205I, 229I, 251I, 271I, 299K, 325I, 349I, 371I, 397I, 421K, 437I, 453K, 471I, 499I, 521K, 543K, 567I, 589K, 609I, 637K, 713I, 737I

classify/categorize: 49D, 521K, 589A–B, 589K, 609I, 667D

compound words: 123A, 205A, 371A

concept development: 49D, 50K, 77A–B, 102K, 123B, 147B, 589A–B, 638I, 667D, 690I

connotation/denotation: 499I, 589K, 689J, 737I

extending vocabulary: S3, S9, S15, S21, S27, S35, S41, S47, S53, S59, S67, S73, S79, S85, S91, S99, S105, S111, S117, S123, S131, S137, S143, S149, S155, S163, S169, S175, S181, S187

figurative language: 39, 61, 173A–B, 205B, 211, 239, 251B, 325I, 349I, 437I, 509, 555, 589D, 677

*See also* **Author's Craft.**

homographs and homophones: 173K, 299K, 499I, 543K

idioms: 349I, 667K

multiple-meaning words: 123I, 349I, 397I, 421K, 437I, 453K, 521K, 567I, 589A–B, 609I, 667D

prefixes, suffixes, and roots: 50I, 76, 102I, 122, 173D, 206L, 271I, 350L, 421K, 437A, 471I, 499A, 737A, S10–S11, S22–S23, S39, T4

*See also* **Decoding/Phonics, prefixes and suffixes.**

selection vocabulary: 20L, 50L, 78L, 102L, 124L, 150L, 174L, 206L, 230L, 252L, 274L, 300L, 326L, 350L, 372L, 400L, 422L, 438L, 454L, 472L, 502L, 522L, 544L, 568L, 590L, 612L, 638L, 668L, 690L, 714L

synonyms and antonyms: 77A–B, 77K, 123B, 123I, 147B, 147I, 206, 229K, 251I, 299K, 397I, 453K, 543K, 667K, 689I

syntax, use to confirm meaning: 20J, 300J, 371I, 590J

word origins: 101I, 173K, 213, 251I, 471I, 499I, 638I, S39

word relationships: 147I, 229K, 271I, 543K, 637K, 638I, 666, 690I, 712, 737I, S170–S171, S182–S183, T176

*See also* **Word Study.**

**Vocabulary Power:** 20, 50, 78, 102, 124, 150, 174, 206, 230, 252, 274, 300, 326, 350, 372, 400, 422, 438, 454, 472, 502, 521K, 544, 568, 590, 612, 638, 668, 690, 714

**Vocabulary Strategies:** 20, 20L, 50, 50L, 78, 78L, 102, 102L, 124, 124L, 150, 150L, 174, 174L, 206, 206L, 230, 230L, 252, 252L, 274, 274L, 300, 300L, 326, 326L, 350, 350L, 372, 372L, 400, 400L, 422, 422L, 438, 438L, 454, 454L, 472, 472L, 502, 502L, 522, 524L, 544, 544L, 568, 568L, 590, 590L, 612, 612L, 638, 638L, 668, 668L, 690, 690L, 714, 714L

**Vowels, Words with Long and Short.**

*See* **Decoding/Phonics; Spelling.**

**Web Sites:** 78E, 124F, 150B, 171, 172, 173G, 206B, 206F, 219, 228, 230B, 230K, 250, 251C, 251E, 252B, 419, 454F, 469, 497, 502F, 590E, 668F, 714F, 721, S159

**Web, World Wide.**

*See* **Technology, Internet/*The Learning Site.***

**What Good Readers Do:** 20J, 50J, 78J, 102J, 124J, 150J, 174J, 206J, 230J, 252J, 274J, 300J, 326J, 350J, 372J, 400J, 422J, 438J, 454J, 472J, 502J, 524J, 544J, 568J, 590J, 612J, 638J, 668J, 690J, 714J

**Word Analysis.**

*See* **Decoding/Phonics; Systematic Vocabulary Development; Word Study.**

**Word Attack.**

*See* **Decoding/Phonics.**

**Word Bank:** 21, 51, 79, 103, 125, 151, 175, 207, 231, 253, 275, 301, 327, 351, 373, 401, 423, 439, 455, 473, 503, 525, 545, 569, 591, 613, 639, 669, 691, 715

**Word Choice.**

*See* **Vocabulary and Concepts.**

**Word Families.**

*See* **Word Study, related words.**

**Word Identification Strategies**

decode using structural analysis: 50J, 55, 65, 69, 83, 124L, 150J, 155, 161, 174L, 206L, 252L, 271I, 350L, 400L, 422L, 472L, 502L, 522J, 529, 531, 535, 568L, 612L, 668L, 714L

develop automatic word recognition through rereading.

*See* **Rereading for Fluency.**

use context to confirm meaning: 20J, 27, 33, 35, 50L, 157, 230L, 274L, 300J, 305, 309, 311, 326L, 372L, 438L, 454L, 544L, 590J, 590L, 638L, 690L

use reference sources: 78L, 102L, 150L, 300L, 522L

use syllable patterns: 49C, 229C, 251A, 271A, 325A, 421C, 453C, 471A, 521C, 543C, 567A, 689A, 713A

*See also* **Decoding/Phonics.**

**Word Knowledge.**

*See* **Vocabulary and Concepts; Word Study.**

**Word Order.**

*See* **Written English Language Conventions.**

**Word Relationships.**

*See* **Comprehension, word relationships; Vocabulary and Concepts.**

**Word Sorts:** 49I, 77I, 101G, 123G, 147G, 173I, 205G, 229I, 251G, 271G, 299I, 325G, 349G, 371G, 397G, 421I, 437G, 453I, 471G, 499G, 521I, 543I, 567G, 589I, 609G, 637I, 667I, 689G, 713G, 737G

**Word Study**

analogies: 205I, 229K, 397I, 567I, 713I

animal names: 224

antonyms: 77A–B, 101I, 123B, 147B, 229K, 567I, 589K

clipped words: 220

connotation/denotation: 499I, 589K, 737I

context clues: 371I, 479

dictionary/glossary use: 101I, 123I, 689I

etymologies: 173K, 213, 479

figurative language/simile: 173A, 211, 239, 437I

foreign words: 101I, 251I, 471I, 499I, 609I

homographs: 49K, 543K

homophones: 173K, 299K, 637K

idioms: 349I, 667K

jargon: 521K, 637K

multiple-meaning words: 349I, 421K, 437I, 567I, 609I

regionalisms: 667K

related words: 77K, 147I, 737I

# Acknowledgments

For permission to reprint copyrighted material, grateful acknowledgment is made to the following sources:

*The Afro-American Newspapers:* "Anansi and Turtle," adapted by Matt Evans. Text © 1997 by The Afro-American Newspaper Company of Baltimore, Inc.

*Atheneum Books for Young Readers, an imprint of Simon & Schuster Children's Publishing Division:* "Before the Game" from *That Sweet Diamond: Baseball Poems* by Paul B. Janeczko. Text copyright © 1998 by Paul B. Janeczko.

*Debby Boone and Gabriel Ferrer:* "Flying Kites" from *Tomorrow Is a Brand New Day* by Debby Boone and Gabriel Ferrer. Text copyright © 1989 by Resi, Inc.

*Estate of Arthur Bourinot:* "Paul Bunyan" by Arthur S. Bourinot.

*Boyds Mills Press, Inc.:* "A Walk Through My Rain Forest" from *The Distant Talking Drum* by Isaac Olaleye. Text copyright © 1995 by Isaac Olaleye.

*Curtis Brown, Ltd.:* "Eleanor Roosevelt" by Rebecca Kai Dotlich from *Lives: Poems About Famous Americans*, edited by Lee Bennett Hopkins. Text copyright © 1999 by Rebecca Kai Dotlich. Published by HarperCollins Publishers.

*Carolrhoda Books, Inc., a division of the Lerner Publishing Group:* "What's a Puffin?" and "Meet the Puffins" from *Puffins* by Susan E. Quinlan. Text copyright © 1999 by Susan E. Quinlan.

*Cobblehill Books, an affiliate of Dutton Children's Books, an imprint of Penguin Putnam Books for Young Readers, a division of Penguin Putnam Inc.:* "Blue Jeans" and "Pencil" from *The Kid Who Invented the Popsicle* by Don L. Wulffson. Text copyright © 1997 by Don L. Wulffson.

*Dell Publishing, a division of Random House, Inc.:* From *The War with Grandpa* by Robert Kimmel Smith. Text copyright © 1984 by Robert Kimmel Smith.

*Dial Books for Young Readers, an imprint of Penguin Putnam Books for Young Readers, a division of Penguin Putnam Inc.:* From *Back Home* by Gloria Jean Pinkney. Text copyright © 1992 by Gloria Jean Pinkney.

*Ghost Town Publications, P. O. Drawer 5998, Carmel, California:* From "Gold!" (pp. 9–11) in *Tales and Treasures of the California Gold Rush* by Randall A. Reinstedt. Text copyright © 1994 by Randall A. Reinstedt.

*Harcourt, Inc.:* "Breaks Free," "Waterless Shores," and "If the Earth Were Small" from *Cactus Poems* by Frank Asch. Text copyright © 1998 by Frank Asch. From "Cricket" in *Big Bugs* by Jerry Booth. Text copyright © 1994 by The Yolla Bolly Press. "Apple Orchard" (Retitled: "Apple Picking") by Erich Hoyt from *Down to Earth* by Michael J. Rosen. Text copyright © 1998 by Eric Hoyt; compilation copyright © 1998 by Michael J. Rosen. "Tortillas Like Africa" and "Nopales" from *Canto Familiar* by Gary Soto. Text copyright © 1995 by Gary Soto.

*HarperCollins Publishers:* "School" from *Childtimes: A Three-Generation Memoir* by Eloise Greenfield and Lessie Jones Little. Text copyright © 1979 by Eloise Greenfield and Lessie Jones Little. "My Journals" from *Hey World, Here I Am!* by Jean Little. Text copyright © 1986 by Jean Little. "My Uncle Looked Me in the Eye" from *Something BIG Has Been Here* by Jack Prelutsky. Text copyright © 1990 by Jack Prelutsky. From *Home* by Michael J. Rosen. Text copyright © 1992 by Michael J. Rosen; compilation copyright © 1992 by HarperCollins Publishers. "Dividing the Horses" from *Stories to Solve: Folktales from Around the World* by George Shannon. Text copyright © 1985 by George Shannon. From *Wolves* by Seymour Simon. Text copyright © 1993 by Seymour Simon.

*Highlights for Children, Inc., Columbus, OH*: "Bugs, Beware!" by Pat Kita from *Highlights for Children* Magazine, September 1991. Text copyright © 1991 by Highlights for Children, Inc.

*Felice Holman:* "Who Am I?" from *At the Top of My Voice and Other Poems* by Felice Holman. Text copyright © 1970 by Felice Holman.

*Lee & Low Books Inc., New York, NY 10016:* "Children of Long Ago" (21 lines) and "Children of Long Ago" (9 lines) from *Children of Long Ago* by Lessie Jones Little. Text copyright © 2000 by Weston W. Little, Sr. Estate. "Words Free as Confetti" from *Confetti: Poems for Children* by Pat Mora. Text copyright © 1996 by Pat Mora.

*National Wildlife Federation:* "Old Notch" by Ruth Kelley from *Ranger Rick* Magazine, October 1998. Text copyright © 1998 by the National Wildlife Federation. "Reader Riddles" from *Ranger Rick* Magazine, September 1996. Text copyright © 1996 by the National Wildlife Federation.

*Orca Book Publishers, Box 468, Custer, WA 98240-0468:* From *Prairie Born* by Dave Bouchard. Text copyright © 1997 by Dave Bouchard.

*Marian Reiner:* "We Could Be Friends" from *The Way Things Are and Other Poems* by Myra Cohn Livingston. Text copyright © 1974 by Myra Cohn Livingston.

*Scholastic Inc.:* "The Case of the Gold Brick" from *Still More Two-Minute Mysteries* by Donald J. Sobol. Text copyright © 1975 by Donald J. Sobol.

*Misty Stands in Timber:* "As I Walk Along the Hillside" by Misty Stands in Timber.

*Estate of James S. Tippett:* "Hang Out the Flag" by James S. Tippett.

**Pupil Edition Acknowledgments**

## Teacher Notes